THE BANK OF ENGLAND

1891–1944

Appendixes

THE BANK OF ENGLAND 1891–1944

R. S. SAYERS

Appendixes

CAMBRIDGE UNIVERSITY PRESS
CAMBRIDGE
LONDON · NEW YORK · MELBOURNE

Published by the Syndics of the Cambridge University Press
The Pitt Building, Trumpington Street, Cambridge CB2 1RP
Bentley House, 200 Euston Road, London NW1 2DB
32 East 57th Street, New York, NY 10022, USA
296 Beaconsfield Parade, Middle Park, Melbourne 3206, Australia

Library of Congress catalogue card number: 75-46116

ISBN 0 521 21067 4 Volume 1
ISBN 0 521 21068 2 Volume 2
ISBN 0 521 21066 6 Appendixes

First published 1976

Printed in Great Britain
at the
University Printing House, Cambridge
(Euan Phillips, University Printer)

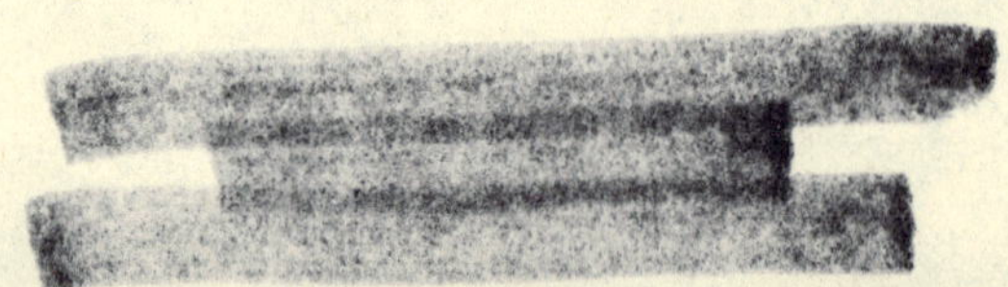

AUTHOR'S NOTE

The nature of the content of this volume varies greatly from one Appendix to another. The documents reproduced originate from various sources and are various in date. Some originated in the Bank, some in the Treasury, some in other Government Departments or elsewhere. Some of them are formal and some are not. The amount of editorial matter thought appropriate has also varied greatly. The variations in printing style serve as a reminder of these variations in the nature of the material.

CONTENTS

Appendixes

APPENDIX I

METHOD OF ELECTION OF GOVERNORS: EXTRACT FROM COURT MINUTES, 10 FEBRUARY 1848

The Governor laid before the Court the Report of the Committee of Treasury which, at the last Court, was referred back for re-consideration, and it was

Resolved,

That the Report, as amended be adopted, viz:

'The attention of the Committee of Treasury having been directed by recent occurrences to the subject of the constitution of the Court of Directors and of the system hitherto pursued in the selection of Candidates to be recommended to the Proprietors for election as Directors and Governors, they have given this important question their mature consideration, and make the following Report thereon to the Court.

The Court are aware that it has been the custom to expect each Director in rotation to offer himself to fill the offices, first of Deputy Governor and afterwards of Governor; – and Directors not willing so to offer themselves, have, with few exceptions, retired from the Direction, – The Committee of Treasury consider that this practice has proved prejudicial to the interests of the Bank, and ought to be abandoned; – They consider that it has occasioned, (and might again occasion) the withdrawal from the Court, of many valuable Members, able and willing to act as Directors, but whose health or occupations have rendered them averse to undertake the more onerous duties of Governor and Deputy Governor. For this and other reasons to which it is not necessary more particularly to allude, The Committee of Treasury are of opinion that Gentlemen should be selected to fill the Chairs upon some other principle than that of rotation, They think that the Court should select out of the number willing to serve, the persons who may be deemed most qualified, without regard either to their seniority in the Direction, or to the fact of their having served in the Chairs at any former period, or to the number of years they may have served; – but the Committee are of opinion that no Director be recommended to the Proprietors for Governor till he shall have actually served in the Direction 5 years, and that the selection should be determined by ballot.

Should this change in the system of Nomination for the Chairs be approved by the Court, The Committee are of opinion that it would no longer be necessary to pay the same regard as heretofore to the age of Candidates for the Direction. – It has hitherto been considered requisite that such Candidates should be below the middle age, lest on reaching the Chairs in their rotation, they should have attained a too advanced period of life. But, under the proposed system, this precaution would not be required, and the field for the choice of suitable Candidates would be enlarged. – With a similar object, the Committee propose no longer to require as an indispensable condition that Candidates should be actually engaged in business, although, at the same time, they are still of opinion that persons who have been Members of Commercial Houses should alone be selected.

The wish having been expressed by several Proprietors that greater publicity should be given to the names of the Candidates recommended to them for election, it is proposed that they be advertised in the newspapers twelve days before the day fixed for the ballot, and, that the *new* Candidates should be distinguished from those recommended for re-election.'

APPENDIX 2

TREASURY MEMORANDUM ON THE GOLD RESERVES, 22 MAY 1914

[The memorandum here reprinted is that referred to in the concluding paragraph of Chapter 4. The best available copy is a printed copy in the Public Record Office, and is reproduced here by kind permission of the Controller of H.M. Stationery Office. This (its P.R.O. reference is T.170/19) is marked, on a covering page not reproduced, 'Sir J. Bradbury' and 'Proof'. The only date it bears is 22/5/14 at its end, and this date appears also with Blackett's initials in the covering note. No later printing is known, and it seems likely that final copies would have been printed only if the Chancellor had put to the Cabinet the bankers' request for a Royal Commission, which had occasioned Blackett's writing the memorandum.

Apart from one trifle in the covering page, and the correction of 'VII' to 'VIII' for the heading over paragraph 73, this copy bears no manuscript corrections. The insertion in square brackets in paragraph 9, all other parentheses, and the footnotes attached to paragraphs 60 and 72 are all exactly as in the copy. In paragraph 68 Holden's speech at the London City and Midland Bank is dated 'March 5th, 1914'; in fact it was on 23 January.

Blackett's covering note says that the memorandum arose from the Chancellor's request 'for a statement of the views of the Treasury'. Blackett acknowledges the contributions of Bradbury, Blain and Hawtrey (all of the Treasury) but none from the Bank, and indeed any co-operation from the Bank in producing such a memorandum would not at this date be expected. The insertion in paragraph 9 suggests that Governor Cunliffe was consulted on a particular point. Although close knowledge of the Bank's techniques is suggested by paragraphs 34, 40, 41 and 42, it is the opinion of Sir Ralph Hawtrey (on 29 November 1974) that this would have been drawn from Bradbury's personal store of knowledge rather than from any *ad hoc* consultation with, say, Nairne or Harvey at the Bank. Though memory at sixty years' distance does not allow him any absolute certainty, Hawtrey agrees that the memorandum must be regarded as a purely Treasury statement of views. The Bank was not given, at this date, to producing such papers, and the Treasury memorandum therefore serves as the only authoritative official survey of the problem; nevertheless it may probably be taken as indicative also of the Bank's general views in the pre-1914 years.]

GOLD RESERVES

I.—The Bank Charter Act, 1844, and the Cheque System.

1. The Gold Reserves of the United Kingdom are very largely conditioned by the Bank Charter Act of 1844, and by the corresponding Bank Acts of 1845 relating to Scotland and Ireland. Prior to 1844 there was no statutory provision for the maintenance of any central reserve of gold in this country. The main purpose of the Act of 1844 was not, in fact, to provide a central reserve, but the creation of such a reserve was its most successful achievement, and, although most of the hopes which were entertained by the authors of that Act have been falsified, the successful accumulation and retention of a central Gold Reserve at the Bank of England, which was an incidental result, have been enough to maintain the Act on the Statute Book unrepealed and unmodified for 70 years.

2. On this point paragraph 104 of the Report of the Royal Commission on Indian Finance and Currency, 1914 [Cd. 7236] may be quoted: "In this "country the intention of the framers of the Bank Charter Act of 1844 was "to prevent the abuses attendant on the issue of notes without the backing of "a metallic reserve by securing the retention in reserve of coin against every "single note issued over and above a maximum amount which was allowed "to be covered by securities.... Its result has been to reduce notes to a very "insignificant position in the British Currency system. The complete "inelasticity imposed by the Act of 1844 upon the currency of notes... has "only been tolerated because of the discovery in the cheque system of an "alternative means of obtaining an elastic paper currency which could not "be obtained through the note issue under the Act. The main paper currency "of the United Kingdom now consists of cheques, and the Gold Reserve of "the Bank of England, though nominally supporting a comparatively small "note issue, is really the ultimate support of a gigantic currency of cheques "and other credit instruments of which the notes of the Bank of England "form only a small portion."

3. In normal times indeed the notes of the Bank of England are nothing more than gold certificates, for in such times the notes in reserve in the banking department are seldom of less value than 18,450,000*l*., the amount nominally issued against securities.

4. The panic of 1847, only three years after the passing of the Bank Charter Act, made it clear that the belief that the Act would prevent commercial and monetary crises was ill-founded. The suspension of the limit on the fiduciary issue during the crisis did not, however, lead to any modification in the Act. Its operation was still too new and knowledge of financial theory too limited to permit of a clear perception of what was amiss. So enlightened an economist as Stanley Jevons actually propounded the theory that commercial crises recurred every decade or so under the influence of sun-spots,

according to some law analogous to the connection between the moon and the tides. The theory secured a wide acceptance, and the recurrence of panics in 1857 and again in 1866 seemed to lend it the support of experience.

5. But before the panic of 1857 a great discovery was made. This was that the most potent instrument for conserving and replenishing the Gold Reserves of the country was to be found in the rate of discount.

6. The country had thus by a series of accidents provided itself with a not unsuccessful banking and currency system. More or less incidentally the Act of 1844 had established a central Gold Reserve, and an instrument had been found in the shape of the discount rate for regulating that reserve. In the cheque system the country had a paper currency far superior to the legal tender notes which had been regulated into relative insignificance by the Act of 1844, and finally, in the extra-statutory power assumed by Government in a crisis to suspend the Act, a means of creating an emergency currency had been invented by which to overcome the worst terrors of such a period.

7. Thus though the Bank Charter Act was again suspended in 1857 and 1866, and in 1857 for the first time and last time fiduciary notes were actually issued in excess of the legal maximum, bankers and merchants have remained ever since fairly well satisfied with the system of Gold Reserves which experience had built up and sanctioned, and apart from Mr. Goschen's unsuccessful attempts in 1891 to introduce £1 notes after the Baring crisis of 1890, no serious effort has been made to remodel that system.

II.—Agitation for Increased Gold Reserves.

8. For the last 30 years, however, the question whether the amount of our Gold Reserves is adequate has been continually canvassed, and it seems to be almost a commonplace among bankers to-day that those reserves are now inadequate and ought to be increased. It is possible, no doubt, that the persistent efforts of Sir E. Holden (the Chairman of the London City and Midland Bank) to rouse his fellow-bankers to a sense of this inadequacy, and the support which has been given to this view by the more vocal portion of the banking community represents less unanimity than appears on the surface, and that the comparative inaction which has so far attended these efforts is due to the effective inertia of the unconvinced, and not solely to the difficulties which stand in the way of any scheme of distributing the burden of increase.

9. Sir E. Holden has, however, had some success. A strong committee of bankers, under the chairmanship of Lord St. Aldwyn, has been studying the whole subject with a view to formulating proposals, and it is believed that most of the big London banks have in recent years accumulated special Gold Reserves of their own apart from the central reserve at the Bank of England. Whether these special reserves are important in the aggregate or not is diffi-

cult to determine, because (as also the proceedings of the Committee) they are kept secret. Only the London County and Westminster Bank publish figures of their average daily cash in hand and at the Bank of England (the London City and Midland Bank have promised some fuller particulars from December 1914), but even these figures, which in nearly every case lump together till money, special reserve, and cash at the Bank of England, do not help much for the purpose now in question. That the special reserves are not absolutely negligible is certain, but whether they are important additions to the available gold resources of the country or not is unknown. [The present Governor of the Bank of England says that they are not, and he ought to know.] In any case, so long as they are kept secret and in the sole control of the banks which have created them, they contribute nothing to the real strength of the central reserve, and are important only if they are a preliminary to the strengthening of the central reserve upon some prescribed scheme.

10. However this may be, the activity of Sir E. Holden and his demand for a Royal Commission on the subject make it worth while considering with some care whether or not the present reserves of this country are adequate.

The case put forward by advocates of an increase of the Gold Reserves may be grouped as follows:—

(i) Comparisons with foreign countries.

It is urged—

(*a*) that in proportion to the volume of our banking and exchange transactions our Gold Reserves are smaller than those of foreign countries.

(*b*) that the Gold Reserves of foreign countries have of late years been increased to an extent out of all proportion to the very small additions made in this country.

(ii) Comparisons with former periods—

It is urged that, regard being had to the enormous growth of our banking and exchange transactions, our gold reserves are relatively very much smaller than in the past.

(iii) Complaints of the fluctuations of the Bank rate.

It is said that British commerce suffers from the frequency of the changes in the Bank rate, and the steadiness of the Bank of France's discount rate is contrasted to the disadvantage of our own, it being contended that the size of France's Gold Reserves is the cause of her steady Bank rate.

(iv) The agitation also touches on other points, including complaints of the management and methods of the Bank of England, in its regulation of the Gold Reserves;

(v) And suggestions are offered as to the distribution of the burden of the cost of making additions to the reserves, a not uncommon cry being that the Government, as holding the deposits of the savings banks, should make a substantial contribution.

It will be convenient to begin with a discussion of the first two heads, comparisons with foreign countries and with former times.

(i)—*Comparisons with Foreign Countries.*

11. There is no need to produce statistics to prove that our Gold Reserves are small in comparison with those of most foreign countries. The proofs are indeed so convincing that people are apt to accept them unquestioningly as proving the truth not merely of the propositions that our reserves are smaller in proportion to the turn-over than those of foreign countries and that such proportion is even smaller to-day than 20 years ago, but also of the conclusion which these propositions are intended to establish, namely, that our Gold Reserves are smaller than they ought to be. It is, however, quite fallacious to accept them as proving the inadequacy of our Gold Reserves. This conclusion would follow only if it can be shown that conditions here and elsewhere have been and are sufficiently similar to justify close mathematical comparisons.

12. How far then are such comparisons justified? As already shown the great bulk of the internal exchange transactions of this country, so far at any rate as aggregate totals are concerned, is carried on very largely by means of cheques, and only to a very small extent by means of legal tender, whether coin or notes, except perhaps in the United States of America, where conditions are otherwise very dissimilar, the cheque system has not obtained a vogue in any way comparable with its vogue in this country in any of the foreign States with whose Gold Reserves comparison is usually made. In most foreign countries legal tender currency forms the main basis of internal exchange, and a considerably larger Gold Reserve is required to maintain the convertibility of a currency of legal tender notes in normal times than is necessary as a support for the cheque system. [This statement may seem a little dogmatic, but is really not questionable, and in a memorandum of this sort a certain amount of dogmatic assertion is inevitable if reasonable limits are to be observed.] In other words, if we confine attention to internal exchange alone and regard the Gold Reserves as the working balance necessary to maintain the convertibility of the circulating medium, so far as it does not consist of full-value coin, the working balance of gold required in the United Kingdom is smaller than the working balance needed in countries with a large legal tender currency in circulation. The prevalence of the cheque system here, therefore, justifies relatively smaller Gold Reserves, and makes mere arithmetical comparisons of the aggregate amounts held here and elsewhere quite valueless.

13. It is equally impossible to draw valuable conclusions as to the adequacy of our Gold Reserves from statistics of comparative increases in this country

and in others during recent years. Each extension of the cheque system economises gold and justifies a reduction in the ratio between the working balance and the total transactions, and a very great increase in the latter may involve no actual increase, or only a very small one, in the size of the Gold Reserves. On the other hand, where the currency consists mainly of legal tender notes, an expansion in the volume of transactions involves a proportionate increase in the amount of gold in reserve. This may be the direct result of statutory enactments relating to legal tender, &c., as, *e.g.*, in Germany or the U.S.A., or it may be a necessary measure of prudence as, *e.g.*, in France.

14. Again, the insular position of our country and our comparative freedom from fear of foreign invasion, and the fact that for many generations a state of war has been unknown within the British Isles, have all encouraged the banking habit to an unprecedented degree, so that to all appearance the hoarding habit is entirely eradicated. All over the Continent of Europe the reverse is the case; in almost every European country there are people living who have experience of war within their country's borders; and every crisis in the foreign relations of one state with another is immediately reflected in the books of the banks as the result of hoarding on an indefinite scale. Prudent banking cannot neglect to make special provision against difficulty at such times in the shape of a relatively large Gold Reserve, whereas in this country the very prevalence of the cheque system is a symptom of the absence of any such tendency to hoard on a large scale, and hoarding as such is a danger which does not enter into the calculations of any banker.

15. Now the effect of hoarding in a country where legal tender notes are mainly used is that, instead of being deposited at banks large sums are retained by individuals in the form of such legal tender notes, and in order to provide for keeping such notes convertible, banks of issue are compelled either by statute or by their own rules or habits to increase their holdings of gold in reserve proportionately. A general dearth of liquid resources and a danger of a currency famine ensues. At such a moment it is of great importance that the central banking institution of a country should be willing to support any concern which is intrinsically sound by granting liberal credit during temporary stress, and this naturally involves a heavy strain on the reserves of the bank, which is reflected, not necessarily so much in an actual decrease in the amount of gold, as in a fall in the ratio between gold in reserve and notes in circulation.

16. It is permissible to believe that undue importance is attached to the dangers of such a situation, seeing that the hoarded notes when they are eventually released will not to any considerable extent be presented for encashment in specie, but will simply be redeposited with the banks from which they have been withdrawn or withheld, and the excessive amounts of notes in the hands of the public are thus only nominally in active circulation, and do not really constitute any large addition to the probable demands on

the central Gold Reserves or involve much risk of inflation or of a depreciation of the currency. So long as they are hoarded indeed there is no inflation. The danger arises when the hoards are let loose, and some precaution is undoubtedly needed to provide against this danger and to secure the rapid withdrawal of notes at this moment, and a prior increase in the Gold Reserve is, no doubt, effective for this end. Even so, it is still open to question whether the precautions taken are not excessive.

17. But, however this may be, the fear of hoarding is undoubtedly one of the reasons which accounts for the relatively large Gold Reserves of countries other than Great Britain, and wherever the ratio of banking reserves to liabilities is dependent in any way on statutory regulation, the banks have no option but to provide against hoarding conditions by keeping large Gold Reserves.

18. Finally our position as a lending nation gives us a power of attracting gold from abroad whenever we require it such as no other country, with the possible exception of France, can command. This is a further justification for the relative smallness of our Gold Reserves, while the enormous increase in our investments abroad in recent years justifies the relative smallness of the additions we have made to those reserves during that period. Moreover, the fact that London is the greatest free market for gold in the world and the clearing house of the world's trade, and as a money market is rivalled, if at all, only by Paris, enables London very quickly to replenish her Gold Reserves. It is true that the freedom of her market for gold makes London more liable to demands for gold for export than, *e.g.*, Paris, but this is far more than counterbalanced by the advantage which the free gold market ensures in obtaining and retaining gold.

19. It may be urged at this point that these last arguments are of little force in justifying the great disparity between the holdings of gold in England and France respectively, seeing that as a creditor nation and in importance as a money market, France is at any rate not far behind this country. It must be conceded at once that the disparity is very striking, and the case of France, therefore, perhaps deserves some special attention. The legal tender note system prevails in France, and on this ground some disparity in the size of the Gold Reserves here and in France is explicable. French people again have not quite grown out of the hoarding habit. But on the other hand, the ratio of gold reserve to notes in circulation is not in France subject to any legislative restriction, and the directorate of the Bank of France has practically a free hand in the matter, its notes being issued against the general assets of the bank in such proportion as the directors think fit and the limit on total circulation which is fixed by statute from time to time being always placed at a figure which is considerably in excess of any probable demand. If the hoarding habit is not as dangerous as is generally believed, according to the view put forward in this memorandum, why should the Bank of France keep a very high Gold Reserve for fear of hoarding? Is it not clear that, compared

with the Gold Reserves of France, our own Gold Reserves are inadequate?

20. I think that, however much stress is laid on the value of our cheque system in economising gold and whatever allowance be made for the special reserve needed for maintaining the circulation as unlimited legal tender of the French five-franc piece—this coin is in practice equivalent to an inconvertible note printed on silver,—it is undoubtedly true that the disparity between the two Gold Reserves is partly attributable to the deliberate policy of the Bank of France, and that, if that policy was adopted here, the British Gold Reserves would need to be very considerably increased.

21. No doubt the size of the French Gold Reserves has a commercial value in steadying the bank rate (a point to be discussed later) and a national value as a precaution against the contingency of an European war. But it is far from impossible that a smaller reserve would secure these ends with equal success and that the economic waste involved in keeping so large an amount of barren metal is too heavy a price to pay for these advantages.

22. It is undeniable that the Gold Reserves are often excessive in some other countries where the proportion of cash to liabilities or of gold to notes (when legal tender notes are largely used) is regulated by statute. The most striking case is that of the United States of America where in spite of a colossal Gold Reserve, and, although cheques have a very considerable vogue, the country went through a terrible financial crisis in 1907 due to shortage of legal tender. It is not suggested that the crisis was caused by the size of the Gold Reserves, but that it could have been met successfully with very much smaller reserves had the banking and currency system been a rational one, the moral being that the system is at least as important as the size of the Gold Reserves. The statutory regulations under which American banks work thus make comparison between the Gold Reserves of the United States of America and of this country quite valueless.

(ii) *Comparison with former periods.*

23. What has been said in regard to comparisons with foreign countries is enough to show the uselessness for proving inadequacy of comparisons between the relative increase of Gold Reserves and commercial and banking activities in this country during the last few decades. It will suffice here to give one illustration of the operation of the cheque system in husbanding the central Gold Reserve of the Bank of England, and, though this illustration belongs to a much earlier period, it is representative of less striking but equally active changes which are continually working in the same direction. About the year 1854 the London Clearing House was remodelled, with the result that all the daily settlements between the big banks, which had previously been effected by means of Bank of England notes, were thenceforth made by cheques drawn on the accounts of the banks at the Bank of England.

By this means something not far short of 1,000,000*l.* worth of banknotes were released and the immediate effect of the change was equivalent to the addition of an equal amount to the real reserve of the Bank against special demands.

III.—Are our Gold Reserves Inadequate?

24. Instead of proceeding to deal on argumentative lines with the remaining parts of the case of the advocates of increased Gold Reserves, which contain complaints of the operation of the bank rate and of the methods and capacity of the Bank of England in conserving the Gold Reserves, it is perhaps preferable to approach the question of the adequacy of the Gold Reserves from a more detached standpoint. In order to determine this question, it is necessary to consider—

(*a*) The possible causes which may deplete the Gold Reserves and

(*b*) The means available for meeting such depletion and the time required for making these means effective.

(a) *The possible causes which may deplete the Gold Reserves.*

25. The Gold Reserves may be depleted either by increased demands for legal tender currency for internal use or by demands for gold for export. In either case the demand may be either normal or abnormal.

Internal Demands for Gold.

26. Well-ascertained seasonal demands for gold for internal purposes, such as occur at holiday times, &c., do not, strictly speaking, deplete the real reserve against emergencies. They are, however, of importance if an abnormal demand happens to coincide with a seasonal demand.

27. Apart from seasonal demands, a normal demand for additional legal tender arises whenever there is an expansion of trade, additional cash being required for payment of wages, &c. In this country, owing to the inelasticity of the fiduciary portion of the note issue, such a demand for additional legal tender can only be satisfied by an outflow of gold from the central reserves, or by the attraction of gold from abroad. In practice the latter means of supplying a demand operates only through the channel of the central reserves.

But here again it must be remembered that the cheque system operates to confine such normal demands within narrow limits, the effect of a period of expanding trade being much more marked in the figures of the clearing-house returns than in the demand for gold coin. Still provision for some strengthening of the Gold Reserves is a necessary accompaniment of expanding trade.

28. An abnormal internal demand for additional legal tender arises only at a time of financial crisis and collapsing credit. A general and enduring collapse of credit (which would mean a revival of hoarding and is scarcely thinkable) would involve a demand for legal tender so enormous as to make any conceivable Gold Reserve altogether inadequate. A reserve in such circumstances would be a mere drop in the ocean, and recourse to a fiduciary note issue, *i.e.*, an effective suspension of the Bank Charter Act, would be inevitable, and would probably require to be followed up by the issue of a forced currency of legal tender notes. The whole credit system of this country is based on the assumption that credit itself will not completely collapse, and it is useless to think of reconsidering this premiss.

29. A temporary collapse of credit due to over-trading or over-speculation is the contingency against which the Gold Reserves are really required, and the question of the adequacy of those reserves, so far as internal demands are concerned, is simply whether they are sufficient to make such an emergency rare and to prevent it from developing into a complete collapse when it arrives. As a matter of history there has been only one occasion (1857) since the passing of the Bank Charter Act of 1844 on which the Government's undertaking to suspend the Act, or the knowledge that this emergency method of relieving the situation was available as a last resort, has not been enough to restore sufficient confidence and prevent an actual breach of the law as it stands. In other words on only one occasion has the Bank of England's Gold Reserve proved actually insufficient to meet demands on it at times of maximum stress. Even in 1857 the fiduciary notes issued in excess of the legal limit did not exceed 1,000,000*l.* in value on any one date, and the period of actual excess issues lasted less than a fortnight.

30. In the past then our Gold Reserves have never proved entirely inadequate. At the present date our position as a creditor of other nations is so strong that a temporary collapse of credit at home, so far from leading to an efflux of gold, would give rise to a calling in of foreign loans and a consequent influx of gold from abroad. It is therefore highly probable that any such abnormal internal demand will be met without absolutely exhausting the existing gold reserves on the existing statutory basis. Even if the worst happened and our means of securing gold from abroad proved to be too slow in effecting this purpose—and as will be shown presently this is contrary to all reasonable probability—such a demand can be met by a temporary excess issue of legal tender notes against security, a temporary suspension of the Bank Charter Act as in 1857, and no likelihood exists of a suspension of cash payments.

31. As the law now stands suspension of the Bank Charter Act assumes the appearance of an heroic extra-statutory expedient dictated by an appalling and overwhelming danger. It may be well that the adoption of this expedient should be protected against abuse by such restrictions—this must be discussed later—but, apart from the historical one, there is no particular reason why

suspension of the Bank Charter Act in emergencies is not regulated by statute in advance, in which case it would be regarded as a normal and natural means of meeting a situation, which, though abnormal in the sense that it is happily rare, is, on the other hand, normal in the sense that its recurrence from time to time surprises nobody. Most foreign countries which have copied or adapted the British example have not imitated this particular feature of our system, but have made statutory provision in advance for the application of special remedies in similar crises.

Demands for Gold for Export.

32. Normal demands for gold for export occur every autumn, and the resulting hiatus has to be filled in the same way as that caused by normal internal demands. In either case our unrivalled power of attracting gold from abroad is unquestionably sufficient, and the real point of any complaints as to the inadequacy of our reserves is not that they are actually inadequate, but the idea that the means adopted for strengthening and preserving them, viz., the raising of the Bank rate, could be more evenly and more sparingly applied if the reserves were larger.

33. Abnormal demands for gold for export result from financial crises in other countries. Here, as in the case of internal demands, whatever the amount of our Gold Reserves, we must in the long run rely on the power to attract gold from elsewhere. No one questions that we have power ultimately to attract an ample supply, and the important question is whether time is available. This question will be more conveniently discussed under the next head.

(b) *The means available for making good depletion in the Gold Reserves and the time required for making these means effective.*

34. Gold required to make good a depletion in the reserves must be obtained either direct from the mines or from existing stocks in other countries. London, as the great free market for gold, is the centre to which most of the world's gold production is shipped. Many mines, including those of India, West Africa, and most important South Africa, send their raw gold to London to be refined, so that this gold necessarily passes through the London market. On arrival here the gold is sold to the highest bidder. Any that remains finds its way to the Bank of England at the fixed price of 3*l.* 17*s.* 9*d.* an ounce. If, therefore the Bank of England is specially anxious to increase its Gold Reserve it can always compete in the market with other buyers for the new gold. This involves offering more than 3*l.* 17*s.* 9*d.* an ounce for it. Bankers and merchants constantly grumble because the Bank does not adopt this course more frequently, but the Bank's reluctance to do so is as natural as is the desire of the bankers and merchants that it should be

done, for the result is to throw the whole cost of strengthening the reserves on the Bank of England and to avoid any raising of the rate of discount or disturbance to the money market and to trade. It is equivalent, in fact, to the sale by the Bank of England of exchange on the foreign country to which the gold would have gone at a rate of exchange somewhat less favourable than the ruling rate of the day. The main use of this expedient is in cases where the foreign demand for gold is very temporary and can be thwarted by this means, but in the nature of things this expedient can be applied successfully only to a very limited extent, and it is therefore of small importance.

35. The normal method by which gold is obtained is the raising of the bank rate. A rise in the rate of discount operates (i) to check the demand for credit in this country and thereby the demand for legal tender, and (ii) to increase the remuneration of capital employed in London and so to attract surplus funds from employment elsewhere. Each of these results has a tendency to move the foreign exchanges in London's favour. The second of them works very quickly if only because of the profitable arbitrage business which a high rate in London and a lower rate elsewhere makes possible pending the adjustment of the exchange rates. The exchanges accordingly begin to move towards the point at which it becomes advantageous to make remittances to London by means of gold. Once the import specie point is actually reached, gold begins to come in (mainly in the form of sovereigns or to a lesser extent other gold coins) from the central reserves of other countries, and before that point is reached, it usually becomes unprofitable for other countries to purchase for export the new gold coming to London from South Africa, &c., and the Bank of England is thus enabled to secure a large share of the weekly arrivals.

It is true that most foreign countries place such restrictions on the outflow of gold that the specie point may be exceeded without gold flowing to London, *i.e.*, they prefer to let their internal currency go to a discount. And to a certain extent they may even continue to compete for the new gold in London regardless of the rate of exchange and the heavy cost to themselves. But as shown later, their interests will usually prevent them from taking such action if London's need is urgent.

36. The annual interest on the enormous sums invested by this country abroad is largely paid for in normal times by the export to this country of local products of the countries where the money is invested, but even so there remains a very large surplus still owing which would have to be remitted to this country in cash if it were not for the fresh investments of British capital which are made abroad year by year to assist and stimulate the development of other lands. Thus by merely checking the rate of fresh investment abroad, the people of this country can, at some sacrifice no doubt, but without serious inconvenience, at once draw to an extent that may be regarded as for present purposes absolutely sufficient on the gold resources of such places.

The regulation of the rate of discount provides, therefore, an extremely effective lever for attracting gold to replenish a depleted reserve here.

37. Furthermore one of the most noticeable phenomena of the currency history of the present century has been the rapid rate at which Gold Reserves have been accumulated by countries which formerly had little or no gold. The Argentine, Brazil, India, the Straits Settlements, have all built up special funds to secure the stability of the exchange value of their local currencies while Chile and other countries are on the point of following suit. Twenty years ago a temporary withdrawal of British financial support from one of such countries was reflected almost entirely in a sudden drop in the exchange, so that the only adjustment possible occurred without the passing of metal or at least of any appreciable quantity of metal. To-day the exchanges in these countries move only within or around the comparatively narrow limits of the two specie points, and adjustment can always be effected by the passing of gold out of the local reserve. Indeed this is the object for which the reserves exist. By their means India, Brazil, &c., have gained the enormous advantage of a stable exchange, while the United Kingdom has been enabled to invest ever increasing amounts in the development of these countries with full confidence that the funds so invested will not, as in former days, be locked up in times of need at home, but that a sufficient amount of liquid assets convertible without ruinous sacrifice into sterling money will be available in this country at a pinch.

38. Here then in the conversion funds of the South American Republics, and the Gold Standard Reserves of India, the Straits Settlements, &c., are new stores of gold which exist for the direct purpose of being available at times of need for export to the older monetary centres of the world. The successful efforts made by these countries are often held up to the admiration of the people of the United Kingdom as an example of what we ought to have been doing for our own Gold Reserves. But (apart from the fact that the special demands of these countries have naturally been reflected in a reduction of the surplus available for building up Gold Reserves here), it is quite evident that the creation of these new reserves has greatly strengthened the position of London's reserves. For good and sufficient reasons in their own interests, these countries have, in fact, relieved London's Gold Reserves of part of their former burden, and *pro tanto*, these new reserves take the place of corresponding additions to our reserves and furnish a strong presumption that our present reserves are adequate, seeing that they have increased, if but slightly, above the figures of twenty years ago when none of these new external reserves existed at all.

39. Our means of attracting gold have been shown to be enormously powerful. It remains to consider whether there is any reasonable doubt that they can be made effective within the interval required to prevent a drain of gold whether for internal or external purposes from resulting in a collapse.

In the case of normal demands, there is little doubt that ample time will always be available. The point for consideration is whether the means used to replenish the reserves will operate quickly enough to meet either an exceptionally strong normal demand which threatens to become abnormal, or to stem the tide of an abnormal demand when it comes.

40. The interval within which gold can be attracted from abroad depends ultimately on physical conditions, such as the time required to ship gold from Berlin, Rio, New York, Cape Town to London. Thus the increased rapidity of transit and improved communications generally provide an additional justification of the slow growth of our reserves in the last few decades. In times of peace, an internal crisis, due to over-investment or over-trading, ought to be capable of being dealt with very quickly. Gold arrives in considerable parcels from South Africa weekly, and the whole of this could readily be secured by the Bank of England. In addition, although it is part of the hypothesis that prudence has been insufficiently exercised, commitments abroad can always be rapidly reduced, and gold made to flow in from the reserves of other countries. It is difficult, therefore, to believe that replenishment from these two sources will not be rapid enough to keep the gold in the issue department of the Bank from falling below the legal limit.

41. It is, no doubt, possible that the rate of new gold production may fall off suddenly, and probable that it will not continue at the high figures of the last decade. The ultimate effects of such changes are too controversial to discuss here, even if space permitted. It is enough to assume the existing conditions, so long as they exist, remembering that a definite slowing down of the rate of new production would naturally permit of gradual adjustment, while a sudden stoppage of the mines, though it might conceivably hasten the arrival of a crisis, could hardly coincide with the moment of crisis, and arrangements would have been made for speeding up the attraction of gold from elsewhere, if it were known that no gold was coming from South Africa. In any case the actual rate at which gold is produced is not in itself vastly important from the point of view of Gold Reserves.

42. Again, foreign countries are too much interested in the stability of the London money market to regard a threatened collapse with equanimity. At the time of the Baring crisis of 1890 the Bank of France actually lent the Bank of England three million sovereigns. In the American crisis of 1907 (which is now the classic instance of a demand for gold for export) the Bank of England did not respond to tentative suggestions made by the Bank of France that similar assistance should be offered. But this country secured a considerable amount of gold from Paris, and this could not have happened without the goodwill of the Bank of France, which can apply very effective checks on the export of gold when it desires to do so. Now an internal crisis, with London as the storm-centre, would be world-wide in its effects, but the surest way in which other countries such as France could protect themselves would be by supporting London, just as London by maintaining a free market for gold is always supporting the Gold Reserves of all other countries.

43. The action of France in 1890 and 1907 was not purely philanthropic, and it is only by co-operation, whether between rival bankers in London or rival nations all over the world, that the modern system of credit can be sustained at all. When, therefore, it is urged that it is derogatory to this country's dignity, and, indeed, dangerous in view of possible unfriendliness, that we should be dependent on French assistance, it may be answered that this is the natural state of things wherever a crisis occurs. Moreover, French assistance, even in 1890, was probably not essential to prevent a complete collapse, as is shown by the contrast of 1866, when London had great difficulty in making a 10 per cent. Bank rate effective in securing gold, although the Paris rate was only 6 per cent. What French assistance in 1890 did was to enable the crisis to be promptly mastered, to the great relief of Paris. The same conditions are bound to hold good at the next internal crisis, so long, at least, as peace prevails, since even a temporary collapse of London as a free market for gold would dislocate the machinery of all the money markets of the world.

44. It is perhaps permissible to mention, while considering the question of the interval required for measures for the attraction of gold from other countries' reserves to become effective, that, in her own interests, India, as also other countries, keeps much of her gold reserve in London, entirely separate from the Bank of England's Gold Reserves, just because when a crisis occurs, whether in India reacting on London, or in London reacting on India, the gold will be needed in London. Physical questions of transit are, therefore, entirely eliminated in these cases. This is no doubt an argument which must be cautiously advanced, for political reasons, particularly in regard to India, but while the justification for the location of India's Gold Standard Reserve in London is that it is to India's advantage to keep it there, the presence of that gold in London instead of in India might in given circumstances be of immense value to this country.

45. Abnormal demands for gold for export differ little from abnormal internal demands from the point of view of the interval available. The position of London should, on the whole, be slightly stronger when the demand is for export. The problem is in the first instance to prevent the development of an internal crisis whereas an abnormal demand at home implies the actual presence of critical conditions amongst us. It may be said generally that it is on the whole always easier to prevent or check the drain of gold abroad than to prevent or check the drain of gold into internal channels. Moreover when the demand is for export, the raising of the bank rate can be made so to influence foreign exchanges that gold may flow from, say Buenos Aires to New York as well as to London, whereas an internal demand can only be satisfied by shipment to London.

46. Here also the creation of the new Gold Reserves already mentioned and the enlargement of the gold reserves of some of the older European countries are obviously of assistance to London, the stronger position abroad

reducing the weight of London's burden, so that from this point of view so far from being a reason for increasing our reserves the efforts of other countries might be held to justify their reduction.

IV.—Effect of War on our Gold Reserves.

47. Something should perhaps be said at this point as to the possible position as regards the Gold Reserves in the case of a first-class European war in which this country was a participant. It is often said that suspensions of cash payments would be an inevitable result, unless our Gold Reserves are greatly strengthened. The expectation of a suspension of cash payments is probably derived from knowledge of the fact that during and after the Napoleonic wars cash payments were so suspended for a long period. But the Crimean War did not involve suspension and there is no strong ground for believing that such a result is inevitable to-day. The first effect of a war is naturally to increase, not to decrease, the amount of the Gold Reserves of the country engaged in war, gold being attracted by the high rate of discount and as a result of preparations for a big Government loan to finance the war.

48. It is of course impossible clearly to forecast what would be the effect of a general European war in which most of the continental countries as well as Great Britain were engaged, leaving only New York (assuming the neutrality of the United States of America) among the big money markets of the world available from which gold could be attracted to the seats of war. A general collapse of credit is far from inconceivable in such circumstances: but in that case no Gold Reserve, not even that of the Bank of France, would suffice to prevent immediate suspension of cash payments. It is, however, not less probable that our position as a creditor nation would suffice to make emergency measures unnecessary and that at worst an extension of the fiduciary issue of notes would be enough to meet our needs. In the absence of actual invasion of the country, the natural check on the export of gold which would result both from the height of the discount rate and the risk of capture run by ships containing specie would make the problem mainly one of meeting excess internal demands. Mobilisation would naturally involve some considerable increase in internal legal tender requirements, especially at first, and if it came during the holiday season of the late summer. But even in the latter case the reduced autumn demand for export would help to counterbalance this special cause of outflow. So long therefore as credit held, the abnormal demands should not be unmanageable. It is therefore quite reasonable to hope that the country would get through the first and, from the money market point of view, the most dangerous stages of the war without exhausting the Gold Reserves.

49. Finally, the disadvantages of a forced currency in so rich a country as this are often exaggerated. In normal times the acceptability of "banker's money" rests on the belief that debts due in gold can be satisfied in gold to

the full extent of actual requirements for gold. It is only one step further for people to be compelled by law to accept legal tender notes at a time when it is known that, though gold is not immediately forthcoming, such notes rest on sufficient valuable assets capable of being turned into gold at some future time when normal conditions are restored. Gold, after all, is not absolutely indispensable, and even a forced paper currency would provide the country with a very fairly workable temporary medium of exchange; for in the last resort it is not a coin with an intrinsic value equal to its face value that people need, even for foreign commerce, but a token which gives a command over commodities such as is now given by gold. The real danger is that the currency will be depreciated and that the Treasury would not be strong enough to insist on the measures needed to prevent this and restore specie payments after the war.

50. A big European war in which Great Britain stood aside might possibly prove in the end no less troublesome to our Gold Reserves, owing to the strong demand for export of gold entailed, and the actual size of those reserves is perhaps more important in such a case than if we were actually at war. In the latter case the question is rather whether any reserve, however large, would be large enough, and little would be gained by increasing our existing reserves if they are sufficient for all other contingencies but this. The former case would be a special form of abnormal demand for export of gold. If, however, the arguments already set out to prove that our reserves are adequate in time of peace to meet all demands for export are sound, there does not appear to be any ground for holding that this special form of demand would be too much for them.

51. The conclusion seems to be that, regarded as a preparation for war, our Gold Reserves are either adequate in amount or else are incapable of being raised to a figure which would make them any more adequate.

V.—The Bank Rate.

52. We can now turn back to the argument of advocates of increased Gold Reserves which finds fault with the frequent fluctuations of the Bank rate and urges that larger reserves would serve to steady it. In regard to the discount rate there is some slight conflict of interests between the banker and the merchant. The banker would perhaps sleep more comfortably in his bed if (at someone else's cost) the level of the Gold Reserves were permanently raised; but he has little desire to effect a diminution in the range and frequency of the Bank rate's fluctuations. On the whole he prefers a fairly high average Bank rate, and he certainly is not prepared to go to expense in increasing the Gold Reserves for the sake of reducing the average rate. What he really wants is a higher average of Gold Reserves which will give him a greater sense of security, and to let everything else go on much as at present.

53. The merchant, on the other hand, believes himself to have a real

interest in obtaining a more stable Bank rate. He is moved to rapturous envy by the straightness of the line in the statistical charts which indicates the French bank rate when he compares it with the jagged line showing that of the Bank of England. At the same time the merchant, no doubt, thinks that with larger gold reserves he will get a lower average Bank rate as well as a more stable one, again judging from French conditions during the last decade; and he would be willing with some cheerfulness to endure a slight increase in the average discount rate for a year or two, if it were definitely due to concerted action to raise the level of the reserves, and nothing was done meanwhile to throw doubt on his belief that the final result would be to give him for the future a stable rate, averaging on the whole rather less than at present.

54. When all these hopes and expectations are examined more closely, it becomes very doubtful whether there is much substance in them. It is curiously difficult for mankind generally when dealing with or thinking about a reserve of any kind to remember that it is a reserve. Once a reserve is set aside, any attempt to use it is likely to be stigmatised as "tampering with the reserve." This is more than ever true in regard to gold reserves. Brazil at the moment supplies a good illustration. Having accumulated a sum of about 20,000,000*l.* in gold in the Caixa da Conversão to secure stability of exchange, Brazil was so loth to use it that not long ago the exchange was allowed to fall considerably below specie point and the country was made to endure great inconvenience due to a dearth of legal tender, mainly to prevent the gold from being depleted; and since the gold has been issued more freely for the precise object for which it was intended, people interested in Brazilian securities have been alarmed by sensational paragraphs in the financial press drawing attention to the dangerous depletion of Brazil's reserve of gold.

55. Now both the banker and the merchant, when they talk of increasing the Gold Reserves of this country, mean by that phrase a permanent raising of the average to a higher level. Once the higher level has become habitual to them, both bankers and the City generally will at once become nervous whenever the reserves show signs of falling below the new level, and steps will be taken to conserve them. The comparative steadiness of the French rate is only in part due to the size of the gold reserves; it is possible only because Paris is not a free market for gold and the Bank of France has other means than a raising of the discount rate by which to check the export of specie. The application of these means must involve nearly as serious a curtailment of credit as does a rise in the discount rate in London. While, therefore, greater steadiness of the Bank rate would certainly assist the British merchant in making necessary calculations as to margins of profit, he envies French conditions only because he fails to see the other side of the picture, and he would strongly resent the increased and, as he would say, arbitrary restrictions on credit which would necessarily have to be applied to take the place of the automatic action of a raised Bank rate.

56. Moreover, it is very frequently the case that the discount rate is high because profits are high and the merchant can afford to pay that rate for bonâ fide business purposes. "It is better to stop a runaway horse by heading him up a hill than by running into a stone wall." The merchant, at any rate, would greatly prefer to be allowed to decide for himself whether he would pay the rate demanded or restrict his business rather than be compelled by his bank to adopt the latter alternative. His present grievance against the discount rate is really a grievance against an economic law. He thinks it hard that the bank should step in and take away a bit of his profit just when he thought he had done really well, but the bank's action is dictated not by covetousness but by prudence and recognition of the fact that high profits are tempting people out of their depth, and that inflation will result unless the bank intervenes. It may, therefore, be regarded as certain that, to however large a total the average level of the reserve be raised, the Bank rate would have to be moved up and down fairly frequently to maintain that average, and the average Bank rate would not be lessened, and that a successful approximation to French stability in the matter of discount rates is not compatible with the retention of London's position as a free market for gold.

57. All that the merchant could really hope for from the increased reserves would be that the changes in the discount rate might be a little more gradual, the range remaining as at present. This result would be a consequence of the more comfortable night's sleep which bankers would have gained from the increase. But very much the same result could be obtained without any increase in the permanent level of the reserves, if preparations were made a little earlier each year against the autumn drain, and the Bank rate raised in anticipation of the demand before its effects become seriously felt, so as to avoid a sudden and steep rise in the rate when depletion actually takes place. This means nothing more than a temporary strengthening of reserves against seasonal demands with a view to allowing them to be depleted more readily and involves none of the cost attaching to a permanent raising of the level. The difficulty in the way of this course of action at present is probably the uncertainty of the Bank of England whether it could carry the other banks and the market with it and make a higher rate effective at an earlier period than according to present practice. This question leads naturally to the next point, the complaints sometimes heard as to the Bank of England's management of the machinery which controls the Gold Reserves.

VI.—The Bank of England's Position as Guardian of the Gold Reserve.

58. The Bank Charter Act of 1844 had the effect of increasing the importance of the Bank of England as the central banking institution of the country and in giving it a practical monopoly of note issue in England and Wales strengthened its position as guardian of the only important Gold Reserve in

the British Isles. As other banks grew in importance the Bank of England became more and more what it is to-day, the bankers' bank. The few branches which it possessed in the provinces in earlier years have lost in importance and some of them have been closed, the Portsmouth Branch being the latest among them to be extinguished.

59. Up till the 80's of last century the Bank's sway in the London money market was held undisputed, and it was able effectively to exercise the sole responsibility for watching over the country's Gold Reserves. The other big banks held, and hold, their reserves either in the form of Bank of England notes or, more largely, in the form of cash deposited at the Bank of England. The growth of the London Clearing House and the extension of the Clearing House system to the provinces tended in the same direction, because it became an essential condition of membership of the London Clearing House that a balance should be kept at the Bank of England by means of which debits and credits at the daily clearance could be adjusted. For a long time, therefore, the Bank of England, intimately related to the chief banks in London and through them to the country banks, and sufficiently their master to compel their attention to its wishes, had no difficulty in making the Bank rate effective, and the open market rate of discount responded unquestioningly to any move in the Bank rate or any other indication of the wishes of the autocratic Old Lady of Threadneedle Street.

60. From the 80's onwards this supremacy has been more and more challenged. The large London banks, which have not only absorbed the majority of the older private and provincial banks, but have constantly tended to amalgamate between themselves, as for example the London and County with the London and Westminster Bank, now somewhat overshadow the central Bank.* To-day the total of the deposits of other banks with the Bank of England probably approaches in the aggregate or even exceeds the total of that bank's Gold Reserve. The Bank of England is compelled therefore to show more deference to the wishes of the great banks and must rely on their ready co-operation to make the Bank rate effective. Mutual assistance and consultation between the big banks and the Bank of England have become more imperatively necessary, and the centre of gravity has shifted to some extent from the Bank parlour to the Committee of the Clearing House as representing an alliance of all the most important banks.

61. This gradual change has moreover led to a certain amount of friction.

* *C.f.*—Mr. Cole's evidence on behalf of the Bank of England before the Royal Commission on Indian Finance and Currency, questions 3348–3352, and 3372–3 [Cd. 7069 of 1913] in which objection was taken to the practice of the India Office in lending out its London balance in the City, on the ground that loans are made regardless of the interests or wishes of the Bank of England in the matter of the Gold Reserve. This objection has been largely met by the undertaking recently entered into by the India Office to keep a minimum proportion of its balance (one-fifth or one-sixth, according to amount) with the Bank of England free of interest. This arrangement is doubtless satisfactory for the Bank and for this country, but is open to objection from India's point of view, especially as no such restrictions are placed on the activities in the matter of lending of foreign Governments many of which lend out balances in a similar way.

The directorates of the big banks, perhaps not unnaturally, are inclined to be very critical of the Court of Directors at the Bank of England, and are no longer willing to credit that court with the possession of all the financial wisdom of the City, urging that specialisation and the hurry of modern commercial life make it difficult to keep the Bank Court thoroughly representative and up to date. The big banks tend therefore to resent anything like dictation from the Bank of England. Meanwhile the Bank of England's directors and shareholders look with natural jealousy on the large dividends paid by other banks as compared with the 9 per cent. or 10 per cent. which is all that they themselves can earn so long as they pay due regard to the responsibilities of the Bank's position as the bank of the Government and the guardian of the country's credit, responsibilities which fortune thrust upon them in days when they had no rivals.

62. In these circumstances the power of the Bank of England to make the Bank rate effective is much less than it was up to some 30 years ago. Yet the responsibility remains and ostensibly no change has occurred. Several significant features show the reality of change. The secret Committee of Bankers under Lord St. Aldwyn's chairmanship to consider the whole question of the Gold Reserve, the special gold reserves which the big banks are said to be creating for themselves, and the fact that syndicates of banks come into existence when special measures are required for supporting a firm which has got into temporary difficulties, whereas in old days the Bank of England would have taken on such a task alone, are all symptoms of the shifting in the centre of gravity. But so far no practical steps have been taken to readjust the situation on a considered basis.

63. It would, no doubt, be a mistake to over-estimate the dangers and difficulties of the situation, but there is perhaps ground for thinking that the merchant's interests do suffer to a small extent thereby. It is fairly clear that the large banks have got off cheaply hitherto in regard to the cost of maintaining the Gold Reserves. The Bank of England cannot be expected to endanger its modest dividends by heroic measures, and the merchant, who cannot escape paying whatever rate of discount the Bank of England, the big banks and the money market between them may make effective, will provide his share of the burden without special provision. The big banks, on the other hand, while reaping a large share of the profits, are under no definite obligation to assist in paying their share of the cost of maintaining the reserve. Self-interest and the obvious need for co-operation may prevent them from flagrant abuse of their power and good fortune, and full credit must be given them for the absence of any serious grounds of complaint against them. But when in small things their interests conflict with those of the merchant, there can be little doubt that the Bank of England is likely to pay somewhat more attention to them and somewhat less attention to the general interests of the merchant than would otherwise be the case. As already suggested, this may be the reason why efforts have not been made to

secure a more gradual raising of the rate in preparation for the autumn drain, and the habit of window-dressing for balance sheet purposes, which would be purely childish if it did not also involve some slight but real inconvenience to the merchant owing to the temporary tightening of the market which results may be instanced as a further symptom of the undue preponderance of these banks in the scale.

64. It is not impossible that the agitation for increased reserves is largely the result of a recognition of these unsatisfactory features in the present situation, and that, while mistaken as to the need for such increase, the movement may lead to a clearer perception of the seat of the trouble, and so to the application of an effective remedy. Sir E. Holden has actually included in his programme several proposals which would assist to this end, such as statutory definition of the obligations of big banks in the matter of gold reserves and publication by all banks, both British and foreign, which accept deposits in this country, of fuller accounts, showing, in particular, the real amount of the cash reserves. As already stated, only the London County and Westminster Bank now publishes figures of its average daily cash holdings, though the London City and Midland Bank, of which Sir E. Holden is chairman, has promised some further figures in December 1914 with the object of inducing other banks to follow suit; but, even where window-dressing does not vitiate the available figures, they do not help very much. The creation of special gold reserves by these banks might prove really valuable if it were made a step towards the handing of them over to the Bank of England on agreed terms and subject to some well-considered scheme of a central control in which the big banks would, for the first time, secure a recognised voice. But for the moment these reserves are equally capable of being used to hinder the policy of the Bank of England, and tend only to intensify the divergence between the seat of responsibility and the seat of power.

65. It is not proposed here to develop this subject further or to attempt to work out a scheme for restoring a perfectly effective central control. There is no reason to suppose that the big banks are anxious to usurp the functions and with them the responsibilities of the Bank of England: they are too well aware of their existing advantages. Quite possibly, therefore, some very slight modification of existing conditions will suffice, if once the big banks recognise, as they seem to be doing, the necessity for regularising and defining their practical participation in the responsibility. The essential point is that the control should be single and central, and that the responsible authority should have adequate powers of effective action.

VII.—Emergency Measures.

66. If this question, which seems ripe for settlement quite apart from any question of an increase in the aggregate reserves, should involve the inter-

vention of Government or require legislation, the further question of a revision of the Bank Charter Act will probably arise again. As shown above, suspension of the Act is the recognised safety-valve in an emergency, but instead of being automatic it requires a Deus ex machina to open it. Many people hold that this condition of things is right and desirable. It is certainly difficult to substitute a good automatic safety valve. The simple German method of a tax on excess fiduciary issues of notes beyond a given maximum has the disadvantage of being too rigid. The rate of tax is fixed, but the rate of discount at which an emergency currency becomes desirable is one which varies widely according to circumstances: 6 per cent. might be famine rate in one crisis, while 10 per cent. might not be excessive for a time in another. This difficulty could, no doubt, be got over by leaving the rate of tax to be settled *ad hoc* by the Chancellor of the Exchequer on each occasion. But this might not be acceptable to the City, and its only advantage over present methods is that, though the Deus ex machina would still be called in, he would not be influenced (for good or ill) by the knowledge that a subsequent statute of indemnity must be obtained from Parliament.

67. The late Lord Goschen's scheme for 1*l.* notes had many points in its favour, but was wrecked on the rock of popular prejudice in favour of gold coins. It would have secured some economy of gold by centralising the store of gold in the country and thus made available for emergencies some part of the gold now in the pockets of the people where it is of small value when a demand arises for export. Possibly the country would accept some such solution if it were confined by statute to emergencies, but this involves the disadvantage that the emergency currency would not be, as it ought to be, indistinguishable from the currency in use in normal times.

68. Sir E. Holden has suggested (speech on March 5th, 1914, at the annual general meeting of the London City and Midland Bank) that the joint stock banks (and presumably all banks receiving deposits in this country) should be compelled to keep 6 per cent. of their liabilities in gold, showing the figures in their balance sheets, and that an amendment to the Act of 1844 should empower them, in the case of a breakdown in credit, to send into the Issue Department of the Bank of England 20,000,000 sovereigns and 40,000,000*l.* worth of bills of exchange and take out in exchange 60,000,000*l.* of bank notes. He further suggested that the Government should, by way of a gold reserve against the Savings Banks deposits, pay off their debt of 11,000,000*l.* to the Bank of England, gold being accumulated in its place.

69. Apart from the question, to be discussed later, how far, if at all, the Government should contribute to the cost of keeping gold reserves, the latter suggestion would extinguish the Bank's charter (unless fresh legislation were passed), and would cost the Bank $2\frac{1}{2}$ per cent. on the whole 11,000,000*l.*, and would cause the Government to lose the difference between the redemption of Consols at 75 instead of at par, without in itself strengthening the Gold Reserves in any way. For the danger to be faced is not the presentation

of part of the fiduciary issue of notes for encashment in gold, but a shortage of legal tender currency. Some scheme for an emergency issue of notes must obviously be framed before the 11,000,000*l.* gold thus provided could be of any conceivable use to any one, and whatever scheme were chosen there is no real connection between the 11,000,000*l.* of Government debt to the Bank and the problem at issue.

70. The first part of Sir E. Holden's scheme seems to contain one idea which is on the right lines, viz., the power which it is suggested should be given to the Bank of England to issue notes against bills of exchange. Modern doctrine on the subject of note issues, as illustrated in the Federal Reserves Act of the U.S.A. in 1913, is becoming more and more firmly favourable to the view that bills of exchange are the most suitable cover for notes. Apart from this idea, the scheme does not appear to be very useful. So long as the banks, other than the Bank of England, have gold remaining in their special reserves, why should resort be had to an emergency currency? All that is needed is for them to use their gold, either directly or by exchanging it for Bank of England notes in ordinary course. There is clearly a tendency here to forget that reserves are meant to be used, as appears still more strongly when Sir E. Holden adds that "the remaining portion of the banks' gold" (after the 20,000,000*l.* had gone to the Bank of England) "would be retained "in the vaults of the various banks."

71. Apart therefore from the suggested use of bills of exchange, Sir E. Holden's scheme does nothing to solve the problem of the machinery to be used in an emergency. It contains no suggestion as to the authority with whom should rest the decision to issue emergency notes or the criterion for determining when the moment for such issue has arrived, nor is the question of the utilization of the profits of such issue discussed. Finally, it suffers from the very serious disadvantage of introducing into this country the system of statutory reserves against banking liabilities which proved so disastrous in the United States in 1907, and is objectionable always because a reserve loses all value if it cannot be freely used.

72. It is much easier to criticise other people's suggestions than to frame a satisfactory scheme of one's own, and I shall not do more here than state my own belief that a good scheme for an emergency currency thought out in advance and authorised by Parliament in advance would be an improvement on the existing arrangement and should not be incapable of being devised. On general grounds extra-statutory action is always undesirable, and the fact that the emergency is one which must necessarily be sudden when it arises, and may well occur during a state of war, seems to afford good ground for preparing and arming ourselves against it at leisure and during peace.*

* So long as 5*l.* notes remain the lowest normal denomination of notes the emergency currency should probably conform to the normal unless the inconvenience of a 5*l.* note and the obvious desirability of a 1*l.* note when change is scarce force the adoption of the latter. It seems clear that a tax equal to the rate of discount at the time at which the crisis becomes so acute as to demand the emergency measure must be imposed and continue so long as the emergency

VIII.—The Incidence of the Cost of Maintaining Gold Reserves and the Question of a Government Contribution.

73. It remains to consider certain questions as to the incidence of the cost of maintaining the Gold Reserves which are always raised when any proposal is made for their increase, and in particular the suggestion that the Government ought to contribute. No more need be added here to what has already been said incidentally on the question of the incidence of the cost as between bankers generally and the Bank of England, but there are one or two further questions into which it may be well to go a little more deeply.

74. For what purpose is a gold reserve required? Ultimately the answer is, it is required to prevent the banker from going bankrupt. It is a condition of the banker's existence as a banker that he must at all times be able immediately to meet his liabilities in legal tender money to the full extent of any demand that may be made on him, and the Gold Reserves exist solely in in order to provide him with a working balance against all possible demands, whether normal or abnormal. So far as normal demands are concerned, no one will dispute that the full cost of maintaining the Gold Reserves should fall on the banking community, taking it as a whole, and ignoring for the moment any distinction between the Bank of England and other banks. It is of course the case that the banker can pass on the cost to his customers, just as a wholesale dealer passes on the cost of maintaining stocks in reserve to his customers. But in the sense that the keeping of reserves diminishes gross profits, the banker must clearly pay the whole cost of keeping reserves against normal demands.

75. But is the same argument wholly valid in the case of abnormal demands? The answer is surely in the affirmative. Perhaps the easiest way of arrival at that answer is to show the impossibility of any alternative. There seems to be only one, that the tax-payer should bear or share the cost of keeping a reserve against other than normal demands. The question here is not for the moment concerned with Government's position as holding savings banks deposits. The claim that the Government should share the cost in that capacity rests on the assumption that the Government is a banker, whereas the question now asked is whether the taxpayer should assist the banker in bearing the cost.

76. Now it may be conceded at once that the regulation of banking and currency is one of the primary duties of the State and that the Government

currency circulates. If there were real objections to leaving the sole responsibility with the Chancellor of the Exchequer, possibly an ex-officio Committee, consisting of, *e.g.*, the Governor of the Bank, the Lord Mayor of London, and the Permanent Secretary to the Treasury for the time being, might be established by the Amending Act to advise the Chancellor of the Exchequer, the Act containing provisions for a written statement of reasons for decision and a written record of advice tendered to be laid before Parliament. The main difficulties would arise in framing regulations as to the time-limit, if any, during which excess notes should be legal tender, and the maximum amount, if any, to which such excess notes should be restricted.

should look after the interests of the banking community as well as those of other industries. It is true again that the Government by giving a practical monopoly to the Bank of England for Government business, instead of putting that business out to competitive tender, make the taxpayer contribute something out of his pocket to the maintenance of the Bank and thus to its power to maintain the reserves. Mr. Cole, ex-Governor of the Bank, mentioned in a speech on the subject of Gold Reserves about two years ago the higher average of Government balances in recent years (which is largely due to chance) as a contribution by the Government to the cost of increasing the reserve, but the contribution is so indirect, being accidental rather than intentional, that it is impossible to found any argument upon it. Again, the Government recognise that it is their duty, within somewhat indefinite limits, to manage their balances with some regard to money market conditions and the Bank's control of the Gold Reserves, but this is done, so far as it is done, in much the same way as any big customer consults and defers to the wishes of his bank when his own interests are but slightly affected by meeting his bank's convenience.

77. None of these facts or arguments afford any ground for saddling the taxpayer with any charge in relief of the banker's burdens in respect of the Gold Reserves. Banking is a commercial enterprise in this country conducted for private profit. If the taxpayer were to contribute to the expense of the Gold Reserves he would be giving a bounty to a particular industry, that of banking, and though some of the benefit might accrue to industry generally so far as the whole profit was not absorbed by the banker, no modern-day Government is likely to view with favour a proposal to subsidise the banker and the capitalist out of the taxpayer's pocket.

78. The function of the Government is rather to secure that the banker shall conduct his business on lines that will not threaten disaster to the country and to compel him to keep an adequate reserve and to observe other necessary precautions, if he cannot be induced to do this without compulsion. The necessity for any such governmental action would usually arise from the desire to protect the many sound bankers from unfair or unscrupulous competition by the few. In the matter of gold reserves it seems very doubtful whether any such protective action is called for, unless it be the enforcement of more frequent and more detailed statements by the banks of their cash position. If further specific action is eventually needed, it will probably be in order to carry out in practice some scheme for modernising the central control of the reserve on which the considered opinion of the banking and mercantile community has reached some sort of unanimity. This can hardly be said to be the case yet, though the report of Lord St. Aldwyn's Committee may assist in this direction, unless the Committee is led astray by the endeavour to make out a case for Government's assistance, by laying stress on the Government's activities in regard to savings banks.

79. The claim that the Government should keep a special Gold Reserve or

make a special contribution to the central Gold Reserve in order to provide against the liabilities to savings banks depositors is a specious one, and the strength of the claim has undoubtedly been somewhat increased by the introduction of the system of withdrawal on demand. It should be noted, however, at once that the claim whatever its value is for a contribution not from the taxpayer but from the Savings Banks Fund, and the cost of contributing would logically fall on that fund alone. If as a result its power of paying its way were permanently impaired, the proper way of meeting the loss would be by a reduction in the rate of interest payable to depositors.

80. The arguments used in support of the claim are mainly (*a*) that Government should as a banker share the burdens which other bankers have necessarily to carry and (*b*) that there are special risks of panic among the class of persons to which the savings bank depositor belongs. There is this amount of truth in the second argument that, if ever hoarding on a large scale were to reappear in this country, it would undoubtedly be most likely to occur among the class of savings banks depositors. But no Gold Reserve less than practically the whole of the aggregate amount of deposits would suffice to pay the depositors in such circumstances, and even then the reaction of such a run on credit generally would be enough to bring down the whole credit system of the country. For dealing with a small run, the savings banks are better off than commercial banks, because ample notice is required for all but very small withdrawals, and their life and death do not, as with commercial banks, depend on being able to meet all liabilities on demand. The whole credit of commercial banks depends on belief in their ability to do this; the savings banks depend not on prompt payment but on the knowledge of the security of the Government.

81. There is nothing in the history of savings banks which would support the demand for a special gold reserve. Adequate arrangements are made for till money and such runs as have occurred have always been easily met by the sale of securities. Inconvenient as heavy withdrawals are to the Government's finance, they do not cause any drain on the Gold Reserves. In fact when they do occur it is usually because depositors want the money to spend owing to the encroachment on their savings caused by unemployment and trade depression, and just at this time the banks are always likely to be embarrassed not by shortage but by congestion of their reserves. Withdrawals of money to be immediately spent or deposited with other banks leave the Gold Reserve question untouched.

82. The truth is that there is almost no community of interests between the savings banks and commercial banking, and it is a mistake to call the Government a banker in its capacity as holding savings banks' deposits. The reason why hoarding is slightly less improbable among savings bank depositors than elsewhere is precisely that such people are comparatively unacquainted with banking. Money is usually placed in a savings bank in order to be kept there, and the liabilities of the Savings Banks Fund are

completely covered by Government securities, whether in the form of stocks or of a direct charge on the Consolidated Fund. Money is placed in a commercial bank in order to be drawn out, and the very essence of commercial banking is that only a small part of the assets is immediately realisable at any given moment or in any way so well secured as are the assets of the savings banks. The kind of crisis against which a banking reserve is necessary arises directly out of the operations of the commercial banks, and there is nothing in those of the savings banks which could conduce to such a crisis. People do not rely on the savings banks for securing legal tender money at a moment when credit money is not in favour, nor do the savings banks make their profit out of the arrangements for the supply of credit which render crises possible. This is what commercial banks do, and on the principle, therefore, that the reserves should be kept up at the cost of those who reap the profit, it is the commercial banks and not the savings banks which should pay for the precautions necessary to secure the realisation of such profits.

22/5/14. B. P. B.

APPENDIX 3

SIR JOHN CLAPHAM'S ACCOUNT OF THE FINANCIAL CRISIS IN AUGUST 1914

After the publication of his two volumes, *The Bank of England* (Cambridge 1944), Sir John Clapham continued to work on the more recent history of the Bank, and the following pages are an account he wrote of the 1914 crisis. There was no programme of publication, and Clapham had not made his final revision when he died suddenly in March 1946. As much more material has become available, particularly in the Public Record Office, since Clapham died, it has been thought best to avoid any attempt at revision. What is here printed is virtually as he left it, a colourful account of the actions of a generation relatively close to Clapham's own.

THE TRANSITION FROM PEACE TO WAR

There is no reason to think that the Bank of England or anyone in it anticipated war in a fortnight, or indeed war at all, on 20 July 1914. Three days earlier the Chancellor of the Exchequer (Lloyd George), at dinner with the bankers, had told them brightly that there were 'always clouds in the international sky', and that there were clouds 'even now'. But he was confident that we should 'pull through the difficulties',[1] which were, he said, less serious than those of a year earlier. Bankers did not always trust that Chancellor; but every instinct and wish would encourage them to believe him. He had access to the red boxes of the Cabinet and he ought to know.

The Bank had closed its Portsmouth Branch in the spring,[2] for business reasons valid enough in a world at peace. Only in that spring also the Deputy Chief Cashier had left the official quarters at the Bank where Chief Cashiers had used to live, including Abraham Newland who signed the £1 notes when Pitt was fighting the French. Bank Rate in July was a quiet 3. A rise to 4 came on Thursday, the 30th, when fear of war among continentals – and probably some planned financial preparation for it – had brought 'enormous sales of securities'[3] on the London market and a rush for gold in Paris.

[1] *Times*, 18 July 1914.

[2] On 30 April.

[3] *Times*, 30 July.

With its 3 per cent, the Bank remained in organisation and spirit Victorian. Its Governor (Walter Cunliffe), first elected in 1913, would expect to leave the chair in April 1915. He was a big, brave, sporting, English man of affairs, experienced in the City but not a financial thinker – not a Goschen; not a George Warde Norman. He had never written pamphlets on the exchanges or on currency. He was assisted by a Committee of Treasury of the traditional sort, nearly all ex-governors: only two had not yet served in 'the Chairs'. The Committee's minutes for 29th July, and those of the Court for 30th July, are correct, formal and, but for the rise of 1 per cent, empty.

No doubt some members of the Court, by that time, were bracing themselves for a possible war. One of them had fought, and many must have been in touch with soldiers who believed that Germany meant trouble and knew that, in the case of trouble, her armies would march through Belgium. *The Times* had written on the 27th about the possibility of having to 'vindicate' our international friendships 'with the whole strength of our Empire'. On the 28th it called on the jarring political parties – Germans looked for civil war in Ireland – to 'close the ranks'. On the 30th it was harking back to memories of the great French Wars. *The Economist* of 1st August called these articles 'poisonous' and Winston Churchill's precautionary orders to the fleet – whereby 'the King's ships were at sea'[1] – 'deplorable'. 'The City, of course, is all for peace', it wrote; 'the nation' will support 'strict neutrality'. 'Of course' the City was all for peace, if peace was to be had. There had already been commercial failures, and on 31 July, when more than £1,500,000 of gold was taken for export, other business was 'at a standstill'.[2] How many people in the City, how many Directors of the Bank, believed that peace could be preserved with honour or wisdom on a platform of 'strict neutrality' banking history is not required to discuss; nor can any history learn. But, according to Lloyd George, the Governor of the Bank told him on the Saturday 'that the financial and trading interests in the City were totally opposed to our intervening in the war'.[3] That may well be correct.

There is nowhere a suggestion that the Bank had been instructed, or had thought it expedient, to make special preparations for the strain of war. The Committee of Imperial Defence had prepared that 'War Book' of which ex-ministers write; but there was no War Book at the Bank. Instructions from the then Chancellor of the Exchequer, a man of peace almost to the last, would have been both unlikely and improper. Someone in the Treasury may have dropped hints: if he did they have left no splash of ink.[4]

For years the Bank had been carrying more substantial reserves of gold than were usual in the nineteenth century – but as a general precaution.

[1] Churchill, *The World Crisis*, I, 213.

[2] *Times*, 31 July.

[3] Lloyd George, *War Memories*, I, 40: Lloyd George kept no diary and his memory was not infallible.

[4] I do not think anyone did. I am informed from the War Cabinet Secretariat that the War Book contains nothing about notes or financial expedients.

Bagehot's ideal of £13/15,000,000 had become Goschen's ideal of £40,000,000. On 27 July 1914, the total in hand was £38,100,000. Some, perhaps all, bankers had also increased their gold stocks, with a view to financial emergencies and that possible–impossible tragedy of a European war into which England might be sucked by some conceivable–inconceivable mischance. What use was made of these reserves will appear.

The Court of the Bank did not meet between 30 July and 10 August, nor the Committee of Treasury between 29 July and 12 August – and for two years of war the minutes of that once dominant Committee are astonishingly empty and barren. During the shattering interval when neither body met, decisions were taken by Walter Cunliffe, the Governor, and such colleagues as he was able, or cared, to consult. He raised Bank Rate from 4 to 8 on Friday, 31st July, and from 8 to 10 next day after an informal 'meeting of the Directors'. Before the Court met again, he had moved it down in one big and one small step to 5. The figures show the speed and success with which the money market trouble was handled by the joint action of Bank and Treasury – nine days only from 4 up to 10 and down again to the 5 which became the standard war-time rate.

Saturday, 1 August, had been the most difficult day in the City. The coming Monday was Bank Holiday and there was a big normal demand for holiday cash. The Stock Exchange was shut. The London banks – or some of them – had called in short money from bill-brokers, on the Friday, 'to an extent which appeared to be difficult to justify'[1] – and the Bank had done three millions of discounts. This led to Cunliffe's Saturday 10 per cent – crisis rate – the market being driven hard into the Bank. The public had been driven there too: from the Friday, but especially on the Saturday, there were queues in Threadneedle Street waiting to cash £5 notes. It was more a holiday than a panic demand, as everyone agreed. Its prime cause was not distrust of Bank notes, except perhaps among the rather numerous foreigners to be seen in the queues,[2] but refusals of banks to pay out all the sovereigns demanded, in spite of those accumulations of gold made, one would suppose, for just such an emergency. Clients were given Bank Notes and joined the cashing queue in Threadneedle Street. Over five thousand people took gold across the counter in those two days; and others, but a dwindling number, in the following week. Cunliffe had plain things to say some days later about 'these bankers'; but certain bank leaders recalled that, on the Friday, they had suggested suspension of the Bank Act and a transfer of gold and securities from the banks to the Bank, to support an emergency note issue.

But on the Saturday nothing was settled. The Governor reported to the Chancellor that the Bank had advanced over £27,000,000 in five days and could not count on more than £11,000,000 in the reserve by nightfall; that there was risk either of refusal for well-founded demands on it or breach of the Act of 1844. At once a Chancellor's letter came from Downing Street,

[1] *Times*, 1 Aug.   [2] *Times*, 8 Aug.

with the traditional wording, signed by Asquith and Lloyd George: the Bank was promised indemnity in case it had to break the law for adequate cause, provided that it gave assistance only at the crisis rate of 10 per cent.[1] That rate, sanctioned by Directors the same day, remained in force only until the following Thursday – when the banks were still shut. In the brief interval other expedients had been hit on. Until November 1915, no one troubled to ask or tell in Parliament just what happened under the Chancellor's letter. Technically the Act was violated: notes beyond the legal fiduciary figure and not backed by gold, passed into the Banking Reserve. Some of these were advanced, for a special and temporary purpose, to the banks.[2] The maximum excess issue so occasioned was £3,851,000. But as there was no suspension of cash payment at the Bank, and no passing of 'illegal' notes into general circulation, there was held to be no need for a Bill of Indemnity.[3]

The expedients hit on were, first, a prolongation of that Bank Holiday, that Monday on which, before midnight, Britain went to war: the fall of the Holiday was opportune and its extension gave the City and the Treasury time to breathe and think. Second, the announcement on the Sunday of a month's moratorium – the word was not used – for bills of exchange:[4] here speed was essential because, international remittance having broken down, Tuesday would have brought a crisis in the bill market. Third, the making of postal orders into legal tender currency, and the promise of a swift issue of 'government notes on the security of the Government'[5] for 10s. and £1. These, the Chancellor of the Exchequer promised, on Wednesday, for the Friday; and the first £2,400,000 of the £1 class, flimsy and ugly, appeared a day earlier. Had there been a Bank–Treasury 'War Book', an emergency currency might have been ready. 'The fleet was ready and the expeditionary force was ready. The financial machinery was not.'[6] Hence this improvisation.

These expedients had been blocked out in hasty conferences on the Sunday and Monday, conferences of the Chancellor and Treasury officials with the Bank – essentially the Governor – the bankers and other City leaders. On Friday and Saturday suggestions were made and policies discussed which became superfluous, when what the Governor described to the Chancellor,

1 *A. & P.* 1914.6, XXXVIII.121: Suspension of Bank Act.

2 See pp. 35–6 below.

3 The figure given by Asquith in Parliament in Nov. 1915 was not quite the same: *Hansard*, LXXV.1002. The notes advanced to the banks were in place of the new Currency Notes, of which enough were not then available; p. 35 below.

4 *Proclamation of Sunday, August 2nd, 1914, for Postponing the Payment of Certain Bills of Exchange* (other than cheques or bills on demand) in H. Withers, *The War and Lombard Street*, 1915, App. II.

5 Lloyd George in the House, Wed. 5 Aug. *Times*, 6 Aug.

6 Withers, *op. cit.* p. 32. Withers adds – 'I have good authority for stating that bankers had long ago represented to the powers that be, that a store of emergency currency would be needed if England were involved in a great war.' This is repeated in *The Economist* which Withers was then editing, on 8 Sept. 1917.

five days later, as 'this arrangement of yours', the new note issue, was decided on. Late on the Sunday a meeting consisting of representatives of the Clearing Banks and the two principal Discount Companies suggested the extra Bank Holidays, from Tuesday to Thursday, and the month's moratorium. They favoured suspension of the Bank Act and of cash payments also. The proposal for a transfer of gold and securities as basis for an emergency note issue was put aside; but the meeting definitely recommended an issue of 'Bank Notes of the value of £1 and 10s....as soon as possible'.[1] This Cunliffe would presumably have preferred to the 'arrangement of yours'. Certainly his Court voted a few days later that, if the new notes became a permanence, the Bank ought to issue them – a wish not met for fourteen years.

The plan for government notes, embodied forthwith in an Act (4 & 5, Geo. V c. 14 of 6 August), made the Bank their distributor. It would do the work free. They were to be issued as loans to the banks with interest payable to the Treasury. Banks might take them 'as and when required' up to 20 per cent of their liabilities on deposit and current accounts. Cash payment was not suspended. Cunliffe had snorted at the notion. He had cashed his own notes and would cash these. But the Chancellor, when making his announcement, begged the public not to press for gold.

The Bankers had been worried about their frozen assets – with a shut Stock Exchange and a petrified bill market. They also feared withdrawals of deposits and their transfer to the Bank. This fear had some foundation. On the Wednesday an account of over £100,000 was offered to the Bank – and refused by the Governor. 'I thought it was not cricket', that sportsman said.

All the considerations that led to Treasury rather than Bank issue are not on record: 'it is a pretty lengthy argument on both sides',[2] the Chancellor told the House, an argument into which he would not go. The need for small legal tender notes, not merely more notes, had been present in the minds of men in the Treasury from the first; and so had the notion of postal orders as legal tender *ad interim*. Then there was the time question. The Bank, an exact and methodical worker, could not have promised quick delivery. With the limited printing equipment, that would have been a mechanical impossibility. Messrs de la Rue, using postage-stamp paper, turned out the first rather shoddy £1 notes in three days. Cunliffe brought one in to Lloyd George all rubbed and discreditable, with a 'far better have left it to us';[3] so he may have fancied that the Bank could have delivered in time. One reason why they were not asked appears to have been that, as the note was to be legal tender throughout the United Kingdom, which Bank of England notes at present were not, Scottish and Irish susceptibilities had to be considered. There was also, as the Chancellor put it, 'an advantage to the

[1] In a letter dated 2.0 a.m. 3 Aug. quoted to me by Mr Hawtrey of the Treasury.

[2] *Times*, 6 Aug.

[3] Lloyd George, *War Memories*, I, 69. The first 10s. notes were printed by Waterlows.

Government from a Revenue point of view' – that interest payable to the Treasury. And perhaps a desire at the Treasury, of which Gladstone once wrote, for 'financial self-assertion' in dealing with the Bank, may have had some influence.[1]

The advances of Currency Notes to the banks were repayable at any time, and also renewable. Notes repaid might either be cancelled or kept in a distinct account at the Bank with a view to cancellation. Scottish and Irish banks might use the notes as cover for those extra issues which under existing law could only be made against hard cash. As all banks soon found that they had no need for notes up to anything like the permitted maximum, an amending Act (of 28 August) allowed them to take certificates of the right to receive notes in place of the notes themselves, a new and odd sort of asset.[2]

In the interval between the decision in favour of Treasury Notes and the Chancellor's announcement of it in the House, a series of financial conferences was held to crystallise banking opinion. The Governor would confer with the Chancellor; the Chancellor with the bankers; the three parties together. Holden, of the Midland Bank, acquiesced in the Treasury Note plan because he thought the Bank could not give him help enough: 'it will kill them'. But, anxious and emphatic, he declared that the Notes would 'go to a discount'. 'At once', Felix Schuster of the Union and Smiths added. They might have to ration customers with cash, they said. (They already had.) But under this plan, the Chancellor urged, you can get gold at the Bank which does not fear a run. A 'round-about' way, they grumbled. 'We don't want to make it easy', the Chancellor very sensibly retorted.

In the absence of the bankers, the Governor, nearly as cool as the Chancellor but angrier, endorsed the convertibility of the new notes at the Bank, and of the postal orders *ad interim*.[3] 'The banks', he said, 'have declined to part with £5 as against a £5 note. That is the trouble amongst the crowd.' Bradbury of the Treasury spoke of possible panic. 'The best way to avoid a panic is to meet the situation like lions', growled Cunliffe: he had shot big game in his time and his 'massive strength' remained in the Chancellor's memory, though none of his few words did.[4]

The bankers returned. They had talked of telling clients that anyone might draw up to 10 per cent of his account. Don't, said Cunliffe, or they will all do it. Aren't you fighting shadows? 'Directly we get these £1 notes out, I do not think there will be any difficulty afterwards.' You seem to want some measure 'to protect yourselves against yourselves', he told Holden – a Napoleon of banks not often so plainly put in his place.

In the bankers' absence, the Governor advised the Chancellor not to be too

[1] I have had the advantage of discussing the matter with Lord Bradbury and Mr Hawtrey, with Sir Otto Niemeyer who at that time was also at the Treasury, and with Sir Ernest Harvey and Mr Catterns of the Bank of England. The last suggestion is my own.

[2] All summarised in the Parliamentary paper 'Treasury Assistance to Banks and Discount Houses' of 27 August: *A. & P.* 1914, L.501.

[3] The postal orders ceased to be legal tender 3 Feb. 1915. They were all printed at the Bank.

[4] Lloyd George, *Memories*, I, 68–9.

hard on them – their money was out in overdrafts to traders and they did not care to admit it. I want to tell them that I refuse to rob them of clients: I already have refused. But they are hoarding gold. Ours is low. Tell them it would be damned awkward if we have to suspend while their vaults are full.

At the next stage in the conferences, the bankers present, Cunliffe mentioned his self-denying policy. 'Mr Governor, we are very much obliged to you', Lord St Aldwyn, the statesman-director of the London Joint-Stock Bank replied: and that ghost was laid.[1] Then the Chancellor spoke about the gold. The banks must set a good example. St Aldwyn, in defence, referred to the suggested transfer to the Bank, a suggestion which had not been given its due credit. They 'entirely agreed' to an anti-gold-hoarding passage in the Chancellor's coming speech. So far, good.

But at what rate was the Treasury to advance the new notes? At Bank Rate, of course, Cunliffe argued. (When these conferences began Bank Rate was at 10; when they ended, at 6.) If lower, the banks would in effect fix the rate. Holden, his overdrafts in mind, said that anything above 5 would 'upset the whole industry of the country'. Cunliffe, thinking of a possible spell of 6, reminded him that industry had done very well 'over the best part' of 1913 when bankers had charged 5.[2] Holden explained that he now had 'fixtures' – long-term agreed overdrafts, no doubt – at 4 and 4½. When he learnt that Bank Rate might be got down to 5, as it actually was by the Saturday, he sank into temporary rest with a 'well and good'.

On Friday, 7 August, the banks had reopened. Much gold taken from the Bank in the previous week was repaid. The Governor could report to the Chancellor a complete absence of pressure everywhere, except at Manchester: the clearing bankers agreed with his report.[3] Calm continued on the Saturday. And so, with 5 per cent five days after the declaration of war, the first phase in the adjustment to unknown conditions was over. Suspension of the Bank Act, that decisive central event in earlier less grave crises, was sidetracked and neglected on its siding. All had passed with wonderful smoothness, *The Times* wrote. And when, just three months later, Walter Cunliffe was raised to the peerage, the Prime Minister, who had served for years at the Exchequer, reminded the City how 'in time of great emergency' the Governor had 'shown the utmost courage and resource'. The courage no one ever questioned. If resource implies invention, there may have been less of that.

The new Currency Note was legal tender to any amount. So were the Scottish and Irish notes in Scotland and Ireland, whether fiduciary or based on the Currency Note. As the old fiduciary issues were relatively small, this new British note became – in time – the basis for important extensions of

[1] St Aldwyn (Hicks-Beach) led the bankers and showed 'all his old tact and mastery'; *ibid.* I, 65.

[2] Bank Rate was 4½ from April to October 1913, after that 5.

[3] Lloyd George in the House: *Times*, 8 Aug.

issue in Scotland and Ireland.[1] And as it might be paid out in exchange for bank notes – two new 10s. for an old Scots £1 – it soon got into circulation. This was the easier because the original character of a loan at interest was early modified. While it existed, the loans might be repaid and the whole episode closed – a possibility which the Court of the Bank evidently faced when it voted its 'if the notes became permanent', on 13th August. But, by Treasury Minute of 20th August, Currency Notes might be got from the Bank by other banks in the ordinary way of cash withdrawal, and without payment of interest. And as the Bank had exceeded its legal issue by passing to them £5,500,000 of its own notes, to take the place of the promised Currency Notes as an asset before these were ready; as all such abnormal 'issues' were restored by 28th August; and as by that time the flow of Currency Notes, at first slow, was steady, the banks could take them from their cash at the Bank at will.

Most of the original loans of notes at interest were quickly paid off. They had in fact proved small. The 20 per cent of their liabilities which the banks were entitled to take would have come to about £225,000,000. The amount taken came to less than £13,000,000. 'The mere knowledge of these currency facilities being available gave confidence',[2] the Chancellor said later.

The first Currency Notes were technically bad and very easily forged. The second series which came in October, was not much better. At the end of the year some two thousand forgeries had been detected. By that time there were £38,162,000 of the notes outstanding; but only £38,162,000 – a very reasonable figure so far, when it is remembered what quantities of gold had been carried in pockets and how steadily this carriage declined.

At the Bank, and for the Treasury, a Currency Note Redemption Account was opened on 21 August. The debit side showed the notes themselves; on the credit side stood Bank Notes, gold and silver, and – predominantly – Government securities, mainly Ways and Means advances and Treasury Bills. The Government was beginning to circulate its promises to pay on the security of its other promises to pay; but then the Bank, which for these purposes was all but the Government, had for decades circulated some notes on the same basis, many of them on Government promises two centuries old.

The management of the Currency Notes was undertaken by the Bank free of charge, and so remained throughout the war years – and after – except that a partial test examination of those Notes that came in for cancellation, and their ultimate destruction, were done by the Post Office, whose Orders and paper had been so handy at the start.

A 'Postponement of Payments Act', a moratorium, had been hurried through on the Monday. It covered in retrospect Sunday's emergency proclamation; and as its name suggests, it was wide: among things that

[1] The Currency Notes set aside and held as cover by Scottish and Irish banks against excess note circulation, for which gold had formerly been necessary, stood at £2,120,000 in 1914; £16,930,000 in 1916; and £36,980,000 in 1918.

[2] *Times*, 28 Nov. 1914.

might be postponed was 'any other payment in pursuance of any contract'. Between Monday and Thursday further action was discussed in the financial conferences. Cunliffe thought that now there had been moratorium enough.[1] The ablest financial critic of the day wrote later that 'a Bank Holiday extended for a week or more'[2] would have been better than any general moratorium, especially for banks. But the critic was not at the conferences, and Cunliffe was overruled. On Thursday, 6 August, a second proclamation under the new Act dealt with 'bills of exchange (being cheques or bills on demand)' dated before 4 August, negotiable instruments other than bills, and contracts 'made before that time'. All these were given a month's moratorium – later extended to three months.

There were payments and liabilities excluded; but most of these did not much affect bankers or the Bank.[3] The main objects of the exclusions were to protect small creditors, the legal rights of wage earners, and the right of government – central or local – to collect taxes or rates. But one thing that might not be postponed was 'any liability of a bank of issue in respect of bank notes issued by that bank'. Cunliffe could not instruct his cashiers to postpone cashing, but Holden might cling to his deposits for a month, if he thought this expedient. The small man got well-deserved protection: the high body corporate perhaps got rather too much.

Cunliffe had presumably thought that suspension of the Bank Act gave all necessary facilities: he could extend credit without breaking the law and help anyone in difficulties. The Currency Notes Loan policy relieved him of the liability, but he had it in reserve. He had tried to convince the bankers that nothing more was needed. In the event, as has been seen, they made a very limited use of their second line of defence. It is most doubtful whether they really needed a third; but they wanted security and more security, and it was given them. Having got it they acted, for the most part, as reasonably as might have been expected. Depositors were not kept waiting for a month. The second and third months were not utilised by the banks at all. The extended moratorium they left to people in greater need of it. 'At the beginning of September they credited their customers again with the balances which were due to them on August 4th';[4] and for them the thing was over. But they did not easily live down the criticism which hesitations and timidities in the crisis had brought upon them. In *The Economist* of 29 August a correspondent, an economist himself and in touch with Government,[5] said what a pity it was that 'when the Bank of England has stood staunch and other elements in the money market have done their best...the

[1] Cunliffe's opposition to a general moratorium is recorded in his retiring speech in 1918: a bankers' moratorium 'was never in my opinion really necessary'.

[2] Withers, *The War and Lombard Street*, p. 34.

[3] The payments were – of wages and salaries; all under £5; rates and taxes; maritime freights; payments under Workmen's Compensation or National Insurance Acts; payments by trustee savings banks; and a couple more. The Proclamation is printed in Withers, *op. cit.* App. B.

[4] Withers, *op. cit.* p. 37.

[5] J. M. Keynes (Lord Keynes).

joint-stock banks should with some signal exceptions have failed, as they so signally have failed, in courage and public spirit'. Bankers retorted that the failures were the exception not the rule. But a measure of failure was admitted; and the correspondent rejoined by asserting that bankers as a group had 'abstained from every form of bold or definitely public-spirited action'.[1]

Trouble in the bill market over the weekend that preceded war was due in no way to any distrust of British financial strength, whether Britain went to war or not. She was still the great creditor nation, and besides that, the safest place outside America in which to have money. Business men everywhere – except in Paris – were only too eager to get bills on London with which to pay their debts or make their remittances. The Parisian bankers had large balances in London which they naturally wished to repatriate. Bills on London were not in request there. The pound fell from 25.17 francs to 24.50. 'Gold was shipped to Paris as fast as its transport and insurance could be arranged for.'[2] In the week before the war £1,762,000 of sovereigns were sent to France and £1,486,000 more to Belgium and 'The Continent', mostly it is reasonable to assume on French account.

But, everywhere else, eagerness to get money to London drove the exchanges so hard in London's favour that, as has been said, it 'broke the machinery'.[3] In spite of the withdrawals to Paris, the half-panic fear that Britain might be drained of her gold was, at bottom, unreasonable. War risks made shipment of gold over long distances costly in insurance and freight. That told both ways; but arrangements could be made in Britain's interest, and were made very promptly. India was a regular debtor. The Indian Government had gold at the Bank, backing for India's 'gold exchange standard' currency.[4] From this store £3,400,000 was released temporarily. It acted as a gold import, an extra free stock in London. The United States and Canada also were debtors. Some gold was shipped: much more, by speedy arrangement, was bought and stored at Ottawa for the account of the Bank – in bars and United States gold coin. In South Africa, the Bank undertook to buy at 77s. 9d. the ounce and to credit 97 per cent of the whole to the account of the mining companies in London: the gold was to be deposited with the Treasury of the Union or at certain specified banks. Several days before August was over the Bank could report £43,500,000 of gold, though not where it all was.[5]

The gold arrangements were completed in the week following 8th August, and they helped the Bank to carry the very heavy liability which it accepted in that week – the liability for what came to be known as the pre-moratorium

[1] *Economist*, 12 Sept.

[2] Withers, *op. cit.* p. 46.

[3] Withers, p. 41.

[4] A currency in which gold does not circulate freely, but in which the relation between the circulating currency, in this case rupees, and gold is kept steady by the manipulation of a reserve of gold and exchange at the selected gold centre, in this case London; an early type of 'managed' currency.

[5] See p. 44 below.

bills. The liability was made necessary by that general moratorium which Cunliffe had opposed – the moratorium announced originally for a month, but prolonged by proclamation from month to month until 4 November.[1]

Forty years before 1914 regular bankers had not done much bill accepting. They had left that to the accepting houses. But they had been doing more and more of it, so that now they were deeply interested both as acceptors and as discounters of bills. 'The greatest difficulty', the Chancellor of the Exchequer noted in a Notice issued in his name on 13 August,[2] 'arose from the stoppage of remittances to London both from the provinces and from... all parts of the world.' (The extended Bank Holiday should have sufficed for the provinces, and with the gold situation described the world would have got back into its stride – but there was the delay-making moratorium at home.) 'This caused a breakdown in the foreign exchanges and deterred bankers from discounting bills in the normal way.' (Though why they should have been so much deterred is hard to see.) Therefore he or, as those who took part in the negotiations recall, Lord Reading acting for him, held 'close and constant consultations with the Governor...the bankers, the accepting houses and the principal traders,'[3] in search of a way out.

The way hit upon – how and by whom is nowhere written down – was a great operation by the Bank and a guarantee to it against loss on the operation by the Government. The Bank would discount any approved bill of exchange, 'either home or foreign, bank or trade', that had been accepted before 4 August 1914. And this was to be done 'without recourse' to the holder of a bill who, at law, accepted liability for it when he endorsed. Further, if acceptors were not in a position to pay when the bill matured, the Bank would lend to them at 2 per cent above Bank Rate, and it would not claim balances not recovered by the acceptor for a year after the war – a date which proved far more remote than anyone then fancied: this was announced at the end of the first month on 5 September. An 'approved' bill was one such as the Bank usually discounted, or one accepted by 'such foreign and colonial firms and bank agencies as are established in Great Britain'.[4]

The rush to discount, at 5 per cent, may be imagined. The maximum day's business at the Bank was £9,448,000 on 14 August; from 10 to 31 August, both included, the figure was £77,455,000. A special committee of Directors appointed on 13 August to watch the business was kept busy enough. And when, towards the end of the three months, dealings with acceptors became imminent, another committee was set to sift 'applications...from acceptors to provide funds'. Most holders of bills had been eager to discount. As there was no 'recourse' there was no risk anywhere – except ultimately to the

[1] In connection with the first extension, 8,256 firms were consulted; 4,653 voted for it – bankers, export merchants and stockbrokers overwhelmingly; the Bank voted against. *A. & P.* 1914, L.501: papers on Government assistance to Banks, etc.

[2] Printed in Withers, App. II, B.

[3] All from the Notice of 13 Aug.

[4] Withers, App. II, C: the Treasury Statement of 5 Sept.

Treasury. Bills were poured in to the Banks in most abnormal quantities and largely by small traders. The absence of 'recourse' must have secured discount for some doubtful paper. Bankers took what was offered and the Bank could not well refuse to take from them paper which they, the local and central experts in the 'standing of parties', had seen fit to handle. It did the duty undertaken steadily, few questions asked. The total of bills discounted under these special arrangements, and with the help of the Treasury guarantee, was a round £120,000,000. What exact proportion this was of the bills out on 4 August is not known. It was certainly not more than a third, for estimates of the August figure varied between £350,000,000 and £500,000,000. The remaining two-thirds or three-quarters were settled in the ordinary way.[1]

But the handling of this quarter or third was a big affair at the Bank as the income from it – at 5 per cent – indicates. Compare it with the discount income in earlier years. In 1911–14, a period of active business, it had averaged £344,000 a year, rising a little from year to year. (For the years 1908–11 it had been £186,000).[2] In the half-year 1 September 1914–28 February 1915 it was no less than £877,000. For the next half-year it fell away to £71,000; and discounting was never of first-rate importance again. The business was nearly all done in London: the days of active discount at the branches were, as it was to prove, over.

Though the bulk of the moratorium discount income had been collected by the end of February 1915, there remained that derived from advances made to acceptors who were not in a position to honour their signatures at the ultimate maturity of the accepted bills. Acceptors had undertaken to pay in England, and their correspondents – mainly in enemy or enemy-occupied territory – were unable to put them in funds at the appointed date. The Bank had agreed to make advances to meet all good bills accepted before 4 August 1914 and still not covered in November; but it also made advances on some accepted later. Charging 7 per cent as announced, it had taken £159,000 from this business by the end of February 1915. During the next six months it took no less than £1,470,000.

This episode, followed by the long-drawn-out closure or disorganisation of international commercial relations, marked the beginning of the end of the old accepting-house business. There was recovery, but 'never glad confident morning again'. With the accepting houses, commercial firms up and down the world suffered, firms who for war reasons could not collect genuine debts. Some advances to both groups passed into what came to be known at the Bank later as cold storage. The existence in 1932 of an old 'cold storage' debt of £700,000 from a single firm illustrates the character of the store.

There were cold storage debts that could be traced back to other sources – a shut Stock Exchange at the height of the City crisis and arrangements made

[1] Lloyd George in the House, 27 Nov. *Times*, 28 Nov.

[2] Vol. II, App. C.

subsequently by the Government for Stock Exchange relief and relief of embarrassed exporters. The Exchange had shut on 31 July and it did not re-open until 4 January 1915. Its shutting helps to explain the hesitations of the banks. They had lent to stockbrokers and also to customers against securities: they held securities themselves as assets. Nothing was marketable, and loans in the least injudicious became most doubtful assets. Fortunately the Exchange had been in a 'slow fever...for several miserable years'.[1] Economic and political anxieties 'had taken all the heart out of the speculator, and it was generally agreed by most active stockbrokers in the middle of July that... they had never seen so little stock being carried over [from settlement to settlement] on borrowed money'.[2] Yet the stockbrokers owed about £80,000,000, though not all to the banks. What the banks had lent to customers with Stock Exchange securities as collateral is less certainly known: it has been put at £250,000,000.

The Exchange was kept shut and dealings during the moratorium, when resumed, were at officially controlled prices mainly for political reasons: the risk of the enemy unloading through a neutral intermediary on to the London markets had to be avoided. Once more the Government took the ultimate liability for losses and left the Bank to do the work of relief to lenders on Stock Exchange securities – other than the banks who had been fully provided for already. Taking the making-up prices of 29 July as basis, the Bank agreed to advance to such lenders as requested it 60 per cent of the value of the securities upon which they had lent, at 1 per cent above Bank Rate. As with its advances on bills, the Bank undertook not to insist on payment of the debt until a year after the peace, or until the expiry of an Act passed to protect debtors which was expected to remain in force almost as long.[3]

Less closely connected with the Bank was a parallel scheme for the relief of exporters whose debts from abroad were frozen, temporarily or for what came to be known as 'the duration'. A committee whose members were drawn from the Treasury, the Association of Chambers of Commerce, the bankers and the Bank sifted their claims.[4] An approved claimant might draw a six-months bill on his banker, which the committee would guarantee. If in the long run loss resulted, the Exchequer was to bear 75 per cent of it, the accepting bank the balance.

'A fine load of liabilities, on paper has thus been taken by the broad shoulders of the British taxpayer', a fighting and acute financial critic wrote in December, 'but, unless the war lasts longer than seems likely, he need not fear that he will have a big bill to meet.'[5] What the critic's mental estimate of

[1] Withers, p. 120. [2] Withers, p. 121.

[3] The Courts (Emergency Powers) Act 1914, 31 Aug. It was determinable at any time by Order in Council. A committee to handle the Stock Exchange business was appointed on 29 Oct.

[4] Sir Henry Babington Smith, Sir Donald Maclean, Sir Algernon Firth, Sir William Plender, Brien Cokayne and G. H. Pownall.

[5] Withers, pp. 125–6.

'the duration' was that December is not on record. *The Economist*'s was 'a few months'.[1] Before leaving his readers, the critic noted that the highest figure of the Bank's 'other securities' during the moratorium (2 September) had been £121,820,692 against £33,623,288 on 15 July. Wonderfully efficient and adaptable, this old Bank, he concluded: 'it bought bills, including those of the agencies of foreign banks, that it would not have looked at in ordinary times. It made advances with similar lack of prejudice...and it was ready with a supply of tea and buns for Belgian refugees who brought Belgian money to be turned into sterling.'[2]

There would have been a money market crisis at the weekend of 1 to 3 August even if England had kept out of the war on that Bank Holiday. Bourses and Stock Exchanges were shut; gold was being hoarded at several points; trade routes were interrupted; the business of international remittance was upset. A month's moratorium for bills and a suspension of the Bank Act would have been the necessary minimum, a minimum already agreed to before Edward Grey's Monday speech, and the facts behind it, decided the House of Commons to accept war. (Up to luncheon-time on the Sunday 'it looked as if the majority' of the Cabinet 'would resign', rather than accept.)[3] If England had stayed out of the war for a little longer, the use of an emergency currency might perhaps have been postponed. It was adopted in principle, so far as we can tell, on the Sunday – but after luncheon-time. The Chancellor of the Exchequer, now convinced of a terrible necessity, turned his back on his past, took all the best advice he could get, and plunged into City matters that were not entirely familiar to him with darting, adventurous, open mind.

His next task was the to him quite unfamiliar and inappropriate one of financing a great war. But in this sort of thing the Bank had helped before. Just under a century back, an ex-Governor had very correctly said that it 'was instituted for that express purpose'.[4] The Chancellor's first application to the Governor recalled its much earlier days, though certainly the Chancellor did not know this. He asked for 'Ways and Means' Advances – 'Ways and Means', by leave of Queen Anne the family motto of William Lowndes of Winslow, Bucks., Secretary to the Treasury in William's and Marlborough's wars, and the Bank's very good friend. Cunliffe gave the Chancellor £6,000,000 at once, in two instalments, and had his gift approved by the Court on 13 August. When the war of 1914 began an advance of £6,000,000 would carry fighting on for quite a time; but as it was certain that more would soon be needed, the Court gave general authority a week later for advances as required, at such rates not exceeding the Bank Rate of 5 as might be agreed on between the Treasury and the Governor. Before the year was over heavy advances were agreed on at 2½.

[1] *Economist*, 14 Nov. 1914.
[2] Withers, pp. 130–1.
[3] Churchill, *The World Crisis*, I, 218.
[4] Jeremiah Harman, II, 11.

War also brought some novelties in the 'Private' Drawing Office. On the day that the first Ways and Means Advances were sanctioned, the opening of a drawing account for the Bank of France was approved. Then, on 20 August, an account was opened for the Banca d'Italia. Presumably the Foreign Office had been consulted and perhaps the Foreign Office knew that Italy, though allied with Britain's enemies, had a secret clause in her treaty that excluded the case of war with England: she had already professed neutrality in this war. In September the name of the National Bank of Switzerland appears. The ally, a potential ally, and the most honourable and resolute of neutrals are linked with the world's second greatest reserve of wealth and credit, in London. Before the end of the year, the governments of France, Belgium and Serbia, allies, and of Chile, a friendly neutral, all have drawing accounts; and so have the National Banks of Belgium and Serbia, with those of Norway and the Netherlands – both neutrals well disposed but, for geographical reasons, not always able to be openly helpful.

APPENDIX 4

DOCUMENTS CONCERNING THE SETTING UP OF A LONDON EXCHANGE COMMITTEE, 1915

1. LETTER FROM THE TREASURY TO LORD CUNLIFFE, 20 NOVEMBER 1915

TREASURY CHAMBERS
20th November 1915

My Lord,

I am directed by the Lords Commissioners of His Majesty's Treasury to transmit for your information and guidance a copy of Their Minute of the 17th instant constituting an American Exchange Committee and approving arrangements which have been made with certain Banks in connection with the measures proposed for regulating the American Exchange.

I am to add that the Minute is to be read with the Chancellor of the Exchequer's letter of the 18th instant which further defines the powers and duties of the Committee.

Copies of the Minute may, if your Committee think fit, be communicated to the various Banks concerned.

I am,
My Lord,
Your obedient Servant,
(*Signed*)
JOHN BRADBURY

Lord Cunliffe of Headley,
Bank of England, E.C.

2. TREASURY MINUTE, 17 NOVEMBER 1915

The Chancellor of the Exchequer states to the Board that in connection with the arrangements which are being made for the purpose of regulating the rate of exchange between the United Kingdom and the United States of America the Banks named in the First Schedule of this Minute have arranged to borrow from a Committee of American Bankers the respective sums therein specified to a total amount of fifty million dollars ($50,000,000) and to deposit with the Bank of England 4½ per cent War Loan Stock to the respective nominal amounts therein mentioned to a total of £6,900,000 together with a 10 per cent margin; and that the Banks named in the Second

Schedule have arranged to deposit with the Bank of England 4½ per cent War Loan Stock to the respective nominal amounts mentioned in that Schedule to a total of £3,100,000 together with a ten per cent margin; the Stock so deposited to be held by the Bank of England on behalf of the Committee of American Bankers as security for the above-mentioned loans, and the interest thereon to be credited or paid over by the Bank of England from time to time as it becomes due to the Banks by which the Stock has been deposited.

It has further been arranged that the sum of Fifty million dollars borrowed under this arrangement shall be placed under the control of an American Exchange Committee to be established in London to be employed by that Committee for the purpose of supporting the American Exchange in such manner as they may in their discretion think fit.

The American Exchange Committee will be constituted as follows:—

Lord Cunliffe of Headley,
Sir Edward H. Holden Bart.,
Sir Felix Schuster Bart.,
Brien Cokayne Esq.,

with power to add to their numbers subject to the approval of Their Lordships and the Banks named in the First Schedule and with power to appoint agents abroad. The American Exchange Committee will act on behalf of the Lords Commissioners of His Majesty's Treasury, who, subject to Their obtaining the necessary Parliamentary authority, will guarantee the performance of all engagements entered into by the Committee.

The American Exchange Committee will repay the sum of Fifty million dollars above referred to to the Committee of American Bankers for the accounts of the respective Banks named in the First Schedule at the expiration of six calendar months from the date on which the moneys were advanced together with all sums due by those Banks to the Committee of American Bankers in respect of interest upon or commissions and expenses in connection with the respective loans, in so far as the moneys then remaining in the hands of the Exchange Committee may enable them to do so.

In the event of the moneys in the hands of the American Exchange Committee being insufficient to discharge these liabilities in full the deficiency will be provided in the first place by the Banks named in the First and Second Schedules in proportion to the amounts set opposite to their respective names in the third column of the First Schedule and in the second column of the Second Schedule.

Any moneys provided by the respective Banks under the last preceding paragraph will be treated as an advance on behalf of the Treasury to be repaid out of moneys provided by Parliament with interest at Bank rate varying, but apart from such interest no profit will be made by the Banks out of any of the operations above specified.

The Treasury will forthwith seek the authority of Parliament to indemnify the respective Banks named in the First and Second Schedules from all losses, costs, expenses, damages, liabilities claims and demands of every description arising out of or in consequence of the arrangements above referred to.

The Chancellor of the Exchequer recommends these proposals for the approval of the Board.

My Lords approve and are pleased to direct that provision for enabling Them to give effect to the undertakings proposed be included in the Government War Obligations Bill about to be presented to Parliament.

FIRST SCHEDULE

First column	Second column	Third column
Name of Bank	Amount of Loan $	Amount of $4\frac{1}{2}\%$ War Loan Stock to be deposited £
Barclay & Co. Ltd.	5,000,000	700,000
Lloyds Bank Ltd.	7,500,000	1,000,000
London City & Midland Bank Ltd.	7,500,000	1,000,000
London County & Westminster Bank Ltd.	7,500,000	1,000,000
London Joint Stock Bank Ltd.	5,000,000	500,000
National Provincial Bank of England Ltd.	5,000,000	1,000,000
Parrs Bank Ltd.	5,000,000	700,000
Union of London & Smiths Bank Ltd.	7,500,000	1,000,000
	$50,000,000	£6,900,000

SECOND SCHEDULE

First column	Second Column
Name of Bank	Amount of $4\frac{1}{2}\%$ War Loan Stock to be deposited £
Capital & Counties Bank Ltd.	370,000
Coutts & Co.	175,000
Glyn & Co.	175,000
London & South Western Bank Ltd.	210,000

SECOND SCHEDULE (continued)

First column	Second Column	
Name of Bank	Amount of $4\frac{1}{2}$% War Loan Stock to be deposited	
	£	
Martins Bank Ltd.	70,000	
Williams Deacons Bank Ltd.	175,000	
Bank of Liverpool Ltd.	210,000	
Lancashire & Yorkshire Bank Ltd.	105,000	
Manchester & County Bank Ltd.	105,000	
Manchester & Liverpool Dist: Banking Co. Ltd.	210,000	
Union Bank of Manchester Ltd.	70,000	
Bank of Scotland	175,000	
British Linen Bank	175,000	
Clydesdale Bank Ltd.	175,000	
Commercial Bank of Scotland Ltd.	175,000	
National Bank of Scotland Ltd.	175,000	
Royal Bank of Scotland Ltd.	175,000	
Union Bank of Scotland Ltd.	175,000	3,100,000

3. LETTER FROM THE CHANCELLOR OF THE EXCHEQUER, 18 NOVEMBER 1915

Treasury Chambers,
Whitehall, S.W.
18th November 1915.

My Lord and Gentlemen,

You have at my request agreed to act as a Committee for the regulation of the foreign exchanges, and in order to assist you in your operations I undertake to place at your absolute disposal (a) all the Gold which is now in the possession, or may during the period of your operations come into the possession, of His Majesty's Government, (b) all the proceeds still to be received from the recent loan in the United States, and from any further loan or credit to be contracted abroad in any form and from the sale abroad of any Securities by or on behalf of His Majesty's Government during the said period; and (c) any American, Colonial or other foreign Securities which may be bought or borrowed or otherwise acquired by or on behalf of His Majesty's Government during the said period for the purpose of exchange operations.

You are to be at liberty to deal with or dispose of all such Gold, Moneys and Securities either directly or through your agents in any manner that you may think fit, and you are to take charge of and carry into effect all Exchange operations that may be necessary for His Majesty's Government. You are also to respond, for the payment of all debts contracted abroad, or payable to people resident abroad, by or on behalf of His Majesty's Government, for which purpose I shall lay before you from time to time the fullest particulars that I can procure with regard to such debts.

His Majesty's Government will seek the authority of Parliament to reimburse to you any actual out-of-pocket expenses incurred by you and your agents in connection with the above operations, but you will receive no remuneration and any profit resulting from your operations will accrue to His Majesty's Government.

His Majesty's Government will also ask Parliament to indemnify you each and all and hold you harmless for all losses, costs, damages and claims which you may incur on account of anything you may do or omit to do in connection with the operations which you are to undertake as aforesaid.

I am,

My Lord and Gentlemen,
Your obedient Servant,
(Sd.) R. McKenna.

The Lord Cunliffe,
Brien Cokayne Esq.,
Sir Edward Holden, Bart.,
Sir Felix Schuster, Bart.

APPENDIX 5

LIST OF STAFF GRIEVANCES – MEMORANDUM DATED NEW YEAR 1919

[This memorandum, presented to the Court of Directors on 27 February 1919, led to the appointment, on 6 March 1919, of the Special Committee on Grievances and so to the development of staff representation within the Bank.]

<u>Private</u>]

A Memorandum, respectfully addressed to the Governor and Directors of the Bank of England by the staff of the same, at the beginning of the New Year of 1919

SIRS,

It is inevitable, when the whole industrial world is in the throes of reconstruction after the Great War, that so old and conservative an institution as the Bank of England cannot escape the purging process of the time. After the unparalleled stress and strain of the last four and a half years, during which perhaps the human element in Bank life has been unfortunately too little accounted of, there is bound to be a reaction accompanied by unrest, dissatisfaction, and yearning for better conditions of hours and pay: but the constitutional procedure, whereby grievances may be brought to the notice of the Court is so indirect and liable to blockade, that only the adoption of the recommendations in the Whitley Report is felt by the staff as adequate to meet the situation.

The staff have every reason to believe that a great scheme of re-organization is under consideration by the Court at the present time, and in view of that belief they venture very respectfully to draw attention to the following matters which seem to call for special notice:

Standing Committee of Directors and Staff for mutual conference advocated

In accordance with the Whitley Report, it is felt that a Standing Committee, co-operative and representative of Directors, Heads of Departments, Principals, and Staff, should meet periodically to talk over matters affecting the well-being of the employees. In no other way does it seem possible that difficulties can be brought to light and alleged grievances ventilated. Hitherto the staff have accepted the conditions of service with patient resignation, but all over the country industry is organizing itself in its own defence, and the Banking community generally has at last awakened to the fact that it is unorganized and powerless and has taken steps to form a Guild to protect its interests. It were a pity if Trades Unionism in any shape or form should enter within the walls of the Bank of England if it can be obviated now by the establishment of some such Committee as is suggested above.

Banking Hours

There is no doubt that the Banking Day should be definitely fixed, and it should certainly be no longer than that which obtained before the War. It has always been the uncertainty of the time of getting away that has made life so difficult to live in the outside world—as engagements could seldom be made with certainty that they could be fulfilled. Much could be done by more efficient organization and the drawing of definite times for passing work through, to render the hours of Bank men less arbitrary.

Overtime

The hours of the Banking Day being once fixed, any clerk kept beyond the appointed hour of leaving should be paid for overtime accordingly, extra remuneration being given for waitings. Banks hitherto have very cruelly exploited their employees in the matter of extra hours without extra pay, and it is felt that if overtime pay were rigidly instituted new methods of organization or of speeding up the work would soon be forthcoming to enable employees to leave at the appointed hour.

Salaries

Throughout our generation the cost of living is bound to continue very high. It is essential therefore that the old scale of salaries should be appreciably raised, the anomalies of the so-called New Scheme be eliminated, and compensation granted to any sufferers under its defects.

Classes

The system of 'classes' has worked most inequitably as between office and office and man and man—increase in class ratings being dependent on luck, rather than on length of service or merit. Moreover, much bitter feeling has been aroused by the delays in filling up vacancies in offices as they arise. Many men have lost considerably by this procrastination, and the unfairness is palpable. It is an open question whether classes should not be abolished altogether, and 'personal money' introduced as aforetime for special work and special posts over and above an adjusted scale of House money. In this way promotions of junior men over seniors would not penalize the latter by keeping them stationary in their class as hitherto, while their contemporaries, because they happened to be in other offices, went forward. Men with higher qualifications would obtain higher pay without the offence of receiving payment through others' loss.

Delays in filling vacancies

Personal money and promotions

Pricking men in

While recognizing the absolute right of the authorities to promote men as they think fit, attention should be drawn to the fact that much discontent has been justly caused of recent years by the growing practice of pricking men into offices unexpectedly, and so preventing legitimate advancement all down the line. Under the present system it would appear that few men can ever rise in their office above a First Class, outsiders being introduced for senior posts without scruple.

Responsibility unremunerated

The difference in salaries at present in force in the case of Senior Clerks, Superintendents, Chief Clerks, and Deputy Principals, is so absurdly small as compared with the rank and file, as practically to make the increased responsibility unremunerated. Perhaps a subtle cause of unrest in the Bank is the fact that there are so few well-paid posts open to the Staff, and therefore no inducement for men to interest themselves in their profession—more especially as promotion would seem to be due too often to personal influence rather than to recognized merit. There ought to be far more posts with salaries ranging between £400 and £1,000, and in the better offices the maximum salaries ought to be correspondingly higher, instead of being on the same level as any ordinary office.

Income Tax

Whether salaries should be paid free of Income Tax or not is an open question which should be studied in the light of the practice of other Banks, for whose adoption of the system there must be some justification. But on the other hand the salaries of Bank Clerks should be on a scale liberal enough to enable them to fulfil their duties as citizens, and to pay all claims made by the State upon their purse.

Statement of Income Tax deducted desirable

If the Bank continue to deduct Income Tax from salaries, a quarterly statement should be issued by the Secretary's Office to each Clerk showing exactly how much tax has been deducted, and how the nett sum is arrived at.

Overtime Pay

The question of payment for Overtime has loomed large of course during the war, and no answer has been vouchsafed to the anomalies pointed out in the memorandum to the Governors in May last. It is reasonable to expect that a graduated scale of payment on some more equitable lines according to salary should be introduced without delay, and that Sunday work and night work, if ever necessary, should be remunerated at a much more generous rate than prevailed during the war.

Pensions

Pensions henceforward should be calculable on the advanced scale of salaries necessary now to meet the permanent increase in the cost of living. It is thought, moreover, that if possible, retirement should be optional at sixty on full pension, or earlier on a proportionate allowance.

Hitherto the men who have profited most by the Bank in this connection have been the ne'er-do-wells and the invalids. The men who do yeoman service are compelled to serve out their time to the bitter end—as there is no possible escape from the Bank (except by forfeiture of pension) unless under the plea of ill-health. This ought not to be. In special circumstances it should be permissible for any man, after say twenty-five years of service, to be free to resign his position on a proportionate pension. Many tragedies would be averted thereby, and men who realize that their talents might be more serviceable in other directions would not be too old to begin life again. Under the 'New Scheme' the Bank itself forces the resignation of incompetent men at the age of fifty—on pension—but here again legislation is in favour of the 'bad bargains' of the Bank and not of the men who serve during their career the interests of the place most faithfully. A strong reason for putting forward this plea for optional permission to retire earlier on pension is the fact that it has come to be recognized that unless a man is promoted before or soon after he is thirty his future prospects in the Bank are practically *nil*, and hence the not unnatural absence of any real interest in their work on the part of the older men who have no incentive left to stimulate them on. This lack of incentive is one of the saddest phases of Bank life that call for sympathetic solution.

Widows

The pensioning of widows deserves far more generous attention than hitherto has been the case. If a pension be deferred pay, the widows of men who serve the Bank all their lives but die in their late fifties or early sixties ought not to forgo so entirely what was clearly due to their husbands but for their premature death. The present annuity granted by the Bank should be largely increased in such cases.

Leave

The permanent staff have deeply appreciated the recent order that every one this New Year should enjoy a holiday for four consecutive weeks. It is cordially recognized that the Bank during the War were unable to allow the usual leave, and that therefore much that was due has been forgone, but the confidence in the authorities is such that it is believed exceptional privileges will be granted during the next few years whereby the staff may not altogether lose the rewards of their long sacrifice and strenuous endeavour.

Conclusion

In conclusion, the staff would affirm their loyalty and appreciation of the many benefits they enjoy in the service of the Bank, for whose dignity as the leading Bank in the country they are naturally jealous. The foregoing Memorandum has been drawn up not in any spirit of disloyalty or captious criticism, but with the hope in these perilous years of transition from War to Peace that by drawing attention to anomalies and defects in the working system of the Bank as regards its staff, reforms may be inaugurated in due time, a feeling of harmony and goodwill may be restored and mutual co-operation, sympathy, and respect be the hall-marks of the House in the years that are to be.

We are, Sirs,
Your obedient Servants,

On behalf of the Staff.

APPENDIX 6

THE GOLD EXPORT EMBARGO, 1919–25

Throughout the war there was no legal obstacle preventing the export of gold, provided that the export was not for enemy benefit, which would have brought it into conflict with Trading with the Enemy legislation. The policy of the authorities was to make gold difficult to obtain; the steps taken in pursuance of this, and the lack of insurance and shipping facilities, made export virtually impossible while hostilities lasted. After the Armistice, the possibility of export became practicable, and the decision of 20 March 1919 to unpeg the foreign exchange value of the pound made export of gold highly profitable. Immediate steps were necessary to constitute an effective embargo.

This was done by Order in Council of 1 April 1919, issued under the authority of the Customs (Exportation Prohibition) Act 1914, Section 1 of which had, 'whilst a state of war in which His Majesty is engaged exists', extended to all articles Section 8 of the Customs and Inland Revenue Act 1879. Under the Termination of the Present War (Definition) Act 1918, 'the state of war' would cease to exist on ratification of treaties of peace. Before November 1920 there had been ratifications covering Germany, Austria and Bulgaria, and Hungary was about to ratify. This would leave outstanding only Turkey, and the Treaty of Sevres had already been signed; it could not then be foreseen that it never would be ratified. (It was eventually superseded by the Treaty of Lausanne, 1923.) In November 1920, therefore, it looked as though the statutory basis of the gold export embargo might disappear at almost any time. At that moment, although early restoration of the gold standard was unquestioned government policy, nobody regarded it as immediately practicable, and a new statutory basis for the gold export embargo was required immediately.

On 10 November 1920 the Financial Secretary to the Treasury (Baldwin) therefore introduced the Gold and Silver (Export Control etc.) Bill (*House of Commons Hansard*, Vol. 134, 1320–26): this would not automatically forbid exports, but would give a government power by proclamation to forbid exports except under licence. On the Second Reading (29 November 1920) the government was asked, on general grounds of objection to permanent powers, to accept expiration of the proposed law at 30 June 1921 (*House of Commons Hansard*, Vol. 135, 1042–67); Sir Donald Maclean, an opposition Liberal, made the request. During the Committee stage, this request was reformulated substituting a later expiry date, 31 December 1923, simply because the original suggestion would have allowed continuance, under an Expiring Laws Continuance Act, without adequate opportunity for debate. Baldwin, reporting that he had consulted, among others, 'those who are responsible for the protection of our currency and similar matters in the City of London', said that five years, not three, 'ought to be the shortest period', and that he had been thinking of 'a longer period'. The House thereupon agreed that the new law should expire on 31 December 1925 (*House of Commons Hansard*, Vol. 136, 113–24). The Bill became law as 'An Act to control the exportation of gold and silver coin and bullion and to prohibit the melting or improper use of gold and silver coin', 10 and 11 Geo. 5 c. 70.

There is no evidence at the Bank as to what was 'the longer period' Baldwin had in mind, but it may well have been 'the ten years of the reconstruction period' which had become a standard phrase, in the context of the foreign exchanges, during the Cunliffe Committee discussions in 1918. (See especially a committee question put by Cunliffe, and Cokayne's answer: 'It will be some years, probably the full ten years, before...exceptional measures cease? — Yes.') The matter was discussed between Baldwin and Norman at the Treasury on 8 December 1920 (Norman Diary), five days before Baldwin in Parliament rejected three years but conceded five. The ultimate date, 31 December 1925, the proximity of which certainly had some influence on opinion in the critical opening months of 1925, was thus fixed as a compromise between the rather greater elbow-room the responsible authorities would have preferred and the orthodox desire of Parliamentarians to keep special powers under adequate review.

The necessary proclamation under the 1920 Act was duly issued on 7 February 1921. Neither the amendment of the Bill, limiting its life, nor the issue of the proclamation attracted press comment.

APPENDIX 7

THE CUNLIFFE COMMITTEE AND THE CUNLIFFE LIMIT

Discussion on the desirability of a committee to consider financial reconstruction after the 1914–18 war first appears in Treasury records in October 1917. Bradbury and Chalmers (Treasury), Nash (Ministry of Reconstruction) and Cunliffe (Governor of the Bank) participated. It was agreed at this stage that Austen Chamberlain would be the best Chairman, and that the Governor should be a member; other names were later suggested by Cunliffe, in response to Bradbury's request. The proposals were accepted by the Chancellor of the Exchequer (Bonar Law) early in November, with a condition on personnel: W. H. N. Goschen (Chairman of the Committee of London Clearing Bankers) being substituted for another banker proposed earlier.

Chamberlain then (November 1917) declined the Chancellor's invitation, and as a substitute Chairman the Treasury could think only of public figures having no special experience of finance. The trouble was that Cunliffe's membership restricted 'the field and choice for chairman to guns of the largest calibre'. Bradbury thought it better not to put Cunliffe himself in the Chair and Chalmers (who had lately figured in the famous Cunliffe Quarrel – see Chapter 5) took this view 'even more strongly'. Nevertheless, the Chancellor himself took the plunge, and on 19 December Cunliffe accepted his invitation to become Chairman. (This was six weeks after he had been told that from April 1918 he would no longer be Governor.) The committee was appointed in January 1918 by Treasury Minute. In addition to Cunliffe, the members were Sir Charles Addis (not yet a Director of the Bank of England), R. Beckett, Sir John Bradbury, G. C. Cassels, G. Farrer, H. Gibbs, W. H. N. Goschen, Lord Inchcape, R. W. Jeans, A. C. Pigou, G. F. Stewart and W. Wallace. Between the First Interim Report (August 1918) and the Final Report (December 1919), Bradbury and Cassels dropped out, and Blackett was added. Apart from Bradbury and Blackett from the Treasury, and Professor Pigou (Cambridge), all were bankers. (P.R.O. T.1/12238/47228.)

The original terms of reference were:

to consider the various problems which will arise in connection with currency and the foreign exchanges during the period of reconstruction and report upon the steps required to bring about the restoration of normal conditions in due course.

Early in 1918 the following words were added:

and to consider the working of the Bank Act, 1844, and the constitution and functions of the Bank of England with a view to recommending any alterations which may appear to them to be necessary or desirable.

The First (and only) Interim Report was signed on 15 August 1918 and was published at once (Cd. 9182). Thereafter, Cunliffe had great difficulty in arranging further meetings, as members found themselves caught up in activities consequent on the abrupt end of the war in November 1918. Eventually a very brief Final Report was signed on 3 December 1919 (a month before Cunliffe's death). It was published at once (Cmd. 464). No Evidence was published. Both Reports were reproduced in full in T. E. Gregory, *Select Statutes, Documents and Reports Relating to British Banking, 1832–1928* (Oxford, 1929), pp. 334–70.

The Committee's own Summary of Conclusions in its Interim Report, paragraph 47, is reproduced below, including the references to the earlier paragraphs.

47. Our main conclusions may be briefly summarised as follows:–

Before the war the country possessed a complete and effective gold standard. The provisions of the Bank Act, 1844, operated automatically to correct unfavourable exchanges and to check undue expansions of credit. (Paras. 2 to 7)

During the war the conditions necessary to the maintenance of that standard have ceased to exist. The main cause has been the growth of credit due to Government borrowing from the Bank of England and other banks for war needs. The unlimited issue of Currency Notes has been both an inevitable consequence and a necessary condition of this growth of credit. (Paras. 8 to 14)

In our opinion it is imperative that after the war the conditions necessary to the maintenance of an effective gold standard should be restored without delay. Unless the machinery which long experience has shown to be the only effective remedy for an adverse balance of trade and an undue growth of credit is once more brought into play, there will be grave danger of a progressive credit expansion which will result in a foreign drain of gold menacing the convertibility of our note issue and so jeopardising the international trade position of the country. (Para. 15)

The pre-requisites for the restoration of an effective gold standard are:–

(a) The cessation of Government borrowing as soon as possible after the war. We recommend that at the earliest possible moment an adequate sinking fund should be provided out of revenue, so that there may be a regular annual reduction of capital liabilities, more especially those which constitute the floating debt. (Paras. 16 and 17)

(b) The recognised machinery, namely, the raising and making effective of the Bank of England discount rate, which before the war operated to check a foreign drain of gold and the speculative expansion of credit in this country, must be kept in working order. This necessity cannot, and should not, be evaded by any attempt to continue differential rates for home and foreign money after the war. (Paras. 18 and 19)

(c) The issue of fiduciary notes should, as soon as practicable, once more be limited by law, and the present arrangements under which deposits at the Bank of England may be exchanged for legal tender currency without affecting the reserve of the Banking Department should be terminated at the earliest possible moment. Subject to transitional arrangements as regards Currency Notes and to any special arrangements in regard to Scotland and Ireland which we may have to propose when we come to deal with the questions affecting those parts of the United Kingdom, we recommend that the Note Issue (except as regards existing private issues) should be entirely in the hands of the Bank of England. The Notes should be payable in London only and should be legal tender throughout the United Kingdom. (Paras. 20 and 21)

As regards the control of the Note Issue, we make the following observations:–

(1) While the obligation to pay both Bank of England Notes and Currency Notes in gold on demand should be maintained, it is not necessary or desirable that there should be any early resumption of the internal circulation of gold coin. (Para. 23)

(2) While the import of gold should be free from all restrictions, it is convenient that the Bank of England should have cognizance of all gold exports and we recommend that the export of gold coin or bullion should be subject to the condition that such coin and bullion has been obtained from the Bank for the purpose. The Bank should be under obligation to supply gold for export in exchange for its notes. (Para. 24)

(3) In view of the withdrawal of gold from circulation we recommend that the gold reserves of the country should be held by one central institution and that all banks should transfer any gold now held by them to the Bank of England. (Para. 25)

Having carefully considered the various proposals which have been placed before us as regards the basis of the fiduciary note issue (paras. 26 to 31), we recommend that the principle of the Bank Charter Act, 1844, should be maintained, namely, that there should be a fixed fiduciary issue beyond which notes should only be issued in exchange for gold. The separation of the Issue and Banking Departments of the Bank of England should be maintained, and the Weekly Return should continue to be published in its present form. (Para. 32)

We recommend, however, that provision for an emergency be made by the continuance in force, subject to the stringent safeguards recommended in the body of the Report, of section 3 of the Currency and Bank Notes Act, 1914, under which the Bank of England may, with the consent of the Treasury, temporarily issue notes in excess of the legal limit. (Para. 33)

We advocate the publication by the banks of a monthly statement in a prescribed form. (Para. 34)

We have come to the conclusion that it is not practicable to fix any precise figure for the fiduciary Note Issue immediately after the war. (Paras. 35 to 39)

We think it desirable, therefore, to fix the amount which should be aimed at as the central gold reserve, leaving the fiduciary issue to be settled ultimately at such amount as can be kept in circulation without causing the central gold reserve to fall below the amount so fixed. We recommend that the normal minimum of the central gold reserve to be aimed at should be, in the first instance, £150 millions. Until this amount has been reached and maintained concurrently with a satisfactory foreign exchange position for at least a year, the policy of cautiously reducing the uncovered Note Issue should be followed. When reductions have been effected, the actual maximum fiduciary circulation in any year should become the legal maximum for the following year, subject only to the emergency arrangements previously recommended. When the exchanges are working normally on the basis of a minimum reserve of £150,000,000, the position should again be reviewed in the light of the dimensions of the fiduciary issue as it then exists. (Paras. 40 to 42)

We do not recommend the transfer of the existing Currency Note Issue to the Bank of England until the future dimensions of the Fiduciary Issue have been ascertained. During the transitional period the issue should remain a Government issue, but new notes should be issued, not against Government securities, but against Bank of England Notes, and, furthermore, when opportunity arises for providing cover for existing uncovered notes, Bank of England Notes should be used for this purpose also. Demands for new currency would then fall in the normal way on the Banking Department of the Bank of England. (Paras. 43 and 44)

When the fiduciary portion of the issue has been reduced to an amount which experience shows to be consistent with the maintenance of a central gold reserve of £150 millions, the outstanding Currency Notes should be retired and replaced by Bank of England Notes of low denomination in accordance with the detailed procedure which we describe. (Paras. 45 and 46).

The Final Report, except for a few sentences not relevant to the present work, is as follows:

2. *Foreign Exchanges.* – We stated in the introduction to our Interim Report our opinion that a sound system of currency would in itself secure equilibrium in the Foreign Exchanges. We have reviewed the criticisms which have been made upon this part of our Report, but we see no reason to modify our opinion. We have found nothing in the experiences of the war to falsify the lessons of previous experience that the adoption of a currency not convertible at will into gold or other exportable coin is likely in practice to lead to overissue and so to destroy the measure of exchangeable value and cause a general rise in all prices and an adverse movement in the foreign exchanges.

3. The nominal convertibility of the currency note which has been sustained by the prohibition of the export of gold is of little value. The weakness of the exchanges is in a measure due to trade conditions, but an important cause of the depreciation in sterling in New York and other financial centres is, in our opinion, to be found in the expanded state of credit in this country. The existing expansion is not merely the legacy of the stress of war finance and Government borrowings, which even now have not ceased, but also, in part the result of maintaining rates from money in London below those ruling in other important financial centres. The difficulties of the Foreign Exchanges' position are aggravated by the grant of long term loans and credits, whether directly or under guarantee or otherwise by the Government or by private lenders, to enable foreign States or their nationals to pay for exports from this country. Few of these loans and credits will be liquidated at an early date. The large payments which we have to make to America, North and South, for necessary imports of foodstuffs and raw materials from those countries make it essential that we, in our turn, should secure payment in cash for as large a proportion as possible of our exports visible and invisible. We recommend therefore that preference should be given to exports to countries which are able to make payment in the ordinary course of trade.

Increased production, cessation of Government borrowings and decreased expenditure both by the Government and by each individual member of the nation are the first essentials to recovery. These must be associated with the restoration of the pre-war methods of controlling the currency and credit system of the country for the purpose of re-establishing at an early date a free market for gold in London.

4. *Bank of England.* – The principles of the Bank Charter Act of 1844 were fully considered by us in our Interim Report. We have examined with care the opinions there expressed in the light of certain criticisms which have been made with regard to them. We see, however, no reason to alter our conclusions. We have again considered the principles governing the banking systems of the principal foreign countries and we are satisfied that they are not so well adapted to the needs of this country as those contained in the Act of 1844. Certain important alterations which experience suggested to be desirable have been made in the constitution and management of the Bank during the war, and we do not now think it necessary to make any further recommendation.

5. *Government Borrowings on Ways and Means Advances from the Bank of England.* – We desire to draw attention to the extensive use made during the war of the system of Ways and Means Advances from the Bank of England. We referred to this matter in paragraph 16 of our Interim Report and explained its effect in causing credit and currency expansion. The powers given to the Government by Parliament to borrow from the Bank of England in the form of an overdraft on the credit of Ways and Means were, as the name implies, intended to enable the Government to anticipate receipts from Revenue or permanent borrowings for a brief period only. Indeed Parliament by expressly providing that all such advances should be repaid in the quarter following that in which they were obtained showed that it had no intention of bestowing upon the Government the power of securing an overdraft of indefinite duration and amount. Under the exigencies of war finance the Government found it necessary to re-borrow in each quarter on the credit of Ways and Means the amount needed to enable them to comply with the statutory requirement that the previous quarter's Ways and Means Advances should be repaid, with the result that the total outstanding advances remained for a long time at a high figure. We are glad to see that efforts are now being made to reduce this overdraft to more moderate dimensions.

We, therefore, hope, now that conditions are less abnormal, that the Government will confine its use of Ways and Means and Advances from the Bank of England to providing for purely temporary necessities. Such advances afford a legitimate method of tiding over a few weeks' shortage, but are entirely unsuitable for borrowings over a longer period.

... ...

8. *Currency Note Issue.* – We have considered whether steps should not be taken at an early date to impose limitations upon the fiduciary portion of the currency note issue with a view to the restoration of the normal arrangements under which demands for new currency operate to reduce the reserve in the Banking Department of the Bank of England. In view of the fact that demobilisation is approaching completion and that as we hope fresh Government borrowing will shortly cease, we consider that effect should now be given to the recommendation made in our Interim Report that the actual maximum fiduciary circulation in any year should become the legal maximum for the following year, subject only to the emergency arrangements which we proposed in paragraph 33 of our Interim Report. The policy of placing Bank of England notes in the Currency Note Reserve as cover for the fiduciary portion of the issue as opportunity arises should, of course, be continued. We recommend further that the Treasury Minute made under Section 2 of the Currency and Bank Notes Act, 1914, providing for the issue of currency notes to Joint Stock Banks, which is in fact inoperative, should now be withdrawn.

In the text of this work the main references to the Cunliffe Committee and its Reports are in Vol. 1, Chapters 6 (pp. 111, 118, 127–9, 223), 7 (pp. 136–7, 149) and 12 (pp. 285–6, 287–8). Other references are on pp. 99, 227, 307.

Two other matters deserve a little more detail: 'the Bradbury trick' and the Cunliffe Limit'.

1 THE BRADBURY TRICK[1]

This was a device, invented by Bradbury of the Treasury but welcome to Cunliffe at the Bank, whereby changes in the double note issue (Treasury plus Bank) should be brought into the Bank Return. It was accepted by the Cunliffe Committee in paragraph 43 of its First Interim Report:

> 43. It remains for us to consider how and when the present issue of Currency Notes is to be replaced by the Bank of England issue. There would be some awkwardness in transferring the issue to the Bank of England before the future dimensions of the fiduciary issue have been ascertained. We, therefore, recommend that during the transitional period the issue should remain a Government issue, but that such post-war expansion (if any) as may take place should be covered, not by the investment of the proceeds of the new notes in Government securities, as at present, but by taking Bank of England notes from the Bank and holding them in the Currency Note Reserve, and that, as and when opportunity arises for providing cover for the existing fiduciary portion of the issue, the same procedure should be followed. The effect of this arrangement would be that the demands for new currency would operate in the normal way to reduce the reserve in the Banking Department at the Bank of England, which would have to be restored by raising money rates and encouraging gold imports.

The germ of this idea can be found in Treasury papers in April 1916, beginning with a Minute from Bradbury to Chalmers and the Chancellor. Chalmers told the Chancellor that the proposal would be 'highly distasteful' to the Bank, not on any general ground but because, at that particular juncture, its introduction would lead to dearer money and so be fatal to the government's borrowing plans (P.R.O. T.170/106). At what date Bradbury's proposal was first mentioned to Cunliffe is not known, but he had evidently accepted it in time for its inclusion in the First Interim Report of the Cunliffe Committee (August 1918), and the Report of the Bank's internal committee 'on the Revision of the Bank Act', approved by the Court on 12 December 1918, shows that it was by that date part of the accepted doctrine of the Bank.

2 THE CUNLIFFE LIMIT

This was a device originating in the broad notion that a return to normal in monetary affairs implied a return to 1913 prices, or at any rate a very substantial fall below the level reached at the end of the war, and a corresponding fall in the amount of notes required for circulation. It was also ventilated in the context of a deflation required to allow a return to the gold standard at the former parity. It was taken up by the Cunliffe Committee, in paragraph 42 of its First Interim Report:

[1] I believe that I owe the term 'the Bradbury trick' to Mrs S. Howson of Wolfson College, Cambridge. (Cf. *Economic History Review*, XXVII, 1 (Feb. 1974), p. 88.) Certainly I had supposed that the inventor of the device was Cunliffe himself, but since talking to Mrs Howson I have found that there is, in the Treasury records cited below, evidence that Bradbury was the originator of a device that was congenial to Cunliffe even if he had reservations about its adoption at a particular moment in 1916.

42. If these arrangements are adopted, there will be an interim period beginning after the completion of demobilisation during which it is probable that the present issue of Currency Notes will have to be gradually reduced until experience has shown what amount of fiduciary notes can be kept in circulation consistently with the maintenance of this reserve. It was suggested to us in evidence that, until that amount has been ascertained, steps should be taken as soon as possible after the war to reduce the uncovered issue at the rate of not less than 3 per cent per annum of the outstanding amount, and that, subject to arrangements for meeting a temporary emergency, the issue in any period of six months or one year should not be allowed to exceed the amount outstanding in the preceding similar period. We think that it would be highly desirable to aim at a steady and continuous reduction, but we are disposed to doubt whether it will be found to be practicable to work to any precise rule. We confine ourselves therefore to the general recommendation of policy indicated above. We entirely concur, however, in the suggestion that, when reductions have taken place, the actual maximum fiduciary circulation in any year should become the legal maximum for the following year, subject only to the emergency arrangements proposed in paragraph 33.

In the Final Report, the Cunliffe Committee urged (para. 8) that it was time to give effect to this recommendation. The Treasury, urging the Chancellor to make an immediate pronouncement, advised that the Governor of the Bank was 'a strong supporter of the proposal to fix a maximum, and... prepared for the fact that it involves a call on his note reserve to cover any increase in the outstanding total' (P.R.O. T.1/12437/53595). The Governor (Cokayne) was, that is to say, anxious to have both the Bradbury trick and the Cunliffe limit in operation. The combination was entirely congenial to a Bank that was anxious to get the monetary system into its own clutches as rapidly as possible, as the only way of establishing the control whereby the gold standard could be re-established. The Chancellor acted without delay: on 15 December 1919 the formal Treasury Minute was issued (Cmd. 485):

The Chancellor of the Exchequer draws the attention of the Board to paragraph 8 of the Final Report of the Committee on Currency and Foreign Exchanges after the War, which recommends the imposition of a maximum limit on the issue of Currency Notes under the Currency and Bank Notes Act, 1914. The Chancellor proposes to the Board that steps shall be taken to give effect to the recommendation that the actual maximum fiduciary circulation of Currency Notes in any year shall be the fixed maximum for the following year.

The maximum fiduciary circulation during the expired portion of the current calendar year has been £320,608,298 10s. and the Chancellor accordingly proposes that directions shall now be given to the Bank of England restricting them from issuing Currency Notes during the 12 months commencing the 1st January, 1920, in excess of a total of £320,600,000, except against gold or Bank of England Notes, and from issuing in the calendar year commencing 1st January in any year henceforward notes in excess of the actual maximum fiduciary circulation of the preceding 12 months.

From that date until the Currency and Bank Notes Act of 1928, this Treasury Minute stood, almost with the authority of a statute, as the formal constraint on the issue of currency notes. At the outset, with wide support in public opinion,[1] it was intended as an instrument of deflation. The Treasury

[1] Cf. R. McKenna, *Post-War Banking Policy*, p. 1.

intended to put extra teeth into it by secretly holding that the effective limit for any year should be not the previous year's actual maximum but that maximum *minus £m5*, and this was tacitly accepted by the Bank. The only clear evidence of the figure of £m5 as the margin is in correspondence between the Governor and Niemeyer, 10 and 12 July 1920 (Niemeyer was stating the views of the Chancellor and Sir Warren Fisher). This correspondence shows that the margin could be encroached upon, under pressure of circumstances. There were some awkward corners in 1920, but at this time the proximity of the circulation to the Cunliffe Limit merely provided the authorities with an additional argument to quote for policies that would have been the same without any Cunliffe Limit. The slump of 1920–22 then freed the authorities from any concern with the operation of the Limit, for falling prices and activity caused the circulation to decline much faster than the fall in the Cunliffe Limit from £m317 for 1921 to £m270 for 1923. Even in this period of depression, however, the authorities were still sufficiently attached to deflation to wish to avoid any discussion that might force qualification of that policy, and the Cunliffe Limit was left undisturbed. The result was that when the trade slump flattened out and then eased a little, the shrunken Cunliffe Limit became irksome and gave rise to a succession of scrapes as each summer and Christmas circulation peak occurred. The approach of each scrape occasioned, from October 1923 onwards, a scrounging round – though in the dignified terms of Treasury–Bank relations – for some temporising device to enable the authorities to escape opening the subject to Parliamentary controversy. The extreme case was at Whitsun 1926, when the situation was saved by co-operation of the clearing banks, which made extraordinary payments of notes into the Bank to tide over the peak period. (There was a precedent of sorts in 1857, when an excess issue under the Act of 1844 was avoided by the authorities (as Newmarch put it) 'taking the 'at round Lombard Street'.) In each of the years 1924 to 1928 the actual maximum reached was within two millions, and twice within £200,000, of the relevant Cunliffe Limit. It would have been open to the authorities to widen this margin by greater resort to the Bank of England's own Reserve; this device was used to some extent, but when the restoration of the gold standard was in prospect and then achieved, the authorities did not want to force in the Bank's Reserve large movements that would disturb markets unnecessarily. They had in fact accepted the view that the note circulation had become a residual element in the system, though they were unwilling to throw overboard the Cunliffe Limit which had been based on a radically different interpretation. They were not ready to legislate, incidentally putting an end to the Cunliffe Limit, until 1928, a timetable dictated mainly by the timing of the gold standard policy. The legislation of 1928 is discussed in Chapter 12.

APPENDIX 8

MEMORANDUM AS TO MONEY RATES, 10 FEBRUARY 1920

I. GENERAL EFFECT OF THE INCREASE IN RATES

The rise in rates has inflicted no hardship or restraint on the development of legitimate industry which with present profits could well afford even higher rates.

It has discouraged the holding up of stocks of goods and has promoted their quick turnover, thus rendering production and distribution more immediately effective in meeting demand.

It has tended to check the increase in prices and in the cost of living and thereby to lessen the extent of the constant demand for higher wages.

It has afforded an obvious inducement to sell abroad to cash buyers rather than to credit buyers.

It has checked borrowing as well as speculation both in commodities and in securities and by depressing prices of the latter has tended to discourage the sale of securities from abroad to this country which cannot at present afford to take securities in payment for her exports.

It has retarded the inevitable fall in the American Exchange and, in spite of that fall, has throughout facilitated free dealings; in fact it is only since the internal situation in the United States has created for that Country difficulties in financing her exports that trouble has been experienced in selling sterling in New York. It must also be remembered that the operations of our late Allies whose Exchanges have been moving more and more in our favour have been largely instrumental in causing the existing depreciation of our Exchange with the United States.

It has helped to attract foreign capital to London and to retain British capital here.

It has checked the tendency of foreigners – including even Americans – to finance themselves in this market.

It has arrested the currency and credit expansion.

It has shown the intention of this country to face facts and has thus helped to improve our standing in foreign countries.

It has had all the advantages which long experience has rightly attached to a rise in rates – though in a less degree than heretofore owing to this country having ceased to be a large creditor.

II. PROBABLE NEED FOR EVEN HIGHER RATES

It is true that all these effects would be, and probably will eventually have to be, enhanced by a still further rise in rates. In October it looked as though a 5¾% effective rate, although unlikely to achieve great results at the time, would perhaps be sufficient if maintained during the present year. But since then the Federal Reserve Board have raised their official rates to such an extent that it is very probable that a further rise will be necessary here.

It is not true as has been alleged that until the Government has virtually extinguished its floating debt there is no use in paying a high rate for Treasuries. In fact the reverse is the case. For once the floating debt has become sufficiently reduced, the Bank of England will be restored to its position as regulator of money rates in accordance with the needs of the Country and the Treasury's only concern will be to obtain the best possible rate for the negligible balance of floating debt then outstanding.

III. STEPS NECESSARY FOR A RETURN TO NORMAL CONDITIONS

Generally speaking it will be agreed that steps should gradually be taken to appreciate the currency, to bring about a fall in the prices of commodities, to increase the purchasing power of 'money' and to get back to the gold standard; or, in a word, to prevent the continuance of the present inflation.

These steps are necessary to enable the manufacturer to improve the export trade, to stabilise internal conditions, and to restore the balance between (1) commodities of all kinds and (2) money and credit.

The depreciation of the currency is two-fold: first, a general depreciation of say 150% as measured by the rise in prices: second, a specific depreciation as measured by the premium of nearly 50% on the price of gold as bullion, or, what comes to the same thing, by the fall in the foreign exchanges.

The first and most urgent task before the Country is to get back to the gold standard by getting rid of this specific depreciation of the currency.

This end can only be achieved by a reversal of the process by which the specific depreciation was produced, the artificial creation of currency and credit, and for this the appropriate instrument is the rate of interest. The rate of interest is the price of loanable capital and, whatever may be the theoretical advantages of discrimination by the Banks, no other practical means for limiting advances and the concomitant creation of credit and rise in prices has been suggested than the old and well-tried plan of a rise in the Bank rate.

'The existing expansion' – in the words of the Currency Committee's final report – 'is not merely the legacy of the stress of War finance... but also in part the result of maintaining rates for money in London below those ruling in other important financial centres.'

Economic reconstruction after the War involves a high demand for capital, and the normal effect of demand is to raise the price of the thing demanded. The operation of this economic law was suspended during the War by the artificial creation of credit and currency. Now that this has ceased the law again comes into play, with the result that as a preliminary step the Bank of England rate has been raised to 6%. This is not to make money artificially dear, it is to set the rate for money free to find its natural level by the equation of supply and demand. It is to strip the market of the artificial conditions of control in which the rate of interest had ceased to be the measure of the demand for loanable capital.

The validity of this step is not impaired by the circumstance that the export of gold is still prohibited. It is true that in normal conditions the undue expansion of credit would be indicated by the drain or the fear of a drain on the gold reserves of the Bank of England, and that at present this is not possible. It is not, however, the drain on the gold which serves to check the undue expansion of credit but the consequent rise in the rate of interest, and this holds true whether in point of fact the gold be exportable or not. It is the rate of interest that counts.

The process of deflation of prices which may be expected to follow on the check to the expansion of credit must necessarily be a painful one to some classes of the community, but this is unavoidable. It is small comfort to the holders of gilt-edged Bonds to be told that it is only the price and not the value of their Securities which is depressed by a rise in the rate of interest. Per contra, people with fixed incomes and the great body of the working classes will be greatly relieved by a decrease in the cost of living. The Government will have to pay more for their loans but the increased cost to the Nation is as dust in the balance compared with the restoration of free trade and the removal of social unrest and political discontent.

IV. IMPRUDENCE OF REVERTING TO CHEAP MONEY

If rates were now lowered the holders of existing Treasury Bills would indeed secure a profit; the many holders of other Government Securities would be enabled for the moment to write back some of the depreciation already suffered and possibly in some cases to unload holdings at higher than present prices on an unsuspecting public; and Bankers without raising their present Deposit Rates would be able to attract increased deposits from present holders of Treasury Bills and thus further to enlarge their loans and with them the general conditions of expansion. But none of these gains to individuals can be advantageous to the country as a whole, and all the beneficent effects of dearer money on the general financial condition of the Country, both internal and external, would be lost.

It is true that with lower rates for Loans and Treasury Bills the Exchequer would have less money to raise for service of the Debt; i.e., the taxpayers, who consist to a highly disproportionate extent of the moneyed classes, would have less to pay for the use of money borrowed from those same classes by the Government.

But it may be doubted whether the reduced cost to the Exchequer would not be more than outweighed by the increased cost to the Nation of practically all commodities and ultimately by the increase in wages (which would inevitably be brought about by such expansion as would follow lower rates) and in any case the injustice, if any, of the high rate is merely a question between one class and another inside the Country and should not be allowed to interfere with the permanent interests of the Country as a whole.

The Federal Reserve Bank's rate for commercial Bills is already 6%, and in the other principal creditor country, Japan, rates are already much higher than ours. Indeed even now London is to some extent financing American business and any slight reduction in our money rates would intensify this anomaly.

The inevitable expansion of credit which would follow a reduction in rates, would include an increase in the issue of Currency Notes, and once their legal maximum was reached or during the process of reaching it the Bank's Reserve would be so depleted as to demand penal rates.

It is therefore submitted that no fall in rates at the present time (even ignoring the foreign demand for accommodation here, as shown, e.g., by conditions in America) could last beyond a few months; while during that period the financial condition of the State could only be worsened.

It may be debated whether last November was the best moment for an increase in rates: some think that it should have come six weeks later, others that it should have come six months earlier, when the export of gold was prohibited.

But no long-sighted person could doubt but that to reverse the general policy then deliberately adopted, after a partial trial and without reaching the logical and ultimate levels, would be to invite a crisis.

APPENDIX 9

RESOLUTIONS OF THE COMMISSION ON CURRENCY AND EXCHANGE, BRUSSELS CONFERENCE, OCTOBER 1920

The currency of a country, in the sense of the immediate purchasing power of the community, includes (a) the actual legal tender money in existence, and (b) any promises to pay legal tender, e.g., as Bank balances – which are available for ordinary daily transactions.

The currencies of all belligerent, and of many other, countries, though in greatly varying degrees, have since the beginning of the war been expanded artificially, regardless of the usual restraints upon such expansion (to which we refer later) and without any corresponding increase in the real wealth upon which their purchasing power was based; indeed in most cases in spite of a serious reduction in such wealth.

It should be clearly understood that this artificial and unrestrained expansion, or 'inflation' as it is called, of the currency or of the titles to immediate purchasing power, does not and cannot add to the total real purchasing power in existence, so that its effect must be to reduce the purchasing power of each unit of the currency. It is, in fact, a form of debasing the currency.

The effect of it has been to intensify, in terms of the *inflated* currencies, the general rise in prices, so that a greater amount of such currency is needed to procure the accustomed supply of goods and services. Where this additional currency was procured by further 'inflation' (i.e. by printing more paper money or creating fresh credit) there arose what has been called a 'vicious spiral' of constantly rising prices and wages and constantly increasing inflation, with the resulting disorganisation of all business, dislocation of the exchanges, a progressive increase in the cost of living, and consequent labour unrest.

I

Therefore:

It is of the utmost importance that the growth of inflation should be stopped, and this, although no doubt very difficult to do immediately in some countries, could quickly be accomplished by (1) abstaining from increasing the currency (in its broadest sense as defined above), and (2) by increasing the real wealth upon which such currency is based.

The cessation of increase in the currency should not be achieved merely by restricting the issue of legal tender. Such a step, if unaccompanied by other measures, would be apt to aggravate the situation by causing a monetary crisis. It is necessary to attack the causes which lead to the necessity for the additional currency.

The chief cause in most countries is that the Governments, finding themselves unable to meet their expenditures out of revenue, have been tempted to resort to the artificial creation of fresh purchasing power, either by the direct issue of additional legal tender money, or more frequently by obtaining – especially from the Banks of Issue, which in some cases are unable and in others unwilling to refuse them – credits which must themselves be satisfied in legal tender money. We say, therefore, that –

II

Governments must limit their expenditure to their revenue. (*We are not considering here the finance of reconstructing devastated areas.*)

III

Banks, and especially Banks of Issue, should be freed from political pressure and should be conducted solely on the lines of prudent finance.

But the Governments are not the only offenders in this respect; other parties, and especially in some countries the municipalities and other local authorities, have raised excessive credits which in the same way multiply the titles to purchasing power.

Nor will it be sufficient, for the purpose of checking further inflation, that additional issues of legal tender or the granting of additional credits should cease; since the floating debts of Government and other authorities constitute in themselves a form of potential currency, in that, except in so far as they are constantly renewed, their amount will come to swell the total currency in existence. Consequently –

IV

The creation of additional credit should cease and Governments and municipalities should not only not increase their floating debts, but should begin to repay or fund them by degrees.

In normal times the natural and most effective regulator of the volume and distribution of credit is the rate of interest which the central Banks of Issue are compelled, in self-preservation and in duty to the community, to raise when credit is unduly expanding. It is true that high money rates would be expensive to Governments which have large floating debts, but we see no reason why the community in its collective capacity (i.e. the Government) should be less subject to the normal measure for restricting credit than the individual members of the community. In some countries, however, the financial machinery has become so abnormal that it may be difficult for such corrective measure to be immediately applied. We recommend, therefore, that –

V

Until credit can be controlled merely by the normal influence of the rate of interest it should only be granted for real economic needs.

It is impossible to lay down any rule as to the 'proper rates' of discount or interest for different countries. These rates will depend not only on the supply and demand at different times but also on other factors often of a psychological nature. It may, indeed, confidently be said that when once the arbitrary increase of inflation ceases and when the Banks of Issue are able successfully to perform their normal functions, rates will find their own proper level.

The complementary steps for arresting the increase of inflation by increasing the wealth on which the currency is based, may be summed up in the words: increased production and decreased consumption.

The most intensive production possible is required in order to make good the waste of war and arrest inflation and thus to reduce the cost of living; yet we are witnessing in many countries production below the normal, together with those frequent strikes which aggravate instead of helping to cure the present shortage and dearness of commodities. When diminution in the Governments' demands frees more credits for trade and for the recuperation of the world, when inflation has ceased and prices cease to rise and when the general unsettlement caused by the war subsides, it is probable that great improvement will be seen in productive activity. Yet in our opinion the production of wealth is in many countries suffering from a cause which it is more directly in the power of Governments to remove, viz., the control in various forms which was often imposed by them as a war measure and has not yet been completely relaxed. In some cases business has even been taken by Governments out of the hands of the private trader, whose enterprise and experience are a far more potent instrument for the recuperation of the country.

Another urgent need is the freest possible international exchange of commodities. With this another Commission will deal, but we feel that our recommendations here on inflation would not be complete without adding that –

VI

Commerce should as soon as possible be freed from control and impediments to international trade removed.

Equally urgent is the necessity for decreased consumption in an impoverished world where so much has been destroyed and where productive power has been impaired. It is, therefore, specially important at present that both on public and private account and not only in impoverished countries, but in every part of the world –

VII

All superfluous expenditure should be avoided.

To attain this end the enlightenment of public opinion is the most powerful lever. If the wise control of credit brings dear money, this result will in itself help to promote economy.

We pass now from inflation and its remedies to the other points submitted to us.

Without entering into the question whether gold is or is not the ideal common standard of value, we consider it most important that the world should have some common standard and that as gold is to-day the nominal standard of the civilised world, –

VIII

It is highly desirable that the countries which have lapsed from an effective gold standard should return thereto.

It is impossible to say how or when all the older countries would be able to return to their former measure of effective gold standard or how long it would take the newly formed countries to establish such a standard. But in our opinion –

IX

It is useless to attempt to fix the ratio of existing fiduciary currencies to their nominal gold value; as unless the condition of the country concerned were sufficiently favourable to make the fixing of such ratio unnecessary, it could not be maintained.

The reversion to, or establishment of, an effective gold standard would in many cases demand enormous deflation and it is certain that such –

X

Deflation, if and when undertaken, must be carried out gradually and with great caution, otherwise the disturbance to trade and credit might prove disastrous.

XI

We cannot recommend any attempt to stabilise the value of gold and we gravely doubt whether such attempt could succeed; but this question might well be submitted to the Committee to which we refer later if it should be appointed.

XII

We believe that neither an International Currency nor an International Unit of Account would serve any useful purpose or remove any of the difficulties from which International Exchange suffers to-day.

XIII

We can find no justification for supporting the idea that foreign Holders of Bank notes or Bank balances should be treated differently from native holders.

XIV

In countries where there is no central Bank of Issue, one should be established, and if the assistance of foreign capital were required for the promotion of such a Bank some form of international control might be required.

XV

Attempts to limit fluctuations in Exchange by imposing artificial control on Exchange operations are futile and mischievous. In so far as they are effective they falsify the market, tend to remove natural correctives to such fluctuations and interfere with free dealings in forward Exchange which are so necessary to enable traders to eliminate from their calculations a margin to cover risk of exchange, which would otherwise contribute to the rise in prices. Moreover, all Government interference with trade, including Exchange, tends to impede that improvement of the economic conditions of a country by which alone a healthy and stable exchange can be secured.

We support the suggestion that –

XVI

A Committee should be set up both for continuing the collection of the valuable financial statistics that have been furnished for this Conference and also the further investigation of currency policy.

APPENDIX 10

GENERAL PRINCIPLES OF CENTRAL BANKING

FORMULATED BY THE GOVERNOR IN 1921

Early in 1921 the Governor formulated some general principles of Central Banking (purposely of a somewhat negative character) and invited certain authorities to discuss their validity. They were as follows:

1 A Central Bank should not compete with other Banks for general business.

2 A Central Bank should not take monies at interest on its own account nor accept Bills of Exchange.

3 A Central Bank should have no Branch outside its own country.

4 A Central Bank should not engage in a general Exchange business on its own account with any other country.

5 A Central Bank should be independent but should do all its own Government's business – directly or indirectly – including Gold and Currency.

6 A Central Bank should be the Bankers of all other Banks in its own country and should assist them to develop its business and economic resources.

7 A Central Bank should protect its own Traders from the rapacity of other Banks in its own country.

8 A Central Bank may have an Agency in another country.

9 That Agency (if not itself a Central Bank) should do all its banking and all kindred business with the Central Bank of the other country.

10 And should receive the most favoured treatment and information from the Central Bank of the other country.

11 And should do the Banking and kindred business of its Principal's Government in the other country.

To these three more of particular importance in the Federal Reserve System were added at the suggestion of Mr Strong, the Governor of the Federal Reserve Bank of New York:

12 A Central Bank should act as the settling Agent for Clearing House balances arising between the Banks of its own country, and to the widest extent practicable.

13 A Central Bank should handle domestic collections for its members and so regulate the domestic exchanges.

14 A Central Bank should have power to examine Banks which come to the Central Bank for credit and assistance.

RESOLUTIONS PROPOSED FOR ADOPTION BY THE CENTRAL AND RESERVE BANKS REPRESENTED AT MEETINGS TO BE HELD AT THE BANK OF ENGLAND

1 Autonomy and freedom from political control are desirable for all Central and Reserve Banks.
2 Subject to conformity with the above clause a policy of continuous co-operation is desirable among Central and Reserve Banks.
3 Without hampering their freedom, co-operation should include confidential interchange of information and opinions among such Banks with regard to such matters as rates of discount, the stability of exchanges and the movement of gold.
4 Each such Bank should recognise the importance of international as well as national interests in the re-establishment of the world's economic and trade stability.
5 Each such Bank should endeavour to conduct its foreign banking operations with the respective Central or Reserve Banks of other countries.
6 Each such Bank should endeavour to extend adequate and proper banking facilities, without undue regard to profit, to other Central and Reserve Banks: such facilities to include the custody of gold, monies and securities and the discounting of approved bills of exchange.
7 Each such Bank should take such steps as may be possible to ensure at all times the absolute right of withdrawal of all gold, monies and securities held on behalf of other Central and Reserve Banks.
8 Each such Bank should endeavour to assist in the establishment of a free market in forward exchange in its own country when no adequately organised market exists.

APPENDIX 11

MANUSCRIPT NOTES BY THE GOVERNOR FOR MEETING OF COMMITTEE OF TREASURY AND FOR BRADBURY COMMITTEE, 28 JANUARY 1925

The next two pages consist of facsimiles of the notes prepared for himself by the Governor, Montagu Norman, to take to two critical meetings in the debate on a return to the gold standard (see Chapter 7). In order to contain the notes completely within two pages, as in the original, the size has been reduced; this enables the reader to see exactly how Norman set out, for his own use in meetings, his summary analysis.

Reduction of size has, however, destroyed something of the character in the handwriting; therefore on a third page part of the note is reproduced in its original size. The original paper is 20 by 25.2 mm.

For a further specimen of Norman's notes, see Appendix 17.

28 1 25

1.

with Exch 490 . advised freedom at an Early date

4.75 Sh. advice – be during 1925 –

–

for difference in price-level. see Times 25th

– International cooperation for international advantage

2.

Reasons for Cushion. Advice of BS & JPM.

Good will of U.S.

Warning to Speculators

allays fears at home of too drastic rates

May cover S.A & Australia

Assurance doubly sure

" against Cushion. Implies fears as to success.

Undignified

may prevent drastic rate

" " adequate Exports

Parliamentary difficulties

Cost of Cushion to Exchequer covered by smaller cost of service of debt: in itself a reason for Ch. to desire gold parity

3.

Reasons for Apl / May }

Favoured by BS & JPM.

Only different in detail fr Dec 31.

{ Easy to arrange prompt Cushion
{ Impossible to arrange .. 6/8 months ahead

avoid months of waiting & wondering

takes the world unprepared.

May avoid near depreciation of Stg.

Recommend to Com on Wed. 3.pm: Cable 15. 1–9 incl.
.. 16 (2) 1–

Shd. advice – be during 1

: price-level. see Times 25th.

operation for international advantage

2.

. Advice of BS & JPM.

Goodwill of U.S.

Warning to Speculators

allays fears at home of too

May cover S.A & Australia

Assurance doubly sure

bui. Implies fears as to Success.

Undignified

may prevent drastic rate

" " adequate Export

Parliamentary difficulties

APPENDIX 12

ANNOUNCEMENT CONCERNING THE GOLD STANDARD MADE BY MR CHURCHILL IN THE HOUSE OF COMMONS, 28 APRIL 1925[1]

RETURN TO GOLD STANDARD

But before I come to the prospects of 1925 I have an important announcement to make to the Committee. It is something in the nature of a digression, and yet it is an essential part of our financial policy. Ever since the Spring of 1919, first under War powers and later under the Gold and Silver (Export Control) Act, 1920, the export of gold coin and bullion from this country, except under licence, has been prohibited. By the express decision of the Parliament of 1920 the Act which prohibits the export was of a temporary character. That Act expires on the 31st December of the present year, and Great Britain would automatically revert to the pre-War free market for gold at that date. Now His Majesty's Government have been obliged to decide whether to renew or prolong that Act on the one hand, or to let it lapse on the other. That is the issue which has presented itself to us. We have decided to allow it to lapse. I am quite ready to argue the important currency controversies which are naturally associated with a decision of that kind, but not to-day – not in a Budget speech. To-day I can only announce and explain to the Committee what it is that the Government have decided to do, and I will do that as briefly as I can.

A return to an effective gold standard has long been the settled and declared policy of this country. Every Expert Conference since the War – Brussels, Genoa – every expert Committee in this country, has urged the principle of a return to the gold standard. No responsible authority has advocated any other policy. No British Government – and every party has held office – no political party, no previous holder of the Office of Chancellor of the Exchequer has challenged, or so far as I am aware is now challenging, the principle of a reversion to the gold standard in international affairs at the earliest possible moment. It has always been taken as a matter of course that we should return to it, and the only questions open have been the difficult and the very delicate questions of how and when.

During the late Administration the late Chancellor of the Exchequer (Mr. Snowden) appointed a Committee of experts and high authorities to

[1] *Hansard*, Vol. 183, 52–8.

examine into the question of the amalgamation of the Treasury and the Bank of England Note Issues. The inquiry resolved itself mainly into an examination of whether and in what manner we should return to the gold standard. The Committee was presided over by my right hon. Friend who is now Secretary of State for Foreign Affairs (Mr. A. Chamberlain), and then a private Member, and its other members were Lord Bradbury, Mr. Gaspard Farrer, Professor Pigou, and the Controller of Finance at the Treasury. This Committee heard evidence from a great number of witnesses representing every kind of interest: financial and trading interests, manufacturing interests, the Federation of British Industries and others, were heard. It has presented a unanimous Report in which it expresses a decided opinion upon the question of the gold standard, and it sets forth its recommendations as to the manner in which a return to that standard should be effected.

I have had the Report of this Committee printed, and it will be available in the Vote Office as I finish my remarks this afternoon. It contains a reasoned marshalling of the arguments which have convinced His Majesty's Government, and it sets forth a series of recommendations, in which my right hon. Friend, though he ceased to be Chairman on becoming Foreign Secretary, has formally concurred, and which His Majesty's Government are intending to follow in every respect.

So much for the principle. There remain the questions of time and of method. There is a general agreement, even among those who have taken what I think I am entitled to call the heterodox view – at any rate, it is the view which we on this bench do not accept – that we ought not to prolong the uncertainty, that whatever the policy of the Government, it should be declared, and that, if we are not going to renew the Act which prohibits the export of gold coin and bullion, now is the moment when we ought to say so. It is the moment for which the House of Commons has patiently waited at my request – and I express my obligation because I have not been pressed on this matter before – the moment at which it was, after long consideration, judged expedient that decisions should be made and actions taken. This is the moment most favourable for action. Our exchange with the United States has for some time been stable, and is at the moment buoyant. We have no immediate heavy commitments across the Atlantic. We have entered a period on both sides of the Atlantic when political and economic stability seems to be more assured than it has been for some years. If this opportunity were missed, it might not soon recur, and the whole finance of the country would be overclouded for a considerable interval by an important factor of uncertainty. Now is the appointed time.

We have therefore decided, although the prohibition on the export of gold will continue in form on the Statute Book until the 31st December, that a general licence will be given to the Bank of England for the export of gold 4.0 P.M.
bullion from to-day. We thus resume our international position as a gold standard country from the moment of the declaration that I have made to

the Committee. That is an important event, but I hasten to add a qualification. Returning to the international gold standard does not mean that we are going to issue gold coinage. That is quite unnecessary for the purpose of the gold standard, and it is out of the question in present circumstances. It would be an unwarrantable extravagance which our present financial stringency by no means allows us to indulge in. Indeed, I must appeal to all classes in the public interest to continue to use notes and to make no change in the habits and practices they have become used to for the last ten years. The practice of the last ten years has protected the Bank of England and other banks against any appreciable demand for sovereigns or half-sovereigns. But now that we are returning publicly to the gold standard in international matters with a free export of gold, I feel that it will be better for us to regularise what has been our practice by legislation. I shall therefore propose to introduce a Bill which, among other things, will provide the following:

First, That until otherwise provided by Proclamation the Bank of England and Treasury Notes will be convertible into coin only at the option of the Bank of England;

Secondly, That the right to tender bullion to the Mint to be coined shall be confined in the future by law, as it has long been confined in practice to the Bank of England.

Simultaneously with these two provisions, the Bank of England will be put under obligations to sell gold bullion in amounts of not less than 400 fine ounces in exchange for legal tender at the fixed price of £3. 17s. 10½d. per standard ounce. If any considerable sum of legal tender is presented to the Bank of England the bank will be under obligation to meet it by bullion at that price. The further steps which are recommended by the Currency Committee, such as the amalgamation of the Bank of England and Treasury Note issues, will be deferred, as the Committee suggest, until we have sufficient experience of working a free international gold market on a gold reserve of, approximately, £150,000,000. It is only in the light of that experience that we shall be able to fix by permanent statute the ultimate limits of the fiduciary issue. All that will be in the Bill.

The Bill also has another purpose. We are convinced that our financial position warrants a return to the gold standard under the conditions that I have described. We have accumulated a gold reserve of £153,000,000. That is the amount considered necessary by the Cunliffe Committee, and that gold reserve we shall use without hesitation, if necessary with the Bank Rate, in order to defend and sustain our new position. To concentrate our reserves of gold in the most effective form, I have arranged to transfer the £27,000,000 of gold which the Treasury hold against the Treasury Note issue to the Bank of England in exchange for bank notes. The increase of the gold reserve of the Bank of England will, of course, figure in their accounts.

Further, the Treasury have succeeded in discreetly accumulating dollars, and we have already accumulated the whole of the 166 million dollars which are required not only for the June payment but also for the December payment of our American debt and for all our other American debt obligations this year. Therefore – and it is important – the Treasury will have no need to go on the market as a competitor for the purchase of dollars. Finally, although we believe that we are strong enough to achieve this important change from our own resources, as a further precaution and to make assurance doubly sure, I have made arrangements to obtain, if required, credits in the United States of not less than 300 million dollars, and of course there is the possibility of expansion if need be. These credits will only be used if, as, and when they are required. We do not expect to have to use them, and we shall freely use other measures in priority. These great credits across the Atlantic Ocean have been obtained and built up as a solemn warning to speculators of every kind and of every hue and in every country of the resistance which they will encounter and of the reserves with which they will be confronted if they attempt to disturb the gold parity which Great Britain has now established. To confirm and regularise these credit arrangements, which I have had to make provisionally in the public interest, and to deal with the other points that I have mentioned, a short three-clause Bill will be required. The text of it will be issued to-morrow, and we shall ask the House to dispose of it as a matter of urgency.

These matters are very technical, and, of course, I have to be very guarded in every word that I use in regard to them. I have only one observation to make on the merits. In our policy of returning to the gold standard we do not move alone. Indeed, I think we could not have afforded to remain stationary while so many others moved. The two greatest manufacturing countries in the world on either side of us, the United States and Germany, are in different ways either on or related to an international gold exchange. Sweden is on the gold exchange. Austria and Hungary are already based on gold, or on sterling, which is now the equivalent of gold. I have reason to know that Holland and the Dutch East Indies – very important factors in world finance – will act simultaneously with us to-day. As far as the British Empire is concerned – the self-governing Dominions – there will be complete unity of action. The Dominion of Canada is already on the gold standard. The Dominion of South Africa has given notice of her intention to revert to the gold standard as from 1st July. I am authorised to inform the Committee that the Commonwealth of Australia, synchronising its action with ours, proposes from to-day to abolish the existing restrictions on the free export of gold, and that the Dominion of New Zealand will from to-day adopt the same course as ourselves in freely licensing the export of gold.

Sir Fredric Wise: India?

Mr. Churchill: I am speaking of the self-governing Dominions of the Crown. I do not refer to India, but that in no way affects the argument. [Interruption.]

The Chairman: I would appeal to hon. Members not to interrupt the right hon. Gentleman.

Mr. Churchill: Thus over the wide area of the British Empire and over a very wide and important area of the world there has been established at once one uniform standard of value to which all international transactions are related and can be referred. That standard may, of course, vary in itself from time to time, but the position of all the countries related to it will vary together, like ships in a harbour whose gangways are joined and who rise and fall together with the tide. I believe that the establishment of this great area of common arrangement will facilitate the revival of international trade and of inter-Imperial trade. Such a revival and such a foundation is important to all countries and to no country is it more important than to this island, whose population is larger than its agriculture or its industry can sustain – [Hon. Members: 'No!'] – which is the centre of a wide Empire, and which, in spite of all its burdens, has still retained, if not the primacy, at any rate the central position, in the financial systems of the world.

APPENDIX 13

GOLD STANDARD ACT 1925

(15 & 16 Geo. 5. c. 29)

An Act to facilitate the return to a gold standard and for purposes connected therewith.

[13 May 1925]

Be it enacted by the King's most Excellent Majesty, by and with the advice and consent of the Lords Spiritual and Temporal, and Commons, in this present Parliament assembled, and by the authority of the same, as follows:–

1. (1) Unless and until His Majesty by Proclamation otherwise directs –

(a) The Bank of England, notwithstanding anything in any Act, shall not be bound to pay any note of the Bank (in this Act referred to as 'a bank note') in legal coin within the meaning of section six of the Bank of England Act, 1833, and bank notes shall not cease to be legal tender by reason that the Bank do not continue to pay bank notes in such legal coin:

(b) Subsection (3) of section one of the Currency and Bank Notes Act, 1914 (which provides that the holder of a currency note shall be entitled to obtain payment for the note at its face value in gold coin) shall cease to have effect:

(c) Section eight of the Coinage Act, 1870 (which entitles any person bringing gold bullion to the Mint to have it assayed, coined and delivered to him) shall, except as respects gold bullion brought to the Mint by the Bank of England, cease to have effect.

(2) So long as the preceding subsection remains in force, the Bank of England shall be bound to sell to any person who makes a demand in that behalf at the head office of the Bank during the office hours of the Bank, and pays the purchase price in any legal tender, gold bullion at the price of three pounds, seventeen shillings and tenpence halfpenny per ounce troy of gold of the standard of fineness prescribed for gold coin by the Coinage Act, 1870, but only in the form of bars containing approximately four hundred ounces troy of fine gold.

2. (1) Any money required for the purpose of exchange operations in connection with the return to a gold standard may be raised within two years after the passing of this Act in such manner as the Treasury think fit, and for that purpose they may create and issue, either within or without the United

Kingdom and either in British or in any other currency, such securities bearing such rate of interest and subject to such conditions as to repayment, redemption or otherwise as they think fit, and may guarantee in such manner and on such terms and conditions as they think proper the payment of interest and principal of any loan which may be raised for such purpose as aforesaid:

Provided that any securities created or issued under this section shall be redeemed within two years of the date of their issue, and no guarantee shall be given under this section so as to be in force after two years from the date upon which it is given.

(2) The principal and interest of any money raised under this Act, and any sums payable by the Treasury in fulfilling any guarantee given under this Act, together with any expenses incurred by the Treasury in connection with, or with a view to the exercise of, their powers under this section shall be charged on the Consolidated Fund of the United Kingdom or the growing produce thereof.

(3) Where by any Appropriation Act passed after the commencement of this Act power is conferred on the Treasury to borrow money up to a specified amount, any sums which may at the time of the passing of that Act have been borrowed or guaranteed by the Treasury in pursuance of this section and are then outstanding shall be treated as having been raised in exercise of the power conferred by the said Appropriation Act and the amount which may be borrowed under that Act shall be reduced accordingly.

3. This Act may be cited as the Gold Standard Act, 1925.

APPENDIX 14

TERMS OF THE 1925 CREDITS

Extracts from Announcements to the House of Commons

4 MAY 1925

[Extract from the speech of the Financial Secretary to the Treasury, the Rt. Hon. Walter Guinness, D.S.O., T.D., M.P., in the debate on the Gold Standard Bill (*House of Commons Hansard*, Vol. 183, 622–3).]

The second Clause in the Bill gives power to the Treasury to borrow for exchange operations. The credits under this Clause are to be raised during not more than two years from the passage of the Bill, and any credits raised must be repaid within two years from the date of issue. Though the Clause widens the powers of borrowing money, it does not increase the total amount of money which may be borrowed. Any sums which are raised under these powers must come out of the usual provision for borrowing up to the total of the Supply Services for the year which appear year after year in the Appropriation Act. Under these arrangements, two credits have been already conditionally negotiated. First, there is a credit which has been arranged with the Federal Reserve Bank of New York, who have undertaken to give the Bank of England a revolving credit of 200,000,000 dollars for two years from the 10th May or the date of the British Government guarantee, whichever date is the latest. Then there is a second arrangement with a Syndicate headed by Messrs. J. P. Morgan. That is for a revolving credit of 100,000,000 dollars, also for two years, to His Majesty's Government direct. The interest in each of these cases is to be paid as and when the credit is drawn on at 1 per cent. above the Federal Reserve discount rate, with a minimum of 4 per cent. and a maximum of 6 per cent., or, if the Federal Reserve discount rate exceeds 6 per cent., then at the Federal Reserve discount rate. The House will therefore observe that if we do not use these credits no interest will be paid, and, in the case of the Morgan Loan open to the British Government, there will merely be a very small commission on the right of call on the money.

5 MAY 1925

[Extract from the speech of the Chancellor of the Exchequer, the Rt. Hon. Winston Churchill, C.H., M.P., in the debate (*House of Commons Hansard*, Vol. 183, 815).]

So far as our negotiations with Messrs. Morgan are concerned, those are limited to 100,000,000 dollars, on which $1\frac{1}{4}$ per cent. commission will be paid during the first year of the credit, and, if the credit is not used, half the amount will be payable in the second year. That is to say, there will be £250,000 payable the first year, and half that the second year, or £375,000 in all.

APPENDIX 15

EXTRACT FROM LETTER, 11 DECEMBER 1925, FROM EMANUEL GOLDENWEISER TO SENATOR BAYARD CONCERNING THE CREDIT TO THE U.K.

(From Emanuel Goldenweiser Papers, Library of Congress – File: 'Reserves – Gold Reserves (1925–1940)')

(4) *That the Transaction is, in fact, a Loan to the British Government and not a Bank Transaction with the Bank of England.* This question arises wholly from a misapprehension of the transaction. In the discussions it was at one time suggested that the Bank of England might furnish as a guaranty of repayment in gold British Treasury bills payable in dollars. There were various objections to this suggestion, the principal one being that the British Government, having no direct interest in the transaction, would receive no consideration for the issue of its obligations and could not do so. The object of the guaranty afforded under the Act of Parliament was to protect the Federal reserve banks against any governmental act which might operate to restrain the Bank of England from meeting its own obligation either by the shipment of gold or otherwise. The transaction in essence is an agreement to sell gold on credit to the Bank of England from time to time during the two year period with an agreement by the Bank of England to pay in gold in New York any amounts outstanding at the end of the two year period whether represented in the sterling deposit account or in sterling bills bought therewith as explained in detail in Statement C enclosed herewith. The relation of the British Government to the transaction through the Act of Parliament is negatively to insure us that no restraint will be exercised by the Government against the carrying out of the contract by the Bank of England, and affirmatively to insure us that it will be carried out in any event.

APPENDIX 16

EVIDENCE GIVEN BY THE GOVERNOR TO THE SPECIAL COMMITTEE ON THE GOVERNMENT AND ADMINISTRATION OF THE BANK (TROTTER COMMITTEE)

(Private evidence reproduced from Bank file)

WEDNESDAY, THE 29TH DECEMBER, 1926

NOTES OF THE GOVERNOR'S EVIDENCE

The Governor commenced his remarks by saying that the volume of work has grown considerably of late years and will probably increase still further during the next few years; there has been added work in connection with Home and also with Foreign Affairs – the latter being due to reconstruction and Central Banking – and in his opinion there is no hope of any material decrease for years to come.

He then gave the Committee an outline of the present work –

1. *In connection with the Government*

Before the War the relations between the Bank and the Government were more or less formal but now the Governor is in constant touch with various Government Departments and this work occupies perhaps about 2 hours of his time daily.

He advises on issues and on financial policy, how it shall be carried out and how money is to be provided for various schemes in connection with Housing; Local Loans; the National Debt Office; Trades Facilities Acts; League of Nations; the Crown Agents; Development and guaranteed Loans; the payment of External Debts – especially to the United States; the settlement of War Debts due to this Country; collection and settlement of Debts due by Industrial Concerns formerly dealt with by the Disposals Board, but now in the hands of a Division of the Treasury.

Another question which will shortly entail much work is that of the amalgamation of Note Issues.

2. *Visitors*

Speaking generally he takes the attitude that any reputable person in the City is at liberty to see him.

Regular visitors include –

Visitors		Frequency
Representatives of the	Discount Market	once or more every week
,, ,,	Committee of the Stock Exchange	
,, ,,	Clearing Banks	
Representatives of the	South African Gold Producers	at frequent intervals
,, ,,	Bank of Japan	
,, ,,	Bank of Italy	
,, ,,	Imperial Bank of India	
Representatives of the	Country Banks	whenever any special point arises
,, ,,	various Overseas Banks	

Just now there are questions of amalgamations &c. and he is rather more than an unofficial adviser. They come when invited and also because they wish to ascertain the attitude of the Bank.

3. *Other interests include –*

Public issues on behalf of various clients.
Work in connection with the Indian Currency Report.
Anglo International Bank.
Securities Trust.
Armstrong Whitworth & Co. Problems daily and continuous and likely to be so for some time to come.
The money and general policy of the Bank.
Buying of Bills. This is now on a large scale: questions are constantly arising as to the Bills to be taken &c. and the work in this connection is continuous.

He considered that much of what is outlined under the above headings must be done here: it is essential to keep in close touch with the Banks, the Discount Market and the Stock Exchange. Some of the work no doubt is personal but if the Governor were not a professional much would undoubtedly fall away. General Governmental questions would tend either to go to some other Bank or things would be done on wrong lines. There is no prospect of any of this work disappearing until the effects of the War and of post-war conditions have passed away, which cannot well happen for another 10 years.

4. *Central Banking and Reconstruction*

The deliberate plan of the League of Nations as outlined at Genoa is to help reconstruction in Europe by means of Central Banking. The Financial Committee of the League cannot do this work except through the Bank; they have no machinery. They lay down the broad lines of policy which are carried out here. Practically all loans for the League Schemes are arranged here because all concerned realise that the Bank is disinterested. London is and must continue for some time to be the main lending Market in Europe and New York will never take the initiative, certainly not in outlying Countries.

Experience shows that for the present Central Banking work must be centralised, this is not a question of policy but of fact. There is no definite control, but education is necessary; some of the Banks can already be trusted to do what is right but others take every opportunity of trying to break away and have to be corrected. In doing this he has behind him the general policy of the League. Very few of the new or indeed the old Banks – the Reichsbank and the National Bank of Hungary excepted – are directed by men who know anything of the work. The difficulties which arise are mostly the result of pressure, direct or indirect, of the various Governments from which the Banks have to be protected. After some 15 or 20 years these Banks will have built up traditions which will prevent them from breaking away from the orthodox policy as they do now; those who have had co-operation will wish to continue it when they are free.

There will be much work to be done, in the Baltic States, in Poland, in Roumania, in Russia and elsewhere; this means years of work and there is no one but ourselves to do it.

The Imperial side of Central Banking is important; we are in close touch with South Africa through Clegg; we have had many discussions with Australia and now the Comptroller has gone to visit both. India will have its new Bank and much is being done to prepare close contact.

It is vital for the Governor of the day to be in close personal touch with the Governors of other Central Banks and it is necessary to have here one or more professionals who are prepared to visit other Central Banks at any time.

Our relations with Central Banks must increase or the Financial Committee will no longer be able to function; in that case the British Government would probably need to arrange for the work to be carried on and the choice would most likely fall on us. We are thus making a virtue of necessity.

The policy of the League is a continuing policy and must be supported; it is based on the assumption that existing boundaries are continued, or are modified by consent. It seems certain that changes must come, but if made by consent they will not hinder present policy but will on the contrary assist it. We are in close touch with the League through Salter, through those

Members of the Financial Committee who are here and through other Members who visit us from time to time.

All nations are anxious to see a reconstructed Europe and long for a general tariff arrangement through the League Conference, but this cannot be achieved until stabilisation has been effected.

The appointment of a Committee to deal with Central Banking matters and so ease the work of the Governor and spread responsibility is not feasible; these matters are mostly dealt with by the League and are mentioned regularly to the Committee of Treasury. As our Foreign Section increases and develops it will relieve the Governor of much of this work but it is a slow process and will take a long time. There is difficulty in finding linguists and it will be necessary in the meantime to appoint men with the necessary knowledge from outside.

Comptroller

He regards the Comptroller as equivalent to a General Manager and has never envisaged a Comptroller and a General Manager as separate offices.

When the Office was first created the intention was to interpose the Comptroller between the Governors and the Heads of Departments and the main object was to relieve the Governors of some of their work; one trouble has been that much Central Bank work has been thrown on to the present Comptroller and his managerial functions have been in abeyance. When not engaged on other matters the Comptroller is a party to money policy.

The 'Revelstoke' Committee he thought had not in their minds the appointment of a Managing Director, apart from the office of Comptroller.

The Governor gave further evidence to the Committee in answer to the following specific question:—

Do you favour the appointment of a permanent assistant to the Governors who would discharge the duties that might be generally described as those of a 'General Manager' –

(1) in addition to,

or

(2) in place of, the Comptroller,

and should such assistant be drawn from the Directorate or not?

Note In this connection your Committee particularly wish you to read pages 7–8 of the Report of the Special Committee appointed by the Court of the 11th October 1917.

EVIDENCE GIVEN TO TROTTER COMMITTEE, 23 MAY 1927

I have regarded 'General Manager' as synonymous with 'Comptroller' and I suggest the following scheme for the consideration of the Committee –

Of the Court of 26 –

Not less than 18 to continue exactly as at present.

Not more than 8 to be 'whole-timers' drawing £5/10,000 a year each – in effect a permanent Directorium or Body of Professionals within the Court, but drawn from the Staff or from outside or from the Court itself.

This permanent Body of Professionals might include –

One or two Governors (temporarily),

Comptrollers,

1 such Director responsible for Staff Work, and, as a maximum,

4 such Directors responsible for Foreign and Central Banking and other business.

Such Directors, as stated, would be permanent whole-time and highly paid Professionals: otherwise they would be exactly the same as any other members of the Court.

1 This scheme is an attempt to combine the 'Conseil General' with the 'Directorium'.
2 It would leave the power of the Court in the hands of the same class of Directors as at present.
3 It would make it easier to maintain the numbers in that class (perhaps 18 or 20 instead of 26).
4 It would provide a body of professional opinion from which future Governors might, if necessary, be drawn.
5 It would give a status to those whose help seems necessary: a status which is absent from the post of 'Adviser'.
6 It would avoid a certain confusion of standing and authority between the Staff and Advisers which, I think, is more likely to increase rather than to diminish.
7 It is, I think, the best way of modernising the machinery of the Bank without altering the constitution.
8 I think some such scheme may offer a solution to the present difficulties.

APPENDIX 17

MANUSCRIPT NOTES BY THE GOVERNOR ON BENJAMIN STRONG AND ON EUROPE, 3–9 JULY 1927

The next five pages consist of facsimiles of notes made (apparently only for his own use) by the Governor, Montagu Norman, after his talks with Strong, Schacht and Rist in the U.S.A. in July 1927 (see Chapter 15). It is not clear at exactly what date Norman made the notes; it may well have been on the return voyage across the Atlantic. The dating at the top of the first page, in Norman's writing, refers to the dates of the talks, not of the writing.

The size has been somewhat reduced; the original comfortably fills Norman's pages which are 12.7 by 20.3 mm. (See prefatory note to Appendix 11.)

Notes. [3rd to 9th July 27]

B.F. admires S. as a despot or tyrant: no personal sympathy: little personal understanding. He only studies Germany vagudy & leaves whole position to S.G.

—

He takes great interest in B. France & has much personal liking & sympathy with C.R. who always interests him. He wd do anything to help B.F. entirely overlooking misdeeds of Poincaré. — The two have been drawn together by Poland

—

The following have seemed to put me at a disadvantage: 1. No sympathy

2

about Poland. 2. Daily headlines & scares about Italy & disarmament at Geneva. 3 Soreness about London competition agst N.Y. in reducing acc. comm. to 1/8 (hence Cotton Bills likely to be carried in Lon) 4. Continual pin-pricks by Winston: his attitude much resented 5. No sympathy about Italy.

= Day in, day out, I have been in agreement with H.S.

= Between all 4. much talk & increased personal understanding 2 friendliness. But, sooner or later fundamental differences of position.

B.F. awaiting & urging Stabilisation: cold about Ratification: feature of getting more devises from purchases of Secs. on Paris Bourse: feels their position dominates London, as never before: & likes to ask for his stg. balces. to be reduced: wd. like to see higher B.Rate.

H.S. perplexed: uncertain about his devisen: bourse too active: possessed by Transfer-Complex!: maintains he is not free agent as long as no general settlement of Repns. has been made:

-4.

Hopes to borrow regularly abroad - long or short - in order to pay Treasuries till after Elections = Dec. 1928... & then?

— General. How maintain price level? How keep gold out of N.Y?

H.S. & D. say lower BR in U.S. is only help or solution - with lower call money. If not quickly arranged Berlin, Adam, London will be forced up: BR & Wash[n] will consider.

— Little interest in price level

— B.S. will lend to us three cheap. on gold in Europe But CR said he

5.

wanted no more gold - unless in exchange for stg balances & H.S. is forced to get rid of what gold he has - & may be

Also technically difficult to arrange

As alternative B.I must buy gold in Europe, saving perhaps $\frac{3}{4}$% on ship[t] to US & back to Europe someday.

Generally all of us have one or other political background & impediment: all are 'tethered' till general settle[t] of Rep[ns] & debts plus Stabilisation: CBk cooperation meanwhile rather a 'pretence' than deep reality.

APPENDIX 18

NOTE BY H. A. SIEPMANN ON GOVERNOR'S CONVERSATIONS IN PARIS, 27–28 APRIL 1928

[The following is H. A. Siepmann's record, under the original heading, of the discussions between the Bank of England and the Bank of France, referred to on p. 197 in Chapter 8. This record, though presumably seen and approved by Norman, was *not* an 'official' record agreed by both parties; there is no evidence that it was shown even privately to anyone at the Bank of France.

Similarly, the Bank of France did not provide the Bank of England with any note of the conversations. Moreau, however, had written his own account in his diary, and this was published not by the Bank of France but in the Éditions M.-Th. Génin, Librairie de Médicis, Paris, in 1954, under the title *Souvenirs d'un Gouverneur de la Banque de France*. The relevant entries, which may be compared with Siepmann's note here reproduced, appear on pp. 544–7.]

NOTE OF CONVERSATIONS HELD IN PARIS ON THE 27TH AND 28TH APRIL, 1928

1. To explain why he had insisted that the Governor should come to Paris, Monsieur Moreau said that the elections require his presence in a constituency of which he is Mayor, and that in the interval between the two ballots he has been engaged with preparations for the new loan: in the early part of May he will not be available.

2. Monsieur Moreau then raised the question of Roumania, which was discussed for about two hours on the afternoon of the 27th April. The Governor, in reply to what amounted to a cross-examination, made three points only; he said that:

(i) he wished it to be clearly understood that whatever the Deputy Governor had said to Monsieur Moreau in February on behalf of the Bank of England will be implemented in the spirit and in the letter by the Bank and is endorsed by the Governor personally, without any qualifications.

(ii) if any new questions have arisen since then, which now require to be answered, the Governor could not undertake to answer them without first consulting his colleagues at the Bank, because for some time past he has been out of contact with developments in the situation.

(iii) he could however express his own personal opinion on the general questions of principle involved; for example, he could say:

(a) that he has always held, still holds, and will continue to hold, whatever other course events may take, that Roumania is a case for the League, and

(b) that he has championed and will continue to champion the cause of Central Bank co-operation, and wishes to work in harmony with the Banque de France.

3. Monsieur Moreau suggested at the start that the Governor's letter to Monsieur Burillianu, written on the day after Monsieur Moreau's visit to London in February, amounted to a repudiation of the undertakings given by the Deputy Governor. When the Governor replied that he stands by everything which the Deputy Governor said, Monsieur Moreau asked what exactly the undertaking then given was now held to have been. But he quickly passed over any questions of interpretation or definition, after saying that it had never been the intention of the Banque de France to ask for the recommendation and endorsement of the Federal Reserve Bank for the Roumanian scheme. Their intention was to recommend the scheme themselves, and to ask, in the first instance, for the participation of the Federal Reserve Bank, the Bank of England and the Reichsbank severally. Monsieur Moreau said that he is already corresponding with Dr. Schacht on the subject. The Banque de France was now so deeply engaged that there could be no turning back, and the scheme would be proceeded with at all costs. If the Bank of England were to refuse participation, Monsieur Moreau would regard it as an unfriendly act and as confirming the suspicions which it was possible to entertain about the motives and methods of the Bank of England, not only in this but also in other questions. He would then have no further regard to the interests of the Bank of England and would always act with an eye solely to the advantage of the Banque de France. Very often, until now, he had gone out of his way to render services to the Bank of England – a fact which ought to be recognised and admitted. There was no other reason why he should take gold from America and pay the extra expenses; he might just as well have based the franc on dollars as on sterling in the Paris market; and the present strength of sterling was due mainly to the Banque de France which takes American money over London at a fixed price for sterling and allows the whole benefit of the movement to be reflected in the sterling dollar rate.

4. Monsieur Moreau said that in the entourage of the Governor of the Bank of England it had been thought, and even stated, that the Banque de France was actuated by political considerations in the Roumanian affair. He

wished to remove this misconception, and he gave a detailed account of the series of events by which, between Monsieur Rist's meeting with Vintila Bratianu in September and the return of Monsieur Quesnay from Bucharest in the middle of February, the Banque de France had become associated with the Roumanian scheme. He had an absolutely clear conscience on the subject and would prove his case by handing over copies of the relevant correspondence which he had had prepared for the Governor. As a matter of fact, the Quai d'Orsay, so far from initiating, had, as usual, been rather behindhand with its information and knew nothing about the whole affair until it had reached a comparatively advanced stage.

5. Passing then to points of practical detail, Monsieur Moreau said that the Roumanian loan would be for from 65 to 80 million Dollars: the issue was planned for next June, or say in six weeks' time: the credit would be for 20 million Dollars and the Banque de France would proceed to get together an international group of Central Banks in about a fortnight. The Governor asked whether outstanding questions, such as that of the 1913 loan, would be dealt with by the plan. Monsieur Moreau replied that the Roumanians were entirely disposed to make an equitable arrangement on all points which were not already settled by the Treaties of Peace. He had recommended them to do so. In fact, his advice to the issuing bankers had been first, to avoid introducing into a financial operation any questions of commercial privileges or concessions and, secondly, to adopt the policy of the open door and admit all the different capital markets on equal terms (including, apparently Spain). He thought that a Central Bank which valued its independence must preserve an attitude of complete detachment wherever particular interests, public or private, were involved. It was concerned purely with the financial merits of an operation and had no business to champion the claims even of its own market (still less of a foreign market) in extraneous, though possibly related, disputes.

6. The Governor insisted, however, that the 1913 loan is a very real and serious obstacle to participation by the Bank of England. He knew nothing about the figures and details of the case, and he was not in the least concerned (as Monsieur Moreau had seemed to suggest that he might be) with the financial interests of any individual Directors of the Bank. His difficulty arose from the fact that the Stock Exchange Committee, a semi-public body, had struck out the 1913 loan from its official list and had formally notified him of this fact. The Council of Foreign Bondholders had also taken up a definite position. It would be most difficult for the Bank of England to ignore these facts and to take an opposite attitude. Monsieur Moreau could do as much as anybody to promote a solution of this difficulty and the Governor appealed to him to do so.

7. The general impression left on Monsieur Moreau by this conversation, according to the account afterwards given privately by Monsieur Quesnay, was that for the first time the real position of the Bank of England in the

Roumanian question had been disclosed. Until now there had been a kind of smoke-screen of factitious principles, but the real difficulty all the time had been the 1913 loan.

Monsieur Quesnay suggested that a possible way out of this difficulty would be for the Bank of England, when invited by the Banque de France to participate in a Roumanian credit, to give a conditional acceptance, subject to the issue of a tranche of the Roumanian loan on the London market (since the fact of issue would presume a settlement of the 1913 loan dispute to the satisfaction of the Stock Exchange Committee.)

8. Continuing the conversations on the following day, Monsieur Moreau began by suggesting that, as

(1) the Governor had appeared to admit that, whatever might have been desirable, it was now impossible to take the Roumanians to the League, and

(2) the allegations about political motives were now disposed of, (to which the Governor replied that he knew nothing about it)

the one remaining difficulty in the way of Bank of England participation might be removed by stipulating for a London issue. The Governor said that he was not at all concerned to obtain a London issue and that although the Central Banks credit and the loan are interdependent parts of a single operation there is no necessary connection, in reason or in fact, between the several tranches of the loan and the participation of the several Central Banks in whose markets the loan is issued. The difficulty of the 1913 loan arises from the fact that London is an international market which has to help in maintaining certain standards in the common interest of all international markets: it has nothing to do with the claims of British bondholders as such, nor with the claims of London bankers to a part of the issue. He could say no more than he had said already, namely that the Bank of England would have to consider the whole position before entering into any sort of commitment.

9. Monsieur Moreau asked whether the Governor would not agree to help in obtaining the participation of the Reichsbank and the Banca d'Italia, or at any rate inform Dr. Schacht and Signor Stringher that he no longer insists upon League intervention. But the Governor said he could not do this.

10. When it was suggested that besides the difficulty of the 1913 loan the Bank of England would have to take some account of the questions of principle involved in the procedure adopted by the Banque de France, (such as that two names are required to a bill, or that the Bank of England can not participate in a scheme which they would not be content to recommend) Monsieur Moreau lost patience. He said these so-called questions of principle were simply childish and he refused to take them seriously or to believe that they could honestly be thought by anyone else to have any importance whatever. They were a mere pretext and the fact of their being dragged in again at this stage revived in his mind all the unpleasant suspicions about the sincerity of the Bank of England to which he had alluded on the previous

day. He then proceeded to bring a series of charges, supported by detailed accounts of what at various times had been said and done in London and New York. For example, he referred to a letter said to have been written by the Governor to Signor Stringher about Roumania, and he alleged that the Bank of England took part in all the negotiations between Monsieur Markovics and the private bankers about a Jugoslav Loan. He complained that the Bank of England had offended, in the case of Jugoslavia, against that principle of the open door which he had been at pains to recommend to the French bankers in the case of Roumania. He also quoted a story about the impending resignation of Messieurs Moreau, Rist and Quesnay which was said to have been circulated in order to discredit the Banque de France. All these charges were denied in toto by the Governor, who described them as 'tittle-tattle'; but it was clear that to Monsieur Moreau they constitute an overwhelming body of circumstantial evidence against the good faith of the Bank of England. Other examples appeared in the private conversation of Monsieur Quesnay; as when he attributed to the Bank of England a scheme supplanting the Federal Reserve Bank in the leadership of Italian stabilisation.

11. The Governor replied with a general criticism of the attitude of the Banque de France towards the Financial Committee of the League. He said that it was quite unfair to pretend that stabilisation through the League involves control on the Austrian model, or that the League imposes a cast-iron scheme regardless of local conditions. Had Monsieur Moreau chosen to do so, he might have helped to establish the League in the position of godfather to all the different countries which, in differing degrees, required help from without: and they would all have been the better for it.

Monsieur Moreau denied hostility to the Financial Committee and cited the fact that he had been consulted a dozen times about the Bulgarians and had always said that they must go to Geneva. He had no regrets about Poland, which (unlike Italy, where nothing had yet been done of what was promised) seemed to be making good progress. He maintained that never in any circumstances could Poland or Roumania have been brought to the League and he did not see that their having taken another course need prevent the Financial Committee from doing useful work in years to come, especially as in any event the period of stabilisation plans is practically over. The choice whether to go to the League or not clearly lay, both rightly and inevitably, with the country concerned. Since Roumania had chosen not to go, the sensible thing to do was not to stand aside and decline responsibility for the consequences, but to render such help as could be rendered with a sound scheme, and at any rate avoid the only alternative, which was that Roumania should borrow money and spend it without any scheme at all. The line of demarcation between countries requiring League intervention and those which could do as well with some other kind of help was both arbitrary and vague. For example, it was not clear what were the reasons for differentiating in this respect between Roumania and Jugoslavia.

12. Finally, Monsieur Moreau asked whether the Bank of England would wish to be formally invited now to participate in a Roumanian credit. The Governor suggested that the formal invitation might be delayed until he had had an opportunity of writing, in 8 or 10 or 12 days' time, a personal letter to Monsieur Moreau on the subject.

In private conversation, after the first meeting of the Governors, Monsieur Quesnay detailed what he said were the five alternative reasons for which the Bank of England might refuse to participate in a Roumanian credit. They were:

(1) because the League is necessary,
(2) because the French scheme is political,
(3) pique, because it is a Banque de France scheme,
(4) German disputes with Roumania,
(5) the interests of London issuing houses.

He did not mention that the Bank of England might reject the scheme
(6) on its technical merits,
(7) for the reasons of principle already given to Governor Strong.

He said that not one of his five reasons could be publicly avowed and that therefore in practice a refusal would be impossible. Monsieur Moreau, he said, holds the opinion that a bondholders' dispute cannot properly be the concern of a Central Bank, and he would not regard any one Central Bank as entitled to make its participation conditional upon the participation of others.

Monsieur Quesnay made it clear that by handing over a copy of the scheme the Banque de France have disposed of any question of the Bank of England coming in blind, which implies that the casus foederis based on Monsieur Moreau's conversation with the Deputy Governor cannot now arise.

Monsieur Quesnay stated the facts about the 1913 loan as follows:– the loan was issued in Paris and Berlin. London took a sub-participation from Berlin, up to £2 millions; but less than £1 million could be placed or were ever quoted on the London Stock Exchange, the balance being returned by Messrs. Schröder to the Berlin market. After the war, it became necessary to identify the bonds issued in London, but the amount traced by the issuing bankers and notified as being entitled to the treatment accorded to British holders fell short of the original issue by some £130,000. The Roumanians refused to give British terms to these untraced bonds; but they would probably now be prepared to agree to do so. What they would refuse, and what the issuing Bankers are suspected of wanting to ask, is British terms for the whole £2 millions originally allotted to London but never placed. He said that a year ago an agreement was almost reached between the Roumanians and Messrs. Schröders and he was confident that on the Roumanian side no obstacles would now be placed in the way of an equitable solution.

Monsieur Quesnay's account does not agree with our information, which is as follows:–

Roumanian Government 4½% Loan 1913

Amount £9,900,000: London issue £1,980,000.
Issued in England, Germany, Belgium, Holland and Roumania.
Bonds of £19:16:–or equivalent, i.e., gold lei 500, fcs.500, M.405.
Repayment in 40 years by half-yearly drawings – Jan. and July.
Principal & Interest payable in London or, at holder's option, in Germany, Belgium, Roumania or Holland.

The whole amount of £1,980,000 was admitted to quotation in the Stock Exchange Official List in January 1914. This total was subsequently reduced to £1,745,093, at which figure it stood in May 1924 when the loan was removed from the Official List by order of the Stock Exchange Committee.

The Roumanian Government have refused since 1914 to pay the service on the full amount. They claim that all British subjects are being paid in sterling in respect of all bonds placed in Great Britain before 1914. No payment is made to holders belonging to enemy countries, on the ground that enemy bonds should rank in the calculations of indemnities and reparations.

The nominal amount of the bonds on which interest in sterling is being paid is £562,577: 8: –. A list of the bonds contained in this amount was made in 1920 and is known on the Stock Exchange as 'Schröder's List'. These bonds have been marked by a Roumanian Stamping Commission.

Certain other bonds of the issue held by British subjects but which have not been in their possession continuously since the date of issue have also been stamped by the Commission and it is stated that payment on these is being made in French francs.

2nd May, 1928

APPENDIX 19

CURRENCY AND BANK NOTES ACT 1928

(18 & 19 Geo. 5. c. 13)

An Act to amend the law relating to the issue of bank notes by the Bank of England and by banks in Scotland and Northern Ireland, and to provide for the transfer to the Bank of England of the currency notes issue and of the assets appropriated for the redemption thereof, and to make certain provisions with respect to gold reserves and otherwise in connection with the matters aforesaid and to prevent the defacement of bank notes. [2 July 1928.]

Be it enacted by the King's most Excellent Majesty, by and with the advice and consent of the Lords Spiritual and Temporal, and Commons, in this present Parliament assembled, and by the authority of the same, as follows:—

1. (1) Notwithstanding anything in any Act –

(a) the Bank may issue bank notes for one pound and for ten shillings:

(b) any such bank notes may be issued at any place out of London without being made payable at that place, and wherever issued shall be payable only at the head office of the Bank:

(c) any such bank notes may be put into circulation in Scotland and Northern Ireland, and shall be current and legal tender in Scotland and Northern Ireland as in England.

(2) Section six of the Bank of England Act, 1833 (which provides that bank notes shall be legal tender), shall have effect as if for the words 'shall be a legal tender to the amount expressed in such note or notes and shall be taken to be valid as a tender to such amount for all sums above five pounds on all occasions on which any tender of money may be legally made' there were substituted the words 'shall be legal tender for the payment of any amount.'

(3) The following provisions shall have effect so long as subsection (1) of section one of the Gold Standard Act, 1925, remains in force –

(a) notwithstanding anything in the proviso to section six of the Bank of England Act, 1833, bank notes for one pound or ten shillings shall be deemed a legal tender of payment by the Bank or any branch of the Bank, including payment of bank notes:

(b) the holders of bank notes for five pounds and upwards shall be entitled, on a demand made at any time during office hours at the head office of the Bank or, in the case of notes payable at a branch of the Bank, either at the head office or at that branch, to require in exchange for the said bank notes for five pounds and upwards bank notes for one pound or ten shillings.

(4) The Bank shall have power, on giving not less than three months' notice in the London, Edinburgh and Belfast Gazettes, to call in the bank notes for one pound or ten shillings of any series on exchanging them for bank notes of the same value of a new series.

(5) Notwithstanding anything in section eight of the Truck Act, 1831, the payment of wages in bank notes of one pound or ten shillings shall be valid, whether the workman does or does not consent thereto.

2. (1) Subject to the provisions of this Act the Bank shall issue bank notes up to the amount representing the gold coin and gold bullion for the time being in the issue department, and shall in addition issue bank notes to the amount of two hundred and sixty million pounds in excess of the amount first mentioned in this section, and the issue of notes which the Bank are by or under this Act required or authorised to make in excess of the said first mentioned amount is in this Act referred to as 'the fiduciary note issue.'

(2) The Treasury may at any time on being requested by the Bank, direct that the amount of the fiduciary note issue shall for such period as may be determined by the Treasury, after consultation with the Bank, be reduced by such amount as may be so determined.

3. (1) In addition to the gold coin and bullion for the time being in the issue department, the Bank shall from time to time appropriate to and hold in the issue department securities of an amount in value sufficient to cover the fiduciary note issue for the time being.

(2) The securities to be held as aforesaid may include silver coin to an amount not exceeding five and one-half million pounds.

(3) The Bank shall from time to time give to the Treasury such information as the Treasury may require with respect to the securities held in the issue department, but shall not be required to include any of the said securities in the account to be taken pursuant to section five of the Bank of England Act, 1819.

4. (1) As from the appointed day all currency notes issued under the Currency and Bank Notes Act, 1914, certified by the Treasury to be outstanding on that date (including currency notes covered by certificates issued to any persons under section two of the Currency and Bank Notes (Amendment) Act, 1914, but not including currency notes called in but not cancelled) shall, for the purpose of the enactments relating to bank notes and the issue thereof (including this Act) be deemed to be bank notes, and the Bank shall be liable in respect thereof accordingly.

(2) The currency notes to which subsection (1) of this section applies are in this Act referred to as 'the transferred currency notes.'

(3) At any time after the appointed day, the Bank shall have power, on giving not less than three months' notice in the London, Edinburgh and

Belfast Gazettes, to call in the transferred currency notes on exchanging them for bank notes of the same value.

(4) Any currency notes called in but not cancelled before the appointed day may be exchanged for bank notes of the same value.

5. (1) On the appointed day, in consideration of the Bank undertaking liability in respect of the transferred currency notes, all the assets of the Currency Note Redemption Account other than Government securities shall be transferred to the issue department, and there shall also be transferred to the issue department out of the said assets Government securities of such an amount in value as will together with the other assets to be transferred as aforesaid represent in the aggregate the amount of the transferred currency notes.

For the purpose of this subsection the value of any marketable Government securities shall be taken to be their market price as on the appointed day less the accrued interest, if any, included in that price.

(2) Any bank notes transferred to the Bank under this section shall be cancelled.

(3) Such of the said Government securities as are not transferred to the Bank under the foregoing provisions of this section shall be realised and the amount realised shall be paid into the Exchequer at such time and in such manner as the Treasury direct.

6. (1) The Bank shall, at such times and in such manner as may be agreed between the Treasury and the Bank, pay to the Treasury an amount equal to the profits arising in respect of each year in the issue department, including the amount of any bank notes written off under section six of the Bank Act, 1892, as amended by this Act, but less the amount of any bank notes so written off which have been presented for payment during the year and the amount of any currency notes called in but not cancelled before the appointed day which have been so presented.

(2) For the purposes of this section the amount of the profits arising in any year in the issue department shall, subject as aforesaid, be ascertained in such manner as may be agreed between the Bank and Treasury.

(3) For the purposes of the Income Tax Acts, any income of, or attributable to, the issue department shall be deemed to be income of the Exchequer, and any expenses of, or attributable to, the issue department shall be deemed not to be expenses of the Bank.

(4) The Bank shall cease to be liable to make any payment in consideration of their exemption from stamp duty on bank notes.

7. Section six of the Bank Act, 1892, (which authorises the writing off of bank notes which are not presented for payment within forty years of the date of issue), shall have effect as if, in the case of notes for one pound or ten shillings, twenty years were substituted for forty years, and as if, in the case of any such notes being transferred currency notes, they had been issued on the appointed day and, in the case of any such notes not being transferred

currency notes, they had been issued on the last day on which notes of the particular series of which they formed part were issued by the Bank.

8. (1) If the Bank at any time represent to the Treasury that it is expedient that the amount of the fiduciary note issue shall be increased to some specified amount above two hundred and sixty million pounds, the Treasury may authorise the Bank to issue bank notes to such an increased amount, not exceeding the amount specified as aforesaid, and for such period, not exceeding six months, as the Treasury think proper.

(2) Any authority so given may be renewed or varied from time to time on the like representation and in like manner:

Provided that, notwithstanding the foregoing provision, no such authority shall be renewed so as to remain in force (whether with or without variation) after the expiration of a period of two years from the date on which it was originally given, unless Parliament otherwise determines.

(3) Any minute of the Treasury authorising an increase of the fiduciary note issue under this section shall be laid forthwith before both Houses of Parliament.

9. (1) For the purpose of any enactment which in the case of a bank in Scotland or Northern Ireland limits by reference to the amount of gold and silver coin held by any such bank the amount of the notes which that bank may have in circulation, bank notes held by that bank or by the Bank on account of that bank, shall be treated as being gold coin held by that bank.

(2) A bank in Scotland or Northern Ireland may hold the coin and bank notes by reference to which the amount of the bank notes which it is entitled to have in circulation is limited at such of its offices in Scotland or Northern Ireland, respectively, not exceeding two, as may from time to time be approved by the Treasury.

10. The form prescribed by Schedule A to the Bank Charter Act, 1844, for the account to be issued weekly by the Bank under section six of that Act may be modified to such an extent as the Treasury, with the concurrence of the Bank, consider necessary, having regard to the provisions of this Act.

11. (1) With a view to the concentration of the gold reserves and to the securing of economy in the use of gold, the following provisions of this section shall have effect so long as subsection (1) of section one of the Gold Standard Act, 1925, remains in force.

(2) Any person in the United Kingdom owning any gold coin or bullion to an amount exceeding ten thousand pounds in value shall, on being required so to do by notice in writing from the Bank, forthwith furnish to the Bank in writing particulars of the gold coin and bullion owned by that person, and shall, if so required by the Bank, sell to the Bank the whole or any part of the said coin or bullion, other than any part thereof which is bona fide held for immediate export or which is bona fide required for industrial purposes, on payment therefor by the Bank, in the case of coin, of the nomi-

nal value thereof, and in the case of bullion, at the rate fixed in section four of the Bank Charter Act, 1844.

12. If any person prints, or stamps, or by any like means impresses, on any bank note any words, letters or figures, he shall, in respect of each offence, be liable on summary conviction to a penalty not exceeding one pound.

13. (1) This Act may be cited as the Currency and Bank Notes Act, 1928.

(2) This Act shall come into operation on the appointed day, and the appointed day shall be such day as His Majesty may by Order in Council appoint, and different days may be appointed for different purposes and for different provisions of this Act.

(3) In this Act, unless the context otherwise requires, –

The expression 'the Bank' means the Bank of England:

The expression 'issue department' means the issue department of the Bank:

The expression 'bank note' means a note of the Bank:

The expression 'coin' means coin which is current and legal tender in the United Kingdom:

The expression 'bullion' includes any coin which is not current and legal tender in the United Kingdom.

(4) The enactments set out in the Schedule to this Act are hereby repealed to the extent specified in the third column of that Schedule.

SCHEDULE

ENACTMENTS REPEALED

Session and Chapter	Short Title	Extent of Repeal
7 & 8 Vict. c. 32.	The Bank Charter Act, 1844.	Sections two, three, five and nine, in section eleven the words from 'save and except that' to the end of the section, sections thirteen to twenty, and section twenty-two, and, so far as relates to England, sections ten and twelve.
24 & 25 Vict. c. 3.	Bank of England Act, 1861.	Section four, so far as unrepealed.
4 & 5 Geo. 5. c. 14.	The Currency and Bank Notes Act, 1914.	The whole Act, except subsection (5) of section one and section five.
4 & 5 Geo. 5. c. 72.	The Currency and Bank Notes (Amendment) Act, 1914.	The whole Act.
5 & 6 Geo. 5. c. 62.	The Finance Act, 1915.	Section twenty-seven.
15 & 16 Geo. 5. c. 29.	The Gold Standard Act, 1925.	Paragraph (b) of subsection (1) of section one.

APPENDIX 20

STATEMENT IN PARLIAMENT, 1928, REGARDING FIDUCIARY ISSUE

[The following is an extract from comments by the Rt Hon. Sir Laming Worthington-Evans, Bt, G.B.E., Secretary of State for War, on possible reasons for an application for a change in the fiduciary issue after the 1928 Act. The comments were made during the Second Reading on 14 May 1928 (*House of Commons Hansard*, Vol. 217, 744–6). After referring to the famous three occasions in the nineteenth century and to 1914, the Secretary of State reminded the House of the exact nature of the historic 'crisis letters'.] One can imagine the hesitancy with which the Governor of the Bank and the Prime Minister and the Chancellor of the day asked for and agreed to the issue of such a letter. But Clause 8 of the Bill makes a statutory provision intended to be used, not reluctantly and with hesitation in time of crisis, but whenever the Governor of the Bank feels that the present limit on the fiduciary issue is unduly restrictive, to be used, not in defiance of the law, but in accordance with the statutory provisions intended for the purpose.

[After an interruption, he continued]:

We are replacing an illegality by a legal power intended to be used, not in a crisis, but before the crisis arrives. I do not pretend to be able to forecast every contingency which may cause the Governor of the Bank to make the application, and which may make the Chancellor of the Exchequer of the day agree to an increase in the fiduciary issue; but let me examine some of the possible eventualities, some of which have been indicated by the hon. Member for West Leicester and others. An emergency of the type of the crises of 1847, 1857 and 1866 may never recur. Just as in 1847 and 1866 the knowledge that the letter had been issued to the Bank prevented a run upon the Bank, so the provision made in Clause 8 may itself prevent the panic from which these crises arose.

But a new kind of emergency has become possible. Now that the foreign banks have adopted the practice of accumulating a large reserve of sterling bills, it is always possible that, owing to a change in policy upon the part of those banks, a large sum of gold might be withdrawn in a short time by the realisation of those balances. The probability is that such a measure would be avoided by co-operation amongst the central banks, as was indeed advised in the Genoa resolutions. But if the withdrawal of gold was insisted upon, it might become necessary to extend the fiduciary issue, and that would be an occasion which would justify the Governor of the Bank in asking for that expansion, and the Treasury in granting it.

A third contingency is the possible competition for gold among the central banks. It is quite true that the absorption of gold by any country of considerable economic importance is a matter of international concern. The supply of gold for monetary purposes can only change very gradually, and the value of gold in terms of commodities is principally governed by the demand. The demand is created by the currency legislation of the various countries. If the central banks were to absorb gold without regard to each other's actions they would find themselves competing for a limited supply, and a rise in the value of gold, or, in other words, a fall in the price level calculated in any gold currency, would inevitably ensue. Should the Bank of England find that, owing to a world demand for gold, credit would be unduly restricted, not as a check on speculation, but to the injury of legitimate requirements, then the Bank can request the Treasury to extend the fiduciary issue and so free gold in the hands of the Bank for further credit operations.

Moreover, the principle of a fixed fiduciary issue itself necessitates some provision being made for normal growth. It was only by an accidental combination of circumstances that the Act of 1844 did not require an expansion of the fiduciary issue from time to time.

As my hon. Friend pointed out, at the time when the Bank Charter Act was passed the bank note was the principal credit instrument of commerce and had it remained so the natural development might easily have raised the paper circulation of £30,000,000 to £150,000,000 or even to £200,000,000 in 1914, and the old fiduciary limit would have become manifestly inadequate. The rise was only saved by the gradual displacement of bank notes by cheques. The net circulation in fact never appreciably exceeded £30,000,000. It remained practically constant for 70 years notwithstanding the immense industrial and commercial development and it may be that in the course of the years to come with an increased population and, as we hope, greater employment, greater earnings, greater expenditure and a higher standard of comfort for the people, the currency of the country will require a permanent expansion. The provision in the Bill for increasing the fiduciary issue is not intended therefore to be a mere legislative substitute for the crisis letter. On the contrary it is intended to be used not in a crisis but before it and to prevent undue stringency arising from any of the causes I have mentioned.

The Bill has this advantage. It allows a tentative change in the first instance before Parliament is called upon to legislate. A period of two years during which temporary changes can be tried and the results watched is allowed and if the reasons for the increase appear to be permanent Parliament can be so advised and by legislation the fiduciary limit of £260,000,000 can be extended. I ought also when I am dealing with elasticity to call attention to the power given under Clause 2 to reduce the maximum of £260,000,000 by the Treasury upon being requested by the Bank of England. Of course though it does not seem likely at the present moment it may be that too much gold may come to London. If at a time when credit conditions were easy there was a large influx of gold an unnecessary number of notes would be issued. In order to check the unnecessary creation of credit the Bank would have to sell securities to take the place of the notes, and it is obvious that the Bank cannot be expected to do this on a large scale or for a long time, and it is in order to relieve such a position that the Bank may apply and the Treasury may agree to a reduction of the fiduciary note issue. I do not want in a matter of this sort to dogmatise in the least but I do think that those who are afraid that this Bill is going to cause restriction on legitimate credit operations and so affect employment have a completely erroneous conception of Clause 8.

APPENDIX 21

EVIDENCE BY THE GOVERNORS AND OTHERS TO THE COMMITTEE ON FINANCE AND INDUSTRY (MACMILLAN COMMITTEE) 1929–31

[The uniquely authoritative Evidence to the (Macmillan) Committee on Finance and Industry, 1929–31, was published in two large foolscap volumes in 1931 (see Chapter 16). These have long been out of print and difficult to find outside a few great libraries. The passages reprinted here, with the permission of the Controller of Her Majesty's Stationery Office, constitute about one-seventh of the total.

The selection is broadly confined to three witnesses – Norman, Harvey and Hopkins – whose business it was to expound to the committee the position, the arrangements and the principal activities of the Bank. All the evidence of the Governor (Mr Norman) and the Deputy Governor (Sir Ernest Harvey) is included. The evidence given by Sir Guy Granet, when he accompanied the Governor, is here. So also is that part of Dr O. M. W. Sprague's evidence which he gave jointly with the Governor; Sprague's other evidence, when he spoke for himself alone, although in the presence of the Governor, is not included. Stewart's evidence, though given in the presence of the Deputy Governor, is likewise excluded. A large part of the evidence given by Sir Richard Hopkins, Controller of Finance at the Treasury, and extracts from a Memorandum he provided for the committee are included as supplementing, especially on arrangements between the Bank and the Treasury, the evidence given by the Governors.

It should be noted that other parts of Hopkins's evidence, among them the famous interchange with Keynes on the effects of expenditure on public works, are excluded, despite its great interest from the viewpoint of general economic policy. As mentioned in Chapter 16 (p. 365) other witnesses particularly connected with the Bank were Niemeyer, Clay, Kindersley and Stamp; their evidence, though interesting in the context of various aspects of economic policy, was not primarily concerned with expounding the ordinary functioning of the Bank, and is therefore not reproduced here. Stewart's evidence (to which the same applies) was reprinted in 1950 in the U.S.A. under the title *Monetary Policy and Economic Prosperity* (with an introduction by Donald B. Woodward).

Wherever in the following pages there is any discontinuity in the reproduction, this is indicated.

Members of the committee

The Rt Hon. H. P. Macmillan, K.C., Chairman, lawyer
Sir Thomas Allen, from the co-operative movement
Mr Ernest Bevin, labour leader and trade unionist
The Rt Hon. Lord Bradbury, G.C.B., formerly Joint Permanent Secretary to H.M. Treasury
The Hon. R. H. Brand, C.M.G., banker
Professor T. E. Gregory, D.Sc., economist
Mr J. M. Keynes, C.B., economist
Mr Lennox B. Lee, industrialist
Mr Cecil Lubbock, a Director of the Bank of England
The Rt Hon. Reginald McKenna, banker and former Chancellor of the Exchequer
Mr J. T. Walton Newbold, former Communist M.P.
Sir Walter Raine, industrialist
Mr J. Frater Taylor, industrial adviser
Mr A. A. G. Tulloch, banker]

EXTRACTS FROM THE MINUTES OF EVIDENCE

Thursday 28 November 1929

Sir Ernest Musgrave Harvey, K.B.E., Deputy Governor of the Bank of England, called and examined.

1. *Chairman*: Sir Ernest, we greatly regret that the Governor of the Bank should be indisposed and unable to assist us to-day. I hope you will convey to him a message of our sympathy and our hope that he will be soon restored to health. In the meantime we count ourselves fortunate in having your assistance. You will appreciate that we have felt that evidence from the Bank of England should naturally be the first evidence to be taken by us. I think you are familiar with the Terms of Reference under which we are sitting. You have read them? — Yes.

2. I think we have all realised that the pivotal position occupied by the Bank of England in the financial system of this country makes it desirable that we should have at the very outset a clear conception of the nature and functions of the Bank of England as the Central Bank in this country. I think, accordingly, we might usefully employ our time this afternoon with your assistance in obtaining some evidence from you upon the position of the Bank. In the first place, would I be accurate in describing the Bank of England as the Central Bank here? — Yes.

3. Would you perhaps expound to us, what, in your view, a Central Bank really is? May I say before you proceed to give us your evidence, Sir Ernest, that you have round this table gentlemen of very varying degrees of knowledge in this matter. I hope you will not refrain from giving information which may to some members of the Committee and yourself appear elementary, because to others of us it will be very instructive; so do not feel in any way deterred from giving explanations which to you and other experts may appear elementary. We want to have a clear picture of the position of the Bank of England in the financial system of the country. Will you in the first place give us a short descriptive account of the meaning and characteristics of central banking? — The term Central Bank is, of course, one that to the uninitiated conveys no really particular significance. They regard it rather as the designation of an institution which is regarded as the head of the banking world, though as to the particular factors which constitute it the head there is in the minds of the general public certainly very often a rather hazy conception. I think it is partly due to the fact that for the sake of brevity the term Central Bank has been used, when if the fuller term Central Reserve Bank had been used I think that the public generally would have appreciated at once what is in fact the main function of such an institution as the Bank of England. The principal duty of the Central Bank is to maintain in the general interest of the community the stability of the national monetary unit, or, in other words, to maintain

and to take custody of the central reserves on which the integrity of the national monetary unit depends. Now, in a gold standard world, the maintenance of the stability of the national monetary unit means, I take it, the maintenance of its stability in relation to gold as the common international denominator. The functions of the Central Bank, therefore, and the limitations on a Central Bank as to the type and class of business which it can conduct, are really determined by their bearing upon this duty of maintaining the integrity and stability of the national monetary unit. For this main purpose there are certain duties which it is, I think, generally recognised that the Central Bank must undertake, and I should put first of those duties that it must have the sole right of issuing notes.

It is obvious, I think – it will be obvious to the Committee – that if the Central Bank is to be responsible for maintaining the stability and integrity of the national monetary unit, it must have power of control over the issue of that national monetary unit in the form in which it is usually current in the country. To attempt to maintain the integrity of that unit where power resided in some other entirely independent body to create that unit in such quantities as it might determine, without regard necessarily to the actual requirements of business, would obviously render the task imposed on the Central Bank as the guardian of the monetary unit an impossible one. I should therefore put first, I think, that the Central Bank should have the sole right to issue notes.

Next to that I should place the responsibility for the custody of the central reserves on which the integrity of that unit is founded; in other words, the central gold reserves, and, at any rate in part, the reserves which form the basis on which the ordinary banking functions of the country are conducted. Next I should say that the Central Bank should be the bank of the bankers, and this for perhaps two reasons. It should, by acting as the bank of the bankers, to the extent to which it is employed for that purpose by the banks, be a means of measuring the volume of credit available from time to time for the conduct of the business of the country. It should act also for them as a clearing agent for the settlement of differences between bank and bank. By acting in that capacity it is able by mere book entries to settle differences, often differences of very large amounts, which must arise from day to day as between bank and bank by the claims which one bank may have upon another as against the claims which exist in the opposite direction. Unless some such arrangement as this exists by which these differences can in fact be settled in this manner by book entry, the banks in question would be under the necessity of holding vast sums of currency for the purpose of meeting their respective obligations to one another.

Then another function which I think it is essential should be performed by the Central Bank is that it should conduct the main banking business of the State. The State is the collector of vast sums of money from the community in the form of taxation, and, of course, those sums are only collected for the purpose of distribution for services rendered to the State and very largely, in our own case at the present time, for the payment of interest on the debt and of sums due to holders of maturing obligations of the State. But the incidence of the receipts and the payments of the State is necessarily very unevenly distributed. Certain revenues are always being received by the State – revenues from Customs, Excise and various other sources of that kind – but vast sums of the revenue received by the Government are only received by them at certain periods of the year. A notable instance is in the early months of the year during the annual collection of income tax and super tax. On the other hand, the State has obligations which are falling due in greater or less degree every day. It has the ordinary payments for services, but it has in particular the payment for interest on the debt and for maturing obligations.

If I may just cite one instance to illustrate what I mean: next week, on Monday, the State will have to distribute in interest for the War Loan alone a sum of about £50,000,000. Well, now, the sudden distribution of £50,000,000 by itself can create an enormous disturbance obviously in the movements in the volume of credit. Clearly it would be wasteful and extravagant for the State gradually to amass a sum of £50,000,000, drawing in this money gradually from the public and keeping it lying idle, in order that they may have the cash in hand to meet such a vast distribution falling due at one given moment. Obviously, therefore, the State has to rely on its banker, whoever the banker may be, to assist it to finance this very large distribution in the form of interest. Unless that duty resides in the Central Bank, the Central Bank will have considerable difficulty in adjusting matters in such a manner as to ensure that there will not be violent oscillations in the volume of credit, which would create great disturbances in the value of money from day to day, and which, in a country such as this with world-wide international connections, would possibly create very wide fluctuations in the value of the national monetary unit. If, however, the arrangements are entrusted to the Central Bank, the Central Bank has notice beforehand exactly as to the amounts which have to be provided. It can lay its plans to ensure that the State shall have the funds it requires, and moreover, that when those funds have been distributed they may be re-absorbed in an orderly and gradual manner without causing undue disturbance, and without leaving a flood of suddenly manufactured credit to disturb the value of money and possibly the value of the monetary unit measured internationally.

There are, on the other hand, certain limitations which are necessarily imposed upon the Central Bank. Its liabilities are all, without exception save only such liabilities as consist of moneys due to its own proprietors, payable on demand. It is essential, therefore, that it should maintain its assets in the most liquid form possible. Its business is to provide that the ordinary commercial trading banks of the country shall have a sufficiency of credit available to form the basis, the backing or reserve, call it what you will, of the amounts of credit that they may find it necessary to create to meet the varying demands of their clients scattered throughout the country. Unless the Central Bank maintains its assets in a liquid form it has no guarantee that it will at all times be able to adjust the position without causing unnecessary disturbance. But the Central Bank has another limitation imposed upon it. Its duties are, and must so be recognised by the institution itself, primarily as duties to the community as a whole. It must not be under the necessity whenever it has to undertake operations of considering whether the operations in question are to the immediate interest of its own stockholders or proprietors. It must not be under the necessity of having to assure itself of earning profits out of all the business it does. In fact, it is often compelled, not only to ignore the question of earning a profit, but even to sacrifice assets of an earning character which it already possesses, and so far from carrying out profitable transactions actually to undertake transactions which will result in loss to it. It must, therefore, be able to hold such a position as to be free from the anxiety and care of having to order its operations from the point of view of earning profits. For this reason it is usually, I think, agreed that a Central Bank should not pay interest on its deposits.

I said just now that its main duty – and it is the duty which it must at all times keep before it – is to conduct its operations in the interests of the community as a whole, and for this reason we, at any rate, have always considered that it should be free from the control of particular groups or interests. By that I do not mean, of course, that it should not have regard to the interests of particular groups or interests – indeed, it must have regard to the interests of every group – but it must balance the interests of one group against the interests of another group, and act in a manner which, in its judgment, it considers to be most in the interests of the community as a whole. For the same reason I think I may claim that it is an accepted principle that it should be free from political pressure. Its duty is, as I say, to the community as a whole. It has duties to the Government of the day undoubtedly, provided it is, as I suggest it should be, the banker of the Government, but its duties in that respect are the ordinary duties of banker to client. It should be free from being required to submit to political pressure and to subordinate sound finance to the dictates of political expediency. For that reason, as I say, we feel that it should be free from political control.

I do not know whether you would wish me to elaborate this question definitely of central banking at greater length. I have touched on what are the principal points. There are, of course, various minor points, but those which I have mentioned may, I think, be taken as the leading reasons for certain duties being entrusted to the Central Bank, and for the Central Bank being subject in its operations to certain definite limitations.

4. Then, Sir Ernest, do you emphasise those features as being the distinctive characteristics of a Central Bank? — I would, yes.

5. Features characteristic of a Central Bank, either in this country or in other countries? — Yes.

6. And differentiating therefore the operations of a Central Bank from the ordinary commercial banking of the country? — Yes. That remark, Mr. Chairman, reminds me that I have overlooked one point on which I ought to say a word. We hold that it is not the duty of the Central Bank to enter, generally speaking, into the ordinary banking business of trade and commerce of the country, and for two reasons. In the first place, in common fairness. It would not be right that an institution which is to be entrusted by the commercial banks of the country with a considerable part of their funds, which constitute a considerable part of their cash reserves on which their business is built up, should employ those funds to go out into active competition with them. But even apart from that the Central Bank has to be the port to which the general community can come in a storm. Other banks may be, I will not say in difficulties, but inconvenienced by circumstances entirely outside their own control, often circumstances which have occurred in other countries, and if the Central Bank enters into the ordinary business of the country it will be obvious, I think, that at the very moment when the general financial community may be feeling some strain – owing to some event possibly thousands of miles away – if the Central Bank is doing the same class of business it may at the very moment when the rest of the banks find a need to seek its assistance find itself in exactly the same difficulties as the commercial banks, and therefore the less able to render the assistance which is required of it. We consider, therefore, that it is no part of the ordinary business of a Central Bank to enter into the ordinary commercial banking of the country.

At the same time, when I have spoken on this subject, as I had to about three years ago in Australia, I had to face there a certain – I will not say antagonistic attitude – but critical attitude from a section of the community, who had the impression that unless the Central Bank – I speak now of that particular country; I am not speaking of this country – unless *their* Central Bank had the power to do ordinary commercial banking the community might find themselves left at the mercy of a body of banks who might levy upon them just such terms as they might think fit. The feeling was very strongly expressed therefore that their own particular Central Bank should have the power to conduct ordinary banking business, in order that they might have some sort of assurance that banking facilities that were really required by the country could always be obtained at a reasonable price from some quarter; in other words, that the existence in the Central Bank of the power to do ordinary commercial banking would be an assurance to them of protection against excessive demands from other banks.

7. I gather that your view, Sir Ernest, is that this differentiation of function between a Central Bank and the ordinary commercial banks of the country is one of very great importance. — Very.

8. And the bank that engages in the business of a Central Bank, while it has certain rights and privileges accorded to it, has to pay for those in certain limitations of its activities? — Yes.

9. Is the system of central banking now general among the nations of the world? — It has extended, of course, very much in recent years, and members of the Committee may be familiar with the cases of Central Banks which have been established in recent years since the War in many European countries. The principles which I have been advocating this afternoon will, I think, on an examination of the statutes of those banks, be found to be embodied in practically every instance.

10. I was only anxious to get some indication of the extent to which that doctrine of differentiation of function had in modern times been found acceptable. Apparently in quite recent times the same principle has been adopted in other countries? — Quite recently. Of course, we must recognise that even here central banking is a plant of comparatively recent growth. The Bank of England itself was founded as an ordinary commercial bank, and for years practised as an ordinary commercial bank, and I think it would be fair to say that the foundation of central banking – although the term central banking was not then used, and certainly the conception of central banking as I give it this afternoon was not then present in the minds of people generally – may be held to have been laid when the Bank Act of 1844 was passed. But even so, central banking as we now understand it, did not exist for many years after. I can remember myself the time when I was young in the Bank, 40 years ago, when certainly this particular suggestion that a Central Bank should take no part in the commercial banking of the country was – well, a debatable point; I will not put it stronger than that. In fact I think possibly some members of the Committee will say that it was not recognised by the Central Bank. But it has become a gradual development, and with the increasing responsibilities which in the case of the Bank of England, for example, have gradually been thrown upon us, we have increasingly come to recognise that it is really an essential part of the banking machinery of this country.

11. That is the very word I was going to use. It is part of the financial mechanism of the country – of course, to be judged by the efficacy with which it achieves its object. The object, I understand, is the maintenance of the stability of the currency of this country? — Yes.

12. You recognise that there are differences of opinion as to how that is best to be achieved, but in your view there is a strong consensus of opinion that this particular mechanism which has been evolved and devised is best calculated to achieve that result? — Yes.

13. And the various functions which you have been describing to us this afternoon are all incidental to that process? — Yes.

14. You referred to your recent experience in Australia, and you were kind enough to hand me before our proceedings a pamphlet which has been issued entitled 'Central Banks,' which contains a short paper, or address, by you, Sir Ernest, on this topic. I have had the pleasure of reading it, and find it a summary of the position very much on the lines of what you have been telling us to-day. This, I understand, is now a public document. It has been published, I gather, rather without your knowledge? — It was published with my knowledge though in no way on my initiative.

15. May I take it that it contains more or less your views still? — Yes.

16. I am going to ask our Secretary if he will be good enough to get copies of it for circulation among our members. Would that be agreeable to you? — Certainly. I almost blush to offer it to certain members of the Committee. I am afraid I am rather offering 'A Child's Guide to Knowledge,' and I should like to explain that it was merely a rather impromptu little address delivered after dinner one evening to a meeting of bank clerks and others in Melbourne. It was never intended to attain any wider notoriety than the particular hall in which it was delivered, but somebody appears to have secured the shorthand notes, and, as you have just said, the document was ultimately published here, but not at my wish.

17. But whatever its genesis, in this case it does represent in summary form your views? — Yes.

18. I think it would be useful for us to have it. I notice in the course of your address on

that occasion you referred to various sources of information on central banking, to reports of previous Committees, and so on. Are there any of those to which you think it might be useful for the attention of the Committee to be directed? — If I remember right, I referred to a Report of Evidence that was collected by the Aldrich Commission.

19. Yes. — Senator Aldrich's Commission, prior to the establishment of the Federal Reserve System. That was authoritative. They submitted to us a questionnaire to which we gave answers, and, as a picture of the practice at that time, I think it certainly may be regarded as an absolutely authentic and accurate account. It is, perhaps, in some respects a little bit out of date, because things have altered a good deal since that evidence was given – I think it was about the year 1907 – though it still has interest, because many of the facts in it are still unchanged, the practices are still unchanged. I do not know whether it would interest the Committee, but it goes fairly fully into the question of types of bills of exchange which are acceptable to the Bank, and rather detailed matters of that character, the practice of the bank in regard to granting advances, and various matters of that kind, but I am doubtful whether you would be able to obtain it. It was a State Paper.

20. You referred to the relatively recent evolution of the conception of a Central Bank, and its function in the State. I thought it might be useful to some of us to pursue the history of its evolution in various State Papers. — I am doubtful whether you would be able to do so really in published papers. I think another document I referred to was the Report of the Genoa Conference.

21. Yes, you referred to that, I think. — I referred to the Report and Act in connection with the establishment of the Reserve Bank of South Africa. I think I referred also to the Report of Dr. Vissering and Professor Kemmerer in connection with the establishment of that bank.

22. Yes; that is mentioned there. Now, you have given us, Sir Ernest, a very clear picture of the functions and characteristics of a Central Bank, and the features in which it is differentiated from the ordinary bank as popularly understood. I think now it might be useful if you would pass to the Bank of England itself, and tell us how it is organised as a Central Bank. — Yes.

23. *Lord Bradbury*: I understood you, Sir Ernest, to say that the Bank of England, in its initiation, was largely created for the purpose of an ordinary commercial bank. There is no doubt that through history the Bank of England has done business to a very large extent of a similar character to that which is now done by the joint stock banks? — Yes.

24. I take it that according to your conception of central banking the tendency now is to reduce the volume of that business, and, so far, say, as ordinary traders and manufacturers are concerned, the volume of ordinary banking business that the Bank of England does at present is a rapidly decreasing amount. Is that a correct view? — Certainly.

25. It is not entirely eliminated, even as regards ordinary traders and manufacturers? — No. Of course, there are the remains of old connections, where we do not want to turn people into the street, as it were, but we do not encourage anybody in that category to come to us.

26. The general tendency is to eliminate that policy? — The general tendency is to let it die a natural death, and not replace it.

27. But I think the Bank of England has certain large current accounts for customers other than bankers? — Undoubtedly.

28. They would not necessarily come under your embargo – for instance, the Stock Exchange? — Well, the Stock Exchange, no. The number would be quite limited, because we do not provide them with the facilities which they require. We have large accounts, but they are principally accounts of, for example, Insurance Companies; in many cases they do not come to us for ordinary banking facilities; they seem to have a feeling that the vaults of the Bank of England are a particularly safe place in which to deposit very large volumes of securities; and for that purpose they like to keep an account with us. It gives them the right to leave their securities; they leave with us merely a balance which provides us with adequate remuneration for all the services we render in the custody of their securities. That would constitute quite a considerable amount in the way of balances, but we do not, as a general rule, do their ordinary banking business. We have also many mercantile firms. There are many firms who have had accounts with us for years, and I dare say – in fact I know, that on many of them there has been no operation for possibly 20 or 30 years; but they like to feel that in case of a rainy day they have the power to come to us for shelter.

29. The reason is very largely sentimental? — Very largely sentimental.

30. From the point of view of the Bank of England as a Central Bank, the functions of the Bank could be discharged adequately if its current accounts were limited to bankers' accounts. Is that putting it too baldly? — I do not quite follow.

31. I mean, if its only customers were banks in the wider sense. I only want to get at the theory – whether you think there is, in connection with a proper system of central banking, any necessity for the Central Bank to have accounts with customers other than banks – purely on the theoretical ground? – I will not say that there is any necessity, but I did say a little earlier that we consider that it is desirable – and again I want to make it perfectly clear I am not speaking now particularly of this country – that a Central Bank should

not be restricted in that respect; in other words, that it should have the power to afford banking facilities at reasonable charges – subject, of course, to their being fundamentally of a sound description – if for any reason they are not available elsewhere. As regards the amount of the actual balances, you will realise that if Mr. X keeps £1,000 with the Bank of England, and if he transfers his £1,000 to, let us say, the Bank of London, and the Bank of London is a customer of the Bank of England, it merely involves in the Bank's books a transfer of £1,000 from Mr. X to the Bank of London; it involves no alteration whatever in the total of deposits in the Bank of England.

32. *Chairman*: I think the point, if I may say so, that Lord Bradbury wants to emphasise is, whether the Central Bank should be exclusively the Central Bank – whether there should be a self-denying ordinance excluding it from ordinary banking business. That is the purely theoretical idea? — Yes.

33. You think that they should have a liberty to engage in ordinary banking business? — They should have a liberty which they should not necessarily exercise.

34. *Lord Bradbury*: But the existence of that liberty you do not regard as essential to the proper discharge of the functions of the Bank as a Central Bank? — No. I should not say it was essential to the proper discharge of the functions of the Bank as a Central Bank.

35. *Chairman*: The Central Bank should do no ordinary commercial banking. It should simply do its duty to the State? — No, I must except – of course more particularly in this country – certain classes of private customer. You are talking now, I presume, of the ordinary private bank customer or the ordinary commercial or trading firm. You are not including such people as, for example, the discount market?

36. *Lord Bradbury*: No, I purposely left them out. I was referring primarily to manufacturers and traders, and, secondly, to people who are engaged in what may be called ordinary finance business in London, such as Issuing Houses, the Stock Exchange, and even Insurance Companies? — Yes. Certainly, so far as the Stock Exchange is concerned, and also as regards commercial firms, they are not essential in my judgment to the working of a Central Bank. I am not quite sure when you touch upon Issuing Houses whether there might not be circumstances in which the absence of a relationship with Issuing Houses, the ordinary relationship of banker and client, might not at times be a disadvantage.

37. Well, I speak with a considerable amount of ignorance as to the practice in these cases, but I think there is quite a large number of large Issuing Houses that in fact have not accounts with the Bank of England? — I should say not a large number of large Issuing Houses. I should say that the majority of large Issuing Houses have accounts with the Bank.

38. *Mr. Brand*: Might I ask one question arising out of Lord Bradbury's questions? When Lord Bradbury says the Bank, as a Central Bank, should only have banking accounts, in the term 'banking' would you include the Discount Houses? — Well, for that purpose I should.

39. As firms which should have an account? — Certainly, because that is an absolutely essential part of the machinery, an absolutely vital part of the machinery.

40. *Mr. McKenna*: Sir Ernest, you have recently altered the form of the Bank Return, and give more information than you used to give. You discriminate in that Return now between the deposits of the Clearing Banks and what, for this purpose, are called private customers' deposits? — Yes. I was proposing, Mr. Chairman, if it would be agreeable to the Committee, a little later to hand round copies which I have here of the last issue of our Bank Return, and to make a few remarks on the very point which Mr. McKenna is now raising, to explain exactly what we include under all the various headings of the Bank Return.

41. Do those figures show for a number of years – I understand you have taken them out for a good many years – any decline in the total of the deposits which I will call the deposits of private customers? — No, not a decline, because, of course, the total of the Bank's deposits since the outbreak of the War shows a very considerable increase, as do the deposits of every bank. Taking them simply and comparing them as figures I should say that they would not exhibit a large decline; and for another reason, that since the War – and that was one of the notes which I had down here to mention in connection with the functions of the Central Bank – we hold that a Central Bank should cultivate with the Central Banks of foreign countries that are established on a gold standard as intimate relations as possible for the easing and smoothing out of the variations upwards and downwards that may take place in the position as between countries. In point of fact, as foreign Central Banks do hold funds with us which are included in this figure, if you were to ask me whether the accounts of ordinary commercial firms, private customers, and so on, have decreased, I should say yes, most decidedly.

42. Ordinary commercial firms have decreased but other business of private customers, such as foreign Central Banks, has increased? — They have actually increased in figures. I should say, as I shall say when I come to the subject presently, that that figure which we now segregate from what are termed the bankers' balances includes the balances of a great many other businesses, all the banks, for example, in this country whose operations are not primarily conducted in this country although they may be British companies – their head offices may be here – all the Australian banks, Indian banks, South African banks,

South American banks, Canadian banks, any foreign banks that may have branches in London who have accounts with us, although even in that case the practice of the Bank now is not to open accounts for any foreign institution other than the Central Banks.

43. All the banks that you have named are customers of ordinary banks, are they not? — Certainly. And their accounts with us are in a great many cases, no doubt, merely subsidiary accounts.

44. I understand that in no case do you allow interest on deposits? — In no case.

45. In the case of the Central Banks whose deposits you use for them? — Not even in their case.

46. — You charge them a commission for using their deposits and lending on the market. Is not that correct? — We charge them no commission.

47. You give them a full return, you employ their money for them? — We employ their money for them in such form as they may direct us to employ it; it may be in Treasury Bills, it may be in commercial bills; in some cases it is in longer securities; in some cases they direct us to invest it in gold, and to hold the gold for them.

48. Do such deposits appear in your books as deposits? — No, not to the extent to which they are employed; only the free deposits. They do hold considerable free deposits with us, on which they get no interest, and which appear in our Returns.

49. Then so far as you are the banker for Central Clearing Banks whose deposits are used by you in the market those deposits do not appear in your figures? — When you say used by us in the market you mean invested in the market by us on their behalf?

50. In which you act as their agent? — They are not in our deposits.

51. That would materially reduce the total of deposits? — Certainly, but it still leaves a considerable margin of free balances which are included in that category.

52. You say it is desirable for a Central Bank to conduct private business in order to meet a case in which all the other ordinary commercial banks conspire, or, in fact, do not give credit in a particular instance? — Well, I say they should have the power to do so.

53. Do you know of any such case in this country ever having arisen? — No, I am not aware that in this country it has. In making my remarks I had not this country in mind.

54. Yes, I understood that. I hope to have the pleasure of reading your address. It is a fact, as you explained to us earlier, that the sole source and the basis of credit on which the joint stock banks can act is the Bank of England? — That is so.

55. If the joint stock banks feel that the Bank of England does not supply a sufficient basis of credit they have no other institution to which they can go, have they? — They have no other institution to which they can go. They have, I suppose, the means of forcing the Bank of England to create additional credit, as they do now.

56. *Mr. Bevin*: How? — By calling in their short funds from those who employ them they compel those persons to have recourse to the Bank of England, and thus to create the credit which has been called in.

57. *Mr. McKenna*: It would be a very limited power that they could exercise? — It is not very limited at times.

58. Well, for make-up purposes I know it is not limited, but for a continuous purpose it would be a very limited power? — I agree it would and it might create considerable disturbance inevitably.

59. *Mr. Lubbock*: Those principles that you have laid down, I imagine, are evolved out of the experience and practice of the Bank of England, broadly speaking? — Yes.

60. You spoke of the creation of a great number of Central Banks. The functions of those Central Banks are prescribed for them by statutes? — That is so.

61. Statutes that embody the principles which you lay down and by which they are strictly limited? — That is so.

62. The Bank of England is not regulated in its practice, I believe, by any statutes of that kind? — The Bank of England is practically free to do whatever it likes with one exception. Of course, the arrangements regarding note issue, for example, are all very clearly defined by statute. There are certain other provisions as to what it may do in its relations with the Government as regards lending money to the Government and so on, the form in which it must publish an account, but, apart from that, there is only one real prohibition that is imposed upon the Bank, and that is in the Tonnage Act of 1694 which says that in order not to oppress His Majesty's subjects the Bank is to be debarred for all time from using any of its funds in dealing in merchandise or wares of any description. Really apart from that I believe that there is no restriction on the business which the Bank of England can perform.

63. Although these principles have not been worked out in a laboratory and imposed upon you——? — No.

64. They may be regarded as a process of life and growth and adaptable to changed circumstances? — They have been adopted by the Bank of England by voluntary and free acceptation. *Chairman*: It is like the definition of the Common Law and the Statute Law – the one is a process of evolution and the other is a process of imposition.

65. *Mr. Lubbock*: In some of the Banks they have found it necessary to vary their statutes? — In certain cases, I believe, where they have hampered them, they have already had to go.

66. *Chairman*: You did say in passing that other countries also had their Central Banks.

It may at some stage of our inquiry be of interest for comparative purposes to examine the system of some of the other countries, possibly the United States, but so far as you know, do any of the Central Banks in existence outside this country exemplify those features to which you have alluded, or do they suffer from various qualifications or limitations imposed by statute? — They have undoubtedly certain limitations, certain obligations, which are imposed upon them by their statutes in many cases, especially in recent cases. In most of the recent cases I think I am correct in saying that the statutes have been drawn up for them by the League of Nations. The League of Nations have adopted a more or less general scheme of statutes. Then they have imposed restrictions in some cases which are not imposed in others, and the object of those restrictions it is often clear has been the protection of the Central Bank against control by its Government.

67. Then may we take it that the Central Bank conception has grown up in this country, so to speak, out of the natural financial design? — Exactly.

68. Whereas, in other countries it has been imported? — That is so.

69. Therefore, in other countries where it has been imported it has naturally emerged as a full-grown entity in a written form? — In a written form.

70. Contrasting our unwritten Constitution in this country with the written Constitution of the United States, where the country has adopted a Constitution which has been evolved for it by us? — That is so.

71. But the Central Bank system as you have described it seems to have evolved itself in order to meet the requirements of its environment? — The restrictions, so far as there are restrictions, under which the Bank works in its operations are restrictions which the Bank has imposed upon itself and which, of course, it has the power to alter.

72. And the organism will show an increasing adaptation for the purpose which you have in view? — Exactly.

73. Whereas you were originally engaged in commercial banking like other banks, the specialisation of your function has developed and you are now to an increasing extent becoming a Central Bank? — That is so. I may cite as an instance of that in my early days we had a certain number of branches in the country, and they were actively employed in the commercial business of the districts in which they were situated.

74. Like any other bank? — Like any other bank. Now, I think, they may be described as centres for the collection of balances from the banks in the towns in which they are situated. They hold balances for the banks, they settle the clearings for those banks, they hold a certain number of Government balances, but, apart from that, they are little more really than currency centres for the conduct of the currency arrangements, for the distribution of currency, for the receipt of currency, for the collection of worn coin, and so on. They are little more than that.

75. The result of your general account, and what has impressed me, is that you do not think the Bank of England – or the Central Bank, if I may use that term – should be debarred necessarily from engaging in ordinary business, but you do think that its primary function is not ordinary banking business but those specialised functions which you have described? — Certainly.

76. And the success will be judged by the extent to which it satisfies those special functions? — Yes.

77. *Professor Gregory*: I think we ought to clear up the point as to precisely what is meant by the argument that the Central Bank should not compete with the ordinary commercial bank. I take it that what you have really in mind is that the Central Bank should not be debarred in certain cases from having commercial customers, and that as a principle the Central Bank should be allowed to hold commercial assets, even though it may not be allowed to compete for them? — Yes.

78. You would not agree to the principle that the Central Bank should not hold bills of exchange? — No, it is essential that it should.

79. In other words, some form of competition between the commercial bank and the Central Bank is really inevitable so long as the Central Bank holds trade bills or commercial documents of any kind? — Yes, a certain amount of competition, but the major part of the bills which the Bank receive are brought to the Bank at a time when they cannot be taken elsewhere.

80. I mention this because, as you are probably aware, a considerable amount of agitation on the position of the Federal Reserve System is taking place in the United States, and I am rather anxious to secure the Central Bank from the implication that competition between the commercial banks and the Central Bank is something to be avoided at all costs. It seems to me to be inevitable so long as the Central Bank holds commercial assets. — To that extent, certainly. When I was speaking of competition I was meaning the attraction of banking customers for the conduct of ordinary banking business, commercial accounts, trading accounts, ordinary private customers, and so on.

81. *Mr. Keynes*: Does it not really come to this, that it is rather difficult for you to give us a clear-cut answer because there is a slow evolution going on, of which we are in the last uncompleted stage, so that the Bank of England might in the past have assumed responsibilities that it would not undertake *de novo* if it were a matter of starting afresh. There has been, in effect, a change of practice of the Bank of England, even over the last

25 years? — That is so. There has undoubtedly been a very large change of practice and I think it quite correct to say that it is still in process of evolution.

82. *Chairman*: The general point is that, in so far as the Bank of England has accounts of a commercial nature, they are to be regarded as a survival of past history? — Yes.

83. *Mr. Keynes*: On the other hand, the Bank of England is still inclined to enter into transactions when there are special reasons such as rationalisation in the general interests of the country? — There, again, we do feel that, if we can help in the rationalisation of industry, it is our duty to do so.

84. *Chairman*: There is a change of orientation in the Bank, is there not? The Bank outlook has been changed? — Certainly; it has been changing for years.

85. *Mr. Brand*: You said that the Bank of England regarded itself as having a duty to the community as a whole. Is your view, when you say that it ought not to be prohibited from having commercial accounts, that the object of those accounts would be to enable the Bank to perform duties to the community as a whole and not to any particular firm? — I should say that, as regards the ordinary sections of the community, the commercial community or the private community, our view that the Bank should have the power is, that we may render services if the services are legitimate services and cannot be rendered, or will not be rendered elsewhere; but nothing further than that.

86. *Mr. Bevin*: I do not know whether this matter of conflict between the Central Bank and the commercial banks is going to be dealt with presently, but I would like to ask one or two questions from the point of view of the ideal Central Bank. In your reply a moment ago to a question put by Mr. McKenna, you said that the Bank is all-powerful and, therefore, is the sole decider of the issue of credit. Then we got the answer that, as regards the joint stock banks, there is no appeal against the Bank of England except through the disturbance of business caused by the calling in of funds by the joint stock banks and so putting pressure upon the Bank of England. Would you agree, Sir Ernest, that that is a real weakness? — No; I should not, and for this reason. Somebody has got to decide, and I am doubtful whether, if the responsibility for deciding were distributed, you would, in fact, get as satisfactory, or a more satisfactory arrangement: provided, of course, that the responsibility is discharged properly. I agree that it is a large power to put into the hands of an institution.

87. But you did say that there had been conflict, because, when I asked how, you said 'The joint stock banks have brought pressure to bear upon us by calling in their funds and compelling people to have recourse to the Bank of England.' Now, if it is essential for the joint stock banks to bring pressure on you to issue more credit to meet what they regard as necessary, they cannot do that very well, can they, without causing disturbance in industry? — I did not say there had been disagreement.

88. I thought you said 'as had been agreed' or as you had done. I took down your words? — No; I said it is a normal practice of banks, not for the purpose of increasing credit, but when they wish to improve their own figures for the publication of accounts.

89. *Chairman*: I think that what the Witness had in mind was that that was the ultimate sanction – that that was the breaking point – that if the commercial banks could not supply credit and they had to call in their money, then the only other reservoir was the Bank of England; but that was the ultimate sanction. Is that a fair way to put it, Sir Ernest? — Yes; I think I would accept that.

90. The thing must reach an end at some particular point, and you are, so to speak, the terminus. Is not that so? — Yes. (*Chairman*): Whether it should end there is another question.

91. *Mr. Bevin*: Assuming a joint stock bank is limited in giving credit, owing to the restrictions imposed by the Bank of England, that is reflected in the joint stock bank's attitude to the customers and there is a restriction of trade. The joint stock banks say to the Bank of England, 'The credit you are allowing us is not sufficient to meet the demand upon us.' I will assume that, in the main, the Bank of England is ceasing commercial business, therefore industry is in the state that it is driven to the joint stock banks. Now, there is a conflict. There are the needs of industry; there are the joint stock banks who cannot supply the needs of industry because of the restriction of this almighty power. At present, according to the suggestion, the only way is to cause a crisis, in some way, in order to bring pressure upon the Bank of England. Now, is that an ideal or satisfactory state, to put such pressure on that middle factor as to produce a crisis in the third factor, on which we all live? — There is another factor, and that is that, whilst the Bank of England have no desire whatever to restrict the supply of credit, and can have no object in restricting the supply of credit, seeing that, even from selfish motives alone, it would simply be a source of profit to them, they have what I have described as their fundamental responsibility, which is to safeguard the stability of the monetary unit of the country.

92. *Chairman*: May the position be that there is not any more credit to give...? — Without risking the loss of the credit which already exists.

Chairman: That is the point. You may reach, I suppose, a breaking point, that commercial banks cannot give advances; they in turn come to you and ask if you can assist, and you may find yourselves, in turn, in a position in which you cannot give credit facilities because, if you were to do so, you would destroy the stability of the economic system of the country. *Mr. McKenna*: I am bound to make an observation on that. You say they could not, without endangering the stability of the currency. That is surely a question of opinion. *Chairman*: Certainly. *Mr. McKenna*: What we do not understand yet is the ground on which the opinion is formed from time to time, or the policy which actuates the Bank in saying 'You shall go thus far and no farther.' *Chairman*: The Bank of England is the repository of that information. *Mr. McKenna*: The sole repository. We do not know why they act. That is our trouble at the moment. We know their motives are unimpeachable, they are the most disinterested institution in the world, but we want to know – I would like to know – why they do these things. *Chairman*: I do not think that we can enter into that topic at the moment; Sir Ernest is giving us a description of the existing system. The Bank of England is, as matters stand at present, the ultimate repository of information, upon which it delivers its judgment on the question of credit. *Mr. Bevin*: And that is recommended to us by Sir Ernest as the future state. *Chairman*: And, in his opinion, rightly so. Whether it is rightly so or not, we can discuss later. Have we got your point, Mr. Bevin? *Mr. Bevin*: Yes, I think I have the point. I have the Witness's answers. It stands, like the Bank of England, where it stood.

93. *Chairman*: You were going to tell us, Sir Ernest, something of the organisation of the Bank of England which will illustrate to us a Central Bank in being, and how it functions. Will you illustrate it in your own way? — Well, as regards the particular functions which I mentioned as appropriate to a Central Bank, I may instance the following as actually discharged by the Bank of England. It holds the reserves, the main gold reserves of the country. It is the bank of the bankers, and it holds, on behalf of the bankers, a considerable proportion of the bankers' own cash reserves. It manages the note issue, apart from certain subsidiary issues of banks in Scotland and Northern Ireland, though, even there, it is, for the major part of those issues, ultimately responsible, seeing that, out of a total average circulation for those districts of about $28\frac{1}{2}$ millions, about $24\frac{1}{2}$ millions is secured by the backing of Bank of England notes. It is important, in considering the total of the note issues of the country, to bear in mind the fact that if the issues of the Bank of England are added to the issues of Scotland and Northern Ireland, allowance must be made for the fact that some 25 millions–30 millions is duplicated, seeing that notes for that amount issued by the commercial banks are covered by notes issued by the Bank of England. The Bank of England holds the gold reserves and it is under compulsion to buy any gold that is offered to it at a certain fixed statutory price, subject to certain conditions as to melting and assay, and it is further compelled to sell gold at a certain statutory price. It has the custody of the Government balances and, as the banker of the Government it also manages the National Debt, it pays the interest on the National Debt, receives subscriptions to the national issues, and pays off the maturities of National Debt. In those respects, therefore, it is actually discharging functions which I have suggested properly form part of the functions of a properly constituted Central Bank.

94. As to its own actual organisation, Sir Ernest, will you turn to that now? — As to its own organisation, it is divided, roughly, into two main departments, though there are other subsidiary departments, the two departments being the one engaged with all the banking functions of the institution, including the issue of notes and all matters of an ordinary banking character, the other being concerned with the management of the Public Debt, with the payment of the dividends on the Public Debt, the registration of transfers and all the ordinary duties which the Registrar of any ordinary Stock has to perform.

95. That division dates, does it not, from the Act of 1844? — No, that division does not actually date from then. The division which I think you have in mind, Mr. Chairman, as dating from 1844 is the division within the Banking Department which divides the Issue Department from what is described as the Banking Department. When I come to the Bank Return I will refer to the exact nature of that division.

The Charter under which the Bank is constituted leaves the Bank a very free hand, subject to that one particular provision which I have mentioned. A Supplemental Charter was granted in 1892, but it deals only with matters of internal routine. The Charters define how often the Court of Directors is to sit, the appointment of Committees for dealing with various matters, how the cash is to be held, and matters of that kind. In point of fact the Court of Directors meet weekly. In order to constitute a Court it is required by the Bye-laws that there shall be present the Governor or Deputy Governor and 13 out of the 26 Directors. There are various committees also appointed to deal with various sections of the Bank's work. There is what is known as the Committee of Treasury; that I might describe as being a sort of Inner Cabinet of the Bank. It is a body of nine members, and except that the Governor and Deputy Governor are ex-officio members, it is elected by ballot of the whole Court, by secret ballot. They act as a special body with whom the Governors can consult regarding all the more important business of the Bank, and can consider matters to be submitted to the Court and make recommendations, it being, of course, open to the Court to question any recommendation made and to open a discussion on any matters submitted to them. There are other Committees to which I think perhaps it is hardly necessary to refer in detail, for they deal with various matters such as staff matters, matters of the buildings, and various matters of internal organisation.

As regards the actual establishment of the Bank, in addition to the Governor, the Deputy Governor and 24 Directors who form the Court, there is the senior member of the official establishment termed the Comptroller, who acts as a sort of liaison between the Court and the clerical and official staff. He attends to various domestic matters on behalf of the Governors in order to afford them some relief from the work which they have to perform and he attends all Committees, so that an official view is always at hand on any subject that may come up for discussion. In addition there are others to whom I cannot exactly give any particular designation. They are generally spoken of amongst ourselves as advisers, people with special knowledge who are concerned with many of the developments of the Bank's business which are matters of more recent history, such, for example, as the relations with foreign Central Banks, their relations with the rationalisation of industry and matters of that kind. Also, members of their staff are in the habit of travelling at frequent intervals to interview the Governors and higher officials of foreign Central Banks, and we receive in turn visits from the Governors and officials of the foreign Central Banks. They have under them what is a new creation of recent times, a department which is entirely concerned with conducting the relations with foreign Central Banks. There is an office that is concerned with the preparation of statistics, statistics regarding industry, prices, every matter affecting the trade of the country and the trade of foreign countries. It receives information from foreign sources and collates it and compares it with our own. There is a Secretary's Department which, as its name implies, deals with secretarial matters, and matters connected with the staff and so on. There is an Audit Department which is perpetually engaged in conducting audits of various portions of the Bank's work, which is independent of all other officials in the Bank and is the direct servant of the Governors and Directors, and reports to them direct regarding the position which is revealed by its various examinations of the business and the control and custody of the Bank's assets and so on. There is in addition a large printing factory but that, of course, is not situated actually in the Bank, and is primarily maintained for the production of all the Government dividend warrants and so on and the notes issued.

To give you some idea of the size of the institution and of the extent to which it has grown as the result of the great additional work which has been imposed upon the Bank as the result of the War, I may say that apart from the printing factory, the staff which before the War was approximately 1,000 is now about 3,700 to 3,800. The Governors and Directors alone are responsible for policy and direction, though, of course, they are in constant consultation with the officials who are entrusted with the task of carrying out the policy which is laid down by the Governors and Court of Directors. It may interest you to know, just as a guide, to give you some idea of the magnitude of the work which the Bank has to undertake in connection, for example, with the administration of the National Debt, that there are on the books of the Bank upwards of three million separate stock accounts, quite apart from the very large holdings, of course, of bearer securities. Those are not only Government stocks; they include also Colonial Government, Corporation Stocks, and so on, and during the course of the year it is probable we have to record between nine hundred thousand and a million transfers. We pay from 4½ to 5 million dividend warrants and probably upwards of 5 million coupons, whilst the number of notes – I give you these figures because it is under these heads, the management of the National Debt and the extent of the issue of notes, where the very large increase has been necessitated in our establishment – the number of notes that we issue in the course of the year and consequently pay, because the amount remains more or less stable year by year, is about 650 millions. The whole of these warrants, coupons, notes and so on, is printed in our own factory.

96. *Mr. Keynes*: We are told there are 24 Directors beside the Governor and Deputy Governor, and it is common knowledge that many of those Directors are in active business as merchant bankers connected with the money market. How far do those Directors who are themselves in active business take part in the inner councils of the Bank, and how far are they merely, as it were, an advisory body whose wisdom can be called upon by the more active people? — Well, there is no rule which governs the subject, but in practice it is rare, I think I should be correct in saying, for more than one or two from that type of firm to be members of the Committee of Treasury.

97. *Chairman*: I gather that they are elected by ballot, the Committee of Treasury? — It is a secret ballot.

98. But the ballot might, of course, fall upon a person of the type that Mr. Keynes suggests? — That is quite true, but it is generally understood that on that Committee there must not be a preponderance of members of the Court of that description.

99. *Mr. Keynes*: Would the ordinary Director, who is not on the Committee of Treasury, have knowledge of an impending change in the Bank Rate before the actual morning on which the recommendation of the Com-

mittee of Treasury was made? — When you speak of the 'ordinary member,' do you mean the ordinary member who is not a member of the Committee of Treasury?

100. Yes? — No. He might know, he would probably know the direction in which things were tending. He would not know definitely that a decision had been arrived at to make a recommendation either one way or the other.

101. So the recommendation for a change of Bank Rate would come from the Committee of Treasury? — Yes.

102. I should like to know whether, in the opinion of Sir Ernest, this class of business man, the class of merchant banker from whom the Directors of the Bank are largely drawn historically, by reason of ancient tradition, is suited to modern conditions? — There again, you ask me a question that is rather difficult to answer. I think, if you review the elections of Directors, you will find that the recent tendency has not been to follow quite what was the old historical tradition, but that there has been a tendency to break new ground in recent years.

103. *Mr. Newbold*: On what principle are they elected? Are they selected as stockholders, are they selected as experts, or as representative of certain phases of economic life? — They are elected as men of good credit, first-class credit in the City, who are associated with some form of actual trade, be it foreign trade or be it home trade. They are not selected at the time as bank stock proprietors, though they must be bank stock proprietors before they can be elected, but as men who not only have knowledge but can bring to the Court information and knowledge as to what is proceeding in various spheres of commercial business, who can keep the Bank well posted with reliable information as to questions of credit, questions of industry, as to the prosperity or otherwise of industry, as to the trend of business as between this country and certain foreign countries.

104. I went through the lists of Directors over a period, 1889, 1899, 1909, 1919, 1929, the other day, just to see what was the general trend, the general line of business or of economic activity in which they were engaged. I noticed that there had been quite a considerable change of composition in the last 10 years but still the industrialists are very weakly represented. The Directors of railway companies and shipping companies, I notice, are very prominent. There is one representative of the steel industry, but I think that cotton, engineering, and many other branches of industry are quite unrepresented. I notice that the brewing and distilling industry is not as strongly represented as it used to be, still it is not quite as representative of the modern development of industry as one might have expected? — There has never been any idea that members shall be chosen strictly as representatives of a particular industry, or particular class, or particular trade, definitely as representatives; that is to say, that anybody should be chosen to come and represent that industry as a recognised representative of the industry. If he is informed regarding the affairs of a particular industry, so much the better, but not to come as a recognised representative.

In connection with that, I should like just to make one remark because one knows that there have been recent cases where, in connection with Central Banks, it has been laid down in one or two instances that the Board shall consist of so many representatives of, say, agriculture, so many representatives of, say, finance, so many of industry, so many of commerce, and I have been told that, in some of those cases, the experience which they have had is – as it was put to me once – a vicious principle. For this reason. We will say that an industry – I will not particularise the industry – is to provide a representative. The tendency for that representative – and I am told that this was experienced over and over again – is always to look at every question that comes up from the point of view 'How does that affect my industry, is it in the interest of my industry, or is it not?' and to judge the question from the point of view of his industry and from that point of view alone. Now, the whole theory of the Bank of England is to get a body of men who are in a position to take a detached view, who can afford to take a detached view, who are of such standing and credit that they can be relied upon to sink all personal feeling in taking a broad view of the problems which may be submitted to them, and I have been told – I have been advised, I should say – 'So far as you may be able to do so, do not encourage the appointment of representatives of particlar classes of industry.'

105. But, do you not think that, acting on that principle, there is the same danger of the over-stressing of the point of view of the merchant bankers? — I do not think there is the same danger, no.

106. Why? — They are not appointed by the merchant bankers. If you are the nominee of a certain class or group, you feel that you must serve the interests of that class or group, or that class or group may say, 'Make room for someone else.' That does not apply to any merchant banker, and I think I can say, as one who stands entirely outside this, not having been appointed from outside the Bank, that, in my experience, I should doubt whether it would have been possible to have collected, by any other method, a body of men who do, in fact, as I can bear testimony, bring so absolutely unbiased and disinterested a judgment to bear on every question that is put before them.

107. *Mr. Keynes*: There is an ancient tradition, mentioned, I think, by Bagehot that there are certain firms of merchant bankers

who consider themselves more or less entitled to serve by virtue of heredity. Is there any truth in that? — None whatever.

108. *Mr. Newbold*: I had that statement made very definitely to me by a critic of the Bank of England yesterday? — It is absolutely untrue.

109. But it is very strange how certain merchant bankers have members of their firms appearing on the Court of the Bank over a period of 50 years. As fast as one goes off, another comes on. That is the kind of thing that is likely to lodge in some people's minds? — I think, if you will examine the records, you will find at any rate so far as recent years are concerned that it is not true in more than one case that the member of one firm has ever been succeeded by another member of the same firm. During recent years, certainly.

110. There has been a continuity in the merchant banks since 1889, I believe. I checked this the other day? — No; pardon me; there has always been an interval, except once, so far as I can remember. Mr. Lubbock may be able to support me. I think I am correct in saying that there is only one instance that I know of in which there has been an immediate successor, and that was where a deceased Director was succeeded by another who had previously been a Director of the Bank of England, but he had had to retire on joining a firm which already had a partner a member of the Court. That is the only occasion, I think you will find, so far as I am aware, certainly in recent years.

111. I took my selection over 10 year periods; that is probably how I came to that erroneous view, but I wanted to have it cleared up quite definitely? — You must bear in mind that, if the names of representatives of certain firms do appear, it is generally the result of seeking for somebody who is of the very highest financial standing in the City of London, whose sources of information which he can place at the disposal of the Bank are of the widest possible description.

112. *Chairman*: Heredity may be of some value? — Heredity may be of some value in the case of a firm. *Chairman*: Hereditary attributes may be transmitted.

113. *Mr. Keynes*: When a man has once been elected a Director, does his re-election depend upon whether he has proved himself useful or capable? — I do not know that I ought to be asked to sit in judgment on a Court of Directors who have recently done me the honour to elect me one of their number under exceptional circumstances.

114. Is there a retiring age for Directors? — There is. That was introduced some 12 years ago. It is 70.

115. There is another ancient tradition of which, I think, Professor Gregory also has heard, that former Governors and Deputy Governors are members of the Committee of Treasury. I gather from what you have told us that that is untrue - or erroneous? — I think you will find it mentioned in Bagehot.

116. That is not the case now? — Now the Governor and Deputy Governor are ex-officio, the rest are elected by ballot. It is customary to elect the last occupant of the Chair; if a Governor has just retired naturally it is customary for him to obtain re-election in the ballot in order to retain the value of his advice and experience gained during his recent service as Governor, but in point of fact the only two ex-officio members are the Governor and the Deputy Governor for the time being.

117. *Professor Gregory*: In previous Parliamentary and other inquiries on the constitution of the Bank, I think it was always understood that the Directors were elected from young men before they had very much experience of the City, in order that they might acquire the necessary experience by the time they came to serve their term in the Chair. Is that more or less the practice of the Bank of England, or has it been abandoned? — No, it has not been abandoned but it has been modified; that is to say, that some are elected under those conditions, some are elected in order to bring a maturer experience gained in other service, as has been the case in recent years.

118. *Mr. Brand*: I suppose anybody before he becomes a member of the Committee of Treasury has to be proposed? It is not open to the Court of Directors to vote for anybody they like? — It is open to the Directors to vote for a certain fixed number. Each member of the Court is invited to vote for a certain fixed number; it is a secret ballot.

119. *Mr. Bevin*: All the members stand nominated really? — Any member may be regarded as a candidate.

120. *Mr. Keynes*: The organisation which you have described to us of the Comptroller and Advisers, a sort of higher Civil Service inside the Bank, is a very new thing? — It is. It is a matter of a few years and is still in course of development.

121. It is a very important development of the Bank since the War. They have been gradually developing and evolving what you might call a higher Civil Service, which previous to that scarcely existed in the Bank? — There was formerly no need for it. What has brought the need into existence was the intimate relations which we were in the course of establishing with foreign Central Banks, the need of paying frequent visits to them and receiving visits from them.

122. But I think the duties of the advisers are not limited to foreign affairs, are they? — Primarily foreign affairs, but not entirely; they are also engaged in the matter of statistics and so on, the application of statistics, advising on questions connected with rationalisation of industry and so on.

123. *Sir Thomas Allen*: Would the department also embrace research on credit? — No.

The collection of data to enable research to take place – undoubtedly; and they take part in the application of the data collected.

124. *Mr. Lubbock*: You have not mentioned the Chief Cashier – of course, the Chief Cashier goes on as before? — Yes. The Chief Cashier, I think I may say, even though I am an ex-Chief Cashier, is really the senior active official of the Bank, seeing that he is in charge of the department entrusted with the task of carrying out all the responsible banking duties of the Bank, the duties which are not defined by more or less definite rules as, for example, the duties of the Accountant's Department which is concerned with the management of Stocks.

125. *Mr. Keynes*: Is there any expert of the Bank who studies prices at home and abroad, wages and so on? — Yes.

126. *Chairman*: Is that in the Statistical Department? — That is in the Statistical Department.

127. *Mr. Keynes*: Not merely an official who compiles figures for the use of the Governor, but who interprets them? — Who interprets them. Quite.

Friday 29 November 1929

Sir Ernest Musgrave Harvey, K.B.E., Deputy Governor of the Bank of England, recalled and further examined.

128. *Chairman*: Sir Ernest, we are obliged to you for returning to-day. You had just reached the stage when we adjourned yesterday of placing in our hands a copy of the Bank Return, and were about to expound its meaning to us. I think you might take up the thread of your evidence at that point? — Before I begin, Mr. Chairman, I should just like to say that I saw the Governor after I left the Committee yesterday, and that he asked me to convey to the Committee an expression of his very great regret that he had been unable to attend, and to thank you for the message that you conveyed to him through me. I am glad to say that he has been able to go away to-day. Certainly when I saw him last night he was in no condition to attend to any business, but he is in great hopes that after an absence of four or five weeks he may find himself sufficiently recovered to be able to come and see you at some future date, and deal with the major questions of policy which no doubt you might wish to talk to him about.

129. We are much obliged, Sir Ernest; I am sure we all sincerely hope that he will speedily recover. — There was one question which was dealt with yesterday, and it is a question which obviously, I think, is one to which the Committee attach very great importance – as naturally they must – to which I should like to refer again this afternoon, the question of the creation of credit by the Bank of England. But before I do so I should like to deal with the statutory Bank Return, because I think when I have just run over the Return and explained it in some detail for the benefit of those members of the Committee who may not be very familiar with it, it will enable me to make more clear the remarks which I should like to make with reference to this question of the creation of credit.

130. If you please? — Now, if I may take the copy of the Bank Return which has been circulated, the Return, as no doubt the Committee know, is really based on a form of return which was prescribed by the Act of 1844. As published at the present day it differs in one or two respects from the form there laid down, partly as the result of the legislation which was passed last year when the currency note issue came to an end and was transferred to the Issue Department of the Bank of England, and partly as a voluntary act on the part of the Bank, to which I will refer later. Now, the Act of 1844 was the first occasion on which it was decreed that the Bank of England should be divided into two Departments – the Issue Department and the Banking Department. It ordered that the whole of the gold held by the Bank should be placed in the Issue Department, except such moderate amount as might be required for the ordinary day-to-day needs of the Bank in its Banking Department in connection with the business between itself and its customers. The provision included in the Gold Standard Act, which relieved the Bank of the necessity of cashing its notes in current coin, left the Bank really without the need to carry any gold in its Banking Department, except possibly just the trifling amounts of gold which are always being received from the public. At the present day gold is constantly trickling in from circulation, and a certain amount passes into the Bank, but it only passes *through* the Banking Department. The Committee may therefore take it that the amount of gold coin and bullion which is recorded as being held in the Issue Department is to all intents and purposes the whole of the gold coin and bullion which the Bank now hold, the amount in the Banking Department being quite trifling.

The original Act of 1844 fixed the amount of notes which the Bank might create at a figure of £14,000,000, plus the amount of gold held in the Issue Department. That figure of £14,000,000, generally termed the fiduciary issue, was allowed to be covered by securities. The nature of the securities was not limited in any way, except that the Act provided that the

Government debt, which is a book debt due by the Government to the Bank, should form part of the securities of the Issue Department. As regards the remaining securities which the Bank may hold, the Bank was at that time authorised to hold a limited amount of silver bullion at its current market value, but that provision became almost immediately a dead letter and it was not the practice of the Bank to hold silver bullion. Apart from the Government debt and such silver bullion as the Bank might have held, which was strictly limited in amount, the nature of the securities held was left to the discretion of the Bank, and the only limitation which the Bank have felt to be imposed upon them arose from the provision to which I referred yesterday as being contained in the Tonnage Act, which precluded the Bank from dealing in wares and merchandise. The Bank were advised that this would probably be held to exclude them from holding shares or debentures of any company so dealing. Apart from that they were left an absolute discretion as to the securities held.

I ought, of course, to mention that, when the currency note issue was amalgamated with the bank note issue the amount of the fiduciary issue was increased from the original sum of £14,000,000 (plus certain small sums which the Bank under that original Act had been authorised to add to the £14,000,000 in respect of the lapsed issues of other banks which originally had the power of issue) to £260,000,000. Therefore, at the present time the total of notes which the Bank can create is limited to £260,000,000, plus whatever amount of gold coin and bullion the Bank may from time to time hold in the Issue Department. The new Act made provision for possible increases and decreases of that sum of £260,000,000. Such increases or decreases may be effected on the request of the Bank, subject to the assent of the Treasury, and it is stipulated under that Act that in the case of an increase the consent of the Treasury, which must in each case be for a period not exceeding six months, may be renewed, provided that consecutive renewals do not extend the period beyond two years. If the period of two years were reached it would then be necessary for the matter to be submitted to Parliament for Parliament to decide whether the increase should be continued or whether it should cease.

131. I observe, Sir Ernest, that any Minute of the Treasury authorising an increase of the fiduciary issue has to be laid before both Houses of Parliament. — That is so.

132. That is in Section 8, Sub-Section (3) of the Currency and Bank Notes Act of 1928. — That is so. Now, on the liabilities side of the accounts of the Issue Department the amount of the notes created is divided into two figures, the total in circulation and the total in the Banking Department. I should like to make it clear that the total of notes in circulation means, in fact, all notes that have passed out of the custody of the Bank of England; that is to say, it includes not only the notes that are actually in circulation amongst the public, but also all the notes that are in the tills and the reserves of the banks, and notes which are set aside as cover for the issues of banks in Scotland and Northern Ireland, to the extent to which those issues exceed limits prescribed by Parliament. At the present time the average amount of the notes so set aside is about £24,500,000.

133. *Mr. Keynes*: That is for Scotland? — Scotland and Northern Ireland.

134. The two together? — The two together; that is the average of recent figures. The other figure, of £37,000,000 odd, is the notes which remain in the custody of the Bank and form part of the assets which the Bank is entitled to hold in the Banking Department as a reserve against their liabilities in that Department.

135. *Chairman*: The figure is carried down? — The figure, you will notice, is carried down into the Banking Department as notes. As regards the assets of the Issue Department, the Government debt, I think, has remained at that figure since 1834; it is the remains of a rather larger debt which at one time existed, the debt having prior to that date been approximately equivalent to the amount of the proprietors' capital.

136. What is the form of the voucher that you hold for that? — We have no voucher; we have no document which represents security for that debt. It is entered as a book debt in the accounts of the Public Exchequer, and it is referred to in certain Acts as a debt due by the State to the Bank, but there is no actual document that is held as security. It is merely a debt in account.

137. *Mr. Tulloch*: May I ask whether it is an interest-bearing debt? — It is an interest-bearing debt. When the Bank was founded it was founded for the purpose of lending money to the Government, and the whole of the capital subscribed was really for the purpose of making a loan to the Government. The interest at first commenced at eight per cent., but it remained at that figure for a very brief period. Within 15 years it had sunk to 6 per cent. It rapidly sank further, and in the earlier part of last century it had practically fallen to 3 per cent. In 1903 it was reduced to 2¾ per cent., and 11 years later to 2½ per cent., but the rate of interest is a matter of no concern nowadays to the Bank, for this reason, that in the Act passed last year it was provided that the whole of the net profits of the Issue Department should be paid over to the Government. Consequently whatever the rate of interest paid it is merely a payment by the Government of money which they take from one pocket and put into the other; it does not concern the Bank of England any longer.

Other Government Securities, the second item, consists of any sort of direct obligation of the British Government. There may be long-dated securities, short-dated securities, Treasury Bills, or Ways and Means advances, but at the present time the bulk is in the form of Treasury Bills. To that extent, therefore, I may mention that when there is talk about the high rate of interest that the Government pays on Treasury Bills it is not all money paid away by the Government to the public; whatever the rate may be it is received back by the Government in the profits of the Issue Department to the extent of the Treasury Bills held in that Department, and, as I say, by far the larger proportion of that item consists of Treasury Bills.

Other Securities consists of all other securities of whatever nature other than the following item of Silver Coin to which I will refer in a moment. As I say, it is left to the discretion of the Bank to decide the securities which it will hold, although under the Act passed last year the Bank are required to keep the Treasury informed as to the nature of the assets held in the Issue Department and of the transactions which take place in regard to those assets, which, of course, are really for account of the Government who are the recipients of the profits of that Department. That item consists at the present time entirely of bills, partly domestic, partly foreign.

The other item which appears here is Silver Coin. When the transfer of the currency notes took place to the Bank the Government were the holders in the currency note account of a very considerable sum of silver coin which they had had to take out of circulation owing to the great redundancy of silver which at that time existed as the result of the very large issues which had been made during and shortly after the War. It was in order really to find a home for that silver that authority was given by the Act to the Bank to hold a sum not exceeding £5,500,000 of silver, but that item is gradually being reduced as the circulation of the country requires additions of silver coin. It will gradually disappear but, of course, as it disappears its place must be taken by other securities. The securities are a fixed amount and, therefore, any operations in the securities of that Department cannot affect in any way the volume of credit which exists, seeing that if securities are sold they must be replaced by other securities.

138. *Chairman*: In order to maintain the £260,000,000? — In order to maintain the £260,000,000.

139. *Lord Bradbury*: Is there anything definitely prescribed as to the division of the securities items between Government Securities and Other Securities, or is that entirely within the discretion of the Bank? — It is entirely within the discretion of the Bank.

140. The bulk of them here are Other Government Securities. It would be theoretically in the discretion of rhe Bank to reverse those figures and make the Other Securities £235,000,000 and the Other Government Securities £8,000,000? — It would.

141. *Mr. McKenna*: You spoke of issuing the silver coin held. It is issued to the customer at its face value? — At face value.

142. And you transfer from the Issue Department silver as it is required for currency? — As our stock of silver coin in the Banking Department falls by demand from the community we restore it by transfers of coin from the Issue Department to the Banking Department.

143. At its face value? — At its face value, replacing the silver in the Issue Department by securities which we transfer to the Issue Department.

144. Last year that amount was taken into the Exchequer for full credit, thus forestalling the profit that would be made from the issue of silver currency in future years? — That profit had already been forestalled when this silver coin was originally issued.

145. It had already been forestalled? — It had been issued and the Government had then had the profit.

146. The Exchequer had already forestalled it? — That is so.

147. *Mr. Keynes*: Are the securities in the Return taken at cost? — At cost, and at the close of every half-year, they are valued at current market prices. If there is any depreciation, provision is made out of the income of the Department for them to be written down to the new prices.

148. *Professor Gregory*: At the expense of the Bank? — At the expense of the profits of the Issue Department.

149. *Mr. Keynes*: Are they written up? — Well, I am sorry to say that the occasion has not yet arisen when there has been appreciation, but that, in fact, is the intention.

150. *Lord Bradbury*: You said that Other Government Securities included a certain amount of Ways and Means advances. I take it that is comparatively small – the bulk of the Ways and Means advances are made by the Banking Department, is not that so? — That is so. The Ways and Means advances in the Issue Department are trivial, and are merely for the purpose of easy adjustment for Government purposes in securing the equalisation of the maturities of their Treasury Bills and for other similar purposes.

151. *Sir Thomas Allen*: Would you regard the present fiduciary issue as providing a sufficient basis for our modern English banking system? — The sufficiency of the fiduciary issue is dependent in very large measure upon the extent to which the bankers of the country may elect to hold their reserves either in notes or in balances at the Bank of England. If the bankers, for example, were to decide that they would prefer to hold a very much larger proportion of their balances in notes, it would mean that in reducing their balances in the Banking Department and withdrawing an

exactly corresponding amount of notes in the Banking Department, it would leave the Bank with possibly at times a reserve which might look small having regard to the remainder of the Bank's liabilities. But the very reduction of the bankers' balances would, of course, very largely reduce the need of reserve by the Bank, because it is mainly in the bankers' balances that the Bank are liable to meet with withdrawals from their deposits. Government deposits, for example, cannot vary very largely. The Government does not accumulate money for the pleasure of seeing a large balance in its pass book. It only takes in money as it requires the money to pay out and the Bank might, therefore, confidently rely on the fact that so far as the public deposits are concerned a more moderate proportion of reserve might be sufficient than would be sufficient in the case, say, of the bankers' balances which are subject to withdrawal by the bankers to meet the withdrawals which they may incur from their own clients.

152. I have it in mind that the Cunliffe Committee considered that the gold reserve should not fall below £150,000,000, yet we note than on the 20th November the gold coin and bullion totalled £132,000,000. On or about that date the bank rate was reduced. Would you, therefore, think that the figure quoted by the Cunliffe Committee was too high or too low, and what would you consider to be a minimum of the gold reserve of the Bank? — I think it is fair to say that the Bank of England do not carry any fixed figure in their mind as at all times an adequate figure of gold. It must be obvious that the sufficiency of the gold held must depend upon the changing circumstances of the moment – what is the period of the year? – is it a period of the year when we may be subject to considerable withdrawals from abroad? – what are the liabilities which we know to lie ahead of us? – what, so far as we can measure, are the claims upon us by foreign countries which they might enforce at any moment? We have never considered, I think, that the Cunliffe Committee in mentioning £150,000,000 did more than consider a figure which in normal circumstances and having regard to the fact that gold in the pockets of the people had been replaced by notes would be a fair average figure, may I say. It is obvious that at one moment £150,000,000 might be sufficient, whereas at another moment it might be insufficient. We are not wedded to the figure of £150,000,000 in the least. I think there is good evidence of that in the fact that we have allowed the figure to be brought down. There is, however, one fact which must always be borne in mind. Whatever the figure named as the minimum below which we should not fall, the lower you put it the less our power of resistance in case of any crisis. The lower, therefore, you allow the figure to fall the more necessary it may be at times to take rather drastic measures for the curtailment of credit – for the maintenance of a comparatively high, or at any rate effective, rate. But we are not wedded to any figure. We judge the figure according to the circumstances of the moment, and in our judgment so far as we were able to estimate the circumstances of the time we considered that it was not unreasonable to allow that figure of £150,000,000 to be reduced to the figure at which it now stands.

153. *Lord Bradbury*: This question of the Cunliffe Committee's recommendation and the £150,000,000 is likely to be a matter of some importance, and I think it is very desirable that we should be clear in our minds as to what the Cunliffe Committee's recommendation was. Might I ask that Paragraph 41 of the Report should be read?

Chairman: Shall I read it?

Lord Bradbury: If you would be so good.

Chairman: Paragraph 41 reads: 'The pre-war gold reserves were about £38,500,000 in the Bank of England and an amount estimated at £123,000,000 in the banks and in the pockets of the people. If the actual circulation of gold coins ceases and the whole of the gold is concentrated in the central institution, some economy is permissible in view of its increased mobility. On the other hand the aggregate amount of currency required will undoubtedly be larger. We accordingly recommend that the amount to be aimed at in the first instance as the normal minimum amount of the central gold reserve should be £150,000,000, and that, until this amount has been reached and maintained concurrently with a satisfactory foreign exchange position for a period of at least a year, the policy of reducing the uncovered note issue as and when opportunity offers should be consistently followed. In view of the economic conditions which are likely to follow the restoration of peace, it will be necessary to apply this policy with extreme caution and without undue rigidity. When the exchanges are working normally on the basis of a minimum reserve of £150,000,000 the position should again be reviewed in the light of the dimensions of the fiduciary issue as it then exists.'

Sir Thomas Allen: My difficulty on this is to know how far on questions of policy we should proceed with Sir Ernest or how far we should leave them to be dealt with when Mr. Norman comes before us. I do not want to pursue this matter unduly if at some later date we are going to take up all questions of policy with Mr. Norman. If you think it advisable I would rather hear what Sir Ernest has to say in a general way and deal with this question of policy later.

Chairman: I think it would be better to postpone these questions because the considerations which animate the Bank in altering the bank rate are naturally questions of policy on which Mr. Norman will give us his evidence.

154. *Mr. Frater Taylor*: May I ask, Mr.

Chairman, how the figure of £260,000,000 was determined?

Witness: I think, Mr. Chairman, I may say it was the figure that recent experience had shown to be necessary with a small reduction made in consideration of the fact that Southern Ireland would cease to employ our currency and would adopt their own currency, and that there would on that account be a return from circulation of notes no longer required. I may mention in passing that, although I have not got the latest figures before me, the reduction that was made at that time, which, if I remember right, was approximately £4,000,000, has already been exceeded by the notes which have been returned from circulation in Ireland. This shows that the allowance made has been more than met by the facts and notes are still returning from Ireland.

155. *Chairman*: The £260,000,000 was a figure based on experience? — Based on experience, yes.

156. *Mr. Keynes*: You said, Sir Ernest, that Other Securities included some foreign bills. Does that mean bills payable in foreign currency? — In foreign gold currency in a country on a free gold standard.

157. Is that an important part of the £8,000,000 or £9,000,000? — It is quite a considerable part.

158. *Mr. Newbold*: Have you any idea what proportion? — It varies. I might tell you the figure for last year which might be inaccurate for the figure of this year, because there is a constant variation. I could not state any proportion, for the simple reason, as I say, that it might be 30 per cent. one week, it might be 40 another, 50 another, or 60.

159. *Chairman*: Perhaps it would be sufficient if you gave a rough indication. (*Mr. Keynes*.) I am quite satisfied with Sir Ernest's reply that it is an important proportion. — It is an important proportion, sometimes more than 40 per cent., sometimes less.

160. *Mr. Brand*: Are these bills commercial bills? — Commercial bills such as would be acceptable for discount here, or in the case of a foreign country, such bills as would be acceptable for discount by the Central Bank of that country.

161. *Mr. Keynes*: You told us that the active circulation of notes as shown here includes notes held as reserve in their tills by clearing banks? — Yes.

162. Has the Bank of England any information as to the amount of notes so held? — No.

163. Can they form any estimate? — The only means we have of forming an estimate is to take the published figures of the banks and aggregate the figure which they give of cash in hand and at the Bank of England and then deduct from it the amount of cash which they held at that date at the Bank of England.

164. Would it be possible to ask for a weekly return from the bankers? — Certainly. Obviously this is a matter in which the relationship of banker and client arises, and even if the Bank can form an estimate it is not the Bank's business to state what the bankers hold in their tills. If the bankers like to disclose it, well and good, but we feel it is for them to do so and not for the Bank of England.

165. It is very difficult for the Bank of England to form accurate conclusions if they do not know what the active circulation of notes is. — We should welcome the information. As I say, we can form an estimate to that extent, although it is only approximate.

166. *Mr. Keynes*: Is there any reason why the joint stock banks should not be required to make a return?

Chairman: Is not that for the customer to say? — I should like to hear the bankers.

167. *Mr. Keynes*: The Bank of England would welcome it? — Certainly; we should be very pleased to have the figures before us.

168. As an ultimate determiner of policy you are being deprived of very important data? — Even if we were given the figures we should not know how much of those notes was necessary for current business and how much for reserve.

169. No, that would have to be calculated over a period of time. The fluctuations, anyhow, would be important. Supposing a joint stock bank is varying the proportion of its reserves which it holds in notes and in Bank of England deposits respectively, that throws you out in the inferences which you ordinarily make from fluctuations in the latter? — Yes, in theory it may; in practice I should be inclined to think that so far as our knowledge goes the holdings, certainly so far as they are notes held in reserve by the banks, are of a fairly constant character. But that is merely an opinion again; it is purely a guess.

170. There is no reason of public policy so far as you are aware why you should not know? — I know of none.

171. You said that the whole of the profits of the Issue Department now go to the Treasury, and the profits of the Banking Department alone go to the Bank. If the Bank were to ask for an increase in the fiduciary issue of £20,000,000, the first effect of that would be to transfer £20,000,000 of notes from the Issue Department to the Banking Department and £20,000,000 of securities from the Banking Department to the Issue Department? — That is so.

172. Therefore, assuming interest at 5 per cent. it would transfer £1,000,000 per annum from the pockets of the Bank to the pockets of the Treasury? — That is so, but the need would not arise until the banking reserve of the Bank was already low, and in consequence probably the Bank's holding of securities would have already increased. Thereby the Bank would have gradually accumulated securities which would be available to provide for the transfer.

173. You told us yesterday, with which I

agree, that it was very important for the Central Bank not to be troubled by the necessity of earning profits, it should be beyond care in that respect. Is it conceivable that the fact that the increase in the fiduciary issue would transfer a large amount from the pockets of the Bank to the pockets of the Treasury might lead the Bank to delay increasing the fiduciary issue longer than they otherwise would? — No.

174. It is conceivable? — I should say, speaking for the Bank of England, that it is quite inconceivable that that factor would receive a moment's consideration.

175. *Lord Bradbury*: On that may I put quite a simple proposition to you? Assuming there were an increase in the fiduciary issue and the Bank of England transfers £20,000,000 of securities from the Banking Department to the Issue Department and receives £20,000,000 of notes into the Banking Department, I assume that those £20,000,000 of notes have, from the point of view of the Banking Department, a certain earning capacity when they get there? — None.

176. If they go into reserve they have not, but if you did not get those notes into the Banking Department and had to strengthen your reserve by selling securities, you would obviously lose the earning value of those securities? — I am afraid I do not follow your question. I understood you to say that the notes when transferred to the Banking Department——

177. The Banking Department has £20,000,000 more cash which presumably it can use either to strengthen its reserves and so avoid parting with a revenue producing asset in order to strengthen its reserve, or if it does not want to strengthen its reserve, it might use it to earn money? — But the notes must remain there unless they are withdrawn by the public. (*Lord Bradbury*): True, but the reason of asking for it is to strengthen your reserve instead of parting with securities on the market.

178. *Professor Gregory*: If you were suddenly to increase the fiduciary issue from the present figure of £260,000,000 to £280,000,000 and to replace £20,000,000 of the assets of the Banking Department by notes, transferring the securities to the Issue Department, you could, if you wanted to do so, having a larger reserve, lend £20,000,000 more than you did before? — That is true.

179. *Mr. Keynes*: Supposing this year there were large withdrawals on account of the Christmas Holidays, the Bank's reserve might look, from the point of view of the public, low. Therefore, it might be better to show more reserves in the Banking Department and less in the Issue Department. There is no reason why this change should not be adopted if the profits of the Bank of England are so large that a million a year is no concern one way or the other? — I do not admit that.

180. If that is not so, is it not saying rather too much to say that the Bank might not be influenced? — No, for the reasons that I have mentioned. If I may take your instance that the reserves at Christmas might be drawn down to a figure which would look undesirably low, let us say instead of £37,000,000 at the present time in notes it were drawn down to, say, £17,000,000, in the meantime the Bank would have acquired £20,000,000 of earning assets. Whilst that £20,000,000 of notes had been withdrawn, unless the Bank acquired £20,000,000 additional earning assets the market would be deprived of £20,000,000 of credit.

181. If it allows its published reserves to fall it will still get these profits. The Bank regularly derives profits from the deposits at the end of the year. It would not get any more revenue from increasing its fiduciary issue; this would normally represent a transfer from the Bank to the Treasury. It is therefore perhaps injudicious for the amount of fiduciary issue to be linked up with the question of division of profits between the Treasury and the Bank of England. I see no reason why the contribution of the Bank of England should be reduced or increased because of the fiduciary issue. (*Professor Gregory*): I should like to follow that up by putting the question that Mr. Keynes put to you, rather more positively, and asking you your own personal opinion as to whether it would not be better in the interests of the Bank of England generally that you should pay a franchise tax to the Government on your net profits, rather than on the profits of the Issue Department? (*Witness*): Are you speaking of the total profits derived from both Departments?

182. *Professor Gregory*: Yes. At the moment it is not on the net profits that you pay tax to the Treasury, but on the profits of your Issue Department. Suppose you stopped with that and subsequently paid the franchise tax on your net profits rather than on the profits of the Issue Department? — That is a question, Mr. Chairman, that I think I should like to have time to consider. It is a question of high policy, which I should hardly feel at liberty to deal with this afternoon.

183. *Mr. McKenna*: The question raised arises as the result of a bargain with the Treasury, does it not? — Quite.

184. That bargain could be altered at any time by agreement between both parties? — It is in an Act of Parliament; what Parliament has passed, of course, Parliament can undo.

185. *Chairman*: The question has been raised and it will be on record. I think we might proceed now? — If I might now take the items of the Banking Department, the capital of £14,500,000 - that, as I said before, is really a figure which was arrived at by sums which were contributed from time to time by private citizens for the purpose of making advances to the Government. The Govern-

ment Debt was originally almost identically the same figure; I think part of it was repaid by the issue of three per cent. stock to the Bank in place of a corresponding amount of old book debt. The Rest consists of undistributed profits, and the normal practice is not to allow it to fall below a figure of £3,000,000.

186. *Professor Gregory*: Is any proportion of the capital, to the knowledge of the Bank, held by the joint stock banks at the present moment? — I do not know. I should doubt it.

187. Would the Bank have any objection to the holding of Bank stock by a joint stock bank? — No, I do not think so. There is no limitation of the holding of Bank stock, and I do not know that the Bank, who regard it as more or less an ordinary trustee investment, would object to anybody holding the stock. If the idea in your mind is that by the purchase of stock a joint stock bank might obtain a measure of control, that is not possible unless it buys the whole of the stock. (*Professor Gregory*): The idea in my mind was whether there might not be a tendency in this country towards the situation in the United States, where the Central Bank is in fact owned by the Member Banks.

188. *Mr. Frater Taylor*: Is the stock generally held just in the same way as the stock of any joint stock bank is held? — Entirely. There is a very large body of holders.

189. *Mr. Lubbock*: 14,000, I think? — 14,000.

190. *Mr. Newbold*: Must all holders be British subjects? — No.

191. You may have foreign stock holders? — Certainly.

192. Have you any knowledge of what proportion is foreign, because it is extremely important in the national interest? — I should say it is extremely small. I cannot tell you the proportion, but no holder, whatever his holding, has more than one vote – no matter how much he holds. He has no vote at all unless he holds £500, and if he holds £5,000,000 he has one vote.

193. Is it usual for the stock to be held in small blocks or large blocks, or does it vary; there is an impression that it is in great blocks? — No. There are a large number of small holders.

194. *Chairman*: On the figure you have given us of roughly 14,000 holders it works out at an average of about £1,000 each. (*Mr. Newbold*): I know it works out at that average, but I have spent the last 15 years in searching stock lists and, frankly, those averages do not impress me at all. — (*Witness*): No; it is very well spread.

195. I was wondering whether there was a large number of small holders and large ones embedded among them, as in the case of joint stock companies? — No, I should say that was not the case.

196. Would you have any objection to the list of your proprietors being made known? It would clear up a lot of trouble in the country, you know. (*Chairman*): Is it not at Somerset House? (*Mr. Newbold*): No; it pre-dates that by hundreds of years! (*Mr. Lubbock*): You could probably give some figures about it. (*Chairman*): It would be undesirable to give actual names of the holders, but the kind of information that might be given would be, first of all, the number of holders, secondly the average holdings, then the maximum and minimum holding, and, if you please, the percentage of nationalities. That would not disclose the actual names of individuals. (*Mr. Newbold*): No. I only want the composition. (*Witness*): I think figures could be prepared which would give Mr. Newbold the information he wants.

197. *Mr. Newbold*: If we could have some figures of the comparative interests and proportions, what is held by merchant bankers, what is held by private individuals. The latest stock list I have seen is somewhere in the thirties; there seems to have been nothing since? — I should say the great majority, from my recollection of reading the list of accounts, is in the hands of private persons.

198. *Chairman*: We should be glad if you could have a table drawn up in which, without committing any breach of confidence, you could put the number of holders up to £1,000, £1,000 to £10,000, something of that kind. You will turn that over? — Yes. I think I had reached the Proprietors' Capital, and the Rest which, as I stated, is usually kept at a figure of not less than £3,000,000. The Public Deposits – these include all the Government balances at the Head Office and at the branches. The Exchequer, the Paymaster-General's Account, Savings Banks monies passing through the account pending investment, and so on. The Commissioners of National Debt have considerable accounts through which the monies of the various funds which they administer are passed and through which the monies are invested. There are the Dividend Accounts of Government dividends, that is, monies which have been provided to meet dividend warrants which have been issued and not yet presented.

199. Are these various accounts in the nature of current account balances? — Yes.

200. They are among your customers, so to speak? — They are.

201. And this represents the amount of some of their credits? — Yes; all public monies. I should say that 'Public Deposits' includes accounts the funds to the credit of which are public monies, and for the opening of which accounts authority has been given to the Bank by the Treasury. No public officer can walk into the Bank of England and say that he wishes to open an account and place money to the credit of that account and have it regarded as a public account. Every account must be authorised by the Treasury. There are various accounts into which tax monies are placed as collected, through which

they are passed and from which they are transferred to the Exchequer.

202. *Lord Bradbury*: These are exclusively home Government accounts. If you have accounts of Governments of other parts of the British Dominions you put them under 'Other Deposits'? — Yes.

203. *Sir Walter Raine*: Will you to-morrow transfer £50,000,000 for the dividend you have mentioned as payable on Monday morning? Will you transfer it at once? — No; not £50,000,000. From the experience we have as managers of the National Debt, we can estimate to a very close figure what sum will be required to meet dividend warrants presented on Monday, and it will be the business of the Treasury, in arrangement with us, to supply to the credit of that Dividend Account such a sum as will, according to our experience, be sufficient to meet the dividends presented on that day. They will not put the whole of the dividends, they will only provide such sum as we know from experience when the dividend date falls on a Monday will probably be presented on a Monday. If it were a Saturday, we should know that the amount of dividends cashed would be less, and they would not require to make the same provision.

204. *Mr. Frater Taylor*: Will that mean a temporary increase in Public Deposits then? — No; because the money will be paid in in the morning and will be paid out to the holders of dividend warrants in the afternoon.

205. *Sir Walter Raine*: What will happen next Wednesday when you draw up this Balance Sheet again. The cheques for the £50,000,000 will have been sent out by Monday morning. Supposing £40,000,000 have been paid by Wednesday, what will happen to the other £10,000,000, so far as this Balance Sheet is concerned? — Nothing; it will not figure there, the other £10,000,000 which have not been provided will not figure in the Balance Sheet.

206. Unless the Government provide the wherewithal, it does not figure here? — Unless the Government have provided themselves with the money in order to meet it and have kept it on their own Exchequer Account and have not yet transferred it to the Dividend Account to meet the dividends; but, seeing that always, at these periods, it is necessary for the Government to have recourse to the Bank of England for a certain amount of Ways and Means advances, they will not borrow that money until the day on which the money is required to meet the dividends. To the extent to which they have required to borrow money from the Bank to meet the dividends, there would be an increase in the Government securities and an increase in the bankers' deposits because they will, as I say, not borrow the money until they need to pay it out.

207. *Mr. Frater Taylor*: Is the Exchequer Account to which you have referred a separate item altogether and apart from the Banking Department? — It is a separate account in the 'Public Deposits.'

208. So this is not really the Balance Sheet of the Bank that we are looking at; it is merely of a department? — Oh! no; this is the Balance Sheet of the Bank. The Exchequer is one of the accounts included under the head of 'Public Deposits.' 'Other Deposits' is now, as you see here, divided into two items – Bankers and Other Accounts. This is not a statutory requirement, but was a voluntary disclosure of information which was made with the consent of the bankers who, when consulted by the Bank of England, very readily gave their consent to the publication of these figures, which it was felt would be of value to the market in estimating the position as between the bank and the market.

209. *Mr. Tulloch*: May I ask you if these are only Clearing Bank balances, or are any other balances included? — These bankers' accounts are all of British banks whose main functions are conducted in this country – the Clearing Banks and banks in the Provinces, if they are British banks, that have accounts with the Bank of England. It includes the balances which they all hold at our branches. It does not include banks which, though British banks, are in the main operating in the Dominions or in foreign countries, such as the Australian, Indian, Canadian, South African and South American banks.

210. *Mr. Keynes*: It includes Scottish banks? — Scottish banks too.

211. And Northern Ireland? — And Northern Ireland.

212. *Professor Gregory*: But not the Bank of Ireland? — No; not the Bank of Ireland.

213. *Chairman*: Does not the Bank of Ireland operate in Northern Ireland as well as in the Free State? — It does, but it is not now a British bank in the United Kingdom.

214. *Mr. Frater Taylor*: The fact that these other banks bank with you means that they come under your reserve. It is a convenience, in a way, is it not? — Yes. I should say that practically none of them are solely customers of the Bank. They are far more active customers of the other banks. They keep accounts with us, they keep substantial balances with us; as I think I described yesterday, possibly, as a tradition from old times, they like to feel that they have got a safe port in a storm, somebody to whom they can go in times of difficulty, to whose bank parlours they have the right of entry and the right to come and ask for accommodation, if the accommodation is not available to them elsewhere.

215. *Chairman*: And their balances will be under the head of 'Other Accounts'? — Their balances will be under the head of 'Other Accounts' – the Bank of Ireland, for example, all the banks which have just been mentioned, any London office of a foreign bank which happens to have an account, though they are

few, any Colonial bank, and also the Indian Government which has been mentioned.

216. Foreign Central Banks? — Foreign Central Banks. They are all included in 'Other Accounts.'

217. *Mr. McKenna*: Arising out of the discussion yesterday upon the deposits of the Central Banks: in certain cases you have taken money for deposit privately and then used those deposits for your clients on the market. Take the case of a particular bank; for instance, you have an account for the Bank of X? — Yes.

218. The Bank of X places with you £100,000, with the request that you use that money for them, and you return to them all the profits made upon the £100,000. Either in practice or by express obligation, or implied obligation, can the Bank of X get that £100,000, or any part of it, on demand? — They have the right to come to us, to bring to us the assets which have been acquired on their account, and to invite us to discount those assets.

219. In practice, has that right ever been exercised by any of your customers? — Certainly.

220. If that right is, in practice, exercised, do these accounts really disclose the whole of your deposit liabilities? — Yes; I should say so most undoubtedly.

221. On paper certainly, but do they really? — What about a discount market broker who is a holder of bills and who has the right – an acknowledged right – to bring them to us to discount?

222. That is rather a different case; that is recognised in the ordinary course of business. If the Bank of X were banking with an ordinary commercial bank, this £100,000 would have been placed on current account with the ordinary commercial bank and it would appear as a deposit liability of that bank. The Bank of X lodging the money with you, uses that money in precisely the same way as it would use it if it were deposited with a commercial bank. The commercial bank would show it on its liabilities; the Bank of England does not. Is it not really in the nature of a current account? — I am trying to get the point to which your remarks are directed. Is there a fear in your mind that the total of the deposits put together – the deposits, for example, of all the banks – does not really show the total deposit liabilities because, in some way, these investments are taken out of the Bank of England deposits? I do not see why, because the Bank of England makes the purchase of the bills on behalf of the Bank of X, the position is in any way altered by that fact from the position which would exist if the Bank of X made the purchase itself and lodged the securities for safe custody with the Bank of England. We merely act as agents for the purchase.

223. If the Bank of X had made a deposit with you and it appeared in your accounts and you paid the Bank of X the precise return which you obtained on that money, that would be following, would it not, the ordinary course of business, except that instead of paying a fixed deposit rate you would pay what the deposit actually earned. Now, you do not adopt that course if you do not include the Bank of X money as a deposit, although it is repayable on demand, and you hold both the deposits and the securities outside your accounts. Have you not really got a greater liability than your accounts disclose? — Not a greater liability, it seems to me, than the liability which always rests upon us to discount practically the whole of the bank bills in the London market – a liability that may be imposed upon us at any moment.

224. All the bankers' deposits may be demanded, must be paid on demand, but they are all expressed in your balance sheet, and we know that you are under a liability to pay £58,000,000 to the bankers on demand. We know, further, that you are liable to pay £38,000,000 on 'Other Accounts' on demand. Your accounts do not disclose the fact that you are liable to pay, on demand, all the money which you hold from the Central Banks? — Subject to our first having discounted those bills and created out of them the deposits.

225. You discount the bills yourselves——? — Yes.

226. It is really a demand from them? — No.

227. You discount the bills and meet the claim. You do not go to the outside market to discount the bills; you discount them yourselves? — Not necessarily.

228. You may? — We may.

229. *Professor Gregory*: I should like to ask you, Sir Ernest, whether the Central Bank, lodging monies with you and instructing you to invest them in bills, can draw on the existing deposit? — Not without discounting the bills.

230. *Mr. McKenna*: But the bills are discounted by the Bank of England on demand? — The money is sent to the Bank of England for the purpose of being invested in bills, and the instruction will be to invest in bills acceptable by the Bank of England, and those bills they expect to be able to discount, in case of need, in exactly the same way as every other holder of acceptable bank bills in the London market expects to be able to come to the Bank of England and discount bills.

231. *Mr. Keynes*: Is not the substantial point that the fluctuations in the amounts which are held by foreign banks is one of the most important factors determining the conduct of your business? If the amount of the foreign banks' balances is going down you draw different inferences from what you would draw if they are going up. Your accounts are so drawn up that that piece of information is only in the hands of the Bank of England and is withheld from me? — But if those funds are with another bank the information is only in the hands of that bank. It is not in the possession of either the Bank of England or anybody else.

232. Oh, yes. There are many other pieces of information which are withheld both from you and from me? — Undoubtedly.

233. But the main effect of this way of treating the account is that the information is withheld from me, but not from you? — Well, of course, to a certain extent we know a certain amount of the foreign claims upon the London market. Their inclusion here would be an indication possibly on which students of the market might be able to form some sort of estimate as to the volume of foreign claims on this market.

234. It is a very important point. I think I am right in saying that the Federal Reserve Banks of the United States have a precisely similar arrangement for receiving money from foreign banks and then investing for them in bills, but the Federal Reserve Banks publish the figures. Is not that the case? — Well, I did not know it; I was not aware that they did.

235. *Chairman*: Do you say they do? (*Mr. Keynes*): I believe they do. I shall have to verify that. (*Professor Gregory*): They certainly do in regard to the volume of business in bills conducted for foreign correspondents. (*Witness*): I had forgotten that.

236. *Mr. Keynes*: Publication has certain advantages, has it not? Some people criticise this bills of exchange system for foreign Central Banks mainly on the ground that the volume of securities held for a particular Bank can fluctuate without producing an effect on the market, whereas if it is a movement of gold it produces an effect. Some people say it is undesirable that you should be able to have changes in the amount of foreign balances without its producing an effect on the market, that it is a positive weakness to the Bank of England that the rest of the market should be unaware of fluctuations of this description. — But what of the position of the Bank of England who are entirely unaware of the extent to which foreign balances are held by other banks?

237. It would enable you to form accurate inferences if you had a statement from the bankers of their foreign balances, and I have no reason to think that you could not get that. Would it not be much better if we knew the fluctuation in the foreign balances? — Well, I should not like to commit myself to a definite answer.

238. *Chairman*: I think that is a question for Mr. Norman. It will remain on the record. — Yes, I should like him to answer that.

239. *Mr. Keynes*: Would it be possible to give us any indication in rough proportion of how the £38,000,000 of Other Accounts is divided between the four categories of British banks operating abroad, foreign banks, Dominion Governments and other accounts? — It would be possible, but I am afraid I cannot give them to you, because I have not got them in my notes and I have certainly not got them in my head.

240. *Mr. Keynes*: Would Sir Ernest consider whether it would be possible for him next time to tell us roughly what the average would be over a period of time? (*Chairman*): Information may be given to us, but it is a question of policy whether the publication of that information is desirable in the public interest as being likely to affect the market. (*Mr. Keynes*): I will put it, if you like, in the form of two questions. Could we be given confidentially roughly the proportion for last year and, secondly, is there any reason of public policy why it should not be published? (*Chairman*): We have a note of that and I will see that that point is considered. (*Witness*): I certainly could not commit myself to the production of that information. I am afraid I have been taking no notes; if I could be supplied with notes of these various points——(*Chairman*): A transcript of the shorthand note will be transmitted to you in the course of the next few days.

241. *Professor Gregory*: In the case of any foreign correspondent – dealings in bills or any other earning asset, this figure of unspent balance would be included in the Other Accounts? — Certainly.

Thursday 5 December 1929

Sir Ernest Musgrave Harvey, K.B.E., Deputy Governor of the Bank of England, recalled and further examined.

242. *Chairman*: Have you been furnished with a print of the evidence that you have given us? — I have, thank you.

243. I am sorry it has been so late in coming. It has been delayed. — I have not been able to look at it yet. I received it to-day.

244. You were engaged, you remember, when we adjourned, in your analysis of the weekly account of the Bank of England and explaining the different items in it. I think you had more or less exhausted your comments on the return, and we asked a number of questions upon it. Will you resume at the point where you left off in your exposition? — Before I resume on the Bank Return, may I deal with the answers which I reserved last time to three questions?

245. If you please. — The first answer I reserved simply because I had not the facts before me. I was asked a question about the holders of Bank Stock.

246. Yes, I remember. — I see no possible objection to quite full information being given if the Committee think fit. I have had a careful analysis made of the existing holders of Bank Stock. The only information I could give last

time was that the number of holders was 14,000. I find that the exact number is 14,378 at the present time. Of those holdings, 8,796 – that is considerably more than half – are holdings of £500 and less; 2,583 are holdings of from £500 to £1,000; 1,980 are from £1,000 to £2,500. Thus between 13,000 and 14,000 out of the whole number of holdings are of £2,500 and less. There are larger holdings, but if I skip the intervening figures, there are 30 holdings of amounts over £25,000. Then I was asked a question regarding bankers' holdings of Bank Stock. There, of course, whilst we may see bankers' names or the nominees of bankers on our books we do not know the purpose for which they hold it. It may be their own, it may be simply held on customers' account, e.g., as security for an advance, but whatever the purpose, the total held by bankers – I am only speaking of bankers as we define them in the Bank Return – is under £500,000. I was asked a question about foreign holders. Of foreign banks there are none; of other accounts of foreigners if we may judge from the registered addresses, there are holdings for a total of about £57,000.

I said that I believed that a good deal was held by trustees. I find that of the amount held by British holders – and I include in that category holders within the Empire – the amount held in single names and the amount held in joint names which we assume are trustees, excluding amounts held by nominees of banks, are practically identical – sole names £6,000,940, and in joint names, £6,000,944.

247. *Mr. Brand*: Are those the nominal amounts? — The nominal amount of stock, yes. As regards the powers of the holders, under the Charter as it stands, no holder has more than one vote whatever the amount of his stock, but trustees are empowered to vote, holders in joint names having power to authorise one of their number to vote. At the present time, therefore, the voting control is enormously widely spread. Further – I think I mentioned last time; if not, I do so now – no holder can vote unless the stock has been in his name six months. That is really the extent of the protection which we have against control being obtained by anybody; the widely held nature of the stock and the fact that if anybody wishes to get control they have got to purchase from a vast number of holders and they have got to have held the stock for six months. I do not know if there are any other questions on this subject on which the Committee would wish for information?

248. *Sir Thomas Allen*: Is there a vote for each trust account? — One vote for each trust account. They may authorise one of their number to vote.

249. Do we take it that any holding in the Bank of England, either individually or collectively, would carry with it one vote? — There is no vote for a holding of less than £500.

250. *Mr. Newbold*: Is any proxy voting allowed? — Proxy voting is not allowed.

251. Quite definitely? — Only to the extent that in a joint account the holders may authorise one of their number to vote.

252. *Mr. Tulloch*: Have you power to refuse to register a transfer to a holder of whom you do not approve? — No.

253. You are bound to register? — We are bound to.

254. *Chairman*: We are very much obliged to you for that information. — That answers that question. Then I was asked a question which arose in connection with the discussion as to what might influence the Bank, in the case of the need for an increase in the fiduciary issue; whether they might be influenced by the fact that such an increase would reduce profits. In connection with that discussion I was asked whether it might not be preferable that instead of the Government receiving the profits of the Issue Department they should receive some proportion of the total net profits of the Bank, leaving the Bank to receive all profits of issue and banking and then to pay this proportion to the Government. I have given a good deal of consideration to that point, and I am bound to say that my conclusion is that such an arrangement would be undesirable for the reasons which I will state. For myself I am satisfied that bearing in mind the principles which guide the Bank at the present time – whilst I am not going to say that such a question as was put to me last time as to whether the loss of, say, a million of profits is a matter immaterial to the Bank, which, of course, it is not – the question of profits, as I have said before, never influences us. I endeavoured to explain then why, in the case of an increase of the fiduciary issue there would be no need for the Bank to trouble itself about profits. I was not satisfied after I had left the meeting whether I had really made my meaning clear. What I said was that the need for an increase in the fiduciary issue could only arise owing to the fact that there had been such a heavy demand upon the Bank reserve that the Bank would, in order to keep the market supplied with funds, have been obliged to create other earning assets – to buy securities – or even if the Bank took no action, that the reduction in their reserve would have entailed such a reduction in the bankers' balances that the bankers would have been forced to call in call money, and thus to drive the market to the Bank to borrow and compel the Bank to create additional assets in the form of advances to the market. So that when that need arose the Bank would already have acquired a corresponding *additional* amount of earning assets, and would thereby have been put in possession of the assets to transfer to the Issue Department, and they would not in fact be losing profits.

255. *Mr. Keynes*: In any given circumstances, at any given level of deposits of the Bank of England, an increase in the reserve of

the Banking Department diminishes the profits of the Bank? — That is true, but the question we were considering was the reverse question, should we refuse or should we hesitate to increase the fiduciary issue because we might lose profits. I say no, not for one moment.

256. *Mr. McKenna*: For the reason that you would, before that moment arrived, have been making exceptionally large profits? — Exactly. We should be foregoing profits which we might otherwise have made. I hope I have made that clear now, because I was not satisfied after I left last time whether I had made that point clear.

257. *Mr. Keynes*: You accept the point that at this moment if the fiduciary issue were £20,000,000 more than it is the Bank of England would, taking the value of money to be 5 per cent., lose £1,000,000 net profits? — Well, if the fiduciary issue were £20,000,000 larger, we should undoubtedly do so, assuming all other things to remain the same. Certainly. But the reason that convinces me that there are dangers in an arrangement under which the Government would participate in the total profits is this. Is it inconceivable that some future impecunious Chancellor of the Exchequer, let us say, badly in need of funds, might not seek to exercise some sort of pressure on the Bank to make the Bank increase its profits in order that the Government might get an increased benefit and share of those profits? Even if he did not do that, is it not possible that he might one day say, 'We are increasing taxation all round, we will take more of the Bank's profits,' and thereby compel the Bank, perhaps, to embark on profit-earning activities for the sake of keeping their profits level. I do not believe myself that you could have such an arrangement under which the Government participate in the total profits without sooner or later running the risk of the Government intervening to try and control the profit-earning activities of the Institution. That is my feeling.

258. *Professor Gregory*: Might I ask you one question which does not arise out of what you have been saying, but out of a remark which I have heard elsewhere? Has the Bank taken legal opinion on the particular point whether they could not have a limit for their fiduciary circulation without actually issuing up to that limit? — No.

259. Supposing you took power to issue up to £280,000,000, but you actually issued only £260,000,000? — I think not. Under the Act the fiduciary issue is the fiduciary issue for the time being authorised, whether by Parliament or by an additional minute of the Treasury, and the Act says that we must put into the Issue Department securities of a value equivalent to the total of the notes representing the fiduciary issue.

260. In your opinion you are not allowed to have a margin of the fiduciary issue unissued? — No.

261. *Mr. Keynes*: I see the great force of your argument about the Bank of England having autonomy in regard to its profits. I also agree very much with what you said previously, that it is very important that the Bank of England should have enough profit not to be worried on that score. Do you think it would be easier to maintain the existing system, from the public point of view, if the dividend to the existing shareholders were fixed for all time at a certain figure so that there would be no question of the profits earned by what is really a public institution going into private pockets? — Personally, I should prefer to allow that matter to stand until the Bank has given any evidence that they are distributing unduly large amounts among their shareholders. Unless the Bank gives evidence that the Institution is being used for the distribution of unjustifiable profits amongst its shareholders I cannot see that any action is necessary. Of course, I have heard it said that the Bank has already increased its dividend. True! But people are apt to forget that though we increased our dividend we used in the old days to pay our dividend free of deduction of tax, and we took the opportunity when we increased our dividend to throw the tax on to the stockholders, so that, although on paper the rate per cent. may look bigger than it was, in fact the stockholder has had to pay a heavy income tax on his dividend. I think myself that unless we show signs of distributing excessive profits the position is better left as it is.

262. *Mr. Brand*: Do you know what other Central Banks do – the Reichsbank, for example – as regards the Government sharing in profits? — I cannot tell you exactly what the Government share is; of course, it varies for each Central Bank.

263. There is not a fixed dividend in the case of other Central Banks? — No. There are cases in which there is a fixed minimum dividend of a certain amount, first payable to the shareholders, and then any profits over and above the fixed dividend are distributed in certain ways.

264. *Mr. McKenna*: There are occasions, are there not, when the Bank of England cannot help making very high profits. Take, for instance, the case of the War. It was unavoidable during the War that the Bank should make far larger profits than it ever made in its history, and I am right in saying that you solved the difficulty then by handing the surplus over as excess profits? — That is perfectly true; we did make large profits.

265. And you handed over all the excess? — At the end of the War and I may say that it was an absolutely voluntary act on the part of the Bank; we delivered to the Government the whole of our excess profits.

266. I take it that, should circumstances arise again – they might arise in times of peace – in which the Bank might make exceptional profits, the Court would not regard it as un-

reasonable that the same procedure should be adopted? — Well, I will put it this way. I think you may take it that that indicates the attitude of the Court in these matters. There is more than one way in which the Bank can temper the wind to the shorn lamb, if we may call the Government the shorn lamb, but I think you may take that as a fair indication of the attitude of the Bank in this matter.

267. *Mr. Keynes*: If the point of your evidence is that it would be very unlikely that the Bank would use its position to put money into the pockets of the shareholders, is it not foregoing a real advantage in regard to public opinion, to keep up the formalities of the former system when the reality no longer exists? — The former system?

268. The former system by which the dividend fluctuated in accordance with the profit-earning capacity of the Bank. That was so? — That was so, undoubtedly. That was a long time ago. The Bank having existed for nearly 250 years has had time to build up a strong position, but I for one should never fear that any inquiry would reveal that the Bank had not shown an absolute public spirit regarding the manner in which it may use the strength of its position for the public benefit.

269. *Chairman*: I think we understand the position. There is no suggestion that there has been any abuse; it is merely a suggestion that the public might prefer that there was not even a possibility of abuse. Your suggestion, on the other hand, is that the public need have no apprehension in the matter? — They should not have at the present time.

270. And your point is that it is a question whether there should be any interference until the need has been demonstrated? — Until the need arises.

271. That a change would not confer any practical benefit on the public because the public have not suffered? — I should be reluctant to see any step which in any way seemed to affect the fact that the Bank is a private Corporation.

272. We appreciate that? — If it abuses its position as a private Corporation, then by all means let the Government step in.

273. I think we understand entirely? — But until it abuses it, I would much rather it were left as a purely private Corporation.

274. Were there any other topics you wished to pick up from the last occasion? — The other one, Mr. Chairman, was in connection with the item in the Bank Return with which we were dealing. Perhaps I might now go straight on.

275. Mr. Keynes asked some questions as to the proportion of the constituents of Other Deposits, Other Accounts? — I think I told the Committee the nature of the accounts which were included. I am not sure whether I included quite all of them because one or two have occurred to me since, and I want, therefore, just for a moment to run over them again, if I may. They include, as I said, all bankers' accounts that are not in the item 'Bankers' in the Return. They include foreign Central Banks, they include people like the merchant banking houses and various financial houses, discount companies, insurance and trust companies, Indian and Colonial Governments. There is one item which sometimes bulks fairly largely, which I did not mention. It includes dividend accounts of all non-Government Stocks, of which the Bank manages a very considerable number, that is to say, the monies in our hands to pay the dividends on Colonial Stocks, Corporation Stocks and so on, Government Guaranteed Stocks – anything that is not a direct charge on the Exchequer.

276. *Mr. Keynes*: Local Loans? — Local loans; and it includes also the accounts of some public bodies, which are not Government; such accounts, for example, as the International Financial Commission, Greece, who at times have quite a considerable balance, the Caisse de la Dette, Egypt, who at times have quite considerable sums of money, the Agent-General for Reparations Payments, who at times has considerable sums. They vary, they fluctuate a good deal. And, of course, it includes all the Bank's own internal accounts. As to the details, that is to say, the exact proportion in which they are divided, I prefer, with the permission of the Committee, not to state the details. I honestly do not believe it is necessary; they relate to matters of our private clients and I should prefer not to state them.

277. *Lord Bradbury*: You said that you included in 'Other Accounts' money to pay dividends on Local Loans. You do not mean Local Loans Stock? — No, I think the Local Loans Stock Dividend Account is a Public Account.

278. *Mr. McKenna*: You say that the total of these accounts fluctuates widely? — Individually. When I say widely, of course that is a matter of degree. The total of them does not fluctuate very widely.

279. *Chairman*: *Inter se*, they do I suppose? — *Inter se*, there are considerable variations from time to time.

280. *Mr. McKenna*: To what extent might the total fluctuate – between what sort of limits? You see why I ask the question? — Yes, quite! I should doubt whether it would fluctuate more than say, perhaps £4 millions or £5 millions. You must not pin me down to that, because I am not quite sure.

281. *Chairman*: We can easily get that? — You can get it by comparing the published returns.

282. *Mr. McKenna*: I can get recent figures, but I cannot get figures over a long period. Would £4 or £5 millions be reasonable? — A comparison of the published returns would show you. I expect you have got them.

283. *Chairman*: Of course, this division of the Bankers' and Other Accounts in Other Deposits dates only, I think, from 1928? —

From November of last year, on the amalgamation of the currency notes with the bank notes. (*Chairman*): I notice that from November 1928, when the separation began, the total of 'Other Accounts' seems to be remarkably constant. The range seems to be between £36 millions and £38 millions. Of course it is a very short period that I am looking at here.

284. *Mr. Brand*: I do not know whether this question was asked last time: What proportion of the total of Other Accounts represents balances of foreign Central banks? — No. If the Committee really feel that it is important – I do not like giving part of the figures; they might be misleading unless I gave the whole details.

285. *Mr. Newbold*: Do the accounts of foreign Central Banks vary very much? — No, they are very steady. I will explain to you the reason why they are steady. As I think I have told the Committee before, we do not work for foreign Central Banks for commissions. We always tell them we do not look upon them as clients from whom we wish to earn profits, but we wish to be repaid for our trouble and work, whatever we do for them. We simply ask them, therefore, to keep adequate free balances to compensate us for what we do, and the total of their balances is the aggregate of those free balances which they maintain with us. They may keep other free balances for their own account, and they may therefore vary to a certain extent, but by and large they are a fairly constant figure.

286. *Mr. Brand*: And all the rest of their money is in the form of bills, I suppose – more or less? — Bills, yes; principally bills. They do sometimes buy British Government securities, short securities.

287. *Mr. Keynes*: Last week I made allusion to the foreign bank deposits of the Federal Reserve Banks. Is Sir Ernest aware that the Federal Reserve Banks publish separately every week their foreign bank deposits, any sums which foreign banks owe them, and also as a separate heading the amount of bills purchased for foreign correspondents? The latest weekly record that I have for the last is 455,000,000 dollars. — Yes, I know they do. They publish the bills, they do not publish the short Government securities. On that very question I have had the opportunity of a talk to an American who is pretty well-informed on these matters. I asked him whether he considered that the figure which they publish is really a useful figure, and he told me that he regarded it as misleading and he doubted whether it served any really useful purpose.

288. Would it not be a useful figure? — If it were all the foreign balances it would be a useful figure, I dare say.

289. Would the publication of all the foreign balances not be useful to the Central Bank? — Take our own case: The foreign moneys placed with us by Central Banks, as I said last week, are – I will not say a very small proportion, but they are a small proportion of the total foreign balances held in the London market if we are to believe the estimates we see of the holding of foreign countries in the London market.

290. Might it not equally well be argued that your deposits were a very small proportion of the total deposits of the country? — No, because they can be aggregated with those of other banks. The rest of the deposits are all published, but not the foreign holdings, they are not published.

291. Obviously it is a very important item in judging the situation whether the foreign bills which the Bank of England hold for foreign correspondents are increasing or decreasing. It is a very important barometer. — It may be. I am doubtful.

292. You were saying that it was the susceptibilities of foreign banks that made you hesitate. Now, the publication of bills as distinct from Government Securities by the United States must be as offensive to their susceptibilities as similar statistics here would be? — If we were to publish the figures of foreign balances, of course, the foreigner would know that it was only the foreign balances that were with us, but I think the figure we published would be exceedingly misleading to the British public. It would give no indication whatever as to what is the total.

293. Would not moves up and down give any indication? — None.

294. I was not merely suggesting that the Bank of England should be required in isolation to give these figures, but that all banks should be required to publish them. Would not that make this information of very great importance even to the Bank of England itself? — Well, I think if we possessed the information it would be useful undoubtedly as a guide to us. I think it would. But that is a different question. The publication of ours by itself, I am convinced, would be simply misleading and would be of no use whatever.

295. *Chairman*: The question has two aspects, first, the value of the information and, secondly, the question of the expediency of publishing it. The information may be of less value because it is not complete, but would you get yourselves in trouble with other countries if you published, or if all the banks published, these particulars? — I do not see why we should. If it were an aggregate figure, I do not see why that should create trouble.

296. Without discriminating between individuals? — Absolutely. Now, if I may come back to the Bank Return, the Banking Department, and deal with the assets, the right-hand side: 'Government Securities' includes all securities of the Government.

297. *Mr. Frater Taylor*: Any foreign Government securities? — Only British Government, that is to say, all direct securities of the British Government. It does not include, for example, Trades Facilities Stocks if we hold any, or

anything that has merely a guarantee of the British Treasury. They are all direct obligations.

298. *Mr. Keynes*: It includes Treasury Bills and Ways and Means advances? — It includes Treasury Bills and Ways and Means advances when there are any, long-dated Government stocks or short-dated Government stocks. 'Discounts and Advances,' of course, speaks for itself, but I ought to make this point clear, that 'Government Securities' includes Treasury Bills, that is, Treasury Bills bought by the Bank where the Bank initiates a transaction. If a Treasury Bill is brought in by anybody for discount at the Bank it is treated as a discount and goes into 'Discounts and Advances.'

299. 'Discounts and Advances' are entirely a thing which is done on the initiative of the client? — On the initiative of the client, absolutely.

300. *Mr. McKenna*: Do you never buy commercial bills, bank bills? — Yes, we do occasionally. They are not in 'Discounts and Advances.'

301. They appear in 'Other Securities'? — I was coming to that.

302. *Mr. Keynes*: The distinction between the two is not really the category of the document, but the way it came into the Bank? — The way it came into the Bank, as to whether it was an action by the Bank or an action by the Bank's client. 'Other Securities' includes, as I say, any Government guaranteed stocks, any Indian, Colonial or foreign securities, miscellaneous securities, and it may include bills which the Bank has gone out and purchased.

303. *Mr. Frater Taylor*: Would it include ordinary shares, for instance, of a commercial company or anything of that kind? — No. The Bank does not buy ordinary shares, not as investments, ever.

304. You passed over the word 'Advances.' That represents advances to whom? — To clients, any client who may come in and deposit security. I may say that we do not make any advance without security, a good margin of security, of the highest class quoted on the London Stock Exchange. We make no advance on a security where there is a liability and, of course, we make no advance against our own Bank stock.

305. *Mr. Brand*: Would all advances to the bill market come in there? — They would all come in there, and the object with which we separated those two items, which we did in November last, was that the public, and especially the financial public, might be able to gauge to what extent the market were in the Bank and see to what extent the market were indebted to the Bank; to gauge the variation in their indebtedness.

306. *Mr. Keynes*: Are all the items in that total effected at Bank Rate? — In 'Discounts and Advances'?

307. Yes. — Are you talking of discounts or advances?

308. Either? — Discounts for the market, yes. If a private customer did bring in say a Treasury Bill, as he might do, and ask us to discount it, and he were a valued private customer, we might allow him what we considered was the fair market rate. But that business is unimportant.

309. *Professor Gregory*: Advances are at a half per cent. over the Bank Rate, as a rule, are they not? — To the market. To customers the rate varies according to the account and character of the securities; as a rule, little as to the character of the securities, because we always insist on the best, with ample margin; it is determined more by the value of the account.

310. 'Discounts and Advances' under the head of 'Other Securities' includes any advances that you might make to your private customers, as well as to the market? — Absolutely every advance, except an advance on Ways and Means to the British Government.

311. *Mr. Keynes*: Would it not show more accurately how the market stood if you had two items, one the discounts and loans to the market at or above Bank Rate, and the other the business with your clients of other categories? — Generally speaking, we think that the variation in the combined total is quite a close enough indication. It is a reliable indication. It might happen, though it is rare, that some public body or some Government for whom we could not at the moment issue Stock might say, 'Will you just carry us on for say a month, until we can issue Stock'; we might make them an advance, but for all practical purposes you can ignore the private advance and discount business of the Bank; apart from the business which the Bank does with the market, the advance and discount business is small and varies little, and the variations do show——

312. The variations rather than the actual amount? — The variations rather than the actual amount, because there is always some business done for other people though, as I say, it is small.

313. *Sir Thomas Allen*: When you speak of an advance to a client, does that mean that any type of would-be client is prohibited, under certain circumstances, from getting an advance, or are you applying it strictly to certain individuals or shareholders? — Anybody who is a banking client of the Bank. He must have a banking account and a banking account that is a genuine account and of such a character as to entitle him to get accommodation from the Bank.

314. That is to say, that, if I had not an account with you, I could not come to your Bank with proper security and get an advance? — No, we should say, 'Go to your own bank.'

315. *Mr. Frater Taylor*: Do 'Securities' include foreign securities? — They may, yes.

316. Are any of those 'Other Security'

items earmarked against particular deposits? — No.

317. *Professor Gregory*: The answer which you have just given to Sir Thomas Allen, that you would normally not make an advance to somebody who had not got a definite bank account at the Bank, would not apply, I take it, in a national emergency? — Well, during the War, for example, if we considered it to the public advantage to assist, for instance, when the Government were making an issue of stock and so on, if we felt we could do something to facilitate matters, I do not say that we drew a hard and fast line, but I cannot call to mind at the moment any case in which we have made an advance to anybody who was not a banking customer.

318. May I put a case – a purely hypothetical one? In the crises, for example, of 1857 and 1866, it was rather the boast of the Bank, was it not, that it did assist the City to an almost unlimited extent? Would you, in a case of that sort, really seriously inquire if a merchant who wanted accommodation had been in the past a regular customer, or not, before you extended credit? Is the rule as inelastic as that? — No, I would not say it is absolutely inelastic, but, in pursuance of our policy not to compete with other banks for private bank business, it is our practice to say, 'Why not go to your own bank?' If the other bank were unable to do it, or if the other bank said, 'We should be obliged if you would help our client,' and so on, I do not say we should not do it, we probably should, if it were in the national interest, but, ordinarily speaking, we would not deal with anybody not a client, nor would we open an account for the avowed purpose of making an advance. If a customer came to us, for example, and said, 'We want to open an account with you, will you make us an advance?' our answer would probably be, first of all, 'Why do you come to us?' They do, from time to time. Even in the presence of two bankers, I am bound to say the answer we receive is very often, 'Well, my bank is so unreasonable.' Our answer always is, 'You will find us very much stiffer than any other banker, and you had much better stay where you are.' I have done it myself on occasions. That is the practice we follow.

319. Of course, you realise I am not asking about the practice of the Bank in normal times, but in times of national emergency? — I agree, in times of national danger or crisis, I am not prepared to say that there is anything that the Bank would not do if it were really in the national interest and consistent with its primary duties to the community.

320. *Mr. Frater Taylor*: Is that figure of £29,952,000 a net figure, after providing reserves? — Do you mean by that, is the figure of securities the present market value, or the value at which they stand in the books, and is the latter less than the market value?

321. No. Is that figure the realisable value? If it is necessary to provide a reserve, is the reserve deducted before that figure on the assets side is arrived at? — If we consider it wise, and I think you may take it we do, to keep our securities below market value, then that is the figure at which they stand in our books.

322. Which brings me right to the question of 'Rest' on the other side. Is that, in effect, the Bank's reserve? — It is part of it.

323. *Mr. McKenna*: Might we not presume that, like many other banks, your securities stand at a written down figure? — Well, I think if sold they would realise more than the figures standing in the Bank's books.

324. *Lord Bradbury*: The arrangement by which the Bank undertook to make advances to holders of 3½ per cent. War Loan was only for a period? — That was only for a period.

325. But, if any advances were made, they would come under this item, even though the holders were not clients of the Bank? — Certainly.

326. *Chairman*: Our next item is 'Notes'? — The Notes I have already dealt with, in dealing with the Issue Department, and as regards the gold and silver coin, I have already explained that that is practically entirely silver.

327. I want, particularly, to have the benefit to-night of your account of the relations of the Bank with the discount market. I think that is a matter where you can help us very much? — Would you like me to take that next? Because there was one point which I thought might be of interest to those members of the Committee who are less familiar with the Bank Return. It is a question that I know bulks rather largely in the minds of some. It has already been referred to. Perhaps I might just explain for their benefit, for a moment, what exactly happens on certain occasions in the figures of this Return. It is a question that I think Mr. Bevin was particularly interested in. Imagine that the Bank are creating £5,000,000 of credit; how is it done, what is the effect on the Return? Of course the only way in which the Bank itself can create credit is by the purchase of securities which would fall under the head of either 'Government Securities' or 'Securities' in 'Other Securities,' or by the making of an advance or advances, or by the discounting of bills. The creation of that £5,000,000 of credit would, therefore, increase one or other of the first two figures on the right-hand side of the Banking Department, and the credit created would automatically increase the total of the bankers' balances on the other side of the Return. It is often said that one of the causes of our troubles is the failure of the Bank of England to create sufficient credit. Now, I want the Committee just to bear in mind the sort of thing that we have to consider when it is a question of creating credit. What happens to that credit we have created? I say it goes on to the bankers' balances. But, of course, nobody wants to take £5,000,000 for the

purpose of keeping it idle. It is true that the bankers may themselves, if they like, use that £5,000,000 as an additional basis for the creation of still further credit, by increasing their advances, the £5,000,000 enabling them to maintain their proportion of cash. But either that £5,000,000, or the credit which is created against it, will be used. It may go to this bank, that bank, or the other bank, but, in effect, what happens is this, that, no sooner is that £5,000,000 of credit created than, as a rule, some bank, or, it may be, other firms, private firms, sometimes financial houses or other persons, find themselves in possession of additional money. What do they do? We may feel the reaction of it at once in the fact that somebody wants to lend more money on call in the market. There may immediately be – I do not say it always happens; I am only saying what may happen – this additional money may be offered in the call market, with the result that the discount market may take the money on call. If so, they want bills, they want to invest their money; there will be a keener demand for the bills available; rates will immediately begin to sag, and it is not impossible that the gradual sagging of the rate of discount may have an adverse effect on rates of exchange, and what may happen is that the very creation of that credit will bring about a set of circumstances through exchange depression in sterling as measured in foreign currencies, that will lead to a loss of gold. It may even result, in the long run, in the loss of the whole of the £5,000,000 in gold. What then results? So far as our figures are concerned, we are restored to where we were, but we have exchanged £5,000,000 of Notes for £5,000,000 of securities; our position is weaker, and we have done no good.

Therefore, when we are urged to create credit – whilst, of course, we are anxious to do anything that is possible as likely to be of benefit, say, to industry – we have always got to bear in mind the position of the exchanges and their tendency, whether it is weak, whether the additional creation of credit is likely perhaps by a lowering of the rates in our own market to weaken the exchanges to a point at which, having created £5,000,000 of credit, we may lose it or a good deal of it in gold at once without actually having done any good. As I said at the commencement, our primary duty is the maintenance of the stability of our currency unit and, therefore, when we are asked to create credit we cannot blindly create credit without bearing in mind what its effect is likely to be on our other and primary function. I merely say that because I want those members of the Committee who are perhaps less familiar with this subject to realise the sort of consideration which we have to bear in mind when it comes to a question of creating additional credit. This is rather trespassing, of course, on the domain of higher questions of policy which it has been agreed should be reserved for discussion later. I do not want to get into an abstruse discussion on the subject because there are minds here much better qualified to deal with it than my own; and I would much rather that it were left for discussion later, but I did just want to mention the point.

328. *Mr. McKenna*: Before you leave this subject – I do not want to enter into any controversy upon the matter; I want to ask one question – when you speak of your duty to maintain the integrity of the currency I understand you to mean to prevent depreciation of the currency? — Yes.

329. Do you pay equal attention to avoiding an appreciation of the currency? — Certainly.

330. How do you do that? — I am speaking, of course, of our ordinary normal procedure. Our endeavour is to watch the ordinary indices of price levels and exchanges.

331. Have you made efforts during the last four or five years to prevent the fall in prices which has taken place? — Well, I do not know that I really should care to pursue this question at the present moment. It is, of course, a very difficult question, and a question which honestly I do not claim to be particularly qualified to discuss.

332. *Mr. Lubbock*: Is Mr. McKenna going back to the whole question of the restoration of the gold standard? — *Mr. McKenna*: No, I am only dealing with conditions since the restoration of the gold standard. *Mr. Lubbock*: Resulting from it? — *Mr. McKenna*: Well, I should not agree to that. The actual fall in prices has been roughly 10 per cent. in the last five years. It is the appreciation of the currency by 10 per cent. *Chairman*: I think what the Witness has done has been merely to sound a note of warning to some of us to remember that an increase of credit created by the Bank of England may have repercussions, if you follow it through to the end, which might render it less advantageous than it otherwise would be. *Witness*: Undoubtedly.

333. You must follow it through to the end, and if we follow it through to the end we may find that the results which we anticipated at first are possibly in the end defeated? — I simply want the Committee to bear in mind that there are circumstances, or may be circumstances, in which——

334. The last state may be worse than the first? — The last state may be worse than the first. *Chairman*: We will bear that in mind as a warning. *Mr. McKenna*: I wish to put in a proviso that this is the crux of the controversy.

Chairman: Quite. Sir Ernest is merely sounding his own note of warning, that in his opinion those other considerations should be taken in view, and in his opinion those other considerations may in some circumstances outweigh the advantages.

335. *Sir Thomas Allen*: I should like to mention in this connection that when Sir Ernest speaks of the creation of credit which might

involve a removal of gold from the country, some of us are thinking about the creation of credit in respect to our own national industries that would not involve the removal of gold to some other country. I merely want to mention that, that the thought in some of our minds is quite distinct from the expression given by the Witness to what he understood was in the minds of other members. — I think, Mr. Chairman, that that aspect of the question will arise more naturally when I come to deal with the Bank's relations with, let us say, Rationalisation, on which I shall have something to say which I hope may be, at any rate, comforting to some of those present.

336. *Professor Gregory*: I think that in pre-War days, if I am not mistaken, the Bank of England in deciding whether or not to raise or lower Bank Rate decided primarily on the relation between the reserve in the Banking Department and the outstanding liabilities in the Banking Department. That is to say, the ratio? — You are talking of pre-War days?

337. In pre-War days. — Yes, I should say, broadly speaking, that is correct.

338. Would I be correct in assuming, without questioning the expediency of the Bank of England's policy in any way, that the first consideration so far as it bears on the figures in the Bank Return is no longer the ratio, but the amount of gold coin and bullion in the Issue Department? — No, I would not say that. I would say it was the ratio in the Banking Department having regard to the amount of gold which we hold in the Issue Department and to the state and tendency of the exchanges. All three have got to be taken into account.

339. *Mr. Keynes*: The 'Government Securities' and the 'Other Securities' fluctuate to a fairly great extent, they fluctuate a little every week. Those represent, I understand, what are called the open market operations of the Bank. What are the governing considerations in the mind of the Bank in regard to their daily operation in respect of these securities? — It is true that the fluctuations in Government securities are sometimes large, but the reason for them can generally be seen by a glance at the reserve and at the figures of the other deposits. There are various things that may lead to a considerable increase. Take for example the payment of a War Loan dividend. The Bank may be asked by the Government for money for payment of War Loan dividends. That may obviously create a considerable movement in Government securities. But if you mean, is there any consideration that may decide us to make an increase in the Government or in the 'Other,' as to which it is to be, it is not a question that arises in our mind.

340. *Mr. Lubbock*: You are governed really by the amount of money in the market? — When Government balances are running very high, other deposits will be short; when Government balances are running low other deposits will be high – and if it is not necessary to keep market rates very firm we may in the first circumstance buy bills in order that the market may have enough money with which to carry on until the Government have disbursed their money.

341. *Mr. Keynes*: Does not the Bank deliberately govern the amount of its open market operations, so as to maintain the total of the bankers' deposits round about some predetermined figure? — No; I could not say that; because we find by experience that ease in the market may exist at one time with the bankers' balances at a much lower figure than at another time when money seems scarce.

342. Would it be correct to say that you are governed by whether you think the open market rate of discount wants stiffening up or can be allowed to relax? — I am afraid I do not quite follow what is exactly your question.

343. Each day you have to decide what the volume of your open market operations shall be? — Yes.

344. That will affect the aggregate of the bankers' deposits in the Bank of England? — Yes.

345. I was asking whether you were mainly influenced in making your decision by the desire to keep the bankers' deposits at some figure that you fix in your mind as desirable, or whether you are thinking of the open market rate of discount? — It depends entirely upon whether we think the circumstances require that we should give our principal attention to the rate of discount or if we think that the circumstances are such that we need not worry about the market rate of discount; in the latter case our policy would be to keep the funds of the market at a figure which is not going to cause them disturbance.

346. *Professor Gregory*: And how would you arrive at what you considered to be a suitable figure of bankers' deposits? — We know more or less by experience, although it is true that the figure varies from time to time, what amount of bankers' balances should mean ease and what a shortage.

347. You are thinking mainly of the effect of fluctuations in that item on the condition of the money market in the next week or two? — In conjunction with the need for watching the rate of discount in relation to the trend of foreign exchanges and our holding of gold, either the need to attract it or the absence of any need to attract it at the moment.

348. You would not take into account the state of employment or the price level? — We always have before us the price level, certainly; but if we are well supplied with reserve, and having regard, let us say, to the season of the year, to the likelihood of the exchanges, owing to the season of the year, turning in our favour or against us, if we are well supplied with reserve we should not enter into market operations simply to keep the bankers' balances down to some particular figure. We should not mind if they went £10,000,000 up or

£20,000,000 up, so long as it was not going to threaten us, as I said earlier this afternoon, with a possible reaction which might bring us into a position which would be painful to industry. If industry can get benefit without the threat of our having to submit them to a very painful operation at a later date, there will always be the means for them to get credit as far as we are concerned.

349. Are you constantly trying the experiment of easing them out, and then seeing what are the consequences of that? You cannot predict the consequences, can you? — We cannot predict them; we can only judge to the best of our opinion, according to our experience of what happens at certain times of the year, and having regard to such operations as we happen to know have got to take place, say, between this country and other countries.

350. That is to say – again it is a question of fact – you have those wider varying considerations in mind, but you judge from your experience and do not take action directly upon those considerations? You take the money market indices into account, although you are aware that behind those money market factors you have the industrial and unemployment situation? — I would say that we do not overlook the question of unemployment and the needs of industry.

351. *Mr. Lubbock*: Is it your experience that any increase of credit carried beyond a certain point always has the same result; it results almost immediately in the weakening of discount rates? — Yes. Always, in point of fact, if we go beyond a certain point.

352. Therefore, any additional credit that the Bank of England creates hardly has time to reach industry before it is taken away in the form of gold? — Undoubtedly. If we are in a weak position where we cannot afford to lose much, of course the risk is greater, but directly we create credit it almost immediately finds its way outside to the call loan market, with the effect that it depresses discount rates.

353. *Mr. Brand*: When the Bank this summer lost, say, £20,000,000 of gold to France and other countries, did the Bank take measures to counteract the effect of that loss on the market, so as to keep the same amount of money in the market? — You will find if you look at a succession of Bank Returns that the amount of gold that we have lost has been almost entirely replaced by an increase in the Bank's securities. After all, you must remember this, that it takes very little, really, to swing over from a shortage of cash in the market to a tightness of cash. One man in the market with £250,000 to lend when everybody has got what they want can go round, as we know has been done, and try to lend it here and there all round the market, and nobody will take it, and we are then told, 'Money is unlendable.' In fact it is the same £250,000 which has been offered all round. But another day you may have one man who wants £100,000 and who goes to one lender after another and says, 'Please can you give me £100,000?' And in every case receives the same reply, 'Impossible.' The story soon gets round, and people say, 'Money seems tight to-day.'

354. *Mr. Keynes*: If we make a foreign loan of £5,000,000 that, presumably, will turn the balance of trade against us and in some proportion that will react, will it, on the amount of bankers' deposits which the Bank of England can safely create? — If the loan is made and the proceeds are drawn away we shall see its effect in the movements of the exchanges.

355. So that if the attractiveness of foreign lending increases, that means that you must take steps to reduce the market's balances at the Bank of England? — If the attractiveness of this market to the foreign borrower is increased, is that what you mean?

356. Yes, is increased. — It may, if our position is already, in our judgment, weak enough, having regard to impending circumstances.

357. So that we are very much at the mercy of fluctuations in foreign centres with which we may have very little to do directly? — Undoubtedly, in certain circumstances.

358. You agree that the dear money which prevailed in New York until fairly recently would have the effect of diminishing the amount of bankers' deposits which you could allow safely to exist in London? — Undoubtedly.

359. Your evidence rather suggests that the total effect of all foreign influence of this kind remains the determining influence on the amount of credit that can be created? — Yes, and I think it must be so if we wish to be a real international financial market.

360. You regard us as being at the mercy of all these foreign demands? — At their mercy, to a considerable extent.

361. *Mr. Brand*: Other centres also being to some extent at the mercy of other nations? — Yes.

362. *Mr. Keynes*: Those with the largest quantity of free gold relatively less at the mercy, and those with the smallest quantity of gold more at the mercy? — If they will use it.

363. *Mr. Newbold*: Why do they not use it? — Ask them! That is a conundrum I cannot answer.

364. *Mr. Keynes*: Perhaps this is a question of policy which should be left until later. Has the Bank of England considered whether there are any changes that could be made that would put us less at the mercy of fluctuations abroad? — I do not think I should like to answer that question now. I wanted to speak quite shortly about our relations to the discount market which, after all, is the pivot of the machine here. I do not know that I need do it at any length. The discount market, of course, really exists as a sort of buffer between the Bank of England and the commercial banks. It is

obviously necessary for the commercial banks in addition to whatever they may decide to hold in the form of cash, whether cash in their own tills or balances at the Bank of England, to have a second very liquid line of defence to meet any sudden demands that may come upon them, and that line of defence, of course, is their call money, which is lent from day to day. The discount market really lives by dealing, broadly speaking, in bills of exchange.

365. *Chairman*: Commercial bills? — And Treasury bills. To a limited extent it may carry a few short bonds, because Government bonds when they become short are practically the same as bills of exchange, but, broadly speaking, it deals in bills, either commercial bills or Treasury bills. The funds with which the discount market operates are derived practically from two sources. They have their own funds to start with, their own capital on which they start to do business, and then they borrow from the commercial banks on day-to-day loans. They may borrow other moneys, but a large part of the money which they borrow is these day-to-day loans from the banks, and they are liable every day to have this call money called from them by the lender. Of course, it is common knowledge that the banks publish every month figures which are the average of their figures on, let us say, four Tuesdays in the month, or four Wednesdays in the month, or four Thursdays in the month, whatever the day is on which they decide to take their averages. Banker 'X' may go to a discount broker and may call the money, or part of the money, which he has lent him. The broker who is carrying bills of exchange on that money necessarily has to replace the money, and so he goes round to other banking friends, and possibly Banker 'Y,' who has no particular need of funds on that day, because either he is not making up or he has no big demands on him, or he may have received funds, will lend to the broker. Thus the discount market brokers are working with their own capital as a basis to which they will add very considerable sums borrowed from the banks, but they knew that, supposing calls should come on the banks simultaneously, or the banks should make up on the same day – to take the extreme case, viz., the last day of the year when every bank is making up its Balance Sheet and desires, quite legitimately, to show a good cash holding and that it is keeping its funds liquid – the discount market must be able to feel assured that they can replace the money from somewhere. Well, there is only one place to which they can go then to borrow money in any quantity, and that is the Bank of England. Therefore, they must be sure that the type of bills in which they deal are bills which the Bank of England will accept from them when the need arises. So far as their own funds are concerned, funds which cannot be called from them, of course, they can hold bills of a different character if they choose; that is their own concern entirely; but, so far as their relations with the Bank of England are concerned, they can only come to the Bank and demand – I say 'demand' advisedly because it is an understood thing that they will always get accommodation within certain limits and on certain terms – they can only demand accommodation from the Bank against a particular class of security or bill. Of course, it may mean that at certain periods, if the market have apprehensions that the Bank Rate is going to rise, if they see ahead a possible lengthy period of high rates, they may say to themselves: 'Well, we had better clear out some of our bills before the rates go up; we will take them to the Bank at once and discount them; it is better to go there and get rid of them, release our funds and be able, when the rate has gone up, to replenish our portfolio at the higher rate.' There the Bank has to protect itself by limiting the currency of the bills which it will take. It may say: 'Yes. Whilst we will give the discount market the accommodation it requires, we will only advance to it ordinarily for a minimum period of a week, or we will discount bills, it may be, having two or three weeks to run.'

Of course, at the Bank our regulations as regards the bills we accept, though they are not governed by any statutes or anything of that kind, are, in fact, quite definite, and have been taken more or less as a model by most foreign Central Banks. They are, that the bills shall bear at least two good British names, one of whom must be the acceptor. The discount market know that. Of course, the bills may represent, let us say, a sale of cotton by the United States to Great Britain; they may represent movement of produce from the East to Great Britain; they may also represent movement of produce between two foreign countries which is financed by credit obtained from a British house, and where they accept the bill, although the bill relates to a movement of goods abroad, it is a British acceptor. The market knows that it can always get its accommodation at a price. Of course, I do not mean to say that any member of the discount market can come in and get accommodation to an unlimited extent. The relations between the Bank and the discount market are exceedingly intimate. Seeing the sort of obligation that the Bank accepts towards the discount market, we claim the right to be kept fully informed regarding their position; if need be, to see their balance sheets, and the right – of course, in the strictest confidence – to the very fullest information.

366. *Chairman*: What is the size of the market? — The number?

367. Yes? — Do you know, Mr. Brand?

368. *Mr. Brand*: The number of firms – about 20. — More than 20, I should think.

369. *Mr. Lubbock*: About 20 discount accounts? — I should think it is over 20. I should think it is somewhere about 23. I could

not tell you exactly. Of course, they vary from private firms of moderate size to the big discount companies, but they do provide a piece of machinery which enables the bankers, with the minimum of disturbance, to adjust their own positions to meet their daily needs, and the discount market know all the time that they have the Bank of England on which to rely. The machinery is practically peculiar to London.

370. *Chairman*: It does not exist in any other country? — There have been attempts to copy it, but it exists nowhere else really as it exists in London. The rate paid by discount houses to banks for short money, call money, of course, has nothing to do with us at the Bank; that is a matter for the banks themselves. Whilst I do not know that they have any established rule, it is generally understood that they charge a minimum of about 1 per cent. below Bank Rate, but that is not a question upon which I can speak; that is a question for the bankers themselves.

371. That is known as call money? — That is bankers' call money. Of course, there is a lot of other money that is lent on call. What the proportions are, it is difficult to say. I have often asked people and I should estimate – I may be quite wrong; Mr. McKenna probably knows much better than I do – that the bankers' call money is probably about 50 or 60 per cent. of the call money in the market. The other call money is call money in the hands of private lenders, and if they cannot get such a rate as the bankers will expect to get – let us say, their minimum rate of 1 per cent. under Bank Rate – they will cut the rate at once and they will begin to lend money more cheaply, and that is the call money which may act as a depressing factor on discount rates. But, of course, that is a factor over which we really have no control. We have to take it into consideration, but, as I say, it is not a matter that we can control. The rate at which the discount house can generally sell its bills to the Bank is what is known as the Bank Rate, that is the Bank's minimum rate of discount to the discount market. I have already explained it is not the Bank's minimum discount rate. If a private customer, who is a valued customer, brings a Treasury Bill or even a commercial bill to the Bank and asks us to discount it, the Bank Rate is not necessarily the rate charged; we may charge what we consider is a fair rate, having regard to what is the actual rate in the market at the moment. But that business, as I said before, is of no importance; advances to the discount market are usually made for periods of a week and at a rate of one-half per cent. over the Bank Rate. I say usually. There is no rule that absolutely governs it, but that is the usual practice.

372. *Mr. Keynes*: Have you any statistics as to the volume of acceptances outstanding? — No.

373. Might the Bank of England make it a condition of regarding an acceptor as first-class that he should send them a weekly return of his acceptances? — The acceptors do keep the Bank furnished with very full information regarding their positions and we do claim the right to see their balance sheets.

374. *Professor Gregory*: You refer to the acceptors' balance sheets? — Yes.

375. *Mr. Keynes*: I am not thinking so much of their credit – whether individuals are overdoing it or not – but what the aggregate is from the point of view of the market as a whole. Would it not be useful if they let the Bank know, from week to week, the aggregate amount of acceptances outstanding? — Well, I think it might be useful, if it could be done without hurting the susceptibilities of acceptors, and so long as no fear got into the minds of drawers that acceptors were passing on confidential information regarding their business.

376. *Mr. McKenna*: Banks do publish the total of their acceptances? — Banks do, I agree, and, of course, the balance sheets of all the accepting houses show them, but they are not all public property.

377. *Mr. Brand*: You could not write and ask the Credit Lyonnais for details, for instance, could you? — No. But then we do not take the acceptances of the Credit Lyonnais. (*Mr. Brand*): Those acceptances are on the market.

378. *Mr. Keynes*: Has the Bank of England any statistics of the volume of bills which the money market brokers are carrying? — If you ask as to the bills in existence which the Bank might be asked to discount, is that what you have in mind?

379. The total amount of acceptances, excluding a certain proportion outside, which would be in the hands of the market? — Certainly.

380. Have you any statistics as to the amount in the hands of the market? — No.

381. Have you no statistics as to the amount of call money which is being used for the purchase of bills? — No.

382. Would it not be useful to have that information? — It would be interesting, and it might be useful.

383. I ask it because in the United States they pay very great attention to the figures? — We have no complete information on that point.

384. *Mr. McKenna*: Would you have any objection if the Committee were to make a recommendation that the Bank of England should get information as to the aggregate amount of acceptances? — No. I do not think I need say anything more about the discount market. I had also down 'Bank's Relations with Issuing Houses,' but I can deal with that almost in two words.

385. *Mr. Keynes*: One rather important question before you leave this point. It was alleged in the Press quite recently that the Bank

of England put pressure on the discount market not to deal in bills except at a stated figure? — It was stated in the papers, I believe, that the Bank of England actually told the market the rate at which they should tender for Treasury bills. I know it was absolutely untrue.

386. There was no attempt on the part of the Bank of England to get the discount houses to keep to a particular market rate? — There was a suggestion at the moment that the Bank thought it desirable that the Bank Rate should be allowed to be effective, and that the discount market should not be allowed to slip away, but as to any idea that the Bank said to the market – as it was openly stated – that they were to tender for bills at a certain rate, there was absolutely no foundation whatever for that. I was present myself at the interview, and I know it was not said, or anything to indicate it.

387. It was stated by a very reputable organ of the Press as a fact? — We are said to be very reserved in our attitude towards such statements in the Press, but if you start to contradict such statements where are you going to stop?

388. *Chairman*: You said you could tell us in a couple of sentences the relations of the Bank with the Issuing Houses? — There I merely wanted to say this, that our relations with the Issuing Houses are absolutely informal – that is to say, the Issuing Houses that undertake the issuing of the higher class issues. It is the practice for them to keep us informed; it is simply a practice. They are under no compulsion to come, no obligation whatever and we have no right to demand that they shall come, but they do in practice come and tell us what their intentions are. They come to consult us obviously, partly for their own advantage and partly for ours. It helps to the orderly issue of loans. That is to say that too many loans of a particular character are not thrown on to the market at any given time, and if the British Government has an operation in view it gives us the opportunity, without disclosing the fact in any shape or form, to exercise some sort of restraining hand so that the operations of the British Government will not be prejudiced by other people coming out and blocking the way. The relations are purely informal, absolutely unofficial, but I think I can claim that they work pretty efficiently and that they are really to the advantage of the community and everybody concerned.

389. *Professor Gregory*: When you use the word 'efficiently,' are we to understand that the Bank has sometimes suggested that there should be a delay in the issue of a loan? — We have asked that it shall be delayed. I am not talking about the terms of the loans, I am talking about the times and effects of issues.

390. I was not implying for a moment that you expressed a view about the goodness or badness of the loan, but you have expressed ideas informally as to the desirability of postponing the issue? — We have suggested, 'Perhaps you had better postpone it.'

391. *Mr. Brand*: Has not the Bank gone further and taken a stand against all short-dated loans? Ever since the War the Bank has expressed a strong opinion against short-dated loans? — You are talking of foreign loans; that is a different matter. I was thinking more of the loans of the class of municipalities and Colonial Governments and British Government and issues of that sort.

392. *Professor Gregory*: I take it that your approval, or your unofficial expression of opinion, we will say, is expressed more decidedly when it is a question of a foreign loan than when it is a question of a domestic loan? — Yes. They come as a rule and ask us if there is any objection, and if we see obvious objections we say so, and I am bound to admit that as a rule, as a general rule, they accept our word and act very loyally.

393. *Mr. Keynes*: It is generally believed that what is called the unofficial embargo on foreign loans has played a dominant part in this country. Can we hear about the method of the unofficial embargo on foreign loans? — I think I am right in saying it was a pure matter of moral suasion. When it was decided that it was not to the advantage of this country that foreign loans should be issued we did let it be known, or if anybody came to us or if we heard of cases where an operation was pending we did, on occasion, send for the people and say, 'We think that on the whole it is to the advantage of the community that this operation should not take place just at this time.'

394. Can you tell us whether the wishes of the Bank of England are generally observed? — Yes.

395. *Mr. Brand*: Would you say that they are observed far more than the wishes, for instance, of the Federal Reserve Board? — I should say undoubtedly so; it is quite the exception for the wishes of the Bank of England not to be observed.

396. *Mr. Keynes*: You do not think that the firms who wish to act in the public interest would be at a disadvantage in comparison with those who are less well disposed? — I do not think so.

397. The present practice works sufficiently well? — I think it does.

Thursday 12 December 1929

Sir Ernest Musgrave Harvey, K.B.E., Deputy Governor of the Bank of England, recalled and further examined.

398. *Chairman*: Professor Gregory has one or two questions he would like to ask you, Sir Ernest, in connection with the discount market before you proceed to other matters. *Professor Gregory*: You stated in your evidence that the Bank does not, in fact, determine the price which the discount market shall charge for discounting bills. I take it that we are not to infer from that that the Bank of England does not sometimes itself, directly or indirectly, operate in the market. I take it the Bank does operate in the market? — Yes, certainly.

399. Do you think it would be possible to throw some light on those operations? They are mysterious, but I think they play a very distinct part in the economy of the market? — Do you mean as to the circumstances under which we operate, or the manner in which we operate?

400. I should like you to elucidate both those points? — As to the circumstances, I think they are governed primarily by the volume of credit existing, considered in conjunction with the state of the foreign exchanges, their tendency at the moment, and the condition of the Bank's reserves, as to their sufficiency or otherwise, and as to the likelihood of their being increased or decreased. That would determine the time of operation. As to the manner of operation, it is simply conducted through a broker who operates as any other broker.

401. Do you generally, when you operate in the open market, operate through bills or through Government securities? — Generally through bills. When I say 'generally' I do not wish it to be thought that we do not operate through Government securities. We may operate through Government securities, but, of course, at a time like this when the volume of bills is so much larger than in, let us say, pre-War times, owing largely to the great volume of Treasury Bills, the proportion of operations in bills is larger in comparison with securities than used to be the case.

402. I think it used to be said by experts, and it was repeated in the interviews between the Directors of the Bank of England and the representatives of the National Monetary Commission of the United States, that you sold Consols for cash and bought them back for time when you operated in the open market. Is that a relic of by-gone days or is it done at the present time? — I should describe it as a relic of past history.

403. *Chairman*: Will you kindly resume, Sir Ernest. I think you were going next to deal with the relations of the Bank to the clearing banks? — The relations of the Bank with the clearing banks are, of course, fundamentally those of a banker and client. That fact naturally imposes on me the need for exercising considerable discretion as to what I say, because naturally there have got to be very confidential relations between bankers and clients, and certain operations if they are to be discussed or described, are better described by the client than by the banker.

404. Yes. Of course, we are going to have representatives of the banks here. It is for them, if they wish, to disclose information on their side. They are not, of course, under the seal of confidence that you are? — No. The Bank acts, as I say, as an ordinary banker towards clients. That is to say, we supply them with currency as they may require it and, of course, in this connection the Bank have special obligations, being the controllers of the issue of currency. They issue currency, they receive currency, simply according to whatever the banks may choose to demand or pay in. The decision as to that rests entirely with them. We exercise no control over what they choose to draw out or pay in. Our aim is to allow currency operations to work absolutely freely according to the requirements of the moment. Then the Bank acts as the agent for the Clearing House for the settlement of clearing differences between bank and bank. The banks present their claims on each other in the Clearing House. A balance is struck at the close of the day, certain banks have balances to receive, others have sums which they have to pay. The Bank is advised by the Superintendent of Clearing House of the amount which each bank has to receive or pay and settles those sums by mere transfers to or from the accounts of the several banks.

405. A concentration of the day's activities? — Exactly. It has no effect whatever upon the total of the bankers' balances, the aggregate remains the same, but the distribution between banks may vary considerably.

406. *Sir Thomas Allen*: That is, the bankers' balances with you? — That is the bankers' balances with us. Those balances, of course, that the bankers keep with us are regarded by them and by the world at large as part of the cash holdings of the bankers.

407. *Chairman*: Liquid assets? — Liquid assets, cash assets. Of course, they have in addition their own cash holdings. These consist of till money, the sums required to meet the ordinary operations of the day between themselves and their own clients, and may consist in addition, and no doubt do consist, of a certain reserve over and above till money requirements to meet exceptional contingencies. As I said before, the Bank have no means of measuring the extent of any reserves of that category which they hold except on one day in the year, the 31st December, when the bankers all

publish balance sheets on the same day, and by aggregating these cash balances and deducting from them the amount of cash which we know they hold with us we are able to arrive at a fairly correct figure as to the total amounts of cash which they themselves hold. But we only know, of course, the amount they hold on the last day of the year; if they do hold such reserves as I describe they may vary considerably during the year; those variations we have no means of measuring. In pre-War times a good deal was written and said about the cash reserves held by the bankers in addition to the central cash reserves held by the Bank of England. In addition, of course, there was the further cash reserve which consisted of coin in the pockets of the people. Well, since those days I am inclined to think that opinion has rather inclined towards the view that centralisation of reserves offers, perhaps, an opportunity for greater economy in the amount of unremunerative cash which exists. Of course, so far as the old cash reserves in the pockets of the people were concerned there was always the danger – not, I think, always realised – that if an attempt were made to mobilise them there was always a risk, and I think we proved at the outbreak of War that it was a real risk, that there might be a leakage; those cash reserves would not all find their way to the central reserve if an attempt were made to mobilise them.

408. *Sir Thomas Allen*: Would that involve a leakage out of the country? — Out of the country, or, in hoarding. Now, as regards surplus reserves of cash held by banks I do not wish to discuss the question as to whether and to what extent they are desirable, but I wish to point out just one or two facts. In the first place, if there is a demand by the public for increased currency, to the extent to which that increased demand may be met by bankers out of their reserves, there is no indication to us certainly, or to the public, that there has in fact been an increased demand for internal circulation. In the same way if notes are returned from currency and are used to add to a banker's internal cash reserves, the fact is not indicated. We realise, of course, that in an emergency – such an emergency, for example, as an interruption of communications or any other cause – banks must be assured of being able to obtain sufficient currency to meet the demands of their clients. For that reason the Bank of England do, at their branches distributed about the country, hold considerable reserves of notes which are available for bankers in times of need.

One question has occurred to me from time to time, and it was brought home rather forcibly to us a little while ago when we had representations from the North of Ireland, currency notes being legal tender there, that the currency notes in circulation there were deteriorating as to condition very seriously, and that the only way that the banks there could remedy the situation would be to send the notes to the Bank of England and withdraw new notes in their place. But such an operation, of course, involves the banks in considerable expense. They are live notes. They have got to be insured; in addition to freight they have insurance to pay, and the Irish Banks did represent to us that they considered it rather a hardship that a currency which had been made legal tender by the Imperial Parliament, if it was to be kept in a fit condition, was to involve banks at a distance in expense which was not incurred by banks nearer home. Well, we have overcome that difficulty. We have sent representatives from time to time to Northern Ireland and are continuing to do so. They are collecting the worn, dirty notes which are unfit for circulation, we send over supplies of fresh notes, we take from them the old notes, and by that means we are gradually restoring the condition of the currency. But that has raised in my mind the question whether now that the Bank of England notes of £1 and 10s. are legal tender in Northern Ireland and Scotland, it may not be desirable for the Bank to establish in Northern Ireland and in Scotland – I will not say branches, or even agencies – depots of currency to which the banks can have access, to which they can return their worn and dirty notes, from which they can obtain supplies of clean notes and even supplies of additional currency when required. Of course, there might be a little expense involved. That does not concern the Bank; that would concern the Treasury as the receivers of the profits of the Issue Department, but I am sure from the conversations I have had with representatives of the Treasury that no obstacle would be raised in that quarter.

There is another fact to bear in mind as regards these reserves of banks. When these notes are held by banks they form part of our published figures of notes in circulation; they are live notes, they are idle cash, serving a useful purpose, I admit, and a necessary purpose as a cash reserve. But when notes are held by the Bank of England in store they are merely pieces of paper, and I am not sure whether a greater reliance on stores of notes within the Bank might not perhaps lead to some economy and I have a feeling that it would, at any rate, enable a truer estimate to be formed as to the real volume of currency needed for the day to day requirements of the public.

As to the relations of the Bank with bankers, I am happy to say that looking back over a long period of years I think I can claim that there has been a steady improvement in the relationship existing between them. I think the co-operation steadily improves. We are in frequent informal intercourse with the representatives of all the important banks. We have even, by the kindness of the banks, an arrangement now by which once a quarter the meeting of the clearing banks is held at the Bank of England with the Governor, just for that occasion, in the Chair. I do not say that the meetings are always occasions when great subjects are necessarily discussed, but they do maintain regular touch between the bankers as a body and the Bank which formerly did not exist, and I think that their effect has been good.

As regards the functions which the Bank performs for other banks, I have said that the relations are fundamentally those between banker and client, but with one important exception certainly. It is not ordinarily the practice of the other banks to come to the Bank for accommodation. I do not say that it is not done, but that is not the ordinary practice. As I explained before when referring to the discount market, the normal practice when a bank requires to improve its cash position is for that bank to withdraw call money from the discount market, to leave the representative of the discount market from whom the money has been called either to find it elsewhere in the market, or, if it cannot be obtained there, to come to the Bank of England. Ordinarily speaking, clearing banks cannot reduce the total of the balances which they hold at the Bank except by drawing notes or gold. They may, of course, be called upon to provide moneys taken in by the Government, say, for taxation, they may have to provide money because the Bank itself has effected some operation which shortens the volume of money which they hold, but, ordinarily speaking, the banks cannot themselves affect the aggregate of their balances except by drawing notes or gold.

Well, Mr. Chairman, I really think that that more or less exhausts, so far as I am concerned, the relations between the Bank and the bankers, but if anybody wishes to ask any questions I will do my best to answer them.

409. *Professor Gregory*: I would like to ask some questions which Sir Ernest may not care to answer as they are questions which in the long run involve policy. The first question is whether Sir Ernest thinks that any public purpose could be served by formal representation of the joint stock banks on the Board of Management of the Bank of England? So far as the absence of representatives of the joint stock banks is concerned I think the system differs from any other central banking system in the world? — I am not prepared to answer. I cannot quote the instance, but I have a feeling that in one case at least where that arrangement existed it has been terminated as the result of experience. I cannot name the case at the moment, but I have a feeling that that is so.

410. The next question that I should like to ask is this: Assuming that the character of the London money market alters somewhat in the future, that the supply of bills coming forward for discount becomes rather smaller and that the discount market loses some of the importance which it has had in the past – I think there might be a tendency for that – do you not think something might be said for the development of regular borrowing arrangements between the joint stock banks and the Bank, particularly at the termination of a quarter or some such period as that? — Well, I have always regarded the advantage of the existing system to be that it does enable the banks to meet their own requirements with the greatest economy. Whether if there was a regular practice by which the banks came to the Bank, it might result in possible overborrowing I do not know.

411. As things actually are, do you not think that there is some danger of the course of rates in the London money market being quite unnecessarily upset when a fairly large number of joint stock banks are calling in money? — I think I can say on that point if any operation of that kind occurs the Bank are generally careful unless the protection of the currency of the country is involved, of the gold reserves which constitute the foundation of credit – unless there is danger to them the Bank usually take pains to arrange that the operations of the banks shall not unduly inconvenience the money market.

412. May I ask you a question with regard to a field of possible activities of the Bank of which you have not spoken, but which, I think, is important; that is, in regard to the supply of statistical information. I should like to ask you, Sir Ernest, whether you have ever considered the possibility of the Bank issuing an Annual Report on the lines of the Annual Report of the Federal Reserve Board, for instance? — I will not say I have not considered it, but I cannot honestly say that I have considered it to the point of coming to any definite conclusion. I should like to say this – I shall come to it a little later – that we already do supply purely statistical information to our foreign Central Bank friends monthly. It is at present circulated only to them. Whether it would be an advantage to circulate it elsewhere I do not know. After all, it is really a collection of information which is already available, most of it, in other directions, and is merely collected for the convenience of our foreign correspondents who have not possibly the same means of turning to the sources from which we get it. I have a specimen of it here. I will tell you the type of thing it deals with. It deals with the Bank of England itself, its own figures, with those of clearing and other banks, money and bill rates, foreign exchanges, bank clearances, public finance, floating debt, security prices, gold, overseas trade, commodity prices, indices of wholesale prices, retail prices, cost of living, unemployment, trade disputes, British postal receipts, production of staple commodities, building, shipbuilding – the information may vary according to whatever is most important at the moment – capital issues, railways and shipping, and information of that description. With Empire Central Banks, of course, we have specially intimate relations, and to them we write every fortnight a rather voluminous letter which is a general review of

conditions here in this country, of foreign conditions as we view them where there has been any marked change or any occurrences of special importance in Continental and foreign countries, and if we may judge by the letters we receive from these banks the information is much appreciated. When it comes to the question of the Bank itself publishing an Annual Report I confess I am sometimes nervous at the thought of publication unless it is historical. The question is whether, when it is merely historical it is of any particular value, or whether from the fact that it is issued from the Central Bank undue importance may be attributed to certain things which are stated, more importance than perhaps they merit.

413. I suppose you yourself are quite familiar with the publications of the Federal Reserve system? — I am.

414. *Mr. McKenna*: Amongst the causes of variation in the aggregate of the clearing bankers' balances at the Bank of England we may reckon, may we not, the currency demands by the public and, secondly, the transfer of money from customers of the banks to a customer of the Bank of England who is not a customer of the banks, such, for example, as the Government? — Certainly. I think I stated that.

415. You stated the latter, but did not refer to variations in the currency in circulation? — No.

416. In your experience it is a fact, is it not, that at certain seasons of the year there are unusual demands by the public for currency? — Certainly. When you say 'unusual'——

417. I mean exceptional. — They are, as a rule, 'usual' when related to particular seasons.

418. They are usual at that season; they are seasonal demands? — Yes, seasonal demands.

419. It is also within your experience, is it not, that in the first three months of the year there are exceptional demands by the Government upon the customers of the clearing banks? — Yes.

420. It follows, does it not, that when there is this seasonal demand for additional currency and when there is an exceptional demand by the Government for taxes, at all those periods the clearing banks have less than the usual balances with you? — No, I cannot admit that. Let me take the first three months of the year. The Government is receiving the revenue from income tax, super-tax and so forth. The Government does not take that money to keep it lying idle. As it takes in the money its practice is to reduce its offerings of Treasury Bills, and so as the money comes in the money goes out and the position is kept fairly level.

421. I agree with you that ultimately there is no change because the money goes out again, but I put it to you whether from your experience it is not a fact that there is always a lag in the return of the money, both from the public so far as the circulation is concerned and from the Government so far as taxation is concerned? — I should say that as regards that lag, if the circumstances of the Bank's reserves, the exchanges again, and the various matters I have referred to before warrant it, it is the practice of the Bank of England to try and minimise that lag.

422. I am not saying what the Bank of England do. I only want to know, does the Bank of England in practice watch from day to day at these special seasons whether the banks are maintaining their usual balances? — Absolutely.

423. *Mr. Keynes*: Arising out of Mr. McKenna's last question, is it not a statistical fact that the balances of the clearing banks are less in February, for example, than the average of the year? — It may be.

424. What reason is there that year after year the Bank of England should not rectify that position? — We have to judge as to whether the balances, though less than normal, are sufficiently less to need adjustment by the Bank, or whether the comparison is due to the fact that at other periods the balances may be in excess of requirements.

425. If the balances of the clearing banks were £2,000,000 less, that would mean that the banks could lend approximately £20,000,000 less to industry. Is there any reason why the requirements of industry should be less in the Spring than in the rest of the year? — Not that I know of.

426. I have heard the argument expressed – I do not say that I support it – that one of the reasons why we often see reaction in trade in the second quarter of the year after a rather promising beginning is because banks habitually have to curtail their accommodation during the period of income tax collection for no obvious reason except that the Bank of England has refrained from rectifying the position? — I cannot admit that the Bank does so refrain.

427. Well – does not. There is no difficulty in rectifying it, is there? The Bank simply has to buy £2,000,000 of bills? — That is quite true. You must remember this, that there is much of taxation which comes in on certain days of the week, and while you may have over a period the Government taking a considerable sum of money, you may have a week in which they take in a considerable sum, say, on one day, and then there is a period when things are easy again, and then you will get another day——

428. I am not speaking of days; I am speaking of a period; a month, for example; or two months? — The Bank does its best. If it does not succeed, well, I can only express regret. That they do attempt to do it I can definitely say.

429. Would it be possible to give us figures showing the average of the clearing banks' aggregate balances in the Spring, month by month, as compared with the average of the year? — From the banks' published returns? They only publish averages, of course. I do not

know whether we ought to publish their figures. After all, here we are in the relation of banker and client, and we do not publish any of their figures. We leave it to them to publish what they think fit; if they see fit to do it I see no objection.

430. *Mr. McKenna*: I think you do now publish the aggregate? — We publish, of course, our total every Wednesday night. Those figures are available; they are already available.

431. You publish the aggregate of our balances every week? — Undoubtedly, on one day of the week.

432. *Mr. Keynes*: Of course we have not got those figures for back years. *Mr. McKenna*: If we had those figures for back years I think I could show you that the aggregate is always lower in the first quarter. *Chairman*: Is it an erratic fluctuation? I rather gather from Sir Ernest it is not a question of a rapid diminution. *Mr. Keynes*: No. During the period of income tax collection there is a constant transfer from the clearing banks to the Treasury which is not rectified by the Bank of England. *Mr. Lubbock*: I have all the published figures of the banks since November, last year, and I cannot see that February shows any great decrease, so far as the past 12 months are concerned. *Mr. Keynes*: The only figures I have been able to examine are the reserves which the clearing banks themselves publish over a period of years. *Chairman*: It is a pure question of fact, that can be cleared up perfectly easily by the bankers themselves. The question put to Sir Ernest is this: Whether, that phenomenon existing, and possibly having repercussions on the industrial position, appropriate steps have been taken by the Bank to obviate what we may call the seasonal diminution of credit. I rather gather from him that their effort is to smooth out the irregularities. The question how far they have succeeded in doing that is a different question? — We endeavour to do it with the co-operation of the Treasury, who, as I say, are receiving the money, and are repaying Treasury bills. The matter is governed to a certain extent by the maturities of the Government bills.

433. *Mr. Keynes*: There is no need to depend on the Treasury, is there? The Bank can itself purchase bills, and habitually does so? — That is so, but if we go into the market to-day and purchase bills, and the Treasury happen to have a large maturity which they are very anxious to reduce in order to even their maturities within a day or two days——

434. I am not speaking of day-to-day fluctuations? — No.

435. Arising out of Professor Gregory's questions, is it a practice of the Bank of England never to explain what its policy is? — Well, I think it has been our practice to leave our actions to explain our policy.

436. Or the reasons for its policy? — It is a dangerous thing to start to give reasons.

437. Or to defend itself against criticisms? — Because the reasons very often are based on information which has been obtained in the strictest confidence, sometimes from foreign countries, and which we should not feel ourselves at liberty to publish. As regards defence against criticism, I am afraid, though the Committee may not all agree, we do not admit there is need for defence; to defend ourselves is somewhat akin to a lady starting to defend her virtue. *Chairman*: I think Mr. Keynes will agree with me that this is a general question. If you decide to rely on the discretion of a person then you must accept his decisions. They are not examinable.. Where you leave the decision of a matter to a man's discretion and he gives no reason for his decision, then you must accept that decision. Take the case of a company. Share transfers may be rejected by a company without reasons being assigned. The decision as to whether or not they will accept a transfer is left to the discretion of the directors. If they do state their reasons, then these reasons become examinable. The question whether you should repose discretion in a person is another matter, but if you do repose discretion in a person then you must accept his decision.

438. *Mr. Keynes*: The policy of the Bank of England very often requires the co-operation of the joint stock banks and the rest of the money market and issuing houses. Is it easy to rely on that co-operation if those bodies have no means of knowing what the policy of the Bank of England is? — They have means – quite informal, quite unofficial.

439. They may know what the wishes of the Bank of England are in respect of particular actions, but do they have an authoritative statement as to what the policy of the Bank of England is over important periods of time? — They have no formal statement of policy, no.

440. Does it not, perhaps, sometimes prevent the success of any policy, that whereas it is being perpetually discussed in public no one knows on which side of the discussion the Bank of England itself stands? — There is one objection. I should hesitate to bring a charge against anyone, but, if we state a definite policy, we may give the opportunity to certain people to take advantage of what our intended actions may be, and with that knowledge enable them to take advantage of the situation for their own benefit, and it may mean that if we have to take a certain course, it may have to be a longer course than if we take it without any previous announcement. Do you understand my meaning?

441. Does not the policy of secrecy as to its intentions deprive the Bank of what I might call the collective wisdom of the community? These questions are very difficult and very novel. They require a great deal of co-operative thinking by all people who are competent to contribute to the common stock. Does not the policy of secrecy of the Bank mean that no one

outside the Bank can express an opinion which is founded on sound information? — These are difficult questions to answer without time for more consideration.

442. *Professor Gregory*: Even half a generation ago, banking policy was a matter which did not intimately concern the lives of millions of the population. At the present time the Central banking policy has a very intimate relationship with social and political policy; it necessarily must have. Do you think there is a danger of the Bank of England being misunderstood even more by publishing no information than it would be by publishing partial information? — This seems to be rather a question for others to answer. *Lord Bradbury*: Is there not a difference between the publication of information or figures that are not published now and a general discussion of the credit situation, and the Bank of England giving reasons why, at any particular time, it lowers Bank Rate? I think myself that would be a very different thing, but the publication of a good deal more information than is published now and the general discussion of the credit situation might be useful. *Chairman*: These are different points. I think we are probably all inclined to agree that the information available for public discussion is inadequate at present, and it may be necessary to give more data. *Lord Bradbury*: I can back up Sir Ernest Harvey in one thing, the Federal Reserve System, when I was last in America, made a public announcement which led everybody to think that the rate would be raised; then there appeared to arise an internal difference of opinion and the rate was not raised. Meanwhile, the whole market took certain steps thinking that the rate would be raised, and it was not raised, and the Federal Reserve System came in for a great deal of blame.

443. *Sir Walter Raine*: Does the Bank of England settle the amount of Treasury Bills that is to be issued each week? — The Treasury settle that figure.

444. *Mr. Keynes*: I should like to ask a question on the first part of Sir Ernest's evidence. Is there any minimum figure of bankers' deposits which you expect them to carry? — None.

445. Do the bankers, in fact, keep with you more than is necessary for their convenience, or more than is necessary for obtaining an emergency supply of notes? — On some days, certainly.

446. But on an average? — Well, I think they should be asked that question, because I do not know what kind of obligations may come upon them, and they do.

447. Does not the Bank of England deliberately aim at a given figure at any given time for the aggregate of the clearing banks' balances? — No.

448. Does the Bank ever suggest to the clearing banks that they should maintain rates at an agreed level, for example, for call money? — I have never known of it being done, but the question had better I think be addressed to the Governor; I do not know whether he has ever suggested such a thing to them at some time when I have not been present.

449. It is commonly alleged that the balances which the joint stock banks keep on the day of the week on which they make up their accounts is an artificial figure higher than the average. Is that correct? — Am I at liberty to answer a question like that? I think you should ask the bankers that.

450. *Sir Thomas Allen*: I would like to ask Sir Ernest if he would care to state definitely whether it is his view that the demands of the Government at certain periods of the year definitely affect the amount of credit available for industry? — Well, that is a point I was coming to when I touch on the relations between the Bank and the Treasury.

451. You spoke of the closer relationship which now exists between you and the commercial bankers and the improving co-operation which has taken place. Would you care to elaborate that a little further for our assistance? — I do not know that I can add much to what I have said. It is general in tendency, it is not specific in any way, but I think I can claim that there is really a complete contact with them and that every banker recognises that he can come at any moment to the Bank and consult them on any matter of any importance, and that he will find the Bank responsive.

452. You spoke of your relationship with the bigger banks. I take it you mean what is called the 'Big Five'? — No; I include all the clearing banks, all the bankers, in fact, who are described as bankers in the Bank Return.

453. Any banker may come to you and apply for information? — Certainly. May I pass now to the relations with the Treasury?

454. *Chairman*: Please? — Here, again, of course, the relations are fundamentally those of banker and client. The Bank of England keeps the main Government balances. It is in daily touch with the Treasury, sometimes many times a day. Probably twice in the week - if circumstances require it may be oftener - the Governor himself will pay a visit to the Treasury, sometimes accompanied by myself. When he is away, I pay such visits in his place. We have no secrets from them, we keep them fully acquainted as to the general trend of affairs in the City and the outlook, as we see it. We, on our part, never venture to interfere on any question that can be considered a political question, unless we are asked to express an opinion as to what the financial effect of a certain political operation may be. If we are asked, we give our advice, but we never seek to interfere in politics. The Treasury, on the other hand, are good enough to reciprocate; that is to say, that, whilst we keep them fully informed as to the general trend of affairs in the City, as to any occurrences of importance affecting the position of finance and credit, they do not seek to dictate any alternative line

of financial policy if we, in our judgment, consider a particular line of policy essential for the protection of the country's main reserves. As regards other Government Offices, we have no direct contact without the knowledge and approval of the Treasury. In fact, it is with few of them that we have direct contact at all. If other Government Offices desire the opinion of the Bank on any subject, as a rule they obtain it through the Treasury.

Apart from these visits that I have spoken of, it is the practice for the Governor to visit the Chancellor of the Exchequer at fairly frequent intervals, and to keep him also fully informed. And I suppose I need hardly say that the colour of the Government of the moment has absolutely no influence whatever on the nature of these relations. The Bank undertakes the issue of all Government loans, including Government guaranteed loans. It manages the stocks, pays the dividends, conducts any drawings, registers transfers and performs all the ordinary work which a Registrar would perform. We conduct the weekly issues of Treasury Bills, but always in the presence of a representative of the Treasury. That representative determines the amount of the Bills to be sold. He determines the amount to be offered for the following week, but, of course, our advice is always freely at his disposal. The Treasury tell us their views as to probable income and expenditure in the near future, and, in the closest collaboration, we endeavour to ensure that the ebb and flow of those movements in Treasury finance shall not cause any unnecessary or avoidable disturbance in market conditions.

Now, the Chancellor of the Exchequer has declared it to be his policy to reduce the floating debt, a policy with which the Bank are in entire concurrence. But in this connection there are just three points that I want to mention. If the floating debt is allowed to become unwieldy, it entails a very large offering of Bills every week, and if that weekly offering is allowed to become too big, it is obvious that certain dangers may arise, certain difficulties for the Bank, for example, in the control of the situation in any time of doubt and difficulty. If the amount gets too large and the market has doubts as to the future course of rates, it may be difficult to issue the Bills. On the other hand, at a time when there is, perhaps, a shortage of commercial bills, especially having regard to increased deposits of the bankers, who must find liquid employment for a certain proportion of their funds, a reasonable amount of bills does provide a convenient medium for maintaining the efficient working of the Money Market and enabling the banks to preserve that degree of liquidity which they regard as essential. A moderate amount of Treasury Bills also provides a convenient medium for enabling the Treasury to adjust its own position, having regard to the inequalities as between the volume of receipts from revenue and the volume of payments for services, debt and other purposes. A reasonable amount of Bills thus affords the Treasury a means by which they can avoid the necessity of being forced, at times when they are receiving money, to carry unnecessarily large idle balances. Therefore, although it is sometimes said that the floating debt – the rate of interest on which is not fixed but varies with market rates of discount – may, if rates are high, be expensive – which I do not deny for a moment – nevertheless if kept within manageable limits, it does, on the other hand, provide a means whereby the Treasury can and does secure a fairly effective degree of economy in operation.

If we want a tribute to the efficiency of the system, I do not think we need look further than this week's newspapers, where we see that the United States, for I believe the first time in their history, have made an issue of Treasury Bills on lines precisely similar to those followed here. They have embarked on this – I do not think it is indiscreet for me to say so – after long talks to us about the system, and, for all I know, after similar talks with the Treasury, regarding the working of the system, and I think we are entitled to take that as a tribute to its efficiency.

The Bank acts, of course, as the financial adviser of the Chancellor of the Exchequer. It does not seek to impose unsought advice, but, as I have already explained, its advice is always freely and fully at his disposal and, at the same time, it is able to act on occasions as a mouthpiece of the Chancellor to the City. That is a brief outline – for I feel I must be brief if I am to finish within the time available to me – of the general relations between the Bank and the Treasury, completely close, completely cordial, and I think the Treasury would bear me out in saying that, in the Bank's attitude, and in their relations with them, they do help the Government to secure the maximum of economy. I do not know, Mr. Chairman, whether anybody wishes to ask a question before I proceed?

455. *Mr. Keynes*: Would Sir Ernest agree that, the larger the volume of Treasury Bills outstanding, the easier it is for the Bank to make Bank Rate effective? — Not beyond a certain volume, no. I think when you have sufficient for the purposes I have mentioned, anything further is undesirable. For, remember, we have a fiduciary issue of £260,000,000, and with that large amount any addition to the floating debt should, in my judgment, be kept within manageable proportions, and you must bear in mind that, if this form of debt is allowed to get too large and the weekly offerings of bills become too great, you do run grave risk of creating difficulties.

456. *Mr. McKenna*: Could you conveniently let us have figures showing the average cost to the Government of Treasury Bills for the last seven years, from 1923 to the present day? — Yes, if you mean the average cost of public issues.

457. You would not mind? — Certainly

not. *Mr. McKenna*: One figure only will be needed, which will be the average cost of public issues of Treasury Bills over the whole period. I am leading up to the point that I think events will show that it is the cheapest form of borrowing that the Government has had for the last seven years. *Sir Walter Raine*: Might I suggest that it would be more interesting to have a figure for each year? *Mr. McKenna*: Well, it will be prepared for each year, but we can divide it by seven for ourselves.

458. *Mr. Keynes*: I gather that it is your opinion that the idea of a large volume of Treasury Bills being dangerous is a fallacy and that the opposite is the truth, namely that a substantial reduction of Treasury Bills might be a very grave danger to the present method of regulating the effective rates on the market? — I think that, if the reduction was too great, you would run a risk, perhaps, of clogging the machinery of the market, and you would deprive the Government of a convenient method of adjusting their accounts.

459. We understand that some of the Treasury Bills are held by Government departments, some are held by the Bank itself, some by the money market, some by the joint stock banks and some by other holders. We have no figures of those five items separately; I do not know whether they could be given. Whether they can be given or not, would it not be the case that any material reduction in the amount held otherwise than by the Government and the Bank itself might very soon produce the effect which I am fearing? — It might. As I have indicated, it might if the reduction was too rapid or too great.

460. If the reduction of the floating debt merely means that the Issue Department of the Bank of England holds more long-dated securities and fewer short-dated securities, then, obviously, there is nothing in what I am saying; but if it had the effect that the supply of bills to the outside market was materially reduced below its present level, would you not very soon reach the danger point? — That is the point I had in mind, that you have, in my judgment, got to have sufficient to keep the market working. But even in recent times the market worked quite well on considerably fewer bills than exist at the moment.

461. *Sir Thomas Allen*: Would not Sir Ernest agree that it is of enormous importance to the banks that they should have considerable short-dated securities in order to keep a certain amount of assets liquid, and that the real rate of interest is not the most significant factor? — They must indeed. That is partly what I have in mind when I say that in my judgment, whilst there are not enough commercial bills you must have a certain volume of Treasury Bills to keep the market working. When I say the market I have not in mind just the discount market, I have in mind the banks and their need to maintain the requisite degree of liquidity. *Sir Thomas Allen*: I would not care for too much emphasis to be laid on the rate of interest for these short-dated securities.

462. *Mr. Frater Taylor*: Does the Treasury budget ahead with you, or is it somewhat hand to mouth? — We form our estimates generally about three or four weeks ahead; we can of course form reliable estimates of major operations like maturing debt and so forth; as regards such items as income and payments on Government account we generally form estimates for about three or four weeks ahead, and, of course, we revise those estimates from week to week. So that we are always estimating about four weeks ahead, but revising estimates previously made for a particular week as it draws nearer.

463. *Sir Thomas Allen*: Do you know of any definite cases where money has been kept off the market arising out of a certain expectancy that the Treasury will be wanting money which otherwise might reasonably have gone into industry? — Do you mean, kept off the market by the Treasury?

464. No, kept off the market by the bankers in anticipation of Treasury issues? — No. We have nothing but the total of the bankers' balances to judge by. We do not know for what purpose those balances may be allowed to increase and have little means of judging the question.

465. *Lord Bradbury*: Might I put a question of a rather general nature? I think it would be rather useful to get a reply for the information of the Committee generally. I believe that before the War the normal maximum of Treasury Bills outstanding was something in the neighbourhood of £30,000,000. The present total, I think, is somewhere in the neighbourhood of £800,000,000? — That is so.

466. To what general cause has it to be attributed that the present needs of the market for a security of that kind should be so very much in excess of the pre-War needs? I take it there is general agreement that although £800,000,000 is a very high total there would be no question of a reduction to anything like the pre-War figure? — In looking at the present total of £800,000,000 you must not forget that, as I have said before, the Issue Department has a fiduciary issue of £260,000,000, and, as I mentioned when going through the Bank Return, a very considerable proportion of the Government Securities in that Department consists of Treasury Bills. Therefore, £800,000,000 must not be taken to be the total of the active volume of bills. Then, again, there are other factors. We know that some foreign countries which were in the habit in pre-War days of holding considerable amounts of gold against their notes now hold Treasury Bills to some extent in lieu of gold. There are other similar classes of special holders. Therefore, the volume of £800,000,000 that you see published must not be taken as the measurement of the volume of Treasury Bills in active circulation in the market. But, even allowing

for all special holders, I recognise that the volume is vastly greater than it was. For one thing, the volume of commercial bills is, I should say, less. There has been perhaps a tendency in commerce to replace financing by bills by financing by overdrafts, which has accounted for some of the reduction. Then it has to be remembered that the volume of the bankers' deposits is enormously greater, and that their need for cash or absolutely liquid security is therefore much greater; I should say that much of the increase is due to those causes. Take foreign holders of balances in our market. I do not know how their holdings compare with foreign balances of pre-War days, but I should judge that foreigners are considerable holders of Treasury Bills at the present time. My point, therefore, is, that though the total volume does look enormously greater, the actual volume in what I may call live circulation probably has not increased to anything like the extent to which it might appear to the casual observer.

467. It is sometimes a little difficult in these complicated matters, when you have cause and effect, to say which is the cause and which is the effect. Is it possible that what I may call the decay of the commercial bill may be to some extent the effect of the existence of a large number of Treasury Bills? — I think not. If you ask me why I think not, my opinion is based on the experience which I had when I visited Australia about three years ago. Exactly the same thing has happened there – the bill has gone out of favour and the overdraft has taken its place. It is a question I went into pretty closely when I was out there. There were various reasons, but exactly the same phenomenon has occurred out there.

468. Do you make the same reply in regard to bankers' deposits? May not the enormous growth of bankers' deposits be due to a very large extent to the floating debt? — Well, of course, if it enables bankers to keep additional reserves of liquid assets, such as call money which the market can invest in bills, it may give the bankers the power to create more deposits by advances. I should not like to attempt to determine which is cause and which effect. *Lord Bradbury*: I do not want to pursue the question now. It is a very abstruse question. I rather wanted to get Sir Ernest's *prima facie* opinion.

469. *Mr. Brand*: When you say 'diminution of commercial bills' you mean diminution of internal commercial bills? — Yes.

470. Not commercial bills financing foreign trade? — No.

471. *Sir Thomas Allen*: Have you any fear that the overdraft is superseding the commercial bill? — I think it is doing so and that it is regrettable. I did my best to persuade the bankers in Australia to attempt to revive the use of bills. There were in that case fiscal difficulties in the way. I discussed it with the Prime Minister and the Treasurer, and I think they appreciated the desirability of securing a revival of the use of bills. The reason I think it regrettable is that an overdraft is not a very liquid asset, unfortunately. A bill can be bought and sold at any moment, and a bank that holds bills can pass over its assets, if it requires, with much greater ease and facility than assets in the form of overdrafts.

472. Would you say it was equally regrettable for Great Britain as for Australia, in view of our better industrial security and the more secure industrial situation? — Of course, within certain limits I should always prefer the bill to the overdraft, as the more mobile instrument.

473. *Sir Walter Raine*: May I ask if the reason for the overdraft coming into favour, as against the commercial bill, has not been because the various trades insist on the buyer making his arrangements with his banker, instead of, as used to be the case in many trades, giving a bill? — I am told that in many cases the reason is the fear of the debtor that if he finances by means of a bill he will have to pay interest for the whole currency of the bill, whereas if he obtains an overdraft he simply pays interest on the fluctuating debit balance from day to day. He usually pays a higher rate, of course, in the case of an overdraft.

474. But is it not a fact that the various trades have considerably shortened their credit? I just mention the coal trade. In pre-War days in South Wales we used to pay in a month, in the north of England we used to pay in 14 days; now, by Government order, everybody has to pay for export coal in seven days. Now, in the pre-War days, of course, you got your money in without giving a bill. I just mention it as an illustration, and I believe, from what I know, it is a fact in other trades that the trader says to the buyer, 'You must make arrangements with your banker and not ask us to take bills'? — I am afraid I do not know enough about that subject to answer.

475. *Chairman*: Has the incidence of the stamp duty had anything to do with the replacement of the bill by the overdraft? — It had in Australia, certainly, but not here.

476. Now, perhaps you will pass to the subject of your relations with foreign Central Banks? — I have told you earlier that in our relations with foreign Central Banks there is absolutely no idea in our mind of seeking to secure relations with foreign Central Banks for the sake of profit. Our object is entirely to establish close and friendly relationship, which we think may enable us, in co-operation, to find means of minimising some of the causes of international financial disturbances, which have been experienced in the past. It is perfectly true, and I admit it perfectly frankly, that with a foreign Central Bank if they approach us with a view to establishing business relations we say, 'Yes,' always assuming that the applicant is in fact either a properly constituted central bank or in the way of becoming a properly constituted central bank, or

if we think that by establishing relations we can encourage them to become a properly constituted central bank. With any other foreigners we decline to entertain any business. We open no accounts, unless in some very exceptional circumstances it is represented to us say by the Government that it is expedient to make an exception; otherwise we open no accounts, and have not done so for some years past, for any foreign institution or person. Foreign Governments apply to us from time to time with a request that we will open an account for them. I have had one such case within the last fortnight. Our answer is always the same – we decline to open accounts for foreign Governments, but add that any proposals that come to us through a Central Bank will receive our careful and sympathetic consideration. Our object, I think, will be obvious to the Committee. Holding, as I said earlier, the opinion that a Central Bank should be the banker of its Government, our endeavour is always to guide the foreign Government into the arms of its Central Bank. We think it makes for the establishment of the right financial position.

We endeavour to cultivate the closest relationship we can with the Central Banks, not merely by correspondence, but also by personal visits. We started this policy in a humble way; in fact I am not sure that I was not, except for one or two visits paid by the Governor, the first emissary that went abroad for the Bank. I paid five or six visits to foreign countries. After a time we realised that it was necessary to develop this practice much more fully if we were to make a success of it, and we took into the Bank of England – a matter to which Mr. Keynes has alluded, I think, and to which he seemed to attach importance – several people of what he described as of the standing of the Higher Civil Service, who were able men, had knowledge of finance, and in some cases a knowledge, theoretical or practical, of central banking, and who, above all things, had a knowledge of languages. But I should be sorry if the Committee were to get an idea that the mere engagement of people of this type is all that is necessary for the betterment, if betterment be necessary, of the organisation of the Bank. I say it with diffidence, having regard to the avenue through which I have reached my present position, that there is certain knowledge, certain tradition – and by 'tradition' I do not mean a hidebound objection to development – and an instinct which can only be gained by long service in a Central Bank. These are supplied by officials who are brought up in actual contact with the daily business which the Bank conducts in connection with its daily operations, its market operations, its relations with the discount market, and so on – officials such as the Chief Cashier, and so on – and in my judgment the ideal arrangement is to have both classes, and to weld them together into a real unified team working in the closest co-operation. That is what we have been aiming at for some time, and, I think, with considerable success. Even from the staff which we have recruited in the ordinary way, we are sending members abroad for months at a time to foreign Central Banks who are kind enough to take them in, and allow them to see the sort of business they are doing, the lines on which they work – they are young men, who have had experience in the more important fundamentals of our business – and the arrangement gives them an opportunity to perfect their language qualifications. That has been going on for some considerable time. Then, of course, our higher officials pay visits, and we receive visits from representatives of other Central Banks. During the past year, for example – I had the curiosity to take out the figures – we have visited – and when I say 'we' I mean the higher representatives of the Bank – 20 Central Banks. We have received visits, on the other hand, from Governors and higher officials, of 30 foreign Central Banks during the past year. We place rooms at their disposal; we tell them anything they want to know about our scheme, our methods, without, of course, revealing actual figures which we are not at liberty to disclose, or any information that is of a confidential nature regarding our clients, or the Government, but generally informing them as to our system. They seem to appreciate the visits; we give every encouragement and believe that the arrangement is doing good.

. . . .

Saturday 14 December 1929

Sir Ernest Musgrave Harvey, K.B.E., Deputy Governor of the Bank of England, recalled and further examined.

791. *Chairman*: You will recall, Sir Ernest, that when we parted last you had been dealing with the overseas and foreign Central Banks and your relations with them. I do not know whether you have anything further to say on that topic, or whether you would wish now to pass first to your relations with the Stock Exchange and other bodies, and then to the topics of banking reconstruction, new financial machinery and rationalisation, upon all of which you have something to say. (*Professor Gregory*): May I ask one question upon the relationship of the Bank of England with other Central Banks? Those relations, the interchange of visits and so on, do not impinge on the international policy of the Central Banks, do they? When policy is being discussed you have rather more formal meetings between the Governors and the representatives of the Central Banks? — Yes.

792. *Chairman*: I wonder if you could tell us anything about the Commonwealth Bank of Australia. I see in the papers that a new Bill is now passing through the Legislature? — Yes, I will say something about that, if I may. Before I actually resume where I left off, Mr. Chairman, there are just one or two remarks that I should like to make with reference to the subjects dealt with last time.

793. Please. — I thought it might interest the Committee if I circulated to them copies of the information which I think I then stated we issue to the Central Banks. We do not claim for it any particular value; it is nothing more than an attempt to collate in a convenient form information which is already available in this country, though from a lot of different sources, and therefore, perhaps, rather difficult for foreign Central Banks to collect.

794. Convenient compilation? — Yes. I thought the Committee might like to see the type of information and the form in which we send it out, so I have brought some copies with me. (*Copies distributed.*)

795. *Mr. Lubbock*: Although, as you say, the information is drawn from sources available to everyone this summary is not published in this country? — It is not published in this country, no.

796. *Professor Gregory*: Do you think that there would be any objection to the Bank issuing a bulletin something like that issued by the Federal Reserve Bank, not expressing any views, but summarising its operations? — If it were considered of use I do not really see why something of the kind should not be done.

797. You would not like any statement of opinion to be inferred from such publication, and you think it might be difficult to avoid that? — It might be difficult, I think.

798. *Chairman*: This is a very interesting publication; full of meat, if I may say so? — I was asked further to produce figures as to the average rate at which issues of Treasury Bills have been made by tender during the last seven years. I have brought those with me, and I will pass them round, if I may. It should be borne in mind in looking at the figures that the first two years, of course, were years prior to our return to the gold standard, and the conditions, therefore, are not strictly comparable. (*Copies distributed.*)*

799. *Mr. Keynes*: Might I ask you one question on these figures? I think you told us that the Treasury Bills held in the Banking Department were not necessarily discounted at market rate. Are they included in these results or excluded? — To the extent to which they are Bills that may have been tendered for by the Bank, just as the public tender, they would be included, but to the extent to which they may have been bought in the market, they are excluded from that calculation, having originally been issued in response to tenders received from the public.

800. It would exclude bills which were taken by the Issue Department at special rates? — Yes.

801. *Mr. McKenna*: This is a summary of the weekly published figures of tender rates? — Yes, taken from the published results of the weekly tenders. Then Mr. McKenna asked a question as to whether it was not a fact that the bankers' balances during the first quarter, when the Government are drawing in large sums from the public in the form of taxation, are not, as a rule, less than the bankers' balances in the succeeding quarter. I have had figures taken out for seven years; they are the averages of the weekly Wednesday night figures of the bankers. I ought to say that, in the days before November of last year, when we commenced the publication of the bankers' balances, the figures of bankers' balances, which we always had before us daily for consideration, were the London balances. Since we published these figures we have included the country balances, because we feel that the figures we publish ought to tally with the figures which the bankers themselves regard as their cash with the Bank. In point of fact, the country balances hardly vary, they are extraordinarily stable, for the reason that London is the centre where the bankers naturally employ their balances. They have facilities as regards accounts at country branches, by which, if a balance runs down at a Provincial Branch, they can arrange with us to telegraph money down for their credit at that branch. Similarly, if currency comes in to them in the country, they can pay it into one of our branches, and if, by that means, their balance at any branch is increased to a figure which they think is unnecessarily large, they can have the surplus transferred by telegram to London. For that reason, as I say, the country balances remain very stable. The variation is remarkably small. Therefore, in drawing up this comparative statement of bankers' balances, we have had to estimate the figure for the provinces in the years before November of last year, but I think you may take it that, substantially, these figures are correct. I have not had time to have figures extracted for seven years based on the daily balances of the bankers. There would not have been time. I have only taken the Wednesday night figures.

802. The daily amount is essential to my purpose. May I explain what I mean? You take every Thursday from the banks the money

---

* *Average for each year of the average weekly rates at which Treasury bills issued by tender were allotted*

	£	s.	d.
1923	2	12	5.33
1924	3	7	10.52
1925	4	1	10.73
1926	4	10	3.79
1927	4	5	1.51
1928	4	2	9
1929 (50 weeks only) ..	5	5	4.65

which they have accumulated for the payment of taxes. That money is used by you in repayment of part of the weekly Treasury Bill issues which fall due for payment on Thursday, Friday, Saturday, Monday, Tuesday, Wednesday. Now it follows from that that the money which the Government have got in hand for repayment of the Treasury Bills only comes back to the banks in the course of the week, and, consequently, they are deprived of the use of the funds from Thursday to Wednesday in a diminishing quantity as you repay the Treasury Bills. Now, my contention would be that your figures would show that, during the first quarter of the year, the bankers have got a minimum balance with you on Thursday, a slightly larger balance on Friday, a slightly larger balance on Saturday, a slightly larger balance on Monday, and only get back to their normal figure on Wednesday, the day on which you publish your figures. So that, in the first quarter of the year, we are regularly deprived of bank cash. It is only the daily figures that show that? — I do not want to be held too strictly to this, but I think I am right in saying that, not very long ago – it may be a year – it is a question which possibly a Government representative could answer with more authority than I can – the Government did, in fact, make a change as regards this taking in of taxation, and, instead of leaving money with the bankers for a week and taking it, say, once a week, they do, in fact, take it in now more frequently in order to secure a quicker transfer of the money to the Exchequer. I believe I am correct in saying now that the old arrangement under which the bulk of the money did come in on a Thursday has been considerably modified. Of course, in so far as there is a variation between the Government's receipts from Treasury Bills and their payments of Treasury Bills, that is a matter that is not in our hands. It is in the hands of the public who tender for the Bills. They may tender for the Bills payable on any day they like. If the bankers, as tenderers for Bills, have any expectation that they will be deprived of money, say, on Thursday, Friday and Saturday, they can arrange their tenders for new Bills accordingly, so that they will be receiving payment for maturing Bills in the earlier part of the week and not have to meet a heavy balance of payments during the latter part of the week.

803. But the clearing banks are comparatively small tenderers? — I should not put it too small.

804. Well, they could, to some degree, mitigate the trouble, but they could not remedy it entirely, or anything like entirely. (*Chairman*): Are there not two questions, Mr. McKenna? First of all, does this phenomenon exist, namely, the fact that you only see the Wednesday figures does not give you a fair reflection of the week? Secondly, if that phenomenon exists and is detrimental, how it can best be remedied, if it can be remedied? — I think I can give the Committee a satisfactory answer. Here are the results based on the figures of each Wednesday night. I propose to circulate them. I am going to say a word on this. I have said that I have not had time to have the daily figures taken out over a period of seven years. These are the Wednesday nights' figures, but there was time to supplement them by taking out the absolute daily average for three of the seven years, and the daily average confirms the weekly average in its general effect in all three cases.

805. *Mr. McKenna*: In the first quarter of the year? — In the first quarter of the year, and in only one of these seven years were the balances actually smaller in the first quarter than in the second; in all the other cases they were larger.

806. That is not my point. It is not the relationship between the first quarter and the second quarter, it is the relationship between the Wednesday of the first quarter and every other day of the week in the first quarter. — Yes, I appreciate that, but, as I say, I have had taken out the averages of the daily balances for three of those years; there was no time to do more; and in those three cases the daily average confirms the result shown by the weekly average of the Wednesday night.

807. Well, it is unintelligible to me, if all the banks pay over the tax money on the Thursday and that money is accumulated in the Bank of England to the credit of public deposits, how the public deposits on the Thursday are not higher than on the Wednesday. (*Chairman*): Let us see a sample of the figures. — These are the weekly averages. (*Copies distributed.*)

808. *Chairman*: The real point is whether the Wednesday night figures are a fair reflection of the week during the first quarter of the year. Do I understand that you have examined not only the weekly balances during the seven years, but you have examined the daily balances for three years? — That is so.

809. And as the result you find that the Wednesday balances, in point of fact, do afford a fair reflection of the position on each day of the week? — For those three years they do.

810. *Mr. Keynes*: From the point of view of bankers' reserves, what matters to the bankers is the aggregate of their holding of notes and of their balances with the Bank of England? — Certainly.

811. When the bankers' total reserves are diminished, it may be more convenient for them to reduce their holding of notes rather than their Bank of England balances by sending in notes to the Bank of England. In so far as they do that, the reactions on their total reserves due to extreme stringency, while very real to them, would not be reflected in the Bank of England's figure of bankers' deposits, which is only one part and not the total of the bankers' reserves. Therefore, while your examination of the bankers' balances does not disclose much day to day variation, that alone

is not conclusive as to the market situation, since the bankers may have chosen to reduce their holdings of notes rather than to reduce their balances at the Bank of England? — Yes. Whether it is by design on the part of the bankers that their notes are reduced I cannot say, I think it may be in large measure compulsion when the public are paying their taxes – I do not know; it is for the bankers to say; they may be forced to reduce their reserves of notes to meet the demands of customers for currency with which to pay taxes. We do know that the circulation of notes falls in the first quarter; it falls steadily until withdrawals begin again to meet the Easter demand.

812. It comes to this, that it may be that the Bank of England is short of a very vital piece of information, namely, the note holdings of the bankers. It may be that the alleged failure of the Bank of England to mitigate the severity of tax collection in the Spring is to a large extent due to the Bank of England being deprived of essential data? — Yes, I think that is very possible. Then I was asked a question, last time, Mr. Chairman, to which I am afraid I did not give a very definite reply, viz., did I feel there was objection to the other banks being represented on the Court of the Bank of England. Well, I must confess the more I have thought of it the more convinced I have become that such a thing would be most undesirable. In the first place the functions of the Central Bank and the functions of the ordinary banks are entirely different. Many problems arise which they must approach from entirely different angles, and I question very much whether anyone trained in either of those two schools would be a fit person to attempt to direct the other. I should be sorry myself, I confess, for the commercial bank that asked me to take control of the administration of its affairs. My approach to current problems has always been from an entirely different angle, and I confess I should probably feel quite lost in attempting to deal with the problems of a commercial bank. But, whether I am right or not, I think it is interesting to look at what has happened elsewhere. There are two cases. You may say they are not of outstanding importance, but still there are two cases where provision was made for bankers to be represented on the Board of the Central Bank – two cases within the British Empire. In both cases that policy has been abandoned. One is South Africa, the other is Australia. Then, again, we want to feel that we have the complete confidence of every banker, that he can feel perfectly free to come to us and to tell us his secrets in absolute confidence that they will go no further. I have some misgivings as to whether if the other bankers were represented on the Court that confidence might not perhaps diminish. We might not be made to the extent to which we are now the free recipients of the confidence of the other bankers. In this connection it is a noticeable thing that South Africa when they abandoned the representation of other banks on their Board did what perhaps the Bank of England does not often do; they gave their reasons. They said – I have the words here – 'The Board found it difficult to discuss certain aspects of banking policy before representatives of the banks.' That is exactly my feeling. It is true that there are countries where it is provided that representatives of the other banks shall be on the Board of the Central Bank, but there are several where it is definitely provided that such representatives shall not be on the Boards, and most of the latter are cases of Central Banks that have been most recently established – not on the advice of the Bank of England, but presumably on the advice of those consulted, people who have given wide study to the subject. There are eight such cases.

813. I think that what you have told us now is very interesting, but have you considered a more limited proposal, namely, not that the bankers should be represented on the Board of Management, but that there should be much more regular and habitual consultation as, for example, weekly joint meetings with representatives of the Treasury Committee or something of that kind? The impression made on my mind by your evidence on the last occasion was that while consultation has increased and is greater now than it was before the War, it is still in rather an elementary state? — I would say that it is in an informal state, and I am not sure it is not better for being informal.

814. *Mr. McKenna*: Does consultation of the kind of which Mr. Keynes is speaking exist at all? — Not in the form in which Mr. Keynes is speaking of it. No.

815. Of the kind; not of the form? Formal or informal, does consultation of that kind exist at all? — With some banks.

816. With some banks. — Yes, but not with a formal body of bankers.

817. That is to say, anybody communicating with the other banks on any question of policy that is proposed to be adopted or should be discussed. — I do not wish to suggest for a moment that we should allow, or that we ought to allow, our policy to be governed by something that might be said to us by the bankers, but in framing our policy we are always willing to give consideration to any representations that may be made to us by bankers. Any banker who ever seeks an interview is never refused it, and I think never fails to find a willingness to discuss matters. As I said before, I would not admit for one moment, speaking for the Bank, that there is any idea in our minds that we should allow a policy which we think is necessary in the public good to be abandoned simply at the suggestion of a banker, but to any representations made to us from such quarters we always give the fullest consideration.

818. That I certainly agree is the actual fact. Any banker who asks to see the Governor of

the Bank can always see him; the Governor will always receive him with the greatest courtesy and listen to anything he has to say, but I think you will agree with me that that does not constitute discussion of the question, nor does it necessarily imply that the Governor of the Bank of England will give an answer or even discuss an answer? — No, I agree it does not follow. We should not always hold, I think, that it would be right that we should give an indication of our policy in one particular quarter.

819. That is entirely my view also, and I am suggesting, therefore, whether it might not be desirable – I have nothing to say in opposition to your argument against representatives of the banks being admitted to the Board – might it not be desirable that there should be some opportunity for free discussion between the Governor of the Bank of England and representatives of the banks? — I would have no objection, provided it was not to be understood that the Bank had necessarily to produce its arguments in favour of a particular policy, or was under any compulsion to shape its policy according to the opinions expressed by the bankers.

820. *Chairman*: I do not think that is what is suggested. It is rather suggested that there may be a need for greater confidence between the Bank of England and the other banks, and that the other banks might feel that their views should be put before you in collective fashion – not necessarily that they should come to you, but that you should have their views before you and there should be more definite opportunities of contact. That is the suggestion. (*Mr. McKenna*): That is the suggestion. (*Professor Gregory*): I think I was responsible for raising this question originally. While I should not like to be taken as a supporter of all the practices of the Federal Reserve system, it so happens that the constitution of the Federal Reserve system includes one body which might act as a precedent, namely the Federal Advisory Council. The Federal Advisory Council answers questions which may be put to it by the Federal Reserve Board, although, as I understand the practice, the ruling authorities at Washington are under no obligation to follow the advice or adopt the views they express. Assuming it may not be in the public interest for a couple of representatives of the joint stock banks to be on the Board of the Bank of England, is not there something to be said in the present state of things for the constitution of something like an Advisory Council – without necessarily following their advice – with a view to eliciting the opinion of the banking and the business world generally? — Of course, Mr. Chairman, we are getting very near the plane of high policy, and I do not know that I really feel justified in committing the Bank in any shape or form.

821. *Mr. Keynes*: Might not this give an opportunity for the Bank to influence the policy of the joint stock banks quite as much as the other way round? For example, it would give the Governor of the Bank an opportunity, without doing anything that looks sensational, to say on a particular day to the bankers, 'I am thinking of easing out the credit position a bit, but I do not want you to let that weaken bill rates and call money rates in the next week or two. If I allow your balances to increase somewhat may I be assured that you will not let that be an occasion for weakening the bill rate?' — Yes, certainly.

822. One would have thought it would have been quite as important for the Bank of England to get understandings of that sort with the clearing bankers as a whole, just as important that that should happen as that the clearing bankers should have an opportunity of putting their views to the Governor of the Bank. Or again, when it was thought undesirable that there should be certain foreign issues, the clearing bankers are at least as important a factor in that connection as are the issuing houses. If the Governor had the assurance of the whole body of clearing bankers assembled in the presence of one another that they would assist him in the matter in the regular way of business without causing anything in the way of a sensation, might that not be a desirable thing? — Yes. In point of fact, I do not think when it is a question of foreign issues being considered undesirable that we have ever hesitated to express our opinion to the other bankers. It is true, as I say, that the relations have been informal, but they are fairly constant with most of the bankers. What you want is something rather more formal I gather.

823. More regular rather than more formal. — More regular. Please understand that I am speaking for myself without having consulted a single one of my colleagues. Anything that tends to promote contact, co-operation, understanding, I welcome myself.

824. *Professor Gregory*: I think you understand that we are all of us rather feeling our way in this matter. We are very anxious to obtain your personal views without in any way committing the Bank, but it does strike one that machinery is provided in foreign countries which may have some bearing on the problems which we have to discuss as a Committee. (*Mr. Keynes*): It is true that this bears on high policy, and I have matters of very high policy in mind. It appears to me that perhaps the greatest dilemma of the banking system at the present time is that what is the right policy from the internal point of view may be the wrong policy from the external point of view. Well, now, if we depend upon *laissez faire* and automatic working and inscrutable actions it may be impossible to avoid something that is done for external purposes having unfavourable internal reactions. But if you had a joint policy between the bankers and the Bank of England by which an act of the Bank of England was allowed to have its full effect

externally and was prevented by the bankers from having an unfavourable effect internally, currency management might be put on a different plane. Perhaps our chief difficulty is in keeping the bankers from pursuing a different internal policy from what suits the external policy, but I cannot see how that can be avoided if the Bank, which primarily depends upon the working of economic law consequent on its acts, has no definite understanding with the individuals who by their daily actions determine what happens internally fully as much as, if not more than, the Bank of England itself. (*Chairman*): Mr. Keynes has formulated a very large issue and I would suggest that it should stand on record until the Governor comes before us. You will give him notice of that question, Sir Ernest? — Yes.

825. *Chairman*: I do not think Sir Ernest is called upon to answer at present. I think we might pass to the next class of your evidence. — I was dealing with relations with foreign Central Banks. The question is sometimes raised: Most foreign banks have statutes or definite regulations, why should not the Bank of England have the same? I say the cases are not comparable. I think I have said much of this before. We are the product of evolution. In the case of many foreign countries, most foreign countries, central banking is a new plant; in some cases they have not the people trained up in the tradition of central banking, the work has often to be placed in the hands of people whose only knowledge of banking has been gained in ordinary commercial banking and who, therefore, have not only got to learn what central banking is, but have got to unlearn a great deal of the objects which they have pursued as commercial bankers. We do our best to help them, but the work must be slow. For myself, I am satisfied it is making progress. We meet with a remarkable degree of friendly co-operation in some quarters, in others we find still an attitude of reserve and I might almost say some appearance of suspicion as to our motives. It has even been alleged, it was alleged in the Press at one time, that the object of the Bank was to set up a Federal Reserve system in Europe, with the Bank of England and the Governor of the Bank of England at the head of it. Well, of course, the suggestion was and has always been ridiculous. I think we are convincing our friends abroad.

You asked me, Mr. Chairman, whether I would say something in this connection regarding Australia. There, I confess I am in a little difficulty. I went to Australia as an invited guest, with no prompting from this side, but I had not been there long before I discovered that there was a feeling abroad in some quarters that I had been sent by the Bank of England in order to secure some object for this country at the expense of Australia. It was often being brought home to me, and I had to use every bit of such discretion as I may possess in order to try and allay that feeling. In talking about Australia I am in this difficulty. The Commonwealth Bank treated me very frankly, they gave me absolute access to everything, and it would be difficult to discuss the subject without perhaps revealing matters which I have no right to reveal. I should prefer to be excused at this moment from saying anything on the subject.

826. I think we respect your difficulty, Sir Ernest? — I have great hopes that things are really moving in the right direction at last, though I confess that progress has been slow.

827. *Professor Gregory*: You are probably familiar with the fact that the conversations between the Governor of the Bank of England and the various personalities connected with the Federal Reserve system have been very freely handled by Committees of Congress from time to time. Do you not think that that rather strengthens the case, I will not say for immediate publicity by the Bank of England, but for something like an Annual Report in which the British point of view can be put? I would entirely agree with you that American opinion is extremely suspicious of international co-operation, but assuming that international co-operation is inevitable and is in itself desirable, is there not something to be said for the views of American politicians as expressed in published documents in America being corrected by published documents or a statement of facts by the Central Bank in this country? — Your question reminds me of another point that I had intended to touch upon, this very question of the suspicion which seems to attach to any movement of a Bank of England representative outside this country. When the Governor goes abroad all sorts of wild rumours immediately appear in the Press, that he has gone to arrange for a credit or something special of that character, when the visit is probably nothing but a visit of courtesy to discuss questions of mutual interest on terms of equality. What worries me is the thought that if we embark on a policy of explaining matters of a character so simple, ordinary, and I should say necessary, where are we to stop? There might be circumstances in which questions of real importance and yet unsuitable for publication were involved, and if we then offered no explanation, what would the result be? The matter is full of difficulties I assure you. But I think, Mr. Chairman, if I were really to discuss the subject very fully I should keep you beyond the limits of the time which I have still left to me.

828. *Chairman*: I think we have pursued this topic adequately. I am particularly anxious now to hear what you have to tell us about your new financial machinery and rationalisation. That is an extremely practical side? — I am just coming to that, but before I pass to that I have something to say that may interest the Committee merely as one illustration of the way in which we try to perfect our own internal organisation. With the object of ensuring

that our Executive shall work as a combined team with a single purpose, meetings are held twice weekly of about ten to twelve of the senior members of the Officials with the Governor presiding and the Deputy-Governor also present. At these meetings everyone present is free, and indeed is invited, to report on any matters of importance which may have occurred since the previous meeting in the particular branch of the Bank's work with which he is connected. Everyone is free to ask questions, to express comments and to obtain explanations. In this way we try to secure co-ordination of the Bank's various business activities, and the Governor has regular and frequent opportunity of giving such directions as he may think necessary to ensure that everything is proceeding in accordance with the policy which the Bank may for the time being have in view. In addition to such meetings frequent daily intercourse is, of course, maintained between the Governors and the Officials.

Now, Mr. Chairman, if I may come to industry – and that is the last subject on which I hope I shall have to ask you to listen to me – I said at the commencement that we hold it to be one of the primary functions of a Central Bank to maintain its assets in the most liquid state possible. We do not ordinarily consider it, in these times, to be any part of our duty to finance industry directly, but to safeguard the Central Cash Reserves and so make secure the basis on which the commercial banks may be able to discharge that function, in so far as it is the duty of commercial banks to do so. There must, therefore, be a limit to the extent to which the Central Bank can give direct assistance. But desperate diseases need drastic remedies sometimes, and for quite a long time past the Bank has been trying to discharge its part, as a special operation in these difficult times, to assist industry. For some time our operations consisted mainly of interviews with representatives of many important industries, people of real weight in their respective industries, who could give us really reliable information. Out of those interviews other steps have gradually developed. Various industries have approached us through different channels. We engaged, spasmodically at the start, perhaps, people whom we believed to be versed in the difficulties of industry and competent to act as advisers to the Governor. But, of course, the moment came when we realised that our efforts had got to take a more definite shape, and a short time ago we registered a private company, in which we hold the whole of the capital. Our object was to make it quite evident that this business was something distinct from our normal functions. We obtained the whole-time services of various experts, technical, accountancy, legal, and one who we thought, having had very close contact with labour and labour questions, would be able to voice in the discussions the views and feelings of a responsible and well-informed representative of labour. Well, up to the present, four such experts have been definitely engaged, who are Directors of this company and are devoting the whole of their time and energies and enthusiasm to the company, and I think I can claim that they are each of them worthy representatives of their respective spheres. We find that very often there is need for somebody to give a financial lead. The root of the trouble is often financial. I am not going to attempt to say where I think much of the blame lies, but in essence the trouble is often financial, and, obviously, if the Bank of England itself is to find money, or if it is to be able to go to other financial quarters and induce them to find money, there are certain conditions which the Bank is entitled to lay down. The Governor is Chairman of this company, and the Bank Court has other representation on the Board.

829. What are the objects of the Company, as set out in its Memorandum? — In the first place, to advise industries. You have one of the Company's Directors here; perhaps he can tell you more about it than I can myself, but the main objects are to advise industry, to examine schemes for reorganisation, rationalisation, and so on, to advise where we think schemes may be unsound, if we do think so; to the extent to which it is legitimate for us to do so, to provide in some cases some of the initial money, to ensure that schemes are of such a nature as to justify appeals for financial assistance in other quarters; and all with the object of getting these industries into a position in which they can appeal to investment credit. There is a lot of talk, of course, about credit for industry, but there is a tendency to think only in terms of bank credit. The difference between the functions of bank credit and investment credit is too great a subject for me to attempt to deal with, but our object is to try and get such distressed industries as come to us to recognise that, as a first condition, they have got to put their own house in order. We are not going ourselves to provide money, nor are we going to try and induce others to provide money simply to bolster up any industry which in the absence of adequate reorganisation is in itself obsolete and inefficient, or uneconomical, and which has no chance of meeting on a proper competitive basis the competition of new and reorganised industries in foreign countries.

I am glad to say – and I take this to be evidence in support of the existing character of the Bank Court – that we have, through representatives on our Court, access to varying and important financial circles; we know, therefore, that on the financial side we start with goodwill, and many of the members of our Court have given an immense amount of time and trouble to the consideration of these matters. We have, in principle, their absolute support. If schemes are brought to us, they are examined by the Directors of this company, who are experts, who are our advisers; they are then considered by the full directorate of the company, with the Governor and other representatives of the Court, and thus have to pass through another sieve, that we may be quite sure that, on the financial side, they are sound, that their capital position is not top heavy, over-weighted with prior charges, and so forth. If, then, they are considered to be really in the public interest, the Court of the Bank are, within the limits which we must of course maintain, prepared to find, if necessary, moderate amounts of initial cash, and we have already secured in principle the sympathy and support of various financial circles who are prepared to help when help is shown to be justified, but always with the ultimate view of trying to engage the sympathy, the interest and the support of investment credit. I want this to be clearly understood because, here again, I have had responsible people, whose word I can accept, come to me and say that it is alleged that the Bank of England, in entering the industrial field, is in fact trying to secure permanent additional business. I mention the point, though I need not, I am sure, tell this Committee that, of course, there is not a word of truth in it. It is clearly recognised amongst ourselves that the amount of money we are prepared to employ in this class of business, bearing in mind the need for the maintenance unimpaired of our ability to discharge efficiently our primary functions, has to be regarded as a revolving sum, and that as soon as we have put an industry on its feet and can feel assured that it is in a condition in which it can fairly appeal for investment credit, it is for us to withdraw and to secure the release of our money so that it may be available, if necessary, for the help of other industries.

830. Have you had a number of schemes of that sort? — Well, of course, we started with a case which has already been mentioned, though it does not really come into the picture because that was a matter affecting one of our own old banking clients; that was the case of Armstrong's. Another which perhaps hardly comes into the picture either, because it was of a different character, was when the Government of the day decided to embark on a scheme to provide credit on moderate terms for agriculture. Now, if I may take that case: the Bank of England had no interest in agriculture, had not a penny piece embarked in agriculture, and never regarded it as their duty to give direct assistance to agriculture; but, at the request of the Government, they did call the bankers together and invite them to join in supporting the scheme. I think, very largely owing to the appeal which was made to them by the Governor of the Bank, general agreement was secured. The scheme did not, I believe, command support in every quarter, but the proof of the pudding is in the eating. I have not the figures before me, but quite considerable applications, I understand, have been made for assistance under the scheme, and are still being received in some volume. And what is perhaps more remarkable still – I do not know whether there are any Scotsmen present, but a Scotsman generally is as quick as anybody to discern on which side of the bread the butter is – Scotland is I understand clamouring to be brought into the scheme.

831. *Mr. McKenna*: The bankers or the farmers? — The farmers, the agricultural interest; they are demanding to share in the scheme. There are difficulties, of course, owing to the differences in Land Law between Scotland and England, but efforts are being made to find a way round them.

The first real case, perhaps, which occurred was the Lancashire Cotton Corporation. That was a case where we were approached by the industry. We went very fully into the scheme and we realised that wherever the fault lay for the condition into which the industry had got – and I am not going to attempt to apportion the blame – there was a number of bankers interested also and, therefore, it was obvious that we ought not to go forward without moving in conjunction with them. The Governor invited the bankers to meet him and we had many discussions. They found us, I am afraid, sometimes rather hard, simply in our anxiety to ensure that the new undertaking would start without a top-heavy capital position. But, even there, there are limits to what we can do. It is no business of ours what money any commercial bank may have in any field of industry, and it must be for the commercial banks to determine entirely for themselves, with a knowledge of their own obligations, their own positions and so on, and, bearing in mind their primary obligations to their depositors, what they can do, how far they can go. Therefore, we have in such a matter to act with a certain restraint. But at the same time, I will say, it is fair that I should say this, that the bankers as a body have, generally speaking, given us their very loyal support and help. Now, the progress of the Lancashire Cotton Corporation – some of you very possibly know more about it than I do – has been slow, but we are assured by those whom we can trust that it has been sound, that it is steadily going forward, and that it is going to be a success.

Another case we went into was Beardmore's. We followed exactly the same procedure there. We had the representatives of the company, we had our own technical advisers, representatives of the banks interested, and just the same sort of discussions took place, and a scheme was eventually devised. I believe there are those who criticise it, but, of course, it does not mean necessarily that, when we have devised a scheme for a particular concern, that is the end of things. The Governor is a man of vision, and it is remarkable how often his visions come true. I know it is in his mind – I believe it is in the minds of those who are working loyally with us – that these schemes are only one step on the road. It may be that you put on its legs a Company which is engaged in doing all sorts of diverse operations which could be performed much better if they were severally linked up by the process of what is called rationalisation, with corresponding work in other Companies. Therefore, in some of the steps we take, we do not regard them necessarily as complete operations in themselves, but merely as stepping-stones to further operations at a later stage. I said that, of course, if we were to put up money, or if we were to invite other financial quarters to find money, we impose certain conditions. As one of them, I mention the degree of promise afforded by the schemes for the reconstruction of works, the reorganisation of the capital position, and so forth. Then we claim the right to assure ourselves that those who are to be in charge of the industry are qualified, that the technical people are really qualified from the technical point of view, that there are representatives of accountancy who can really keep a proper watch, and control and give advice on the side of the accounts, that there are financial advisers who can be relied on from the point of view of finance. In that way, we do claim a right to a certain measure of control, but only so long as we have our own money there or money put there at our instigation, or on our invitation. I do not know that I can enlarge further, Mr. Chairman, on the subject.

832. *Chairman*: I suppose this system is designed to bridge the gap when the investing public will not take up an industry which is in a depressed condition? — That is our intention.

833. It may be induced to assist it if, by your intervention it is put on its legs? — That is so, the industry having its own part to do in really facing realities and being prepared to cut out dead wood. It is a painful process, and, of course, we are sometimes met by a reluctant attitude, not unnaturally, but it is an operation that has got to be gone through; inefficient or uneconomic industries have got to face it.

834. *Mr. McKenna*: Would it be correct to say that the existence of this company has been a matter of secrecy? — No, it would not. It is registered. It is a private company. As a matter of fact, I have a cutting from a newspaper dated last Saturday, containing a reference to the fact, giving the names of the Directors. It does not mention it as a company actually, but calls it an Industrial Council. It was referred to there. We have no desire to make any secret of it whatever.

835. *Mr. Keynes*: Who are the Directors? — The Directors are at the present time the Governor, Sir Andrew Duncan, Mr. Frater Taylor, Sir James Cooper, Mr. Bischoff and Mr. Frank Hodges. We may add to the number. Obviously, if you have an expert in one particular industry and you decide to tackle another, you may want to enlist an expert in that particular industry. We place no limit on the number.

836. *Mr. Newbold*: What is the name of the company? — The Securities Management Trust.

837. *Mr. Frater Taylor*: You used the name of Armstrong's a short time ago. Should not that have been Vickers-Armstrong? — Well, Vickers-Armstrong. It is true we were concerned in Vickers-Armstrong, but for the reason that we were primarily concerned in Armstrong's; the latter were our clients; we had no connection with Vickers, and our connection with Vickers-Armstrong arose out of our connection with Armstrong's, when it was decided to cut off the armament sections of the two concerns and amalgamate them into a single unit.

838. *Mr. McKenna*: What is the capital of this company? Is it a nominal or a large capital? — Nominal. We finance it entirely.

839. You may remember that, at the time of the formation of the Agricultural Mortgage Corporation, there were communications between the Government and the heads of the commercial banks. Was any communication at that time made by the Bank of England to the commercial banks saying that they were helping in the formation of the Agricultural Corporation? — Undoubtedly.

840. Was any indication given at that time of the formation of this company? — The company at that time did not exist. The need for this company has arisen owing to the extent to which this work has increased, and our desire is to put the principal part of the duties into the hands of experts, merely retaining for ourselves a sort of supervisory position, and that degree of control which must rest with those who find the cash. The company is of recent formation.

841. *Chairman*: What is the date of registration? — I do not suppose it is more than a month or two ago.

842. *Mr. Lubbock*: I take it that the formation of the company was to a considerable extent made for technical reasons? — For technical reasons.

843. And the work could just as well be carried on with the gentlemen you have mentioned as expert advisers of the Governor? — Obviously there are certain classes of security which we may have to hold with our money for a time which are not suitable securities for a Central Bank, and we decided that it would be better that it should be a separate concern severed from the Bank of England *qua* Central Bank.

844. *Mr. McKenna*: I understood from your previous evidence that it was through this company that the Bank of England had operated? — No; not until recently.

845. As I was engaged in discussion with the Bank of England at that time with regard to the subject I could not understand it. — No, I am sorry if I misled you.

846. It is of quite recent formation? — The company is of quite recent formation.

847. *Mr. Newbold*: Is it concerned entirely with British industries? It is not going in for foreign reconstruction as well as British? — None at all.

848. You have done a great deal of that with foreign Central Banks, have you not? Take the Anglo-Austrian? — It is true if you refer to the National Bank of Austria.

849. No, the Anglo-Austrian Bank of Vienna. — Yes, we have; but there were special reasons. You will remember that when the War broke out the Bank of England, at the request of the Government, undertook very large obligations in connection with acceptances in the London market, and that forced us into certain positions which we have been engaged ever since in gradually liquidating. It is that alone which has established any connection between ourselves and such an institution as the Anglo-International Bank.

850. *Mr. Bevin*: Sir Ernest, you were very careful in your evidence to say that you did not apportion blame, but take the cotton industry, or any other industry you like, would you agree that one of the real difficulties that has brought them to their present position was over-capitalisation following the War? — I think it is one. Of course, it has been brought home forcibly to us that the War did compel certain industries to embark on large capital expenditure to meet national requirements, to incur large indebtedness and – I am thinking now more particularly of armament firms – they were left afterwards with this load of debt on them, none of which was productive, because the product of that expenditure is no longer required, of course.

851. I appreciate that, but to what extent do you think, for instance, Lancashire cotton was brought to its parlous condition by the dissipation of reserves owing to bad finance after the War? — I would rather answer that another way. I do not profess to be a profound student of various industries, but I have been told by people who have studied the facts that, in regard to many of the most successful industries of the present day, industries which are often the target of very hard words from the ordinary uninformed critic, as regards their wealth, their present distribution of profits and so on, if the history of those industries is studied – I am told – it will almost invariably be found, that for years, in their initial stages, the owners of those industries were contenting themselves with very modest drafts on the profits and were pouring profits back into the industry the whole time and building it up.

852. That is a good thing? — Undoubtedly, but it has put them into a position, unfortunately, which does make them a target now for uninformed critics.

853. I am not thinking of those who have distributed profits as being the target; I am thinking of those who have got hold of firms like Lancashire cotton, who had done what you say they had done, poured their money back into the industry over a number of years; somebody comes along – names are well known – gets hold of the shares of those companies, pays a low price for them, and, in a short time, disposes of those reserves. That is what has happened in many of these firms? — I am told it happened. I do not pretend to have studied particular cases.

854. The Bank of England, through this company, is seeking now, after all this has happened and whatever the cause may be, to put these firms or put these industries on their feet. When the Bank has got the industry going again, it then leaves it without that parental control and guidance, and so the industry goes back to the ordinary management. I think that is what you say? — Our idea is that, having put an industry on its feet, it is no part of the Central Bank's duty to keep a permanent interest in industry, and we should like to be out of it.

855. One of the ways you have put it on its feet is to take a very conservative view so far as reserves are concerned, is it not? — Yes.

856. We may get a boom in that industry. Do you think it would be wise that there should be legislation or some other protection of that industry against the possibly unscrupulous city financier who sets out to get hold of the industry for the purpose of getting hold of the reserves? — It is a very big question that; I am afraid I have not considered it.

857. I want to put it another way. You start off with a prosperous business, with good reserves that have been built up for two purposes, to equalise dividends and, further, to stand the strain even of wage costs when you have to cut prices during a slump, or something of that kind, and so you tide over the breach. Since the War our experience has been that those reserves have been wickedly dissipated. Then the workmen associated with the industry have to face a demand – they are told it is a purely temporary adjustment to meet a difficulty – for heavy reductions of wages in that industry, and then the industry goes along the long weary road of five, six or seven years to bankruptcy. The bankers pour money in, having so much there they pour in more in the hope that they will not lose what they have already there, and so the industry goes along that weary road until we get to the crisis we are in now, with no reserves and no means of readjustment. Then your company steps in. But the workman has had six or seven years along the weary road to bankruptcy. That is our problem, and in 90 per cent. of the cases our experience is that there is wicked dissipation of reserves. I agree that pouring the money back into an industry, after reasonable interest has been paid, is sound finance. Looking at industry with the experience that you have gained as a result of your expert knowledge, do you think that this Committee ought to recommend that some steps should be taken to protect industry itself against these, shall I say,

unjust custodians, who might dissipate its reserves, and so prevent the industry standing the strain in a cycle of depression? — Well, I cannot honestly say that I have considered the point.

858. *Chairman*: The point which impresses me too is this. You step in in the most beneficent fashion and you rehabilitate the industry. Then, very properly, it not being your business to conduct an industry, you retire. Now that the business is rehabilitated, what security is there against a repetition of the same class of operation as has undoubtedly been disastrous in some cases in the past? But I think that is more a matter of the form of the company rather than the finance. (*Mr. Bevin*): I was rather wanting to get some information on the subject from somebody who has had experience of the reconditioning of these industries. I quite appreciate Sir Ernest saying that he does not want to criticise anybody, but I think we must find a witness who will tell us and who will criticise somebody. (*Chairman*): I think we will get that. (*Mr. Bevin*): We will get somebody, but probably not those who have been engaged in the actual reconditioning. If this expert body has been looking into the affairs of an industry, nobody else can give us such valuable information. (*Chairman*): I think Sir Ernest must, in the course of his investigations, have discovered the symptoms to which you allude, Mr. Bevin, and it may be that he has been engaged in finding a remedy for such a process? — (*Witness*): May I say, if an expression of opinion on that point is wanted from the Bank, I think you would get a much better informed and more authoritative opinion from the Governor, who has been much more closely connected with this branch of the Bank's work than I have. (*Chairman*): It is obviously important, because if the Bank of England takes its part in rehabilitating an industry, one does not want its work thrown away. (*Mr. Bevin*): In 90 per cent. of the serious labour disputes that you can select in the industries of this country, you can place the blame in large measure on the dissipation of reserves and on bad finance and on the change of attitude towards the control of the industry as it existed prior to the War. (*Lord Bradbury*): Might I ask Mr. Bevin exactly what he means by 'dissipation of reserves'? Does he mean the waste of the substance of the company by mismanagement or by distribution of excessive dividends? (*Mr. Bevin*): By distribution of bonus shares for example. (*Mr. Tulloch*): The bad finance in the Lancashire Cotton Trade is admitted, but that is not the cause of the trouble to-day.

859. *Mr. Keynes*: To an outsider it would appear that the obstacle to rationalisation is not so much the difficulty of obtaining finance once a fairly sensible scheme has been framed by the industry itself, but the difficulty in framing this scheme, either on account of the obstinacy or the old-fashioned ideas or the selfishness of Directors, contrary to the interest of the industry as a whole, or of a desire of the banks to exploit the full value of any securities on which they have a lien or perhaps of reluctance on the part of the banks to put pressure on their customers in what is not purely a banking matter. Has the Governor of the Bank of England any hope that reorganisation through the company which he is building up will help in the solution of those problems, that is to say, knocking together the heads of the Directors and knocking together the heads of the clearing bankers? — Yes. Undoubtedly a good many heads have been knocked together already.

In closing my evidence on this subject I should like to suggest to the Committee that the fact that the Bank has been able to undertake this work in the field of rationalisation ought to be regarded as striking testimony of the wisdom of the arrangement under which the Bank is permitted to operate free from restrictive Statutes or Regulations other than those which they may make for themselves, for it seems to me hardly conceivable that had such restrictions existed the Bank would have had the power to intervene as they have done with a view to the betterment of industry.

860. *Chairman*: I think, Sir Ernest, on behalf of my colleagues and myself, I ought to express to you our indebtedness for the valuable evidence that you have given us. You have given us a great deal of information and, if I may say so, you have shown great candour. (*Witness*): I should like to express my gratitude to the Committee for the kind and, if I may say so, gentle way in which they have handled me. I have tried to give a really frank picture of things as I see them. If, in your later discussions, there are any other points on which you would like further information as regards methods, practice and so forth, of course I am always at your service. (*Chairman*): I think in your case our gratitude will take the form of a lively sense of favours to come. We shall have to resort to your assistance again. In the meantime we can give you an interim dividend of thanks.

... ...

Wednesday 26 March 1930

The Right Hon. MONTAGU COLLET NORMAN, D.S.O., Governor of the Bank of England, called and examined.

3317. *Chairman*: Gentlemen, this morning we have the advantage of the presence of Mr. Montagu Norman, the Governor of the Bank of England. I may say, as I think you know, that I have had the advantage of one or two informal conversations with the Governor with a view to deciding in what way we might best avail ourselves of his assistance. We came to the conclusion, as I reported to you before and I think you agreed, that the best plan would be in the first place to ask the Governor to come, as he has come this morning, to survey the position with us generally. He has been good enough to say that he will be happy to come on subsequent occasions and discuss with us other aspects, perhaps more detailed aspects of our problem, as they develop in our hands. The purpose of this morning's meeting is really, if I may say so, introductory. I propose to ask the Governor to give his general survey of the position in which we find ourselves in relation to finance and industry, the approach which the Bank has made to those problems, and the outlook as he conceives it.

Mr. Norman, I think you are familiar with the Terms of our Reference which I may just recite once more. Our Committee was appointed 'to inquire into banking, finance and credit, paying regard to the factors, both internal and international, which govern their operation, and to make recommendations calculated to enable these agencies to promote the development of trade and commerce and the employment of labour.' Our inquiry, as you will appreciate from the Terms of the Reference, is of a very wide character. The operative part of our Reference is to make recommendations, if we are able to do so, which will promote the development of trade and commerce and the employment of labour, and those recommendations, of course, will relate themselves to the financial aspect because the inquiry is into banking, finance and credit. This morning we should much appreciate an account of your own survey of the position in which we find ourselves just now. We all recognise the exceedingly grave position in which commerce and industry find themselves. The papers this morning remind us of the steadily growing volume of unemployment and the difficulties which industry and commerce are experiencing in re-establishing themselves under post-War conditions. We realise that the relation of finance to these problems must necessarily be intimate, and we appreciate that no one is better able than you are to assist us in ascertaining the true relations between finance and industry and the nature of the problems which arise. I think that in the first place we would like to have from you a statement as to what we may call the financial presuppositions of the position as you conceive them to be just now; how far in your opinion finance has to do with the present emergency; how far it is possible for finance to assist in the present emergency; how far the existing regime has proved adequate under the strain and stress to which it has been exposed; and how far it may be necessary to develop or alter the policies that have hitherto been pursued.

I have given this rather rough outline of our position to you in order that you might see where we are. We have already had a considerable amount of evidence more or less of an expository character descriptive of the existing system. We have also had a certain amount of critical evidence, and we have had among ourselves a good deal of discussion, but we are now approaching the stage when we wish to get closer to the questions before us, having in view that it will be our function ultimately to make recommendations. We recognise that whatever be our recommendations, the Bank of England, owing to the position which it occupies, will necessarily be the prime instrument for carrying into effect any recommendations which we may make in relation to finance so far as they may commend themselves to Parliament and to the Executive. It is therefore most desirable that at every stage of our progress we should keep in touch with you and ascertain how far you can assist us, not only in formulating our proposals, but also in indicating to us how far they are practicable, and how far in your view they would be of public advantage. Would you be good enough to start our meeting by giving us, in the first place, a short statement of your approach to the present problems? — Well, Mr. Chairman, the first thing I wish to say is that I owe you perhaps and the Members of the Committee some apology for not having appeared before you at the end of last year, when you were good enough to invite me to do so, and I regret that the circumstances which prevented my coming were beyond my control. I hope you will take it at that. Next, I am glad to make this first appearance before you, and I hope you will give me the opportunity so often as I can of coming again in order that I may attempt with you, if you will, to disentangle some of the difficult problems which undoubtedly lie ahead of us, as perhaps we have in one way or the other disentangled some of those problems which are behind us, because that, I believe, to some extent has been accomplished. I should like to do that because I believe that we can all help one another, and I do not believe it is possible to have a position in which one section of us will benefit and the remainder will be harmed. It is all either up or down together, broadly speaking.

Before I try to go into that very complicated outline which you sketched for me, and which I doubt if I shall achieve in one attempt, I would like to give you in a few minutes some sort of picture as to what over the last few years I have been trying to do, because just the same as all things have a background so I – by which I mean the Bank which I represent – have a background. If I look back a certain number of years during which time I have been working at the Bank, without attempting any exact chronological review, I see that, running throughout the whole of that period, we have had to deal with certain special problems in addition to normal questions. There was, for instance, the troublesome question of perpetual maturities of Debt occurring practically from year to year and giving us no respite. That has been a more or less continuous trouble, internal problems of that kind. But there are two other things externally to which over those years I have really devoted the greater part of my time.

The first of those – long, troublesome, and in some ways disappointing – was the stabilisation of the European countries which had lost what they had possessed before the War. That, which I thought, and still think, was necessary, although difficult in many ways, is to-day, and has been for some time in the main achieved. The second thing was in many ways more difficult, and to some extent has been less achieved, but is in process thereof; that was to bring about co-operation among the Central Banks of Europe and the world on the sort of lines which were originally sketched at Genoa. The latter followed the former. The second was difficult; many personal questions have arisen and still arise in connection with it, but, after all, in my view a great deal has been achieved by the work that has been done in one way and another, by one person and another. It was not in all instances carried as far as one hoped it would have been; it was not always possible to carry it through with the assistance of the League of Nations as at one time one had hoped would be the case, but by and large a great deal has been done and the so-called B.I.S. which is about to be set up is in many ways the climax of our efforts. Those two endeavours have been to that extent accomplished.

A year or two ago we were forced, as I think, to look closely at the position of industry in this country with which previously we had practically no direct contact, and with which as a Central Bank many persons think that even now we should have nothing to do. Nevertheless, owing to the special difficulties and uncertainties in which industry has been, and I think in many ways still is, and having accomplished, so far as one could, the two external operations which I have described to you, we turned to industry, and, unusual as it may be, we have devoted during the last year or so and are still devoting efforts to an attempted study of industry, mainly the heavy basic industries of this country. I do not know whether, technically speaking, we were right or, technically speaking, we were wrong to do such a thing, but I do know that the situation in industry appeared to be such that if our action was theoretically wrong it was in the circumstances a trifling sin that we committed and well worth doing, and I do not regret for one moment having attempted to become interested in this subject. To put it in a nutshell, the information which I have received leads me to believe and hope that the salvation of industry in this country, without which commerce and finance cannot long, or indefinitely, continue, lies in the process of rationalisation, as it is called, which I am not going to attempt to define, which has been defined in many varying ways, but to which I am a strong adherent,' and it is towards the goal of rationalisation, however it be precisely defined, that I hope the Bank of England will contribute as much as it can over the times to come. Now, there are many in this room, I feel sure, who know far more about the industries of this country than I know or shall ever know, because I do not claim any special knowledge about them in detail, and it would ill become me, therefore, to attempt any sort of an essay or to make any dogmatic statement on a subject which is so complicated and difficult and obscure, but, broadly speaking, I believe, if I may say so, that the salvation of industry in this country lies first of all in the process of rationalisation, and that is to be achieved by the unity or unification or marriage of finance and industry. I should like to think, Mr. Chairman, that one of the chief objects and results of your Committee will be that you will bring about that unification between industry mainly in the North, and finance mainly in the South, each of which I believe can contribute enormously to the benefit of the other and to the benefit of the whole of this country. That is how I should look, in a word, upon the object which I hope you will achieve and in which I should like to be allowed to help.

Now, I must say, if I may continue for a moment on this question of industry and our part in it, that just as it is no proper part of a Central Bank's normal business to investigate or have directly to handle industry as such, so a year or so ago, having already made some short progress in the investigation of industry, we planned to form as a matter of convenience a small company in order to segregate these particular operations, and it is through that company we have been endeavouring to deal with such of the difficult and wide questions which have arisen to which as yet little contribution has been made. I wish to say right away, too, that although we did establish that small company in our crusade for segregating such industrial investigations and activities as the nation might need, so I looked upon that as merely a stepping stone, and I am now about to take another step in which I hope sooner or later we shall have your assistance and goodwill, Sir, to establish another company which will unite the City as a whole in showing a willingness for the time being and over a certain period of years to assist industry towards the goal of rationalisation. Now, have I said enough, or do you wish me to go any further, or what do you want me to do? I have given you a picture.

3318. I think we appreciate what you have in prospect. I should like, however, first of all, to have from you your view of the existing interaction of finance and industry; how, in your view, does finance influence industry; how do the two come into contact, what is the relation between the two; because, in my lay mind, I do not understand clearly yet how the operations of finance affect industry. You have very responsible duties in connection with the regulation of the financial system of this country. I think everyone agrees that those decisions have very important repercussions upon industry. I should like to know from you how you figure the interactions between what you do in high finance and the actual practical commercial and industrial position. Because if you take these important decisions as you do from time to time and they have consequences throughout the length and breadth of the land affecting every employer and employé, it is very important that we should see how you conceive that your decisions interact with the industrial position. You see what I mean? — I think I see what you mean; but if you would ask me a more precise question perhaps I could better give you an answer. I have not in mind a method by which I could answer satisfactorily so general a question.

3319. Let me put it in this precise form. You have from time to time to consider whether you will raise or lower the Bank Rate, which is one of the chief functions of the Bank of England. Have you in view when you raise or lower the Bank Rate what are or may be the consequences to the industrial position of the country? — I should answer by saying that we have them in view, yes, but that the main consideration in connection with movements of the Bank Rate is the international consideration, and that especially over the last few years so far as the international position is concerned – certainly until the last few weeks – we have been continuously under the harrow.

3320. It would be interesting for you to tell us how far you are a free agent in this matter and how far you are under the compulsion, on the one hand, of the legislative scheme under which you work, and, on the other hand, of the international position over which you have not got control. How far are you a free agent? — I should say, so far as the legislative position goes, we are a free agent, but so far as the international position goes, if I judge the second part of your question rightly, we are not at all a free agent, but that the whole of the international machinery is bound together and that however much or little it may be recognised, it necessarily works as a whole, as, indeed, it should do, and that in point of fact what is called the gold standard is the cement by which it is bound together.

3321. And, accordingly, if the international position is dislocated or not working harmoniously you are really at mercy? — Not only if it is not working harmoniously – though that may make matters worse – but we are subject to whatever conditions may dominate the international position, certainly.

3322. Therefore, we may take it that when you have to consider the question of raising or lowering the Bank Rate, the predominant consideration in your mind is the international position? — At times it would be the predominant consideration. At times it might cease to have that importance, but over the last period of years the international situation has undoubtedly been the predominant consideration.

3323. Then carrying it a step further, is it because international movements are depleting the stock of gold in this country that you find it necessary to arrest that course by increasing the Bank Rate? — It may come down to that ultimate question of the stock of gold, or it may come down to the general question of rates of interest and confidence. There are many other precise forms that it takes, but, generally speaking, that is true.

3324. Of course, the power which resides in the Bank of England of raising or lowering the Bank Rate is an instrument of the very greatest possible significance, I think you will agree. If that instrument is used for the purpose of preserving the stock of gold, is it effective for that purpose? — It is effective.

3325. How far is the instrument with which you are equipped effective for the purpose? — It is effective.

3326. For that purpose? — It is effective in my opinion.

3327. Equally you will recognise, I think, that while that instrument so used by you may be effective in achieving the particular object you have in view, it must simultaneously have internal consequences upon the credit of the country. You have to look both outwards and inwards? — The two are parts of a whole, I agree.

3328. Yes. One of the problems to which we have been addressing ourselves is whether the use of the instrument of the Bank Rate, effective it may be in achieving the purpose you have indicated, may not be accompanied internally with unhappy consequences. You may be effecting an operation of great value from the financial point of view which has nevertheless unfortunate repercussions internally by restricting credit and enterprise. Your instrument may be doing good in one direction and harm in another. I should like to have from you your conception of the internal effect of the alteration of the Bank Rate. Externally you say it achieves its purpose of arresting the flow of gold if you raise the Bank Rate. Internally, how do you conceive that it operates? — Well, I should think its internal effect was as a rule greatly exaggerated – that its actual ill effects were greatly exaggerated and that they are much more psychological than real.

3329. Yes? — Much more psychological than actual.

3330. The same would apply to a reduction in the Bank Rate – the benefit accruing from a reduction in the Bank Rate? — Yes. I do not mean to say that a large variation in the Bank Rate, a difference of three points or whatever it may be, does not bring about a wider change than that, but I have always thought that in the process of change from one rate to another, the difference is much more largely psychological than it is actual.

3331. But even if it has psychological consequences they may be depressing consequences, and may be serious? — Yes, but not so serious as they are usually made out to be, and I think that the benefit on the whole of the maintenance of the international position is so great an advantage at home, for industry, for commerce, for——

3332. You take the large view. In your opinion, I gather, the advantages of maintaining the international position outweigh in the public interest the internal disadvantages which may accrue from the use of the means at your disposal? — Yes, I think that the disadvantages to the internal position are relatively small compared with the advantages to the external position.

3333. What is the benefit to industry of the maintenance of the international position? — This is a very technical question which is not easy to explain, but the whole international position has preserved for us in this country the wonderful position which we have inherited, which was for a while thought perhaps to be in jeopardy, which to a large extent, though not to the full extent, has been re-established. We are still to a large extent international bankers. We have great international trade and commerce out of which I believe considerable profit accrues to the country; we do maintain huge international markets, a free gold market, a free exchange market – perhaps the freest almost in the world – and all of those things, and the confidence and credit which go with them are in the long run greatly to the interest of industry as well as to the interest of finance and commerce.

3334. One of the criticisms which has been made is that while the policy pursued may have been excellent from the point of view of the financiers of the City of London, it has not benefited the industries of this country – that the considerations which have moved that policy have been directed rather to the financial side than to the plain man's industry? — I know that is said. Of course, industry has had ill luck, shall I say, and has been in a very unfortunate position and from one reason and another has suffered particularly. I agree; I am sure that is true.

3335. There has been no doubt a conspiracy of causes at work? — Almost; yes.

3336. But among the causes at work many minds apparently maintain the view that the deficiencies in our financial system are at least partly to blame and that some revisal of financial policy is necessary. You referred a few moments ago, Mr. Governor, to the project of rationalisation. That, if I may say so, speaking for myself, seems to be merely the sort of thing that people ought to do in any circumstances, put your house in order, see that your business is right and so on. We have always known that good organisation and good management produce better results; in one sense there is nothing new in that; it is a new phrase, a new word, and these long words become very attractive to popular imagination. Now, rationalisation means nothing more than putting businesses in order when they have got out of shape. But that does not seem to me to go to the root of the matter. It does not really deal with the kind of problems to which we have got to address ourselves, namely, the pre-suppositions of the whole system on which we work, the control by the Bank of England of the Bank Rate as the main instrument of policy. It is a question whether those things are working at the present moment for the public advantage, or whether it is not necessary to devise some new expedients. May I put this to you? The very fact that the Bank of England has recently, for the first time in its history, embarked upon entirely new activities seems to me to indicate that the Bank of England has realised that this country is at this moment in a quite unusual position calling for unusual remedies, else why has the Bank, so to speak, left the seclusion of Threadneedle Street and gone down into the streets of the City? It must be because something is in the air, something is happening just now which has never happened before which calls for a review of that position, and even in your case has caused you to emerge from your seclusion and embark upon courses which, whether attractive to you or unattractive to you, you felt it your public duty to engage in. All that is symptomatic and indicative of something being at work just now which has not been in our experience before. How far do you think that position in which we find ourselves, the position of abnormality, is attributable to financial considerations? Have you thought out how far the existing financial structure provides adequate means of dealing with this abnormal position? Finance is no doubt needed to enable a business to re-equip itself and rearrange its working. That has always been going on on a larger or smaller scale; we were familiar before the war with amalgamations of bodies that desired to achieve economy and efficiency. But apart from the finance of rationalisation it is the pre-suppositions of the financial structure of our country upon which our attention at the moment is concentrated, and we are anxious to scrutinise it to see whether it is at that door that the present distress can be laid, and then to see how far it can be aided by any financial expedient. You see how I am looking at it? — I think it is not our financial system which is the cause of our difficulties.

3337. You think it is not a financial question? — I think it is not a question where finance is the difficulty.

3338. May I just add one other thing to your consideration of the problem, because it is important. We are now, I think, round this table, fairly familiar – thanks to Sir Ernest Harvey's admirable exposition – with the normal working of your system and, indeed, all are prepared to pay tribute to the marvellous efficiency of its working within what I may call a normal range. But all instruments are devised to work within given conditions and I gather that in the view of many experts your system has got jammed – in short, that it has been asked to do things that it was not intended to do and that it is breaking down under the strain. The very fact that you have moved out into new spheres is itself symptomatic of a sense of uneasiness that the present system is inadequate and that new systems must be devised. You say you think that the present system is still adequate. Is it still adequate in a world in which the elasticity of adjustment which I should have thought was essential to the adequate working of your system is not attainable for either economic or political or other reasons? If a machine gets jammed it will not work, and may it not be that some of our troubles at the present moment are due to trying to deal with financial problems with an instrument which was designed to deal with other and more normal conditions? Speaking for myself – I do not know in the least whether my colleagues would approve of the way I am putting it – that is the kind of problem that presents itself to me? — Broadly speaking, I do not think that the financial machine is at fault. I think, to use your expression, that industry has had a series of – misfortunes, was it?

3339. Yes. — Or mischances over the last few years and, as it were, has jammed. I think that although rationalisation is a new word, it is an old process; it is an old process which has largely fallen into disuse and it is also, as intended to-day, on a different scale, so different a scale that it is almost a difference in kind as well as in degree from what was originally had in mind. I have never been able to see myself why for the last few years it should have been impossible for industry starting from within to have readjusted its own position. I have never been able to see it on broad lines, taking not companies but industries practically as a whole, which is what I have in mind. I have never seen, and I do not see to-day, why that should not have been done. I know many who are interested in industry who believe that it might have been done. I believe that had it been done the whole face and prospect of industry would look different to-day. It is this long period of mischance, of being in a jam, which seems to have disheartened industry. I do not think myself that that is the fault of finance, except in so far as finance is dependent on a certain international position and certain international liaisons from which it cannot and should not detach itself or attempt to detach itself.

3340. Of course, industry is largely affected by the price level? — I agree.

3341. And one of the most amazing experiences through which we have been passing has been the fall, if I may use the journalistic word, the phenomenal fall in price levels? — Yes.

3342. Has not financial policy something to do with that? — I believe practically nothing in so far as the most recent and heavy falls are concerned.

3343. *Mr. Bevin*: I would like at this particular point to ask Mr. Norman whether or not he does not think that the action of 1925 just made that jam in industry complete, when we as industrialists were given a task of adjusting to the point of 10 per cent. without notice and without any chance of even considering the question? — I think that the change of 1925 – and I have no doubt we are both referring to the same change——

3344. Yes. — was inevitable, made at the right time, but, as the Chairman has said, certain misfortunes of one kind and another have subsequently intervened and have made any effect which that change of 1925 might have had far more difficult and serious, but I do not attribute the ills of industry in the main to that change, and had that change been made and not been succeeded by other things which have happened, I do not think——

3345. But in view of the fact that it did involve facing the workpeople of this country with a proportionate reduction of wages, did it not make the misfortunes that you describe absolutely inevitable? — No, I do not think so.

3346. That is what happened? — I do not think as a necessary consequence.

3347. How could it have been done? You are Governor of the Bank of England. I am a Trade Union Official. That is the point we had to face across the table. I am taking from 1921 up to the point of 1924; I am meeting the industrialists who do not know anything that is in the mind of the Bank of England on the financial policy of this country. They have no knowledge that you are going to interfere, that you are going to restore the gold standard, that you are going to do anything. We met morally the first period of deflation in 1921 when the first step to deflation was taken. We knew that we had to face a heavy reduction of money wages to get a post-War adjustment. We proceeded from 1921 onwards meeting employers across the table and getting that post-War adjustment to a new price. Contracts have been fixed on that new price, new standards have been worked out, men are becoming accustomed to that, to that level of earnings, to everything on the new basis. Suddenly the whole thing is upset by the steps taken in 1925 which throws every bit of work that the two parties in industry had done out of gear. We are faced with rising unemployment, bitter disputes, and a new level of wages to be fixed, without notice, without consideration, without guide, without any indication as to what its object is. I ask you, Mr. Norman, if industry is placed in a position like that, whether or not you do not think the misfortune of the jam is absolutely inevitable? — No, I do not, Sir.

3348. *Mr. Newbold*: Why? — So far as I can tell you – of course, this is a very technical matter which I——

3349. *Mr. Bevin*: No, it is a question of broad policy. You used the term 'marriage.' If industry had been married to finance and we had known how the two minds were moving and what we had to face, that is one thing, but we are left ignorant of this secret operation which is one of the prime factors of industry, and we get this sudden jam? — Action has to be sudden when it comes.

3350. *Mr. Newbold*: Why? — Because it must take effect from a certain date.

3351. Can you not give an indication in advance that it will take effect? (*Mr. Bevin*): I am anxious, Mr. Chairman, to test this point that finance has had nothing to do with the misfortune of the jam. As an industrialist constantly having to handle the problems of nearly half a million men my difficulty has been that while the industrialists and I may build up the best relations possible, suddenly this third unmarried factor in industry – if I may use the term – can operate in a way which destroys all the domestic relationships that exist between us. That is the point I wanted to get at. (*Chairman*): I thought it was more or less accepted that what happened on the reversion to the gold standard did subject the industrial machine to a very severe strain, but that in your view and the view of those who had charge of the policy, the considerations in favour of the reversion to the gold standard were so dominant as to make it worth while to incur even those jolts and strains. I understood that was your view? — That is quite right, and had it not been for other factors which have intervened as I believe since, that would not have given you, Mr. Bevin, the reason to complain as you have done.

3352. *Chairman*: Let us examine that a little. It is an interesting point. It may be that the consequences of the reversion to the gold standard have been greatly aggravated by other conspiring causes. Everybody would agree that it is not the sole culprit, so to speak, and that other causes have unfortunately aggravated the result. May I take it that at the time when the big change over was decided upon it was thought that the time was apposite? — It was thought as I remember it that the time was apposite.

3353. Was that because the circumstances as they were then conceived were thought to render the change as little disturbing as possible? — As little disturbing as possible, and the fact that a decision at that moment had to be taken to go either to the right or to the left.

3354. But were not the hopes that the change would be made with the least possible disturbance to a large extent falsified – in short, those who thought that the time was apposite and who prophesied that the change could be made with comparatively little disturbance were out in their calculations, because it turned out in the event that it did cause very considerable disturbance, either by itself or in association with those other causes. You see what I mean? — Yes.

3355. It may be quite true that a person says now is the moment to do a thing, now is the most favourable moment, and that is, of course, a judgment proceeding upon a survey of the whole position. Those who came to that decision may have been wrong in their survey, or things may have occurred to falsify their prediction? — I should think it was true that some of the events which occurred in association with or subsequent to that change were unexpected in regard to time and extent, and have made the position of industry as you have described it more difficult than was foreseen. I have not the exact sequence of events very clearly in my mind; it was some years ago – but that is the impression I have.

3356. That is how it appeals to me following up Mr. Bevin's point, that if all had turned out as was expected, or shall I say, hoped, the disturbance with which he and those associated with him were confronted would have been much less serious? — I agree.

3357. But in consequence of the other causes that have conspired since that time to falsify that expectation the result has been, in fact, very serious? — Very serious for industry.

3358. And if these circumstances which have supervened had been foreseen it may be that you would not have reverted to the gold standard at the time you did? — I will not say that.

3359. That is, of course, speculation? — Yes.

3360. *Mr. Keynes*: May we ask what those other circumstances were? — I think they were very largely France and Belgium – the stabilisation of France and Belgium.

3361. Their return to the gold standard? — Yes, at certain levels. Germany, for that matter, too. As I remember it those were the principal questions.

3362. You mean their stabilising their money at a low level rather than at a high level? — At a very low level.

3363. *Mr. Newbold*: What do you think induced them to do that at a very low level while we did it at a high level? — I do not know. I think the levels they chose were largely fortuitous.

3364. *Mr. McKenna*: Following Mr. Bevin's point, can you tell us what are the conditions which you would regard as opportune for reverting to the gold standard? — I could not deal in general terms with a matter which might be subject to such varying conditions.

3365. Would you not regard the external value of sterling at the time as a major condition? — As a condition, certainly.

3366. As a major condition? — Maybe as a major condition.

3367. If you found that the external value of sterling, say, the value of sterling in relation to the dollar, was such that the price level in this country was considerably higher than in the United States, would you not regard that as an unfavourable condition for returning to the gold standard? — I should not take that as an argument itself in favour of it. By and large, taking all the considerations into effect, at the time it was considered, I was then, and I am now, of the opinion that the right step was taken.

3368. It would be very interesting if you could recall the considerations to mind now? — There was a Commission, or Committee, which sat on this question for some time.

3369. Yes. Were you acting upon the recommendations of the Committee, then? Were those the considerations which guided you? — I should say so. I think Lord Bradbury was on the Committee.

3370. *Lord Bradbury*: Yes. The phenomenon to which Mr. McKenna refers, the approximation of the rate of exchange to the old gold parity of the dollar, took place while the Committee was sitting, before any recommendations were made. I think, if I remember rightly, the actual difference at the time the Committee reported, as regards the exchange parity, was only something like 1½ to 2 per cent. The exchange had gone up to pretty nearly the old parity. (*Mr. McKenna*): I do not want to go back upon the circumstances of that time, but I am rather under the impression that the sterling exchange was forced up in relation to the dollar at that time. (*Mr. Brand*): I should imagine that when committees were sitting to discuss this question there was speculation by everybody in the world? — Not speculation by me or by anybody connected with me.

3371. *Mr. McKenna*: I put my question in the wrong form; I should have said artificial, that is to say abnormal, means were forcing it up – the anticipation that the Bank of England was going to do it gave an opportunity to the speculator which left him speculating upon a certainty? — He took a view, not a certainty.

3372. If he knew that the Bank of England was going to press this policy he was speculating on a certainty? — First of all, he cannot have known that, and secondly, he cannot have known that even if the Bank of England were in favour of a certain view it would be adopted.

3373. *Lord Bradbury*: Is it not true also that American prices were rather on the up grade at that time, and the difference of something like 10 per cent. between British and American prices was likely to narrow? — I have no exact recollection on this point.

3374. *Mr. Bevin*: In fact the disparity that was created for industry by that act of 1925 has not yet been got over? — I am told that it has just about been got over. I cannot give you chapter and verse for it.

3375. Would I be right in assuming that whatever were the circumstances that led to the decision to return to the gold standard on that basis in 1925 the effect of that act upon industry has been to leave us with a million and a half unemployed, or more, for five years? — No, I am not aware that that is a true statement. I do not think that that has been the cause, or the sole cause; I should imagine that a great many other things have contributed to it.

3376. But even in inquiries that have recently been held, with one of which our Chairman has been associated, I think it has been argued that the cost of production, as expressed in wages, must come down 10 per cent. even now to get to the level? — I am not aware of that.

3377. *Mr. Keynes*: Might I go back to points rather of detail arising out of one or two of your earlier answers? You told us that in your opinion the internal effects of a rise in Bank Rate are largely psychological? — Yes.

3378. Is there any relation between the level of Bank Rate which might be forced on you by international conditions and the volume of credit which can be made available at home? — I do not think one necessarily governs the other.

3379. If you had to-day to raise Bank Rate, say, to 5 per cent. for international reasons, do you think that you could make that Bank Rate effective without altering the volume of credit at all? — I do not say that you could for certain, but you might be able to do so.

3380. How would you do it? — Very often, or at times, the Bank Rate makes itself effective, and no steps are taken. It is largely a question of the outlook of the market, and appreciation of the technical position of the market. It does not necessarily follow, I think, that a rise in the Bank Rate has to be made effective by any special measures.

3381. But it is very frequently the case, is it not? — Frequently the case, but not by any means always the case.

3382. If it is frequently the case, do you say the effect of the curtailment of the volume of credit is merely psychological? — No, but I should say that the effect of the curtailment of credit was very small relatively to the whole mass of credit; that it mainly affects short money.

3383. What would you call 'small'? Do you mean if securities at the Bank of England were reduced by, say, £5,000,000 you would call that 'small'? — I cannot name a figure of that kind, because the conditions change so often, and the whole volume changes so often, but what I mean is that the amount of security operations necessary to make a Rate effective is as a rule very small compared to the amount of securities which are in the market.

3384. Of course £5,000,000 would be small in relation to that? — Very small. I am not thinking of £5,000,000 as an absolute figure.

3385. If the amount of assets held by the Bank of England were reduced by £5,000,000 by how much would that reduce bank credit throughout the country? — I think your neighbour would tell you that best.

3386. *Mr. McKenna*: About £50,000,000 – ten times the amount? — I do not know that that is necessarily so.

3387. *Mr. Keynes*: You do not know? — Ten to one is an arbitrary reckoning based on the bankers' normal percentage of cash.

3388. Would the curtailment of credit by £50,000,000 have no effect of any importance on industry? — I do not think it would; I would be surprised if it had much effect beyond the money market unless of course it had to be continued over an extended period.

3389. In some discussions we have had in this Committee I began by setting forth what I believed to be the orthodox theory of the Bank Rate, the theory that I thought all authorities would accept. What you have been telling us to-day very nearly amounts to a repudiation of that theory? — I did not mean to repudiate it, as I understand it.

3390. What I thought was the more or less accepted theory of Bank Rate was that it works two ways. It has the effect on the international situation that has been described today, and its virtue really is in its also having an important effect on the internal situation. The method of its operation on the internal situation is that the higher Bank Rate would mean curtailment of credit, that the curtailment of credit would diminish enterprise and cause unemployment, and that that unemployment would tend to bring down wages and costs of production generally. We should then be able to increase our exports, with the result that the high Bank Rate which was put on to check foreign lending would no longer be necessary. How very essential that double action is I can illustrate in this way: we are an old country, it may be there is not much investment worth while in this country that would yield, say, more than three per cent.; other countries might offer, say, six per cent. Our balance of trade would not be sufficient to discharge all the foreign lending which we should like to discharge, all the foreign lending which we should like to do at six per cent., therefore the Bank Rate would be raised to something in the neighbourhood of six per cent. That would stop investment at home which, by hypothesis, would only yield three per cent. If the sole effect of the six per cent. Bank Rate was on the internal situation we should never recover our equilibrium, because we should always be stopping enterprise at home, we should always be throwing men out of work who were previously engaged for home investment and we should not be getting men into work in order to provide more for export or get more foreign investment. The virtue of Bank Rate is that, while it would have a quick effect on the international situation, it would also have a slow and perhaps more important effect on the internal position, by setting up tendencies to bring about a new level of money costs of production, so as to enable us to have more nearly that level of exports which the international position requires of us. If the effect of Bank Rate on the internal position were of a negligible character all that would not happen. Am I right in thinking that you would agree with that, what I call, perhaps wrongly, orthodox theory of Bank Rate? — I should imagine that, as you have stated it, that is the orthodox theory, taking a long view, and as such I should subscribe to it – I could not dispute it with you.

3391. If that is so, half the point of Bank Rate is that it should have an effect on the internal situation? — Well, I do not think so necessarily apart from the short money position.

3392. And that internal effect would work through the chain of depressed enterprise at home, and unemployment, and it would be only in that way that you could put on the necessary pressure towards the reduced level of money costs in this country? (*Mr. Brand*): May I just intervene for one moment? Would you say that that orthodox theory took account in the old days of the very large supply of floating capital that now moves about? (*Mr. Keynes*): I should say that was one part. (*Mr. Brand*): Would you say that that element is much bigger now than it used to be, and that consequently you might be able to readjust the situation more quickly? (*Mr. Keynes*): That would be only a temporary help to the external situation. The next point in my mind was, that during the nineteenth century the amount of reduction of money costs which one asked the Bank Rate to effect when we were getting out of adjustment internationally was very small, and probably not more than was accounted for by the normal increase of efficiency. Consequently it was very seldom necessary to force money wages down, it merely meant one had to hold back a little from increasing money wages at a time when increase of efficiency would otherwise have justified that. By that means we could keep ourselves in equilibrium internationally. But in the course of the last four or five years we have been asking Bank Rate to effect a much greater readjustment, and asking it to do this at a time when, for various reasons which I need not go into, the level of money wages is very sticky. One of the suggestions put to this Committee was that this stickiness in money wages was interfering with the traditional operation of Bank Rate. When we returned to the gold standard I myself was of the opinion that this would require the reduction of money costs and that that would provoke trouble, but I certainly never contemplated that it would be as difficult as it has been. I should certainly have forecast that by the year 1930 we should have overcome the maladjustment. It is essential to all this argument that Bank Rate does have an internal effect, otherwise we should never get back to equilibrium. If internal prices were changed to an important degree, as they were changed, and if Bank Rate had no internal effect worth mentioning, it seems to me the whole thing would break down. How far would you agree with that? — Applied to a long period I think I should agree with it. I should think there had been that stickiness in respect of wages in this country, and I should think there had been this great variation for the last year or two in the price level quite apart from Bank Rate or financial causes, or largely apart from it – world causes.

3393. I am not saying that financial influences at the time we are discussing would necessarily reduce real wages, I am only saying that they do require us to take the position in the outside world into account; if our relation with the outside world is changed, as it was when we returned to the gold standard, that means that there must be a change of money values in this country. One might effect that change of money values by decreeing, as they have in Italy and in Russia, that money values should be changed; but our method in this country is not to rely on that, our method is to rely on Bank Rate, and Bank Rate operates, as I understand it, precisely by a depression of enterprise when one wants to put values down, by an encouragement of enterprise when one wants to put values up. So it is of the essence of the case that Bank Rate should have an important effect; that when it is raised it should have an effect in the direction of unemployment. That is what you want. Am I right? — Yes, I should think it was, but is there not the question of how far Bank Rate is relative in regard to all the other countries coming into this position?

3394. Oh, from the international position, very much. If we are forced, for international reasons, to a rate which is depressing to enterprise in this country, then all this sequence of events which I have been describing is set up? — Yes, but the rates being relative in the various countries, their effect on the industries of the various countries should be more or less similar.

3395. Except that there might be local conditions in some countries which would support higher rates, either because they are new countries, or because, like Germany, they have greater efficiency? — Yes, or because they have readjusted their industry.

3396. Yes, or it may be that the rate at which they stabilised their currencies made their real wages for the time being so low that their industrialists could easily afford a higher rate of interest than our industrialists – we having stabilised at a higher rate – could afford? — Yes. The instances mentioned a few moments ago I think apply particularly to that – France and Italy.

3397. *Mr. Keynes*: Yes; that I took to be the force of your remarks. (*Chairman*): I do not think the Governor would suggest that an alteration in the Bank Rate would have no ultimate repercussion in this country. I think he must be thinking of the immediate reaction? — I am thinking of the market position in so far as it immediately affects the exchanges.

3398. Would you agree with Mr. Keynes' view, which I think is generally accepted? — Yes.

3399. That that is the ultimate effect of an alteration of Bank Rate in this country? — Yes, I think I should. (*Chairman*): That is the important point.

3400. *Mr. Keynes*: From the psychological point of view there might be a tendency for the business world to expect something that is not going to happen, or it might be because of intelligent anticipation. Is it rather in this instance a case of intelligent anticipation? —In which case?

3401. The immediate psychological influence of Bank Rate is an intelligent anticipation of the market of the result that will flow from Bank Rate in due course? — I do not think the market looks as far as that.

3402. Do you think that if the market were influenced by current delusion, rather than by vision, it might be intelligent all the same? — Yes; almost unconsciously intelligent. (*Mr. Keynes*): Very likely.

3403. *Mr. Bevin*: Having regard to the fact that the workpeople at home have to suffer the biggest blow of unemployment and the depression of their standard of life, can you see any way to separate the national and the international policies, so that the effect of restoring the gold position internationally can be in some way modified in its effect upon British industry? — I believe it is absolutely impossible to have two separate policies.

3404. *Chairman*: Let us follow that up; that is interesting; that is one of the problems – whether you can, so to speak, dissociate your national and external policies. Is it not possible that you can maintain your international policy outwards and by some of those devices which you have no doubt considered, and others have considered, mitigate the internal consequences of your outward policy? — I think not.

3405. *Mr. Bevin*: Supposing, for instance, you have to stop your gold flowing out, and therefore restrict credit, is it not possible to have a conscious direction of credit under those circumstances to the home market? — And to maintain, as it were, two separate supplies of credit at different rates?

3406. Yes? — I do not think so.

3407. Let us assume that it could not be supplied at two different rates. Could the volume of home credit be maintained? — In some circumstances, yes.

3408. Could that be reduced to any sort of method? For instance, assuming your external trade is good, and credit flowed to your external market until you got to a point where gold began to go out, and then you had to restrict credit, and that produced unemployment, is it possible to have, for instance, some direction through public bodies, municipalities, of the whole operation of credit, and therefore while you restrict one form of credit you maintain the volume of home credit to prevent the blow falling upon the workpeople? — I should say it is impossible. I can see no practical way in which that could be done.

3409. Have you tried to think it out? — I have heard it discussed.

3410. *Mr. Brand*: You started by saying that you had to use Bank Rate to regulate the international position. That, in other words, means to maintain stability of our exchanges? — Certainly.

3411. And the maintenance of the stability of our exchanges is not purely an international question; it is a matter of vital importance to our industry? — Of vital importance to all the questions with which Mr. Bevin is dealing.

3412. Would it not be true to say that there are two quite distinct problems, one is the international and the other national? It may be true, and I think is true, that Bank Rate may have very unfortunate effects on industry in one direction, but it may be necessary for industry in other directions in order to maintain the exchanges. It is not purely for the benefit of other countries? — Far from it. They are two parts of the one question, most essentially, and, as I think I tried to say, it is impossible for one part to benefit without the other.

3413. And the real question is whether you can maintain the supply of credit here and at the same time maintain the exchanges? — Quite right. It is.

3414. *Chairman*: You have, I think, tried some expedients, have you not? Were you not a party to an embargo on foreign investment? — Foreign issues.

3415. Foreign issues? — An embargo?

3416. Well, shall we say a deterrent on foreign issues? — Yes; I was.

3417. Was not that policy on the lines of what Mr. Bevin has been suggesting; was not that intended to mitigate to some extent the effect of the international position? — No, I do not think it was.

3418. What was the object of that? — The particular purpose of that was – and it was not very effective, really – to prevent money being lent to foreign countries and exported at a time when the exchanges were adverse or likely to be adverse.

3419. And, carrying it further, to divert that money to internal uses, was it not? — No; it was an exchange question.

3420. If it had the effect of diverting money that would otherwise have gone abroad to internal issues, would it not consequentially assist industry in this country; money, being deterred from going abroad, would be available for domestic industry? — If it were retained in this country and if the rates were equally attractive in the one place as in the other, but I must confess to you that the purpose of that was an exchange purpose right along.

3421. *Mr. Newbold*: And you say it was not successful? — It was successful to the extent that those who were interested in this business were good enough to forego such opportunities of issues as they had, but it did prove impossible, I believe, not to prevent public issues, but to prevent money going away.

3422. *Chairman*: They found other methods of evading it? — Many.

3423. *Mr. Newbold*: Do you not think we might make a similar appeal to their public spirit for renewed regulation? — I think it would be virtually impossible to be successful.

3424. *Mr. Brand*: Do you mean, Mr. Newbold, the whole public? (*Mr. Newbold*): No. I am wondering whether we could not make an appeal to the issuing houses. (*Mr. Brand*): It has nothing to do with the issuing houses; it has to do with every investor. — Mr. Brand will agree that the question which arose, to which the Chairman has alluded, is a question that a small body of people, all very well known to us, and known to one another, were good enough to fall in with such wishes and views as we expressed; but the matter covers a wider field than issuing houses and includes you and me and Mr. Bevin.

3425. *Mr. Newbold*: You do not think it would be possible to make an appeal? — It would be possible to make an appeal, but I do not think it would be possible to make it successful.

3426. I do not think you could, but I thought that was one channel to be explored. (*Chairman*): The selfish interest of the individual naturally predominates? — Yes; and we must remember this is not British, but European, to a large extent. We are doing a great deal of this for Europe. A great deal of the complaint of what happens is with regard to the business we are doing for Europe, which is largely done in London; when we complain that such and such things are passing over the exchange, it does not mean that they are simply passing over on account of this country; they may be passing over for all kinds of countries – Germany, or Switzerland, or other countries. That is the advantage or disadvantage we get from being a free international market.

3427. *Chairman*: Let me put one or two broad considerations before you. It is, of course, the case that the volume of credit in this country is, to a very large extent, in your hands, is it not? — Yes, I think it is.

3428. And that the volume of credit available in this country from day to day must necessarily have some relation to the enterprise of this country? — Yes, some relation.

3429. After all, money has its price, like everything else; you look at money as a commodity which is bought and sold on given terms, but money is just as essential to enterprise as the raw material of that enterprise. Therefore would you not agree that the question of the extent of the volume of credit at any given moment must necessarily relate itself to the encouragement or the discouragement of enterprise at that moment? — Yes.

3430. I really put this quite elementary position for the moment as a basis for discussion? — Of course, from many angles I should wish to distinguish between short money and long money – there is an essential difference between the two.

3431. Again, when the international position requires, in your view, a raising of the Bank rate, that in turn is made effective by restriction of credit, is it not? — Maybe.

3432. And may it not, therefore, have, as Mr. Keynes was bringing out, a consequent deterrent effect upon enterprise in this country? In your view, I take it, that is inevitable, and, possibly, salutary? — I think it may be inevitable.

3433. And again, speaking in the broadest terms, is it your view that the consequences of that internal restriction of credit, unfortunate as they may appear to be, are outweighed by the advantages of the maintenance of the international position? — Yes, there is very large benefit.

3434. I want to get the theory of the thing. The maintenance of the international position, in your opinion, because of its effect upon the internal position is all important? — Yes.

3435. *Mr. McKenna*: Might I put one or two definite questions on quite recent matters? — Practical questions?

3436. Quite recent matters if you will allow me. You have restricted the quantity of credit by selling securities on balance in the first two months of this year. You had less securities in February than you had in December. Is that so? — I am not sure of the exact figures but I should be surprised if the average of the Bank's total assets in February was much, if at all, below the corresponding figure for December.

3437. You do not remember if you restricted credit? — I am not aware that credit was restricted.

3438. I have the figures for February of this year and February of last year. Between February of last year and February of this year you sold many millions of securities? — Oh, yes.

3439. And you reduced credit? — Yes.

3440. The total amount of credit at the end of February, 1930, compared with February, 1929, represented a reduction of purchasing power of the public of £63,000,000? — You mean that the aggregate of certain banks' deposits——

3441. The aggregate of the clearing banks' deposit was less by £63,000,000? — Yes.

3442. Why did you reduce the amount of credit? — For a reason which I believe to have been sound, as I hope you will agree. I am speaking from memory as to figures; the volume of the bankers' deposits in February, 1929, was abnormally inflated, due to a large extent to the unfortunate fact of the failure of a loan issued two months earlier to deal with certain maturities falling due in the early months of 1929. You will remember that an unfortunate event which took place after the issue was announced caused considerable public alarm, and severely militated against the success of the plans which had been made which, prior to that event, had appeared quite promising. In the end the Chancellor was left to find by other means some £60 millions or so to meet in cash maturing obligations which had not been renewed, and in order to do that it was necessary to make special issues of Treasury Bills to that amount, practically the whole of which went to swell the figure of the bankers' deposits by about the sum to which you have referred. Since then, and notably in February, 1930, steps have had to be taken to rectify a position which had been brought about by circumstances which were entirely fortuitous, such steps being intended to deal specifically with an exceptional and peculiar situation and not to form part of a definite continuous policy.

3443. Would you say that the deposits of the banks and the purchasing power of the public to-day are normal? — Yes. I should say that last year's increase, due to the special expansion of the Floating Debt, was abnormal and that it was necessary and wise to correct the position as opportunity occurred, and in my opinion a reduction in the Floating Debt of the Government was essential.

3444. I am not dealing with the Floating Debt? — No, but it has been due to the special operations in connection with the Floating Debt that there has been an apparently abnormal reduction in the bankers' deposits during the period to which you refer.

3445. I am dealing with the deposits of the banks and the purchasing power of the public. In your view, should the deposits of the banks and the purchasing power of the public remain constant year by year, or diminish year by year or increase year by year? — I do not think that is a question to which it is possible to give a general answer. As I have said, the particular fact to which you have drawn attention resulted from a special and unexpected change in the volume of the Floating Debt, and I think it was essential to rectify the abnormal position thereby created and to withdraw the special issues of Treasury Bills then made as soon as opportunity offered.

3446. I am not dealing with the Floating Debt. I am asking about the deposits of the banks and the purchasing power of the public. Is it, in your judgment, right for the industry of this country that the purchasing power of the public and the deposits of the banks should increase year by year, remain stationary year by year, or diminish year by year. One of the three they must do? — As I have said, I do not think that is a question to which it is possible to give a general answer. I certainly expect to see a tendency for deposits to decline rather than increase during the first quarter of the year when the heavy payments of taxation are taking place.

3447. You think that the deposits of the banks do diminish in the first quarter? — I think they are apt to, and often do.

3448. But deposits only increase or diminish according to your action? — Surely payments for taxation diminish deposits?

3449. Yes, payments through taxation go into public deposits out of the other deposits, but you can immediately put them back into other deposits if you like? — Yes, and frequently do.

3450. If you failed to do that, I agree that deposits would be diminished in the first quarter of the year, but if you do not fail to do that the deposits would not be diminished in the first quarter of the year. Is that right? — That may be true but I should approach the matter differently. I look – the Bank looks – to keep the market supplied in normal circumstances with adequate funds. One of the criteria by which we judge the matter is the amount of funds which the Discount Market may have or may need. One of the unique facts about the London market and its position is the existence of the Discount Market. I should never think that there was real pressure for money unless I saw indications that, in the absence of action by the Bank, the Discount Market might find it necessary to apply to the Bank for advances.

3451. Do you not, in considering the quantity of money required, look at the position of industry and the price level and the number of unemployed – do not these considerations come into your mind in considering the quantity of money, as well as the condition of the money market? — All these things are continually in one's mind. They are, I am sorry to say, matters which, it is quite true, must always be present to one. So far as money is concerned, however, the state of the money market is largely the factor by which the position must be judged and generally speaking I should not say that the volume was inadequate in the absence of some indication from the money market that money was in short supply because they after all are the source from which any bank can replenish its needs.

3452. If you saw the price level falling as it has done the last month or so and unemployment increasing as it has done the last month or so, it would have no effect, I gather, on your mind in inducing you to increase the quantity of credit? — Yes, it would have a great effect on my mind.

3453. Only if the money market borrowed? — One of the indications of a shortage of credit would be signs of pressure in the money market, not necessarily expressed by actual borrowing from the Bank.

3454. If the money market did not make it known to you, you would not necessarily by open market operations increase the quantity of credit? — Not automatically; I should consider that the question of price level, for instance, was a factor bearing specially on a review of the international position. I am told and believe it to be true that recent monetary policy in this country, if not in other countries, has had little effect upon recent movements in price levels.

3455. *Mr. Keynes*: If one takes the figures of the deposits of banks with you, apart from accidental events which you have described, they have kept at a very stationary level. Is that by accident or design? — I should say to some extent by design, though not entirely as the result of a definite policy towards that end.

3456. You have been able to keep them at the figures stated? — Parity, let us say, though I do not attribute it to a definite policy of the Bank.

3457. At least 10 per cent. of the productive forces of this country, both men and plant, are out of work and the existing volume of banking accommodation appears to be fully occupied in keeping the other nine-tenths going. Is it not absolutely impossible that that other one-tenth should be employed as long as you pursue what you call the policy of parity?— No, I do not think that is necessarily so.

3458. How could they be? — Perhaps I did not make my meaning clear. It must be remembered that during the last few years there has been no period when we have not had continuously to face difficulties due to the international position, that is, up to a few weeks ago. I do not myself believe that the mere provision of more money to the bankers is all that is needed to meet the difficulties of industry. I believe that industry has a great deal to do for itself in the way of rationalisation.

3459. You would not expect rationalisation to increase employment until a very late date? — Until a late date.

3460. So you look forward to the present level of unemployment remaining for some considerable time to come? — I would not say that, though I agree that the benefits to be derived from rationalisation would not be immediate.

3461. *Mr. Bevin*: And would increase the progress of unemployment? — It is apt to do so temporarily.

3462. You have no suggestion to put to us how the Bank's policy can help us over that interim period? — I am not prepared to make any suggestion at the moment.

3463. *Professor Gregory*: May I come back to some of the earlier points that you raised because I want them to lead up to other matters. Supposing that the Government had offered you in 1925 an immediate return to the gold standard, but at a parity with the dollar 10 per cent. below the pre-War one, would the Bank have been prepared to accept that offer? — I cannot answer that. It is difficult after this lapse of time to answer a hypothetical question relating to the year 1925.

3464. May I take it that the Bank of England was not in 1925 unduly worried by the possibility that the restoration to the pre-War gold standard would unduly interfere with British industry? — I think that is true.

3465. You thought it would be all right? — I cannot now give the precise process of reasoning which one had in mind five or six years ago, but generally speaking what you state is a correct expression of my view at that time.

3466. What have been the main considerations which you have described as mischances? — I think I meant mainly the stabilisation levels in Germany and other European countries and the accompanying circumstances.

3467. I was very much surprised to hear you say that because I should have thought that the real mischances of 1926 and 1927 were not so much by reason of the stabilisation of those currencies at a low rate of exchange, but the continual fall in exchange in France and Belgium. You had two very serious falls in exchange. I can understand that affecting the situation, but would you not be prepared to say that the mischances which affected us in this country were rather the falling currencies in Europe than their stabilisation? — I think so.

3468. Then I think you said the third important point with which you had been concerned was co-operation among the Central Banks? — Yes.

3469. Do you think, looking back over the last few years, you have in fact achieved any positive success through co-operation? — We have laid the foundations for it, I think. I think it is a most interesting and most hopeful thing for the future; a great deal has been achieved and I hope a great deal more will be achieved through the B.I.S.

3470. Would you be prepared to say that the economic situation of the country, looked at from the international standpoint, had in the last few years been at all affected favourably by what you have been able to do? — Indirectly yes, though it would be difficult to point to any direct result.

3471. You are not of opinion that the fall in raw material prices is directly due to anything that we have done in recent months? — No.

3472. I am not certain whether you are of opinion that the fall in raw material prices has aggravated the English economic position? — No, I am not sure that it has; I do not think that it has.

3473. Supposing that British money wages remain constant and coal as an international commodity falls 10 per cent.; then in countries where wages are adjustable as they are in Poland, for instance, they have an international advantage compared with us? — Yes.

3474. Would you in those circumstances be prepared to admit that the fall in coal prices has been a distinct disadvantage? — Yes, I would.

3475. Has there been any attempt among the Central Banks of Europe in recent months deliberately to steer against the tide of falling raw material prices? — There has been no concerted action. Discussion, yes.

3476. There has been discussion? — I do not believe that the value of raw materials can be largely affected, or has been largely affected, by the various banks' recent monetary policy.

3477. Let us go back to your own view as to the effect of Bank Rate, that it is very largely psychological, with which personally I agree. Do you not think that if there is a general prospect of Bank Rate going up that affects the large holders of stocks and raw materials, and that makes them inclined to sell in a panic? Would you not say the Bank Rate works in that direction? — I should have thought so, though I believe on the other hand that low Bank Rates have often been accompanied by low prices of raw materials and I have recently seen expert opinion to that effect.

3478. I should have thought it was inevitable, if I were a carrier of wheat or anything else, that a rising Bank Rate would make me want to sell. May I get back to your view of the relationship between an internal and external rise of Bank Rate? I think you said in answering Mr. Keynes that in your view the effect of a rise of Bank Rate exhausted itself in the open market rather than in industry. What happens is that the volume of credit in the open market tends to fall with the volume of credit generally. It does not tend to fall in industry? — I do not think I said that, did I?

3479. *Mr. Keynes*: I do not think you said that. I understood you to say that the effect fell on the short-term market first? — The short-term market first.

3480. *Mr. McKenna*: I want to have this perfectly clear. Am I right in understanding from you that you do not consider industry requires more credit unless the market borrows from you? — No, I do not say that; I think industry now requires a great deal of long credit subject to———

3481. That is, a particular borrower requires a long credit instead of a short credit. I am dealing now with the total quantity of money. You do not conceive that you need create a larger base for credit unless the market first borrows from you? — No, not exactly that; I said the indication I have that there is a need of credit comes from the market and the market is mainly the buffer between the Bank and——

3482. The indication to which you pay attention, may I put it that way? — One of the indications to which I pay most attention.

3483. What are the other indications to which you pay attention? — I cannot tell you in general terms as they may vary in different circumstances.

3484. I think we may take it that it is an indication to you that an increase of credit is desirable if the market borrows from you? — Not necessarily borrows.

3485. You look to the money market, and if they want to borrow you are satisfied that more credit is needed; if they do not want to borrow you are satisfied there is enough credit? — No, I do not go quite so far as that. That is one of the indications; I cannot say there are hard and fast facts which would guide me in all circumstances.

3486. I take it that the process of reasoning by which you would know would be that if the commercial banks were required to give more credit they would call in more money from the market, which would be consequently driven into the Bank of England? — I should feel it, though not necessarily by the receipt of applications for accommodation from the market.

3487. You would feel it before they came in? — That is what I have endeavoured to convey.

3488. You feel the market. My observation is that it is equally desirable to feel industry? — And we are endeavouring to do so.

3489. Do you have the same contact with industry – no, I think you told us earlier you did not? — Certainly not the same, but I am continually having more contact.

3490. *Mr. Keynes*: The object of international co-operation would be to relieve the international struggle for gold? — Largely to pursue a common monetary policy, and do away with the struggle for gold.

3491. How do you conceive that would help our internal position? — I think if it had not been for the struggle for gold over the last few years, that is to say, the flow of gold from one place to another, caused by whatever event it was, we would not have had anything like the difficulties in maintaining the exchanges that there have been.

3492. How would it help the internal situation if it were easier to maintain the exchanges? — I think the internal situation would have been much easier over the last few years if the Rate had been X per cent. instead of Y per cent., say 4 per cent. instead of 6 per cent.

3493. You mean there would have been less unemployment? — I think there would.

3494. *Professor Gregory*: When you have, for any reason at all, to sell securities, at the moment the gap in the total volume of funds is filled by the joint stock banks calling money in from the market; and you supply the brokers with the money that the joint stock banks have taken away from them. If for any reason Bank Rate is falling, or if for any reason you expand your earning assets, then the pressure on industry can be relieved without deflating the market; that is to say, the aggregate volume of money at the Bank goes up. Industry is only given what money it gets in a period of need through the process of putting pressure on the money market. The banks have to protect themselves in order to assist their customers by taking funds out of the money market which you replace? — Which I replace.

3495. Which you replace at a price? — Sometimes, yes; but there are other ways than by direct lending by which I may replace it. It frequently happens that there is an indication that money is needed; I act on it without waiting for the market to come to the Bank.

3496. Quite; I am not saying that the process is as mechanical as perhaps I have indicated, but if you do put Bank Rate up you induce the joint stock banks to take money out of the open market in order to keep their volume of deposits approximately what they were before? — I am not sure that I do. I do not believe it necessarily has that effect.

3497. It is not what you are doing. It is what the joint stock banks do? — I do not believe it necessarily has that effect.

3498. I thought that we were working out the theory of how the Bank Rate is supposed to operate under present conditions, but if I am told it does not work that way I am merely asking for an alternative explanation of how it does work. I always thought that when Bank Rate went up, the Bank sold securities, and the way the joint stock banks protected their customers was by drawing on the money market? — That is the effect if there is a sale of securities.

3499. *Mr. McKenna*: When they reduce credit we get our cash basis back by calling in money? (*Professor Gregory*): My point is, that if the Bank had not got to restrict credit in that way you could feed both the open market and your commercial customers. (*Mr. McKenna*): Yes. (*Professor Gregory*): The immediate pressure of Bank Rate is felt in the open market, merely because of the action of the joint stock banks in protecting their customers, consequently the pressure on industry is delayed through the action of the joint stock banks. (*Mr. Brand*): The Bank acts by the sale of securities. (*Professor Gregory*): If the Bank of England wants to make its rate effective it is obvious it must sell securities. It may attract a certain amount of foreign money, but not in such a way as to make its rate effective? — The rate frequently makes itself effective without action by the Bank.

3500. Under the conditions of practical English banking, when the joint stock banks do in fact try to protect their customers, repressive action by the Bank of England does not have an immediate deterrent influence on enterprise, because the general industry of the country does not lose as much money as theoretically it ought to lose? — I think that is right. What has been called the first line of defence with the various banks is the short money market and the first way they supply any needs for which they may be called is by calling from us through the market.

3501. Does it not follow that if you were able through international action to increase the volume of credit the influence on business would be an indirect one through stimulating new issues, attracting more bills, rather than directly on the volume of credit demanded by business? — I should think so.

3502. *Mr. McKenna*: In your judgment, if you increase the volume of credit by buying securities, would there be any effect upon industry over a period? — Over a long period; not over a short period.

3503. Over a period of three or four weeks there would be an influence upon industry? — I should not have thought so.

3504. Over a long period, would you think so? — I should think so.

3505. Such influence would not begin to operate for three or four weeks? — I am not satisfied that it would begin to operate as soon as that.

3506. It would not operate in three or four weeks but in the long run you would get more employment if you increased the quantity of credit? — I am not at all sure that you would as a matter of course.

3507. You do not think there is any certain relation between fluctuations in the volume of credit and fluctuations in employment? — No, I am not sure that there is.

3508. You do not know? — There may or there may not be.

3509. *Mr. Bevin*: Rationalisation in industry will need the training of a type of mind in management of a very broad view that can take in many more factors than can the management of a single business? — A single unit, yes.

3510. Do you think the time has arrived when some kind of training for the purpose of taking a broader view of banking is not also necessary to link up the same kind of considerations over a wider field than has hitherto operated? — I think we are getting a training.

3511. I have listened to the evidence of the bankers to this Committee, and while industrialists have been urged to get out of their rut and to take a bigger view, I am bound to say that the very ugly feeling left in my mind is that so far as the City is concerned it is still within 'the mile' in the main, that it does not go outside its own financial 'mile' to consider these wider problems of industry, except perhaps one or two individuals like yourself who have been tackling the problem recently. I am wondering what is being done in the banking world in this matter, coincident with the inducement and the urge for industry to move beyond the single unit; how far it has received the consideration of the banking world and the financial world? — I cannot tell you. You are speaking generally, are you not?

3512. Generally, yes? — Are you thinking that the international knowledge of, and information given by, those who have come before has been inadequate; that is to say, they have not had due regard to the international position?

3513. *Mr. Bevin*: No, I am thinking of their industrial knowledge. (*Chairman*): I think that what Mr. Bevin really means is this. Industry is being urged to rationalise itself. Is it not time that the banks rationalised themselves? Is not that the point, Mr. Bevin? (*Mr. Bevin*): Yes; coupled with this, that if you are going to tackle an industry and rationalise it merely by amalgamating its units and that kind of thing, you may leave it in a worse condition than it was before. (*Chairman*): For the time being. (*Mr. Bevin*): It may permanently. To have a rationalised industry without fairly big minds running it who understand the objects of rationalisation, I think Mr. Norman will agree, may mean disaster. I have not seen that there have been any councils of war or indications in the banking world of what consideration they are going to give to the part they are to play when they get into this married state that has been referred to? — I want to understand what you are saying. The complaint against these bankers, of whom I am one, which I understand you to make – is it that their knowledge of international affairs is too little or that their knowledge of industrial affairs at home is too little, or is it that that knowledge is not sufficiently theoretical, not sufficiently technical, as you would have it?

3514. It is not sufficiently collective; each is moving in his own little circle as far as I have been able to see it. For instance, you have made a statement this morning that in approaching the problem of industry in the future you would look at it from the point of view of industry and not of the community. That is what you said, I think, that rationalisation of a whole industry must be the considered factor? — Yes.

3515. As I have listened to bankers, they still talk of their customers in the limited sphere of firms and not industry, and no consideration, collectively or technically, or from the point of view of national economics, appears to have been given to the wider concept of the position and the part they have to play in it? — They are coming to it. (*Mr. Bevin*): That is encouraging.

3516. *Mr. Tulloch*: I do not think Mr. Bevin

is right in relation to the bankers not considering these matters from a broad point of view. In all those cases where the propositions are sufficiently large, there is a consortium of two or three or more banks. My information is that there is a great deal of discussion among bankers in regard to these larger propositions? — Yes, I think there is. May I say a word? Of course, you may complain of me, Mr. Bevin, or of those bankers you have seen, that the evidence they have given you comes through their nose and is not sufficiently technical or expert. Of course, that may in some measure be true; I plead guilty to it myself to some extent, and it is a curious thing, the extent to which many of those who inhabit the City of London find difficulty in stating the reasons for the faith that is in them. Mr. Keynes must know that very well. (*Chairman*): Of course, I suppose even a trade union leader sometimes acts by faith. (*Mr. Bevin*): And finds that it has been misplaced.

3517. *Professor Gregory*: May I ask on a question of fact: At the beginning of your remarks you said that you did not think that existing legislation imposed any limit on your powers of action. Supposing your two Departments were amalgamated, you would have a larger reserve against your liabilities, do you not think that would mean in practice that a wider range of action was possible for the Bank? — I do not think so.

Chairman: It is ten minutes to one; the Governor has been with us for two hours; I think we should release him on this occasion, but only to ask him to come back later on. We have much enjoyed and benefited by our discussion this morning. We have raised a good many topics – I do not say we have settled them. You will be provided with a short-hand note of the proceedings, Mr. Norman, for your revisal. Thank you, Mr. Norman.

... ...

Friday 16 May 1930

Sir Richard V. N. Hopkins, K.C.B., Controller of the Finance and Supply Services Department, H.M. Treasury, called and examined.

... ...

5314. The first matter on which naturally we should like to have a statement from you relates to the position of the Treasury and the Bank of England. We have already had, as you are aware, from Sir Ernest Harvey, a very full account from the point of view of the Bank, and from him we learnt that the relations between the Treasury and the Bank of England fall really under two heads. First of all, the ordinary relations of banker and client – the client in this case being more than usually exalted – and, on the other hand, the general relationship on matters of policy which are discussed between the Bank and the Treasury. I think it would be useful in the first place if you told us shortly what are the relations of the Treasury to its Bank, the Bank of England? — Very well. The State, of course, in its various activities has numbers of small banking accounts around the country which are kept with the joint stock banks. For example, accounts to which Collectors of Taxes pay when it is first received, and accounts out of which drawings for local salaries may be paid and so on. But while that is so, all the main Government accounts are held at the Bank of England. The leading account, as no doubt you will know, Mr. Chairman, is the Exchequer Account into which come and out of which go all the main receipts and payments of Government, both on income and on capital account. The Bank of England hold a number of other important accounts too, such as the main accounts of the Revenue Boards, of the Post Office, and of the National Debt Commissioners. I ought probably to refer also to the position of the Paymaster-General's office. The individual spending departments of the Government do not have separate accounts at the Bank of England upon which they draw. They draw upon the Paymaster-General, who, as he requires it, draws block sums from the Exchequer Account and acts as a kind of intermediate banking organisation inside the Government.

5315. Does he act on precepts from the spending departments? — In effect, yes. He acts on an authority issued to him by the departments, showing the drafts they have issued to payees.

In addition to keeping accounts, the Bank has from time to time to fulfil another function of a bank in providing overdrafts, and those are technically known as Bank of England Ways and Means Advances. Practically it is only at the dates when the War Loan dividend has to be paid, upon the 1st June and on the 1st December, that those overdrafts are of any considerable amount.

5316. That is to put the Government in funds in anticipation of receipts? — Yes, we have to meet on those particular dates an outgoing for dividend, apart from the ordinary outgoings of Government, of £50,000,000. We build up our balances in a certain degree for a number of days before, and for the rest the Bank usually gives us accommodation which is worked off as quickly as possible in the days that follow.

Then the Bank acts as our agent in the sale

of Treasury Bills, and in the general management of the remainder of the debt. The Treasury, of course and the Bank of England keep a charge of the total debt outstanding and the figures are continually agreed. In addition to that the Bank keeps the detailed register of the holders. It pays dividends, deals with the maturities and registers transfers. In addition to that, of course, the Bank are our principal advisers upon new issues and conversion offers.

... ...

5318. That gives us an idea of the function of the Bank of England as the banker of the Government. But are there other matters upon which the Bank and the Treasury consult and co-operate outside the normal function of banker and client? — Of course, there may be from time to time numbers of matters in which the Government from its point of view and the Bank of England from another point of view may be jointly concerned.

5319. Of course, debt policy is a very large matter in which you are both interested? — That is so.

5320. I think you desire to deal with that at a later stage of your evidence? — I think it might be convenient.

5321. The Treasury has certain interests in currency questions, has it not? You have now a statutory position in that matter? — Certainly. Of course, the control of the currency is exclusively a matter for the Bank of England. It is not a matter in which the Government intervenes, but I understand you to refer, Mr. Chairman, to the provisions of the Currency and Bank Notes Act of two years ago, under which in certain conditions Government action may be required. When that Act was passed for the purpose of completing the action of the country in going back to the gold standard, we fixed the fiduciary issue at the figure of £260,000,000, which, upon the one hand, was presented as a rigid figure in order that the world might see that we were upon a firm gold standard, while, upon the other hand, we provided a means of elasticity and alteration by simple action, without legislation, whenever the necessity might arise.

5322. Formerly an Act of Indemnity was required? — Yes, formerly, to begin with there was a letter from the Prime Minister and the Chancellor of the Exchequer to the Bank promising indemnity, followed, if any actual breach of the law occurred, by an Act of Indemnity, as you say. The present provision is that the fiduciary issue may, if necessity arises, be either increased or decreased at the instance of the Bank and with the concurrence of the Treasury.

5323. *Mr. Keynes*: On that point am I right that the profit to the Treasury on the Central Bank reserve is, roughly, the profit on the fiduciary issue? — It is the profit on the fiduciary issue, less the cost to the Bank.

5324. So if the fiduciary issue were increased the profit to the Treasury would be increased? — It would.

5325. If that were done *pari passu* with the loss of gold by the Bank, the position of the Bank with regard to profits would be unchanged? — I think that would be so.

5326. But if it were to take place in advance of the loss of gold, in order that the nation might feel that there was a wider margin, then it would involve loss of profit to the Bank of England? — Yes, but you would ordinarily expect it to take place at a time when the security holding of the Bank of England was high, and any increase in the fiduciary issue would represent a surrender by the Bank of England of securities which were in excess of their normal holdings.

5327. That would only be if it took place after an emergency had arisen. It would not be so if the increase were made in order to make the outside world feel that the Bank had plenty of surplus resources? — No, I think that would be so.

5328. Is it possible that some adjustment might be made so that no question of an alternative division of profits between the Bank and the Treasury is mixed up with the question of the right level of the fiduciary issue? — Of course, I should agree at once that no question of profit ought to govern a question of so much general importance as that. So far as the State is concerned, I can say at once that we should not be influenced by a desire to gain profit or by a fear of losing profit, the amount being trivial in comparison with the other issues that were involved. Upon the other aspect it is rather for the Bank of England to give evidence than for me, but I am quite sure that the action of the Bank would equally be uninfluenced by the question of profit.

5329. Could there be any means of adjusting the question of profit without altering the law? — I think not, because the actual provisions of the law at present are that the Bank has to pay over to the Exchequer the amount of profit agreed between them and the Treasury upon the fiduciary issue as it actually stands and that it must keep the fiduciary issue covered by securities.

5330. *Chairman*: The question is whether it would be possible to eliminate the possibility of motive. It is not suggested that motive operates, but is it desirable to eliminate the possibility of motive being suggested? (*Mr. Keynes*): Quite apart from anything happening as a consequence of the present provisions, it might be very unfair to the Bank of England that they should lose profit as an indirect consequence of something that was done for the general good? — I should certainly agree that this is a thing that ought not to be allowed to, say, 'influence decisions.' I cannot conceive circumstances in which it is likely to arise and embarrass the Bank. Certainly if a contingency arose it ought to be considered.

5331. *Mr. Keynes*: But it would arise – you have agreed upon that – in any case in which the increase of the fiduciary issue took place in advance of the loss of gold in order to make people feel more confident? — It would have the effect of diminishing the profits which the Banking Department would otherwise make, the Bank would suffer to that extent, but whether that would lead to the Bank being embarrassed or placed in a difficult situation or make it alter its decision and take a different course is another matter. I should much doubt whether it would.

5332. The Bank might be so public spirited that they would not be influenced by this in their actions, but it might be an unfair consequence of the existing law that they should lose by it. (*Mr. Lubbock*) Is it ever likely that the Bank would ask for an increase of the fiduciary issue when they had adequate resources, in order to make people feel more comfortable? Are there not circumstances in which the Bank would not wish the public to feel comfortable? (*Mr. Keynes*) I should have hoped that that provision would have been used in advance of the emergency rather than after it. I should have thought that altering the fiduciary issue when the Bank of England was already short of gold would have been rather disturbing, but an alteration in advance, in anticipation of something happening later on, would be less disturbing. It would be very undesirable that the Bank should be under any influence to put off the public notification of the change? — I would agree with the general tenor of that, but that any such action at any time when it might necessarily arise would involve embarrassment of the Bank, or that it would delay the Bank in taking action which it would be wise to take, is a question on which I cannot give definite evidence because it lies in the province of the Bank rather than mine, but I should be very sceptical.

5333. *Mr. Keynes*: No one would wish to interfere with the fiduciary issue for the sake of some trifling amount. It might well be that the change might be £40,000,000; that would affect the profits of the Bank of England by £2,000,000 a year. I do not know what the profits of the Bank of England are, but that might easily be a sum which might be slightly embarrassing to them, might it not? — I feel, if I may say so, very respectfully, this is rather hypothetical and that perhaps the Bank could give you evidence more authoritatively than I could upon it.

5334. *Chairman*: I think one may put it to you this way, Sir Richard. There has been some criticism upon the provision of the Act of 1928, which, as you know, authorised the Treasury by minute to increase the fiduciary note issue. There has been criticism as to whether that is a real thing or whether it is merely paper, and whether it is intended to be used, and in what circumstances it would be likely to be used. I think Mr. Keynes' point is that one of the elements that might affect the resort to the power which the Treasury possesses might be the element of motive, or, even if the element of motive were not present, the financial consequences of it might be regarded as operating unfairly. That is only one of the factors in the situation. (*Mr. Keynes*): Suppose that the policy of certain other Central Banks in the comparatively near future is to absorb gold, and that we decide that that is contrary both to our own interests and to those of the world, and that we must resist it to the utmost extent and not raise our money rates because of that and we come to the decision that we are going to maintain our own policy as long as we can. It may well be that it would be wiser before embarking on such a course that the Bank should show the public that it has £40,000,000 more to play with than it has at the moment, i.e., that the fiduciary issue should be increased by £40,000,000, in order to show that we were in a position to implement the policy which the whole world knew we were undertaking. At present if that were to be done, there would either have to be an alteration in the law – which it might be very inconvenient to make at the moment – or else the Bank would be forthwith losing profits at the rate of £2,000,000 a year. Without imputing any want of public spirit to the Bank, one can see that they might think twice before undergoing a sacrifice of that kind? — Yes.

5335. *Mr. Keynes*: Therefore I suggest that a law that mixes up the size of the fiduciary issue with the entirely disconnected matter of the distribution of profits between the Bank of England and the Treasury is a bad law? — There is no doubt a theoretical point to be made; but what I am in doubt about is whether it is practical.

5336. You think that the sum of £2,000,000 is theoretical but a larger sum would present a practical problem? — No. We are now considering the possibility of an increase of the fiduciary issue amounting to £40,000,000. Presumably that would be a policy which was undertaken with an intention that it should be permanent or that there should be no alteration for a considerable period of time. Under the Act as it is framed at present, increases of the fiduciary issue may only be made by agreement between the Bank and the Treasury for a limited period of time. I think it will be agreed that large increases of the fiduciary issue of a permanent character should, as is provided, be subject to Parliament. This transaction would therefore come before Parliament in a limited period of time, and if in fact embarrassment had arisen, there would be the same statutory opportunity of putting it right. I think that in advance of a contingency of this kind there is no need to contemplate an alteration of law, which after all is in the direct descent of the law of the last century on the question of the fiduciary issue.

5337. That seems to me the only possible reason for it? — I think that is a very strong reason for it, with great respect.

5338. *Mr. Brand*: Do you suggest, Mr. Keynes, that there should be a revision of the law to cover the case where a loss of profit takes place? (*Mr. Keynes*): I think it would be well to amend the Act in advance, to dissociate the question of profit from the question of the size of the fiduciary issue. I should have thought that in the kind of contingency that I was contemplating, of something that might arise fairly suddenly, and that would not be of a character to last more than two years, it might be very undesirable to hang up your policy? — I feel sure it would not be held up. If such a contingency arose, and in the national interest it were agreed between the Bank and the Executive that action ought to be taken, I am sure it would be taken, and an early opportunity would afterwards be taken of going to Parliament if there were specific necessity for alteration of the law.

5339. *Mr. McKenna*: The possible alteration of the law would be two years later? — Not necessarily so. You can go at an earlier time if you find that there is reason to go to Parliament earlier. The two years is only the maximum period within which you must go to Parliament.

5340. Do you think it a reasonable provision of the law that if in the exercise of their judgment the Bank of England think that circumstances have arisen which call for an increase of the fiduciary issue, they should not be able to increase that issue without paying so much a year to the Treasury, whether they make a profit or not? — As I have said, there are many contingencies which could be visualised in which the Bank need not be suffering a diminution of profit but only forgoing an excess of profit. That answers one part of the case. The other part of the case I agree had a theoretical force attached to it, but whether it will ever mature as a practical issue I do not know. I should hardly think that it was worth while burdening Parliament with legislation upon this matter until it arose as a practical issue, unless after hearing the evidence of the Bank you considered it was necessary.

5341. *Chairman*: The authority is to be for six months, I see, and it may be renewed up to two years, but it may not go beyond two years without Parliamentary sanction? — Exactly.

5342. *Mr. McKenna*: The Treasury can demand payment from the Bank of England for two years without redress. Whatever the Bank of England securities are earning in their Banking Department, that rate would be earned by the Government on the transfer of securities to the Issue Department. (*Chairman*.) I see that the Act provides that 'Any minute of the Treasury authorising an increase of the fiduciary note issue under this section shall be laid forthwith before both Houses of Parliament.' So that papers are laid indicating that such a minute has been issued? — When the fiduciary issue is raised.

5343. *Chairman*: So that the matter may be raised on the floor of the House at once? — Yes.

5344. The Chancellor of the Exchequer would be answerable? — The Chancellor of the Exchequer would be answerable, and if circumstances had arisen which in his judgment justified an alteration of the profit arrangement he would therefore make known to the House of Commons his intention to introduce legislation.

5345. *Mr. Keynes*: An implication of one of your replies was that, if the contingency arose, and the Treasury and the Bank of England agreed that the fiduciary issue should be increased, the Treasury would give the Bank of England some sort of undertaking that they would be indemnified in due course? — Subject to an announcement in Parliament at the time, that might be done. If it were necessary I have no doubt the Minister would feel entitled to give the Bank then and there an assurance, which would be announced in the House of Commons, and that assurance would afterwards be ratified.

5346. *Sir Walter Raine*: Would the adjustment of profit not come as an expense against the fiduciary issue? — It would have this result, that a profit which on the increase of the fiduciary issue would otherwise have accrued in addition to the Exchequer, would not accrue after Parliament had passed legislation to that effect.

5347. *Professor Gregory*: There is one question which arises in connection with what you have said, although it is not, perhaps, germane to this inquiry. When the Treasury borrows on Ways and Means it has the alternative of borrowing from the Bank or borrowing from other Government departments? — Yes.

5348. I wish you would complete your evidence on Ways and Means, and explain what moves the Treasury to borrow in one direction and not in the other? — So far as the Treasury has balances available on the various accounts which it holds, it uses them.

5349. What are the other departments available for this purpose? — The National Debt Commissioners, many funds in the hands of the Paymaster-General, and a variety of other accounts.

5350. What rate of interest do you pay? — A nominal rate.

5351. You said in answer to Mr. Keynes that you thought that perhaps the practice of appropriating the profits from the Note Issue Department to Government was based on the tradition of the nineteenth century. Is it not merely a continuance of the principles that you observed when the currency note issue was under the Treasury? — Yes.

5352. This is really carrying on the currency note principle? — Yes.

5353. *Mr. Tulloch*: With regard to borrowing from public departments, that means to say that those borrowings come out of the moneys which are in the public deposits, does it not? — The public deposits of the Bank of England?

5354. Yes. — That would be so, yes.

5355. I was wondering from what other source they came if not from the public deposits at the Bank of England? — The cash would be in some other Government account included under public deposits if it had not been borrowed by the Treasury.

5356. There seems to be a tendency in case of need to borrow from public departments, rather than on Bank Ways and Means Advances. Is that so? If the Treasury wanted to borrow for dividend purposes would they borrow so far as they could from public departments rather than from the Bank? — Certainly. We use all our available spare funds first. Then we sell Treasury Bills to the market by tender. Only rarely and in the last resort do we borrow on overdraft from the Banking Department.

5357. Does this borrowing on Ways and Means Advances imply a very substantial addition to the bankers' balances? — Possibly you would expand your question a little.

5358. What happens to these borrowings on Ways and Means Advances? It is all credit created, is it not, in the books of the Bank of England for the Government? — Yes. So far as they are borrowing from the Banking Department.

5359. And do you not immediately draw upon that credit and does it not immediately come back, necessarily, to the bankers' deposits in the Bank of England? — They would be paid out, yes, and go to the customers of the banks.

5360. Unless the banks keep them in their till as a reserve they are bound to come back in bankers' balances. Does not that imply considerable fluctuations in the bankers' balances with the Bank of England? — It would be so for the time being, but only to the extent that those sums are widely fluctuating sums.

... ...

5362. *Mr. McKenna*: If the Bank of England in its general control of credit is to keep bankers' cash at a constant level when the Treasury borrow on Ways and Means, the only method the Bank of England has got would be by selling securities to an equal amount. Is not that so? — I think so.

5363. If they sell securities to an equal amount the Bank of England will lose the interest on the securities, which presumably may run to four or five per cent., whereas they are receiving from you, I understand, on the first £5,000,000 only one per cent.? — That is so.

5364. So that the Bank of England, unless they are prepared to sacrifice the difference between one and four or five per cent. in profits, cannot help letting the bankers' balances increase as you borrow? — I hesitate very much to think that these transactions, comparatively small from the point of view of the Bank of England, and arising only twice in the year, are judged in the least degree by the Bank from the point of view of profit.

5365. *Mr. Lubbock*: I think the Ways and Means Advances only last for a few days; they are generally repaid in quite a few days by the incidence of Treasury bills? — Yes.

5366. *Mr. McKenna*: The 'few days' experience shows may increase to a fortnight? — (*Witness*): It may be in some cases a fortnight before they have entirely run off. (*Mr. McKenna*): I think I can show two successive banking returns twice a year containing Government Ways and Means Advances. As a matter of fact the Bank of England in practice do not sell securities to counteract the borrowing by the Treasury on Ways and Means.

5367. *Mr. Keynes*: May I go back to the question of the fiduciary issue. Am I right in thinking that the character of the assets held against the fiduciary issue is not limited by statute? — No, it is not limited by statute except by the use of the word 'securities' and by the reference to silver coin, which is a small matter.

5368. Is it actually determined by the Treasury or by the Bank of England? — It is determined by the Bank of England.

5369. They may put what assets they like into the Issue Department? — Yes.

5370. *Mr. Lubbock*: You are fully aware, I suppose, of any changes that take place? — We receive particulars of them, as I think the statute requires.

5371. *Mr. Keynes*: Sir Ernest Harvey, I think, told us that an amount which is fairly small but not quite negligible is sometimes held in the form of foreign bills or foreign balances? — Yes.

5372. If the Bank of England were to go further than it has hitherto gone in buying foreign bills and holding large resources abroad it is quite possible that the Issue Department might be the most convenient place to keep its assets. Would the Treasury have objection to that? — No, I see no reason why we should object, if that were the policy of the Bank of England. At the time when the Currency and Bank Notes Bill was passing through Parliament the question was asked as to whether the word 'securities' covered foreign exchange of the ordinary kind if the Bank of England decided to hold it, and it was stated by the Minister that the word did cover foreign exchange of that character.

5373. I was not on that point; I was on the point whether this pool of resources is at the disposal of the Treasury in practice or at the disposal of the Bank of England. You say the Bank of England has the sole power of regulating it? — Yes, that it so.

5374. Really! I rather thought it was one of the pools of resources along with certain other things which the National Debt Commissioners and the Treasury between them controlled from the point of view of moving backwards and forwards between long and short-dated securities? — No; you will find in the Currency and Bank Notes Act a provision that the Bank of England shall from time to time give information or render returns with regard to the securities held to the Treasury, but the regulation is by the Bank.

5375. *Professor Gregory*: The profit of the Note Issue Department as stated in the annual Finance Accounts is net? — Yes.

5376. Do you think there is any objection from the standpoint of the State to giving more detail? — I would like to consider the question before actually replying, but there is only the interest upon the assets of the fund; the only other expense deducted from it of any substantial character is the cost of printing the notes.

5377. I take it the Bank of England presents you with more detailed figures than that? — Oh! yes, certainly.

5378. Perhaps you would consider whether there is any objection to publishing the details? — I will consider it.

5379. *Mr. Keynes*: It makes a very great difference to the profits of the Treasury at the present moment whether the securities are such things as Treasury Bills or long-dated securities? — Yes, but so far as the assets are Government securities we are of course paying as well as receiving the interest.

5380. But all the same, the Treasury has no right to take an interest in the matter? — No. This is the backing of the note issue, and as I understand the matter, according to the general practice of central banking the backing of the note issue is always managed by the Central Bank.

5381. Is it not very much interlocked with such questions as the volume of Treasury Bills outstanding? What matters in that connection is the amount outstanding to the public. The amount in the hands of Government Departments and the Bank of England is not really relevant? — Yes.

5382. You are saying that the amount of Treasury Bills held in the Issue Department is determined by the Bank of England, but otherwise the volume of Treasury Bills is in the hands of the Treasury. My point is that the total volume of Treasury Bills outstanding is determined by the Treasury? — Yes.

5383. But the amount in the Issue Department is determined by the Bank of England? — Yes.

5384. So that the thing which really matters, that is, the amount in the market, is the resultant of the action of those two independent authorities? — But it is not the case that we should act in discord on a matter of this kind.

5385. *Professor Gregory*: Supposing the Bank was to reduce considerably the volume of Treasury Bills in the Issue Department, would you regard it as within the power of the Treasury to make representations of that sort? — It would be a matter that would be regarded as a subject for friendly discussion.

5386. *Chairman*: With regard to the amount of the fiduciary issue, a certain measure of criticism has been directed to the power to increase it. We had one witness before us who took the view that that power was really nugatory, because in normal times it would not be exercised and in emergency times it could not be exercised. Perhaps you have heard that criticism? — It was a criticism, Mr. Chairman, which was made the subject of questions at the time when the Bill was passing through Parliament. A statement of some length was made on behalf of the Government with the concurrence of the Authorities of the Bank as to the circumstances in which an increase in the fiduciary issue might be contemplated. If you so desire, I could put the whole of the statement in.

5387. It is all recorded in Hansard? — It is all recorded in Hansard. There were four types of case mentioned as illustrations of cases where the fiduciary issue might be increased. One was the old case of the crisis, which was dealt with by indemnity pre-War; another was the requirement of increased currency due to the growth of trade or population; another was the possibility of embarrassment by the withdrawal of foreign balances; the other was the necessity to consider a new ratio, owing to what may be described as a scramble among the nations as a whole for gold.

5388. *Mr. Keynes*: Can you tell us what is the object of fettering in any way the discretion of the Bank of England as to the amount of the fiduciary issue? (*Chairman*): How did you fix this particular amount? — The amount was fixed by reference to the circumstances for a considerable period before the date of the Act. It was a figure somewhat in excess of the amount shown to be required during that period.

5389. *Mr. Keynes*: Shown in what way? — By the actual issue of Treasury notes – they were Treasury notes at that time – unbacked by gold.

5390. How was it shown that that was the amount required? — That was the amount which was in fact required and was in circulation during that period.

5391. Since the fiduciary issue is fixed not by the amount in circulation, but by the amount that need not be backed in gold, it has no bearing on the amount in circulation? — Perhaps I have not made myself clear. While Treasury notes were issued – nominally by the Treasury, though under the control of the Bank – there was a certain total of Treasury notes in circulation, part of which were covered by Bank of England notes, and the actual figure fixed for the fiduciary issue of £260,000,000 was consistent with the net total of Treasury notes issued, excluding those covered by Bank of England notes for the period in question.

5392. In effect it continued the previous amount of the fiduciary issue? — In substance, yes.

5393. What was the justification for that figure? — That it was the amount shown to be required. I do not think there would have been any justification if it had been fixed rigidly without the capacity for alteration from time to time as circumstances might demand. We named a figure in order to give the necessary appearance of solidity to the credit system to satisfy the world. At the same time we provided the necessary machinery for swift alteration if circumstances demanded it. In other words, in fixing a figure there was a combination of rigidity and elasticity which seemed to us the most desirable thing to aim at.

5394. It was one of those things which you would call 'psychological'? — Yes.

5395. Which has no real meaning? — I think that things which are in origin psychological have a very important meaning.

5396. You mean that if the fiduciary issue had been fixed at a higher figure there would have been a flight from sterling – or what would have happened? — Yes, I think that the world at large might have looked very much askance at that time and in those conditions at what we were doing. In addition to that, inasmuch as we knew the amount which was required in circulation in the conditions then existing, if we had fixed a very much higher figure the Bank would then have been obliged to carry a very high reserve, and, in fact, in transferring all that additional sum in securities to the Issue Department, might actually have suffered that diminution of its profits that you were speaking about.

5397. The economists from whom we have had evidence so far I think have treated the figure as a pure point of convention for which they thought there was no support. You think it really is more solid than that? — Surely. It is a long time ago since I was dealing with this matter, and the figures do not stick in my mind as accurately as I would wish, but in effect the actual number of Treasury notes which had been out in any season for the year, for two years previously – after making the necessary adjustment in respect of the Irish Free State because they were going away from our currency to another – was some few million less than the £260,000,000 that we fixed. We therefore fixed a figure maintaining the existing situation, but providing a little ease even at the time when the seasonal circulation was highest.

5398. I understand how that was arrived at, but how it appears to many economists is this, that so long as gold was circulating and notes were the alternative to gold, particularly in the middle of the nineteenth century, there was a great deal of sense in the system by which you were not to increase your volume of notes unless you withdrew a corresponding amount of gold. When the Act was passed in 1844 there was a great deal of sense in it. It seems very odd that when gold no longer circulated and therefore the reason for which the system was introduced entirely vanished, it should then be wise to decree that the greater part of the gold in the hands of the Bank of England should never be used for the purposes for which it would be useful unless there was an alteration in the law? — I am afraid I do not agree with that. The point, as I understand it, at the back of your mind is that we were foolish enough to use the gold as backing for the notes.

5399. No, we were foolish enough to continue it after having made a law that the gold could not be used for the only purpose for which that provision was originally introduced. The gold was formerly held for two purposes: one, for cash needs in the home circulation; the other for meeting a foreign drain. It was divided in this way: a certain amount of gold could only be used for the first purpose, namely, for cashing the notes from the home circulation. That was the origin of the division of gold into two sections. Then came the change of the law by which gold no longer circulated. Therefore, the gold that was previously used for that purpose was thereafter held for no purpose; it could not be used at all. That struck a great many people as odd, that having divided up the gold into two parts to be used for two purposes and having abolished one purpose, you should still go on dividing the gold into two parts as before and thereby sterilise the major part of the gold from being used at all unless there was an alteration of the law? — Whatever system you may decide to have in regard to your reserve law and the relation of your gold to your note liability or other liabilities, it will always be the case from the practical point of view that your gold reserve has got to fall into two sections. There is the gold reserve which you keep available for loss and accretion from time to time according to the ordinary swing of conditions. Behind that, as I should have thought, and I imagine, every Central Bank would think, it must have a second line of defence. In other words, the Central Bank will not ordinarily be treating the whole of its gold reserve as a figure which may fluctuate down to nil. That being so, the only thing I think that is essential is that in regard to your note issue you should have elasticity. So long as you do not tie the gold or notes to some particular unchangeable proportion the note issue can be allowed to increase or decrease without a necessary relation to your gold holding. That being so, exactly how you would express the relation of your gold to your notes seems to me to be a secondary consideration.

5400. One would agree that there would be a certain part of the gold which would not be considered available except for grave financial emergency, but would it be correct to regard more than two-thirds of the gold as being in that category? — I should have expected so.

5401. *Mr. McKenna*: You did not arrive at that figure on the basis of two-thirds or any other proportion. You arrived at that figure solely on the number of notes that you had in circulation? (*Mr. Lubbock*): The number of notes was consistent with holding about £150,000,000 of gold in normal times. (*Mr. McKenna*): At that time of which Mr. Keynes is speaking, when the gold had a double function, when you determined what your holding should be, you determined it not in relation to a proportion of the total, not in relation to the practice of foreign Central Banks, but solely with reference to your volume of currency, with which it could not have any relation? — We took the system as it was. We put it on a formal basis. For some considerable time Treasury notes, although nominally issued by the Treasury, had been issued by and under the general management of the Bank of England. The change that we made was a formal change; we made nothing more than a formal change continuing the old situation, but into the situation we introduced an element of elasticity which would enable an alteration of the fiduciary issue to be made where desirable, with the immediate consequence that the Bank's reserves would be altered also.

5402. *Mr. Keynes*: What it comes to is whether the form that it has taken is suitable and whether it is a system that adds to the prestige of the Bank of England or diminishes it. I put it to you that not so many months ago the gold reserve of the Bank of England was falling to rather a low figure, so that the excess of gold that they had over what they must hold for the note issue was down to little more than £20,000,000. Would not the prestige of the Bank of England with the world at large have been greater if they had had control of a larger quantity of free gold? How does it add to the prestige of the Bank that it can only get control of that gold by what, if it were done in a crisis, would be regarded as an act of despair, appealing to the Treasury to relax the law in their favour? — To take any such action as is being recommended by you at the time when the Bill was introduced would have necessarily involved a definite change over from the situation as it was to a different situation. It did not seem to me then - with respect, it does not seem to me now - necessary to have made any change in the system as we had it, provided only that we gave the system elasticity.

5403. Is your ground that the prestige of the Bank of England before the world with its reserves fallen to £20,000,000 is greater than it would have been if it had power to draw on more gold; or, if not, what is the reason? — No, that is not the reason. The reason is that in taking a formal step in 1928 we thought it right to formalise the position as it was at that time.

5404. Yes, I think that is a complete answer on the issue that at that time you were not wishing to make any substantial change, but it is not an answer to the point as to whether a substantial change should not now be made? — (*Witness*): This is a point, Mr. Chairman, to which I have given no special thought recently, and before I agree to the suggestion made by Mr. Keynes I should like to think carefully about it. I confess to feeling rather sceptical. (*Chairman*): I think you will have a good many questions on which you would like notice. (*Mr. Lubbock*): I think the point of Mr. Keynes' question was whether two-thirds of the gold now held should be held for use only in the last resort; whether that is not too great an amount to hold for that purpose. (*Chairman*): Or, at any rate, would it be better if the world could see the Bank of England in a position to draw on larger amounts than it does now without asking leave of anybody? (*Mr. McKenna*): Whether the Bank of England has sufficient room within the £260,000,000 to meet special emergencies as they arise from time to time, and whether they ought not to have larger freedom.

5405. *Mr. Keynes*: There is another subject upon which I have not yet touched. The amount of gold which is immobilised not only depends upon this total of gold held, but also upon the amount of circulation of notes? — Yes.

5406. And the circulation of notes is partly in the hands of the public and partly in the hands of the joint stock banks? — That is so.

5407. Consequently, if for any reason the joint stock banks vary the proportion of their reserves between balances at the Bank of England and notes it has an important effect on the amount of gold at the Bank of England which is free for export. Is not that entirely irrational? — It could be made to be irrational no doubt by, shall I say, fortuitous action on the part of the banks.

5408. Capricious action? — Capricious action.

5409. Is it not the fact that the banks have very largely varied from time to time the amount of their note holdings? — I do not think we have any knowledge of it; I should assume not.

5410. We have asked for figures, we have not yet received them, but there have been indications, I think, that there have been substantial variations. This has, as a consequence, that the free gold reserves of the Bank of England depend on the proportions in which the joint stock banks divide their cash between notes and balances at the Bank of England, when there is no connection between the two things; is it not *prima facie* foolish? — Mr. Chairman, Mr. Keynes has been kind enough to agree that I should have an opportunity of thinking over the problem; I have not had an opportunity of pondering it for a long time. I would like to think it over.

5411. *Mr. Brand*: I suppose the situation might arise when the note holder would consider that there was some relation between the gold and notes; even in this country if gold were to disappear altogether, whatever the law, the note holder would ultimately begin to think? — Certainly.

5412. *Mr. Keynes*: Supposing there were to be, which is not absolutely unthinkable, some moment of internal crisis in which the public chose to carry about rather more notes than usual, supposing the active note circulation increased by 10 per cent. – which would represent a very small amount – the effect might be for the Bank of England to deplete its reserves, unless you call into being the special powers by decree at a moment when for obvious reasons it might be the very worst possible time to do it? — That is true, assuming you think the powers ought not to be exercised.

5413. Why should the amount of gold which the Bank of England has to keep immobilised depend upon a consideration of that kind? (*Mr. Lubbock*): Is that so? Surely it makes no difference to the Bank of England gold holding whether the bankers hold notes in their tills or pay them into the Bank of England? (*Mr. Keynes*): Yes, it makes a great difference to their reserve. (*Mr. Lubbock*): Withdrawals of gold from the Bank of England always come through cheques drawn on joint stock banks. (*Mr. McKenna*): They come out of your reserves. (*Mr. Lubbock*): We are talking now of the conversion of the Bank of England reserve into gold. (*Mr. Keynes*): No, the reserve is the measure of the amount of gold it can export. (*Mr. Lubbock*): If the joint stock banks wanted to export gold they could always get gold by paying in notes. (*Mr. Keynes*): If the banks were to have £10,000,000 less notes in their tills and increased their balances at the Bank of England by £10,000,000, that would increase by £10,000,000 the amount of gold that the Bank of England could export; in fact, it is probable that the banks do hold a good many million more notes than they strictly need; so that the intentions of the present Act could be, fortunately, defeated by the actions of the joint stock banks. On the other hand, it might operate in the other way, and, so far as the public was concerned, it would seem very undesirable that the Bank of England reserves should sink to next door to nothing because for some reason the public were taking more notes into their pockets. (*Mr. Lubbock*): If the Bank of England reserves sank to nothing, the bankers' balances would sink to nothing. (*Mr. McKenna*): If the public increased their demand for circulation by £50,000,000 and your reserve is £50,000,000, your reserve would become nil. (*Mr. Keynes*): If it were not to provoke a crisis the Bank of England would have to replace the notes by purchasing securities to the amount of the reserve. They would have just as much gold as before, but it would all disappear into the Issue Department. (*Witness*): I should like time to consider this.

5414. *Chairman*: Certain matters have been brought to your notice to-day which are typical of the existing legislation, they fit into the present framework. It is quite proper that this Committee should examine that framework to consider whether in any respects it is susceptible of improvement? — Certainly.

5415. Mr. Keynes and others have raised one or two points which are fundamental to that consideration, and we would like to have your observations; first of all, whether these points that have been brought to your notice are, in your view, practical points, and, if so, whether they are things that should be remedied. No system is perfect, and the criticisms which have been made to-day may be criticisms worth considering. One of the purposes of our Committee is to make recommendations which will facilitate the working of the financial system of this country, and we shall be glad if you will let us have your opinion of those criticisms which Mr. Keynes makes. (*Professor Gregory*): I wish that you would consider, Sir Richard, how it would be possible to implement the undertaking which was given by Sir L. Worthington Evans that the fiduciary issue would be increased from time to time to meet the demand – what would be the criteria which could be adopted? — Yes.

5416. *Mr. Keynes*: I should like to make a constructive suggestion. Accepting your criterion, which I think is a very right one, that there should be a certain amount of gold which ought to be used for emergency purposes, perhaps the right law might be that the gold reserves of the Bank of England held against the notes should not fall below £x millions, whether you put it at £50,000,000, or £75,000,000, or £100,000,000. You would say, 'There is a reserve of gold which is only to be used on occasions of crisis, by agreement with the Treasury, and perhaps by Act of Parliament,' and the rest is to be used for ordinary purposes. (*Mr. Lubbock*): Would there not be a panic when you got near that? (*Mr. Keynes*): You would not get near a panic as soon as with the present system. (*Chairman*): No doubt as part of our Report we shall have to give an exposition of the present legislative position, and in doing so we shall naturally deal with any criticisms which have been made upon it, and either accept or reject those opinions. It is particularly desirable that you, Sir Richard, as a representative of the Treasury, should have an opportunity of expressing the Treasury view upon those criticisms, because part of your duty is to administer the existing system, and if criticisms are made upon that system it is proper that you should consider them and offer observations upon them. You have had the advantage of hearing some fundamental criticism from Mr. Keynes. We should welcome your either coming again or giving us your opinion in writing on that particular point. (*Mr. Keynes*): There is one psychological point, if I have not precluded myself from mentioning a psychological point, that I should like Sir Richard to bear in mind. It is rather generally agreed that throughout the world central banks should not have adopted such a high standard as the minimum amount of gold holding. There is not merely the question of our own situation, but the example we set to the rest of the world, and the precedent that we set to other countries with less prestige? — I entirely agree, as long as I am not asked to suggest that the actual figure to which we work as our gold reserve is an unreasonable one, in the sense that certain other ones elsewhere are, having regard to the extent of our wealth and the winds that blow upon us from all quarters of the world.

5417. *Professor Gregory*: You mean by 'reserve' the total stock of gold? — Yes; I mean the total figure, whatever it may be – Mr. Lubbock spoke of £150,000,000.

5418. *Chairman*: Now may we pass to quite a different point – a practical one? It has been suggested that there are seasonal restrictions of credit in this country in the early part of the year due to tax collection. How far have you observed that phenomenon? Taxes are collected largely at one season of the year? — Yes, that is so.

5419. And people are drawing upon their balances in order to satisfy the demands of the Exchequer. Has that any effect upon the restriction of credit for the time being? — The point, of course, relates to the Income Tax and Super-tax, which come in largely in the first three months of the calendar year. We always read in the newspapers that during the period of payment of taxation a certain stringency must arise. As I understand the matter – it is rather a technical one – the actual process of payment of taxation may in some instances produce a diminution in the bankers' balances, which have to that extent to be replaced.

5420. It is said that that restriction of credit has an effect upon enterprise, that there is a sort of brake put upon enterprise at this season of the year? — Only if a restriction actually occurs; but in fact, as it seems to me, the matter should be looked at from this point of view. The ordinary taxpayer has to save money during the months before the 1st January for the purpose of paying his taxation; he requires a higher amount in his bank, and therefore the bankers' deposits as a whole are much higher until the tax is paid; after he has paid the tax, a lower volume of deposits is adequate.

5421. *Mr. Keynes*: And the deposits are equal to the loans. Is it equally reasonable that the loans should be diminished by that amount? — Do you mean the bank advances?

5422. Yes. The bank advances in the widest sense? — You expect to get a certain mounting up of deposits immediately before tax is due and a certain deflation afterwards. Whether we have to follow the percentage proportions with terrible exactitude or whether it may not be possible to allow for a consideration of that kind and even out the actual advances and other operations of the Bank is, I think, a matter for consideration.

5423. It is quite reasonable that deposits should fall for the reasons you have given; it is not so obvious that the advances should fall? — No, I think means could be devised by which the bankers could allow for that. I notice at the present time that bankers' advances are not showing a decline.

5424. And including investments they could only keep those constant if they break their reserve proportion, and if they were encouraged to break their reserve proportion that would destroy the main instrument of control? — Not if it were done upon recognised principles, within known limits, and in consultation with the Bank.

5425. Would not the easiest way be for the Bank of England to create the necessary small amount of credit? — That is a technical point; if I were to go into it I should be trespassing on the Bank of England's sphere. As a layman, looking at it from outside, I should have thought it was a matter that could be adjusted by the banks themselves.

5426. *Chairman*: You think it desirable that fluctuation should be avoided as far as possible? — Undoubtedly. There was another point which was mentioned to the Deputy Governor, and that is whether the question of paying over taxation to a large extent on Thursdays has an unsettling effect upon the bankers' balances and upon the Government balances in the ensuing week. You might like me to say a word upon that matter. The amount that comes in on Thursday is by no means so large a proportion of the whole as it used to be. The super-tax comes in day by day and that part of the income tax which is collected by deduction from Municipal loans, Government loans and the like, comes in on the actual date when the deduction is made. In addition to that, the collection of income tax in the City of London now comes in on Tuesdays and Fridays, and the collection from a good number of provincial towns comes in day by day. There is, however, a larger payment upon

Thursday than upon the other days of the week, and according to the figures I have taken out it looks as if the excess of the Thursday payment over the daily average payment for the first thirteen weeks of the year is in the region of £3,000,000. It is not a large figure. Sir Ernest Harvey tells me he took some figures out; they did not provide any indication that Government deposits were during this time higher on Thursday and that they then sunk till Wednesday. At the same time, if the Committee thought it worth while to have an altered arrangement in regard to the day of payment in of that part of the collection which now comes in on Thursday, it could no doubt be arranged. Another thing that has occurred to me quite recently, on which I have no definite suggestion to make, but which may be worth looking into, is the fact that we are in the habit of issuing a three months' Treasury Bill as opposed to a thirteen weeks' Treasury Bill. In seven months of the year the three months amounts to 92 days, and the result of that is that bills taken out on Friday are payable on Saturday, bills taken out on Saturday are payable on Saturday, because they cannot be paid on Sunday, and bills taken out on Sunday are payable on Monday, or in other words, none are paid on Monday. You get two days' payment of Treasury Bills on Saturday and none on Monday, and that must have a certain disturbing element in the Government balances. It may be worth while looking into that point to see whether that needs correction.

5427. The object being to keep the balances as even as possible? — To keep the Government balances as nearly as possible constant day by day.

5428. I should like to turn to a very important and large topic, the question of the debt policy. As you are aware, there have been very important conversion operations recently which have partly reduced the Floating Debt. It has been suggested that the reduction in the Floating Debt has made the task of the Bank of England more difficult – more difficult, that is to say, because of the part which they play in the working of the banking system of the country. Have you any views upon that? — Yes; perhaps it would be better if I described in some little detail the nature of those transactions and the objects we had in view. It will follow from what I say that I should not agree with the criticism that you have mentioned.

5429. Do by all means let us have your views? — I will try to be as brief as I can. For some five years now we have been regularly engaged in endeavouring to meet maturities of National War Bonds. They have pressed upon us year after year in very considerable amounts. The total amount, which we have redeemed and converted into other forms of debt in the five years which has just ended, is roughly £1,200,000,000. On the whole it has been difficult to keep pace with these maturities as they came, and there has therefore been a tendency for the number of Treasury Bills to increase. Perhaps I should give a rough picture of the history of the Treasury Bills. In the two years prior to March 1923 they were very greatly reduced from the War level to just over £600,000,000. In the three years following they were decreased by £50,000,000 – that was the three years to March 1926 – and in the three years following they were increased again by a like amount, so that at the end of 1929 the number of bills had mounted up again to the figure in March 1923. In giving those figures I have eliminated disparities due to a mere change of form between Ways and Means Advances and Treasury Bills in the last two years. The figures are on a strictly comparable basis.

5430. *Lord Bradbury*: Those figures relate to the total issue, I suppose, including bills held by Government Departments? — That is so. In the autumn of last year when we were approaching this matter we had to deal with two maturities this spring amounting to £165,000,000. We were looking forward to the possibility of a Budget deficit. We knew there would be borrowings in this present financial year for what is known as the Suspensory Fund and for other purposes, and it was quite clear that there needed to be a new issue unless the amount of Treasury Bills were again to increase. We decided to put out an offer on favourable terms – it was criticised in certain quarters as being much too favourable – the object of which was to get together a substantial sum in cash and in conversions so that, as far as we could, we should make a considerable inroad into our task of meeting maturities. It was contemplated that if matters went as we anticipated there would be a further offer, which in fact was made in the spring, to get a further sum to finish paying the maturities, and to put together a substantial sum of money for the reduction of Treasury Bills. The result of the loans, after taking into account the Budget deficit and the other borrowings that were necessary, was to give us a surplus in the region of roughly £100,000,000 to £120,000,000 for reduction of Treasury Bills.

5431. *Mr. Keynes*: Would that be a temporary or a permanent reduction? — That would be a permanent reduction.

5432. That would be in excess of what you required for the maturities? — Yes.

5433. That brought the total down to £490,000,000 from the £600,000,000? — That would be so; yes. One object, as I have said, was the general one of reducing the bulk of Treasury Bills. The number of Treasury Bills has immensely increased since before the War. They represent almost a new element in the financial mechanism. At what figure they should stand, at what figure they are safe, it may be very difficult to lay down, but in general when they stood at the kind of figure at which they have been standing, it was clear they must represent a source of anxiety to the Government in difficult times when the Bank Rate was inclined to rise. When the situation was difficult last summer, it was always an anxiety to us whether we could get the bills subscribed in the volume required, or whether they might not become an element in forcing up Bank Rate. That is the general argument in favour of the reduction of bills. Apart from that I had this in my mind. This was the time when the American slump in Stock Exchange values had become serious. Lower Bank Rates were in prospect, and possibilities of bad trade were in prospect, although I would say at once that neither I nor any others contemplated the depth of the depression that has since occurred. Trade here was sluggish, and the demands for new capital on the home market were exceedingly small, and it seemed to me that an issue at a favourable price for a purpose of this kind would be likely to attract a good deal of investment money which otherwise would tend to go over the exchange to investment abroad; in other words, that this operation might be regarded as tending towards favourable exchanges. It seemed to me also, that this considerable sum of money being freed upon the short money market – inasmuch as bill holders would be paid off, and those bills would not be renewed – would be beneficial as facilitating a lowering of money rates and that in the course of time as other uses were found for the money, it might tend either to the creation in larger numbers of home trade bills here, or it might be taken up by foreign borrowers on sterling bills and go over the exchange under the shelter of the ease which the capital issue might be hoped to produce. In the end the operation should tend on the whole to strengthen and ease our position in the short money market. Mr. Chairman, I have endeavoured to put before you a general picture of the objects which we had in mind.

5434. *Chairman*: The object was a reduction in the amount of Treasury Bills? — Quite. You spoke in your original question of restriction, and I should not regard the two questions as in any sense the same.

5435. Quite. On the other hand, it is said that it is not easy for the Bank of England to make its rate effective if you reduce the volume of Treasury Bills? — The whole of this operation was carried out in co-operation with the Bank. Obviously if there had been circumstances requiring the Bank to make its rate effective there would have been no case for putting out the second offer: nor do I think the Bank has tried to make its rate effective in recent times.

5436. *Mr. Keynes*: On the statistical point you have given us the aggregate of bills. Could you now give us the aggregate in the hands of the market? — They would always be rather less than £200,000,000 below the total figure.

5437. But the fluctuation between the dates? — The figure of bills that I have given you was corrected for the number of bills which had been exchanged for Ways and Means in the Issue Department at the time of the Currency and Bank Notes Bill.

5438. Were those fluctuations in the total about equal to the fluctuations in the bills in the hands of the market, or were they quite different? — The fluctuations in bills in the hands of the market would about equal the total fluctuations.

5439. The amount in the hands of the market you say now is £200,000,000? — No, it is much more than that; I am sorry, I have not got the figure here.

5440. *Mr. Brand*: £200,000,000 was for the Government Departments? — If you want the existing published figures I can let you have them.

5441. *Mr. Keynes*: That is the total. If £200,000,000 is the amount in the Government Departments, we want also to exclude bills in the Issue Department of the Bank of England? — Yes, I have excluded those.

5442. The reduction would be from £400,000,000 in March, 1929, to about £290,000,000? (*Mr. Brand*): The latest published figure I have is £571,000,000 in April, and in March, 1929, £712,000,000? — The published figures were in March, 1929, £700,000,000 and in March, 1930, £589,000,000.

5443. *Mr. Keynes*: Obviously the figures of what the Government choose to hold in one form or other are of no great importance to anybody; you can convert them at any time? — From the published figure say £180,000,000 has to be deducted.

5444. And what was the total at March, 1930? — At the 31st March, 1930, the total of Treasury bills was roughly £590,000,000.

5445. *Mr. McKenna*: And how much for the Government Departments, including the Issue Department? — I take it in the region of £180,000,000 to £200,000,000.

5446. *Mr. Keynes*: That would give £400,000,000 net. And the year before? — £700,000,000 with a like deduction.

5447. So the reduction is roughly from £500,000,000 to £400,000,000. The reason you gave for your policy was that it arose out of embarrassment which you told us occurred some time last year, whether you could get all your Treasury Bills taken up. But surely these difficulties might be nothing more than an indication that the Bank of England was not expanding the volume of credit to the amount that was compatible with the volume of bills required? — No, I should not have thought it was that: I should have thought it was due to the general apprehension as regards the situation.

5448. If the Bank of England had itself

taken up £1,000,000 of Treasury Bills, which would have increased the joint stock banks' power to take up some kind of asset by £9,000,000 or £10,000,000, then the following week you would not have found that state of embarrassment? — Yes, but there may well be conditions in which the Bank of England would say that a course of that kind would not be a safe or reasonable course.

5449. Is not that because of the state of disequilibrium that the Bank of England had chosen to establish between the volume of credit and Bank Rate? — No, I do not think so. I should have thought that in times when the external situation which the Bank of England has to cope with is an exceedingly difficult one, it cannot afford to increase the volume of credit indefinitely.

5450. But what primarily matters for the exchange is the Bank Rate. I should have thought this was an indication of what many people allege, that the Bank of England were pursuing a perfectly right policy with regard to the Bank Rate, but unnecessarily and unduly starving the volume of internal credit; and what you have told us is a corroboration of that view? — I think on questions of currency policy you must examine the Bank of England rather than me. I am a layman with regard to control of the Bank Rate and control of the currency, but I am at a loss to know how, during the period of which I am speaking, a period of real difficulty, the Bank of England could have made any large increase in the volume of credit without letting the rates run away and becoming in serious danger of a higher Bank Rate.

5451. Your whole object was, that the rates should run away. Your whole object was to get the bill rate a little lower in relation to the Bank Rate; you were afraid you could not get your Treasury Bills adequately below the Bank Rate figure? — No; I was on quite a separate point: that when the Treasury Bills were so large in amount there would come times of strain, times of apprehension, times of expectation on the part of the market that Bank Rate was likely to be forced up by external conditions, it might be in the near future. Then with the large volume of bills offered each week, there must be apprehension that they would not all be tendered for.

5452. That meant that the bill rate would be unduly near to Bank Rate? — Yes.

5453. I ask whether the cure for that is not an increase in the volume of credit; your reply is that that will have the effect of making the market rate fall below Bank Rate. That is the object; to enable you to get your Treasury Bills out at a rate which is not so dangerously close to Bank Rate? — I am sorry; I am afraid I really do not follow. We may, perhaps, be at cross-purposes.

5454. I understood the difficulty was that the tender rate for bills will tend to get practically equal to Bank Rate? — Yes.

5455. Which is obviously an impossible situation? — Yes.

5456. If it got above Bank Rate people could make a profit by tendering for bills and re-delivering them to the Bank. So that the Treasury Bill rate was in danger of being unduly high in relation to Bank Rate? — Yes.

5457. I suggest that that could have been cured by a very small increase of credit by the Bank of England, which would have put more resources into the hands of the joint stock banks which they would have used for tendering for bills and would thus have kept the tender rate at the proper margin in relation to the Bank Rate? — I am of opinion that at the time of which I am speaking, the time of the boom in America, the general conditions under which the Bank had to act were extraordinarily difficult and that course impossible. I am not an expert on these things, and it is not my business, but I would be very slow to agree to anything which would suggest that the Bank could have taken a course of action other than that which they did take. To go back to the first point that I made, with regard to the ground for the recent operation: at any time if you have a very large volume of Treasury Bills they may constitute a real anxiety to the Government, as to whether in times of difficulty you can get them subscribed, and that anxiety will remain, whatever the action taken by the Bank of England.

5458. Do you really alter that in the least by reducing the volume from £500,000,000 to £400,000,000? Supposing that the market is adjusted to any given volume of Treasury Bills and then something of a dangerous kind happens in the outside world, you will have simply the same situation arising, once the market is adjusted to the situation, whether it is £400,000,000 or £500,000,000? — You will have the same situation arising in regard to the £400,000,000 as to the £500,000,000, and, as I said, what may be the optimum number of Treasury Bills, having regard to the needs of the market on the one hand and also the desire of the Government to adopt a cheap form of borrowing, and the safety of the situation on the other hand – all this may be very difficult to determine, but the volume as it stood was in our judgment an excessive volume, and it was desirable to take opportunities as they presented themselves to reduce the number.

5459. I am suggesting that that was a wrong diagnosis; that the real trouble was that the Bank of England wanted to have a credit policy which was not in equilibrium with Bank Rate, and I say when those circumstances arise you will have exactly the same difficulty, whatever the volume of Treasury Bills. It is not a function of the volume of Treasury Bills it is a function of the Bank Rate having a relation to the credit policy which is not in equilibrium? — I think that with a smaller volume of Treasury Bills it will be easier for the Bank to carry on a fight against a rise of rate in difficult conditions if the number of bills is small rather than if the number of bills is large.

5460. Of course, if the Bank of England had adjusted itself to the new policy there might not be very much danger. Might I come to the second point, of the effect on the exchanges of the policy which has actually been pursued? The reduction of about £100,000,000 in the outstanding volume of Treasury Bills has happened to take place simultaneously with a very important reduction in commodity prices? — Yes.

5461. *Mr. Keynes*: So that the volume of trade bills has been reduced at the same time? (*Mr. Brand*): Not a great deal. (*Mr. Keynes*): We have had evidence to that effect. (*Mr. McKenna*): Finance bills have increased, but trade bills have fallen. (*Mr. Brand*): I should say that bills in the market outside Treasury Bills have not fallen. (*Mr. Keynes*): Of course, there is the complication of the shift between London and New York, and the question which is getting the acceptances, but the evidence down to two months ago was that there was a shift to New York away from London, and we were told by witnesses that a fall in commodity prices of 12 per cent. meant a reduction in the produce bills on the London market of a very large amount. On the other hand, whence comes the demand for bills of this kind? Partly it comes from central banks and other bodies wanting to keep liquid funds in London? — Yes.

5462. Partly it comes from the demands of oint stock banks, partly for their own direct use and partly through the bill market. We have been told that it is the practice of the joint stock banks to keep a rather rigid proportion of their total assets in the shape of bills, partly in the shape of trade bills and partly in the shape of Treasury Bills, and partly in call money, perhaps 16 per cent.; so that for every £100,000,000 of deposits that the joint stock banks hold there has to be in existence something of the order of £20,000,000 in instruments of this kind, putting trade bills and Treasury Bills together. Supposing that nothing has happened to alter the volume of deposits in the joint stock banks, the shortage of bills arising from the action of the Treasury has to be met in some other way; therefore the first effect of reducing the volume of Treasury Bills would be to cause London rates to be very weak? — Yes.

5463. Until London acceptances become more attractive than New York acceptances? — Yes.

5464. With the result that what Mr. Brand has been telling us is happening now, that the volume of bills has been brought up again to something like the figure that it was before. That means that if the Treasury reduce Treasury Bills by something approaching £100,000,000 they are throwing a burden on the exchanges of the order of £100,000,000, because that particular kind of asset has to be attracted, and, broadly speaking, can only be attracted from trade bills, the home bill having fallen to negligible dimensions. Was it taken into account, when that was done, that it was throwing a burden on the exchanges? You told us that one of the motives was that it would help the exchanges? — Certainly it was taken into account. I suggested that the raising of a substantial sum of money by long-term Government loan in conditions in which there was a very small demand on the home market and a strong tendency for people to send money abroad, on the ground that America was a better place in which to invest their money on long term, would save a very considerable sum from going over the exchange on long-term. It seemed to me likely to create a favourable condition on the exchanges, in the shelter of which a considerable amount of short-term money could go, and surely if it can go under such conditions it is when gone a very considerable strength to our position.

5465. Is not that a wildly improbable calculation? So far as the long-dated market is concerned, do you think the new issues would be affected substantially by the fact of a slight difference in yield of long-dated securities - it would be very little - only a point or two? Do you believe that four per cent. Consols, say, being a point or two lower, would have prevented somebody who was thinking of lending his money in America from doing so, and that this would happen on a larger scale than a transfer of those other accounts which would result from the weakening of the bill rate? — Even if it has been on a large scale, I see no reason to think that there would be any great difference between the two things.

5466. Do you seriously think that? The kind of person who is buying Consols at a point or two difference is quite different from the kind of person who is thinking of investing abroad. The two kinds of investment do not compete with each other, do they? — Yes.

5467. Do you think there would be the same effect? — I should think a loan of this kind would divert a good deal of investment money which might otherwise be going——

5468. On a larger scale? — No, I do not say on a larger scale, or necessarily upon an equally large scale. At any rate, there was a favourable element there; I would not try to evaluate it, but it was certainly tending to affect the exchanges. At the same time, a certain shortage of bills would, as you say, create a need for bills on the part of the public seeking them. Personally, I wish it would create a demand for home bills, for I think it would be admirable if home lending on cheap terms would revive; so far as it will not, it attracts the foreign bill, and to the extent that it has attracted the foreign bill, and the money has gone abroad, it has gone abroad without any serious weight upon the exchange at all.

5469. You have also got to remember that from the point of view of the home investor, this is simply an exchange. You are wiping away £100,000,000 of Treasury Bills; some of the holders of those Treasury Bills will have to replace them by foreign bills? — Yes.

5470. Some of them will take advantage of the conversion operation that you are making? — Yes.

5471. Probably not to a great amount; they are an entirely different class of securities. I find it difficult to invent the hypothesis in which your view could appear plausible. You say that the rest of the new issues in the long-dated market in which you are operating would be taken up – by whom? This is not new money. This is simply an exchange from one kind of thing to another. You are saying that they would be taken up by people who would otherwise have invested their money in America? — To a considerable extent.

5472. What would the people who formerly held Treasury Bills do with their money? — The Treasury Bills will be paid off; they will be seeking new outlets and natural outlets. If we could begin to create a home demand it would be the home market. I do not see why, if we could get a turn in the home trade, the home bill trade should not revive——

5473. The ordinary view is that if you want to strengthen the exchanges you strengthen the bill market, and that is the most important influence. You are telling us that that is quite wrong, that the opposite is true, that if you weaken the bill market you will cause a greater conversion of long-dated lending than you will of the short-dated? — I have not said greater; I will not attempt to place a quantitative value upon one or the other, but I say that the long operation has tended towards favourable exchanges and that the short operation has tended towards cheaper money rates under which bills will come to London and can, I think, be taken up without strain upon our exchange.

5474. By facilitating lower money rates and a lower Bank Rate you mean the action of the Treasury has forced the hand of the Bank of England? — I am not saying so at all; I am sorry if I was abrupt; I did not mean to appear discourteous.

5475. If the foreign situation allowed it, was there any difficulty to the Bank of England in reducing the Bank Rate? — Certainly not.

5476. When you had reduced the supply of bills I can quite see that it might have made a reduction inevitable. It might have made it extremely difficult for the Bank of England to maintain a high Bank Rate, but how did it make it less difficult to reduce it? — I can but repeat, I think that the raising of the loan in the conditions under which it was raised eased the exchanges, and rendered a fall in the rate easier to accomplish at a time when the rate was coming down. The subsequent paying off of the bills in itself tends, I think, until the shortage is filled up by bills that come from other quarters, to keeping rates low. I should have thought that in these extraordinarily difficult times any tendency which went towards keeping rates low was desirable.

5477. The essence of your argument is that that would enable the Bank of England to reduce its rates because you, by offering conversion loans on attractive terms at the end of last year, drew into them a lot of money which might otherwise have been invested abroad? — I am sorry. In the way you put the question to me you seem to suggest that I was claiming that the policy of the Government has itself produced cheap money. I am not saying that at all. I say that it has been a useful adjunct to other factors which were themselves quite obviously leading in that direction.

5478. I think you claim that it facilitated it? — Yes, I claim that it facilitated it, but not that it was the cause.

5479. I should have thought the Bank of England would have had more control over the situation if it had done it by expanding credit; it would have helped the financial situation if it had produced the lower money rates by expanding credit rather than by the Treasury reducing the amount of Treasury Bills? — I am not an authority on this but is it not the case that credit is expanding? I think it is the case that bankers' deposits have been ascending from December to now.

5480. The point is, that if any expansion were desired by the Bank of England it could very well bring about that expansion without Treasury assistance, and the increase of credit would bring rates down. It is so very easy for the Bank of England to bring the rates down. I should not have thought that it was something that required external assistance? — Well, that in the end must depend upon judgment. That was the argument which led us to think that it was on the whole a useful operation.

5481. Would you hold that if you did it again it would be equally useful? — I think it depends on the circumstances in which it is carried out.

5482. If you reduced Treasury Bills by another even small sum, £50,000,000, you would produce all the same consequences over again, would you not? — I do not know. I prefer not to address myself to a hypothetical question, but it seems to me that for better or worse we have at the present time a position of greater ease; I should be the first to admit that other causes have been more important, but I suggest the action we have taken has worked in with the other factors that have been working.

5483. May I put it the other way round? The view has been expressed that from the standpoint of curing unemployement it would be very desirable if the Bank of England had seen its way to increase the basis of credit and the lending power of the joint stock banks. The difficulty in the way of the Bank of England doing it was that if it increased the volume of credit the first effect would be to increase the resources in the hands of the joint stock banks so that they would have an increased demand for bills; thus the market rate would be weak and we should tend to lose gold, and the whole obstacle in the way of an easier policy on the part of the Bank of England was the fear that that would react on the bill market. You are telling us the precise opposite, that the real fear of the Bank of England was that an insufficient demand for bills would react on the bill market, and the fear of that has prevented the Bank of England from expanding its credit? — I was speaking in quite a different sense, of the difficulty with regard to the expansion of credit which has arisen in the past.

5484. It has all happened in the last nine months. The contention is that over the period during which you were reducing the volume of Treasury Bills the extension of credit was less than would have been desirable? — There was nothing in the policy of reducing the number of Treasury Bills which necessitated a restriction.

5485. What it really comes to is, that you say that the reaction on the exchange market of the demand for long-dated securities which would be brought about by an an easier policy on the part of the Bank of England would be more important than any influence on the exchanges caused by the reactions of their policy in changing the market rate for bills. Is that right? — It seems to me so important in so far as money goes over the exchange, that it should go over on short term because when once it has gone it strengthens our position rather than otherwise.

5486. That is exactly the opposite of what we have been taught to believe, that it was the short rate which was the fundamental thing in acting on the rate of exchange; at any rate, for short periods, that what strengthens the Bank of England is having an effective Bank Rate. It is very paradoxical for us to be told that an act which makes the bill rate fall away from Bank Rate facilitates the task of the Bank of England and strengthens its control over the exchanges? — I confess that I feel difficulty in following you when you say it is a paradox. It would perhaps be a paradox if you asked me to agree that no favourable effect on the exchange had previously been exercised by the raising of the loan, but if in fact that favourable effect has been set up, there is the foundation upon which the short term money can go, and if it can go without influencing the exchanges adversely, surely once it has gone it must strengthen our position. It will strengthen us if and when we call it back.

5487. If the Treasury were to raise an important loan for capital development that would strengthen the exchange? — No. I shall come to that on a later opportunity. I shall want to deal with the question of practicability there.

5488. Your contention is that the new issues of the Government, of other kinds than that do have this strengthening effect? — Yes.

5489. Even though the proceeds are used to pay off Treasury Bills and cause a shortage of bills in the market? — Yes.

... ...

Thursday 22 May 1930

Sir Richard V. N. Hopkins, K.C.B., Controller of the Finance and Supply Services Department, H.M. Treasury, recalled and further examined.

... ...

5539. Now with regard to the supply of Treasury Bills? — I looked through the notes, Mr. Chairman, and I was not satisfied that I had always fully understood, or satisfactorily explained my real meaning, in answering some of the questions of Mr. Keynes last time, and as the discussion was a long one I thought I might try to bring together again the views which moved us, and perhaps expand rather better than I did my view in regard to some of the criticisms which Mr. Keynes made.

5540. Please do? — I said at the outset that we held that there was a very great disadvantage from the point of view of the National Exchequer in having an excessive volume of Treasury Bills, and I said that the Bank of England was liable to be seriously embarrassed when the numbers were too large. It would, I think, be agreed that the Bank of England should always be free to conduct its general credit policy by reference to the state of the exchanges and such criteria as it takes without being diverted by the results of a particular market operation. The way in which the embarrassment arises when the volume of bills is very high is this: the people in the money market who lend money to the Government on Treasury Bills first of all borrow it; they borrow it from banks and others at a rate a given degree below Bank Rate for quite short periods, and they lend it to the Government at a rate higher than that at which they borrow, but below Bank Rate, for a period of 13 weeks. It follows that if, during the currency of a Treasury Bill, the Bank Rate is increased there will be a loss to the money market on the bills which at that time are current, because for the balance of the currency of the bills they will be borrowing from bankers and others at a rate higher than that which is accruing to them upon the bill. It follows from that that at the time when the market anticipates that, because the Treasury Bills are near the Bank Rate or otherwise, an increase of Bank Rate is coming, they may be extremely reluctant to tender for bills in large quantities, knowing that in all probability the tender will produce a loss. When, in fact, there is a refusal to tender for all the bills which are asked for, the Government has only two alternatives, either to take from the Bank of England an overdraft on Bank of England Ways and Means advances for the difference, or for the Bank itself to take up the Bills. Either process is in fact a creation of money; either process on a large scale or long continued may render a situation which *ex hypothesi* is difficult, unsound, and force the Bank to put up its rate. That is the point I was trying to draw out. Really in my view it is not in any way a position which can be countered; it is not in any way due to the Bank having provided less money than is consistent with conditions at the time, nor, I think Mr. Keynes will agree, could it be put right by their letting out a small sum of money such as the £1,000,000 which he suggested. If the Bank had a remedy it would rather lie along the following lines. They have, no doubt, informal means of getting in touch with the money market; they might try to re-assure the market that, in fact, the Bank Rate was not likely to increase, if that was their view; but ultimately the market is bound to judge by reference to severe considerations of likely profit or likely loss. It is quite true that that is a difficulty relating to Treasury Bills, whether they are large in volume or whether they are small in volume, but subject to this that there is always a minimum demand for Treasury Bills which will be tendered for in almost any conditions, and the larger the excess over that minimum which has to be asked for week by week the more difficult the situation is likely to become. I am not speaking in any way hypothetically; this is a difficulty which has been experienced with the existing volume of bills on more than one occasion in recent years. That is my further effort to explain the general reason why we thought the Treasury Bills should be reduced. It does not necessarily cover the question, of course, whether we select an appropriate time for reduction.

5541. *Mr. Keynes*: To what date would that apply? — Any time.

5542. The actual occasion arose when the market feared a rise of Bank Rate last summer? — That was undoubtedly one of the occasions.

5543. But after the American crisis that fear passed away? — Yes.

5544. But your actual conversion operation was after the American crisis? — Yes. I gave the general reason why we thought it desirable to enter upon a policy of reducing the number of Treasury Bills. That was with the old amount of bills. The same difficulty might arise at any time when it was expected the Bank Rate might increase.

5545. That was my difficulty. I do not see how you can remedy that. When the market is nervous of an increase of Bank Rate it would act in this way, assuming it was previously adjusted to the volume of bills of all kinds outstanding, whatever was the proportion of Treasury Bills? — But the difficulty is in much smaller compass when we are asking for £30,000,000 in a week than when we are asking for £40,000,000 or £45,000,000.

5546. I should have thought there was no possibility of dealing with a situation in which the market was forced into that position except by reducing the amount of investment abroad or by raising Bank Rate. If it persists for more than a week or two there is no other way out? — I quite agree that this is a difficulty in the management of policy which cannot be overcome, but it can be, I think, greatly mitigated by a reduction of the number of bills, and it greatly weighed with us in trying to fix the best number of bills, bearing in mind on the one hand the need of the money market for this kind of instrument and also the Government desire for adopting in reasonably full measure a cheap form of borrowing, and on the other hand keeping in mind the safety of the situation.

5547. *Mr. Lubbock*: Apart from money market considerations, I suppose you would wish to reduce Treasury Bills a good deal further – or would you not? — I think the funded debt gives us very much less concern on an average of times. From the Government point of view I think the only other consideration is that, on the whole, Treasury Bills are a fairly cheap form of borrowing.

5548. But every debtor likes to have his debt funded as soon as he can? — I agree.

5549. *Mr. Keynes*: Is that a desirable policy on the part of the State? In many cases what is prudent in an individual is extended by false analogy to the State? — The State has to deal with the same money market conditions as the individual, but it has to deal with them on a very large scale.

5550. *Chairman*: The Treasury would be happier if there were no debt? — Indeed they would.

5551. *Mr. Brand*: Or if the whole of the War Loan were Treasury Bills? — Then the whole method of the conduct and management of the debt would have to be very substantially altered, I am afraid. On the more immediate point, we thought that an operation at the present time would facilitate the introduction of a period of cheaper money. We thought that in the new conditions quite a considerable number of people who previously were buying Treasury Bills in the market would move away under the cheaper money rate to other forms of short-term Government stock, possibly even to War Loan stock. We hoped that new conditions might at any rate gradually, if not at once, tend to the creation of the home trade bill; which, for my part, is a thing which I think, if it could be encouraged, ought to be encouraged. It did not seem to us that by reducing Treasury Bills by £100,000,000 we should produce the result that that £100,000,000 would be taken up in foreign acceptances and therefore that the whole would be a strain upon the exchange. That a substantial part of it would, of course, we recognised. Against that I set off in my mind the ease to the exchange, which would result from the diversion from foreign investment of a substantial amount of investible money which would go directly or indirectly into the conversion issue which was the beginning of this operation.

5552. *Mr. Keynes*: That would only be to the extent that the bills would be replaced by foreign bills, would it? In so far as money was going out of bills into long-dated securities that would be a cancellation? — Yes. It would cancel out.

5553. You would only get fresh money into it if that were not the case? — Yes, that is quite true. I have almost finished what I want to say. We recognised that the increase of foreign bills, while it was taking place, would of itself be, as Mr. Keynes said, a strain upon the exchange. If, in fact, the conditions had been such that the strain could not have been borne, or was unlikely to be borne, the second conversion offer of last February–March would not, of course, have been made, but it seemed to us that if the operation were feasible then once it had taken place our position would be greatly strengthened inasmuch as what money went abroad would be short-term money and could be pulled back as the bills were repaid or could be pulled back even earlier, if necessary, and if conditions moved against us, by an alteration of Bank Rate. It seemed to us also that it would be a contribution – and for my part I should say a contribution of some importance – towards the stirring up again of the general channels of world trade if cheap money in considerable quantity were available in London. I should say that a survey of recent months would show that the money has gone abroad upon foreign acceptances without any strain upon the exchanges. The Bank Rate is low. The reduction in our rate is greater than that in the rate of any other great Bank in the world, and while there have been signs of strain from time to time they have not been more, it seems to me, than could be accounted for by spasmodic resurrections of the spirit of speculation in New York or the removal of French balances. Mr. Keynes asked me whether I was not using an argument which could be extended to apply to the raising of a Development Loan, since that also would divert a lot of investible money from foreign to home investment. I said I should join issue there upon the question of practicability. What I meant was that if such a scheme could work in practice as it would work on paper then I should be in agreement with him.

5554. I do not follow the last point, because the question whether the loan was successful in producing useful objects for relieving unemployment would be quite separate, would it not, from the question of its effect upon the exchange? Why should the effect of raising the loan on the exchange be dependent upon whether you liked the ultimate purpose of the loan or not? — If the general sentiment accompanying it were such as to make people say that this was not a good place in which to invest money and America was a better, I think the object would be defeated.

5555. If you could once get the loan underwritten and be sure it would be subscribed, then it would have the same effect as a conversion issue. In itself a Development Loan would help the exchange, you say, but a Development Loan would so upset public sentiment that it would produce effects which would outweigh the help to the exchange? — Yes.

5556. *Mr. Brand*: Do you think the people who put their money abroad are to any great extent the same as the people who invest in British Government loans? — I think, at any rate, a good deal of money which was awaiting investment and which went into this loan might otherwise have gone into sterling loans for abroad, and a certain residue of money which is available for investment either here or elsewhere would have gone over the exchange.

5557. You mean in foreign government loans? — Yes, for instance.

5558. *Professor Gregory*: Is there any evidence that people who formerly kept their funds in Treasury Bills did, in fact, take up War Loan stock? — No; I think it is extremely difficult to get evidence or facts; one has to form a judgment as well as may be, but I should anticipate that a considerable number of traders holding Treasury Bills as a temporary use for money which they intended to use for trade in a comparatively short time, would tend to go away from it, and probably merchant bankers would tend to reduce their holdings.

5559. Does the Treasury know, in fact, how the holdings of Treasury Bills are distributed? — No.

5560. It only knows the amount held by the Bank? — I do not see the tenders. If I saw the tenders I do not think they would be informative, because in so many cases persons tender on behalf of clients. I do not mean to imply that we are not allowed to see the tenders; I merely say that I do not, in fact, see them, and, if I did, I do not think they would be informative.

... ...

Wednesday 2 July 1930

Sir Ernest Harvey, K.B.E., Deputy Governor of the Bank of England, recalled and further examined.

7509. *Chairman*: Gentlemen, before Sir Ernest begins his evidence this morning I should like just to say a word or two about the position in which he comes before us. You will recall that at a very early stage in our proceedings Sir Ernest was good enough to come before us and contribute what I think we all regarded as a most valuable exposition from the historical and descriptive point of view of the Bank of England. At that stage the more controversial topics which arise in connection with the problems of the Bank of England were designedly omitted from Sir Ernest's statement in order that we might have a coherent view in the first place of the activities of the Bank. He is good enough to come to us this morning to deal with a somewhat different aspect of the matter. I have had the advantage of an informal conversation with him just now and he has indicated a number of topics which he would like to discuss and expound to the Committee. He will hand round copies of the document which contains the heads of his evidence. I am most anxious to secure that we should have a complete statement on each of these topics in a coherent form. Therefore, may I suggest to my colleagues that, however attractive it may be to put questions to Sir Ernest as we go along, it might be well to postpone those questions until he has given us a complete exposition of that topic and then deal with those questions before we pass to the next topic. I think that is the course you would wish to pursue, Sir Ernest? — Yes, Mr. Chairman.

7510. Of course, we realise that these are matters in which much explanation and very close thinking is required. It is difficult for a witness in your responsible position to switch over rapidly, if I may say so, from one topic to another. I think you have with you this morning a *précis* or synopsis of the topics. Copies might be handed round by the Secretary and they will enable the members of the Committee to follow the line of your evidence. (*Copies distributed.*) I observe at the outset, Sir Ernest, you propose to discuss in broad terms the policy of the Bank of England since the return to the gold standard, and no doubt we shall have from you, as you indicate, a statement of the aims and objectives which the Bank has had in view; the difficulties, expected and unexpected, which you have encountered during that period; the measures which have been taken to surmount those difficulties; the means at your disposal for that purpose; and generally the considerations of policy which have animated the Bank. I think you might proceed at once to take up that leading aspect of the matter with us? — In giving my evidence this morning, Mr. Chairman, I want, if the Committee will allow me, to confine myself rather to questions which concern the Bank itself, questions of policy and method of operation, questions which I would describe perhaps as domestic, rather than to deal with questions which are more international or involve economic theory. I do that for two reasons. In the first place, you are to hear evidence from Dr. Stewart, who certainly on questions of economic theory is far more competent to give evidence to the Committee than I am. I am not a trained economist, although, of course, one has to give consideration to economics; my training has been in the sphere of actual practice. Dr. Stewart is anxious to leave for America on Tuesday, and I think it important that I should not occupy so much of your time, in the three sittings which you have set apart for us, that there will not be sufficient time left for him to develop the arguments that he proposes to put before you. If there is anything left unsettled or unanswered in my discussion with the Committee, I am, of course, always at the Committee's disposal to come back again, if necessary.

7511. That is very kind of you. — There is one other point that I should like the Committee to bear in mind: We are dealing, of course, with a period when circumstances and conditions have varied enormously from year to year, frequently from month to month; and whilst I propose to take one or two specific incidents in the history of the last few years as illustrations of certain things which I shall have to say, you must not be surprised if, in the event of my being asked why the Bank did such and such a thing at some given moment, I am not at once able to give you the reasons here and now. It is very difficult to carry in one's mind all the factors which have influenced us from month to month during the past five years. But if any such questions are addressed to me and I am unable to answer them, I need hardly say, if I may be allowed to have a note of them, the Committe shall have a considered reply.

7512. Thank you. We will certainly avail ourselves of that offer. — I start with a broad statement of policy and I wish to put it quite shortly. I am speaking, of course, now of the period since the return to the gold standard. There is no object in going back to previous years when considering the policy of the Bank of England acting under the gold standard. I want to describe to you in quite a few words what has been the broad outline of the Bank's policy during these last five years. I said when I was here before that I regarded it as the principal duty of a Central Bank to maintain the stability of the national monetary unit. If I am right in claiming that as the Bank's principal duty, it is obvious that that must be the fundamental principle underlying the Bank's policy; but as a statement of policy, of course, it needs some amplification if the underlying motives are to be properly apprehended. If I were asked to state in a few words what the Bank's policy has been, I should say that it has been to maintain a credit position which will afford reasonable assurance of the convertibility of the currency into gold in all circumstances, and, within the limits imposed by that objective, to adjust the price and volume of credit to the requirements of industry and trade. I should say at this stage that we regard the Bank Rate as our principal weapon for carrying that policy into effect. Whether it is a sufficiently effective weapon or not can be considered later. I think its efficiency has perhaps been impaired in a manner that has not always been recognised, and I shall have something to say about that presently. In speaking of the weapons which the Bank uses I purposely omit any reference to control of the volume of credit by direct market operations; because, after all, such operations are merely part of the machinery by which the weapon of the Bank Rate is made efficient. Now, what are the guides which prompt the Bank to make use of the weapon of the Bank Rate? I should say they were the state of the Bank's reserves, the condition of the money market, both as regards rates and also as regards the volume and character of the funds, domestic and foreign, in the market, and, thirdly, the position and trend of the foreign exchanges. I may be asked, I have been asked, do we not pay attention to the condition of trade? I say that if the machine is functioning properly the condition of trade should be reflected in the factors to which I have referred. It has been suggested, I think, that the Bank has been inclined to pay too much attention to the foreign aspects of the question and not sufficient attention to the domestic, and that is often held to be synonymous with having paid too much attention to finance and not enough to trade. I submit that the two cannot be dissevered. After all, our trade is not a purely domestic matter; the condition of foreign markets is of vital importance to a trade so international in character as ours, and I repeat what I said before, if the machine is functioning properly the condition of trade should be reflected in the factors to which I have referred. It is only within definite limits of time and degree that we can ignore those factors with the simple desire to achieve some internal domestic end. Credit requirements, whether foreign or domestic, industrial or governmental, are all, I think, if the machine is working properly, in the end brought to a focus in the money market. I should like now to give one or two illustrations of the sort of factors which influence us in our policy. I will take first Treasury requirements.

7513. *Mr. Keynes*: Mr. Chairman, that is the end of the first heading in the *précis*. Is that a convenient point to interrupt, or does Sir Ernest wish to go on? — I have no objection, if you desire to put a question.

7514. In giving a list of the matters which affected your mind in altering Bank Rate you do not include money rates abroad; but doubtless you would include those? — Yes. When I said the condition of the money market I had in mind international as well as purely domestic rates. Certainly we always have regard to the comparative rates; that is to say, we consider the position of the money market in conjunction with the comparative levels of rates in the home and foreign markets.

7515. In pre-war days it used to be maintained – I think truly – that to a large extent we led the world; that is to say, if we reduced Bank Rate it probably brought about a corresponding reduction in the rates in other financial centres. One of the witnesses whom we have had before us has maintained that that is still true to a large extent to-day. Other people have told us that that is no longer the case and that the opposite is true, that instead of our rate affecting other rates we, to a considerable extent, have to follow the rates of other centres. What is your view as to that? — I should say that such leadership as we possessed has certainly been affected by the position which America has gained. We had an example of that in the time of the American boom, when the rates there undoubtedly had a governing effect on our rate policy. We were not free agents. No lead from us would necessarily, I think, have been followed elsewhere. We had really to shape our policy in accordance with what was happening there. I would not claim that our leadership was as complete as it used to be.

7516. Shall I put to you the same question a little differently? If the Bank relied to some extent on that leadership, it would consider what rate for money was desirable in this country and the world at large, and would move in that direction in the hope that others would follow suit. If, on the other hand, it had very little faith in its leadership, it would be watching the exchanges elsewhere and trying to get confidential information from other Central Banks as to what they were doing, and it would then adjust its policy not so much to its own ideas as to what it thought other people were going to do. On which side does the actual bias lie? — I should say we are guided by a combination of the two. I think we may still claim a certain amount of power to give a lead to other countries. They do often communicate with us to obtain our views, and we have many opportunities of bringing influence to bear according to what we may consider desirable in the general international interest. I think I may claim, for example, that in the fall of rates which has taken place in the last few months our influence has been important.

7517. One witness has suggested to us that the Bank of England has not, perhaps, quite enough confidence in the strength of its own position, and that if the Bank had followed more boldly what it would have liked to have done, the results would have been better than they have been, and that this lack of confidence may be partly attributable to the Bank being reluctant to see large fluctuations in its gold reserves. The suggestion is that the loss of leadership as compared with pre-War days is mainly due to the fact that certain other countries are in a position to allow their gold reserves to fluctuate widely, while we consider ourselves not to be in a position to do that. The suggestion is that we might be a little braver about that; that if we were more willing to see fluctuations in our gold reserves we might be able to recover our old leadership? — I do not think there has been any hesitation on the part of the Bank of England to allow comparatively large fluctuations in their gold holding. I think myself that on some occasions they have adopted a policy which many people, if they had been in possession of the information which the Bank possessed, would have regarded as courageous. I should say that timidity has not been a fault of the Bank.

7518. Are you content with the sort of figure which the Cunliffe Committee recommended as the normal gold reserve – the mean between the maximum and minimum – that is, £150,000,000, or would you rather see it a much more substantial figure? — We attach no fixed importance to that particular figure. In changing circumstances the figure that we should consider a fair average would vary very considerably.

7519. At the commencement of your evidence you distinguished between the official Bank Rate and the rate which is effective in the market. I should like to ask some questions directed to the issue of the means which the Bank uses to make effective in the market that rate which seems to it a desirable rate in the conditions. It seems to me that there are three methods to be used, and I should like to know how much importance the Bank attaches to them. The first method of a change in the official Rate produces an effect on the mind of the market, partly because it alters the rate at which they can discount in emergencies, partly because it affects the rate which the joint stock banks allow on deposits, and, I think, to some extent, the rate which they charge for call money. That effect comes into operation without the Bank altering the quantity of credit, or doing anything whatever except making a new notification as to the official Rate. The second method consists in curtailing the volume of credit, in order that the market, being short of funds, may feel that the risk of having to discount with the Bank would be greater, and therefore would raise the market rate as a protection against that risk. The third method would be for the Bank to alter the character of its assets without altering the volume of credit, as, for instance, selling Treasury Bills to the market and buying long-dated securities, the strengthening effect on the bill rate of the sale of Treasury Bills being greater on balance than the weakening effect of the purchase of long-dated securities. Can you tell us how that problem presents itself to the mind of the Bank and the normal way of solving it? — I find it rather difficult to attach in general any order of importance to those methods. As regards the first of which you speak, the mere movement of the Rate, the exact effect cannot be determined beforehand – at least, it is very difficult to do so with any certainty. You know that if you put up the Rate one per cent. you will produce a certain effect upon rates. But the extent of the effect and whether it will hold or not depends upon a great many other circumstances. The relative importance of the different methods is entirely dependent upon the circumstances existing at the moment. What might be the most suitable means at one time might be less suitable at another time. The mechanism of tightening up rates by a market operation of some kind would be the natural method to use if, in our view, the existing Bank Rate which, if effective, would be high enough, had for some reason or other become ineffective.

7520. Which of the two types of market operation would you rely on? Would you normally reduce the volume of credit or would you try to change the character of the Bank's assets? — I think our first operation would normally be to reduce the volume of credit by the sale of bills.

7521. And not buy long-dated securities? — That would depend on the probable reactions of the market, on the information which we had at the moment as to possible changes in the volume of credit owing to other causes, Treasury operations, and so forth: but unless we had clear evidence that there was a margin of credit which could only find employment in the short-loan market, we should not necessarily effect any reduction in the volume of credit. If we do reduce the volume of credit in order to make the rate effective, it is only because we are satisfied that the reason for the weakness of the market rate is an excess of money which cannot find employment elsewhere than in the short market. It is true that an apparent excess of money in the short market may be due to action by the bankers for the purpose of restoring a certain proportion of liquid assets, but at the same time, whatever the operations which have brought about the excess of funds in the short-money market, I see no other means by which we can make our rate effective but by shortening those funds.

7522. Might I take as an illustration the

present position? At the present time the market rate is, if anything, below 2¼ per cent., which is rather low in relation to an official Bank Rate of 3 per cent. Supposing, for the sake of argument, the Bank were to consider that an effective rate of 2¾ per cent. would be advisable, would the natural way be to restrict the basis of credit, or to increase the supply of bills in the market whilst increasing the Bank's short-dated securities? What is the ordinary explanation to-day of the weakness of market rates in relation to Bank Rate? Surely it is the very obvious one that the supply of Treasury Bills in the hands of the market has been reduced by £150,000,000 simultaneously with a fall in the face value of trade bills, due to the decline of commodity values. It would seem *prima facie* that the weakness of the market rate was due to the big reduction in the volume of short-dated securities? — I should say that the present weakness of the market rate is largely due to the fact that the Bank have for some considerable time, ever since the fall in rates began, felt that one of the most serious dangers which had threatened us had passed, and that we were therefore free for the moment to keep the volume of credit on the easy side.

7523. Would you not expect a weakness of bill rates if there had been over a period of about six months or a year such an immense reduction in the volume of short-dated securities in the market? — I agree that the first effect of a reduction of bills would be a reduction in the rate, assuming – and this I challenge – that it is necessary for the bankers to maintain the same proportion of bills under those conditions as they maintained when there was a larger supply of bills. I should argue that the bankers have been much too rigid in their working.

7524. Therefore there should be more bills now? — They have not been sufficiently willing to adjust their portfolios to what I would call seasonal – I agree that this year it is something more than seasonal – but to seasonal declines in the volume of bills.

7525. Is there any reason why the Bank of England should not feed the market in accordance with the market's demand without bringing natural forces to bear, so to speak? — The Bank frequently does so. I think I am right in saying there has been a very considerable increase in the volume of bills in recent months.

7526. Would you ever employ a criterion of this kind: When the reason for having a higher effective rate in the market was the fear of the development of inflation you might possibly want to curtail the basis of credit? Therefore, if that was the reason for making the higher rate effective, the method you would first employ would be the curtailment of the basis of credit? — Yes.

7527. But if your reason for having a higher effective rate had been to stop the loss of gold to other countries without there being any danger to the position in the home market, I should have thought that any reduction in the quantity of credit would have been your very last resort, and that you would have employed every other expedient to make the rate effective? — Yes, I think that would be so, but assuming that we sell bills and that we buy long stocks, what becomes of the money that we put out by the purchase of long stocks? Can you be sure that it will not find its way into the short market, and absorb the bills which we have put out, and so deprive our action of any real effect on the rate in the end?

7528. You would not expect that to happen to 100 per cent., would you? — Perhaps not to 100 per cent., no, but our experience tells us that it may run to a considerable percentage.

7529. Even if you let a little time elapse? — You mean if we sell bills first?

7530. I conceive the first effect of the purchase of long-dated securities would be simply to put the position where it was? — Certainly.

7531. But if you allowed a little more time to elapse, so that those who sold the long-dated securities had time to find an alternative investment, you would not find that result? — That is to say, you suggest that we should sell bills first and allow a little time to elapse before we put the credit out again?

7532. No; buy the long-dated securities at once and not expect to get the benefit of that until after a little time had elapsed? — I beg your pardon.

7533. You see what I am driving at? — Perfectly.

7534. From the point of view of the foreign situation it would appear that the Rate is the fundamental thing; from the point of view of the home situation the Rate is probably of secondary importance, at any rate over a period, as compared with the quantity of credit. Therefore there are two methods, one of which is practicable when you have one reason for tightening the Rate, and the other when you have the other reason for tightening the Rate? — And I should say, generally speaking, we have made use of those alternative methods from time to time. Our natural inclination would be to maintain the volume of credit, or even to increase it, provided that the desired effectiveness of the Rate could be maintained. It is very seldom that we purposely reduce the volume of credit unless we have evidence that there is a considerable margin which will only seek investment in the short-money market and depress rates.

7535. That could only have been the case of recent years if the joint stock banks were unable to find an outlet for additional advances. There might be a short period during which the banks would be putting the money into the short-term market directly or indirectly. The tendency that you are contemplating would only arise in a situation lasting a month or two, if the joint stock banks were finding it difficult to get borrowers for advances? — Which advances would be made on the basis of the cash which we had made available.

7536. Yes? — Certainly, that would be so.

7537. Is it your opinion that there has been any recent time when the joint stock banks were unable to find an outlet for advances? — Well, of course I can only judge by results that one sees in the short-loan money market. If we see that there is a scramble for such bills as are available we generally assume, I think we must assume – always provided that the joint stock banks have the proportion of liquid assets which they require – if we see that in spite of that there is still a demand for bills, we must assume that it is because they cannot employ their money in any other way.

7538. Is there any reason why you should not ask them? — None that I know.

7539. If you found that the banks were inclined to invest what seemed to you rather large resources in the short market why should you not ask them whether it is merely a temporary situation, or whether, owing to the difficulty of finding an outlet in other directions, it is likely to last? — There I think that our difficulties may be in part due to lack of information. Our only method of ascertaining, unless we receive information from the banks, is from the position of the market. The figures that the bankers publish are practically valueless.

7540. I should have thought you could sometimes have said to the joint stock banks, 'At the present moment you appear to have somewhat more than your normal proportion in the short-loan market, directly or indirectly. If this position is likely to last we think the situation requires that we should make some curtailment of the basis of credit. If, however, you have reason to expect that you will find an outlet for those resources in other directions we shall not reduce it.' Why should you not have conferences of that kind? — I see no reason; if they are prepared to give us the information we should be very glad to receive it, but as I said before, at present we are really without information other than that afforded by the market.

7541. It seems to an outsider rather strange that you should be making uncertain deductions on imperfect data? — I agree.

7542. When the gentlemen with whose actions you are insufficiently acquainted all reside within a stone's throw? — If the bankers would be willing to give us figures I for one should welcome them.

7543. I have to confess that if they were to give you information as inconsistent with one another as they have given us you would not be much further forward? — I would go further; I would say that if they gave us information which was so unrepresentative as the information which they publish monthly it would be useless; it would be valueless.

7544. *Mr. Brand*: So far as advances are concerned, it would be very difficult for you to foretell within a period of two or three weeks what they were likely to be? — It has been suggested that we should create credit in anticipation of a demand for advances. If we could feel assured that that credit was really going to be held and used to form the basis of advances we would gladly create the credit, but according to our experience that credit will almost inevitably go straight to the short-loan market, until such time as the demands for the advances come forward. Now, if there were a little greater readiness on the part of the banks to vary their proportions, within certain limits——

7545. *Mr. Keynes*: You mean their proportions between bills and advances, not their proportions between cash and deposits? — No, I was thinking of their proportions between bills and advances at the moment. If we had fairly constant figures, if we knew that they were prepared to allow their proportion to vary between a certain maximum and a certain minimum, and if we saw from their figures that they were getting up towards their maximum proportion, we should know that there was no need for us to create additional credit at the moment. If on the other hand we saw that they were getting down towards the minimum we should see that there was need for us to create the credit, in order to put their proportion further up towards their maximum, and give them a margin of play within which they could work.

7546. Apart from changing their proportions between bills and advances, the banks might change their proportions between bills and long-dated securities, not on considerations of system but on considerations of profit? — That is possible, certainly; I do not know what their policy is. They might, as you say, do it simply for reasons of profit.

7547. When they thought long-dated securities were going to fall they would move to bills, when they thought long-dated securities were going to rise they would move to long-dated securities? — Yes. It has been alleged in the last few days that such variations have been taking place. We have no information on the subject.

7548. *Mr. Brand*: It would be within fairly narrow limits, if they kept to the proportions? — If they kept rigidly to the proportions. I am disposed to think that there is rather too much anxiety to keep strict proportions regardless of even seasonal influences. I will just give you one example, if I may. If the Bank of England, because it loses cash heavily at certain seasons of the year, were to take action at once to restore its proportion, although the demand was merely seasonal, it would be blamed, and justly blamed. It is considered quite right and proper that the Bank of England proportion for instance shall vary during the year, as it did last year, between 60 per cent. and 20 per cent. Nobody pays very serious attention to it if it can be explained by seasonal causes. In the first quarter of the year, when the volume of Treasury Bills is reduced, why should it not be proper for the bankers to reduce their proportion of liquid assets held in the form of bills, knowing, as they must do, that the bills will be re-issued during the succeeding nine months, and that they will be able to restore their proportion? Why is it necessary to try and adhere to, I do not say an absolutely rigid proportion, because I know the proportions vary, but a more or less established proportion of bills at a time when seasonal operations must mean a reduction in the volume of bills available?

7549. *Mr. Keynes*: Is not the difficulty this, that it would not pay them to move from bills into Consols, for example, with the expectation of having to move back again within six months, irrespective of what had happened to the price of Consols, unless the rate on bills had fallen to such a level in relation to the yield on Consols that the difference in yield over a short period would meet their expenses and the change of value; and if there is an insufficient fall in the Treasury Bill rate to induce them on the grounds of profit then you will have all the evils on the foreign exchanges that you want to avoid? It seems to me you would be asking the banks to prepare for a fall in Treasury Bills relative to long-dated securities, and that is precisely the phenomenon that you wish to avoid. You are asking the banks to meet fluctuations in the Government position by taking a risk for which they see no adequate remuneration in the relative rates of interest. I should have thought it was much more the duty of the Central Authorities to see that the fluctuations in Treasury Bills did not take place. There are a good many ways in which they could do that – for example, by bringing the Sinking Fund into play mainly during the period in which otherwise the volume of Treasury Bills would fall in. The Central Authority could take that supply of Treasury Bills, rather than ask the bankers to take the risk without expectation of reward for it? — I should like to think over that.

7550. You have told us that the reason for the change in the Bank Rate would generally be to affect the foreign position and the exchanges by making the different levels effective in the market. That would merely be the first and most obvious consequence of the change of Bank Rate. What remoter effect would you expect, particularly if you were only able to make the new rate effective by reducing the volume of credit? —You say that the first effect would be its effect on the exchanges?

7551. Yes. — It would do one of two things, or both. It would stop money leaving the country, or it would bring money into the country, probably.

7552. Yes? — When you say 'what remoter effect should we expect a change in the Rate to have', I am not quite sure that I follow what you have in mind.

7553. If the higher Rate can only be made effective by some curtailment of the volume of credit would you expect the ulterior consequence to be dearer money and a restricted basis of credit? — Well, a restricted basis of credit necessarily would mean a curtailment of the bankers' power to grant accommodation. That, I take it, is one of the effects which you would have expected.

7554. That is the next stage in the course of events – but what after that? — You wish to pursue it to the question of the supply of credit to industry?

7555. Yes. The point is this: Everybody admits the efficacy of Bank Rate in its effect on the exchanges, but it is argued that against that you have the possible detrimental effect on the home situation? — Certainly if industry is relying to too great an extent upon accommodation from the bankers.

7556. If it is only relying to a normal extent, the results would be the same, would they not? — In kind but not in degree.

7557. If you curtail the basis of credit you would, it seems to me, partly get a further favourable effect on foreign exchanges in that some part of the credit which you have destroyed might otherwise have been employed in purchasing foreign securities. But if you rule out that part, the rest, assuming that people are keeping about the same amount of their resources in the form of fixed deposits with the banks, would sooner or later have to come off the weekly wages bill, would it not? Credit is partly employed for foreign purposes. As regards home purposes it is partly employed for financial transactions and partly for making the wheels of business go round. Undoubtedly part of the curtailment would affect that part of the credit which is used for trade purposes, and you would expect some part to come off what is used for making the wheels of industry go round? — Some part would, I imagine. As to the importance of the part, I think it is possibly magnified at the present time by reason of the fact that – here, of course, I am speaking of matters which are not within my own knowledge, seeing that we have no direct connection whatever with trade and industry – industry has probably borrowed more heavily from the bankers than is desirable, in other words has obtained too large a proportion of its credit in the form of bankers' credit instead of in the form of investment credit, I agree that the effect of a curtailment of credit might be felt more seriously at such a time than when industry is financed, so far as its capital requirements go, more by investment credit than by bankers' credit.

7558. My object in trying to bring out that point was that it would seem that changes in

Bank Rate, while extraordinarily effective for the foreign situation, are very dangerous in the internal situation, or can be so in certain circumstances if they have to be associated with changes in the volume of credit. So it would seem to be of great importance, if it were possible, to develop devices for making a higher level of Bank Rate effective without having to curtail the basis of credit available for trade purposes in this country. I suggest that that is a side of banking organisation which is perhaps inadequately developed? — I agree that if you could make your Rate effective without having to touch your volume of credit, from the point of view of internal trade and so on, it would be convenient; I question whether it is always possible however.

7559. I should not have thought it would have been impossible, because it is the price of a particular kind of security; it is not a universal thing, it is the price of a particular type of asset. If you increase the supply of that particular asset one would expect you to do something to alter its price relative to other types of assets. I am not suggesting that anything should be done on a very large scale, or made effective over a long period, but something surely could be done to prevent short period changes in Bank Rate from having so great a reaction on the internal situation. There may be other kinds of expedients that could be suggested if one's mind were exploring that system of evolution. Our system is peculiar in this respect. I do not know if there is any Continental system in which the method of regulating the foreign exchanges is so intimately mixed up with the flow of credit for home purposes as with us? — (*Witness*): No, but then there are few foreign centres, I should say, with the complete freedom of market which exists here. (*Mr. Brand*): I would like to ask whether Mr. Keynes means that in his opinion the short period changes required to effect the purpose would be brought about purely by influences on the floating balances as between one country and another without having any effect on the industrial situation at all? (*Mr. Keynes*): That is my suggestion. I do not suggest that you could do a great deal, but it may be that something could be done in that direction.

7560. *Mr. McKenna*: I daresay you will have observed, Sir Ernest, that over a comparatively short period of time, the total deposits of the Clearing Banks may vary by as much as £100,000,000? — I think I have the figures here . . . Have you any special recent period in mind?

7561. Well, almost any period that you may take, in any year or at any time, you will see that the total of deposits may vary by as much as £100,000,000 in less than 12 months. (*Mr. Tulloch*): I think in the first three months of this year there was a variation of £84,000,000? — That is quite true; this year there was.

7562. *Mr. McKenna*: I think it has been found to be true that over a comparatively short period of time the total deposits of the Clearing Banks vary by from £50,000,000 to £100,000,000. You will observe that the banks keep an almost invariable cash ratio to deposits? — They publish figures which claim that they do.

7563. Yes. I recognise the distinction. I recognise also that that distinction has certain grounds. But I think you would agree that whatever window dressing may take place once a week in order to show a better cash ratio than the average for every day of the week, that window dressing occurs quite regularly? — That may be true.

7564. And consequently, although it may not be a correct figure, the resultant figure for comparative purposes with other resultant figures in other months will be correct. Its relationship to other figures will be correct? — No; I doubt that.

7565. Very well. I will put it another way. Do you estimate that the variation in the figure of the cash proportion as published by the banks is anything considerable? — Yes; of course, it is difficult for us to form an estimate, because we have no information regarding the bankers' cash holdings, what the fluctuations in their own cash holdings may be, but from such sources of information as are available to us, we believe the day to day fluctuations in the cash proportions of the banks to be substantial. It is difficult for me to give figures as our information is, of course, derived from confidential sources and we have had to assume till money to remain constant, but the Committee could perhaps obtain the actual figures from the Clearing Banks.

7566. I would suggest to you that the practice, which I deprecate very strongly, of window dressing either weekly or annually is so regularly adopted that the true cash ratio would be somewhat less than the published ratio, but always about the same amount less? — That may be so; I could not say.

7567. If that be the case, if over a comparatively short period of time there are variations of £100,000,000 in the bankers' deposits, those variations are caused by the action of the Bank of England in increasing or diminishing our cash basis? — You say the action of the Bank of England. When we were talking of the variation in the bankers' deposits, I think Mr. Tulloch spoke of a variation of £80,000,000 odd – that seems to be the largest movement that I see going back to the beginning of last year; it took place between January and March. A large part of that reduction surely was due to no action of the Bank of England.

7568. I will put the question in a different way. It was action *through* the Bank of England; whether the Bank of England took the initiative or not, it could only be through the Bank of England? — That is true.

7569. And being through the Bank of England, the Bank of England could, if it had wished, have countered the action? — Is it suggested that when the public are paying their taxes we should create an equivalent amount of new credit in order to restore the bankers' deposits?

7570. That would not be the remedy I should suggest, but it is not necessary at the moment to discuss that point. I am only dealing with the point that when our deposits are up £100,000,000 it is due to action by or through the Bank of England, and when they are down £100,000,000 it is equally due to action by or through the Bank of England. I will tell you my purpose in suggesting this. We do not know in advance what the action by or through the Bank of England is going to be. The banks do not know that in advance. When their deposits are up £100,000,000 they do not know but what in the course of the next month the Bank of England will bring them down by £100,000,000. We have no indication of what the policy of the Bank of England is going to be in the way of increasing or restricting the volume of credit? — No, and I must confess I cannot quite see how you could have an indication.

7571. I am not suggesting anything at all. I am merely trying to get at the fact. It is so; we get no information. I do not say whether we should or not. If that be the case, does it not follow that when the deposits of the banks are high they are bound to keep rather an exceptionally liquid position in reasonable anticipation that before many months are over their deposits will be down by £100,000,000 and the withdrawal of deposits must come off their liquid assets in the first instance? Is not that so? — Yes; but we are speaking of a variation of £100,000,000 in the bankers' deposits. I cannot find that there has been anything like that variation, except between January and March, 1930. I have only the figures for 18 months with me.

7572. In March, 1928, the deposits were £1,709,000,000, and in December, 1928, they were £1,843,000,000, an increase of £134,000,000. In 1929 they were £1,769,000,000 in May, and they were £1,864,000,000 in January. That is nearly 18 months. They did not fluctuate by as much as £100,000,000 in that one calendar year, but compared with 12 months in the previous year they fluctuated a great deal more. And so on. You find, confining yourself not to one calendar year but to a period of 12 months, they were always up by £100,000,000. I put it to you, when the bankers' deposits are high they have no knowledge that those deposits may not in a few months' time be £100,000,000 less, and they are bound to keep an exceptional part of their assets liquid in order to meet any withdrawals which may, and which they know from experience do, take place? — Which must take place.

7573. I do not agree with that. They know from experience they do take place? — And must take place.

7574. I am not at all prepared to agree to that. On the contrary, I should be disposed to assume the deposits are continually rising? — Taken year by year they do.

7575. The figures speak for themselves? — I have figures here as to the deposits in February. You spoke at one time about a drop in 12 months of £80,000,000.

7576. I spoke of a drop of £63,000,000 last February compared with the preceding February? — In 1929 compared with 1928.

7577. £63,000,000 between 1929 and 1930? — That is quite true; there was a drop of £63,000,000. During the first three years after 1925 there was an average annual increase of about £17,000,000 per year; in 1929 there was an increase over 1928 of £80,000,000, a purely fortuitous increase, and I should maintain that to compare 1930 with 1929 is hardly a fair comparison of normal figures. In 1929 the bankers' deposits undoubtedly had been very much swollen by repayments of debt temporarily financed by the issue of Treasury Bills.

7578. Surely it is common ground between us that provided the bankers keep a constant cash ratio the quantity of the bankers' deposits depends entirely upon the Bank of England? — Yes, but not the variations. The Bank could not possibly pursue a credit policy which would even out all the variations.

7579. It could not pursue a credit policy which would cancel variations from day to day, or even from week to week? — Or for a longer period than that.

7580. But I would contend that they could pursue a policy which would prevent serious variations from month to month. I am not quite sure that on one point I heard you aright. Am I correct in having taken down the words that you find in the state of the money market your principal guide to the credit requirements of trade – or some words to that effect? — Well, no, I do not think I said quite that. I said that the state of the money market is one of our principal guides and that we should expect the requirements of industry to be reflected in the condition of the money market.

7581. You would expect the credit requirements of industry to be reflected in the money market, and you find in the state of the money market your principal guide to the credit requirements of industry. That is how I interpreted it? — Yes.

7582. *Mr. Keynes*: Is not the seasonal fluctuation in the volume of Treasury Bills a much greater evil than you are admitting? If the volume of Treasury Bills outstanding falls by £50,000,000 at a time when Income Tax is being collected, the demand of the market for Treasury Bills, unless the Bank of England does something to restrict credit, will be unchanged; so that the shortage of £50,000,000 in the supply of Treasury Bills is bound to cause a serious weakening of the bill rate unless the Bank of England restricts credit. If the Bank of England does not restrict credit this weakening of the bill rate is serious, and may be disastrous for the foreign exchanges. Consequently, whenever there is a seasonal reduction in the volume of Treasury Bills the Bank of England must either allow bill rates to fall dangerously low, or else it must restrict the volume of credit. If it restricts the volume of credit, owing to the maintenance of their proportions by the banks, some of that restriction is bound to come off the accommodation to trade, whereas there is no reason to suppose that trade needs any less accommodation at the time when Income Tax is being collected than ordinarily – in fact it is rather the contrary, because they have to borrow to a certain extent to meet those demands. So that the mere fact of the seasonal fluctuation would be quite a good explanation of why, year after year, there has been a set-back to trade in the spring. It has been a matter for jocular remarks in the Press that the bankers in their speeches at the annual meetings, which take place early in the year, say how splendid trade is, and three months later there has always been a set-back. Is it not natural to suppose that there would be a set-back, as a logical consequence of the effect on the market of a seasonal fluctuation of £50,000,000 in the supply of Treasury Bills to the market? — Well, does it not come back to the point to which I referred before? It does follow if the bankers seek at that period to keep up the same proportion in their portfolio.

7583. *Mr. McKenna*: May I interrupt again? As a banker, I put it to you: How can they help themselves? If their deposits are going to come down they must have liquid assets, that is to say, bills, with which to pay off the deposits. Therefore, in anticipation of a reduction of their deposits, they must have an excessive supply of bills, or, at any rate, not less than the normal supply? — I agree they must have before their deposits fall.

7584. *Mr. Keynes*: Would it not mean an enormous fluctuation if the supply of Treasury Bills is reduced by more than £50,000,000? The total quantity of the bill holdings of the banks is something like £250,000,000, so that it would mean a very large alteration in their proportions? What alternative assets could they take in for this short period? — I agree, if the whole of the reduction in Treasury Bills fell upon the banks, but it does not.

7585. If every Spring the joint stock banks were to buy £50,000,000 of Consols or securities they would always be buying at a rising price and selling at a falling price. They cannot put out advances which they can hope to recover in a short time. It is not merely a question of diminishing the quantity of bills; they have to increase something else? — I recognise that. Then how is it suggested that the volume of bills should be kept level – by sales from the Issue Department?

7586. Partly in that way and partly by the Treasury spreading its outgoings more evenly over the year? — Its outgoings? I doubt whether the Treasury can very well even its outgoings, but it may be that it could even its incomings. The manner in which the national income is collected is defined, I take it, by Statute or Regulation. As to the manner in which expenditure goes out, apart from such attempts as can be made to even the distribution of interest on debt – attempts which are always being made – I doubt whether the Treasury could under existing arrangements even its outgoings.

7587. It may be that this is a defect inherent in our system. All that one is suggesting is that it is a defect? — You mean that the revenue should mainly come in at one period of the year?

7588. That we should have a large fluctuation in that particular kind of asset, the price of which is of fundamental importance in relation to foreign trade? — I agree it would assist matters if we could avoid having to increase very steadily the volume of Treasury Bills from April to December and then make a corresponding reduction during the succeeding three months.

7589. At present you are in the dilemma that either you have to let the bill rate fall to a rate which is dangerous to the foreign exchanges or else you have to curtail the basis of credit every spring? — It would, I agree, be an advantage if receipts and payments could be more evenly adjusted.

7590. *Chairman*: Mr. Keynes suggested that the banks might buy securities, but have you any guarantee that it would be securities held by investors that the banks would purchase? In the circumstances you are presuming, might it not be that the purchase would be from the money market or particularly from jobbers? — I do not think that jobbers often carry much stock nowadays.

7591. The point is that it needs to be genuine investment money which would ultimately reach industry? — Yes.

7592. *Mr. Keynes*: I think the difficulty of the Bank of England is precisely the same as the difficulty that I was suggesting in regard to the joint stock banks; namely, that if there were this purchase of long-dated securities every Spring which had to be sold later, the person conducting the operations would always incur a loss on the transaction? (*Mr. Lubbock*): I think Mr. Keynes is suggesting that the loss of profit which the joint stock banks would naturally shrink from, purchasing securities and selling them at a lower price, should be transferred to the Bank of England. (*Mr. Keynes*): When I made that suggestion I had not prominently in mind the fact that there would be a drop. The course of the discussion does suggest to me that the solution is not a satisfactory one, that the solution would have to be found in other ways. If the public were gradually building up balances all through the year with which to pay their Income Tax and then in February paid their Income Tax with money that is used by the Treasury to pay off Treasury Bills, and those Treasury Bills are held by the banks, then if the banks are prepared to allow a temporary variation in their proportion of bills no harm will be done to anybody by their proportion of holdings falling by £50,000,000 and the volume of credit falling by £50,000,000. But that is not the true position. (*Chairman*): You have to operate under certain conditions. You have to pay a tax at a certain period of the year. That is the phenomenon, Sir Ernest? — Yes.

7593. *Chairman*: Whether it would be desirable to alter the nature of this phenomenon, or practicable to do so, is hardly within your province? — That has nothing to do with the Bank of England.

7594. You have to do the best you can with the position with which you are confronted? (*Mr. McKenna*): The collection itself would not reduce our deposits. The reduction of our deposits is due to the fact that we pay the money into the Bank of England, but it does not come back out of the Bank of England for two or three days. There is always a lag. (*Mr. Brand*): Is it always two or three days? (*Mr. McKenna*): Each week. If as fast as the money went into the Bank of England it came out again, there would be no reduction of our deposits. (*Chairman*): Some of the complaints that are made about the Bank of England may not be due to the Bank of England, but rather to the circumstances with which the Bank of England has to deal. Consequently you cannot attribute to the Bank matters which are not within their own province. (*Mr. McKenna*): Well, Mr. Chairman, I think that if the Bank of England advised the Treasury as to the methods by which this lag could be avoided the Treasury would probably adopt them? — I should just like to say a word about the lag, in order that the Committee may realise the efforts that are made to avoid it. The Treasury naturally does not want to keep surplus balances lying to its credit, and in co-operation with them, we are always trying to devise means by which surplus money can be passed out as rapidly as possible. I should like to give you some evidence of the lengths to which we went last year in our efforts to avoid a lag. If we overdo it – that is to say, if we arrange so that the Treasury put out more money than they are taking in – there is only one course open to the Treasury, and that is to borrow from the Bank of England on Ways and Means advances to make up the deficiency. Although it is perfectly true that Ways and Means advances are not, as regards amount, an important factor except (say) at the date of the payment of a War Loan dividend – perhaps for a few days now and then – it is a rather remarkable fact that out of the 300 working days of last year there were Ways and Means advances outstanding on 92 days, which proves that on 92 days the Treasury had paid out money faster than they were taking it in. That is one-third of the year.

7595. *Mr. McKenna*: May I just say, I recognise that efforts have been made; I readily admit that the conditions are improving, but my case is that still further efforts could be made, and the evil could be almost entirely destroyed? — (*Witness*): I doubt whether the evil can ever be destroyed unless a means can be found of evening out the receipts and payments on Government account. (*Mr. Keynes*): I should like to say, without arguing, that I am now persuaded that Sir Ernest Harvey's original argument is right, and that the cure could be brought about to a great extent by the joint stock banks varying their holding of bills.

7596. *Chairman*: Now I think you might resume the tenour of your exposition, Sir Ernest. Some of the facts have been a little bit anticipated? — I think they have. I want next to give one or two illustrations of factors which have influenced the Bank in their policy. I take, as my first illustration in connection with Treasury requirements, November, 1925, because it affords a rather striking instance of how the Bank's hand can be forced in the matter of Bank Rate. Gold had been lost during the later months of that year, and there were apprehensions of a rise in the New York Rate. The market therefore decided, so it appeared, to leave the Treasury Bills rather severely alone. We had difficulty for a week or two, the Bank had to come to the rescue to cover the amounts required, efforts were made to reassure the market, but without success, and eventually, by the end of the month, the last week, the amount which the Bank had to provide in order to cover the required amount of tenders was very substantial. It has been suggested that when there is failure to secure the requisite amount of tenders the remedy is in the Bank's own hands, that by applying for £1,000,000 or £2,000,000 of Bills they will have created the basis of credit on which tenders can be put in the following week for perhaps nine times the amount of credit so created. But on that occasion, in spite of taking additional Bills week after week, we were finally forced, as I say, to provide in one week a very substantial sum despite the earlier expansion of the credit basis. We had been struggling to carry on with a four per cent. rate in the hope that when the New Year came we might get a certain amount of relief as regards the foreign position. But finally we were compelled, simply in order to get the Bills taken up and to avoid our being driven into a very difficult position by reason of the large additions of credit that we were having to create, to raise the rate from four per cent. to five per cent.

We have had other experience of the same kind; I do not say that the rate has often been forced up without there being other contributory causes, but we have had similar experience in other times, and a very remarkable case occurred in the middle of last year. Again we had been suffering gold losses, and the market, which often displays not unnaturally a rather nervous disposition at such times applied very sparingly for new Bills. In three successive weeks, we were faced with the necessity of taking up substantial amounts of Bills because the tenders were deficient. Again the expansion in the earlier weeks failed to induce a sufficiency of tenders.

It is true that, as it happened – and, of course, it was a contributory cause – we were suffering continuing losses of gold; indeed, in one respect it was almost fortunate that we did lose gold at that time, as by that means a great deal of the credit that we had created was offset without action by the Bank. But in spite of the fact that we had lost a considerable amount of gold – I think it was something like £15,000,000 over the three weeks – and in spite of the fact that it was a time of year when a seasonal outflow of currency was making drafts on the bankers' cash, the bankers' balances actually rose to the highest figure at which they had been for some months. A time when we are losing gold heavily is not as a rule one at which we want to be forced to create additional credit. Thus, the Bankers' balances were increased by between £5,000,000 and £10,000,000, in spite of the loss of £15,000,000 of gold in addition to a considerable amount of currency. It was a time when we were anxious not to be forced to put up our Rate; and assurances had been given to the Discount Market that if they would help us it was not our intention if we could possibly avoid it to put up the Rate. At the same time, in order to hold the position and in order to withdraw again some of the credit that we had been forced to create, we had been under the necessity of selling other assets very heavily in an endeavour to keep the position under some sort of control. I think the magnitude of the Bank's difficulties arising out of the volume of Treasury Bills has not been fully recognised, but from what I have said regarding successive deficiencies in tenders, I think the Committee will appreciate that, if the weekly offerings of Treasury Bills are too large, very serious difficulties are sometimes occasioned for us.

Then on the subject of gold imports and exports, and the policy of off-setting, I should like to say a word or two, and I take as an illustration our action in the year 1928. We received during the earlier months of that year, the first eight months, considerable additions to our gold, and I think there was a feeling in some quarters that we should have allowed those imports of gold to have more effect on the credit position.

7597. *Mr. Lubbock*: What was Bank Rate at the time? — Bank Rate was 4½ per cent. We felt that a 4½ per cent. Bank Rate inflicted no hardship on trade, that if we created additional credit it would inevitably compel a reduction of Bank Rate, a reduction which would probably to a large extent not have been passed on to trade. We have always understood that there are minimum rates at which money is lent to trade, and that the minimum in most cases would not be below, if indeed as low as, 4½ per cent. We felt then that if we created additional credit on the basis of this gold we might force down our rate, and we anticipated that the gold would leave us again later in the year, and we, therefore, offset the arrivals of gold. Later in the year the exchanges began to go rather seriously against us. We lost gold very heavily. Our policy was, however, to try and maintain a stable Bank Rate of 4½ per cent., and in doing so we permitted the whole of the gold gained earlier in the year to leave us. Again we did not allow gold movements to affect the volume of credit; that is to say, as the gold went out we created credit to replace it. We deprived the bankers of no basis for credit at that time. We sold foreign assets heavily, assets which we had accumulated on previous suitable occasions when our exchange had been receiving artificial assistance by the flight from foreign currencies and so on; we had taken advantage of the artificial support thus given to us to make provision against the day when we expected that those foreign balances would probably leave us. We were forced to part with a large portion of those assets, and we created credit to replace them also. We were anxious, as I say, not to have to raise the Rate. We were in hopes all the time that steps would be taken to curb what was then our main trouble, namely, the speculative boom in New York, and that we might be able to win through on a 4½ per cent. Rate and avoid any necessity of increase. However, in 1929 there was every sign that the boom was going to continue. We went to the length then of competing for gold at special prices in order to try and maintain the position. In spite of that we lost further gold on balance, exchanges did not respond, and, finally, on the 7th February, by which time we had maintained the Rate of 4½ per cent. for very nearly two years, we were forced to go up. We were partly actuated by the need for protecting our own immediate position, and I will not say that there was not a hope in our minds that possibly our action might have some effect on sentiment in Wall Street. That was an outstanding example, I claim, of an effort on our part to try and maintain a stable rate in face of great difficulties. When we are charged sometimes with not allowing the inflow of gold to have its normal effect on credit, it must not be forgotten that our action is generally prompted by a desire to have the means to withstand the reverse movement when it comes, as come it undoubtedly will, without having then to shorten the credit position again.

Another factor which, of course, has its effect on the Bank of England is foreign investment on British account. It is a subject on which I was asked a few questions, when I was here before, chiefly from the point of view of the efficacy of controlling foreign investment by means of what is known as the embargo. Of course, the embargo has been tried on several occasions, but its effectiveness is limited, certainly in the matter of time. I think it is right to pay a tribute to the loyalty that the leading houses in London have always shown to any views that have been expressed to them in regard to these matters. When an embargo has been put on it has generally been quite effective within its own limitations for, say, two or three months, but I know of no means by which foreign investment on British account can either completely or indefinitely be checked. We have seen again and again how issues have been offered to this market, how, under the system of the embargo, they have been turned away, how they have later been brought out in other markets and how, in a very short time, a large amount of those issues has found its way into the London market by private investment.

The Stock Exchange speculation in New York was, of course, a very serious factor with which we had to contend during the whole of 1928 and part of 1929. We were contending not with an official Rate normally below our own, but with a real effective Rate in New York which was always higher, and sometimes very much higher, than our own Rate, and I think I may not unfairly claim for the Bank of England, that they did, by their policy of last year, assist in the correction of that position. I think that the action which the Bank took then in making it evident to everybody that they were prepared to go to whatever rate was necessary to protect this market was certainly a contributory factor in breaking the speculative boom which was doing so much damage, not only to us but to all other European countries. However, the break was brought about, our policy since has been to get rates down as rapidly as possible, partly so that trade should get the benefit of lower prices for credit, and partly with the idea of trying to stimulate the demand for investment securities. We have, as you know, been interesting ourselves actively in the field of rationalisation, but we have felt that if the best is to be got out of that policy it is necessary that we should get the investment market, if possible, into a condition in which it would be more likely to absorb sound industrial investments issued by concerns after they have been rationalised on a proper footing. There has been no recent attempt to reduce the volume of credit. There has been talk from time to time about the ineffectiveness of the Bank Rate. We have not attempted to make it effective. We have every now and then indicated to the market that we think it desirable that the rate should not be allowed to fall away too much, but that we have no wish to have to take steps to enforce an effective rate. Of course, in a period of generally falling rates there is not the same need to make the rate effective as when rates are rising. The mere fact of rising rates is evidence of the need of an effective rate. But our policy ever since the collapse of the speculation has been to get rates down and, as I say, to stimulate a demand for investment securities in the hope that by that means we might in due time assist the transfer from the banks to the investment market of a certain amount of capital financing of industry.

A good deal has been said from time to time about the Bank's alleged policy of deflation. I know of no such policy and I think it is sometimes forgotten that whatever policy the Bank might adopt, whether inflationary or deflationary, they are without the power to enforce it, except to a definitely limited extent, now that we are working again under the gold standard. The gold standard does place a most definite limit on the power either to inflate or to deflate. Any attempt to deflate must mean, it seems to me, turning the exchanges in our favour and an automatic check therefore exists to any attempts which might be made in that direction. I do not know whether anybody wishes to ask me anything on any of these points, Mr. Chairman, or shall I continue?

7598. *Chairman*: I think that would probably be better; our time is so short this morning that we want, if possible, to get from you your ideas on all these subjects. — There has been a good deal of discussion about the question of changes in the volume of Treasury Bills and their influence on the credit position, and in these discussions I think there has been one fact that has been rather overlooked. Treasury Bills, of course, are a very convenient means of adjusting the credit position from day to day, and I have already indicated that our efforts last year to adjust the position as between the Treasury and the public did result in Ways and Means advances being outstanding on one-third of the working days of the year. I have also said something about the dangers of having too large an amount outstanding. But of all the bills in the market Treasury Bills are the least responsive in some respects to movements in Bank Rate. Treasury Bills have got to be issued whatever the Bank Rate – they have got to be issued by the Treasury, they have got to be taken up. It does not matter whether the Bank Rate is 5 per cent. or 10 per cent. In pre-War days the position was entirely different. A very large part of the bills which were then being carried in the market were on foreign account and an increase in the Bank Rate had the effect of driving away a lot of that financing. It does not matter where you put the Rate now, so far as the market is working on Treasury Bills the Bank Rate has no effect except on the rate which the Government has to pay for their money. Our policy, therefore, has been to favour a reduction in the volume of Treasury Bills. We think it would be much better, certainly it would restore more efficiency to the Bank Rate, if there were a smaller volume of Treasury Bills and a larger volume of commercial bills, and our hope has been that possibly if the volume of Treasury Bills were reduced the bankers would be persuaded to endeavour to restore somewhat the use of commercial bills. That unresponsiveness of the Treasury Bill has been at the back of our mind in our desire to see the volume reduced.

The next point I come to is the control of the Bank of England over the credit base. Of course, the only part of the credit base of which we have direct knowledge is the total of the bankers' balances with us, but the credit base is much broader than the mere balances of the bankers at the Bank of England. We have no information, except twice a year, as to the volume of cash which the bankers are holding in their tills. I understood Mr. McKenna to say this morning that he did not think the volume fluctuated very much. We have never known, we have never been able to form any opinion as to whether it fluctuates or whether it does not. It would, I think, undoubtedly be an advantage to us if we could have real information as to what is the fluctuation of the volume of cash in the hands of the bankers. Whether it would be possible for them to give us that information, I do not know.

7599. *Mr. McKenna*: I see no objection to giving that information. I would give it to you at any time you please. — I think it would be useful, because at present it is only on the 30th June and 31st December that we can arrive at a really accurate figure. We can then, by deducting from the Bankers' published figures of 'Cash in hand and at the Bank of England' the total balances held at the Bank arrive at the amount of cash in the Bankers' own hands.

7600. Your difficulty arises from the fact that we only publish monthly statements, and not weekly? — Monthly statements. They are always historical when they are published; that is to say, they are after the event. We have no means of keeping in touch with what the movements are, if movements there be, whilst they are taking place.

7601. With our figures you can know at any moment. If you take 11 per cent. of our deposits and deduct the amount of our balances with you the rest consists of notes? — If we take the figure of 11 per cent. which you publish?

7602. Take 11 per cent. of the deposits? — That may be so with one bank.

7603. That is the figure on which we work. It would hardly vary – perhaps on one day, 0.1 or 0.2 per cent.? — Well, as I say, we have definite information regarding only one portion of the credit base, and I think it would be a good thing if we could have current information regarding the rest. It would give us more definite figures on which to work.

But even if the position of the exchanges is satisfactory and there is no prospect of loss of gold, it seems to me that we can never have a sufficiently large credit base upon which to build a super-structure of credit which would be sufficient to meet all the credit requirements of industry. I think industry has relied too largely for capital requirements on the bankers, and that it would undoubtedly be advantageous if the bankers could see their way to induce industry to finance a larger part of her short term requirements in the bill market and encourage industry to get into a position in which she can appeal for investment credit as regards her longer capital requirements. I think it is wrong to encourage industry to think that everything rests with the Bank of England. I do not think that is true. It may rest with the Bank of England to create the credit, but I do not think it rests with the Bank of England alone to determine always the moment at which and the extent to which the credit shall be created. After all, our contact with industry must be through the bankers. It is no part of our business normally to have any direct financial connection with industry. In so far as it is a banking function it is the function of the joint stock banks.

That brings me back again once more to the point that I was mentioning previously, and that is the question of whether it is in the power of the bankers to give the Bank of England some better indication than we get at present of what the needs of credit for industry may be. For the Bank of England to embark on a policy of creating credit in advance of the known requirements of industry, I think, would be dangerous. We know, as I have said before, that if we create credit which is not required for industry it finds its way directly into the short market as a rule – almost invariably, I think – and may create difficulties for us, and may even force on us the need to restrict credit that has already been created. I may be wrong – I do not know, after what Mr. McKenna has said this morning – I had always thought that the reason why credit created by us finds its way so rapidly into the market was very largely because the banks had no need for it at the moment for extending additional accommodation to industry; they naturally do not wish to leave the money lying idle, therefore, they find such employment for it as they can, and in order to have it readily available in case of need they put it into the short money market. Is it not possible that the bankers could be a little more elastic in the proportions of the different liquid assets which they retain, that they could work between a maximum and a minimum, keeping us informed of what their real position is so that if we see that they are below the mean between the maximum and the minimum we have the means of restoring their figures without the fear that that money will immediately be put into the short money market and be employed in such a manner as to depress rates, and possibly compel us for the protection of the reserve position to embark on a policy of reducing credit? I do not think myself that the Bank could embark on the policy of putting out credit in the absence of a known requirement for that credit, simply in the hope that it might stimulate requirements for its use. I do not believe it is possible, without running a serious danger to our reserve position. In making these remarks, rather disjointedly, I am afraid, I am merely endeavouring to put on record one or two of the principal points that I had it in mind to mention, leaving more detailed considerations until a later date.

... ...

... ...

Friday 25 July 1930

Sir Ernest Harvey, K.B.E., Deputy Governor of the Bank of England, recalled and further examined.

8797. *Chairman*: I think that the last time we met, Sir Ernest, we had taken up with you the various topics in your outline down to and including the third head, and I understand that to-day you propose to take up the matters dealt with under heads IV and V. Head IV deals with the adequacy of existing financial arrangements, under three branches – the question of the amalgamation of the Issue and Banking Departments, the relation of banking to industry, and the relation of the Treasury to the Bank and the money market. They are all large subjects, and I think we might begin at once with your disquisition on those matters? — I refer first to the question of the Issue Department, more particularly as regards the separation of the Issue Department from the Banking Department, what exactly has been the purport of that separation, and the question as to whether the continuation of the separation is desirable, or whether there are advantages which could be gained from an amalgamation of the two Departments which cannot be obtained by any other means. There is one fundamental point regarding the separation of the Departments which I am not sure has always been quite appreciated. I personally have always held the view, though I have not always found everybody ready at once to agree with me, that the separation of the two Departments undoubtedly made the notes an absolute prior charge on the Bank's holding of gold, ranking before all other liabilities. I think it is obvious if one reads the Act of 1844 that that was the intention of the Act. The Act said that the Bank of England were to transfer, appropriate, and set apart to the Issue Department, an amount of £14,000,000 of securities and all the gold coin and gold bullion which was not required for the purpose of the Banking Department. I think that the direction to set aside all the gold held at that time implied obviously that we were similarly to set aside all future gold acquired by the Bank. That certainly has been the Bank's view of the intention of the Act and the Bank have always acted in accordance with that view. The Act then went on to say that notes were to be created against the whole of those assets, and such notes as might not be required by the public were to be held by the Banking Department. It said further that the whole amount of the bank notes, including those held in the Banking Department, 'shall be deemed to be issued on the credit of such securities, coin and bullion so appropriated and set apart to the Issue Department.' We hold, therefore, that the notes are undoubtedly a prior charge upon the Bank's gold. If the two departments were amalgamated, I suppose that that position could be maintained by some provision in a new law, but I think that the continuation of the separation has the advantage of keeping the position prominently before the public. What would be the advantages of amalgamation? I believe that amalgamation of the Department – Mr. McKenna may be able to tell me if I am right – was first seriously advocated, by the late Sir Edward Holden, about 15 years ago. I remember he directed several of his addresses to the shareholders of the Midland Bank particularly to that subject. I have not had an opportunity of referring to what he said at the time, but my clear recollection is that he advocated amalgamation for one purpose and one purpose only, that purpose being to give elasticity to the currency system. Now, by the Act of 1928, elasticity has been given to the system. I do not stop to discuss at the moment whether the provisions are adequate, but merely wish to make the point that it has been possible to give clasticity to the system without departing from the traditional method of separation of the two Departments. I do not know whether there are other advantages which are claimed for amalgamation. Personally, I do not see what those advantages would be. The continued separation certainly has the advantage of following tradition. That is not without considerable value. At the same time, of course, adherence to tradition for tradition's sake could not be allowed to stand in the way of an improved system, but the Bank for their part would certainly not favour amalgamation unless it could be shown that there were manifest advantages to be obtained by amalgamation which could not be obtained by some other method more conforming to the traditional system in the same way that elasticity has been secured without departing from that system.

8798. *Mr. Keynes*: May I put some questions on the possible advantages? The present method of reckoning the Bank of England ratio is quite different from what obtains in any other country, and may, therefore, be to a certain extent misleading. It has been claimed for the amalgamation of the Departments that the true strength of the Bank of England would appear more clearly to the world if its gold were calculated as a percentage of its note issue, than if we followed the present rather curious system of reckoning the ratio by the surplus over the legal tender requirements of the nation and its proportion to the liabilities of the Bank otherwise than on notes? — Yes, but if the notes are in fact a prior charge upon gold, would it be right to act as if the gold was held *pari passu* against the deposits and notes, that is to say, so far as the deposits are concerned, to an extent which exceeds the amount of the notes in the Banking Department, which at present is the measure of the direct claim of the deposits against the gold.

8799. I should not have thought that the publication of the ratio would have implied that, because what one would publish would be the proportion of gold to notes. It would not be the proportion of gold held against notes and deposits. Is it not undesirable that anyone should think that the deposits of the Bank of England are less well secured than the notes? Those deposits now mainly represent the ultimate reserve of the joint stock banking system. The banks already hold a large amount in notes. You would not suggest it would be more prudent for the joint stock banks to keep their ultimate reserve in notes rather than in deposits, would you? — I was intending to refer later to a point which has some bearing upon that. Perhaps this would be a suitable moment at which to deal with the question which has relation to the present figure of the fiduciary issue, £260,000,000. We estimate that at the close of 1928 – and it is only on the last day of the year that we have the requisite bankers' figures to enable us to arrive at a close estimate – the amount of notes actually in circulation in the hands of the public was £263,000,000——

8800. They were in the hands of the public? — They were actually in the hands of the public, excluding bankers' tills, and that total of £263,000,000 included the notes at that moment circulating in Southern Ireland, but actually in course of withdrawal, so that the amount of the fiduciary issue slightly exceeded the total of notes circulating in the pockets of the people in the United Kingdom. In other words, the notes held by the bankers, assuming that the amount of the notes then in the hands of the public may be regarded as the approximate amount necessary for carrying on the ordinary transactions of day to day business and unlikely therefore to be presented for payment, could have been paid in gold.

8801. How much of that was in the hands of the bankers? — We estimate that the amount of notes in the hands of the bankers was about £132,000,000; the total outstanding being £395,000,000. To arrive at that figure we took the total of 'Cash in hand and at the Bank of England' as published by the bankers on the last day of the year, and having deducted their balances at the Bank of England we further deducted an estimated amount of subsidiary coinage based on the returns which the banks make to the Mint every June.

8802. Would there not be a great deal to be said for a system by which the bankers would not keep more notes than they really required and would keep the rest of their deposits with the Bank of England, those deposits reckoning equally with notes as security? The Bank of England's real strength compared with other countries would then become apparent. Under the American law, as you know, banks may not regard as part of their legal reserve any part of their till money. Their legal reserve must be kept on deposit with the Federal Reserve Banks. On the other hand, in France where there is no law on the matter the banks have gone to the other extreme. They keep with the Bank of France only what they require for clearing, and they keep their reserve on a very substantial scale in notes. I should have thought that modern opinion would have approved the American system rather than the French system, and that the English system, which lies between the two, might be expected to move in the American direction rather than otherwise. If half of those notes held by the bankers were to come back to the Bank of England, and if the Bank of England were then to calculate gold as a percentage of its active note issue in the way that all other Central Banks do, it would show a position of extraordinary strength? — Are you speaking of the proportion of gold to notes alone, or to notes and deposits?

8803. To notes alone. — There is no difficulty in showing that proportion now, is there?

8804. No. It is not, for that reason, a very

substantial point. The point is to show the ratio which is in accordance with world practice rather than a somewhat eccentric figure, which I think everybody would agree the present ratio is? — Would not that be met by publishing two proportions, a proportion of gold to notes for the Issue Department and, as now, a proportion of reserve to deposits for the Banking Department; that shown for the Issue Department to be the proportion of gold to notes other than notes in the hands of the Bank.

8805. I think the existing Bank of England ratios have such historical weight behind them that you could not get people to pay attention to the new ones until you drew attention to them. That, however, is an unsubstantial point. The substantial point is that if stress is laid on the greater security of notes as against deposits, would it not be unreasonable to expect the bankers to hold more in the Bank of England and less in the form of notes? That would be a substantial point if, in bringing the system into conformity with the American system, the joint stock banks were required to keep such part of their reserve as they do not require for till money with the Bank of England. I should have thought that it was a disadvantage in modern conditions that there should be any suggestion that the security of notes is in excess of the security of deposits? — The return of the bankers' excess notes to the Bank of England would increase the Bank's liabilities in the form of bankers' deposits and the Bank's assets in the form of reserve by the same amount.

8806. Yes. — And would increase the proportion of security against deposits.

8807. Yes. — And so far as your object is to show a strengthened position you would obtain your end by that means.

8808. Yes. It would not be only showing a strengthened position, it would be an actually strengthened position? — It would.

8809. Because without any alteration of the fiduciary issue the Bank of England would then have enormously larger reserves at its disposal? — Yes.

8810. It seems to me that in a way the suggestion for the amalgamation of the two Departments is an unsubstantial thing insofar as it is a mere form, but it might be a convenient occasion for the resettlement of the fiduciary issue. It might be that if the banks were to agree to keep more of their assets in the form of Bank of England deposits there would, without any change of the fiduciary issue, be a wide margin. If that were not so this would be a good opportunity for giving the Bank a maximum degree of latitude without appearing to do such a weakening thing as would be involved by an alteration in the fiduciary issue. We had a discussion with Sir Richard Hopkins, who told us that one of the arguments for the existing law was that it meant a minimum breach with tradition and we were not weakening the existing safeguards. If you had a change of this sort it would give an opportunity of bringing uniformity to the system without giving to the world the appearance that we were weakening the fiduciary issue. (*Lord Bradbury*): What is the change that you desire on merits? (*Mr. Keynes*): The change that I should desire on merits would be this. I do not think I should lay stress on the amalgamation of the Issue and Banking Departments, except so far as it would give an opportunity for doing something. The other changes which I should like to see would be first of all an increase in the amount of gold which the Bank of England could export if necessary in its own judgment, without appealing to the Treasury authority for alteration in the fiduciary issue. That you could bring about either by the bankers preserving a larger amount of their reserves in balances, or it could be done by a change in the system, such as a law that the Bank of England must hold a minimum quantity of gold, and that any gold in excess of that minimum quantity is to be at the Bank's free discretion. (*Mr. Tulloch*): But the question does arise as to the ability of the banks to transfer cash from their domestic reserves to the Bank of England, because the whole basis of holding this cash is to meet emergencies. (*Mr. Keynes*): I am going on the assumption that the amount of the banks' holdings of notes is very much greater than they require. (*Mr. Tulloch*): I am not sure that that assumption is well founded. I do not know how it is in the case of the majority of the banks, but there is no reason for holding in our own special reserve at our head offices and so on any more than we think is desirable to meet possible emergencies. There might be an occasion when you would wish to rush cash from one part of the country to another. You never know what may happen. You cannot tie yourselves down too much in relation to that consideration. I think it would be a rash assumption that the banks did hold more than is necessary in their view, having regard to possible emergencies. I should like to hear Mr. McKenna's view on that. (*Mr. McKenna*): We certainly hold a great deal more than we should ever regard as likely to be wanted, but then, I think we hold a great deal more in notes than other banks. (*Mr. Tulloch*): In reserve at various centres? (*Mr. McKenna*): Our reserve consists of our balances at the Bank of England, our till money and the notes which we hold in reserve in our vaults. Those notes are very considerable, much more than we could ordinarily require in such a hurry that we could not get notes from the Bank of England. (*Mr. Keynes*): One of the reasons why I should like a movement towards the American system, by which the lawful or conventional reserve of the banks should be Bank of England deposits rather than notes, is that at present the adequacy or inadequacy of the fiduciary issue largely depends on the policy of the joint stock banks. If the joint stock banks turn in a large amount of their notes they can render the Bank of England's position very flush. On the other hand, if they withdraw a large proportion of their deposits they can embarrass the Bank of England. Is it not undesirable that the joint stock banks should have an influence in either of those two directions? — They would not embarrass the Bank if they were to draw on their present balances and hold the amount as reserve, except to the extent to which such action might disturb the public mind through an apparent weakening of the Bank's position.

8811. *Mr. Keynes*: Not long ago the Bank's published reserves were down to below £30,000,000. Supposing that instead of being below £30,000,000 they had been below £15,000,000 it would have been a cause of anxiety at any rate to the public. The Bank of England has much more absolute control over the whole position if the field within which it can operate without asking for a mitigation of the law, or calling public attention to it, is the widest possible? — Personally, I am sometimes tempted to regret that the need has not already arisen to exercise the provisions of elasticity afforded by the Act of 1928. I could almost wish that had occurred in order that the public mind could be educated to regard such action as not necessarily indicating any cause for alarm.

8812. But you can never get the public to do that if you only exercise the provisions in case of need. If you did so the suggestion would be conveyed to the public that there was a need, even at a time when it was quite obvious to you that you did not need it? — But if there was a provision that we should not draw gold below a certain fixed figure, we should obviously have to keep our gold normally at a considerably higher figure.

8813. As you do now? — As we do now, and surely we are entitled to some direction from the State which is responsible for the laws governing the currency system as to the figure to be regarded as appropriate in normal circumstances?

8814. I should have thought not in normal circumstances; I should have thought you would have required directions from the State as to what the ultimate reserve for exceptional circumstances ought to be – say, for the sake of argument, £75,000,000. Part of the gold would be kept for ordinary purposes, the rest would be held at the discretion of the Central Bank to meet fluctuations in the foreign position? — But if you had not accustomed the public in some measure to increases in the fiduciary issue by the exercise of some such discretionary power as that given under the present arrangement, might you not as you approached any fixed minimum such as £75,000,000 intensify any feeling of alarm seeing that the minimum would probably have come to be regarded as the figure which Parliament had considered as indicating the actual point of absolute danger.

8815. I do not think anyone could reach that conclusion. But you would have a very much wider margin than you have at present. You could have much more discretion than you have now and still have as your working minimum £25,000,000 or more. You see we have an object lesson now in the case of the Bank of France. It would be very easy for the State, thinking of a particular set of circumstances, to tie up the Central Bank to the greatest possible extent so as to avoid even the thought of abuse. Is it not much better, when times are quite good and there is no great emergency, to accord to the central institution as much latitude as you can, rather than have to wait to see whether the emergency powers should be exercised? — But I should like that power regarded not merely as an emergency power, implying necessarily by its exercise a position of actual danger.

8816. You could never get it regarded as not an emergency power if you only use it in emergency? — Perhaps it is right that I should tell the Committee that last autumn we did in fact open negotiations with the Treasury with a view to a possible increase in the fiduciary issue. The position was this: On the 1st October our reserve had fallen to £28,000,000. We did not apprehend that there would be any immediate need to increase the fiduciary issue because at that time of year the flow of currency is inwards and we had, therefore, every reason to expect for a time a steady increase in our reserve. At the same time, according to the experience of previous years, we had to contemplate a probable net increase in the demand for currency between that date and Christmas of £20,000,000, which meant that unless there had been meanwhile additions to our gold holding our reserve would have been drawn down to £8,000,000 at Christmas. We therefore opened negotiations with the Treasury and informal arrangements were practically concluded under which the Bank would have made application and would have been granted the right to increase the issue. As it happened, the need never arose. As expected, during the succeeding weeks currency returned in fairly large amounts from circulation, and during the same period considerable amounts of gold which we had had no reason to expect began to reach this country from South America, from Australia and later from the United States. In the result at Christmas our reserve did not fall below a minimum of about £25,000,000 – the minimum occurred on a day which was not a Wednesday evening and, therefore, was not published – and that at a time of year when currency requirements are at their maximum. Even then our proportion only fell to about 25 per cent. Thus the actual need to put the Act in force never arose. But do you consider that if we had had to increase the fiduciary issue under those circumstances and at that time of year it would have had an alarming effect on the public mind?

8817. Very likely it might have had the opposite effect, but I think it would have confirmed the feeling that these powers when used are an indication of anxiety? — But in past history, even in times of real anxiety, whenever the fixed amount of the issue has been departed from, the mere announcement that the Bank has obtained authority to depart from normal legal requirements has usually been sufficient to re-establish confidence, and I should have thought that at least an equal degree of confidence might be looked for on the employment of the provision for elasticity included as part of the normal system in the Act of 1928.

8818. *Mr. Brand*: Does not the Act itself regard it as rather an emergency provision? It can only last for two years. After that you have to get legislative covering? — At the end of two years, and I take the object of that provision to have been that if the increase were due to causes of a more permanent character Parliament should be given the power to reconsider the normal figure established in the Act.

8819. *Mr. Keynes*: I think there is great force in that, but it still seems to me that you cannot expect the public to regard it as a non-emergency measure if, in fact, you only use the power when your statistical position is one which everyone would interpret as one of anxiety? — Well, we have to consider the effect on the minds of the public here, but not only here. We have also to consider the effect on the mind of the foreigner. I am not convinced that the foreigner would not prefer a system under which the need, if and when it arises, has to be met by a step taken formally by the Bank in co-operation with the Treasury, with notice to Parliament, rather than that the matter should be left to the sole discretion of the Bank of England.

8820. Why should the foreigner think that? — I think he might consider that by the import of the Treasury into the matter at the instance of the Bank he would have double assurance that the circumstances in which the alteration of the fiduciary issue took place had received the fullest consideration in all its bearings, and that the justification for it was for that reason perhaps more certain.

8821. I should have thought that he might have had more confidence in the Bank of England alone than in the Bank of England in conjunction with the Treasury? (*Mr. Brand*): I may be absolutely wrong, but my view would not be the same as Sir Ernest's; my view would be that the foreigner would regard consultations between the Bank of England and the Treasury and the sort of formal steps that have to be taken as showing that it was a very exceptional act, brought about by exceptional circumstances. If the Bank on its own were able to have more freedom they would take no notice of it. (*Chairman*): After all, it is equivalent to the suspension of the Bank Act, which was always regarded as indicating a crisis, was it not? The 1928 provision is to avoid the necessity of an act of indemnity, and to make it seem less of an emergency character. Mr. Keynes suggests that if there were amalgamation a greater degree of elasticity might be attained. That elasticity might be attained by other means than amalgamation, might it not? (*Mr. Keynes*): Yes. I do not think it comes anywhere in Sir Ernest's programme. (*Chairman*): The point, however, was not so much the question of the mere formal separation of the Departments as the advantages to be obtained. (*Mr. Keynes*): The effect on foreign opinion. What is the right and responsible action in these matters has, I think, been tremendously affected in the past, and is now, by the policy of the Bank of England. If the policy of the Bank of England in the laws which it puts forward gives rise to the view that it is the right thing to lock up a very large part of your gold reserve by tradition, that will tend to be imitated by other countries. Now, it is very undesirable that other countries should do that. It is very desirable that there should be as much freedom as possible, that we should not have two-thirds of the gold in the world absolutely unused. The Bank of England has locked up for it by law a very high proportion; it has set a very bad example; if it were to go in the other direction it might be the beginning of a general trend on the part of Central Banks to have a larger quantity of free gold? — Is not part of the gold locked up the result of the arrangement under which, so I understand, one bank at any rate holds a large amount more notes than is necessary?

8822. *Mr. McKenna*: That cannot lock up gold, can it? — Certainly, so far as the Bank of England is concerned.

8823. No, it does not lock up gold. It affects the reserve of the Bank of England? — And therefore locks up gold.

8824. No, because that is only the surplus over the locked up gold? — The measure of the Bank's free gold is the reserve in the Banking Department of the Bank of England.

8825. It will affect your reserve? — A reduced holding of notes by banks would increase our reserve, and thus increase the free gold. The measure of our free gold is the size of the Banking reserve.

8826. *Mr. Keynes*: I think I began by agreeing with you that if we pursued the American practice under which the banks keep most of their reserve in the form of deposits, that would be an alternative way of moving in the direction I have indicated? — Quite.

8827. With regard to Mr. Tulloch's point, supposing it were found that a very large part of this was required as till money, that could be met, as I think it is in France, and certainly in Germany, by the central institution having depots from which the joint stock banks could withdraw notes without undue delay if they required them? — That I suggested, with special reference to Scotland and Ireland, when I was before the Committee on a previous occasion.

8828. *Mr. Tulloch*: It was not the till money; it was a kind of second line reserve? — I did suggest that we might open depots, and I hold the view that such a policy might improve the apparent strength of the Bank and increase their holding of free gold.

8829. *Mr. Keynes*: If you did that, then the last reason for the joint stock banks keeping a large amount of notes would vanish. There is one other set of advantages. At present the division of profits between the Bank of England and the Treasury is very much mixed up with the size of the fiduciary issue. We discussed that on previous occasions when you were here, at some length? — Yes.

8830. And we also discussed it with the Treasury. It seems to me that one advantage of the amalgamation of the Departments would be that it would make possible the resettlement of that issue on lines which would prevent any overlapping in regard to the division of profits, which would be entirely separated from such considerations as the appropriate size of the fiduciary issue. I would suggest that it might be a preferable arrangement if the payments of the Bank of England to the Treasury were fixed at a given sum, subject to revision, no doubt, at fairly long intervals, but that on the other hand the payment of the Bank of England to its own shareholders should also be fixed at the present figure, and then all further questions about the division of profits would be got out of the way. It would be easier to do that if there were a general re-arrangement of this sort going on than if it is to be re-opened in any other way. If you assume that the present division of profits is quite right you just stereotype it? — As regards the fixing of the rate of dividend on the Bank of England's stock, whilst the rate has for some time been to all intents and purposes, stabilised, we should not wish to surrender the right to increase or reduce the dividend. As regards the profits as a whole I, for my part, prefer the present system. I have always thought even in the days when the Bank received some of the profits of issue, that it is difficult to contest the right of the State to receive the whole profits of issue. The responsibility for defining the currency, establishing its security, and conferring upon it the status of legal tender, rests with Parliament, and it seems to me that that undoubtedly implies the right of the State to receive the resulting profits. Under a profit-sharing system applied to all the activities of the Bank, I can conceive of circumstances in which pressure might be put upon the Bank to have regard to profits to an extent which does not obtain at the present time.

8831. But you could arrive at the payment to the Treasury as a result of the calculation of what the profits on the note issue would normally be. The profit on the fiduciary issue fluctuates now with the holdings of securities? — It does very largely. There have been considerable variations even since the amalgamation.

8832. That, again, raises the point, which might or might not be desirable, that the Bank has a certain quantity of assets to use for its various purposes, a very important part of which is in the Issue Department? — That is so.

8833. Suppose the Bank, in its management of the market, varies its holdings of long and short-dated securities, at present it has a choice whether it varies them in the Issue Department or in the Banking Department, and the profits of the Treasury may be affected by something which is technically the right thing for the Bank to do, whereas the effect on profits is rather irrelevant to the considerations which ought to move the Bank. Is there any rhyme or reason really in the payment to the Treasury being reached by this traditional means? — I do not say that some other means could not be found, but I think there is great convenience in the present system and that it works equitably.

8834. You remember that when we were talking about this matter before, we agreed that an alteration in the fiduciary issue might become desirable in certain conceivable circumstances, and in so far as the Bank had not lost gold the difference in the profits of the Bank might be very material? — I have never been convinced that it would deprive the Bank of anything but abnormal profits.

8835. But it would if it took place in advance of the loss of gold? — Not unless it took place unnecessarily long in advance of the loss of gold.

8836. It might take place in order to re-assure public opinion, and there might be no loss of gold taking place at any time. I should have thought that circumstances might have arisen for increasing the fiduciary issue where it was not so much a question that the Bank of England with all its knowledge thought it was going to lose gold, but that in view of the lack of knowledge of the public outside it was necessary to re-assure them that you had a strong position. But you cannot re-assure the public without handing over to the Treasury what might be an embarrassingly large sum? — But the anxiety in the mind of the public would not arise unless the Bank's reserve had been drawn down to a small figure, and if the Bank's reserve had been drawn down to a small figure their earning assets must have been increased, assuming that they had not correspondingly reduced the volume of credit available in the form of bankers' balances.

8837. Could not the public anxiety arise from outside events; for instance, from the fact that there was a war somewhere in the world, or because some event had taken place weakening the position of the gold reserve? Supposing, as at the present moment, the public see fresh gold going away from the Bank of England; the Bank does not take steps to re-assure the public; surely, it might be well that the Bank should show a position in which it could meet the fresh gold going out without anxiety? — But would the Bank re-assure the public by increasing the fiduciary issue without ostensible need? Would they not rather disturb confidence by giving what would amount to notice that they were expecting a heavy drain of gold?

8838. If you were moving in the direction that you are advocating, of getting the public into the habit of not being unduly alarmed when the fiduciary issue was increased, that would mean that the Bank would have to increase the fiduciary issue sometimes when it was not expecting to lose gold. You come back to the point that, if you only increase the fiduciary issue when you really are menaced yourself, your action would always be interpreted as an indication that there was a time of strain? — We should not increase the fiduciary issue merely for the sake of getting the public accustomed to it; but I cannot convince myself that in any circumstances in which an increase of the fiduciary issue was necessary it could seriously affect the Bank of England from the profit-earning point of view.

8839. *Mr. Brand*: Because you think your earning assets would always be bigger? — I think so.

8840. Unless bankers' balances were reduced? — Yes.

8841. *Mr. Keynes*: Take the case of last autumn, when you might quite well have extended the fiduciary limit: in fact, the gold drain did not take place. Therefore, if you had to suspend it at that date – and I gather that you very nearly did——? — No. I have not said that. We made provisional arrangements; of course, we did not contemplate that the need would arise for some time afterwards, but we made our arrangements in good time so that if the need did develop we could then increase without undue delay.

8842. We are legislating for all sorts of circumstances the consequences of which cannot be foreseen. It might be conceivable that an increase of £20,000,000 – I do not know what figure you had in mind; that would not be a very large increase, and if a change were made at all, it would hardly be for less – if it had continued in force for six months would have cost the Bank of England £500,000? — Yes, but it would not have continued for anything like that period unless necessary, in which case our earning assets would have been increased correspondingly.

8843. *Chairman*: There is one point made against amalgamation in the Cunliffe Report upon which I should like your view. The Committee say: 'We think that the amalgamation of the two Departments would inevitably lead in the end to State control of the creation of banking credit.' I do not quite follow that statement? — Well, it coincides with our view. As I said a short while ago, we fear that if the Government were to share in the profits of the Bank as a whole, it might lead to attempts on the part of Government to exercise control over the banking activities of the Bank.

8844. Suppose that the suggestion of a fixed dividend were adopted and that the State received the profits of the note issue on some new principle such as Mr. Keynes has suggested, what would happen to the balance of the profits; would they all go to reserve, or are they to be shared by the State and the Bank on some basis? — (*Witness*): Well, I should be afraid of a system under which, having paid X per cent. on Bank Stock, and having paid to the Treasury the profits of the issue, the balance of profits had to be divided in a fixed proportion. A Central Bank should always be free to maintain a position which will permit it to shape its policy without the need to pay regard to mere profit making. (*Mr. Keynes*): I did not intend to suggest any change on that point. My idea was that at present dividends are in effect fixed, and therefore the surplus goes to reserve. It seems to me very desirable that the Bank of England should control very large reserves, and that the building up of those reserves is not a thing that one should object to. I think that system has been adopted in many countries, and I see nothing against it.

8845. *Chairman*: I was, perhaps, not quite fair in suggesting in an earlier question that the provisions in the Act of 1928 were intended to obviate the suspension of the Bank Acts. It was at least the intention, was it not, that the legislative powers there given were intended to be used as and when required for economic reasons? — Yes.

8846. As, for example, to assist in the economy of gold, or to meet the increasing demands of production. The power of expansion has not, in fact, been utilised for either of those purposes yet, has it? — No.

8847. If it were utilised with a certain degree of freedom in circumstances which were not necessarily panic circumstances, the public might be inured to it, as a useful expedient; but is not the apprehension attendant on the use of this measure such that you are not likely to revert to it other than as an expedient in circumstances of emergency? — That is not our intention.

8848. I would like very much, passing from that, to come to a matter which is very much our concern – your sub-heading 'The Relation of Banking to Industry.' It is a large topic, but I have no doubt you have certain ideas to place before us on that matter. Let us hear your approach to the problem? — Ordinarily, the Bank, of course, has no direct financial contact with trade and industry. The contact of trade and industry with banking is normally through the joint stock banks. We are not bankers for industry now, whatever we may have been in the past. It is to the joint stock banks, therefore, that we have to look for guidance as to the needs of industry for an increased volume of credit or for signs that the volume of credit is in excess of requirements. The question then arises how are the banks to give us that guidance? I almost ought to apologise for referring again to the point but as I have said, on several occasions, the barometer to which we look is the volume of money that is seeking investment in the short market, presumably for the reason that, except in so far as additional short assets may be necessary for the restoration of bankers' proportions, the funds in question cannot find employment elsewhere than in the short market. We have also, of course, the figures that are published by the banks, but those, in their present form, are not of much value, except on two days in the year. It has been suggested that we ought to measure the adequacy of credit by the volume of our securities. But the securities alone afford no indication whatever; if we are to judge by assets obviously we must consider the total assets of all kinds, not only securities, but also the reserve. But even that figure affords no reliable indication, because the volume of credit created in respect of the Bank's securities and reserve is divided between the public deposits and the private deposits and the public deposits vary considerably from time to time. We therefore have to look to the volume of the private deposits considered in conjunction with conditions in the money market, and we have to measure on that basis the adequacy of the volume of credit – always, of course, having regard to the external position, the state of our reserve, the position and trend of the exchanges. I say that the division of the volume of credit between the public and private deposits varies considerably at times, and I told the Committee when I was here last as evidence of the efforts which we are constantly making in co-operation with the Treasury to ensure that the bankers are not deprived of too great a proportion of that volume by reason of there being excessive public deposits, that we always endeavour to ensure that surplus moneys which come into the public deposits shall be released as quickly as possible. I cited, as evidence of the extent to which we have been making such efforts, that last year on 25 per cent. of the working days of the year so far from the Government having excess balances their balances were deficient and they had to borrow from the Bank on Ways and Means. I have taken out similar figures for this year up to date. Of course, in the first half of the year we do not ordinarily expect the Government to borrow frequently on Ways and Means advances, because it covers the first quarter of the year, during which they receive heavy amounts by the ingathering of the revenue, but I find that so far this year, including the first quarter of the year, they have borrowed on Ways and Means advances from us on more than 25 per cent. of the working days. I repeat then that it is to the bankers' balances, considered in conjunction with the state of the short market, and with such knowledge – I admit it is not much – as we are able to obtain from bankers' published figures as to whether their holdings of liquid assets of a short character are adequate – that we must be guided as to whether the demands of industry on the bankers are such as to require a larger volume of credit. We are not, as I have said, in direct touch with industry and therefore have no first-hand information.

8849. You have spoken of your barometer, but would your means of knowledge be improved, and would you have a check upon that barometer, if you were able to get additional information from the joint stock banks? — I think that is possible.

8850. What kind of information would you desiderate which you think might be given without undue prejudice to the interest of the joint stock banks? Putting the matter in a general form, do you desire to create more of a liaison between the Bank of England and the joint stock banks in order to give you better means to gauge the industrial position? — I speak with some hesitation as to this, because I realise that in asking the joint stock banks for more informative, more frequent, figures I may be asking for something which it may be difficult for them to supply, such as, for example, weekly figures consisting of the average of their day to day figures.

8851. *Mr. McKenna*: There is no factor or figure known to us in our bank that we are not absolutely willing to give you at any time? — I am sure of that. My only doubt is as to whether you could give us a weekly average of all daily figures.

8852. We make out a weekly abstract of all the figures of the bank; that abstract is open to you at any time you like? — Would that abstract distinguish between cash in hand, cash at the Bank of England, gold and silver coin, money at call and short notice, investments, acceptances?

8853. Yes. We have the day to day figures of our cash, our call money and our bills, but we would not have a daily figure for our deposits and advances. We could give you that statement from week to week? — If we saw a demand for bills in the market we should then be perhaps better able to judge whether it was due to the bankers trying to restore their normal proportions or whether they were merely endeavouring to employ surplus credit for which there was no demand.

8854. It may be said that the first use of additional money held by the banks is invariably in the discount market, either for the purchase of bills or for lending in the market. That operation is effected at 10 o'clock in the morning, before anything else is done, in order to make use of the surplus money for that day. Any other demands that come in during the day will be dealt with in the knowledge that there is this additional money in the market, some of which may be available for next day, or that, on the ensuing day, bills which will run off need not be renewed because of the additional supply of bills bought at 10 o'clock in the morning. Therefore, it is true to say that all additional cash is always in the first instance in the market; it is, nevertheless, available during that day or any subsequent day for use elsewhere? (*Chairman*): That is what is done with the money, but the point that Sir Ernest is really on is the statistical information, whether he has got sufficient information to enable him to gauge the industrial position. (*Mr. McKenna*): I understood Sir Ernest to ask whether we used our surplus money where we could, in order to get our statistical ratio correct? — Yes.

8855. *Mr. McKenna*: We do use it in that way. Having been used in that way it is very liquid? — The idea I had in mind was whether the information you could give us could be such as to indicate whether you had money which was not required for the maintenance of normal ratios of liquid assets and was not needed to meet the requirements of industry.

8856. That could be extracted, I think, from the existing published bank figures, regard being had to the ratio of their advances in trade? — But how often are they available?

8857. Every bank has those weekly. That ratio is very high; the newspapers have recently looked at the latest figures and have commented upon the reduction of the advances in trade, but they have not had regard to the effect of the new Companies Act, under which the Balance Sheet has to show under a separate head certain figures that used to appear under advances. If all the same items were called advances to-day as were called advances last year, there would not be anything like the supposed reduction in total? — Of course, the furnishing of real weekly averages would have another advantage, in so far as it removed or diminished the practice of window dressing on one day a week?

8858. Oh, undoubtedly! — It would have this advantage: At the present time tenders for Treasury Bills by bankers and by the market are entirely governed by the bankers' window dressing days, with the result that we get enormous maladjustment in the bills taken from day to day. If, on the other hand, the Bankers worked on a real weekly average and did not merely build the required cash position on one day a week, tenders for bills could be spread more evenly over the whole of the week, those both of the bankers and of the market, and we should get a much more even adjustment between the Government's incomings and outgoings on Treasury Bill account. That would be a great advantage to us.

8859. Speaking for myself, I am as opposed to window dressing as you are. My Bank published on 30th June our cash ratio as 9.7 per cent. Our average for the month was over 11 per cent. I have observed that some banks published ratios at the 30th June almost double ours, although their cash ratio throughout the month and throughout the year has been considerably below ours. Why they do it I cannot understand, because nobody would be so foolish as to be taken in by these window dressing figures? — Take our own figures, which are merely a statement of our position on Wednesdays. Those figures form the basis for comparisons which are frequently made between some period of the year and the same period of another year, and yet they may be totally unreliable for that purpose. Our figures vary much from day to day, and such a comparison might be between the minimum in a week in one year and the maximum in the corresponding week in another year, and there might on the average be in either case as wide a difference as perhaps £10,000,000 between the figure published and the average of the week. If the Committee think it would be of any value, the Bank, I feel sure, would be quite prepared to publish every week their day to day average. I do not say that in some weeks there would be much variation, but there would be some weeks in which there would probably be considerable variation, and the average figure would afford a more reliable basis for comparisons.

8860. *Chairman*: Surely a common policy adopted both by the Central Bank and the joint stock banks in this matter would tend very much to the public interest? — I think it would...I think, Mr. Chairman, I have now dealt with all the matters of which I intended to speak.

8861. I am very much struck by this discussion. Perhaps I might just summarise the position as I understand it. If you are to assist industry as you would wish to do you must have further sources of information than you possess just now. On your side you would be prepared to advise that more information be supplied by the Bank of England than is available at present in the existing weekly return, but you would expect equally on the side of the joint stock banks that they would co-operate with you by providing on their side further information, and you would anticipate that if that further information were obtainable you would have an even more sensitive guide to the credit policy which the Bank should adopt, and so be better able to adjust your policy to the needs of industry from time to time. Does that represent the position? — Yes.

8862. The essential thing seems to me to be to secure information which will afford closer liaison between those who are in contact with industry and the Central Bank? — Of course, there is other information that we should like to obtain. We cannot forget that, with every wish to provide adequate credit for industry, we must always have regard to the foreign position.

8863. You face two ways, of course, inwards and outwards? — We must. At the present time, for example, I think it would be an advantage if we could have fuller information regarding the foreign balances held in London. We have very little at the present time.

8864. Is that obtainable? — That is a question upon which one has some doubt. I have no doubt that the British houses in London would be prepared to give us information – aggregate figures, of course; we do not ask for details; if they could give us totals which we could aggregate for the whole market it would be useful.

8865. *Mr. Keynes*: You want figures for the different kinds of foreign investments, to show the distinction between bills held for correspondents and deposits? — Yes. In totals.

8866. *Mr. Brand*: Not by countries? — Well, I think that would be necessary, but the question is, could we get such information from the foreign houses? I do not know.

8867. Except by legislation? — I do not believe you could, except by legislation.

8868. *Chairman*: Legislation is very dangerous; it might discourage the very things you want? — That is what I am afraid of.

8869. Would you formulate for us the exact respect in which you feel yourself deprived of information which you think would be useful? There are two stages: First of all, what in an ideal world you would like to have if you could get it for your guidance and assistance, and secondly, what it is practicable to get. It would be very interesting to hear from you where you feel yourself handicapped for want of information, and what information it might be possible to get. For the completion of your equipment of knowledge could you say what would be the ideal set of information for the Central Bank? — I think undoubtedly the bankers' figures, as I have described them, the weekly averages of the bankers; and that, from what Mr. McKenna has told us, would probably be obtainable.

8870. *Mr. McKenna*: The weekly average of the cash being based upon the daily figure? — Yes; but could we get other figures besides the cash?

8871. On some items, yes, but not on all, I am afraid. But would it matter? (*Mr. Keynes*): The banks must know most of the items. The only doubtful thing would be the advances. You could reach the deposits by adding up the other figures. They must know their investments, their cash and the amount of money at call. (*Mr. McKenna*): We have 2,000 branches; we cannot get daily figures for every item. We make them up week by week? — I realise your difficulty, but then, after all, advances probably do not vary from day to day to the same extent.

8872. *Mr. McKenna*: The published monthly statement is the average of the weekly statement. We make out the weekly statement every Wednesday night. — If we had a weekly statement with the daily average statement of the cash and other liquid assets I think that would be sufficient.

8873. The weekly statement and the average daily statement of cash. That we could give you, and we could also give you the average daily statement of the market position; that is to say, bills and call money; that we could give you daily. — I think if we had that we should not need to ask for more. Then we should very much like to know the total of the acceptances outstanding. Some of the banks publish their figures now on certain dates.

8874. *Mr. Brand*: To be complete you would have to get that information from the foreigner also? — We should; and that again introduces a doubtful factor.

8875. *Mr. Keynes*: The Bank of England is prepared to discount certain types of bills. Could it not make a condition that no one who had not complied with this request for information was an acceptable acceptor? — We do not take foreign acceptances, though we should like to know what they amount to.

8876. Could you ask them? — We could ask.

8877. *Chairman*: Mr. Brand, how far do you think, apart from the information coming from the banks, your kind of organisation could assist? (*Mr. Brand*): The figure that the Bank would like from our side would be, I suppose, foreign balances and acceptances? — Yes.

8878. *Mr. Brand*: I do not think the British banking houses would object to sending their figures to the Bank confidentially. Of course, we might hold bills on behalf of a Central Bank abroad. I suppose you would put them as an aggregate. (*Chairman*): Sir Ernest wanted them country by country. (*Mr. Brand*): I think it would be difficult to do it in some cases unless you got the leave of the client concerned. — That we should have to leave to the custodians.

8879. *Chairman*: What would be the practical effect; suppose you were equipped with all that knowledge, what actual practical effect will it have? — The variation in the total of foreign balances would be an important thing for us to know – whether they were increasing or decreasing. It would assist us in estimating the position as between London and foreign centres.

8880. Would it help you to avoid the possibilities of mistakes that might be injurious to our credit? — It might enable us to measure better any changes taking place in the foreign position. I think it might enable us to formulate more reliable estimates as to any need for taking action.

8881. It might enable you, for example, to avoid a restriction of credit which otherwise you might feel it your duty to enforce? — Possibly, though I do not wish to exaggerate such possibilities.

8882. I am thinking of it all in terms of its practical effect? — We have already been endeavouring to get information from other quarters, such as the retail trades, and I am glad to say that so far our efforts have generally met with a favourable response. I think that undoubtedly we shall get reliable indices of such matters as the rise and fall of the turnover in the retail trade and obtain a better indication as to the trend of trade in general. In regard to retail trade in particular practically all the big houses have agreed to supply us with figures.

8883. Then, may we take it that it is now part of the considered policy of the Bank of England that it should, to the best of its ability, get further information regarding the state of industry and commerce than it has hitherto possessed? — Yes. We have been endeavouring to do that for some time past, but it takes time.

8884. It is a policy which the Bank has adopted and desires to pursue? — Yes.

8885. With a view to becoming more efficient in its service of credit? — With a view to having better knowledge, more exact knowledge, on which to base its actions.

8886. And thus avoid unnecessary restriction of credit, possibly? — Possibly.

8887. Would the Bank wish further powers conferred upon it to enable it to obtain that information? — I would rather act without powers; I would rather get it, if possible, by the goodwill of those concerned. If you are granted powers to demand certain things there is always the possibility that you may be refused anything which is not definitely within the scope of those powers. The more you can rely on goodwill the greater the extent of the information you are likely to get, in my judgment.

8888. *Mr. Keynes*: There is an important point I should like to be reassured about. While all the details should be confidential, it seems absolutely essential that this information, when it is centralised at the Bank of England, should be published in the aggregate? — Certainly, if the fullest value is to be derived from it, I think it should be so far as we had been accorded the necessary permission to publish.

8889. I think the building up of a state of affairs in which the information at the disposal of a comparatively well-informed public, and the information at the disposal of the Bank of England, is entirely different, will always tend to create the maximum of friction? — Possibly.

8890. You want, as far as possible, to have a well-informed public and the Bank studying the same data? — There is every advantage in that, because the more fully the data upon which the Bank base their actions is known the less opportunity will there be for uninformed criticism of the Bank's actions.

8891. Yes, and any act of the Bank would be much less violent in its effect because it would to some extent be foreseen. That state of affairs would be much better than that the Bank should be suddenly doing something which is quite inexplicable to people who do not know the exact truth. (*Chairman*): How far would you wish the Bank of England to make available the information? (*Mr. Keynes*): I think the more they can make public in some monthly publication or otherwise those essential elements in the situation which are needed for a rational judgment, the better. (*Chairman*): Supposing, Sir Ernest, as the result of your diplomatic approach, you do get a much greater amount of information on these topics, could the results of it be provided in the form of a Bulletin such as Mr. Keynes suggests? — Yes, I think it might; if it were a mere collection of statistics. The Bank would not be prepared to add comments on the various figures other than such explanatory notes as might seem necessary. As you know, we do already prepare a summary of statistics for foreign Central Banks. I thought it might interest you to see – I am afraid I have only one proof of it to-day – a special half-year summary which we are proposing to send out to Central Banks in the course of a few days. If you think it would interest the members of the Committee to receive copies, we shall be very happy to supply them. It gives many more statistics than are contained in the ordinary monthly summary of which I gave a specimen to the Committee at a previous visit.

8892. *Chairman*: Is that a confidential document, or could it be made available to the public? — It contains for the most part information which is already available, though not in so handy a form. In so far as it contains tables which are new, such tables are based on information which is already available.

8893. *Mr. Keynes*: Are your retail trade figures in that document? — They are not yet completed. The intention is to supply the figures to the Board of Trade, who will publish them. If they publish them there is no reason why they should not also be included in this document, many of the figures in which are taken from such sources as Board of Trade Returns and publications of the London and Cambridge Economic Service.

8894. *Chairman*: How far will you be in liaison with the Board of Trade? It is undesirable that the Board of Trade and the Bank of England should both be collecting the same kind of information? — We are working in close co-operation with the Board of Trade.

Chairman: I think we have had a very profitable discussion, Sir Ernest. We are very much obliged to you for coming again.

... ...

Wednesday 18 February 1931

The Right Hon. MONTAGU COLLET NORMAN, D.S.O., Governor of the Bank of England, and Sir W. GUY GRANET, G.B.E., called and examined.

9027. *Chairman*: This Meeting of the Committee has been called for the purpose of further discussion with the Governor of the Bank of England and certain of his colleagues on one or two topics on which it is desirable that our evidence should be amplified. There were also some matters upon which we have not yet received evidence which it is desirable to cover before we proceed to the completion of our Report. In particular, realising as we do that the practical end of our Report is to make suggestions whereby the financial system of this country, and indeed of the world, might subserve the recovery of industrial prosperity, we are anxious to have further evidence from the Bank of England with regard to the efforts which we know that they have recently been making in that direction. This morning we have the advantage of the presence of the Governor of the Bank once more, and with him Sir Guy Granet, who has been particularly associated with this aspect of the Bank's work. We propose to discuss with the Governor and Sir Guy Granet the experience of the Bank in relation to the Bankers' Industrial Development Company Ltd. I understand that Sir Guy is fully conversant with the details of this matter and will be able to assist us there, and possibly the Governor would wish to add some general observations upon the policy of this development.

I think, Mr. Governor, I might ask you this general question first of all. The Bank has, I have no doubt, realised the very difficult times through which industry is passing just now in this country, and it has been as an outcome of that realisation that the Bank has addressed itself to the question of how finance, represented by banking interests and particularly by the Bank of England, could best assist in the process of recovery. Would that be a fair statement of the general outlook of the Bank? — (*Mr. Norman*): I think that would explain the setting up of this company.

9028. Perhaps you would tell us, Sir Guy, what were the general lines that were indicated to you that you should follow when you were approached with this project? — (*Sir Guy Granet*): I do not really remember that. The idea was, as far as I can recollect, that the Bankers' Industrial Development Company was formed as an instrument in abnormal times for dealing with finance in respect of industry, having regard to the fact that, the times being abnormal, it was difficult for the ordinary issuing house or financial agency to find the money.

9029. Could you give us some sort of account of what you have been doing, something like a Chairman gives at a general meeting of his company; he tells the shareholders who are interested in it what it has been doing and what progress has been made? — Perhaps I had better, for the sake of order, explain the constitution of the Bankers' Industrial Development Company. That is a company which was brought into being by the efforts of the Governor of the Bank, and it has a capital of £6,000,000. It is a private company and the £6,000,000 is divided into two classes of shares; £4,500,000 are subscribed by practically all the Deposit Banks and Merchant Bankers and Finance Houses of the country and £1,500,000 by the Bank of England. There is a provision, first, that the life of the company is to be for five years only. It can be prolonged by special Resolution, but I take it that that provision is important, because it seems to indicate what was in the Governor's mind, namely, that this was a temporary creation to deal with an abnormal situation. The other point about its constitution is that the capital, though it is for a nominal amount of £6,000,000, cannot be called up to the extent of more than 25 per cent., except in the event of liquidation, and that the capital which is subscribed by the Bank of England is put behind the other capital; that is to say, the whole of the £1,500,000 subscribed by the Bank of England has to be paid up before the rest of the subscribers can be called upon to pay anything in excess of that 25 per cent. So that the Bank of England has taken not only a very substantial part in the finance of the corporation but has deliberately put itself in a worse position than any of the other subscribers.

9030. Yes, I follow that. — Then the Board of the company consists of six gentlemen, with the Governor as Chairman. The other five are Baron Schröder of Schröders, Mr. Peacock of Barings, Mr. Wagg of Helbert Wagg, Mr. Bruce Gardner and myself. Mr. Bruce Gardner is the Managing Director of the Securities Management Trust, which is a creation of the Bank of England. It is an organisation which the Bank created in order to enable it to deal with problems arising out of its connection with the rationalisation of industry, and it has the advantage of having on its organisation experts on law, labour, industry and economics, so that it is very well equipped to deal with all industrial problems, and Mr. Bruce Gardner in his capacity of Managing Director of the Securities Management Trust is able to give us the benefit of the presence and the work of all those gentlemen of the Securities Management Trust, from which we have derived great advantage on occasions.

9031. When did this Securities Management Trust come into existence? — About two years ago. (*Mr. Norman*): In the latter part of 1929.

9032. Was that the first movement that was made in this direction of having, so to speak, a co-operative council? — (*Sir Guy Granet*): I think so, but that was before my time. I cannot speak as to that, except from hearsay. I cannot give definite evidence.

9033. As regards the Bankers' Industrial Development Company, its purpose and policy would, I suppose, be set out in its Memorandum in the usual way? — Yes.

9034. I have a quotation from it here. — Might I say a little more about that, just to show you how it works?

9035. Please do. — I will not be long. I have given you the Board. Most of those gentlemen have an alternate whom they designate to do the work for them. The Governor has designated me as his alternate and, in that capacity, I take his place in the Chair at the meetings. The other alternates are Major Pam for Baron Schröder, Mr. Nigel Campbell for Mr. Wagg, and Mr. Keefer for Mr. Peacock. As a matter of fact, the Board which regularly works is composed of Mr. Peacock, Major Pam, Mr. Keefer, Mr. Nigel Campbell, Mr. Bruce Gardner and myself. So that there are two members of the Board and four alternates. We meet every week regularly, but over and above that we have informal meetings and, of course, we are in daily touch, not only with one another but, I think I can say, with some industrialist or other. Then, as regards the purpose of the company, that was advertised, and I had better quote it. The purpose and policy of the company is 'To receive and consider schemes for the reorganisation and re-equipment of the basic industries of the country when brought forward from within the particular industry, and, if approved, to procure the supply of the necessary financial support for carrying out the scheme.' So that the position is that we have got, not to suggest ourselves what industries should be grouped, or on what lines they should be grouped, but to wait until something happens. Of course, that is the theory; as a matter of fact, one has to do a good deal of work by conversation and intercourse and so on. We do not suggest, but we discuss things before they come up to us in the form of a scheme, and that goes on all the time. In theory, we cannot do anything except receive something which is submitted to us.

9036. The initiative is supposed to come from the industry? — Yes - and more than supposed; I venture to think it ought. It would be a dreadful thing if industry thought that here was a body of bankers or economists who were going to tell industry how they ought to be organised; that would at once get their bristles up. And, besides, obviously it ought to come from the industry. We have not the knowledge. You asked me, with reference to the company, whether, in my opinion, the company had justified its existence. That is a very difficult question to answer, but I think that we have done a great deal of good and, in order to answer that, I would just like to point out the sort of difficulties that we have had to deal with. First of all, apart from the fact that we cannot produce schemes ourselves, when we do get a scheme, obviously that scheme has got to be very carefully investigated, not only generally, but from the point of view of detail, costings and so on. The essence of a scheme is really very often the costings, whether, in point of fact, if you get a certain grouping, you are going to be able to effect economies in production. That takes a long time to check properly, and I want you to realise that we have not got a whole group of experts whom we can put on to schemes so that we can be examining three or four schemes at one time; we have got to do them one by one. Another difficulty that we have found, and in regard to which I think we have done some good, is this. When we began we got various schemes, especially in the Steel Industry, for putting companies together and so on, and some of them seemed pretty good, but we had nothing whatever to show us whether, if we found money for a scheme of rationalisation in one place, we were not really going to do harm somewhere else. We had not a picture before us of the lines on which the Steel Industry should be reorganised in this country and we were entirely in the dark. That became apparent to us very soon and, as a result, we had a meeting of persons representative of the four principal districts in Great Britain and we put the thing before them and had a discussion. We invited persons representative of Scotland, of the North-east Coast, of the Midlands and of South Wales, and we had a long discussion with them and pointed out our difficulty; they quite agreed and they also agreed that the only useful thing to do was to try, on behalf of the Steel Trade, to produce some Report as a guide to the lines on which rationalisation should take place in the Steel Industry. Having agreed to do that, they then agreed to ask Mr. Bruce Gardner to act as their Secretary in the matter. That meant that he had to do the work and he spent a very great amount of time on producing the Report; it was done piecemeal and submitted, step by step, to those gentlemen, and finally he has produced a Report which I think is a very valuable one and which has the complete approval of those gentlemen. To the extent that they are representative of the Steel Trade of Great Britain, it has the approval of the Steel Trade; it is not a public Report yet, but it is approved by four very representative groups of steelmakers in the country, and I think if we had done nothing else, we have done something there which is extremely useful to industry, because otherwise you were bound to go wrong as regards the Steel Industry.

9037. But a survey of that sort is obviously

the preliminary to some practical steps, is it not? — Yes, I agree.

9038. With a view to ascertaining the possibilities of the business and how far it is wise or proper to supply further finance to it? — Yes. I see I have omitted one thing. I ought to have said what we had actually done in point of fact, apart from our difficulties. We have, in fact, actually floated only one scheme, but we have one more which is just ready; practically everything has been done except the Prospectus. It is ready. Another scheme has been fully investigated and practically approved, another has reached almost that stage, and then, beyond that, there is quite a large number of schemes which are simply in the process of discussion. It takes a long time before you get even two people to agree.

9039. Suppose you have had a thorough investigation of a particular branch of industry and have been able to assess its position and its possibilities with that guidance which you receive, how does the company proceed to do its own job, that is to say, give financial assistance? Once you realise that the proposition is one which deserves your support, what form exactly does your assistance take? — Then we try to construct a security which we can offer to the public with our backing, something to which we think it is legitimate to ask the public to subscribe, with our backing and with the knowledge that we have gone into it. But I agree, our conception of our duty is that we have got to take certain risks which an ordinary issuing house could not afford to take.

9040. Quite. — That does not mean that we do not investigate, but I think we have got to be prepared to deal with a less complete security and ask for subscribers for a less complete security than a private issuing house could do.

9041. *Mr. Brand*: By 'your backing' you do not mean your guarantee? — No, we have not thought of our guarantee yet, and I hope we shall not have to.

9042. *Mr. Keynes*: What is the purpose of your capital, called and uncalled? — It is in order to create a credit machine, so to speak. That is what I understand. In the event that Mr. Brand has just mentioned, where we thought it was a case in which we would have to guarantee, or to take private steps to finance, it puts us in the position of being able to get any money within reason offhand.

9043. You have not intended, in the case of rather small propositions, to take up the securities yourselves and then issue to the public a security which would be covered by your own holding of a variety of smaller issues? — I think that is certainly in contemplation, but that case has not yet arisen. That certainly is one of the things I would contemplate doing.

9044. One of the criticisms that has been made is that while, if a very big concern wants a large sum of capital, it can usually get it, the present methods of issuing capital for concerns that want, say, £100,000, are very expensive? — Yes. That has nothing to do with the B.I.D. You mean generally in business?

9045. I did not know whether or not that had anything to do with you. You are only looking at very big things? — Yes. We of the B.I.D. deal with big propositions *ex hypothesi*. They have got to be schemes of rationalisation. Are you suggesting that we ought to deal with little things?

9046. No. I was merely asking whether the little things come within your purview or not. You say they do not? — No, not the little things. Smaller things than are contemplated by that declaration, I think, must. That is my personal opinion. I do not know whether my colleagues on the B.I.D. agree, or whether the Governor agrees, but I have that feeling that we must deal sometimes – certainly where it is a case which is not inconsistent with ultimate rationalisation – with the smaller unit.

9047. *Mr. Tulloch*: You use the expression – I think it is contained in your Memorandum – that you receive and consider schemes of reorganisation, and so on, of basic industries? — Yes.

9048. Do you confine yourselves to the basic industries? — Well, no; I do not think so; but that is the charter, that we are only to consider basic industries. If a case came before me in which I had to decide whether a thing ought to come before the Board of the B.I.D. or not and I thought it was a scheme which was beneficial to industry, I would not care whether it was a basic industry or not. But, again, that is my own particular view.

9049. I should like to understand this, if I can. You used the words that you have to take certain risks which an ordinary issuing house cannot afford to do. Could you expand that a little and tell us exactly what you mean by risks; you do not guarantee, I think you said? — No. An ordinary issuing house doing an industrial issue would have to be very careful when it makes an issue to see that, so far as it can, it produces a security which is a good one, and stands the test not only of a valuation of assets but of a good record of earnings. A private issuing house would not dream of issuing a debenture on a new prospect, however attractive, a mere – I will not call it speculation, but something which was all in the future. We must, I think, issue or find money for something – assuming we find it is a good thing – which is based, to a certain extent, on estimates of what is going to happen in the future. Again, I am speaking for myself; I do not want the B.I.D. to find money recklessly, of course; also I do not want the B.I.D. to take the whole of the risk and leave the company without any responsibility at all. I think the B.I.D. ought to try and get some sort of security from the company that it is financing; though, as I say, I do not think that the B.I.D. could properly be expected to require such security as a private issuing house.

9050. It would really mean this, that you would be asking the public to take certain risks which an ordinary issuing house would not ask the public to take. That is the reply, is it not? — Asking the public?

9051. Yes. You are not backing the scheme by guarantee. You are putting the issue out? — We always try to put a thing out, because that is a test as to whether it is a good thing or not.

9052. Putting out an issue, which perhaps an ordinary issuing house might not venture to do having regard to the security behind it? — I agree. We have got to issue securities which though, in our belief, entirely good and for the benefit of the industry, are not such as a private issuing house could afford to issue.

9053. *Chairman*: The advantage of the B.I.D., I take it, is this, that, while the risks might be of a character which an ordinary issuing house might not care to put on the market, the public has this assurance in subscribing, that it is a scheme which is – to use a colloquialism – vetted by a responsible body and put forward on their responsibility, if not with their guarantee? — Yes.

9054. And that, from a financial point of view, is of very great importance to the investing public? — It is; and, of course, that, from our point of view, puts a very great responsibility upon us too.

9055. *Mr. Brand*: On the other hand, you would say that first-class issuing houses would be performing the same function in respect of issues? — I agree.

9056. *Mr. Keynes*: You would be prepared to offer securities which, in your judgment, were perfectly good, although, perhaps, rather less conventional than the ordinary issuing house. You could afford to be less conventional? — It is not only convention. I am putting myself in this position, that I am an issuing house in one aspect and I am the B.I.D. in the other. I do not mind being unconventional. I want to get the issue off my hands. I know perfectly well there are certain issues which I would recommend the B.I.D. to issue which, as a private issuing house, I could not get away with – I could not get rid of them. There the convention would come in on the part of my clients.

9057. You could not get away with it in the long run? — No, not more than once, anyhow.

9058. *Chairman*: Then it is quite obvious that you think you have a function that you can usefully perform? — Oh! I do. I am not in the dark at all about the B.I.D. I think we have got a function which we can usefully perform. I think we have done good work, but I do not think we can go ahead and produce a scheme a week. The more one goes into it, the more one finds that it is really necessary to act slowly, from our point of view, and, over and above that, the difficulty of getting people together is very great.

9059. *Mr. Brand*: Then your success will depend upon whether your judgment has been shown to be good, because if the public in fact lose by these issues, the B.I.D. will be rather in the position of the private issuing house. It could not do it again. (*Mr. Keynes*): The B.I.D. only lasts for five years. (*Mr. Tulloch*): It may go on. — I hope it will last less!

9060. *Chairman*: I think it is exceedingly interesting. What strikes me about it is this, that a body of this sort is not created unless it is felt that it is wanted. You have told us of the nature of your activities and you have assured us that, in your view, those activities can be useful. Something, apparently, has been wanting hitherto in the present emergency, which you are able to supply? — In the present emergency.

9061. Of course, one of the main purposes of our investigation is to assist, if we can, in the present emergency. We recognise that we are in a period of abnormality and the question is, what assistance can be given? This movement of yours is one of the forms in which finance has endeavoured to come to the rescue. What we are anxious to know is, how this new device is functioning, how far it is functioning usefully and what purpose it can serve; how far it is one of the recovery agents, so to speak? — I think it has done useful work and it has justified its existence. But I question whether it is going to do more than give a little help. I would not put too high the influence of the Bankers' Industrial Development Company. I do not think you can regard it as something which is going to cure the present discontent. It is one of the things which is going to help. I think there are other things.

9062. *Mr. Newbold*: You seem to be very pessimistic about the whole position. — Well, I must have got out the wrong side of my bed. I am a convinced optimist. All I want is not to pretend that we are going to cure all the ills of this country by the Bankers' Industrial Development Company.

9063. I hope not. — We are doing our best.

9064. *Chairman*: We are only regarding it as contributory to the general objective, and one would like to know to what extent it is contributing. You very wisely caution us not to put too much reliance on it. — I do not want to put it too high, but I think it has made a contribution and is making a contribution.

9065. *Mr. Keynes*: Have you, in the case of any important industries, made an estimate as to what is the order of magnitude of the capital requirements for a thoroughly good rationalisation scheme, assuming that the attendant conditions were satisfactory – that is to say, that you had got all the parties together and had a scheme that seemed to your mind sound and so forth? What sort of amount is it going to cost? Will the steel industry of this country, in order to be set properly straight, need £10 millions, £50 millions, or £100 millions? — To put things straight? I would like to think that over. It is very difficult to say, but so far as I have gone it is quite clear to me, from what I have seen myself, that £10,000,000 could be spent straightaway profitably. By 'profitably' I do not mean that you would necessarily get a return on it immediately, but that it is profitable from the point of view of the country and industry. That money could be usefully spent; I think you could put it higher than that and say that that money ought to be spent in order to make production as efficient as it can be made.

9066. *Mr. Brand*: You are talking about one industry? — Just at the moment I am thinking really of only one industry. That is what I have come across myself.

9067. *Mr. Keynes*: It might be £10,000,000, £20,000,000 or £30,000,000, but that would be the outside of what you imagine would be required? — It is very difficult to say. I have only dealt with five or six things in the sense of understanding a lot about them. We have talked about them, but I have only had experience of five or six; therefore I give you the £10,000,000, but there might be a lot more.

9068. I am quite willing to believe you. I want to get your idea of the order of magnitude. Have you formed any impression of how much new capital would be wanted in the Lancashire cotton industry? — No, none at all. I am just beginning to learn a lot.

9069. Is there any source whereby we can ascertain the sort of sum that would be involved in rationalising the cotton industry? — I could not give it to you.

9070. The point in my mind is this. It is often said that sooner or later we are going to need a very great deal of capital for that purpose, and that that is a reason for being rather strict towards other ways of using capital. The savings of this country used to be estimated at about £400,000,000 a year. That was no doubt accurate up to a fairly recent date – it may be, for all I know, not so accurate now – but in anything like normal times we are saving something like £400,000,000 a year. The requirements of rationalisation would inevitably be spread over some fairly long period, because even when you had made your plans you could not at once spend the money that was necessary. I was wondering whether there was any probability of a very large proportion of the national savings being required in any one year for purposes of rationalisation. If the requirement of the steel industry is £10,000,000, £20,000,000 or £30,000,000, and the requirements of the others are on that sort of scale, it looks as though the most that would be required for rationalisation in any one year would be a very small proportion of the available savings of the country? — I should have thought so.

9071. You think it is not a very serious financial problem, it is a problem of organisation; that the amount of money in relation to the sort of amount that the public is saving is not large. Is that right? — Yes.

9072. *Mr. Brand*: It is a problem of profit making. The money may be there but you cannot get it for a particular industry unless it can be shown to be going to make profits? — That is the difficulty we are in now, and that is the difficulty which the B.I.D. has been created really to meet, that the ordinary issuing house in times like these, except in building up a security of its own, cannot get the money for industry.

9073. *Chairman*: And it cannot get the money because industry does not see profits in sight? — Partly because of that and partly because the investor is like a fish, he is on the feed sometimes and sometimes he is off. You cannot really lay down the law about that, except that you know that he does not feed sometimes.

9074. From your statement of the functions of the B.I.D. it seems to me that this is one of the contributory agencies by which finance can usefully come to the aid of industry. It is a new device and whether it is a device which should be encouraged or not depends upon whether it is functioning satisfactorily. You are the person who can tell us, administering it as you do, whether you think it is a valuable thing which ought to be encouraged in the public interest? — My opinion, for what it is worth, is very definitely yes.

9075. *Mr. Brand*: The B.I.D. is a temporary institution as at present framed? — Yes.

9076. You mean that your experience with the B.I.D. would make you feel that institutions of that character should be added to our existing financial machinery? — I do not think so now. I admit I have wobbled in my mind over that, but I have come pretty clearly to the conclusion 'No,' in answer to that. I think as an emergency measure dealing with abnormal times an institution like the B.I.D. – whether the B.I.D. is the ideal form or not – is a good thing. For times which are not abnormal I would really come down on the side of the fence against any special institution.

9077. I would like to be quite clear. Does that mean that you think the City of London performs for British industry all the functions that ought to be performed? — No.

9078. My question was directed to the needs of industry in normal times? — I should say that the City of London performs for industry more than anybody else performs in normal times. If you say everything that ought to be performed – I do not know. No, it cannot, obviously; but it performs its duty generally to industry extremely well. I agree with you. Look at Germany and other Continental countries; you see that there the banks have a closer liaison with and control over industry than we have here, and I have been rather attracted by that. It looks as if possibly the foreign banks were able to do something to help industry from the management point of view that we do not do here, but I cannot see any evidence that that is so. After all, abroad there is nobody else but the banks to help industry. There are no issuing houses or brokers or people like that. There is nobody but the banks. It is quite true the banks would have a liaison hold over the management, but they have made some appalling mistakes within one's own experience in industry, and while admitting that normally they may do good, in abnormal times like these I do not see that they have done industry any good whatever.

9079. Perhaps I do not make my meaning quite clear. I personally have no intention of suggesting that the banks or the City should in any way manage industry. The question that I have in my mind is this:– is the machinery of the City of London perfect in the assistance that it gives to industry to raise long dated capital? So far as raising money for foreign Governments or institutions and so on, there are, as you know, various issuing houses in London that devote themselves very largely to that. Take the year 1928, when large sums were raised from the British investor for what was called British industry. What guidance had the British investor from the City? There was a very large number of very bad issues and on each of those prospectuses the name of one of the Big Five appeared in large letters. I think your reply confined itself very largely to Germany. In fact, in New York, the recognised institutions take a much closer part in raising long-dated capital for industry than practically any other concern except yours and one or two others in London? — I have heard you say that in other places. I do not quite agree with you. Generally speaking, I think that industry is well served by the City of London in normal times. You come to the question of 1928 and what was called the industrial boom then. That raises a totally different set of questions. Of course, one knows that that was a very unfortunate period in the history of the City; it had nothing to do with the ordinary financing of industry by the City, and the question of responsibility of the banks for allowing their names to appear on prospectuses is one which is of great importance. I am not prepared to deal with that to-day. I have not really come here prepared to deal with it.

9080. Then you consider really that the relations between British industry and whatever issuing institutions they go to, if there are any, are adequate? — Yes.

9081. That British industry does not want any closer contact or more continuous contact with issuing institutions than it has now? — No, I think not. If you think that things are not right in the sense that there is nothing to connect the issuing houses with the management of the company for whom it makes an issue, I agree, but I have thought a lot about it and I do not see how you can secure a really effective connection between the institution that finds the money and the management. You may think you have got it, but you have not really. You may have a representative on the Board, you may have weekly or monthly reports and so on, but you do not really get a check. You cannot. It is not your function really to supervise management, and when I am told that the German banks have done it I wonder really whether it is effective.

9082. What I have in mind is not the supervision of the management? — Oh, I beg your pardon.

9083. It is a closer, more continuous connection, not only from the point of view of giving overdrafts, which they do now, but from the point of view of acting as financial advisers to British industrial companies, assisting them in the raising of long dated capital and so forth? — I really think that they are pretty well served now in normal times.

9084. *Chairman*: The question is whether we need any additional institutions in this country. It is a very interesting thing to see how the finance of London has evolved and specialised itself in various departments. We have the Bank of England, we have the big commercial banks, the issuing houses, the discount houses, those have all evolved themselves by the process of evolution to meet the requirements of the country. The question is whether in our present state of industrial development it may not be necessary to call into being some additional specialised bodies to assist in the present state of the country's financial needs. What strikes me as interesting is that here is an example before our eyes of something of this sort that has happened that has not happened before in the City of London. These things grow up because they are wanted. A genius, some person such as the Governor, has an idea. At first it may be very inchoate, it takes shape. The question which concerns us as a Committee is whether we ought to recommend a development along the line of this new departure, whether it is a thing that should have a permanent place and be developed, or whether, on the other hand, it is only a device to meet an emergency, serving its purpose, and disappearing. May I put it to you as it occurs to me as a mere layman? Of course, it is essential for large industrial undertakings that they should have an adequate supply of finance. At present there are three sources available to them. They have their own reserves, undivided profits, which they may have put back into the business. Then they can have recourse to the ordinary banks; but the banks' primary function is really seasonal assistance, it is not intended that they should provide permanent capital. Then, lastly, there is the investing public which is reached by various instrumentalities, by the ordinary prospectuses of the issuing houses, and so forth. Those are the sources which a manufacturer who has a good project before him looks to when he wants money. He may have some resources of his own or he may go to the bank. The bank say, 'We cannot assist you. We would be glad to assist you on the commercial side of your work, but this is not a matter for us. We advise you to go to the public.' He says, 'I cannot go to the public because I cannot put forward a prospectus with an accountant's certificate saying that the assets are so much and the profits for the last five years have been so much. Yet here is something which would be a very valuable addition to the country's activities.' What agency exists with our present financial organisation to assist a man of that sort? Where can he get his money? — I think there are all sorts of ways for a man like that to find his money. The provincial broker is a very good source of supply for small amounts which are needed for an industry which is well thought of in the locality, and so on.

9085. Where personal credit is involved? — Yes, if the thing is well known and esteemed I do not believe there is any difficulty in finding a small sum of that sort locally – £50,000 or so. When it comes to a big amount I agree unless he has got something to show for it he will find it difficult. But then, I am not sure that that is a bad thing for him. He ought to go by steps rather than embark on a very large expenditure simply on prospects.

9086. It has been suggested to us that there is room for a new type of institution in the City which would fill the gap. Whether there is a gap or not is, of course, one of the questions in dispute, but it has been suggested that there is a difficulty in obtaining money for quite useful enterprises through any of the existing agencies. It has been suggested further that we might have finance companies of some sort which would be prepared to supply funds to suitably vetted undertakings, not quite on your line, but a more or less permanent institution to which resort could be had for that kind of assistance. Whether it is a practicable suggestion or not I do not know, but it has been put forward that there is something wanted between the ordinary issuing houses and the ordinary bank. (*Mr. Lubbock*): The Agricultural Mortgage Corporation has been quoted to us as an analogy. (*Chairman*): Yes, that is an example of the sort of thing. Various experimental ideas have been mooted before us. One would rather like to have the benefit of your view, whether there is a need in the City of London for new developments in view of the changed situation to-day, not merely for emergencies, but as part of the financial structure of the country? — You mean a financial institution created solely for the purpose of finding money for new schemes which they may regard as suitable?

9087. *Mr. Brand*: No, I did not mean that. (*Chairman*): Not for entirely new schemes? — I would rather like to know what you do mean.

9088. *Professor Gregory*: What we have in mind is a means for providing the appropriate mechanism for long period issues. — I say definitely, rightly or wrongly, my opinion is very clear that the mechanism exists and functions well.

9089. You say the mechanism exists and functions well. Let us exclude for the moment quite small issues which you say could be handled through provincial brokers. Do you regard the existing issuing houses as in a position to handle very large propositions which are likely to become more normal as industry becomes more integrated? — I am a prejudiced person, but my answer is yes.

9090. *Mr. Keynes*: Most of the existing issuing houses are also accepting houses. The accepting house must necessarily keep its assets extremely liquid? — Yes.

9091. Therefore, it must not be in the position of having to nurse an issue, and everything it takes it must take in the expectation of being quit of it at an early date. It might be well to have a house with large resources of its own, but without any other responsibility, which would be prepared at times to nurse an issue, to have subsidiaries which would be prepared to take up smaller issues. Would that be a proper activity for an accepting house? — (*Sir Guy Granet*): I quite agree from the point of view of an ordinary Issuing House. If it is an accepting house it has to be very liquid. It has no business to make an issue unless it is possible to hold the baby to some extent. But I agree one must look to being liquid if one is an accepting house, and, therefore, one could not as part of one's ordinary business engage in financing enterprises as to which we felt sure we should have to hold some part, and to that extent I do not think there is any question that there is no institution in London at present. (*Mr. Norman*): And ought not to be.

9092. *Mr. Brand*: I do not want to be persistent, but as I understand it, Sir Guy's answer is that, being, as he is, senior partner in Higginson & Co. and also Chairman of the B.I.D., in neither of these capacities is he performing functions of any value whatever? — (*Sir Guy Granet*): I have been extraordinarily unfortunate in my capacity for making myself understood, if that is your understanding; because I thought the whole of my evidence had been directed to saying that I have been of extreme value in both capacities.

9093. But only, I understand, in abnormal circumstances? — In abnormal circumstances, such as affected my capacity as Acting Chairman of the B.I.D. As that, in abnormal circumstances, I say I have been useful. Then in my normal capacity as senior partner of my firm in normal times, I again humbly, but certainly, say I have been useful.

9094. The functions that your firm performs for certain industries I would like to see very much extended? — So would I.

9095. Those are the functions that I think are in general not performed adequately in the

City of London except to the extent that you, and perhaps one or two other institutions, do it? — Well, you have told me that before, and I do not quite agree with you. As regards Mr. Keynes' suggestion, I agree with him that there is no house or institution in London which performs the functions which he suggests it might be desirable that some house should perform.

9096. *Mr. Keynes*: If I might follow up the Governor's remark, that there should not be such an institution, you explained to us some minutes ago how the mood of the public fluctuates very much as to their willingness to take securities which the expert thinks equally good at one time as at another time. If there is no such institution, if the issues are made by houses which must keep themselves liquid, it must mean that the ability of industry to get its capital will vary very much according to the mood of the public – it will be starved at times, and at other times it will be much too easy to get money? — Yes.

9097. Surely that must be very detrimental to the stability of business in all ways? — I think, as you very rightly point out, it is not on the whole beneficial to business that you find it easy to get money at one moment and not at another; and that at certain times an issue house, such as we are talking of here, would be less inclined to finance an issue than at other times. If an institution such as you suggest existed, I suppose that you could theoretically say that, even in difficult times, it would finance a thing, because it was part of its duty to hold the baby. My own belief, you know, is that in practice that sort of business would tend more and more not to finance businesses which meant a long lock-up; but that is just my belief.

9098. *Professor Gregory*: Every issuing house, whether it has other functions or not, naturally wants to keep itself as liquid as possible? — Yes.

9099. Do you not think such special institutions, while not handling lame ducks, but handling perfectly normal, sound capital propositions, would be less embarrassed than the existing issuing houses, which have first of all to take care of long-established connections with Foreign Governments and institutions, and have to handle their acceptances, and, therefore, find themselves torn between a good many different motives? — Subject to what I have said, I agree that would be so; but I would not personally like to subscribe to the capital of such an institution.

9100. Why not? — I think they would perform a very useful function while their money lasted.

9101. Special institutions of this sort would have to use exactly the same sort of criteria and standards as the existing issuing houses? — No. I understand the hypothesis is that the special institution is to deal with issues which the existing issuing houses do not want to handle as a rule, namely, issues which involve a long lock-up.

9102. *Mr. Brand*: That is not my basis. — Well, I am sorry. I cannot keep up with the variety of questions. I thought I was being asked one question; but apparently I was being asked another – I am very sorry.

9103. *Mr. Keynes*: Shall I give a background to what I say? One of the major beauties of our present system is that only when there is a boom, and too much development, do you get very high profits. Therefore, it is only possible to make sure then of getting things off quickly, i.e., just when development ought not to be taking place, because there is already too much. On the other hand, when you get a slump like the present occasion, when there is far too little going on, it must necessarily for that reason be a time of loss, and therefore a time when, if you leave it simply to the private man, who wants to make a certain profit within a short period, it cannot be worth his while to do it: so our arrangements are so made that it is precisely when we do not want things done that it is easy and profitable to do them, and when we do want things done it is difficult? — Well, I do not know. I would like to have your question down on paper and consider it. I really do not know what my answer should be.

9104. *Mr. Brand*: I would like to put one further question about New York, because you know New York better than I do. Would you say that, apart from the private issuing houses, there are a good many which have certain relations with industry, such as companies which are attached to the big banks? — Yes.

9105. Would you say that they have no closer connections in any sort of way with American industry than ourselves? — Yes, of course they do; and very often they have got control.

9106. Then your answer would be not that they do not have a closer connection, but it is not a good thing? — No, I say very often they have closer connections; but very often, having got closer connections, they make mistakes – really bad mistakes.

9107. I know they do. — By professing to be in a special position as regards industry, they make their mistakes all the more detrimental, because people think they really are on the inside track as regards a certain industry.

9108. Your answer is not that it does not exist; but that it is a bad system? — I would like to make the somewhat absurd answer that it does not exist and that it is a bad system also. I agree to some extent that it exists; and I will not say it is a bad system; but I will say I have not seen it work well.

9109. A short time ago I asked a very experienced New York banker this question: Was ever an issue for an industrial company made in New York without the issuing responsibility – you know what I mean by that –

of a recognised bank or financial institution; and his answer was that it was never done? — No, I should think not.

9110. That is what I mean? — That is what I should have thought.

9111. You do not think that that is an advantage over our system, where, in general, industrial issues are not made by any such recognised banking house? — Well, I do not know. The recognised backing that you talk of in New York is simply recognised because they have done business before. They are supposed to have some holding in the company, or something of the kind. It is not a backing that I attach any importance to, from the point of view of giving me confidence in the issue, unless I happen to know the firm issuing; then I know: 'Well, anyhow they are careful people. They make mistakes, no doubt, like other people, but anyhow they are careful and honest; and, therefore, I am sure I will get a run for my money.'

9112. Is not that exactly what the investor wishes to know – what I would wish to know, for instance? — (*Mr. Norman*): May I say a word to Mr. Brand? Within my experience these issues in New York, which are made like that, are frequently made because the person who brings them about has not yet been able to sell his shares. Very often that is so. I think it is most questionable if, in many cases, you can attach any responsibility to that issue in the sense you are now trying to attach to it, if you will allow me to say so. You can exclude from what I say, of course, certain eminent concerns; but I have known of instances there when the purpose of the issue has been simply to carry on a position until the person who brought about the issue could dispose of his interests.

9113. Would you say, Mr. Governor, that that has happened with a great many Syndicates and Trust Companies which make issues in this country? — No, I would not say that.

9114. I am not talking of reputable ones? — I was speaking of New York, not this country, when I gave my answer.

9115. But take the 1928 situation here? — I was only talking about New York.

9116. *Professor Gregory*: May I put a question of fact, and not an inference? As things actually are, Sir Guy, the amount of issues which the existing issuing houses are capable of taking up with their existing international obligations is surely limited? — (*Sir Guy Granet*): Clearly it is limited.

9117. The capital needs of industry in consequence of reorganisation and the growing scale of industry, are much greater. The amount that English industry needs to obtain in the long period capital market to-day is surely greater than it was 20 years ago? — I do not know at all, but it is a very considerable sum, I should imagine.

9118. Do you think that the existing agencies, in view of the fact that the issuing houses can only do a limited amount of work, are satisfactory in dealing with the increased demands of British industry? That is the real point, I think? — You asked a question as regards the increased demand. I do not know whether they are increased or not, but obviously there comes a time when an issuing house cannot do more than a certain amount. Whether that time has been reached or not is a question of fact on which I do not know enough.

9119. I should have thought that, with the change from private enterprise to joint stock enterprise, the capital market is called upon to supply, through some form or other, a larger amount of capital to-day than it was in times before that development – I am not raising the question as to which is the agency? — Yes, but I am a comparative new comer to the City, so that I cannot carry my mind back very far. It may very well be so. I am not fencing with you on that. I simply do not know.

9120. If one takes a simple case like the Lancashire cotton industry, which has become a joint stock concern compared with what it was 30 or 40 years ago, it does make an increased demand for capital? — (*Sir Guy Granet*): I will accept any evidence on that that you give me, because I do not know. (*Mr. Norman*): May I say a word about that? The Lancashire cotton case which you mention was a case which is an illustration of this particular and curious process through which we are now going; and insofar as the B.I.D. can deal with it, it will do so. I agree with Sir Guy; I feel rather more strongly, I think, about some of the things than he does; I think he has not given you a sufficiently definite idea of the capacity of London, based on past experience, to supply money for long purposes. I think it is very, very large indeed. As to your suggestion, Dr. Gregory, for instance that it depends on the issue house, I can only say that is one tithe of it.

9121. Quite so? — (*Mr. Norman*): You have spoken several times as if the issue houses could be filled up; but their business is only a very small business, and certainly only a part of the whole. I imagine in industry the mass of money is really found through some broker or another; and their capacity for finding money is very big. I myself feel, if we succeed in getting through this period, for which the B.I.D. was intended to function, we shall return to conditions in which the capital demands of industry, even if it should require large sums of money, will be supplied with no more difficulty than they have been supplied before. I am perfectly clear about that. I think there may be less investment abroad, but in future I think there will be adequate investment at home. I should think that the criterion whether or not that is to happen will be whether or not an industry can promise reasonable profits; and if it cannot, it is better without the money.

9122. I quite understand that? — That is my view. I do, therefore, believe – I quite agree with what Sir Guy said right back at the beginning – that the B.I.D. is only intended to fill a gap, not intended to make any permanent alteration in the structure of the City, or of credit. We have always found in the past, as I have been told, that, wherever the occasion for business existed, some institution or concern would find its way in and grow towards it. That has been the great difference between, for instance, ourselves and America. One has grown and the other has been made. Without any question, I believe that we shall grow again to fill any increasing needs.

9123. *Mr. Brand*: The B.I.D. performs, as Sir Guy has explained to us, certain very valuable functions of investigation and so forth in this abnormal period, but I would say that those functions should be performed in normal times. You contemplate that the broking firm is really best, or quite sufficient? — Quite sufficient. I do not mean only the stock-broker, or members of the Stock Exchange, though I think they do a great deal. There are a great number of other firms.

9124. *Mr. Newbold*: What type of firms have you in mind? I ask that because some of us are not so well acquainted with the City as others? — A large amount of this has been done by stock-broking firms. Then there are a certain number of firms and businesses connected with trust and investment companies, in one way or another, who do a considerable amount of this business – quite a large amount.

9125. *Mr. Brand*: This is a slightly different point; but, for instance, if the British electrical industry has to compete with the American or German electrical industry, you find the big German and American firms supported by enormously powerful financial institutions, with whom they are closely in touch. The broking firms cannot possibly do that. It may be that the British electrical companies would go and get for the time being the support of one of the joint stock banks; but that is the sort of function which cannot be performed by a broking firm? — No, it is on a different scale.

9126. That is one of the results of having more intimate connections between the big industries and banking institutions, and other big institutions, than I think exist in England. (*Mr. Newbold*): What have you in mind for financing such an organisation as a big electrical enterprise? — I should have thought the big electrical enterprise would have no difficulty in arranging its finance through its bankers.

9127. *Chairman*: Really the upshot of it is that the existing agencies, in the opinion of both of you, are quite adequate for normal times; but the present times being abnormal, it has been necessary to resort to some abnormal expedient, and the B.I.D. has been adopted as an expedient to assist in getting rid of the present abnormality. That is really the position? — That is my view. (*Sir Guy Granet*): It is mine, too.

9128. It is a remarkable feature of B.I.D. that it should have been associated with the Bank of England, which is a great Central Bank, and not with one of the commercial banks. Do you think it is the sort of function that is proper to be associated with a Central Bank? — (*Sir Guy Granet*): Well, it would depend on what you mean by 'associated'. The Bank of England is interested in the B.I.D. They have subscribed capital which they postponed to other people, and they gave the idea of the B.I.D., and so on; but I do not think we are associated with the Bank of England in any real degree, because our Board functions entirely independently of the Bank. The Governor is here to speak for himself, but I think he has been particularly scrupulous in making that quite clear. I think the Board would find itself dreadfully embarrassed if there was any sort of suggestion that we were in any way acting under the orders or suggestions of the Bank of England. We have always regarded ourselves as entirely independent; but we are associated in the sense that we owe our origin to the Bank.

9129. The odd thing is that the initiative in this movement has come from a Central Bank rather than from a commercial bank or other agencies? — May I say as to that, in my judgment nothing else could have brought the B.I.D. into existence except the Bank of England. I am quite sure that we could not have been created by anybody else. It was entirely due to the personal influence and power of the Governor that we have been created. There was a very great reluctance on everybody's part about it.

9130. No one else would step into the breach? — No. It is very difficult to say quite what might have happened. There might have been either some other institution formed, or the Government might have stepped in.

9131. My point is, that it is not the function of a Central Bank to do these things in normal times? — No.

9132. But you represent to us that on this occasion the initiative was taken because there was nobody else to take the initiative; and the Bank of England, for the general welfare of the country, prompted a step of an unusual character, not within its normal functions, but with a desire to give a helping hand? — That is so.

9133. And this was the form devised. Is that a fair way of putting it, Mr. Governor? — (*Mr. Norman*): Quite right. (*Sir Guy Granet*): I think so. (*Mr. Norman*): An abnormal effort for an abnormal occasion.

9134. *Mr. Newbold*: Do you think it is an abnormal occasion? — (*Mr. Norman*): Yes, I do.

9135. How long do you think its abnormality is going to last? — I do not know how long it is going to last, but I am quite certain that when this company was formed a year or two years ago the conditions were abnormal in the sense in which I mean them.

9136. I think your abnormality will last a very long time and that it will become a permanent institution? — I do not think so.

9137. *Mr. Brand*: You think in normal times the functions that the B.I.D. perform are absolutely unnecessary and should disappear? — (*Mr. Norman*): Yes. (*Sir Guy Granet*): In normal times I think so.

9138. *Mr. Keynes*: Adam Smith once said that an abnormal condition seldom lasted for more than ninety years? — (*Mr. Norman*): But the abnormal then becomes normal - you must give me that.

9139. *Chairman*: The abnormality of the one day becomes the norm of the later day. Everything is abnormal at first until it has become established? — I would like to believe that Sir Guy Granet and his colleagues on the B.I.D. during the five years ahead of them will produce such an effect on the basic industries that their condition, outlook and mentality will become different from when the B.I.D. started, and that having been done, or mostly done during an abnormal period, the industries will thereafter be able to obtain such finance as they may properly require based upon the reorganisation which the B.I.D. will have brought about. For reorganisation, I ought to say, rationalisation, because that is what I mean, without explaining its precise significance.

9140. Metaphors are dangerous, but I was going to suggest that in your view at present a tonic is required, but a tonic is not good as a normal diet? — I do not call it a tonic. I think a nurse is required, and the B.I.D. is intended to fulfil that function.

9141. You ought to get rid of the nurse at the end of the illness? — At the end of the period. I seem to see this as possible. It has been in my mind for a long time, and the more I look at it the more confident do I feel in myself, without being able to submit evidence to prove it, that some such course as that will be followed.

9142. There is one matter I would like to spend a few minutes upon, Sir Guy. You have said, quite properly, that you have come into existence really on the Bank's initiative, and you have been given your head by the Bank, and you do your own work? — (*Sir Guy Granet*): Yes.

9143. Mention has been made of the Securities Management Trust? — Yes.

9144. What are your relations with it in contradistinction to your relations with the Bank? — I have no relations whatever with it. My colleague, Mr. Bruce Gardner, is managing director of that, and I make use of him in that way to get into contact with anybody on the staff or organisation of the S.M.T., who will be good enough to help me over anything. They have legal and other eminent experts there from whom very often one can get a great deal of information if they will be good enough to let one have a talk. That is the only relation. I have no connection whatever with them.

9145. When did that organisation come into being? — In 1929.

9146. Might I ask, Mr. Governor, is that also one of the expedients that has been born, so to speak, of the present emergency? — (*Mr. Norman*): The S.M.T. was only an expedient in this sense of the word. Owing to the abnormal conditions, the Bank came to be possessed of certain securities acquired for particular purposes. The mere fact of having acquired those securities brought the Bank into contact with industry which is not part of a Central Bank's normal duty. The S.M.T. was established to take over this business and conduct it in another building as a matter quite distinct from the Bank's ordinary functions, the business being entrusted to persons having special qualifications to deal with these and other cognate affairs. If you look at the S.M.T. really as a temporary or industrial adjunct of the Bank of England that is not an unfair description of it.

9147. Is it serving a useful purpose? — Certainly a very useful purpose indeed.

9148. I rather gathered from what Sir Guy said it had now become an intelligence department because it was necessary for it to make investigations which brought it into contact with industry, and in that way was useful to you in turn as a staff of experts? — Yes. The S.M.T. maintains a certain staff of experts who are at Sir Guy's disposal when they are required.

9149. And I suppose at the disposal of the Bank also? — But they *are* the Bank.

9150. That in itself is a new departure. You had not that before? — That is a five years' growth.

9151. Do you contemplate that also will fade out after it has served its purpose? — Certainly.

9152. During the time of its existence, and it exists now, do you find that the information which it is able to place at your disposal is of value to you in the ordinary conduct of your business? — Not in the ordinary conduct of normal business.

9153. I should have thought, though I do not know, that being able to lay under contribution that expert knowledge in legal, economic or industrial matters might be a useful source of information to you in connection with the policy of the Bank that you had to adopt from time to time. You have not found it useful for that purpose? — No.

9154. Therefore, in your view, it serves a special purpose of a temporary character? — Yes.

9155. You do not contemplate its continuance as an organisation of the Bank? — No.

9156. *Mr. Brand*: Might I ask you one question on that? You contemplate (and I absolutely endorse your view) that Sir Guy and his colleagues on the B.I.D. will bring an entirely new spirit into industry? — Yes, I do.

9157. During the next five years? — Yes.

9158. That is because, apart from personal qualities, they will bring a knowledge of finance and banking and a way of looking at these things from the financial point of view? — Yes.

9159. Do you consider that is not a function in normal times that could be more closely performed for industry than it is performed now? — I think it is a special need arising out of the parlous condition in which industry is at the present time.

9160. You do not think it is a good thing for a banker to give his opinion to an industrialist, and an industrialist to give his opinion to a banker in normal times more than now, so as to establish a closer connection? — Give his opinion, yes; but I do not want to establish ownership between the two.

9161. I agree. — Is not that really the question?

9162. *Chairman*: But falling far short of that, surely a closer liaison is possible. That is one of the major topics we have been considering, namely, whether there has been sufficient contact between industry and the banks from the point of view of the bank being at hand as an adviser on the financial aspects of industry. The banks must study industry to some extent because they supply the sinews of war. How can they give useful help unless they have an authoritative means of obtaining information? That strikes me as a difficulty for the banker? — I should say that the banker (I do not refer to a banker of the type of Sir Guy) requires to have some information – I do not know how he would get it – in order to know in what channels he could usefully, as well as safely, lend money. I should think he would need to know that, but that is mostly short lending. I think the direction in which he may give credit is very important, but otherwise, I do not think that any further link, an incorporated link, so to speak, between industry and banking is needful. But I do believe that as industry has now been somewhat converted by this process which is going on so in the future they will be in a position to obtain their needs and they may have a close liaison with some form of finance or another. But if you are going to try and establish any definite, any incorporated, form of liaison, it is either going to come down to ownership or to conflict with ownership and I am all against that – to conflict with the proprietors. I am entirely against that.

9163. *Mr. Brand*: Take the big American Trust and Security Companies, like the Guaranty Trust Company. Their principle, I believe, is, as a rule, not to have any ownership of industrial shares, but they take responsibility for industrial issues. Do you believe that is a wrong principle? — I would.

9164. Do you think that is an instance of having a relationship with industry that the joint stock banks here never do have? — That, I think, is a private relationship.

9165. You would not like to see anything of that kind here? — No, I would not like it at all. I think it is wholly unsuited to our traditions, mentality and capacity – I really do.

9166. Do you mean our capacity is too little, or too much? — It has developed in other directions. I do not think you could create with safety that sort of thing with the A.B. Bank or the C.D. Bank. There is the great development of trust investment companies and that sort of thing here which does not exist in these other countries. The same in Germany. I rather agree with what Sir Guy said some time ago that the unification between banking interests and industry there has tended, if anything, to go too far.

9167. I agree. — (*Sir Guy Granet*): And in certain other countries even more so – take a country like Italy.

9168. *Mr. Lubbock*: It has been represented to us that the banks have not sufficient knowledge of industry and do not take a sufficiently wide view of industry as a whole when they make their advances to particular firms? — (*Mr. Norman*): That is a different question altogether.

9169. I quite agree. I was going to ask you whether you have anything to say about that. It has been suggested that the banks ought to have some kind of well-developed link between themselves and industry as a whole in order that they should make their advances perhaps on a different principle? — I think that is a different question altogether. I think it is an important one, and certainly a very difficult one. I myself have often wondered on what basis joint stock banks decide in which direction they will most willingly lend their short money. I am not speaking of capital loans.

9170. *Mr. Brand*: Their advances? — Yes. I have often wondered that, and I do not know the answer to it now. I have asked several.

9171. *Mr. Keynes*: So have we? — But this is not the question we have been discussing. We are on a totally different track now, absolutely different.

9172. *Mr. Lubbock*: I am quite aware of that, only the general relationship between banks and industry prompted me to ask you a question about that particular point?—Quite so.

9173. *Chairman*: On that same point I would like to put a further question to you, Mr. Governor, if I may. You have at your disposal under your roof, as you have told us, a certain number of experts who were not formerly housed there. Having returned to a more or less normal period, I suppose it would always be the function of a Central Bank like the Bank of England to take very important financial decisions from time to time, and those decisions must have certain effects upon industry, and upon the general welfare of the country. Would not it be of use to you to have these experts at your hand at ordinary times, so that you may lay their special information under contribution when you are coming to these decisions on matters of policy which from time to time you have to take – I mean as a source of information? — I do not think so. They are specialists you see.

9174. Then have you at your disposal normally, apart from these experts, sufficient material, statistical information, and knowledge of the situation generally, to enable you to proceed to decisions on policy with reasonable comfort? — I do not attach importance to great elaboration of statistical information. In my opinion the requisite information is available.

9175. In coming to a decision upon any large question of policy one wants to be well instructed. One wants to know whether you have at your disposal the sources of information on the point which you have to consider in coming to a decision. What I want to know is this – whether you feel in the organization of the Bank of England you are able to lay under contribution sources of information which you require and ought to possess in coming to these important decisions? — Yes, I do. There is much information, however, which in my view is more valuable for the purpose of testing conclusions arrived at independently than for providing the foundation on which to base conclusions.

9176. *Mr. Bevin*: Are you very hopeful of the initiative in the way of re-organization by the manufacturers showing itself in five years? Judging by Sir Guy's evidence this morning there is a good deal of slowness in these things? — (*Sir Guy Granet*): I did not suggest, if I may explain, that the slowness is universal. I was merely giving illustrations of slowness in certain directions to give you some idea of reasons why one cannot get ahead quite so quickly as some people think we should.

9177. When you are getting these schemes of re-organization one of the most important things to get a re-organization scheme given effect to with any degree of alacrity, once it is decided on, is the adaptability of labour. I think you would agree with that. What consultation is there with the labour organizations when these schemes are going through? — When it come to us, none.

9178. And none before it, as far as I know? — That I do not know, but you see our function is purely financing and, therefore, I do not go into that. When it comes to us we are only on the finance.

9179. May I put it in another way? Assuming you are looking at the finance and getting the scheme, what steps do you take to see that the labour side has been adjusted so that your scheme has a chance of working out satisfactorily? — What steps do we take, or can we take?

9180. You take no steps apparently? — No.

9181. Assume there is a big re-organization scheme in steel and you are going to plan regionally, which means a movement of people and alteration of craft conditions due to new mechanism, it may be after you have agreed financially to support that that you are involved in a dispute with the men because you fail to get adaptability? — Perhaps I have not quite made myself understood. You cannot over-estimate the importance of relations with labour, but it is a part of management. It is nothing to do with the banking side of it. Therefore, we assume, in a scheme brought forward by an industry, as these schemes are, that that side of it has been fully gone into. Insofar as we can criticise at all we look at it in this way, as I think I have mentioned. We look to see whether the scheme is based on a very large expansion of production. We find it is based on pretty well the existing basis of production. Then we ask: Does this scheme involve closing works right and left, or does it involve the modernization of plant, and re-layout of plant? All that we go into. But the ultimate responsibility as to what the effect on labour will be, as to whether it means an immediate reduction, or not, we do not regard as our business. That does not mean to say we disregard it, but we do not look at it as our business.

9182. But you do look on good management as part of it. May I put it in another way? Do you satisfy yourself that good management, in addition to consulting its engineers and consulting its advisers as to lay-out, would have consulted labour? Good management would have had a fairly clear idea of what it could do before it ventures into these schemes. Do you make any enquiries as to whether management has taken any steps with labour? — I cannot say yes to that. We do not take any step to enquire into that definitely for the reason as I say that we regard that side of it as being something beyond our scope, but it is one of the things we ask about informally, and is the subject of conversation all the time, but it is not one of the things on which we lay ourselves out to get a certificate, so to speak.

9183. My experience for what it is worth is this. The management deals with these reorganisations and just dumps them down without any previous consultation or without any attempt to get co-operation and then you have a dispute, or you do not get the scheme to work well? — (*Mr. Norman*): That has not been my experience.

9184. It has been mine in both schemes I have had to deal with. — It has not been mine.

Chairman: I think, Mr. Governor, we have exhausted this branch of our discussion. We are very much obliged to you, Sir Guy. The Governor is kindly coming back after lunch, but I understand you are not. Thank you very much.

(*Adjourned for a short time*)

Appendix 21

The Right Hon. MONTAGU COLLET NORMAN, D.S.O., Governor of the Bank of England, and Dr. O. M. W. SPRAGUE, called and examined.

9185. *Chairman*: This afternoon, Gentlemen, the Governor is accompanied by Dr. Sprague, and it is proposed to turn to rather different topics from those which we were discussing with the Governor when he was accompanied by Sir Guy Granet this morning. I think I might introduce the subject of our discussion by saying that, in the course of our Inquiry, we have frequently heard the view that a solution for many of our difficulties was to be found in international co-operation; that, while we had our domestic difficulties, and our domestic obstacles to recovery, a merely national policy in financial matters was not possible in these days, and least of all possible for a country such as ours; and that the redress for certain of the disequilibria which are afflicting us might be found through the medium of better international understandings and better international management of finance. That is a matter which, from the practical point of view, is hedged about with very great difficulties because it is not within our own control. Then our attention was drawn to the fact that there had come into existence a new organisation in the shape of the Bank for International Settlements – in fact it was during our own sittings – with new functions and new objects, and naturally we are anxious, if we can, to get some light upon the possibilities of that new organisation, how far it may further an international policy and what should be the objectives of that international policy. I think we might look at the general situation; first of all, the earlier period, let us say from 1925 to 1928 before the world causes became so prominent, and then the period since 1928 when there has supervened on the top of our domestic problems a general international situation of great acuteness which has largely increased the whole difficulty. In the presence of witnesses such as we have this afternoon, I at least feel myself in the position of a person to be instructed and informed, rather than a person in the position of asking the questions most likely to elucidate information. I think, Dr. Sprague, we should be very glad if you would, having heard the outlook I have expressed, indicate to us on what lines we might most usefully talk to you this afternoon? — (*Dr. Sprague*): I would suggest that there might be a discussion relating definitely to the B.I.S., followed by a consideration of the more general problems split up into those two periods which you have just mentioned. I think the functions of the B.I.S. and its immediate possibilities can be developed first, and that then, perhaps, it can fruitfully be introduced into a more general discussion of the whole position of the London money market, the Bank of England and other agencies. At first I should think that it was necessary to place before the Committee a picture of the functions of the B.I.S. and the hopes that attended its establishment.

9186. I think that would be an excellent programme. Would it be convenient for you, or the Governor, to give us the evidence about the B.I.S.? We have had very little evidence, practically none, about its constitution and its objectives? — I think quite clearly it should be for the Governor, as he was concerned with its establishment and has had much to do with its functioning up to the present time. My own knowledge of it is very much that of an interested outsider.

9187. Mr. Governor, would you be good enough to give us a little historical survey of the existing situation out of which the B.I.S. has grown? — (*Mr. Norman*): I will do my best.

9188. We are much obliged to you. — The B.I.S., we have to remember first, was born out of the turmoil of The Hague, out of the Young Plan, and in many ways that was a very unpropitious moment for its birth. Before that time there had been a considerable amount of communication and co-operation between the various Central Banks privately. The first ideas defined came, I think, from Genoa, and among other things which the Genoa resolutions proposed was that the Bank of England should summon a conference of Central Banks to do, in effect, what has now become the duty of the B.I.S. It always appeared impossible, during those years when we were waiting, to summon such a conference, for the excellent reason that the people would not come. They would not come, not because they were unwilling to co-operate, but because they were unwilling to face the publicity and the questionings in their own countries which would arise if they attended any such conference, and all the attempts that I made to that end failed. But, notwithstanding that fact, there were at that time outstanding individuals, as I believe, in the Central Banking world who made co-operation possible in its earlier stages, and pre-eminent among them were Governor Strong and President Schacht. They were both dominant men, extremely interested from different sides – and very different they were – in co-operation. They were the most whole-hearted supporters of the idea and did, in its early stages, I believe, a great deal in trying to bring about a common policy as between the various banks. Owing largely to their personalities, they were the two men who were outstanding in that respect, and they are no longer with us to-day.

But the particular object, or one of the particular objects, of the B.I.S. was to get rid of the difficulty of Reparation payments, and one of the successes which I think the B.I.S. has already achieved is that it has largely, if not entirely, taken Reparations out of the political arena and put them into a back room in the B.I.S.; so that a question which for many years had been a difficult and at times rather acute question, and may possibly become so again, has really now dropped into comparative insignificance – nobody thinks about it and the payments have been largely mechanised. Added to the Reparation payments, the international debt questions have been joined up with them and the two are now in the process of being transferred from where they originated to where they belong, with the minimum of comment and the minimum of friction, and to that extent I think the B.I.S. has been wonderfully successful within a limited sphere.

Another point in which I think the B.I.S. has been even more successful than I should have expected is that it has provided a method of conference, or a club, among Central Banks, which, over the last six or eight months, has become regular and useful and, without comment from outside, has allowed many of those who are interested in the common problem of Central Banking to meet regularly once a month, which they do with great persistence, to discuss all those matters of their own as well as of the B.I.S. which happen to come to the surface at the moment.

Those are the two great points. Apart from those, what is the purpose of the B.I.S.? We have to remember, first of all, whence the funds of which they are able to dispose in one way or another are drawn. There are, first of all, the Reparations and Debt funds in which they act really as little more than a trustee, and therefore those are not of any great importance. There are certain further duties of the B.I.S. as regards trusteeship, strictly speaking, for various loans. Those also are purely mechanical and do not give rise to any matters of current interest. You then come to the funds which the B.I.S. controls because it is becoming, or may become, the repository of Central Banks' reserves. A large development has been made in that direction, a great number of the European Central Banks are now keeping their surplus reserves with the B.I.S., and that may prove to be a very large factor in its duties. But those funds also, being reserves, are not free for general uses and they can only be employed by the B.I.S. within the same, or perhaps stricter, limitations as were before observed by the various banks to whom the funds belong. So that, by and large, the only free funds which the B.I.S. has at all are certain long deposits made by various countries – Germany, France, and so forth – in connection with The Hague Agreements. There they have certain funds, not very large, which, although they are debts of the B.I.S., are in their holding for a great number of years. Those are the only free funds which, strictly, the B.I.S. has to dispose of, and for the most part those are now being used, I think, where there is the greatest need for them. For instance, there is a great demand in certain countries for certain middle-term credits, as they are called, for the purpose of assisting exports from one place to another, and a certain amount of those funds is employed in that way. You will see, therefore, from that enumeration of the funds, that the B.I.S. has not got, and never will have, as it is composed and as it has been started, any very large sums of which to dispose. As I look upon it, and as I said at the beginning, the B.I.S. has now made those first steps which it was necessary for any organisation to make. It has taken Reparations and Allied Debts largely out of the political arena, mechanised them, to a certain extent; it has trustee duties which are purely nominal at the present time; and it is holding Central Bank funds; and I doubt whether there are at present any further directions in which as a bank it can advance in the near future. I think it has got to the stage now where, having done what it could do immediately, it has got to go slowly and develop by degrees, watching, so far as possible, where it can be helpful, possibly in certain circumstances not acting with its own funds, but acting in one direction or another as the leader and disposer of funds contributed by various Central Banks for particular purposes. That is conceivable, but no occasion has arisen up to the present. I think it has got to consolidate the position so far as it has gone and it has got a vast amount of internal and more or less troublesome things to decide, especially in regard to details of administration and organisation which, in a concern made up of people representing six or eight nationalities, are very difficult and complicated and give rise to a great deal of trouble. I do not think it will do more than that for some time to come. It is already able to arrange certain conveniences among the Central Banks in the transfer of funds from one place to another, but that is mechanical; it may give a slight economy, but it is not a matter of any general importance. I repeat, therefore, that, so far as its own development goes, I doubt if there are any large economies or changes to be made in the near future; I think it has got to develop slowly, to learn to stand before it can walk and to walk before it can run, and that, I should think, would take a considerable period.

One of the difficulties with which the B.I.S. is always faced is that there are in the Young Plan, which may be said to be the basis of the B.I.S., certain vague references to all sorts of things which might be done towards rebuilding the world. How those are ever to be carried out I have not the slightest idea, what they precisely mean I do not know; they are continually mentioned, especially by those countries who feel the need more than others of some further development. They are continually mentioned, but how and in what direction the B.I.S. can really help to discharge, if at all, those vague promises in the Young

Plan, I do not at present see. Time may show. If one had to sum up what they amount to it would perhaps be something of this sort:– that they are intended to expand and improve international trade and at the same time transfer as much money as possible from the short to the long market. Those are the two broad things which, I think, are implicit in these vague promises. I mention them merely because they are so often in the minds of people, and especially of our German friends, as being the real inducement which led them to adopt as whole-heartedly as they did the idea of the B.I.S.

I must also say one word, if you please, about a matter with which many of you here are familiar, and that is the special difficulties of an international body. We have at the present moment extraordinarily good personal relations, far better than we used to have when it was necessary to make a formal visit to meet anybody. Nevertheless, a Central Bank Governor, when he comes to Basel, is necessarily to a certain extent dominated by the particular state of his own fiscal and economic situation at home, of the mind of his public, of the mind of his Government, and it is a matter therefore, not, as I say again, of establishing personal friendship – which we have done to a marvellous degree, I think, almost intimacy – but of taking up questions which are international and regarding them, as one would say, on their merits. No two or three countries can really regard an international question on its merits. There is no such thing as merits when you come to that. To get the affairs of a country, and possibly the needs of a country, considered on their merits is a thing which has not been achieved, and, I believe, will not be achieved for a very long time. The moment the position of certain countries is mentioned you get a reaction for or against, for particular reasons applicable to the individual in whom the reaction takes place. There will be a new Europe before we get away from that.

That, broadly, is the picture. I could go on a good deal more, but it would be mostly details. I have given you the setting up, the possible objects, the funds that they have at their disposal, the way they work, the possibilities ahead of them, and in particular one of the difficulties which I see, which is the difficulty of judging a question really on its merits.

9189. There is one feature of the B.I.S. to which you allude, which, I think, for our purpose, is particularly important. You said it furnished for the first time a new form of meeting among the representatives of the Central Banks and thus afforded opportunities of discussion and meeting regularly, which were valuable. How far do you think that, through the medium of this discussion at the B.I.S., it will be possible in the future to concert international policy among the nations to greater extent than has been possible in the past, and thus lead to a better adjustment between the various countries in regard to their financial policies? — I have said that the affairs of certain countries whenever they come to be discussed produce entirely different reactions in the minds of the individual persons who discuss them, and I think it is going to be a very long time before that is altered, a very long time indeed. So far as the co-operative relations between any couple of banks or three banks are concerned, there I think already in most instances a considerable amount of progress had been made in the earlier period which I have mentioned. But I think it is easier now to get consideration of a particular problem as between two or three banks than it was before, because one can more easily meet, discuss it, go into it, without making a particular journey and having to state precisely, 'I have come to discuss this or that particular question.' You can take it in your stride, and it is very much easier, and it works in that way extremely well. I will leave to Dr. Sprague to discuss the future more precisely, but I think the prospect of bringing about any change in general monetary regulations – which in the main would be a Governmental question – and the time when they will be brought about, is very remote.

9190. Is the ideal of an international policy one that should be aimed at? Is an international policy really necessary now with a proper financial system? — It is imperative, I think. But so far the attempt has produced innumerable difficulties and few solutions. It has produced solutions in a few cases where two or three individuals have joined together to produce a certain end, but not as a general rule.

9191. Without some such principle of unity of management is it possible to obtain economic stability? — I do not think you will obtain economic stability through unity of management of the Central Banks represented on the B.I.S.

9192. Can they contribute to it? — They can contribute to it and are already personally extremely anxious to contribute to it. There is certainly unity in principle there, but they are swayed by various considerations and also by the policy of their Governments and by their markets; some of them have markets which are venturesome and willing to adopt international measures; others have markets which in these matters are young and untrained, or they scarcely have a market at all. Some of them have Governments whose position is, shall I say, affluent and rich and sound; others of them have a Government which is perpetually struggling to find funds to meet particular payments. So that at the present time it is extremely difficult to get in fact the adoption of a common international policy.

9193. But it would be the objective? — It is the objective among all the individuals there, without any doubt, subject to the reservations which I have made.

9194. And what would that international

policy be designed to achieve? Is it towards greater stability among the nations in regard to price levels or towards the better distribution of gold? To what practical aims would an international policy be directed? — I believe it would be directed towards achieving what I take to be the objects of the Young Plan – monetary stability, the development of trade, and a general transfer of short into long money as and when needed.

9195. And to do that in concert with each other so that the policy of one should not pass over the policy of others? — Quite; and I think the B.I.S. is going to develop by degrees, especially when it is forgiven a few wild oats it may have had to sow. I think it will get into a position where it will at least be an example and enjoy a prestige, and induce people to do this, that, and the other because it is the right thing to do – teach manners and conduct. That, I think, it is going to do. It is not a question of employing funds.

9196. Greater financial comity? — Yes.

9197. *Mr. Keynes*: The bank has to employ all its reserves in some money market other than its own? — It has no reserves of its own. It is unique in that way.

9198. On what principles does it decide how to employ its funds? — If I take the categories of funds which I have mentioned; first of all, the Debt Payment funds and the Reparations funds, those are for the most part employed in the market where payments have to be made. There is really no choice. Then it has other funds which are virtually the deposits of the reserves of the Central Banks. Those for the greater part are given to it in certain forms, and broadly speaking, it will have to account to those Central Banks, if and when called upon, for those funds at a moment's notice.

9199. Whether they are deposited in sterling or dollars, or wherever they may be? — Yes; they are deposited in one form or another and liable to be called in. The B.I.S. does not speculate to any great extent with those funds.

9200. Is there any advantage to the depositor in depositing through the B.I.S. rather than direct in the market concerned? — Perhaps not to the depositor, but if you take the way in which some of the smaller banks have used their funds, I think there is great advantage in it.

9201. You mean that although they would be keeping it in sterling or dollars as the case might be, they might not be employing it in those centres to the best advantage? — Yes. I think the orthodoxy which is being established by the B.I.S. is an advantage. Also I think it will come about that if the B.I.S. has, for instance, 100 in reserves of Central Banks it will find in time that it can keep 80 available and use for the general advantage elsewhere, perhaps 20. That would take some years of experience, but that is a possibility. It may economise in reserves.

9202. It would seem to be a more progressive state of affairs if what was owing by it was on deposit with itself and was transferred to one deposit rather than to a variety of deposits. — I do not know what you mean by 'on deposit with itself' because the B.I.S. has no deposits of its own. The deposit must be in a stated currency.

9203. It might be in fine gold? — It might be in gramme-or – an idea which seems to have been started, although we have not adopted it. Even if you give it a different name, call it Swiss francs at par, it is perfectly well known in what currency it will be wanted.

9204. But if it were in the Clearing House of the Central Banks it would never be wanted; it would put the balances of the Central Banks in one pair of hands. — That is what I hoped would happen. We have not yet had this money for a year. You will have to go through one or two seasonal periods. I believe you will get a Clearing House of reserves, but that will take time.

9205. Is there any risk of the B.I.S. impairing its position as the repository of reserve funds by embarking on too much philanthropy? — Philanthropy in the use of its funds?

9206. Yes. — Not of those funds, I think. Philanthropy might be shown at a later stage, possibly, by the purposes for which it uses its own funds, that is to say, its long funds, which might be used by agreement with others for a particular purpose. There I think it has to go very slowly. I think there is not the least doubt that if the B.I.S. began to use for philanthropic purposes the reserves of the Central Banks they would be withdrawn.

9207. There is no reason why the deposits with the B.I.S. should not in the course of time be suitable, as the reserves of the Central Banks, as an alternative equivalent to gold? — All of those funds are looked upon by Central Banks as the equivalent of gold.

9208. *Mr. Brand*: They are their foreign assets? — Yes. They are what are called metal reserves mostly, nothing else.

9209. *Mr. Keynes*: If that is to be maintained it is very important that there should be no question of their being used philanthropically? — I think there is no question of that; in fact, I think the B.I.S. know quite well that if they were to use those funds philanthropically that would be virtually the end of it. Of course, I am giving you my own view of the administration of the B.I.S., which I do not administer.

9210. Do you think there is any probability at present of decisions being reached by the Board of the B.I.S. which take the form of agreeing that Bank Rates ought to be relaxed or stiffened up, that there ought to be a general tendency upwards or downwards in money rates throughout the world? — I think there is no prospect of the Board of the B.I.S. passing a resolution to that effect. That is a thing which can quite easily develop in the club life of the B.I.S.

9211. Is there any reason why the B.I.S. should not in course of time come to discount the obligations of Central Banks? — The portfolio? No, because they do so already.

9212. I mean obligations of other Central Banks? — The portfolio?

9213. *Professor Gregory*: Yes. — They do so already. They are continually switching from one portfolio to another.

9214. *Mr. Keynes*: That means that they have, in effect, a Bank Rate of their own? — No, it does not. It is appertaining to the market concerned, entirely.

9215. Is there any reason why they should not provide a Central Bank with a deposit simply by discounting the obligation of that Central Bank at their own rate, the rate of the B.I.S.? I am thinking of the B.I.S. standing to the Central Banks in the same position as the Central Banks stand to the home money market? — That is the direction in which they are developing. That is what I mean by the clearing fund; it may clear, not only in cash, but in three months.

9216. *Mr. Brand*: They would grant credit to other Central Banks, would they? — No, I do not think they would grant credit. They would discount the portfolio of the Central Bank.

9217. *Mr. Keynes*: They would create deposits in their own books——? — Against the three months' portfolio, as they are doing now.

9218. Cannot the Central Bank turn a local deposit into the equivalent of gold by making a deposit with the B.I.S. out of its own domestic assets? — The B.I.S. will take certain funds, certain approved currencies as deposits, but I think they have not yet accepted a deposit in the domestic currency of a Central Bank.

9219. Could you take £1,000,000 worth of Bank Bills to the B.I.S., get a deposit against those and then regard that deposit as a foreign deposit? — No, not at present. When I was speaking of the clearing, that is a possibility that I had in mind. You could not at present; you might arrange to do so.

9220. Is not the fact that the Federal Reserve Bank of New York is not a member an important handicap? — Yes, in my view.

9221. And, of course, also, neutral countries are very poorly represented on the Board? — The Board, as you know, is liable to be increased from whatever it is at present – 16 I think – by anything up to 9 other countries who may be selected before long.

9222. Is there a reasonable hope of its developing along the lines you have indicated? — Yes. I am speaking now of short money, am I not?

9223. *Professor Gregory*: Clearing functions? — Clearing functions; yes, it has a great opportunity, I think, and that is where it will develop.

9224. Personally, Mr. Governor, you are hopeful that it will? — I am.

9225. It is not merely a possibility, but rather more than that? — I think it will. I think it will establish a clearing fund for the reserves of the Central Banks in approved currencies, and I hope – though this I say with reserve – that it may be possible to establish a position where a certain number of approved currencies will be interchangeable. That is what I mean by the clearing fund – exchange clearing. Speaking for myself and not for the B.I.S., I do not see any very great difficulty in developing slowly upon those lines, but before it can be done you have got to have the experience of a few years and see what the seasonal changes are. You cannot do it on the experience of a few months; you must see over a series of years what are the season a changes in the exchange position.

9226. *Mr. Keynes*: There would be obvious advantages in this, if it could be developed, over what are called the gold exchange methods? — A great number of advantages.

9227. It would not be an alternative? — I think not. I think it is an improvement on the gold exchange. One has to recognise that the B.I.S., in making an arrangement of this sort, might be taking a risk; they might be called upon, if people got frightened, to deliver at short notice a very large amount of one currency. That is a risk they have to take; they have, therefore, got to see the seasonal changes and, if I may so call them, the possible panic changes that might take place.

9228. *Mr. Brand*: Supposing some years ago the franc had been taken as a good currency and the moment arrived when the franc was a bad currency. Would not that be an extraordinarily awkward thing? — Very awkward, and that is the risk. The B.I.S. has to be very careful which currencies it takes.

9229. *Mr. Keynes*: If the bank itself and the depositor both have the option to require and to pay gold against any particular currency, whether the deposit is made in gold or whatever it may be, you do not formally have to remove a bank from your list, you have merely to assist in keeping the reserves in that currency? — Yes. My idea has been to keep gold out of it as far as possible. (*Dr. Sprague*): I wonder if I might make comparisons with the Federal Reserve Banks of the United States.

9230. *Chairman*: Please do. — (*Dr. Sprague*): I think it should be realised that the various members of the B.I.S. are independent sovereignties; they are not subject to that measure of control which can be exercised over the various Federal Reserve Banks by the Federal Reserve Board. They also differ from the Federal Reserve Banks in that all the Federal Reserve Banks employ their surplus funds in the single money market, New York, where they have acquired their bankers' bills and Government securities, and it is in that New York market that any one of the Federal Reserve Banks will dispose of bank acceptances, or Government securities, if it needs to secure additional funds with which to meet settlements with the other Federal Reserve Banks. In the case of the B.I.S., I see great possibilities of its rapid development in a variety of ways, with a minimum of friction, in a world in which the various members are all in tolerably sound condition and their countries are in a sound economic and financial position. If and when there is a fair approach to financial equilibrium about the world, then the B.I.S. is an agency which can do a good deal of valuable work in facilitating operations in overcoming minor divergencies in the supply of funds or means of payment. When, however, you consider a world which is far from equilibrium, some countries having an abundance of funds, others in a rather needy condition, eager to secure additional funds in every variety of way, then it seems to me you are confronted with a problem which cannot be in large measure solved by means of the B.I.S. Readjustments, in other words, are necessary in each of these various countries, with some assistance from the outside where there is clear evidence that measures of a self-help character are being taken; but co-operation will never take the place in such circumstances of the necessary self-help measures, measures which cannot be enforced effectively by the B.I.S., certainly not now in its present state of development, and, I should be disposed to think, not in the future. For these reasons, I think it would be unwise to express the view that in the present state of the world very much, or the major part of what is necessary, can be accomplished through the agency of this particular institution.

9231. Or through any other international agency? — I emphasise the need of self-help, for I feel that people are disposed to look about for some international agency which will render it unnecessary for them to resort to what I believe to be necessary measures of self-help.

9232. 'Self-help' naturally has a pleasing sound to a compatriot of Dr. Smiles. What do you mean exactly by 'self-help'? — That is the burden of what I may have to say, if you are good enough to listen, after we have finished with the B.I.S.

9233. *Mr. Brand*: Might I ask what would be the effect of an outbreak of war on the B.I.S.? Is it being internationalised? — (*Mr. Norman*): It has been internationalised. Its funds and deposits are exempt from seizure in all the countries signatory to the Hague Agreement. That does not include the United States.

9234. *Mr. Keynes*: So you dare not hold dollars? — We hold them at our peril, but we are brave enough.

9235. *Chairman*: One question I might ask as a practical one. The conspicuous feature in the economic position has been the extraordinary fall of world prices. Do you think that the B.I.S. has any role to play in correction of that tendency? — I do not think it recognises any such role.

9236. Would it have any indirect power to assist or obstruct recovery? — Yes, I think, to the extent that it could achieve some of the objects which I have named, such as facilitating trade and exports, or increasing the supply of long funds. But I do not think the B.I.S. would recognise it has any price fixing duties – for that is what it amounts to.

9237. Have you found that there is any common agreement in the club life or the official life of the B.I.S. in recognising the importance of that aim? — I think everybody recognises its importance, but I do not think they would all agree on what is desirable. I think it would be extremely difficult to get any general view.

9238. If one nation thought that it was important to get the restoration of price levels to some particular point, is that the kind of thing which might be discussed in the counsels of the B.I.S.? — I do not think there would be any agreement on it.

9239. No agreement and no action directed towards it? — No, not towards that object in itself.

9240. Or means which might in the individual case of each country bring about such a state of things? — I do not think anybody there would be willing to devise measures which are intended as price fixing measures. From what I have heard in discussion, I think that is not an unfair statement.

9241. *Mr. Brand*: Does it make a difference that the B.I.S. has no issue power behind it? Take the Bank of England. When it discounts a very large number of bills it can do so with the knowledge that its currency will increase and so forth. The B.I.S. is in a totally different position? — Yes, it cannot create credit.

9242. It cannot create credit. — I do not think it could be made to do so wisely. (*Dr. Sprague*): If I may put in a slight modification along this line, I would say this. If all the Central Banks throughout the world came to hold as a large part of their reserves deposits with the B.I.S., and transfers on its books were the principal means of making settlements between countries, then I should suppose that the increase in the discounts made by the B.I.S. would be credited to one or other of the Central Banks and then would be shifted about among them; just as when the Bank of Engand creates credit generally it increases the deposits of the joint stock banks, and that goes on until gold goes out, or there is an increased requirement for currency. With the small number of Banks in it, with the moderate portion of their reserves held by the B.I.S., and the comparatively small part of the settlement between countries which is made through the B.I.S., I think an increase of, say, ten millions in the loans of the B.I.S. credited to the Central Banks would almost immediately result in a loss of balances by the B.I.S., as the funds when employed by the borrowing Bank would not be re-deposited generally by the recipient Banks – at least not until you have practically the whole business of making settlements between the Central Banks and between countries concentrated in the B.I.S. At present, there is a practical impossibility of any appreciable amount of expansion, just as there is for a single joint stock bank, if the others are not keeping in step.

9243. *Mr. Lubbock*: The Governor said that the question of fixing or raising prices was not part of the policy of the B.I.S. Do you think that if there was such a policy the Central Banks in co-operation could do anything to carry it out? — (*Dr. Sprague*): Very little.

9244. It is so much in the air that the Central Banks should get together and do something to raise prices that that is what leads me to ask the question. (*Mr. Bevin*): Why could they not do so? — That is a very long matter. I shall come to it towards the end, but I would like to say this. If the shortage of credit and the decline in the course of general prices were clearly due to an insufficiency of gold all over the world, if there had been practically no increase in the gold reserves of any of the Central Banks during the last five years, that would suggest a definite cause of price decline which might be remedied by appropriate legislation throughout the world designed to reduce the required reserves. I should think that the B.I.S. might, in the case of such a definite cause of price decline, make investigations and make general proposals; but, at the present time, it is not true that the gold reserves of the Central Banks, taking them as a whole, are failing to increase. There certainly is no general belief about the world that the immediate cause, or that *the* cause, of the decline in the level of prices can be attributed to gold shortage or existing reserve requirements. The decline, I should say, would be thought to be due to a variety of different causes. By some it would be found to be in the monetary sphere, but outside this country that view is not generally accepted. That being the case, it would be regarded in B.I.S. circles as quite inappropriate to attack the price level problem by anything that the B.I.S. could do, or anything that it could appropriately suggest.

9245. *Mr. Keynes*: That was not the question. The question was could they, not would they, do anything? — (*Dr. Sprague*): I should say, distinctly, that it was impossible to do anything, but I should like to develop that at a little later stage. (*Mr. Lubbock*): We will reserve that point. (*Mr. Keynes*): I should like to register the fact that we have heard no reason why they could not. (*Mr. Lubbock*): We are going to hear it.

9246. *Chairman*: Will you now develop for us the points which you wish us to discuss with you? — I should like at the outset to develop a matter which I think might desirably be placed at the very beginning of the Report which this Committee is to formulate. I think that it is most desirable to make a contrast between the position of the London market in the pre-war period as compared with its position in recent years. There is not very much difference so far as the organisation of the market is concerned with its various financial agencies. You have the Bank of England with its powers not essentially and fundamentally modified by the change in the Act of 1844, and you have the clearing banks with somewhat greater concentration than in the pre-war period. Then you have the various financial agencies, issuing houses, bill brokers, and discount houses, as before. But I do not think there is any fundamental change in the organisation of the London market in the two periods.

The essential differences that I see are these. In the pre-war period London developed as the central money market of the world during the long period when there was an abundant supply of funds saved for investment, part of which was invested in this country and part of which found investment abroad. But, generally speaking, throughout the pre-war period, I think, we may say that there was a preference at any given rate in the mind of the investor for British securities as contrasted with foreign securities. That I regard as one of the essential factors in the development of a central money market, whether it be a market which is mainly a national market or one which is mainly a world market. It is a centre in which surplus funds find liquid employment. It is a centre to which borrowers of all sorts, both national and international, resort, but it maintains its equipoise in large part because of the preference for domestic issues as contrasted with foreign issues. If you get a situation in which there seems to be in the minds of investors, for any reason whatever, a preference either persistent or intermittent for foreign issues at any given rate, that is a very serious element of weakness in the functioning of such a money market. So I should say that if people in the United States were to prefer investments in the vicinity of Dallas, or Minneapolis, instead of New York, Philadelphia, or Boston, it would be far more difficult for the New York market to function within the area of the United States.

The second difference I see is this. In the pre-war period, foreign investments more directly, more immediately, and more largely served to stimulate British exports than is now the case. In the pre-war period, the proceeds of large loans were likely to be expended in large part by the borrower in this country because the sort of constructional material which he needed could in general be purchased more cheaply in this market than elsewhere. I judge the position in the post-war period to be that, to a greater extent than formerly, the borrower is disposed to buy his rails, or his electrical equipment, or whatever it may be in some foreign market. That places a direct pressure upon the exchanges which would be in a measure absent if the purchases were made more largely in this country. It brings it about that foreign loans to a greater extent than formerly either lead to the exportation of gold, or compel resort to measures intended to make the short money market more attractive.

I think it is reasonable to say that the market to some extent is living upon the prestige which it gained (and which it deserved from its record) during the nineteenth century and the first decade of the present century. If you were to take a country having a money market with no such prestige and also a country which was not in a position to provide the materials desired by the foreign borrower at low prices, practically all of the proceeds of any foreign loans made by that country would be taken out in the form of gold. The position is obscured in the case of the London market because by a certain amount of management the short market can be made a bit more attractive and can retain or attract additional foreign funds. But I am disposed to think that the country is in a measure living upon the prestige gained in the past under the particular conditions which I have mentioned. It is for this reason that I see no possibility of full employment of labour and capital in this country until conditions are changed in such wise that British industry will seem as attractive an investment relative to foreign investments as was the case in the pre-war period. That covers the essential differences that I see in the function of the money market and I do not think they are of a nature to be effectively treated by any conceivable modification that you might make or suggest in the powers of policy of the Bank of England. If the Bank had larger powers, or is freed from the present restrictions as regards the fiduciary issue, it might permit of somewhat greater withdrawals of gold in any given period of time. But you would always have to bear in mind that the advantage of being able to export £20,000,000 or £30,000,000 or £40,000,000 in gold might be very much more than offset by any weakening of confidence in the stability of the London market throughout the world. That stability must rest in the final analysis, as it would appear to me, upon the ability of this country over the years to develop its industries, and profitably to compete with the rest of the world. It might very well be that some industries may decline, but there must be a development of other industries to take their place. The weakness of the exchanges, as evidenced in recent years, is not anything that could be corrected by the loosening of the restrictions governing the operations of the Bank, unless a slightly greater outflow of gold would lead to the establishment of conditions in this country that would strengthen its competitive position. If you believe that £40,000,000 of gold exported from this country would set in motion an upward movement of prices over the rest of the world and no upward movement here, so as to place the industries of the country in a relatively better condition, why then that might be desirable. But the ability to maintain, for a few months, a given rate of 3 per cent. or 4 per cent. or 5 per cent., or the ability to make somewhat more considerable loans, would seem to me, in the absence of plans for the reorganisation of industry, or the development of new enterprises and reduction of costs, not to get one anywhere. Monetary policy alone cannot correct a weak position. It may be used to remove impediments or to defer the necessary house-cleaning, the self-help which I spoke about a short time ago. I do not believe, in other words, that the economic position of the country, or its financial position would now be quite certainly better if the fiduciary issue had been made considerably greater in 1927, and a considerable amount of additional gold had been exported, and if rates had been maintained slightly lower at certain periods since that time. You are not justified, as it seems to me, unless you have very convincing proof, in assuring that a modification in the structure or powers of the Bank of England would have made any appreciable betterment of the present position.

9247. *Professor Gregory*: May I ask you one question which is relevant to what you have just been saying? Could you possibly give us your view of the argument which has been put to us, that the stiffening of money rates here, whatever effect it may have on British industry, worsens the conditions of the external world from the standpoint of British exports by inducing depression all over the world? — I do not believe that slight differences in the rates charged have a fundamental effect; and certainly I do not believe that this country is a sufficiently large part of the world's economic area or that its operations have a sufficiently direct influence upon the world at large, to warrant that assumption. Moreover, I would point out that certainly a part of the explanation of the present world slump is to be found in the over-development of certain countries and the over-development of the production of certain goods. If rates had been lower in the last two or three years, and a somewhat larger amount of foreign lending had occurred, with a somewhat larger outflow of gold, is it to be presumed that the quantity of wheat, cotton and coffee produced would have been appreciably less? You may, of course, hold that there would have been a somewhat greater consumption of wheat and cotton, and various other commodities; but I am disposed to say that you are living in a period in which certain commodities are obviously being over-produced, and that more liberal supplies of capital would probably have enlarged the production of the things that are now in over-supply, rather than the variety of miscellaneous products the production of which must be increased, as it seems to me, in order to absorb the vastly greater productive power of the world, arising out of modern technical improvements.

9248. The argument that modifications in the constitution of the Bank of England are no remedy for the fundamental difficulties which the country is suffering from is no argument that those modifications may not be useful on other grounds? — For the future. If they are not put as a means of extricating the country from its present position, I am willing to go a long way with you, just as I was with regard to the B.I.S., whose functions can be developed far more widely and usefully when we get back to a situation approaching equilibrium than in the present state of dis-equilibrium. So I hold, as regards the world in the future, when it gets back to equilibrium, that the Central Banks can do vastly more than they have ever done in the past by the exercise of restraint in periods of boom to lessen the unsound developments that culminate in crises and periods of depression. There is no evidence, so far as I know, in past experience that the operations of Central Banks, or of other banks, have done much to extricate the world from a depression. All you can say from past experience is that the banks reached a position in which they were able to make additional loans long before the world extricated itself from the depression, and that consequently the banks were not an obstacle to recovery; but I do not think it can be shown that in fact, by anything they did in the past, they brought about such a recovery.

9249. *Mr. Keynes*: That is the usual accusation against them anyhow? — Yes.

9250. *Mr. Brand*: To return to this country: do I take it that your view is that the fundamental difficulty is that we are out of equilibrium so far as our costs are concerned? — Yes.

9251. *Mr. Lubbock*: Do you consider that the export of £40,000,000 or £50,000,000 of gold, to which you referred just now, at any period during the last few years, would have raised prices in other countries to such an extent as to have helped us? — No, I think it would have had practically no effect, because I think it would all have gone to France and the United States, and I do not think it would have made any appreciable difference in the monetary policies of those countries. It certainly would not in the case of the United States.

9252. *Mr. Keynes*: Nothing has any effect really, you seem to think? — Nothing of that sort. The Federal Reserve Authorities were prepared to neutralise many hundreds of millions of gold, if sent to them. The many modes available for doing so were indicated to people here five or six years ago by Governor Strong. You could not force the expansion of credit by any conceivable amount of importation of gold into the United States. It is perfectly feasible to sterilise as much as £200,000,000 or £300,000,000 in gold.

9253. *Mr. Bevin*: Then the function that the gold standard was intended to perform in the nineteenth century is now played out? — It is played out in a sense, until the world gets back to equilibrium.

9254. What guarantee is there that it will ever play its part then? — That is again a point that I hope to deal with.

9255. It is rather a useless instrument now for the purpose of regulating or forcing the equilibrium? — I think it is. In the case of extreme departure from equilibrium I do not think that through monetary means alone you can either force an equilibrium by pressure or bring about equilibrium by monetary inflation.

9256. Is there any reason why we should remain tied to it? — May I come to that a little later? If you will not forget that question, I shall be greatly obliged. Now I should like to say a word or two about the return to the gold standard and the question whether it would have been advisable to return at a lower valuation of the £ sterling. I think it was reasonable to presume that the country would show a little more capacity for adjustment than in fact it has exhibited. Its capacity for adjustment in the past was always remarkable. Although I do recollect that Mr. Keynes was not confident of its ability to adjust, I still think that it was not an unreasonable view to take that the country could adjust itself.

9257. *Mr. Keynes*: Will you develop what you mean by the word 'adjust'? — I mean some reduction in costs through improvements in organisation, and possibly through a reduction in some directions in salaries and wages; not all salaries and not all wages: by a development of new industries, and so on.

9258. On the question of efficiency, we have had evidence from Professor Bowley that the increase of output per head during the years since the return to the gold standard has been greater than at any other period. There has been no particular disappointment on that head? — No; except that there has been at least as great an increase in other countries; and it is this very increase in output, due to acceleration in production, that I think is one of the disturbing factors of the present situation.

9259. If industry had been more efficient, it would have been worse still? — That is so only if gains in efficiency are not accompanied by changes in the proportion of labour and capital employed in different occupations.

9260. *Mr. Bevin*: Was it reasonable to assume that, with modern inventions all over the world known to be practically equal with Great Britain, whatever we had done we could be expected to maintain equilibrium necessary, by increases in efficiency sufficient to beat the world by another 10 per cent., because that is really what we were asked to do? — That is what my friends in Finland have done during the last year. They have now put themselves into such a state they tell me that they can compete with Soviet timber, and I take off my hat to them.

9261. They carry out in some countries the

policy of shooting people who do not agree with them. We do not do that in England. We have to deal with reasonable people here. (*Mr. Newbold*): And you are taking a very short view of Finland, I think? — There was no shooting in Finland on account of that lowering of costs. But I agree this is socially the most civilised country in the world, more so than my own country. I am willing to take that as a factor in the position, but there are other considerations involved in this return to the £ sterling. Clearly, if you had not returned to the £ sterling at $4.86, but let us say 10 per cent. under, at $4.40, that would have meant a reduction in real wages and salaries in this country. The price of bread and many other things would have gone up, because the prices of imports always do reflect at once the gyrations of the foreign exchanges if they are at all considerable. Now the case for a return to the gold standard at $4.40 rather than $4.86, so far as I see it, is that various people who are interested in social betterment, including labour leaders, are prepared to have a reduction in real wages if it is disguised. They object to a reduction in money wages, but they seem to consider that a reduction in real wages, if it is accomplished without any reduction in money wages, is all right.

9262. *Mr. Keynes*: But you are an economist and you cannot hope to get away with a statement like that. (*Mr. Newbold*): Economists would not say that. (*Mr. Keynes*): Surely the whole difference is that in the one case the burden, in so far as there is a burden, is spread over incomes of every kind, including debts; in the other case there is no machinery in existence for causing an equal change in wages everywhere and in every direction simultaneously so as to make a reduction in the cost of living? — That is largely my objection to this exchange device, that it is an equal reduction, and I do not believe that all wages in 1925 should have been scaled down by an equal percentage, and I do not believe it now. I do not consider that wages in shipbuilding and in Lancashire should come down.

9263. *Mr. Keynes*: It is precisely on those industries that you are putting the pressure if you do that. If, by means of raising the exchange, you raise the value of money it is on the export industries, which are inclined to be lowly paid, such as coal and so on, that you are putting the pressure? — My remedy is for a recognition of the position in all sections of the community and a readiness to make sacrifices not by classes altogether, but in those directions which would seem to me calculated to improve the competitive position of the country. I must say that I do not believe in a wholesale scaling down by a direct ten per cent. cut at the present rate of exchange, and I do not believe in an indirect ten per cent. by establishing an exchange at $4.40. Neither of those broad general methods of meeting the situation seems to me to be at all satisfactory.

9264. *Mr. Bevin*: We had the first deflation in 1921. Then the wicked Trade Unionists and the incompetent Employers' Associations in this country set to work to find out what was likely to be the stable position. I think it can be argued, by the very argument you have been advancing about one class of workers against another, that by the end of 1923 we had arrived almost at an equilibrium in wage levels between what are sometimes described as the home trades and the export trades? — Yes.

9265. Then came along the restoration of the gold standard which fell directly on the export trades and had to be met immediately. The gold standard was restored in April, 1925, I think, and the wholesale demand on miners' wages was in May of that year. It ended up with a subsidy and finally with the upheaval of 1926. You suggest that it was much more preferable to have gone on to the gold standard, and to allow that great upheaval to take place, than it was to remain at the equilibrium which we had already reached as a result of trying to adjust ourselves after the first period of deflation? — No, there are some other elements in that equilibrium or in the lack of it. If you had resumed at $4.40 it is by no means certain that the Belgians would have resumed at the rate at which they did resume, nor the French. It is at least quite possible that the French in that case might have resumed at 136 francs to the £ instead of 124.

9266. *Mr. Keynes*: Might it not have been well to wait until they had fixed theirs? — I think this country has always in these matters taken the lead. The situation was not ripe for an international arrangement. Either things had to be allowed to drift indefinitely or some country had to take the lead. But you are not justified, it seems to me, in assuming that everything that has fallen out during the three years following 1925 would have taken place in exactly the same way and at the same time, if there had been a return to the gold standard at a different period and at a different rate.

9267. *Mr. Bevin*: We would have been able to compete with the United States better, would we not? — I do not think that it matters very much whether one holds that it was unwise or not – it was done. It is nearly six years ago now and the practical question really is what are the appropriate measures for the country to take so that it may, sooner or later, be in a position of effective competition with the rest of the world with generally full employment for all. I think that the most serious difficulty in reaching equilibrium and in maintaining equilibrium in the years ahead is, as I intimated a little while ago, due to the very rapid increase of efficiency in production. The field in which that is most marked at the present time, I should say, is agriculture, which seems to be rapidly becoming more analogous to manufacturing than ever has been the case in the past. With the free use of agricultural implements, fertilisers and appropriate seed, it is becoming possible to produce enormously greater quantities of most agricultural products on a given acreage and with a given amount of labour. But for most of these agricultural products there does not seem to be any elastic demand in the sense that there would be an enormously greater consumption if prices were lower. That means in my judgment, that over the years an increasing proportion of the labour of the world must find employment in other occupations – in providing other goods and services. It is obviously a very difficult thing to get people out of agriculture when once they are in it, especially in the newer countries, because the home is attached to the business unit. Most of these agriculturalists though they are independent farmers, quite definitely belong to the wage-earning class.

Again, as regards any two periods of business activity, there is a larger production of goods in the latter period of activity than in the first period, so when the world gets back to another period of activity there will unquestionably be a very much greater output of goods and services than in the last period of activity – a more considerable increase I believe than between any two periods of activity in the past. That, to my mind, forces the necessity for enterprise and foresight in determining the directions in which the productive forces of the world shall be utilised. In general, I should say, it means an increase in the output of the more highly finished goods and new products. It is reasonable to presume that in the next period of activity, the wage-earner in general will have more consuming power and be able to buy more things than in any period of activity in the past, but it is not to be presumed that he will simply be buying larger quantities of all the things which he bought in the previous period of activity. In general, the wage-earning class in Western countries was well provided in the last period of activity with the simpler forms of goods, food and clothing. He will want better food and better clothing and other things. It is the chief function of business men, of the entrepreneur, to sense the direction of demand for all sorts of things for which there is an elastic demand if the goods can be brought upon the market at lower prices, which is reasonably certain with large production under improved modern methods. But all that seems to me to assume an elasticity of mind on the part of your business men and a readiness to develop organisation, not merely in the field of production, but in the merchandising department, and also a readiness on the part of labour to remove obstacles to the entrance of additional persons into other fields of activity. That is perhaps getting somewhat far away from the question at issue but it impresses me that this is the fundamental objective of any measures whatever designed to extricate the world from its present unhappy state. If I may illustrate it by a case in the United States: When the collapse came in 1929 there was a widespread theory in the United States that it was possible to get back to business activity by forgetting that there had been any collapse, and acting as if things were speedily to go on as usual, and it was generally believed over there that the depression would not be lasting. All sorts of corporations and municipalities continued plans to put into execution schemes for the expansion of capital development and so on as if nothing had happened. The main result of that, as it seems to me, was positively to defer the necessary re-adjustments, for it made for the time being an increased demand in the construction field, both for materials and labour. But it was precisely in the construction field that prices were high and also the cost of labour. I am unable to see that there is any headway made towards re-adjustment when prices of wheat and cotton are cut by 50 per cent. if, at the same time, you maintain the wages of bricklayers, which were among the highest of all wages in the United States at, let us say 15 dollars a day, or if you maintain the price of steel products say with a slight concession of ten per cent. You do not, it seems to me, secure re-adjustments in that way. If one could be warranted in supposing that all the different things that were produced in the last period of activity would be wanted in greater quantities but in the same proportions in the next period of business activity you could do that. But that clearly is not the case. Every period of depression has witnessed a certain amount of pressure which has eliminated from the field numbers of badly organised business concerns, and has scaled down the obligations of a good many concerns that were top heavy, and it has involved some shifting of labour out of certain occupations into other occupations. If the furnishing of credit whether by banks or by Governments contributes to these rather obscure ends, to this rather uncertain outcome, it is helpful, but I am disposed to think that most of the efforts are directed towards trying to get back to the old *status quo*. You attempt to support the price of wheat, cotton or coffee so as to lessen the hardships of those who have produced those commodities, and this would be all to the good if it simply gave a little time for people to get out of those occupations or if, with the mere passage of time, there would be an increased demand. But, unhappily, in most of these instances, these measures simply seem to serve to continue or even enlarge the output of commodities that are already in excess supply. Most of the new developments that will absorb the increased capacity for production are, I am inclined to think, developed by new men and by small men, not by the largest business undertakings that are in operation, although there are exceptions, such as, perhaps the electrical industry. But let me take one instance. The automobile business was not started on a large scale. It was started initially by people with very small amounts of capital and their enterprises were enlarged by putting their profits back into the undertakings.

In this country I should say that clearly one of the obstacles to the development of these miscellaneous industries, upon which I believe the future of the country must depend, is a system of taxation which bears heavily upon the profits of the individual concern until it gets to be large enough to be a public company. It does not very much matter what amount of taxation you put upon people who are over fifty years old. They will probably go on doing the same thing that they always have been doing. But it makes an enormous amount of difference if there is a heavy burden of taxation upon the more enterprising people who are developing undertakings from scratch and who are perhaps thirty-five or forty years old. If you could adjust the scheme of taxation in any way in this country so as to relieve profits and, as an offset, possibly increase the tax upon fixed incomes, something might be said for that on general economic grounds.

... ...

Memorandum on the fiduciary issue handed in by Sir R. V. N. Hopkins, K.C.B.

... ...

6. The absence of any power to increase the fiduciary issue proved on occasion to be inconvenient. In a severe emergency – and such emergencies arose in 1847, 1857, 1866 and 1914 – it was necessary for the Prime Minister and the Chancellor of the Exchequer to communicate with the Bank promising to lay proposals before Parliament for authorising an excess issue *ex post facto* should the Bank find it necessary to adopt that course. The first objection to this procedure is that it is an extra-statutory procedure which might have the effect of shaking confidence rather than restoring it. As a fact in past emergencies the knowledge that the Bank had been authorised to issue excess notes was usually sufficient to restore confidence and only in 1857 was it necessary to issue an excess. But it is clearly better to have a regular machinery. Another objection to this customary arrangement was that in the earlier stages of a crisis the market was left in uncertainty as to whether and when the Treasury letter to the Bank would appear. Another objection was the tradition which has gradually become established of requiring the Bank to raise the rate to 10 per cent. before the issue of the Treasury letter.

7. *From 1914 to 1928.* – No formal change was made during the War as regards the fiduciary issue of Bank of England Notes except that the Currency and Bank Notes Act which became law on the 6th August, 1914, besides granting indemnity for any issue beyond the amount fixed by law which might have occurred since the 1st August, authorised the issue of Bank Notes in excess of any limits fixed by law, so far as temporarily authorised by the Treasury and subject to any conditions attached to that authority.

8. During the War and for ten years thereafter Currency Notes for £1 and 10s. were issued by the Treasury. It is unnecessary to consider the earlier history of that issue and it will be sufficient to indicate the position in its last years. The notes were issued and withdrawn solely through the Bank of England, payments being received or made at the Bank. The actual demand for notes by the public was subject to seasonal variation, reaching a maximum for the year at one of the holiday seasons, usually Christmas. There were no legal restrictions on the size of the issue or on the cover held against it. In fact, however, it was covered in part by Bank of England notes (£56¼ million in 1928) and as to the balance by Government securities and a limited amount of silver coin (£5¼ million in November, 1928). Although the fiduciary issue (i.e., that part of the issue in excess of gold, and/or Bank of England Notes, the equivalent of gold, held as cover) was in theory unlimited, the maximum fiduciary issue had from 1920 onwards been limited by the Treasury rule following the recommendation of the Cunliffe Committee that the issue in any year should not exceed the maximum issue actually reached in the preceding year. The maximum permissible fiduciary issue in 1928 was £244,935,128. The actual fiduciary issue in the last return published was £229,254,130. This return related to the 21st November, 1928; the issue was at that season of the year at a figure considerably less than the maximum.

9. *Position in 1928.* – The Cunliffe Committee had recommended the amalgamation of the Currency and Bank of England issues into a single Bank of England issue. This recommendation became the accepted policy of the Government and was approved by the Committee on the Currency and Bank of England Note Issues, 1925 (Lord Bradbury, Mr. Gaspard Farrer, Sir O. E. Niemeyer, Professor A. C. Pigou). Both the Committees mentioned had expressed a strong preference for the principle of a fixed fiduciary issue. The second Committee had in their report anticipated that the experience necessary to enable the fiduciary issue to be definitely fixed would be obtained by the end of 1927 and that the amalgamation could be effected in 1928.

10. As already explained the issues to be amalgamated differed in many respects. The Bank of England issue was made against a fixed amount of securities and a fluctuating

gold holding. The whole of the notes permissible at any time were created, those surplus to public demands being held as reserve in the Banking Department. The profits on the first £14,000,000 of the fiduciary issue were for the account of the Bank, though in fact expenses and payments to the Exchequer absorbed a great part of those profits. On the other hand, the Currency Notes were issued in part against a backing in Bank Notes (equivalent to gold) and for the rest against a variable volume of securities. There was in theory no limit to the issue, but in practice there was a slowly shrinking maximum fixed in the manner previously described. No more notes were issued than the public called for and the total issue varied seasonally throughout the year. The issue was made through the Bank of England but for the account of the Treasury. The purpose in view in fixing a maximum fiduciary issue in the case of Currency Notes was to secure that any demand in excess of the limit fixed shall fall upon the reserve of the Bank of England who would be under the necessity of setting aside Bank Notes (equivalent to gold) to cover any such excess. In short the two issues, while exhibiting points of difference, thenceforth resembled each other fundamentally in that neither issue could be expanded beyond a fixed limit unless backed by gold. The two issues were thus made alike in being subject to the Bank's control through its credit policy.

11. *The 1928 Act.* – The Act of 1928 provided for the amalgamation of the currency and bank note issues but otherwise continued existing arrangements with the minimum of change. The new combined fiduciary issue was fixed at £260 millions. At that time certain changes were being made in the Irish Free State currency system, the effect of which was to reduce the fiduciary issue required in this country by up to £6 millions. The figure of £260 millions was simply the currency note maximum fiduciary issue of about £245 millions plus the Bank of England fiduciary issue of £19¾ millions less the Irish adjustments, the resultant figure being rounded up slightly to £260 millions.

12. The new fiduciary issue of £260 millions was therefore very slightly larger than the amount actually reached by the old issues during those particular seasons in the immediately preceding years when the active circulation was at its height. It was substantially higher than the amount reached by the old issues at other dates in those years as the fiduciary issue of Currency Notes varied with the demand. The new fiduciary issue being fixed, the additional notes available under the new system at seasons of low circulation constituted an addition at those seasons to the reserve of the Banking Department of the Bank of England.

13. The Act whilst maintaining the system of a fixed fiduciary issue, so long an established principle of this country, gave power to the Lords Commissioners of the Treasury (i.e., in practice to the Chancellor of the Exchequer), on the application of the Bank of England to assent to an increase or reduction of the amount of the fiduciary issue. Reductions could be authorised without specific conditions. As regards increases it was provided (in view of probable reactions upon foreign opinion) that any such authority should run for a period not exceeding six months, and that it might be renewed or varied on the representation of the Bank but not so as to remain in force (with or without variation) for more than two years without the sanction of Parliament. Authorities for increase of the fiduciary issue were ordered to be laid before Parliament. During the debates on the Bill a statement was made on behalf of the Government with the concurrence of the Bank illustrative of the circumstances in which the authority would be exercised. The relative law and the terms of this statement are included in the Appendix to this Note.

... ...

33. The Act of 1928 was deliberately framed so as to alter the existing system only to the extent that experience had shown to be necessary. This course was taken not merely as a matter of convenience but in the belief that it was the best course. So long as gold is the recognised standard of international values, a certain gold reserve has to be maintained to liquidate international balances. The movements up or down of this reserve should have a direct relation to the note issue so that importations of gold should expand credit and losses of gold restrict credit. The amount of the reserve has to be sufficiently substantial to satisfy public opinion, both at home and abroad, as to the stability of the currency, but there is no *a priori* standard by which the precise figure can be scientifically determined. The proportional reserve system favoured by other countries has not yet been effectively tested and it was of more than doubtful expediency for adoption in this country which had to aim at restoring a free gold market on comparatively small gold reserves. It was decided, therefore, to maintain a fixed fiduciary issue backed by Government securities and over and above that, a variable issue backed pound for pound by gold. The amount of the fiduciary issue was based on the circulation which had been actually required in 1928 and which represented the equilibrium then reached. A procedure, however, was provided by which the amount of the fiduciary issue could be modified, either to take account of normal developments which could not be foreseen in 1928 or to deal with any exceptional emergencies that might arise, without resort to the extra-statutory procedure of suspending the Bank Act. It was thought that, upon the whole and given the traditions of this country, the most advantage lay in a fixed fiduciary

issue capable of alteration from time to time as circumstances might demand by an act which on the one hand was formal and on the other was swift and free from complicated procedure. This plan was felt to combine the advantages of continuity with a simple but elastic procedure under which the Bank and the State could co-operate in that sphere which concerned them both.

34. The chief criticism that can be made about the resultant position is that there may be occasions when the system would make the monetary situation appear to the market or to the world more stringent than it really is. If there be an abnormal drain of gold at a season when the internal note circulation is high, the reserve of notes in the banking department of the Bank of England may fall to a low figure notwithstanding that the Bank may feel the intrinsic position to be such as to call for no restrictive policy. The Act, however, contains the remedy for this position, viz., an increase or a series of increases of the fiduciary issue as the reserve falls. If it be thought that the present law unduly conceals this position until the increase is actually made, it may be replied that on any appropriate occasion the joint intention of the Bank and the Government can, if it be desirable, be made known in advance, and further, that the system is at present in its infancy and occasion has not so far arisen to advertise the elasticity of the existing system by an actual alteration of the fiduciary figure.

35. Broadly, it is suggested that to go back now to the pre-1844 arrangements (coupled, it may be, with a law as to the maintenance of some minimum gold reserve) or to change over to other principles such as govern the note issues of other central banks in the world, would involve a great dislocation of settled habits and could hardly be justified except by the most certain prospects of an improved result. It is suggested that no practicable alternative presents such probability of advantage as to justify or even to suggest a change of system.

... ...

36. A further criticism of the system established by the Act of 1928 has to be met, namely that it mixes up the size of the fiduciary issue with the entirely disconnected matter of the distribution of profits between the Bank of England and the Treasury. This is, of course, a separate question. It would be practicable, if it were considered desirable, while maintaining the existing reserve law to substitute a different profit arrangement.

37. Prior to the War the Bank made some profit out of the old fiduciary issue of £19¾ millions. Under the old Acts the Bank, as stated above, paid £120,000 a year to the Exchequer (in addition to £60,000 a year to the Inland Revenue for stamp duties) in respect of profits of the £14,000,000 issue, and in addition paid to the Exchequer the net profits arising from the expansion of the fiduciary issue from its original figure of £14,000,000 to £19¾ millions. Any net profits of the Issue Department after charging these sums remained to the Bank. At the time of the 1928 Act the Bank surrendered this profit and it was prescribed that the Exchequer should receive the whole net profit on the fiduciary issue of £260,000,000.

38. It was during the passage of the late 1928 Bill that reference was first made to a connection between the size of the fiduciary issue and the profits of the Bank. An amendment to the Bill had been proposed in Parliament with the object of increasing the initial fiduciary issue. It was pointed out *inter alia* in the Government reply that this course would be incompatible with the proposed profit arrangement. It is obvious that if the issue had been fixed at some arbitrary increased figure, say £300,000,000, instead of being determined as it was by the actual facts at that time, the Bank of England would, short of some altered arrangement as to profits, have been placed in the dilemma that either they must allow their gold holdings to fall (by £40,000,000 in the instance taken) or they must have faced an annual loss equal to the interest on that sum.

... ...

42. In these circumstances it seems the conclusion can be stated as follows. When the need for an actual increase in the fiduciary issue arises it will ordinarily occur at a time when the securities in the Banking department and the Bank's current earnings are high. The increase will not represent a sacrifice of normal profits of the Bank but will rather correct an abnormal increase of profits. The effect of the extension of the fiduciary issue in anticipation of gold demands would be to diminish securities in the Banking Department and increase the Reserve. The position would not be injurious to the Bank unless the securities in the Banking Department were reduced below normal. But even if a case be assumed where the public interest required the Bank to obtain an extension of the fiduciary issue in anticipation of gold demands at a time when its securities were depleted, the swollen reserve that would result would not presumably last for long. To suppose that it would is to suppose that the increase of the fiduciary issue had not been required and, if so, it would be discontinued.

43. In any case a gain or loss accruing to the Bank from this cause would be very small in comparison with the gain or loss arising from changes in Bank Rate. If the Bank does not hesitate to sacrifice earnings by reducing Bank Rate why is it supposed that it would hesitate to ask for an increase in the fiduciary issue? It appears to the Treasury excessively improbable that the Bank would be deflected from choos-

ing the course most advantageous to the public by any such consideration.

44. These considerations suggest the view that no alteration of the existing law in regard to the profits of issue is necessary. If at any time this view were for some special reason falsified, it would still be open to the Chancellor of the Exchequer of the day to arrange with the Bank of England some altered principle appropriate to the circumstances and to act upon it forthwith, making an announcement to the House of Commons at the time and introducing any necessary legislation to validate the arrangement at the first convenient opportunity thereafter.

July, 1930.

APPENDIX 22

TERMS OF THE 1931 CREDITS

CREDIT FROM THE U.S.A.

Treasury Minute dated 28 August 1931

The Chancellor of the Exchequer states to the Board that he has had under his consideration proposals for the issue in the United States of America of Bills of the British Government expressed in Dollars.

The arrangements contemplated are as follows:

Messrs. J. P. Morgan and Company, New York, will undertake to purchase Treasury Bills in amounts of $10,000,000 nominal or multiples thereof, at such times as they may be called upon to do so by the Treasury, up to an aggregate amount of $200,000,000 (Two hundred million dollars) at any time outstanding.

The currency of the Bills will be 30 days, 60 days or 90 days as may be determined by the Treasury and the Treasury will be entitled upon repayment of any of the Bills to call upon Messrs. J. P. Morgan and Company to purchase further dollar bills up to an equivalent nominal amount so however that no Bill shall mature later than one year from the date of the commencement of these arrangements.

All Bills issued under these arrangements will be payable at the office of Messrs. J. P. Morgan in the City of New York in gold coin of the United States of America of the present standard of weight and fineness without deduction for any British taxes.

Bills will be issued at a rate of discount one per cent above the official Discount Rate of the Federal Reserve Bank of New York for 90 days commercial paper at the date of discount such rate of discount being not less than four and one half per cent per annum nor more than six per cent per annum unless such Discount Rate of the said Federal Reserve Bank exceeds six per cent per annum in which event the rate at which Bills shall be discounted shall be the same as such Discount Rate of the said Federal Reserve Bank.

In respect of the obligation of Messrs. J. P. Morgan and Co. to purchase Treasury Bills as aforesaid a commission of one per cent on the total sum of $200,000,000 will be payable and in addition a managing commission of one quarter per cent on the same sum, such commissions being payable forthwith. It is agreed, however, that the amount of Bills which may be outstanding under the above arrangements at any one time is not to exceed substantially the equivalent of the amount ultimately taken firm of a loan proposed to be raised in France. The Treasury will within one month notify Messrs. J. P. Morgan and Co. of the amount so taken in France and if it should be less than 5,000,000,000 francs the amount of Messrs. J. P. Morgan's undertaking to purchase Bills under these arrangements shall be proportionately reduced and surrendered by the Treasury. In that event the managing commission applicable to the surrendered amount and half of the one per cent commission so applicable shall be returned to the Treasury.

The proceeds of the issue of Dollar Treasury Bills will be paid to an account to be opened for the purpose with Messrs. J. P. Morgan and Co. in New York and will be placed at the disposal of the Bank of England upon payment by the Bank to the Exchequer of the sterling equivalent at the rate agreed and the sterling proceeds will be applied forthwith to the repayment of sterling Treasury Bills or Ways and Means Advances.

The Chancellor of the Exchequer recommends to the Board that arrangements be concluded for the issue of Dollar Treasury Bills accordingly under the powers conferred upon Their Lordships by the War Loan Act, 1919.

My Lords concur.

Let a Warrant authorising the preparation and issue of Treasury Bills to an amount not exceeding $200,000,000 be prepared and forwarded to the Comptroller and Auditor General for countersignature.

Let a copy of this Minute be forwarded to the Comptroller and Auditor General.

Certified to be a true copy.
(Sd.) R. V. Nind Hopkins.

CREDIT FROM FRANCE

Treasury Minute dated 31 August 1931

The Chancellor of the Exchequer states to the Board that he has had under his consideration proposals for the issue in France of Bills of the Government of the United Kingdom expressed in Francs.

The arrangements contemplated are as follows:

Up to an aggregate nominal amount of 2,500,000,000 francs Bills will be issued in France payable to H.B.M. Consul General in Paris or order and endorsed by him or on his behalf in blank. The Bills will be dated the 10th September 1931 and will be payable on the 10th September 1932 at the Bank of France, Paris, the funds necessary for the purpose to be available at that Bank on the 7th September 1932. Bills will be in denominations of 2,000, 10,000, and 50,000 francs and will be issued at a price of 95¾ per cent during such period as may be agreed by the Treasury.

Commission will be payable to the issuing agencies at the rate of one and a quarter per cent on the nominal value of the bills sold. The expenses of issue (including stamp duty and coupon tax if payable) will be borne by the Treasury.

The proceeds of the issue (less commission) will be paid by the issuing agencies to an account of the Bank of England at the Bank of France, Paris, ten days after the agreed date of notification of sales, but the Treasury will be entitled to ask for prepayment of the whole or any part of the Bills so notified as sold subject to discount at the rate of 3% per annum, free of any taxes arising under this arrangement except the Turnover tax.

The Chancellor states further that arrangements are contemplated for the grant of a loan to His Majesty's Government by banks and financial institutions in France up to a total amount of 2,500,000,000 francs, such loan being in the form of a power to His Majesty's Government to draw, at one day's notice to be given to the Bank of France, by way of overdraft upon the accounts opened by the participant institutions up to the said amount during a period of one year as from the 10th September 1931.

The operations will be centralised by the Bank of France which will arrange for the distribution among the participant institutions of all amounts debited or credited to the accounts. Upon any sums so drawn interest will be payable to the participant institutions at the rate of four and a quarter per cent per annum net. Accounts will be drawn up quarterly.

The repayment of any sums so drawn will be secured by the deposit by way of collateral of British Treasury Bills payable on the 10th September, 1932 identical in form and terms with those to be issued in France under the arrangements already recited but in denominations to be agreed upon hereafter. Collateral Bills will be deposited in London as may be necessary for the account of the participant banks and institutions in the name of the Caisse des Dépôts et Consignations in a bank or banks to be specified by that institution, all expenses or taxes (if payable) resulting from the deposit being payable by the Treasury. The nominal amount of the Bills so deposited at any time shall be an amount the discounted value of which at the rate of 4¼% per annum would be sufficient to cover as nearly as may be the amounts drawn and outstanding.

In respect of the obligation of the participant institutions to provide these facilities an engagement commission of one per cent and an over-riding commission of one quarter per cent on the total amount of the maximum overdraft (namely 2,500,000,000 francs) will be payable forthwith on the acceptance by the Treasury of the terms proposed by the banks and financial institutions.

The proceeds of the issue of Franc Treasury Bills and any sums drawn under the loan arrangements will be placed at the disposal of the Bank of England upon payment by the Bank of the sterling equivalent at the rate agreed and the sterling proceeds will be applied to the repayment of sterling Treasury Bills or Ways and Means Advances.

The Chancellor of the Exchequer recommends to the Board that arrangements be concluded in accordance with the above proposals under the powers conferred upon Their Lordships by the War Loan Act 1919.

My Lords concur.

Let a Warrant authorising the preparation and issue of Treasury Bills to an aggregate amount not exceeding 5,111,000,000 francs (of which 2,611,000,000 francs represents bills to be issued as collateral) be prepared and forwarded to the Comptroller and Auditor General for countersignature.

Let a copy of this Minute be forwarded to the Comptroller and Auditor General.

AGREEMENT BETWEEN FEDERAL RESERVE BANK OF NEW YORK AND THE GOVERNOR AND COMPANY OF THE BANK OF ENGLAND

(a) Subject to the terms of this agreement, Federal Reserve Bank of New York agrees, when and as requested to do so by the Bank of England during the period of 3 months from 1st August 1931 to 31st October 1931 to purchase from the Bank of England prime commercial sterling bills; provided, however, that the amount of the bills so purchased under this agreement and owned by Federal Reserve Bank of New York shall not at any time be in excess of the equivalent of approximately $125 million. Payment will be made by Federal Reserve Bank of New York, for the bills so purchased by it under this agreement, by credits in dollars to the Bank of England on the books of the Federal Reserve Bank of New York.

(b) An opening commission of 1/16 of 1% flat will be payable by the Bank of England to Federal Reserve Bank of New York at the date of signature of this agreement on the total amount of $125 million.

(c) The rate of discount at which bills will be purchased by Federal Reserve Bank of New York under the terms of this agreement shall be 3 3/8%.

(d) The bills purchased by Federal Reserve Bank of New York from the Bank of England will be prime commercial sterling bills eligible for discount at the Bank of England and eligible for discount and purchase by Federal Reserve Banks and will not include any renewal bills. They will be accepted by English banking institutions, will be endorsed or guaranteed by the Bank of England and will bear at least one other satisfactory banking endorsement. They will have maturities of not more than 90 days from date of purchase.

(e) The bills purchased by the Federal Reserve Bank of New York under the terms of this agreement will be segregated and set aside and held by the Bank of England for account of and subject to the order of the Federal Reserve Bank of New York. Lists of the bills so purchased and held will be furnished to Federal Reserve Bank of New York by the Bank of England,

and Federal Reserve Bank of New York reserves the right to reject any bills contained in such lists and to require that the Bank of England replace them with other bills of the kinds described in paragraph (d) hereof.

(f) At or before the maturities the Bank of England will pay or repurchase all bills purchased by Federal Reserve Bank of New York which mature prior to 31st October 1931, or the Bank of England may substitute for such bills other bills of the kinds described in paragraph (d) hereof. On 31st October 1931 the Bank of England will pay or repurchase all bills then outstanding. The repurchase of bills as provided in this paragraph will be at the same rate of discount at which they were purchased by Federal Reserve Bank of New York. Amounts due from the Bank of England as provided in this paragraph shall be paid to Federal Reserve Bank of New York in dollars or, if necessary, by the shipment of gold to Federal Reserve Bank of New York.

(g) Amounts due in dollars under the terms of this agreement shall be calculated on the basis of the dollar equivalent of sterling taken at the par of exchange (i.e., $4.8666 per £1).

(h) The Bank of England hereby certify to the Federal Reserve Bank of New York that they have received from the British Government assurances that it will interpose no obstacles to such exports of gold if necessary under (f) and that it will do whatever may be necessary to facilitate any such exports of gold.

(i) The Bank of England hereby assure the Federal Reserve Bank of New York that they have been granted by the Bank of France a substantially similar credit for the approximate franc equivalent of $125 million to be made available by advances against bills.

(j) If and when the Bank of England desire to use any part of either the above-mentioned credit granted by the Bank of France or the credit granted by Federal Reserve Bank of New York under the terms of this agreement, the Bank of France and Federal Reserve Bank of New York will each have the option to require that the amounts drawn shall be divided in substantially equal proportions between the two credits.

For the Governor and Company of the Bank of England.
(Signed) E. M. Harvey.
Deputy Governor.

1st August 1931.

[Bank of France credit to Bank of England 1 August 1931. The letter is unsigned, but evidence shows that it was despatched, signed by Sir Robert Kindersley.]

CONTRACT BETWEEN THE BANK OF FRANCE AND THE BANK OF ENGLAND

(Translation)

I. The Bank of France undertakes to grant to the Bank of England a credit in francs for an amount of three milliards 100 millions of francs.

II. The credit will be opened for 3 months of 30 days from August 1st, 1931, and will be guaranteed by means of a deposit of Commercial bills.

III. The Bank of France will consider any demand which may be made by the Bank of England with a view to a prolongation of the credit for a period of 3 months of 30 days.

IV. The interest on the amounts used will be paid at the rate of 3 3/8 per cent per annum.

V. An opening commission of 1/16 per cent shall be payable by the Bank of England at the date of signature of the present contract on the amount of the credit.

VI. Any portion of the credit which may be utilized shall be for a period of not less than 30 days.

VII. The Bills which are used as cover for the credit shall be Commercial Bills eligible for discount at the Bank of England and shall not include any renewal bills. The Bills shall be accepted by English Banking Institutions and bear the endorsement of first class Banking Institutions.

The Bills shall have a maturity of at least 30 days and not more than 90 days.

The Bills shall be in pounds sterling and shall be calculated on the basis of a parity of 124.21 francs to the £.

The Bills shall be endorsed in blank upon the request of the Bank of France.

VIII. A margin of 5% on the amounts utilized, calculated on the nominal value of the Bills, shall be provided by the Bank of England with a view to replacing any Bills that should not have been accepted or should have been returned for repayment.

IX. The Bank of England undertakes to withdraw 8 days before maturity all the Bills deposited as guarantee and to deposit new Bills in their place, unless a corresponding amount of the credit is repaid.

X. No drawing against the credit shall be made before one working day after the deposit of the corresponding Bills.

XI. The Bills constituting the guarantee of the credit shall all be placed under the dossier of the Bank of France at the Bank of England in London.

All costs and taxes of any kind borne by the Bank of France shall be repaid by the Bank of England, at the maturity of the credit.

XII. The Bank of England shall be responsible when the credit expires for all sums in francs which shall not yet have been paid, and shall take back for its own account the Bills figuring as guarantee.

Paris, August 1st, 1931.

Monsieur Moret,
Governor of the Banque de France,
Paris.

Sir:—

With reference to the credit which the Bank of France has been good enough to open on behalf of the Bank of England to-day, while such credit represents an arrangement directly and solely between the two Central Banks, it is understood that in view of the superabundance of funds on the Paris market the Bank of France reserves to itself the right at any time during the existence of the credit to distribute any portion of the credit to its Bankers.

It is further understood that the Bank of France reserves to itself the right to request that the credit should be utilized pari passu with the credit of the same amount opened to-day by the Federal Reserve Bank to the Bank of England.

We hereby confirm that we have received from the British authorities an assurance that they will place no obstacle in the way of any measures that would be necessary for the repayment of the credit.

I should like to take this opportunity of expressing on behalf of myself and the Institution which I represent my cordial thanks for the courtesy and consideration which I have received from you in connection with these negotiations.

I am, Sir,
Your obedient Servant

Director of the Bank of England.

APPENDIX 23

TEXT OF PRESS NOTICE ISSUED 20 SEPTEMBER 1931

(Suspension of the Gold Standard)

His Majesty's Government have decided after consultation with the Bank of England that it has become necessary to suspend for the time being the operation of Subsection (2) of Section 1 of the Gold Standard Act of 1925 which requires the Bank to sell gold at a fixed price. A Bill for this purpose will be introduced immediately and it is the intention of His Majesty's Government to ask Parliament to pass it through all its stages on Monday, 21st September. In the meantime the Bank of England have been authorised to proceed accordingly in anticipation of the action of Parliament.

The reasons which have led to this decision are as follows. Since the middle of July funds amounting to more than £200 millions have been withdrawn from the London market. The withdrawals have been met partly from gold and foreign currency held by the Bank of England, partly from the proceeds of a credit of £50 millions which shortly matures secured by the Bank of England from New York and Paris and partly from the proceeds of the French and American credits amounting to £80 millions recently obtained by the Government. During the last few days the withdrawals of foreign balances have accelerated so sharply that His Majesty's Government have felt bound to take the decision mentioned above.

This decision will of course not affect obligations of His Majesty's Government or the Bank of England which are payable in foreign currencies.

The gold holding of the Bank of England amounts to some £130 millions and having regard to the contingencies which may have to be met it is inadvisable to allow this reserve to be further reduced.

There will be no interruption of ordinary banking business. The banks will be open as usual for the convenience of their customers; and there is no reason why sterling transactions should be affected in any way.

It has been arranged that the Stock Exchange shall not be opened on Monday, the day on which Parliament is passing the necessary legislation. This will not however interfere with the business of the current settlement on the Stock Exchanges which will be carried through as usual.

His Majesty's Government have no reason to believe that the present difficulties are due to any substantial extent to the export of capital by British nationals. Undoubtedly the bulk of the withdrawals have been for foreign account. They desire however to repeat emphatically the warning given by the Chancellor of the Exchequer that any British citizen who increases the strain on the exchanges by purchasing foreign securities himself or assisting others to do so is deliberately adding to the country's difficulties. The banks have undertaken to co-operate in restricting purchases by British citizens of foreign exchange, except those required for the actual needs of trade or for meeting existing contracts, and should further measures prove to be advisable, His Majesty's Government will not hesitate to take them.

His Majesty's Government have arrived at their decision with the greatest reluctance. But during the last few days the International financial markets have become demoralised and have been liquidating their sterling assets regardless of their intrinsic worth. In the circumstances there was no alternative but to protect the financial position of this country by the only means at our disposal.

His Majesty's Government are securing a balanced budget and the internal position of the country is sound. This position must be maintained. It is one thing to go off the gold standard with an unbalanced Budget and uncontrolled inflation; it is quite another thing to take this measure, not because of internal financial difficulties, but because of excessive withdrawals of borrowed capital. The ultimate resources of this country are enormous, and there is no doubt that the present exchange difficulties will prove only temporary.

APPENDIX 24

EXTRACT FROM CHANCELLOR'S STATEMENT ON SECOND READING OF FINANCE BILL 1932

EXCHANGE EQUALISATION ACCOUNT

(*House of Commons Hansard*, Vol. 264, 1425–9, 19 April 1932)

Before I deal with the matter of that prospective deficit, I want to describe to the Committee certain proposals which will appear in the Finance Bill. During recent weeks the exchange position of this country has been one of considerable difficulty. There has been a great loss of confidence abroad and that loss of confidence has led to large accumulations of liquid capital which can very easily be moved from one financial centre to another and can, therefore, materially assist the operations of speculators. The effect of the transfer of this liquid capital is to exercise a very disturbing influence upon the exchanges – particularly upon sterling exchange, which is no longer linked to gold.

Since we were so successful in repaying the credits which were raised abroad last year and in balancing the national accounts the tide of liquid capital has been setting very strongly in towards these shores. That is flattering to our vanity, but at the same time it is sometimes a serious embarrassment to our trade, and, moreover, in so far as it does not represent a genuine and permanent improvement in the balance of trade it is apt to give rise to dangerous development. In such circumstances nobody can say with certainty that the ebb may not set in presently. Therefore, I have been driven by the force of events to this conclusion, that, if we are to avoid violent and perilous fluctuations in our currency, especially those which are due to these speculative operations, if we are to enable this country to function effectively as the main international centre of the world, then it is essential for us to hold adequate reserves of gold and foreign exchanges, in order that we may meet any sudden withdrawal of short-dated capital and check and repel these speculative movements.

I will try to describe to the Committee the proposals which I have in mind, and I must ask for their indulgence if part of this matter appears to be somewhat technical in character. I propose to wind up the old Exchange Account and to use the assets as the nucleus of a new account to be called the Exchange Equalisation Account. I propose to ask the Committee to give me powers to borrow up to £150,000,000 for this account. The details of assets in the account will not be published, but they may take various forms, either gold, or sterling securities, or foreign exchange. That will give us a very large and extended power of purchasing exchange. The new powers, combined with the powers already possessed by the Bank, upon which, of course, the main responsibility for the management must continue to rest, will enable us to deal far more effectively than we could otherwise have done either with an unwanted inflow of capital or, if the alternative should again arise, with an outflow of capital from this country.

There are certain other purposes for which this Exchange Equalisation Account can be used conveniently. First of all, there is an accounting question connected with the weekly returns of the Bank of England. Hon. Members know that there are two departments in the Bank – the Issue Department and the Banking Department. The Issue Department is liable for the note issue amounting to some £400,000,000, against which it has assets in gold and securities. The Banking Department, on the other side, is the one in which the purely banking business is carried on. The management of the Issue Department is by law entrusted to the Bank, but its profits can concern only the Exchequer, because the Exchequer is entitled to any interest earned or any profits made in the Issue Department. On the other hand, the profits of the Banking Department are for the account of the Bank. My proposals only affect the Issue Department, and I have given this preliminary description in order to show that they do not confer upon the Bank any new privilege or any new profit. The Bank will continue to bear itself any risks which may be involved in foreign exchange operations carried on in the Banking Department. That arrangement is made at the Bank's own desire, and I am sure it is one which will be approved by the Committee.

With the pound divorced from gold the accounting arrangements of the Issue Department present some difficulty. Its liabilities for the Note Issue are in sterling. Those of its assets which may consist of foreign currencies fluctuate in terms of sterling; but so far as its assets consist of gold – including any gold that may hereafter be acquired – the law requires the gold to be valued at the old par. Thus, the Issue Department cannot, with the exchange at $3.80 add £100 to its gold holding without showing an apparent loss of £28; and, in the same way, it cannot sell £100 of its gold holding without showing an apparent profit of £28, while its holdings of foreign exchange fluctuate in value every week. Our currency authorities ought to be free to hold such amounts of gold and foreign exchange in the Issue Department as may be required without being hampered by technicalities of this kind. On the other hand, we must be very careful to keep full cover against the Note Issue. I consider that in order that at all times and in all conditions the assets of the Issue Department – that is to say, the backing of our currency – should be consistently and conservatively valued, the gold in each return should be valued at the old par, and all the foreign exchange assets should be valued at the current rate of exchange irrespective of their purchase price.

In order that the account may at all times precisely balance on this basis, my proposals provide that at any time when a valuation on this basis shows a deficiency resources to the corresponding amount shall be passed from the Exchange Equalisation Account to the Issue Department of the Bank, and that when a surplus is shown that the converse operation shall take place. I ask the Committee to observe that both of these accounts are worked for the credit of the Exchequer, for the use of the Exchequer, and for the account of the Exchequer. Therefore, it does not very much matter whether any particular asset is for the moment in one account or the other, both are for the account of the Exchequer.

There is another point. In connection with the credits which were raised by the Bank of England last year from the Banque de France and the Federal Reserve Bank the undertaking was given at the time, and Parliament was so informed, that any loss arising from the transaction would be made good to the Bank. The Finance Bill, accordingly, will contain a provision charging £8,000,000, which is the outstanding loss on that transaction, to the Exchange Equalisation Account.

I may be asked: Suppose that these powers are given to the Government, will that be the final end to the fluctuations in the exchange; will it mean that the exchange will be kept at a fixed point, or at any rate that it will be maintained within a fixed range of values? I am not going to give any such assurance. When you consider the economic disturbances which are still occurring in the world, and of which we probably have not even now felt the worst, it is perfectly useless to pretend that we can hold our exchange position exactly as we please independent of anything which is going on around us. On the other hand, we can say this, that those who are charged with the conduct of our currency will be much better equipped in the future with these powers to maintain that currency steady than they have been in the past; and that to that extent we should see a great improvement.

There is another question: Will these transactions involve the Exchequer in any loss or in any considerable loss. I think the answer to that question must be that that is a very conceivable possibility. We do not know what is going to be the future of gold prices. We do not know what settlement will be reached as regards Reparations and War Debts, and other matters, which are now disturbing the world. These uncertainties rule out any possibility of our being able to return to gold immediately. We do not know when or in what circumstances we may return to gold, or at what level. If in the long run we were to return to gold in such a way that the pound stood at a higher gold value than the average level at which purchases of exchange had been made, the transactions would inevitably show a loss. This is a possibility, but it is not one which should deter us. If we are merely seeking safety from an accounting point of view, we can proceed as we did in the earlier period of the suspension of the Gold Standard between the years 1919 and 1925. The pound would be allowed, substantially, to take its own course, liable to fluctuations with every seasonal movement of trade or every outburst of speculation, or change of sentiment caused by developments abroad. The problems of the present time are in many ways altogether different from those which faced us immediately after the War. In my judgment, the risks entailed by the uncontrolled fluctuations of the currency today outweigh the possible loss on the transactions which I have mentioned.

APPENDIX 25

FINANCE ACT 1932

PART IV

(22 & 23 Geo. 5. c. 25)

Exchange Equalisation Account

24. (1) There shall be established an account, to be called "the Exchange Equalisation Account," which shall be under the control of the Treasury and shall be used for the purposes specified in this Part of this Act.

(2) The Treasury may, if at any time they think it expedient so to do, cause the Exchange Equalisation Account (in this Part of this Act referred to as "the Account") to be wound up forthwith, and the Account shall in any event be wound up not later than six months after the date on which the Commons House of Parliament resolve that the Account is no longer required for the purpose for which it was established.

(3) The Treasury may cause any funds in the Account to be invested in securities or in the purchase of gold in such manner as they think best adapted for checking undue fluctuations in the exchange value of sterling.

(4) There shall be issued to the Account out of the Consolidated Fund, or the growing produce thereof, at such times and in such manner as the Treasury may direct such sums, not exceeding in the aggregate one hundred and fifty million pounds, as the Treasury may determine, and all the assets of the Exchange Account shall be transferred to the Account at such time as the Treasury may direct.

(5) For the purpose of providing for the issue of sums out of the Consolidated Fund under the last preceding subsection or for the repayment to that Fund of all or any part of any sums so issued, the Treasury may raise money in any manner in which they are authorised to raise money under and for the purposes of subsection (1) of section one of the War Loan Act, 1919, and any securities created and issued to raise money under this subsection shall for all purposes be deemed to have been created and issued under the said subsection (1).

(6) The Bank of England may advance to the Treasury any sums which the Treasury have under this section power to raise.

(7) The Account shall in every year until it is wound up be examined by the Comptroller and Auditor-General in such manner as he, in his discretion, thinks proper with a view to ascertaining whether the operations on and the transactions in connection with the Account have been in accordance with the provisions of this Part of this Act, and he shall certify to the Commons House of Parliament whether in his opinion, having regard to the result of

the examination, the operations on and the transactions in connection with the Account have or have not been in accordance with the provisions of this Part of this Act.

25. (1) There shall be paid to the Issue Department of the Bank of England out of the Account such sum not exceeding eight million pounds as is in the opinion of the Treasury equal to the amount of the net loss which by reason of variations in rates of exchange has been sustained in connection with the credits obtained by the Bank of England from the Bank of France and the Federal Reserve Bank of New York on the first day of August, nineteen hundred and thirty-one.

(2) For the purpose of any valuation of the assets held in the Issue Department of the Bank of England, being a valuation made before the winding up of the Account –

(a) gold held in the Department shall be taken to be of the value of three pounds seventeen shillings and tenpence halfpenny for every ounce troy of the standard fineness specified in the First Schedule to the Coinage Act, 1870 (hereafter referred to as "the fixed value"); and

(b) assets in currencies other than sterling held in the Department shall be valued at the rate of exchange prevailing at the date of each valuation.

(3) Whenever any gold is purchased or sold on account of the Issue Department during the existence of the Account, the amount by which the price of the gold exceeds the fixed value thereof shall, in the case of a purchase, be made good to the Issue Department from the Account, and, in the case of a sale, be made good to the Account from the Issue Department.

(4) Immediately before the Account is wound up, the amount by which the market value (as agreed between the Bank and the Treasury) of the gold then held in the Issue Department exceeds its fixed value shall be made good by the Department to the Account.

(5) If on any sale of assets in currencies other than sterling held in the Issue Department (whether the sale occurred before the establishment of the Account or occurs at any time during the existence of the Account), or on any valuation during the existence of the Account of any such assets, it appears that by reason of variations in rates of exchange occurring at any time after the twenty-first day of September, nineteen hundred and thirty-one, there has been any depreciation or loss in connection with those assets, the amount of the depreciation or loss shall be made good to the Issue Department from the Account, and if on any such sale or valuation as aforesaid it appears that by reason as aforesaid any appreciation or gain has arisen in connection with any of the said assets, the amount of the appreciation or gain shall be made good from the Issue Department to the Account.

(6) Where under this section any amount is to be made good from or to the Account, there may, in lieu of a payment in cash, be transferred from or

to the Account securities equivalent in value, in the opinion of the Treasury, to that amount.

(7) It is hereby declared that in subsection (3) of the last preceding section of this Act and in section three of the Currency and Bank Notes Act, 1928 (which relates to the securities to be held in the Issue Department), the expression "securities" includes securities and assets in currency of any country and in whatever form held.

26. On the winding-up of the Account the assets thereof shall be applied in such manner as the Treasury may direct for the redemption of debt, and the Treasury shall thereupon cause to be laid before Parliament a statement of the sum so applied, and of the sums issued out of the Consolidated Fund to the Account, together with a report by the Comptroller and Auditor-General with respect to such matters in relation to the Account as he thinks fit.

APPENDIX 26

REPORT OF COMMITTEE ON MONETARY AND FINANCIAL QUESTIONS TO IMPERIAL ECONOMIC CONFERENCE AT OTTAWA, JULY–AUGUST 1932

The Committee submitted to the Conference and recommended that it should adopt the following statement:

I

(a) A rise throughout the world in the general levels of wholesale prices is in the highest degree desirable. The evil of falling prices must be attacked by Government and individual action in all its causes whether political, economic, financial, or monetary.

(b) For dealing with the problem in its widest aspects the Governments represented at this Conference record their conviction that international action is urgently necessary and announce their desire to co-operate with other nations in any practicable measures for raising wholesale prices.

(c) The Conference has considered what action can be taken by the nations of the Commonwealth to help towards raising prices.

As regards monetary factors, the Conference recognizes that the central position of the United Kingdom, not only among the countries of the Commonwealth but in world trade and finance, makes the United Kingdom a main factor in anything that can be done. The Conference therefore welcomes the following statement made on behalf of the United Kingdom by the Chancellor of the Exchequer:

His Majesty's Government desire to see wholesale sterling prices rise. The best condition for this would be a rise in gold prices and the absence of a rise in gold prices inevitably imposes limitations on what can be done for sterling. A rise in prices cannot be effected by monetary action alone, since various other factors which have combined to bring about the present depression must also be modified or removed before a remedy is assured. His Majesty's Government nevertheless recognize that an ample supply of short-term money at low rates may have a valuable influence, and they are confident that the efforts which have successfully brought about the present favourable monetary conditions can and will, unless unforeseen difficulties arise, be continued.

(d) The Conference recommends the other countries of the Commonwealth represented here to act in conformity with the line of policy as set out in the statement of the Chancellor of the Exchequer, so far as lies within their power.

In the monetary sphere the primary line of action towards a rise in prices should be the creation and maintenance, within the limits of sound finance, of such conditions as will assist in the revival of enterprise and trade. Among these conditions are low rates of interest and an abundance of short-term money. While regard must be had to the different conditions applying to various types of loans, the rate of interest for all purposes should be kept as low as financial conditions permit. At the same time it is necessary that these favourable monetary conditions be achieved, not by the inflationary creation of additional means of payment to finance public expenditure, but by an orderly monetary policy, safeguarded if the necessity should arise, by such steps as will restrain and circumscribe the scope of violent speculative movements in commodities or securities.

It must be kept in mind, however, that the success of any such policy will be hampered and might be nullified by the failure to modify or remove important non-monetary obstacles. Of the non-monetary factors which are depressing the level of prices many are of international character and require an international remedy. The nations of the Commonwealth should, nevertheless, take all steps that lie in their power to increase public confidence, especially in the field of business enterprise, and to facilitate trade.

(e) The Conference recognizes the great importance to traders of stability of exchange rates over as wide an area as possible. The complete solution of this problem must await the restoration of conditions for the satisfactory working of an international standard as referred to below. In the meantime, and pending such a solution, this Conference has considered the possibility of achieving valuable results in two directions – first by creating an area of stability among countries regulating their currencies in relation to sterling; and secondly, by avoiding wide day-to-day fluctuations between sterling and gold.

As regards the latter, the Conference has noted with satisfaction that the United Kingdom has already established machinery aimed at preventing wide fluctuations in the gold value of sterling caused by speculative movements. As to the former, the Conference recognizes the value of the countries within the Commonwealth whose currencies are linked to sterling maintaining stability between their exchange rates and looks to a rise in the general level of wholesale prices as the most desirable means for facilitating this result.

II

The Conference recognizes that the ultimate aim of monetary policy should be the restoration of a satisfactory international monetary standard. Such a standard should so function as not merely to maintain stable exchange rates between all countries, but also to ensure the smooth and efficient working of the machinery of international trade and finance.

This postulates international agreement among the great trading nations of the world, and while certain of the States here represented hold very definite views on the question of the most desirable standard the Conference refrains from making any recommendations on the subject in view of the fact that the question is shortly to be discussed at an international conference. There are, however, several conditions precedent to the re-establishment of any international monetary standard. The most important among them are: a rise in the general level of commodity prices in the various countries to a height more in keeping with the level of costs, including the burden of debt and other fixed and semi-fixed charges; and an adjustment of the factors political, economic, financial and monetary, which have caused the breakdown of the gold standard in many countries, and which, if not adjusted, would inevitably lead to another breakdown of whatever international standard may be adopted.

It is also in the view of the Conference of the utmost importance to the future working of any international standard that international co-operation should be secured and maintained with a view to avoiding, so far as may be found practicable, wide fluctuations in the purchasing power of the standard of value.

CONFERENCE CONCLUSIONS

The Conference approved the above Report and adopted the statement contained therein and commended them to the several Governments for their consideration.

APPENDIX 27

NEGOTIATIONS FOR TENTATIVE DOLLAR-STERLING-FRANC STABILISATION, APRIL-MAY 1933

This brief episode in monetary history, recounted here on the basis only of papers in the Bank, affords some insight into the attitudes of British, American and French monetary authorities on the eve of the World Economic Conference, 1933; it shows also how inextricably the Bank of England had at this date become enmeshed in economic discussions between governments. Development of international monetary co-operation was interrupted by the unilateral action of the U.S. Administration that summer, but the talks in April and May can be regarded as a foretaste of the negotiations culminating in the Tripartite Declarations three years later. In 1933, as in 1936, whoever was at any moment discussing possibilities with American or French representatives, the Bank of England and the Treasury day by day were working very closely together.

The story begins at or about 25 April 1933. The U.K. Prime Minister was in Washington where discussions, ahead of the forthcoming World Economic Conference, revolved round the War Debts question. On this as on foreign exchange questions Roosevelt at this juncture was being advised by Warburg, a prominent commercial banker. On the War Debts question Warburg had a plan, and it is necessary to avoid confusion between this 'Warburg Plan', under discussion at the end of April, and the foreign exchange 'Warburg Plan' which became a centre of attention in mid-May. This Appendix is primarily concerned with the latter, the exchanges plan, but there was important connection between the two subjects, in that the British were unwilling to enter any complete commitment on exchange stabilisation unless the War Debts question could be settled. Despite insistence on this prior condition, the British had been driven, by Roosevelt's action on the gold status of the dollar, to take the initiative in opening discussion of exchange problems in Washington. There they met little appreciation, as they felt, of exchange problems; particularly they found it important to dispel misunderstandings about the British Exchange Equalisation Account, and to impress on Americans the seriousness of the exchange confusion produced by the President's action.

At this juncture London learned, from Leith-Ross (U.K. Treasury, who was in Washington with the Prime Minister), that the President was avoiding any public commitment on exchange questions but might be persuaded to some co-operation in the management of the exchanges. He (the President) had deputed Warburg to discuss the subject with Leith-Ross. In the ensuing talks Warburg suggested a *de facto* stabilisation, working with Exchange Accounts operated by all three countries, and it was impressed on him that \$3.50 was the highest dollar value of the pound tolerable for Britain. Warburg said that he would discuss these lines with the French, who he thought would warmly welcome action of the kind and indeed might have a plan to suggest (Monick, who was the French representative immediately concerned, has stated that there was not at this stage any French plan, and no evidence has come to light of any basis Warburg had for any expectations). At this stage the U.K. Government, holding strongly that a War Debt settlement was pre-requisite, warned its representatives in Washington that any such term as '*de facto* stabilisation' must be avoided, and that any pre-Conference agreement on the exchanges must be limited to 'an oral gentlemen's agreement'.

A few days later Warburg informed British representatives of the talks he had had with the French, on or about 26–7 April. The French had strongly urged some action to steady the exchanges if the Conference was to have any hope of success. Warburg in reply had informed them of the upshot of his talks with the British. He had put forward no precise plan; it would, he had said, be possible to make Anglo-American arrangements for avoidance of fluctuations in the dollar/sterling rate but that it would be better if the French authorities would join, possibly in the establishment of a joint exchange account or a profit-sharing agreement between three separate exchange accounts. The French reaction to these suggestions had been agreement that avoidance of fluctuations in the exchange rates was imperative, but they (the French in Washington) had not yet had any instructions from Paris as to the machinery for attaining this objective. While, in the next fortnight, the French were believed to be thinking over these questions of machinery (they had as yet no exchange equalisation account) a newspaper canard in Paris put the brake on any development. Difficulties appeared also to be mounting at the American end, partly through incoherent relations between the U.S. Treasury and the Federal Reserve Bank of New York. Unfavourable conditions in the background were that the President seemed fearful of embarrassing by new exchange commitments his various efforts to raise prices in the U.S.A.; and – most importantly from the British point of view – there was ominous lack of progress on the War Debts issue. In the second week of May, the authorities in London learned that the French, contemplating the complexity of any arrangements for joint exchange accounts, had cooled off.

On 15 and 16 May, however, the French suddenly turned to pressing for urgent agreement. They wanted temporary *de facto* stabilisation and expressed willingness to co-operate in some tripartite management. This was put to Warburg in Washington, by Monick. Warburg was ready with a tentative outline plan; Monick, on studying this, said that this was the kind of arrangement his Government had in mind. (Monick has since stated that the French authorities did not have any actual plan of their own.)

Warburg immediately informed a U.K. representative (Bewley) of this *démarche*, and this was reported to London, with this 'Warburg Plan' in all available detail. As formulated by Warburg, this followed closely a plan written by Crane of the New York Federal Reserve Bank, who had been briefing Warburg in these weeks. There were two differences, both of some moment. (1) Whereas Crane had envisaged \$m250 as the contribution of each of the three countries to a joint exchange account, Warburg now said \$m500 each. (2) Whereas Crane had envisaged the period until the final adjournment of the London Conference, Warburg spoke of three months, renewable. Warburg was, in effect, raising his bid.

The British reception of Warburg's plan remained guarded. They looked for clarification of the vague intentions of the other two parties, especially as to the arrangements for joint management and the levels at which the exchange rates should be held. Neither the French nor the Americans were known to have administrative arrangements for exchange accounts that could immediately be geared in with the British, and if the purpose of any agreement was to hold rates pending the outcome of the Conference, immediate initiation would be essential. As the actual operator of the British account, the Bank, with the prospect of becoming the partner in a tripartite management, was acutely conscious of the need for clarification of this aspect. On the rate, the British authorities were fearful that the Americans and French would argue from the current level, which at \$3.91 and 86 francs to the £ was regarded in London as unrealistic. There was a suggestion that Hambro should pay a short visit to Washington, to stress these points, but he did not go.

Instead, the Bank of England on 19 and 20 May had discussions with the Bank of France. In these discussions the Bank also developed its fears that any stabilisation plan, temporary or permanent, would depend on some understanding on internal monetary policies, a consideration that had become more worrisome as uncertainties about the intentions of the Roosevelt Administration developed. These doubts were shared by the Bank of France, and the outcome of the discussions was that the U.K. Treasury informed their representative in Washington that the French and British authorities regarded it as prerequisite that 'the three Governments should make known to each other their several policies', and that 'before technical measures can be undertaken in co-operation there is great need of clear understanding of the policy of the American Government...H.M. Government are quite ignorant of the *steps* in contemplation by the U.S. in connection with credit expansion...and their fear is that if exchange stabilisation is attempted by itself without this knowledge or any agreement between the three countries on the subject, it may be defeated by lack of co-ordination of credit policy'. The British suggested that the American Delegation to the Conference should include or be accompanied by representatives ready to speak for the U.S. Government on this fundamental question. At this stage the British reasons for not agreeing to the Warburg Plan, as it then stood, were set out in an important Treasury memorandum (Phillips, 21 May).

Meanwhile in Washington there was no progress on the War Debt question. Moley appeared to have become the President's adviser on this whole range of problems, and the British were unsure how far it was useful to discuss exchange questions with Moley. They consulted Sprague, who had no plans to offer but informed British representatives, 27 May, that the U.S. Government accepted the French proposal to discuss stabilisation and that Harrison (FRBNY) with a U.S. Treasury official would leave for Europe shortly. On 30 May Sprague reported that *de facto* stabilisation of the dollar could now not be expected at any early date; 'Warburg's scheme is now right out of the picture' and that the most that could be said at present was that the U.S. Government would aim at keeping the dollar as stable as possible until and during the World Conference.

APPENDIX 28

THE TRIPARTITE AGREEMENT OF 25 SEPTEMBER 1936

Statement by the British Treasury, relating to the monetary agreement reached between Great Britain, France and the United States, 25 September 1936.

1. His Majesty's Government, after consultation with the United States Government and the French Government, join with them in affirming a common desire to foster those conditions which will safeguard peace and will best contribute to the restoration of order in international economic relations, and to pursue a policy which will tend to promote prosperity in the world and to improve the standard of living.

2. His Majesty's Government must, of course, in its policy towards international monetary relations, take into full account the requirements of internal prosperity of the countries of the Empire, as corresponding considerations will be taken into account by the Governments of France and of the United States of America. They welcome this opportunity to reaffirm their purpose to continue the policy which they have pursued in the course of recent years, one constant object of which is to maintain the greatest possible equilibrium in the system of international exchanges and to avoid to the utmost extent the creation of any disturbance of that system by British monetary action. His Majesty's Government share with the Governments of France and the United States the conviction that the continuation of this two-fold policy will serve the general purpose which all Governments should pursue.

3. The French Government inform His Majesty's Government that, judging that the desired stability of the principal currencies cannot be ensured on a solid basis except after the re-establishment of a lasting equilibrium between the various economic systems, they have decided with this object to propose to their Parliament the readjustment of their currency. His Majesty's Government have, as also the United States Government, welcomed this decision in the hope that it will establish more solid foundations for the stability of international economic relations. His Majesty's Government, as also the Governments of France and of the United States of America, declare their intention to continue to use the appropriate available resources so as to avoid as far as possible any disturbance of the basis of international exchanges resulting from the proposed readjustment. They will arrange for

such consultation for this purpose as may prove necessary with the other two Governments and the authorised agencies.

4. His Majesty's Government are moreover convinced, as are also the Governments of France and the United States of America, that the success of the policy set forth above is linked with the development of international trade. In particular, they attach the greatest importance to action being taken without delay to relax progressively the present system of quotas and exchange controls with a view to their abolition.

5. His Majesty's Government, in common with the Governments of France and the United States of America, desire and invite the co-operation of the other nations to realise the policy laid down in the present declaration. They trust that no country will attempt to obtain an unreasonable competitive exchange advantage and thereby hamper the effort to restore more stable economic relations which it is the aim of the three Governments to promote.

Statement by the British Treasury relating to the announcement made on 13 October 1936 by the United States Secretary of the Treasury on sales of gold for export.

Arrangements for technical co-operation with the monetary authorities in the United States have now been completed and a new regulation is being published by the Secretary of the Treasury of the United States which will enable gold to be obtained in the United States in exchange for dollars by any country which gives reciprocal facilities to the United States. His Majesty's Government have arranged for such facilities to be afforded in London to the United States authorities. This day-to-day working arrangement should greatly facilitate the technical operations of exchange control; similar arrangements have been made with the Bank of France so as to provide for effective co-operation between the three centres.

APPENDIX 29

CURRENCY AND BANK NOTES ACT 1939

(2 & 3 Geo. 6. c. 7)

An Act to amend the law with respect to the Issue Department of the Bank of England, the Exchange Equalisation Account and the issue and place of payment of Bank of England notes.

[28th February 1939]

Be it enacted by the King's most Excellent Majesty, by and with the advice and consent of the Lords Spiritual and Temporal, and Commons, in this present Parliament assembled, and by the authority of the same, as follows:—

1. The fiduciary note issue shall, unless and until, after the commencement of this Act, it is reduced under subsection (2) of section two of the Currency and Bank Notes Act, 1928, or increased under subsection (1) of section eight of that Act, be three hundred million pounds and accordingly –

(a) in subsection (1) of the said section two and subsection (1) of the said section eight, for the words "two hundred and sixty million pounds" there shall be substituted the words "three hundred million pounds"; and

(b) any Treasury Minute in force at the commencement of this Act under the said section eight shall cease to have effect.

2. – (1) The assets held in the Issue Department of the Bank of England (in this Act referred to as "the Department") shall be valued on the day on which this Act comes into operation and thereafter once in each week.

(2) For the purposes of every such valuation, the assets shall be valued at such prices as may be certified by the Bank of England to be the current prices of those assets respectively on the day of the valuation, ascertained in such manner as may be agreed between the Treasury and the Bank:

Provided that adjustments may, if the Treasury so direct, be made in respect of interest affecting the current price of any securities and, in the case of securities standing at a premium, in respect of that premium.

(3) If, as the result of any such valuation, the value of the assets then held in the Department differs from the total amount of the Bank of England notes then outstanding, there shall be paid to the Department from the Exchange Equalisation Account (in this Act referred to as "the Account") or to the Account from the Department such sum as will counteract that

difference, and separate payments may be made in respect of differences arising from changes in the value of gold and differences arising from changes in the value of other assets.

Any payment required by this subsection may be effected in cash or, by agreement between the Treasury and the Bank of England, by a transfer of gold or securities (whichever is appropriate), or partly in cash and partly by such a transfer.

3.–(1) Gold held in the Department may be sold to the Account and gold may be bought for the Department from the Account, in each case at the price at which gold was valued for the purposes of the last valuation under the last preceding section.

(2) The Treasury shall pay into the Account all sums received by them after the commencement of this Act in respect of the profits of the Department under section six of the Currency and Bank Notes Act, 1928.

4.–(1) Notwithstanding anything in any enactment, bank notes for five pounds and upwards may be issued by the Bank of England otherwise than at their head office without being made payable at the place of issue, and all bank notes for five pounds and upwards issued by the Bank shall, wherever issued, be payable only at the head office of the Bank unless expressly made payable also at some other place.

(2) Section four of the Bank Charter Act, 1844 (which requires the Department to issue notes in return for gold), shall cease to have effect.

5.–(1) This Act may be cited as the Currency and Bank Notes Act, 1939.

(2) This Act shall come into operation on the first Wednesday after the day on which the Royal Assent is given thereto.

(3) The enactments set out in the Schedule to this Act are hereby repealed to the extent mentioned in the third column of that Schedule.

SCHEDULE

Section 5.

ENACTMENTS REPEALED

Session and Chapter	Short Title	Extent of Repeal
7 Geo. 4. c. 46.	The Country Bankers Act, 1826.	The final proviso to section fifteen.
3 & 4 Will. 4. c. 98.	The Bank of England Act, 1833.	Section 4.
7 & 8 Vict. c. 32.	The Bank Charter Act, 1844.	Section 4.
22 & 23 Geo. 5. c. 25.	The Finance Act, 1932.	Subsections (2) to (6) of section twenty-five.

APPENDIX 30

DOCUMENTS ON THE REGULATION OF OVERSEAS ISSUES IN LONDON ('CAPITAL ISSUES EMBARGOES')

[This appendix contains various official statements and regulations selected to show the path followed in the restriction of new issues between 1914 and 1939. The selection signposts the path rather than charts it in detail and for the most part excludes discussion and comment. For a discussion of the embargo and its effectiveness as seen by the Governor of the Bank in 1930, the reader should consult Questions 3414–26 in the minutes of the Macmillan Committee (Appendix 21).]

1 EXTRACT FROM THE TEMPORARY REGULATIONS UNDER WHICH THE STOCK EXCHANGE WAS RE-OPENED ON 4 JANUARY 1915

Committee Room, The Stock Exchange, 23 December 1914

4. (3) No dealings will be allowed in any new issue made after 4 January 1915, unless specially allowed by the Committee and approved by the Treasury.

(*Economist*, 2 Jan. 1915

2 NOTICE ISSUED BY THE TREASURY, 18 JANUARY 1915)

In connection with the re-opening of the Stock Exchanges the Treasury have had under consideration the general conditions under which new issues of capital in the United Kingdom can be permitted during the continuance of the War.

It appears to the Treasury that in the present crisis all other considerations must be subordinated to the paramount necessity of husbanding the financial resources of the country with a view to the successful prosecution of the War. Accordingly they wish it to be understood that until further notice they feel it imperative in the national interest that fresh issues of capital shall be approved by the Treasury before they are made.

Treasury approval will be governed by the following general conditions:—

(1) Issues for undertakings carried on or to be carried on in the United Kingdom shall only be allowed where it is shown to the satisfaction of the Treasury that they are advisable in the national interest.

(2) Issues or participations in issues for undertakings carried on or to be carried on in the British Empire Over-Seas shall only be allowed where it is shown to the satisfaction of the Treasury that urgent necessity and special circumstances exist.

(3) Issues or participations in issues for undertakings carried on or to be carried on outside the British Empire shall not be allowed.

(4) The Treasury will not in ordinary cases insist upon the above restrictions where issues are required for the renewal of Treasury Bills or other short instruments held here and falling due of Foreign or Colonial Governments or municipal corporations or railways or other undertakings.

All applications should be made in the first instance to the Treasury.

The Treasury will not be prepared to approve under paragraph 4(3) of the Temporary Regulations for the Re-opening of the Stock Exchange any dealings in new issues which have not been approved by the Treasury before they are made.

3 ANNOUNCEMENT 27 JANUARY 1915

In connexion with the embargo upon capital issues by the Government, notification of which was given in *The Times* of Tuesday, January 19, it is now announced that the Chancellor of the Exchequer has appointed a committee to consider and advise upon applications received by the Treasury for approval of fresh issues.

The members of the committee, which has held its first meeting, are the Right Hon. the Viscount St Aldwyn (chairman), Lord Cunliffe, Governor of the Bank of England, Sir Frederick G. Banbury, Bart, M.P., the Right Hon. Sir Thomas P. Whittaker, M.P., and Mr G. Stapylton Barnes, C.B., of the Board of Trade. The secretary to the committee is Mr Basil P. Blackett, C.B., of the Treasury.

(*Times*, 28 Jan. 1915)

[*Note:* The following changes and additions in the membership of the Committee were subsequently made:

3 June 1915 Captain E. G. Pretyman, M.P., Parliamentary Secretary, Board of Trade, appointed vice Mr G. Stapylton Barnes, retired.

25 April 1916 Lord Cunliffe, appointed Chairman vice Viscount St Aldwyn, resigned, and Mr Gaspard Farrer appointed a member of the committee.

9 January 1917 Sir H. Llewellyn Smith, K.C.B., appointed vice Captain E. G. Pretyman, M.P.

27 March 1918 Mr J. F. Mason, M.P., and Mr C. T. Needham, M.P., appointed additional members.]

4 STATEMENT, 24 MARCH 1919

[The Chancellor said in the House of Commons:]

I have given very careful consideration to the various representations which have been made to me in regard to Defence of the Realm Regulation 30F. providing for the control of capital issues, and I have now, after consultation with Members of this House who have shown a special interest in the question and with my City advisers, come to the conclusion that, in view of the general movement towards the removal of restrictions upon trade and industry, I am no longer justified in attempting to maintain Government control over the distribution of capital for domestic purposes.

An amending Regulation is accordingly being prepared, which will exempt from the requirement of a Treasury licence all issues by companies established in this country where the issuing company certifies upon the prospectus that no part of the proceeds of the issue is to be applied to capital purposes outside the United Kingdom.

As regards issues by British companies for capital purposes abroad, and issues by or on behalf of persons resident abroad, the position is to some extent altered by the recent decision to set free the foreign exchanges, but, until the full effects of that decision have become apparent and as long as the domestic demands for new capital both for trade and industry and for national purposes, are so pressing, I do not think it would be safe to remove the restrictions upon investment outside the United Kingdom. The new Regulation will, therefore, provide that no such issues shall be permitted except under licence.

The restrictions will not apply to rearrangements of existing capital where no new money is raised, or to the renewal of maturing securities except where the person responsible for repayment is a person resident outside the United Kingdom.

(*House of Commons Hansard*, Vol. 114, 45)

5 NOTICE ISSUED BY THE TREASURY, 25 MARCH 1919

The Lords Commissioners of His Majesty's Treasury give notice that pending the amendment of Defence of the Realm Regulation 30F. in accordance with the statement made by the Chancellor of the Exchequer in the House of Commons on Monday, the 24th instant, they have issued a general licence for issues of capital by companies resident and carrying on business in the United Kingdom, for capital purposes within the United Kingdom, provided that in every prospectus offering to the public for subscription or purchase any issue made under such general licence a statement is included that 'no part of the proceeds of the issue is to be applied for capital purposes outside the United Kingdom or to replace money which has been so applied'.

(*Economist*, 29 Mar. 1919)

6 STATEMENT, 2 APRIL 1919

[The Chancellor announced in the House of Commons the appointment of an enlarged (Capital Issues) Committee with the following terms of reference:]

To consider and advise upon applications received by the Treasury for licences under Defence of the Realm Regulation (30F.) for fresh Issues of capital, with a view to preserving capital during the reconstruction period for domestic purposes within the United Kingdom, and to preventing any avoidable drain upon Foreign Exchanges by the export of capital, except where it is shown to the satisfaction of the Treasury that special circumstances exist.

(*House of Commons Hansard*, Vol. 114, 1206)

7 NOTICE ISSUED BY THE TREASURY, 18 AUGUST 1919

1. Defence of the Realm Regulation 41D, which prohibits remittances from the United Kingdom by way of loan or for subscription to an issue of capital outside the United Kingdom or for the purchase of securities or property other than merchandise or of a foreign currency to be held with a view to appreciation or as an investment, and requires a banker to obtain, before sending a remittance out of the United Kingdom, a declaration in writing of its purpose;
2. The Prohibition of Import (No. 21) Proclamation of 1917 which prohibits the import of bonds, debenture stock or share certificates, scrip, or other documents of title relating to stocks, shares or other securities; and
3. Paragraph 4(b) of Defence of the Realm Regulations 30F which prohibits the purchase or sale of securities which have at any time since September 30, 1914, been in physical possession outside the United Kingdom, have been withdrawn.

The Treasury desire to call special attention to the fact that dealings in securities which have at any time since the outbreak of war been in enemy ownership is still prohibited except under licence. Special precautions must, therefore, be taken by purchasers of securities coming from abroad to secure that this prohibition is not infringed.

The provisions of Defence of the Realm Regulation 30F relating to the issue of capital in the United Kingdom where the proceeds of the issue or any part thereof are to be applied for capital purposes outside the United Kingdom, or to replace money which has been so applied, and to dealings in stocks, shares or other securities, except for immediate payment, remain in force, and Treasury licence will continue to be required as heretofore until further notice for all such issues and dealings.

The Lords Commissioners of His Majesty's Treasury hereby release all undertakings not to sell or pledge for the period of the war or for any longer period, as the case may be, (a) securities imported under licences issued in pursuance of the Prohibition of Import Proclamation (No. 21) of 1917, or (b) British Government securities purchased with the proceeds of sale of such securities or of other securities which have not been held in physical possession in this country continuously since September 30, 1914, but which have been sold by special permission.

Government securities resulting from such sales may be released from any guarantee of a banker or broker and may be transferred into the sole name of the purchaser.

(*Economist*, 23 Aug. 1919)

8 EVENTS SEPTEMBER–NOVEMBER 1919

[In September 1919 the Treasury Committee (see Item 6 above) was dissolved and the administration of Regulation 30F was transferred to the Board of Trade, which acted through a small departmental committee 'on behalf of the Treasury'. Under the Board of Trade regime licences were more freely granted and in November 1919 a general licence was issued, thus in effect abolishing the restrictions on new issues.]

9 EVENTS 1920–24

[About the beginning of 1920 the bankers were told by the Governor that no short-term foreign loans should be issued in the London market. (Short-term loans were defined as being those having less than 20 years maturity whether this maturity was fixed or optional.)

In May 1920, the Governor arranged informally with the three principal brokers for their co-operation in facilitating issues to finance the government's urgent housing programme. This was done at the request of the Chancellor and the Minister of Health. In July 1921 this special arrangement came to an end. (Cf. Norman's Diary, 30 April 1920, 5 May 1920, 11 May 1920, 11 July 1921.)

On 1 February 1922, a fresh definition of short-term foreign loans was made, the Chairman of the Bankers' Clearing House being informed that the 'date for the compulsory redemption of any Loan shall continue as at present to be not less than 20 years from the date of issue, but that hereafter a borrower may reserve to himself an option to effect earlier redemption provided such earlier redemption takes place not less than 10 years from the date of issue'.

On 14 January 1924, in a letter written to the Chairman of the Bankers' Clearing House, the Governor, 'having again consulted the Chancellor of the Exchequer', removed the embargo except as regards 'Treasury Bills or other obligations, the interest on which is paid or expressed in the form of discount'. Moreover, no assistance was to be given to any borrower who had failed to comply with the requirements of the Committee of the Stock Exchange set forth in *The Times* of 12 December 1923. (This referred to certain foreign governments which were withholding payment of some coupons on certain of their loans.)]

10 EXTRACTS FROM COMMITTEE OF TREASURY MINUTES, 1924–5

9 April 1924

The Governor informed the Committee –

* (1) That too many demands were being made to obtain Foreign loans here in the near future and that, in view of the Exchanges and of the over-lending by this Country in 1923, he was strongly of opinion that only applications on behalf of those countries which were in need of money for reconstruction purposes deserved consideration.

* Board of Trade figures published in *Economist* 9 February 1924.

[This is a rare instance of published figures being cited as evidence in Committee of Treasury Minutes.]

22 October 1924

The Governor informed the Committee –

(1) That having been approached, since the closing of the German Loan, as to the issue of foreign Loans in London, he had again replied that all such issues were, and were likely to be, undesirable under present Exchange conditions, except only those guaranteed by the Treasury or supported by the League of Nations; any attempt to issue would probably lead to an immediate rise in the Bank Rate.

25 February 1925

The Governor informed the Committee –

... ...

(4) That, with reference to previous Minutes, he proposed, in spite of recent contraventions of the spirit of the policy, to continue –

(a) ...

(b) to restrict whenever possible the issue of Foreign Loans in London for purposes other than Reconstruction;

and in regard to (b) he saw no difference between a Loan raised openly by prospectus or raised privately with subsequent application for a quotation on the Stock Exchange.

1 April 1925

The following matters which had been deferred for further consideration were considered, vizt:–

... ...

It was agreed that...even after the 'Gold' announcement it will still be necessary to discourage Foreign Issues and investment by all possible means.

27 May 1925

The Governor acquainted the Committee of the following matters which had arisen since the last Meeting –

(1) In view of the large number of recent and impending Colonial Issues he had asked the Chancellor to point out to the Governments of the Dominions and Colonies the strain thus caused on the Exchanges and to request their co-operation in reducing as far as possible demands for further Loans.

II EXTRACT FROM A PERSONAL LETTER FROM THE GOVERNOR TO SIR BASIL BLACKETT, 27 OCTOBER 1925

Personal

27th October 1925

My dear Sir Basil,

... ...

2. You ask why the Embargo on foreign issues is still maintained. The Embargo (with the general agreement of the Treasury) was due to the goodwill of all concerned as a sort of self-denying ordinance of the City. It was at the outset very effective and helped 'the pound to look the dollar in the face' as was intended. But by degrees, and especially during May and June last, it became evident that the real benefits of the Embargo were being seized for themselves by the Dominions whose appetites for new Loans threatened to become insatiable. As we were only just feeling our way through the early days of the revived Gold Standard we asked the Dominions to go slow, or to raise some of their requirements in New York, and, although the Commonwealth Government were very obliging and did as they were asked, others were not so obliging – they even secured the support of the Colonial Office – and we were therefore gradually forced as it were to extend the Embargo to cover Dominion Loans. As you can imagine, from being a mere matter of City policy the embargo thus suddenly became a question of high imperial politics with the result that the whole subject of Overseas Loans (Dominion and Foreign) was referred by

the Cabinet to a secret Committee. As the result of their Report, I hope the Embargo will be removed without notice in the course of a few weeks.

... ...

Yours very sincerely,
(Signed) M. Norman.

Sir Basil Blackett, K.C.B.

12 EXTRACT FROM COMMITTEE OF TREASURY MINUTES, 28 OCTOBER 1925

The Governor then acquainted the Committee of the following matters, vizt:–

(1) The Chancellor hopes that no loan will be floated on behalf of any country which has not settled its Inter-Allied Debts to this Country.

13 EXTRACT FROM A REPORT OF A SPEECH BY THE CHANCELLOR OF THE EXCHEQUER AT SHEFFIELD, 3 NOVEMBER 1925

I am glad, however, to say, and this is an announcement of considerable importance which I thought you would like me to make to you when I was speaking here to-night – that the time has now come when we can take a further step towards the establishment of complete freedom and normal conditions in the money market. From this time forward no objection will be raised on general grounds by the responsible financial authorities to the issue of Dominion, Colonial, and foreign loans on the London market. What has been known as the embargo will now be removed. The old and full freedom of the market will be restored. The City of London must be responsible for using that freedom wisely and soberly. Overlending, that is to say, lending beyond our strength, straining our future credit, lending beyond our savings or our earnings, such overlending will bring its own corrective. I trust with confidence to the corporate good sense of the City to manage its affairs with discretion, to pay regard, not only to the capacities of the market but to the position towards this country of would-be borrowers, and I hope so far as possible without impairing the freedom of the market that preference will be given in the matter of credit to those issues which bring a high proportion of orders for goods immediately to the trade of this country.

14 LETTER FROM THE GOVERNOR TO SIR OTTO NIEMEYER AT THE TREASURY, 21 FEBRUARY 1927

Personal

21st February, 1927

Dear Sir Otto,

For some time past this Market has been governed by your unwritten law; that is to say, no public issues have been made in favour of such countries as had not settled their War debts to this country. Thus, as you well know, France, Greece and Serbia remain to-day outside the pale.

But this unwritten law, which on the whole has been very effective, is beginning to lose its power particularly for two reasons. First, as we were saying last week, Serbia is about to receive quite a large sum in New York either as a State or Municipalities loan – the form is not yet settled. Secondly, France has raised two or three loans in Holland and Switzerland and can, if she wishes, at once obtain a further large loan (say the equivalent of £10 million at least). But these loans, which are nominally issued abroad, are actually, to some extent, sold in London and there is an agreement to that effect.

Thus you see France and Serbia are getting what they want in London in a roundabout way and our embargo seems less potent than it did!!

Please turn this over in your mind.

Believe me,
Yours sincerely,
(Signed) M. Norman.

Sir O. E. Niemeyer, K.C.B.

15 EXTRACT FROM A LETTER FROM THE GOVERNOR TO SIR RICHARD HOPKINS AT THE TREASURY, 4 FEBRUARY 1928

[The letter first points out that France is the only country still debarred from borrowing in London, and that America has now relaxed its attitude to most French issues.]

This may well raise rather awkward questions here: I have been nagged about the embargo (so-called) off and on for a couple of years, as your files to some extent will show you...Quite recently Mr Siepmann has communicated with your Mr Waley, and accordingly wrote on the 17th of last month to one of the Bankers that 'the position in London as regards the issue of French loans has not undergone any change and that there is no reason to expect that the action reported to have been taken by the State Department will lead to any corresponding action here'.

16 LETTER FROM SIR RICHARD HOPKINS AT THE TREASURY TO THE GOVERNOR, 10 OCTOBER 1928

Treasury Chambers,
Whitehall, S.W.
10th October, 1928.

Confidential

Dear Mr Governor,

In view of the considerations urged in your letter of the 2nd instant, I am authorised to say that there is no longer any need for you, on political grounds, to discourage French borrowing in London, as a matter of principle. I take it that you would still watch such proposals from the economic standpoint, and give us an opportunity of considering the matter if any very large scale operation were contemplated?

Yours sincerely,
R. V. N. Hopkins.

The Right Hon. Montagu C. Norman, D.S.O.

17 EXTRACT FROM COMMITTEE OF TREASURY MINUTES, 31 OCTOBER 1928

The Governor acquainted the Committee of the following matters:—

... ...

(3) With regard to a suggested issue in London, he had stated to an enquirer that no public issue expressed solely in Reichsmarks, Dollars or any other foreign currency should be undertaken at the present time.

18 EXTRACT FROM A REPORT OF A SPEECH BY THE CHANCELLOR, 24 JULY 1929

On July 24 the Chancellor of the Exchequer met a large and representative gathering of the banking and mercantile community at a dinner given by the Lord Mayor of London...He referred to the difficult monetary situation which had arisen through the drain of gold during the last few months from the Bank of England to foreign countries, and he appealed to City financial houses to exercise caution in foreign lending where the exchanges were unfavourable to Great Britain.

('The Annual Register for 1929', p. 68)

19 ORDER MADE BY THE TREASURY, 22 SEPTEMBER 1931

[The Treasury Order reproduced below, which was made immediately upon the suspension of the gold standard, was of wide applicability, but is included here because, among other transactions, issues involving foreign exchange were prohibited.]

The Lords Commissioners of His Majesty's Treasury, in pursuance of Section 1(3) of the Gold Standard (Amendment) Act, 1931, hereby order that until further notice purchases of foreign exchange, or transfers of funds with the object of acquiring such exchange directly or indirectly, by British Subjects or persons resident in the United Kingdom shall be prohibited except for the purpose of financing

1 Normal trading requirements.
2 Contracts existing before September 21st, 1931.
3 Reasonable travelling or other personal purposes.

Philip Snowden.
George Penny.
Two of the Lords Commissioners of the Treasury.

22nd September 1931

20 ORDER MADE BY THE TREASURY, 2 MARCH 1932

The Lords Commissioners of His Majesty's Treasury, in pursuance of section 1(3) of the Gold Standard Act 1931, hereby order that the prohibition imposed by the Order made under the said Act by the said Lords Commissioners on the twenty-second day of September, nineteen hundred and thirty one, shall cease to have effect on the third day of March, nineteen hundred and thirty two.

N. Chamberlain.
Victor Warrender.
Two of the Lords Commissioners of His Majesty's Treasury.

2nd March 1932

21 STATEMENT, 30 JUNE 1932

[The Chancellor said in the House of Commons:]

I am sure that anyone who may be contemplating the issue of new capital in the market in the early future will forbear from coming forward for a few weeks while this great operation is proceeding and that the authorities in the City of London will co-operate in this necessary object.

(*House of Commons Hansard*, Vol. 267, 2125)

22 NOTICE ISSUED BY THE TREASURY, 29 AUGUST 1932

On his return from Ottawa the Chancellor of the Exchequer has reviewed the position arising from his request to intending borrowers to refrain from coming on the market pending the completion of the Conversion operation.

Mr Chamberlain gratefully acknowledges the willingness of all parties concerned to accede to his request as a matter of national interest.

In view of the gratifyingly high percentage of assents which have already been received from holders of War Loan, the Chancellor now feels satisfied that some partial relaxation of the present arrangements may safely be permitted; but for the time being he would be glad if not more than the following operations were undertaken:–

(a) A mere exchange of one class of security for another class of security without change of ownership, and

(b) An issue of a new security to replace a security the final redemption of which had prior to July 1, 1932, been fixed for a date earlier than December 1 next,

provided that such operations concern only British (including Empire) sterling issues domiciled in London and involve neither the provision of new cash nor underwriting.

(*Times*, 30 Aug. 1932)

23 EXTRACT FROM NOTICE ISSUED BY THE TREASURY, 30 SEPTEMBER 1932

The following statement was issued last evening from the Treasury:–

. . . .

The Conversion operation having now been completed, the Chancellor feels that no further restrictions in the way of new issues are required with the exception, until further notice, of:—

(1) Foreign issues – i.e., issues on behalf of borrowers domiciled outside the Empire or issues the proceeds of which would be remitted abroad; and

(2) The optional replacement of existing issues by new issues involving either underwriting or an invitation to the public to subscribe new cash.

The Chancellor would ask, however, that, with a view to co-ordinating the requirements of intending borrowers and so preventing possible congestion of the market, no issue ranking as a trustee security may be made without prior agreement with the Bank of England regarding the amount and date of issue.

(*Times*, 1 Oct. 1932)

24 SUMMARY BY THE GOVERNOR, 4 OCTOBER 1932

[In pursuance of the Chancellor's statement, reported in *The Times*, 1 October 1932, the Governor of the Bank agreed the following with the Treasury.]

Bible

1. Any Body domiciled within the Empire may borrow –
   (a) to meet new expenditure within the Empire
   (b) to provide for the final maturity of an obligation domiciled within the Empire.

Such borrowing may be effected by a public issue and can be underwritten.

Before any public issue of a Trustee character is arranged agreement must be reached with the Bank of England regarding the amount and date of the issue.

2. Any Body domiciled within the Empire may borrow new money with which to pay off an optional maturity domiciled within the Empire provided that such borrowing is done privately and does not involve –
   (a) an invitation to the public to subscribe, or
   (b) underwriting, or
   (c) application to the Stock Exchange for a quotation or leave to deal.

4th October 1932

25 NOTICE ISSUED BY THE TREASURY, 13 JANUARY 1933

Now that the series of operations directly associated with the conversion of the Five per Cent War Loan is about to be completed by the repayment on February 1 of the Five per Cent Treasury Bonds, 1933–35, the Chancellor of the Exchequer thinks that the time has come when he may safely withdraw his previous request regarding new issues of capital except in the following cases:—

(1) Foreign issues, i.e., issues on behalf of borrowers domiciled outside the Empire or issues the proceeds of which would be remitted directly or indirectly to countries outside the Empire; and

(2) The optional replacement of existing issues by new issues if those new issues rank as Trustee securities and involve either underwriting or an invitation to the public to subscribe new cash.

The Chancellor still asks, however, that with a view to co-ordinating the requirements of intending borrowers and so preventing possible congestion of the market, no issue ranking as a Trustee security may be made without prior agreement with the Bank of England regarding the amount and date of issue.

(*Times*, 14 Jan. 1933)

26 NOTICE ISSUED BY THE TREASURY, 17 MAY 1933

In a notice issued on January 13 last the Chancellor of the Exchequer, in withdrawing his earlier and more comprehensive request in regard to new issues of capital, asked intending borrowers to refrain for the present from coming on the market, *inter alia*, for foreign issues.

Mr Chamberlain did not attempt at that time to define precisely the scope of the term 'issue', which was used by him, and he now finds it necessary to make a further explanation on one aspect of the matter.

For the present he thinks it is not in the public interest that large blocks of securities, including securities dealt in on the London Stock Exchange, should be purchased from foreign holders, with a view to their sale in this country, either by an issue to the public or otherwise.

With this further explanation he believes that in the majority of instances a judgment will easily be formed whether any particular case should be held to fall within the spirit of his request or not, but he hopes that in future, wherever any doubt arises, inquiry will be made at the Treasury before a transaction is set in hand.

(*Times*, 18 May 1933)

27 LETTER FROM THE CHANCELLOR TO THE CHAIRMAN OF THE STOCK EXCHANGE COMMITTEE, 12 JUNE 1933

Treasury Chambers,
Whitehall, S.W.
12th June, 1933.

Dear Mr Chairman,

From the nature of the enquiries which have been addressed to the Treasury in the last fortnight it appears that the purpose underlying the request which I made in the Press on the 17th May respecting the purchase of foreign owned securities is imperfectly understood by the Stock Exchange.

The large inflow into London during this year of short term money from abroad may have obscured, but it certainly has not removed, the intrinsic weaknesses of our position, and this country is not in my judgment at present in a position to invest large sums at long term in foreign countries.

Though from many points of view it would have been advantageous to do so, I have not thought it possible to make any public request discouraging ordinary private investment abroad by individuals. I kept the notice of the 17th May within the ambit of my previous request by limiting it to the question of the purchase of large blocks of foreign owned securities (whether of British concerns or otherwise) with a view to resale here.

Since this notice was issued I find instances in which brokers or others in this country have been asked by foreign owners to find a market in this country for large blocks of securities by distributing them among a considerable number of buyers without actually making an intermediate purchase. This, of course, equally conflicts with the general object which I have in view, and there may be other technical means for carrying through transactions of a similarly injurious kind. I trust that the members of the Stock Exchange will assist me by discouraging any such transactions by every means in their power.

I shall be obliged if you will convey the sense of this letter to your members, on whose goodwill I am confident that I may rely. Perhaps you would at the same time explain to them that a similar request is being addressed on my behalf to the principal bankers and other firms outside the Stock Exchange who are accustomed to handle business in foreign securities.

Yours sincerely,
(Signed) N. Chamberlain.

Sir Archibald Campbell,
Chairman,
Stock Exchange Committee.

28 STATEMENT, 10 APRIL 1934

[In answer to a Question in the House of Commons, 10 April 1934, seeking 'the principal reasons for the continuance of the existing embargo on foreign loans', Mr Hore-Belisha, Financial Secretary to the Treasury, stated:] among the factors which have been taken into consideration in deciding policy are the need of capital for home development, the effect of foreign lending upon our balance of payment, the position of the exchanges, and the relation between foreign lending and the encouragement of our export trade.

(*House of Commons Hansard*, Vol. 288, 153)

29 STATEMENT, 19 JULY 1934

[In answer to a Question in the House of Commons, 19 July 1934, the Chancellor stated:] I am satisfied that it would not be in the public interest that the existing restrictions should be removed at the present time. But under present conditions I should be ready to consider particular cases especially those falling under the following heads:—

(a) Sterling issues by a country within the sterling *bloc* where the loan is required to increase the sterling assets of that country and so to minimize fluctuations in the exchanges.

(b) Sterling issues on behalf of any borrower where the proceeds are calculated mainly to produce direct benefit to British industry.

(*House of Commons Hansard*, Vol. 292, 1260)

30 ANNOUNCEMENT, 7 APRIL 1936

[On 7 April 1936, the Chancellor announced in the House of Commons the appointment of the Foreign Transactions (Advisory) Committee, to advise him 'both generally upon the scope of the restriction [on foreign issues] and also upon particular applications'.

The membership was announced as Lord Kennet (chairman), the Deputy Governor of the Bank of England, Mr Thomas Frazer, Sir Austin Harris, Mr A. A. Jamieson, Lieutenant-Colonel J. B. Neilson and Mr R. P. Wilkinson. (*House of Commons Hansard*, Vol. 310, 2601)

The 'Terms of Reference and Instructions' included the following paragraphs:]

6. In their task the Committee will be guided in the first place by the general economic situation of the country.

7. The primary object of the present restrictions of foreign lending has been to protect sterling exchange against sudden and dislocating strains. In considering therefore what foreign long-term financing this country can undertake regard must be had not only to the volume of capital likely to be available for the purpose but also to the state of the exchanges and to the different kinds of pressure to which sterling may be exposed. Due allowance will of course be made for new issues on behalf of Empire borrowers, and the movement of international stock exchange securities between London and other markets must also be borne in mind.

8. These considerations would not generally apply to loans the proceeds of which would concurrently be used to finance additional exports from the United Kingdom. This fact has been recognised by the Chancellor in his relaxation of the restriction on foreign lending in favour of sterling issues whose proceeds are calculated mainly to benefit British industry; and the same principle should govern the Committee's consideration of proposals of this nature.

9. The Committee will bear in mind the recommendation of the Committee on Finance and Industry (Section 384) that – 'in the realm of foreign investment it is primarily towards British-owned enterprises abroad that we should wish to see our energies and capital turned rather than merely towards subscribing to foreign Government and municipal loans, which absorb our available foreign balance while doing little for our industry and commerce'. In this connection account should be taken of the treatment accorded to British-owned enterprises by the foreign country concerned.

10. It is of equal importance that the capital required for development in the United Kingdom should not be restricted by excessive lending abroad.

11. In deciding whether considerations such as these at any moment admit of an increase or call for a decrease in the amount of foreign new

issues the Committee should keep in close touch with the Treasury and with the Bank of England.

12. In accordance with the Chancellor's announcement the Committee should give favourable consideration to applications for sterling issues by a country within the sterling area where the loan is required to increase the sterling assets of that country and so to minimise fluctuations in the exchanges.

13. The applications to be considered by the Committee will include (a) financing on behalf of foreign Governments, States or other public authorities, (b) offers of share or loan capital to the public which involve the remittance of funds directly or indirectly to any country outside the British Empire, (c) offers (involving such remittances) made otherwise than to the public in respect of which permission to deal may be sought from the Stock Exchange, (d) the acquisition of foreign holdings mentioned in paragraph 3 of this note.

31 STATEMENT, 16 MARCH 1937

[The Chancellor said in the House of Commons:]

I was recently informed by Lord Kennet that, in their consideration of proposals for new issues by Investment Trust Companies, the Committee felt that the proportion of such new issues invested abroad should be confined to the minimum necessary to the conduct of the business in accordance with the ordinary practice of Investment Trusts, and further that if in the case of the applicant company the proportion of foreign investment should be unusually high the general purpose of the Government should be furthered by a reduction of that proportion as occasion may serve. The Chairman of the Committee has with my approval communicated the substance of this view, which has my concurrence, to the chairman of the representative association of Investment Trust Companies.

(*House of Commons Hansard*, Vol. 321, 1852)

32 STATEMENT, 1 FEBRUARY 1938

[The Chancellor said in the House of Commons:]

I do not consider that the time has come when consents in respect of foreign issues, as defined under the Foreign Transactions Advisory Committee's terms of reference can be given indiscriminately, and I refer in particular to those on behalf of foreign governments, foreign local or public authorities, or state-controlled organisations. Applications of this kind will continue to be considered on their merits, along the lines laid down in the Committee's terms of reference and with regard to the general policy of His Majesty's Government. Greater latitude will, however, be allowed until further notice in respect of applications which do not fall within the class which I have mentioned. I refer particularly –

(a) to the raising of new money in this market on a long-term basis on behalf of British borrowers, in which term I include borrowers in any part of the Empire, for the purpose of acquiring assets or developing enterprise in foreign countries; and

(b) to transactions involving large blocks of foreign-owned securities which were the subject of my predecessor's letter of 12th June, 1933, to the Chairman of the Stock Exchange Committee.

Applications should still be made to the Foreign Transactions Advisory Committee in respect of such proposals, not only because the Treasury will continue to avail itself of the advice so tendered, but because it is essential that we should know what is going on. Such applications will, however, in general receive the sympathetic consideration of the Committee, though I do not, of course, say that in particular cases there may not be reasons of public policy which would lead to their rejection.

What I have just said applies, of course, to long-term lending, and illustrates the desire of His Majesty's Government to encourage a suitable expansion of international capital transactions. I should add that foreign short-term lending of a non-commercial character involves other considerations and raises special difficulties which render it generally undesirable.

(*House of Commons Hansard*, Vol. 331, 41)

33 STATEMENT, 20 DECEMBER 1938

[The Chancellor said in the House of Commons:]

The House will recollect that on 1st February, 1938, I stated that, in view of the condition of our exchanges at that time, greater latitude would, until further notice, be allowed in respect of certain applications to the Foreign Transactions Advisory Committee. In view of present circumstances, the Foreign Transactions Advisory Committee came to the conclusion, in which I concur, that an immediate restriction is now required of the greater latitude then announced, and I have reason to think that the need for such restriction is generally acknowledged. Accordingly, I take this opportunity of stating that the temporary relaxations made in February have been withdrawn.

(*House of Commons Hansard*, Vol. 343, 2678)

34 NOTICE ISSUED BY THE TREASURY, 3 SEPTEMBER 1939

1. Until further notice and unless it falls within the classes of issues exempted by Treasury Order, no fresh issue of capital of whatever nature may be made without the consent of the Treasury.

2. Issues for undertakings carried on or to be carried on in the United Kingdom or in British Countries overseas will be allowed only if it is shown

to the satisfaction of the Treasury that they are advisable in the national interest.

3. Issues or participations in issues for undertakings carried on or to be carried on outside British Countries will be allowed only where it is shown to the satisfaction of the Treasury that urgent necessity and special circumstances exist.

4. The Treasury will not in ordinary cases insist upon the above restrictions where issues are required for the renewal of Treasury Bills or other short instruments held here and falling due of Dominion, Colonial or Foreign Governments or of Municipal Corporations or Railways or other Undertakings, provided that due application is made for consent. Applications for consent in respect of issues in replacement of longer term obligations maturing upon a definite date will receive special consideration.

5. The existing Foreign Transactions Advisory Committee under the title of the Capital Issues Committee will advise upon all applications for consent.

... .

APPENDIX 31

MONETARY RECONSTRUCTION IN EUROPE, 1922–28: ADDENDUM TO CHAPTER 8

The account given in Chapter 8 of the Bank's activity in monetary reconstruction in Europe was limited to events which were either of major concern to the Bank or peculiarly illustrative of the Bank's policy and methods. The files of the Bank on this subject include also much detail on other episodes in European reconstruction, including some relating to the smaller countries. This other material is the basis of the following notes prepared in the Bank by D. J. H. Chetwin. These indicate some of the minor European activities of the Bank in this phase. It should be understood that no attempt has been made, by drawing on sources outside the Bank, to give a rounded picture of any of these episodes.

Throughout these years Norman was Governor and, though it was with unique personal interest, it was in this capacity that he took the steps indicated below; he is referred to by name only to preclude confusion with governors of other central banks involved.

CZECHOSLOVAKIA

The Bank's underwriting application for £400,000 bonds, when a final tranche of the Czechoslovak State Loan of 1922 was issued in London in 1924, was allotted in full: the Bank was concerned that the issue should result in a debt settlement of like amount by the Czechs to H.M. Treasury. Norman had earlier resisted the issue because he viewed the Czechs as obstructing economic rehabilitation in Hungary. When a National Bank was to be established, the Czechs turned for financial help to America.

DANZIG

The Bank of Danzig came into existence early in 1924. Norman gave general advice while the new bank was being planned and offered a credit for which there was some difficulty in deciding on appropriate security and which in the event was not required. The Bank of England and the Bank for International Settlements did, however, make advances of £75,000 each for three weeks in 1931.

There were two loans under League auspices. The £m1.5 Municipality of Danzig 7% Mortgage Loan was issued in 1925 by two London houses and in 1927 the £m1.9 Free City of Danzig 6½% (Tobacco Monopoly) State Loan was issued, £m1.5 being offered in London by the same two houses. Both these London issues were heavily over-subscribed. Norman had been approached for advice before the first issue and had in turn approached Strakosch and the League, insisting that he could give his support only if the loan received League approval and blessing: this was a new departure for the League, as the loan was purely for development, but it was argued that Danzig was the League's child.

DENMARK

Denmark arranged British and American credits during the 1920s from a number of commercial banking sources, mostly in connection with currency stabilisation, but there seems to be nothing in the Bank's files to suggest that the Bank was concerned in any of these.

When, in 1926, Denmark was contemplating a return to the Gold Standard the Bank's advice on the best method was sought, given and followed. The opportunity was taken by the Bank to stress the advantages of Denmark's joining the circle of co-operating central banks. The Bank's advice was again sought when the Gold Standard position came under review three years later.

ESTONIA

Estonia, though not subject to inflationary or economic problems of the same order as other recipients of League aid, had the benefit in 1927 of an international loan under League auspices, the Republic of Estonia (Banking and Currency Reform) 7% Loan 1927. This raised some £1,350,000 net, mainly for the purpose of freeing her central bank, the Eesti Pank, from illiquid assets. Of the loan, £500,000 nominal was issued in London.

In 1925, the Estonian Government had consulted Norman on the appointment of a Financial Adviser. He suggested two names; one of the men, the later Sir Walter Williamson, was duly appointed in 1926. A year later under the League scheme new statutes promulgated for the central bank included the appointment of an Adviser, and to this post Williamson was then appointed. As with other advisers placed in European central banks, Norman assumed the responsibility of keeping Williamson informed by correspondence and otherwise.

The Bank of England (Siepmann and Osborne) was involved when a new central banking statute was under consideration in 1926. At one stage the Bank was asked for a two-month credit but this was in the event not needed. Norman offered general co-operation in the task of putting the Eesti Pank on a sound footing, although he personally cherished an idea that the three Baltic states (Estonia, Latvia and Lithuania) should act together and set up a central bank jointly. He was consulted on arrangements for issuing the loan in London; to this he reacted circumspectly, although he did go so far as to make an abortive approach, for the Estonians, to a London issuing house.

FINLAND

Harvey (in 1925) and Siepmann (in 1929) visited Finland, and the Governor of the Bank of Finland, Ryti, was an occasional visitor in Threadneedle Street. In February 1926, the Bank of England granted the Bank of Finland a £600,000 stabilisation credit for one year (in replacement of a facility extended by U.K. commercial banks): the credit was twice extended in 1927–8, but was in fact never used.

In a forthright letter to Ryti, towards the end of this period, Norman revealed a disenchantment with such credits: 'such credits have become altogether too fashionable. They seem sometimes to be taken when they are not needed, even though they cost money, and I have the impression that the amounts taken have also been on occasion needlessly high. Too much, I think, is made in these days of what is known as the psychological argument. We are told that public opinion would scarcely withstand the shock of any considerable reduction in the proportion of cover held against the note issue. But if this is so, should it not be our business gradually to educate public opinion to become a little less sensitive in these matters? The general standard of reserves maintained against the circulation appears to me from every technical point of view to be unduly high. The consequence is that a considerable part of these so-called reserves is no reserve at all, but merely an expensive, idle sediment, which serves no useful purpose.'

NORWAY

Norway returned to the Gold Standard in 1928. Siepmann had visited the Norges Bank in 1927, and the latter had then suggested a credit from the Bank of England to inspire confidence, coupled with one from the Federal Reserve Bank. In the event, however, because the Norwegians wished to have a credit freely available before *de jure* stabilisation, a credit and a loan were obtained from private sources in America.

PORTUGAL

In 1927 the Portuguese authorities approached two London houses and discussed with Norman the possibility of a London issue: Norman pointed firmly to the necessity for a League plan. Siepmann and Osborne worked on draft bank legislation and later there was talk of Siepmann's going out as an expert on behalf of the B.I.S. to examine Portugal's stabilisation plans, but this fell through.

When the possibility of a London loan was under discussion in 1927–8, there were protests from some contractors and others who were in dispute with various Portuguese authorities, but Lubbock (Deputy Governor) ruled that the Bank of England should intervene only if asked by the Foreign Office.

YUGOSLAVIA

The Bank offered to the Banque Nationale du Royaume des Serbes, Croates et Slovènes its support in general terms in any stabilisation programme, and for several years a scheme always seemed imminent but never quite materialised. Negotiations were conducted concerning both wartime and pre-war debts in the U.K. and elsewhere; Siepmann devoted much time to draft legislation; a consortium of British banks stood ready to make a loan and their representative took up residence in Belgrade for a considerable time – which embittered the French who saw their political influence in Yugoslavia endangered: but stabilisation was delayed and the British market was never quite ready. One London house gave some short-term assistance in 1929, but stabilisation finally came in 1931 without any British loan.

APPENDIX 32

THE BALANCE OF PAYMENTS IN THE INTER-WAR PERIOD

This appendix was prepared in the Economic Intelligence Department of the Bank and combines two articles which have previously appeared in the Bank's *Quarterly Bulletin*.[1] It begins by discussing contemporary knowledge of the balance of payments and gives sources and methods for the figures available at the time: this section should be read in conjunction with Tables A and B. Section 2 then goes on to consider the revisions made to these figures in the light of later information and comments briefly on the trends revealed by the new 'best estimates' as set out in Table C. The appendix concludes with some brief thoughts on the figures' reliability.

[1] M. D. K. W. Foot, 'The Balance of Payments in the Inter-war Period', *Bank of England Quarterly Bulletin*, September 1972, pp. 345–63, and R. G. Ware, 'The Balance of Payments in the Inter-war Period: Further Details', *Bank of England Quarterly Bulletin*, March 1974, pp. 47–52.

Table A. *Contemporary 'current account' estimates published by the Board of Trade for the period 1907–38*[a] (£ *million*)

The first set of estimates for the current account was published in the *Board of Trade Journal* in March 1923. This covered 1920 and 1922 and gave very tentative figures for 1907, 1910 and 1913 for comparison. Thereafter, the Board of Trade published an annual article, between January and March, giving estimates for the previous year and revisions to the two years before that. Subsequent changes were recorded in the annual *Statistical Abstract*.

Two rows of figures are shown for each item in the 'current account' in this table; (i) is the first estimate published for each year, while (ii) shows the final figure produced in the period. Ditto marks in (ii) indicate no revision from the original estimate.

		1907	1910	1913	1920	1922	1923	1924	1925	1926	1927	1928
1 Visible trade balance excluding gold[def]	(i)	−136	−153	−145	−385	−180	−216	−355	−396	−466	−389	−352
	(ii)					−181	−208	−338	−392	−464	−387	,,
2 Net government payments −/receipts +[gh]	(i)								−15	.	.	+13
	(ii)						−25	−25	−11	+4	+1	+15
3 Net national shipping income	(i)	+85	+90	+94	+340	+110	+110	+130	+124	+120	+140	+130
	(ii)					,,	+133	+140	,,	,,	,,	,,
4 Net income from overseas investment	(i)	+160	+187	+210	+200	+175	+150	+185	+250	+270	+270	+285
	(ii)					,,	+200[j]	+220[j]	,,	+250	+250	+250
5 Net short interest and commissions	(i)	+25	+25	+25	+40	+30	+30	+40	+40	+60	+63	+65
	(ii)					,,	,,	+60	+60	,,	,,	,,
6 Net miscellaneous receipts	(i)	+10	+10	+10	+15	+10	+10	+15	+15	+15	+15	+15
	(ii)					,,	,,	,,	,,	,,	,,	,,
7 Balance of invisible exports	(i)	+280	+312	+339	+595	+325	+300	+370	+414	+465	+488	+508
(2 to 6 inclusive)	(ii)					,,	+348	+410	+438	+449	+469	+475
8 **Balance on current account excluding**	(i)	**+144**	**+159**	**+194**	**+210**	**+145**	**+84**	**+15**	**+18**	**−1**	**+99**	**+156**
gold (1+7)	(ii)					**+144**	**+140**	**+72**	**+46**	**−15**	**+82**	**+123**
9 *Excess of gold exports/imports over imports +/over exports −*	(i) (ii)	*−6*	*−6*	*−13*	*+42*	*+10*	*+13*	*+14*	*+8*	*−11*	*−3*	*+13*

Table A (*cont.*)

		1929	1930	1931	1932	1933	1934[b]	1935[b]	1936	1937[c]	1938[c]
1 Visible trade balance excluding gold[def]	(i)	−381	−387	−411	−289	−264	−295	−261	−347	−443	−377
	(ii)	,,	−386	−408	−287	−263	−294	,,	−345	(−442)	
2 Net government payments −/receipts +[gh]	(i)	+22	+21	+16	−25	.	+9	−2	−2	−4	−13
	(ii)	+24	+19	+14	−24	−2	+7	,,	−3	(,,)	
3 Net national shipping income	(i)	+130	+105	+80	+70	+65	+70	+75	+95	+130	+100
	(ii)	,,	,,	,,	,,	,,	,,	+70	+85	,,	
4 Net income from overseas investment	(i)	+285	+235	+165	+140	+155	+175	+185	+195	+220	+200
	(ii)	+250	+220	+170	+150	+160	+170	,,	+200	(+210)	
5 Net short interest and commissions	(i)	+65	+55	+30	+30	+30	+30	+30	+30	+35	+35
	(ii)	,,	,,	,,	+25	,,	,,	,,	+35	(+40)	
6 Net miscellaneous receipts	(i)	+15	+15	+10	+15	+10	+10	+10	+10	+10	.
	(ii)	,,	,,	,,	,,	,,	,,	,,	,,	(,,)	
7 Balance of invisible exports	(i)	+517	+431	+301	+230	+260	+294	+298	+328	+391	+322
(2 to 6 inclusive)	(ii)	+484	+414	+304	+236	+263	+287	+293	+327	(+386)	
8 Balance on current account excluding	(i)	**+136**	**+44**	**−110**	**−59**	**−4**	**−1**	**+37**	**−19**	**−52**	**−55**
gold (1+7)	(ii)	**+103**	**+28**	**−104**	**−51**	.	**−7**	**+32**	**−18**	**(−56)**	
9 *Excess of gold exports/imports over imports +/over exports −*	(i) (ii)	*+15*	*−5*	*+35*	*−15*	*−196*	*−134*	*−70*	*−228*	*−80*	*+70*

. nil or less than £½ million.

[a] The term 'current account' was not used during this period. Up to and including the 1926 article, it was known as the 'income available for investment overseas' and, thereafter, rather more cautiously as the 'estimated total credit or debit balance on items specified above'.

[b] The figures for 1934–5 contain silver transactions which may properly be regarded as capital items. If they are treated as such, the visible trade balance becomes −285 for 1934 and −276 for 1935 and the current balance +9 in 1934 and +22 in 1935. (Source: internal Bank memorandum.)

[c] Alterations to the partially revised figures for 1937, shown in brackets in (ii), and the initial estimates for 1938 were not published because of the outbreak of war.

[d] Imports – cost, insurance and freight. Exports – free on board.

[e] There are small discontinuities in 1923 and 1938 in the coverage of the visible trade balance. The more significant of these, in 1923, resulted from the creation of the Irish Free State.

[f] Up to 1932, the Board of Trade included gold movements in the visible trade balance and, consequently, in the current account. From 1932 on, they were excluded – the practice adopted here – on the grounds that they were often related to capital, rather than current, account transactions.

[g] Both current and capital items were included.

[h] Included before the 1926 article in 'net income from overseas investment'.

[j] 25 of this revision results from the change in the treatment of 'net government payments/receipts' (see *h* above).

Table B. *Contemporary published estimates of items outside the 'current account' for the period 1907–38*[a] *(£ million)*

	1907	1910	1913	1920	1922	1923	1924	1925	1926	1927	1928
1 New overseas issues in the London market:											
(a) Midland Bank series[b]	−91	−207	−198	−53	−135	−136	−134	−88	−112	−139	−143
(b) Kindersley series[c]											
2 Sinking funds on and repayment of outstanding overseas issues[e]										−134[d]	−108[d]
3 Change in other long-term private investment abroad (increase −)[f]											
4 Change in net external short-term liabilities (increase +)[g]											+75
5 Change in the level of the Bank's gold reserves (increase −)[h]	−2	+1	−5	−37	+1	−1	.	−16	−7	−1	−2

Table B (*cont.*)

	1929	1930	1931	1932	1933	1934	1935	1936	1937	1938
1 New overseas issues in the London market:										
(a) Midland Bank series[b]	−94	−109	−46	−29	−38	−43	−21	−26	−32	−25
(b) Kindersley series[c]	−96	−98	−41	−37	−83	−63	−51	−61	−60	−29
2 Sinking funds on and repayment of outstanding overseas issues[e]	+49	+39	+27	+48	+67	+42	+81	+107	+61	+39
3 Change in other long-term private investment abroad (increase −)[f]		.	+10	+5	+5	−20	−50	−50	.	.
4 Change in net external short-term liabilities (increase +)[g]	−59	−11	Known to Bank but not published until 1951							
5 Change in the level of the Bank's gold reserves (increase −)[h]	+8	−2	+27	+1	−71	−1	−8	−114	−13	.

. nil or less than £½ million.

[a] Estimates for 1a and 4 were also published for the years not shown in this table.

[b] The nominal value of new overseas issues raised in the United Kingdom excluding issues for the purpose of conversion and refunding. (Source: *Midland Bank Review*.)

[c] This is the Midland Bank series adjusted by Kindersley to include conversion and refunding issues. Allowance was also made for the purchase of these new loans by non-residents. This was done by assuming that the percentage of new loans taken up by non-residents equalled their share (which could be estimated from tax data) of existing loans. (Source: annual articles by Kindersley in the *Economic Journal* 1929–38.)

[d] These figures for 1927 and 1928 are those given by Kindersley (*Econ. Jnl* 1931, p. 383) as the difference between his 'New issues' figures (line 1(b) above) and 'Sinking funds...' (line 2 above). For 1929 and subsequent years he gave separate figures; thus corresponding to his −108 for 1928 the net figure for 1929 would be (−96+49, as in lines 1(b) and 2, =) −47.

[e] Kindersley's estimates. (Source: as for line 1b.)

[f] Source: as for line 1b.

[g] Source: for 1928–30, the Macmillan Committee's Report.

[h] Source: the weekly Bank Return. Changes in the Bank's holdings of foreign currency and in official assistance are excluded. The valuation of the gold is that adopted by the Bank namely £3.89½ (approximately) per standard ounce; this differed markedly from the market price for most of the period in which the United Kingdom was off the gold standard (see Chart 2). The only information published on other official holdings of gold and foreign currency (those of the Treasury up to 1932 and of the Exchange Equalisation Account thereafter) were for the Account's gold stocks. As only end-March and end-September figures (for the period March 1937–March 1939) were given, they are not shown here.

Table C. *The balance of payments 1920–38 (£ millions)*

	1920	1921	1922	1923	1924	1925	1926	1927	1928	1929
Visible trade										
Imports (f.o.b.)	1,812	1,022	951	1,011	1,172	1,208	1,140	1,115	1,095	1,117
Exports (f.o.b.)	1,664	874	888	914	958	943	794	845	858	854
Visible balance	−148	−148	−63	−97	−214	−265	−346	−270	−237	−263
Invisibles										
Government services and transfers (net)	+1	+25	−11	−4	−7	+8	+10	+15	+15	+14
Other invisibles:										
Private services and transfers	+214	+117	+76	+85	+81	+53	+57	+91	+82	+78
Interest, profits and dividends:										
Private sector	+252	+183	+200	+202	+222	+254	+254	+251	+251	+250
Public sector	−4	−3	−21	−24	−24	−19	−14	−9	−7	−3
Invisible balance	+463	+322	+244	+259	+272	+296	+307	+348	+341	+339
Current balance	**+315**	**+174**	**+181**	**+162**	**+58**	**+31**	**−39**	**+78**	**+104**	**+76**
Capital movements										
Official long-term capital (net)	−97	−63	−18	−18	.	−5	−4	−6	−3	−5
U.K. new investment overseas	−53	−116	−135	−136	−134	−88	−112	−166	−143	−96
Sinking funds and repayments on existing issues	+15	+15	+15	+15	+15	+15	+27	+34	+35	+49
Other long-term investment abroad										
Net short-term liabilities / British Government stocks									+136	−84
Acceptances[a]									−61	+25
Total identified capital	−135	−164	−138	−139	−119	−78	−89	−138	−36	−111
Balancing item[b]	−132	−10	−46	−11	+67	+45	+151	+78	−86	+27
Currency flow	**+48**	**.**	**−3**	**+12**	**+6**	**−2**	**+23**	**+18**	**−18**	**−8**
Official financing										
Reserves (drawings on +/additions to −)	−48	.	+3	−12	−6	+2	−23	−18	+18	+8
Assistance	.	.	.	.	.	.	.	.	.	.
Total official financing	**−48**	**.**	**+3**	**−12**	**−6**	**+2**	**−23**	**−18**	**+18**	**+8**

	1930	1931	1932	1933	1934	1935	1936	1937	1938
Visible trade									
Imports (f.o.b.)	953	786	641	619	683	724	786	950	849
Exports (f.o.b.)	670	464	425	427	463	541	523	614	564
Visible balance	−283	−322	−216	−192	−220	−183	−263	−336	−285
Invisibles									
Government services and transfers (net)	+19	+10	−8	−9	−9	−12	−12	−12	−19
Other invisibles:									
Private services and transfers	+60	+31	+30	+24	+25	+22	+34	+80	+40
Interest, profits and dividends:									
Private sector	+220	+169	+149	+160	+169	+183	+198	+208	+197
Public sector	−1	−2	−17	−1	+3	+3	+3	+3	+2
Invisible balance	+298	+208	+154	+174	+188	+196	+223	+279	+220
Current balance	**+15**	**−114**	**−62**	**−18**	**−32**	**+13**	**−40**	**−57**	**−65**
Capital movements									
Official long-term capital (net)	−2	−1	−7	−1	+5	+2	.	−4	+10
U.K. new investment overseas	−98	−41	−37	−83	−63	−51	−61	−60	−29
Sinking funds and repayments on existing issues	+39	+27	+48	+67	+42	+81	+107	+61	+39
Other long-term investment abroad	.	+10	+5	+5	−20	−50	−48	.	.
Net short-term liabilities	−26	−293	+37	+52	+15	+12	+113	+84	−196
British Government stocks			+20	+18	+27	+8	+8	+3	−14
Acceptances[a]	+15	+41	+29	+12	−2	−4	+1	+1	+8
Total identified capital	−72	−257	+95	+70	+4	−2	+120	+85	−182
Balancing item[b]	+64	+337	−4	+70	+38	+68	+131	+101	−21
Currency flow	**+7**	**−34**	**+29**	**+122**	**+10**	**+79**	**+211**	**+129**	**−268**
Official financing									
Reserves (drawings on +/additions to −)	−7	−48	+85	−122	−10	−79	−211	−129	+268
Assistance	.	+82	−114	.	.	.	.	.	.
Total official financing	**−7**	**+34**	**−29**	**−122**	**−10**	**−79**	**−211**	**−129**	**+268**

. nil or less than £½ million.

[a] Between 1928 and 1931 these figures show only changes in acceptances given on foreign account: for subsequent years the figures show the net movements in these acceptances together with those given by foreigners on U.K. account.

[b] Before 1928 this includes changes in short-term liabilities and acceptances; these are thereafter covered separately.

Chart 1. *Contemporary estimates by the Board of Trade of the balance on current account 1907–38*

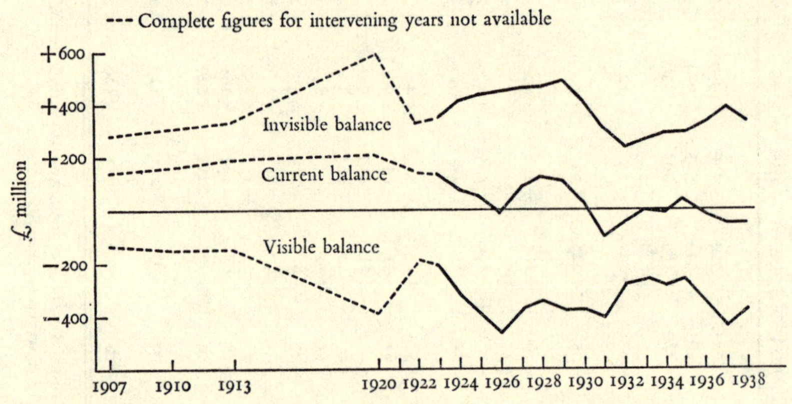

SOURCE: figures for 1907, 1910, 1913 and 1920 Table A lines 1, 7 and 8; figures for 1922–38 Table A lines 1(ii), 7(ii) and 8(ii).

Chart 2. *Sterling and the gold price*

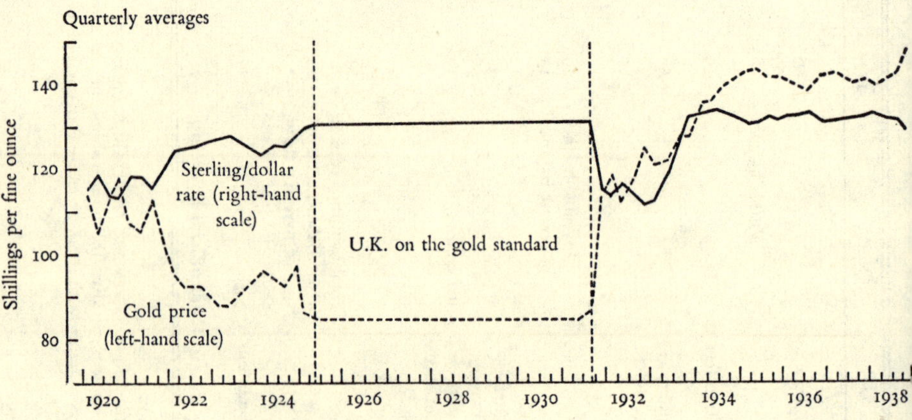

SECTION I, PART I

The picture given by the material presented here is, at first sight, surprising. At the beginning of the period virtually no statistics on the balance of payments were collected at all and, even by 1939, coverage was still very inadequate. We have become accustomed to having a wide range of reasonably accurate and up-to-date information readily available. But this multiplicity of figures is essentially a post-1945 phenomenon. In contrast, when the Royal Statistical Society petitioned the then Board of Trade (B.O.T.) in 1919 for an improvement in the quality and quantity of official data, one of their complaints in a different field of economic information was that nothing had been gathered on wages for thirteen years.

BEFORE 1914

The only official statistics on the items making up the balance of payments collected before 1914 were the monthly import and export figures. Private surveys also provided a few very tentative estimates of some of our invisible earnings in particular years, as well as series showing the volume of new loans raised on the London market by overseas borrowers.

In a sense, there was no need for further figures. What little evidence is available suggests an immensely strong balance-of-payments position before 1914. For the best part of a century, the United Kingdom seems to have earned a surplus from its invisible exports sufficient to finance a regular deficit on visible trade and still allow heavy investment overseas. As the volume of this investment grew (much of it in the form of U.K. holdings of loans issued by foreigners in London) so too did the income subsequently earned from this source. U.K. exports also benefited, at least in the short term, because much of the money raised by foreigners in London was used to buy British capital goods.

It also seems (judging from later statistics and a very tentative estimate of the effect of the First World War) that the United Kingdom's short-term financial position was very strong before 1914. Certainly, because of the strength of the current account position and the central role played by sterling in the international monetary system, pressure on sterling (fixed, on the gold standard, in its parity with other leading currencies) was occasional and rarely serious.

1919–25

Because of the lack of statistics, it was – and is – impossible to gauge accurately the impact of the First World War on the United Kingdom's external position but it must have been considerable.[1] Trade was severely disrupted;

[1] D. E. Moggridge, *British Monetary Policy 1924–1931*.

and many overseas investments were either liquidated to meet the foreign exchange costs of the war or were in default. There was also a serious deterioration, of perhaps £m250–300, in the United Kingdom's net short-term financial position.[1] General confidence was greatly weakened and the war also left the difficult question of war debts and reparations to be settled. This uncertainty was reflected in an increase in the volatility of private capital after 1918, a development which affected sterling not only because it was so widely held, but also because it was no longer the currency automatically sought in times of crisis.

When, therefore, the B.O.T. published their first current account figures (see Table A) it was not surprising that their estimate for the surplus in real terms in 1920 was down on that shown for 1913.[2] In nominal terms, the surplus was thought to have risen slightly but between 1913 and 1920 the general price level had increased sharply; the figures for 1920 were in any case bolstered by a number of temporarily favourable factors (notably, heavy world demand for U.K. shipping services). The effects of the war and its aftermath on sterling were even more evident; by early 1920 the pound sterling had fallen to about $3.30, nearly one-third below its pre-war parity with the U.S. dollar of just over $4.86.

The few available balance-of-payments figures suggested that a surplus was being earned on current account and encouraged the hope of a recovery in the sterling exchange rate. But capital outflows, mainly caused by foreign pressure to raise loans in the United Kingdom, were a frequent source of concern to the authorities, who sought to restrict access to the London market.[3] Substantial amounts were raised by foreigners in this period (see Table B, line 1), largely offsetting the surplus earned on current account. The reserves rose only slowly and it was not until 1925 that sterling regained its pre-war exchange rate with the U.S. dollar.

The rough and ready nature of these early statistics cannot be too strongly emphasised, as can be seen from the detail in Part 2 of this section. Aware of these inaccuracies, the B.O.T. endeavoured to err on the side of caution in their estimates; and indeed, through the 1920s, the view that the current account surplus was being understated was widely held. As late as 1931, the argument is found in the Macmillan Committee's Report.[4] However, evidence from the late 1920s and early 1930s casts doubt on whether this was in fact so; it certainly seems likely that, particularly in the second half

[1] E. V. Morgan, *Studies in British Financial Policy, 1914–25*, pp. 303–67.

[2] 'Shipping Earnings and the Balance of Trade', *Board of Trade Journal*, 3 February 1921, pp. 115–17. Previous articles, the earliest being in the *Board of Trade Journal* for 12 August 1920, had covered one or two items in the invisibles account. Not until 29 March 1923 was a set of current account figures published; very tentative estimates for 1920 and 1922 were then given, with even less firmly based figures for 1907, 1910 and 1913. The basis for this material is discussed below.

[3] Sir Henry Clay, *Lord Norman*, Chapters IV and VI.

[4] *Report of the Committee on Finance and Industry* (Macmillan Committee), Cmd. 3897, June 1931, para. 263.

of the 1920s, the income from investment overseas – the main source of invisible earnings – was, at that time, being overestimated.

1925–31

The trade figures apart, the few balance-of-payments statistics available received virtually no consideration in the deliberations preceding the return to the gold standard in 1925, as recent research has shown.[1] Indeed, in contemporary discussion, the external position was mentioned in only the vaguest of terms. To most people the benefits of a fixed parity seemed obvious and a rate against the U.S. dollar other than that of 1913 unacceptable. If this left sterling overvalued, then the classical remedy under the gold standard – enforced deflation at home, inflation abroad – would induce the necessary readjustment of prices and costs.

But unemployment was already so high that, when it came to the point, the authorities could not willingly contemplate further deflation and, as the 1926 General Strike demonstrated, it was difficult to achieve a reduction in money wages. Therefore, although the United Kingdom remained on the gold standard until 1931, the maintenance of external balance was an unrelenting problem, impinging upon domestic policies. The relative weakness of the reserves during much of this period, for example, made sterling particularly vulnerable to outflows of capital. As a result, interest rates in this country were kept above those in the United States for long periods, to discourage outflows of funds and to make London less attractive than New York for foreign borrowers.

The current account figures published for these years made fairly encouraging reading, with a recovery from near balance in 1926 to a moderate surplus averaging about £m120 a year between 1927 and 1929. As noted earlier, however, these estimates overstated the surplus being earned; in any case, most of it was being absorbed (see Table B, lines 1 and 2) as before by foreign loans. In 1929, despite an apparently healthy current account surplus of over £m100, the combination of a number of influences (including a boom on Wall Street and the Hatry crisis at home) caused a run on sterling almost sufficient to drive the United Kingdom off gold.[2]

Rather more is known about the external position after 1925 because the quality and range of the statistics available gradually improved – though the extent of the improvement should not be overestimated. A number of changes were instigated by the Trade Figures Committee, set up in 1925.[3] The value of some of the items on the invisibles account (for example 'net short interest and commissions' – see Part 2.5) was examined for the first

[1] Moggridge, *British Monetary Policy*.

[2] Clay, *Lord Norman*.

[3] The committee consisted of Lord Bradbury, S. J. Chapman, R. H. Brand, W. T. Layton and Sir Otto Niemeyer. Its terms of reference were 'to report on the existing estimates of the annual balance of payments, with particular reference to the power of this country to make overseas investments'. The Report is dated 28 April 1926: it is unpublished but may be found in the Public Record Office (P.R.O. T.160/244/F9390).

time in some detail. The committee's Report in April 1926 clearly shows, however, that although the principles of balance-of-payments accounting were fully understood, the statistics were still very limited in practice. As Keynes complained in 1927, invisibles remained so in the literal sense.[1]

From 1928, new light was thrown on a number of aspects of U.K. investments overseas, first by annual private surveys by Sir Robert Kindersley and later by *The Economist* (see Part 2.4).[2] Kindersley's early results seem to have been misleadingly optimistic. Similarly, when the Macmillan Committee made the first attempt, during the period 1930–31, to collect figures for short-term financial assets and liabilities, the estimates derived were markedly at variance with later evidence.

Events quickly demonstrated, moreover, that these estimates were incorrect – a year later Keynes put the net liability at about £m500 – and within a few months of the committee's Report a number of complex considerations forced the United Kingdom off the gold standard.[3] A major liquidity crisis in Central Europe had a serious effect on the U.K. financial position, the impact of which was compounded by the emergence of a sizeable deficit on current account (a result of the rapidly deepening world recession). Confidence, already frail, was further jolted by the publication of several government reports which were interpreted abroad as emphasising the weakness of the economy.[4] The repatriation of French sterling balances had been a persistent worry to the authorities for some time and to this was now added an increasingly large outflow of other foreign funds. Between July and September, the authorities used some £m200 of gold and foreign credits to support the sterling exchange rate; but the outflow continued and the United Kingdom was forced off the gold standard in September.

There is no doubt that the extent of the flight from sterling took the authorities by surprise. But, at the time, only the Macmillan Committee's estimates offered an indication of how serious the crisis might turn out to be. Indeed, the general state of ignorance is well evidenced by an internal memorandum produced in the Bank's Statistical Section in September 1931:

> We estimate an adverse balance on Income [i.e. current] account for the year 1931 of £70 to 80 millions in Gold values...
>
> In view of the enormous Capital movements taking place this year, an estimate based purely on Income items may, at first sight, seem of little use. Efforts are being made to estimate the more important *Capital* movements but information is not at present sufficiently up to date to justify even the broadest hint at a figure.

[1] J. M. Keynes, 'The British Balance of Trade, 1925–27', *Econ. Jnl*, Vol. XXXVII (Dec. 1927), pp. 551–65.

[2] Sir Robert Kindersley, 'A New Study of British Foreign Investments', *Econ. Jnl*, Vol. XXXIX (March 1929), pp. 8–24. See also subsequent annual articles up to 1939: 'New Light on Savings – Sir R. Kindersley's Calculations', *Times*, 9 May 1928, p. 22; 'British Capital Abroad – III', *Economist*, 1 Nov. 1930, pp. 799–801.

[3] J. M. Keynes, 'Reflections on the Sterling Exchange', *Lloyds Bank Review*, April 1932, pp. 143–59.

[4] Reports by the Macmillan Committee, the May Committee on National Expenditure (Cmd. 3920), and the Royal Commission on Unemployment Insurance (Cmd. 3872).

1932–38

The Macmillan Committee made a number of recommendations on the improvement of the available balance-of-payments statistics. Of those taken up, the suggestion that a regular and comprehensive review should be made of the short-term financial position was the most significant. The Bank started collecting these figures from the end of 1931 and although initially accuracy was probably not high, the series proved a welcome aid in policy making.

There were few subsequent improvements in balance-of-payments statistics between 1932 and 1939. This was not because the current account position improved dramatically. Indeed it appears to have remained in deficit, 1935 apart, with invisible earnings suffering, in particular (see Section 2, Part 2). Nevertheless, the freedom given by a flexible exchange rate reduced the impact of external conditions on domestic policy and, therefore, concern with the balance-of-payments position. Capital inflows in various forms relieved the pressure on sterling which the current account deficit would otherwise have caused.

Summary

The main conclusion to emerge from the material presented above and in Part 2 is fairly clear. Although considerable improvements were effected over time, the collection of balance-of-payments statistics in the inter-war period could never be described as 'adequate', in the sense we would use that term today.

Even if the current account statistics for the period are accepted as having been roughly correct, the gaps in information about capital movements left a very unbalanced picture. This point is demonstrated in Chart 1. Up to 1930, the current account seems generally to have been in surplus, and yet the maintenance of external equilibrium was an almost constant problem, which impinged on domestic policies. From 1932 onwards, however, although the current account was apparently in slight deficit, it became markedly less difficult to maintain external balance.

SECTION 1, PART 2: CONTEMPORARY SOURCES AND METHODS

The description of each component of the balance of payments is divided into two:

A lists the items covered.

B discusses the method and accuracy of estimation.

It should be stressed that the following definitions relate solely to items as they were then known. Any changes made to these to conform to current usage or in the light of later, more complete, knowledge are not given until Section 2 below.

1 *The visible trade balance (excluding gold)*[1]

A Imports c.i.f. (i.e. cost, insurance and freight).
Exports f.o.b. (i.e. free on board).

B In contrast with current practice imports were recorded c.i.f. rather than f.o.b. This resulted in the foreign exchange cost of imports being overstated – because part of the import value recorded was in fact the result of services provided by U.K. shipping and insurance. Conversely, the foreign exchange earnings of U.K. shipping and insurance were overstated in the current account estimates, because they included payments by U.K. importers.[2]

The current account as a whole was unaffected by this approach and, in other respects, the total estimates for visible trade were probably fairly accurate. Recording errors apart, there was no reason, until the late 1920s, for goods to be valued incorrectly. The existence from then on of widespread tariff barriers may have encouraged false recording, and so adversely affected the accuracy of the figures; but it is impossible to say how important this may have been.

2 *Net government payments and receipts*

A All current and capital items on government account including:[3]
Payment of war debts and receipt of reparations (both interest and capital).
Admiralty and War Office expenditure abroad.

B The size of this item was known with a fair degree of certainty throughout the period, but it was not shown separately until the Board of Trade's 1926 article.

3 *Net national shipping income*

A Gross earnings by U.K. shipping on all but purely domestic routes, minus U.K. payments to foreign shipping.

Bunkering and stores bought in the United Kingdom, and U.K. port dues paid for by foreign ships, less similar costs borne abroad by U.K. vessels.

[1] For the treatment of gold see Table A, note *f*.

[2] A further small difference between practice then and now is that imports and exports before 1939 were recorded at the time when it was estimated that payment was made; but they are now recorded at the time declaration is made for customs purposes. In Section 2 below, the trade figures are estimated according to current practices.

[3] Capital items would now be recorded as 'official long-term capital'.

B Early in 1921, the B.O.T. published two estimates (arrived at by independent methods) of net national shipping income in 1913 and 1920 (see p. 316 n. 2). The difference between the two figures for 1920 was some £m30 (a little under 10 per cent of the total involved) and an average of the two was included in the current account for that year.

Estimates for subsequent years were compiled by reference to changes over the previous year in freight rates and the volume of traffic. This procedure created the possibility of a cumulative error, and there was also the problem that the various freight-rate indices available did not always move in the same way. However, periodic checks were carried out to ensure that the figures were 'of the right order of magnitude'. One such survey was made by the B.O.T. for its evidence to the Trade Figures Committee in 1926. Independent surveys were also carried out in 1931 and 1936 by the Chamber of Shipping and the Liverpool Steam Ship Owners' Association.[1]

The Bank also calculated the net value of this item – independently of the B.O.T. It is not clear when this separate calculation began; but in a brief prepared in September 1931 by the Bank's Statistical Section, a comparison was made for 1924–30 between the Bank and the B.O.T. series, which broadly agreed over that period. This, in conjunction with the surveys noted above, suggests that contemporary B.O.T. estimates for this item of the current account can be accepted with some degree of confidence.

4 *Net income from overseas investment*

A Interest and dividends due to U.K. holders of investments overseas, minus similar receipts by non-residents on their holdings in this country.

That part of the undistributed profits of British companies operating overseas which was transferred (into sterling) to boost company reserves in the United Kingdom, minus similar profits made by foreign companies operating in this country.[2]

Government receipts and payments, both capital and current, before this item was shown separately.

B In every year except 1920 in the period under consideration, income from investment overseas provided the largest net credit to the current account. The method of estimating this very important item, however, left much to be desired, especially before 1930. The freedom allowed to the movement of capital before 1914 and during the inter-war period meant that, in the absence of voluntary surveys, no obvious machinery existed through which the information required could be obtained.

[1] This was the first example of an industry establishing a regular survey of overseas receipts and payments, at the request of the B.O.T.

[2] The rest of the undistributed profits was effectively ignored; had full capital account estimates been published, they would have been included as capital receipts subsequently reinvested. Present balance-of-payments practice is to regard all profits as income (i.e. a current account receipt) and ploughed-back profits, as before, as capital reinvestment.

Until 1928, the B.O.T. had very little source material from which to derive annual estimates. Sir George Paish had published some limited research, in 1909 and 1911, on the total value of and income from investments abroad.[1] But, as the Trade Figures Committee noted in 1926, his work 'was by no means free from many elements of doubt'; there was the additional problem of revising it to take account of items such as the capital movements which occurred during the First World War. Tax returns provided some help in updating Paish's work; but these returns inevitably covered the recent past rather than the present and were based on a definition of income for tax, rather than national accounting, purposes.

Despite these known inadequacies and the fact that until the 1926 Trade Figures Committee's Report there appears to have been no real attempt to estimate the debits in this category, the B.O.T. and outside observers throughout the 1920s regarded the figures entered in the current account for this item as being a conservative statement of the true surplus. The evidence available to the Trade Figures Committee supported this view and a subsequent enquiry by Sir Robert Kindersley, in 1928, gave further weight to the argument (see p. 318 n. 2).

Kindersley's contribution was based on a private survey which estimated the gross income from British-owned capital invested abroad excluding:

(1) shareholdings in financial trusts investing money abroad;[2]
(2) certain private receipts; *inter alia* those of private U.K. companies operating abroad and those from holdings of real estate etc.;
(3) receipts from holdings by U.K. residents of securities of foreign companies and governments not officially dealt in on U.K. markets; and
(4) some U.K. companies who operated both at home and abroad.

Largely because of problems of identification, therefore, Kindersley's survey did not count a considerable amount of the income from overseas investment. Even so, his preliminary figures for the gross income (which he put at nearly £m300) slightly exceeded the Board of Trade's estimate for net income in the same period. Because it was felt that the credits which Kindersley had not counted at least equalled the gross debits on this item, the official estimates for each year from 1926 onwards were raised by £m15 in the 1929 *Journal* article. The justification for this change appeared even stronger during the course of 1929, because Kindersley's detailed estimates for 1926–7 supported his preliminary results: and the 1930 B.O.T. article included a further upward revision of £m20 a year.

However, *The Economist* conducted its own private survey, for 1928, of

[1] Sir George Paish, 'Great Britain's Capital Investments in Other Lands', *Journal of the Royal Statistical Society*, Vol. LXXII (Sept. 1909), pp. 465–80; see also 'Great Britain's Capital Investments in Individual Colonial and Foreign Countries: With Discussion', *Journal of the Royal Statistical Society*, Vol. LXXIV (Jan. 1911), pp. 167–87.

[2] This was done to avoid 'double-counting'.

Table D

Source of income	*Economist*'s estimate for 1928 (published November 1930) (£ million)	Kindersley's estimate for 1929 (published September 1931) (£ million)
1 U.K. holdings of foreign and colonial governments' and local corporations' stocks	61.7 (figure provided by Kindersley)	64.7
2 Interest and dividends from U.K. holdings of shares in companies registered in this country but operating wholly abroad	65.3	86
3 Interest and dividends from U.K. holdings of foreign and colonial companies' stocks and shares	56.7	61.7
4 Income from other private assets (including real estate)[a]	At most 70	Not estimated
5 Undistributed profits in sterling of U.K. companies operating abroad, head office expenses etc.[b]	Not estimated	Not estimated
Total of gross income from overseas investments	At most 254	212 plus at least 19 for unidentified credits

[a] *The Economist* put the capital in this category at £m700 and the rate of return at 10% at the most. In judging whether such a high figure could have been achieved, it may be noted that the rate of return on capital from sources 2 and 3 in Kindersley's study of 1929 was only 7.3%. Kindersley's later surveys provided very tentative estimates for this category in the mid 1930s (but, by this time, the amount of capital involved had probably been greatly reduced); these suggested an income then varying between £m15 and £m25 a year.

[b] The only part of this item which was measured at all before 1939 – head office expenses in the United Kingdom – was put by Kindersley at £m6 in 1938.

the United Kingdom's overseas investments, which suggested a rather more pessimistic estimate of the resulting income than Kindersley's (see Table D and p. 318 n. 2). The latter's next survey (published in September 1931 and relating to 1929) was also more pessimistic, identifying a gross income of only £m212. To this Kindersley felt at least £m19 could safely be added for unidentified credits; but even so, this total was some £m60–70 below his figure for 1927. There was no evidence to suggest that world trading and investment conditions had worsened markedly between 1927 and 1929 and the implication, given the *Economist*'s independent survey, was that his initial estimate for 1926–7 had been too high.

It is not possible to compare the *Economist* and Kindersley surveys for the same year but Table D gives an idea, for two years where conditions overseas were roughly comparable, of which credits were being measured, which guessed and which left unquantified.

The B.O.T. reacted cautiously and perhaps inadequately to this additional

Table E. *Official and private estimates for income from investment overseas in the years 1928–9 (£ million)*

Estimate by	Estimate for:[a] 1928	1929
Board of Trade: net income	285 (Feb. 1929)	285 (Mar. 1930)
	285 (Mar. 1930)	270 (Feb. 1931)
	270 (Feb. 1931)[b]	250 (Feb. 1932)
Economist: identified credits only	At most 254 (Oct. 1930)	N.A.
Kindersley: identified credits only	N.A.	At least 231 (Sept. 1931)

N.A. = not available.

[a] The date of publication is shown in brackets.

[b] This estimate was published in the *Board of Trade Journal*, and in later issues of the *Statistical Abstract* it was brought down to £250 million (Board of Trade, *Statistical Abstract for the United Kingdom 1924 to 1938*, Cmd. 6232, July 1940, p. 434; see also earlier annual publications in this series).

information. What revisions were made had not been completed before the 1931 crisis (see Table E).

An additional feature of the work by Kindersley and *The Economist*, which largely escaped notice at the time, was the indication it gave of how the timing, or indeed the size, of the cash inflow of income across the exchanges may have varied from the current account entries, even assuming these entries to have been correct. The Board of Trade's normal practice, then as now, was to record income when it was earned. But, of course, because of what we would now know as 'leading and lagging' there was a good deal of freedom as to when (or whether) the income was brought into the United Kingdom.

Though this was true for all the components of the current account, the detail of the private surveys on overseas investment made it possible to estimate roughly the importance of 'leading and lagging' for this one item. All the income from source 1 and and almost all from source 2 in Table D was apparently payable only in the United Kingdom. For the rest, greater freedom of movement was possible. Some of the income may have been reinvested in the country of origin; while payment of income from source 3 was often possible in any one of a number of financial centres. This last fact made it possible for some U.K. residents to receive dividends and maintain balances in Paris or New York. The sums liable to 'leading and lagging' on this one item may, therefore, have been considerable. For example, only about £m150 can be taken from Kindersley's figures for 1929 as definitely payable solely in London, out of an identified total of £m212.

After the downward revisions made by the B.O.T. between 1930 and 1932, little additional information became available. Kindersley's annual surveys continued and, as these developed, a couple of new credit items were tentatively estimated for the first time (see notes *a* and *b* of Table D). By comparison with the 1920s, the coverage of this category was now fairly extensive. As the Bank's Statistical Section commented in 1936, 'The figures published by the Board of Trade are therefore subject to a margin of error, but the year to year movement is probably fairly reliable.'

5 *Net short interest and commissions*

A Commission on acceptance credits, brokerage and merchanting transactions
Discount on foreign bills
Short interest (i.e. interest on banks' short-term deposits and liabilities)
Commissions, stamp duty and expenses on new issues paid by overseas borrowers
Insurance remittances from abroad
Earnings on exchange transactions

B In 1903, Sir Robert Giffen valued the commissions earned by bankers, brokers etc. at £m20 a year after making a number of crude assumptions.[1] Using this as a starting point, for want of a better, the B.O.T. put the net figure for this item in 1920 at £m40 on the argument that, 'although some business had been lost during the war, what remained was transacted on a higher level of prices'. Earnings for subsequent years were estimated by judging how much better/worse business had been than in the previous year – an approach which, of course, created the possibility of a cumulative error.

The Trade Figures Committee's own estimate in 1926 was rather more closely reasoned and £m60 was suggested as 'a more probable minimum'. The Board of Trade's figure for 1925 was therefore raised from £m40 to £m60 and entries for the years up to 1930 remained of this order.

However, an internal Bank memorandum of September 1931, using figuring independent of the B.O.T. methods, suggested that the net credit was being overstated, a comment which by then may well have been valid for some time. Late in 1934 this opinion was repeated more strongly (the overstatement being put at £m15 a year) and a committee was tentatively suggested to review the problem. It is not clear if anything came of this suggestion but the published estimates for this item were certainly not lowered. (But see Section 2 below.)

[1] Sir Robert Giffen, 'The Present Economic Conditions and Outlook for the United Kingdom', *Economic Inquiries and Studies*, Vol. II (1904), pp. 405–30.

6 *Net miscellaneous receipts*

A Tourism
Sales and purchases of second-hand ships
Film royalties
Remittances by emigrants and migrants
Other (miscellaneous)

B The Trade Figures Committee saw no reason to disagree with the sum of the entries made by the B.O.T. for these items; but the entries were described in 1932 by a retired B.O.T. official as purely conventional. Only for second-hand shipping and tourism (after 1932–3) was any serious attempt made to estimate accurately the sums involved. More typically, the figure for emigrants' remittances, at least in the early B.O.T. articles, was based on a survey carried out (apparently) in the late 1870s.

As with 'short interest and commissions' the Bank took the view during the 1930s that the small net credit of £m10–15 a year traditionally ascribed to this item was an optimistic interpretation of the few statistics available.

7 *New overseas issues in the London market*

A The total of new issues made by foreigners in the London market net of sinking fund payments on, and repayments of, outstanding issues.

B Through the period, several non-official series of the total of new loans being raised were compiled. The most widely used of these was produced by the Midland Bank which covered all new loans except those for the purpose of converting or refunding existing issues.[1] From 1927 a rather more useful set of figures was compiled by Kindersley from the same source as his estimates for income from investments overseas. He adjusted the Midland series to make allowance for subscriptions to new loans by non-U.K. residents (see Table B, note *c*). By also including conversion and refunding issues and estimating (as an offsetting capital credit which had not previously been estimated) sinking funds on and repayments of existing loans, Kindersley's figures gave a much closer idea of the true balance-of-payments cost of these loans.

The Macmillan Committee recommended that the figures collected by Kindersley should 'be regularly and precisely ascertained from the banks and issuing houses concerned [and that] the net proceeds to the borrower of new foreign issues currently made in London should be supplied in every case by the issuing houses'.[2] However, this recommendation was not followed up and it is therefore impossible to gauge the scope or accuracy of Kindersley's statistics.

[1] From March 1928 onwards, the Bank published its own series in the *Summary of Statistics* but, although rather more comprehensive, the series seems to have been little used.

[2] Para. 417.

8 *Change in other long-term private investment abroad*

A Changes in the value of U.K. investment overseas other than that covered in 7.

B Kindersley's surveys from 1930 on also provided a very tentative estimate for annual changes in the nominal value of capital involved in this item. The assets covered were a heterogeneous collection, ranging, for example, from security investments on Wall Street (for which, after 1935, there were at least some official American estimates) to purchases of real estate in the Empire.

Kindersley's figures do not appear to have been used in official commentaries on the external position but they have been included in contemporary and subsequent private studies.[1]

9 *Net external short-term liabilities*

A U.K. external short-term liabilities and assets.

B Despite the intermittent and often heavy pressure upon sterling after the First World War, no statistics for this very important and volatile item were collected until the Macmillan Committee's investigation. The resulting figures, compiled by the Bank and published in Appendix I of the committee's Report in June 1931, were taken from returns made by selected offices of the London clearing and the Scottish banks, and from a number of other banks and accepting houses.

10 *The reserves*

A Changes in official holdings of gold and foreign currencies and of assistance given by and extended to this country.

B Very little was published on this item in the period up to 1939 although, of course, the details were available to the authorities. The weekly Bank Returns showed the Issue and Banking Departments' holdings of gold. But, as no information on the Bank's foreign currency reserves or on what we would now call official assistance[2] was published to supplement them, they were of limited value to the public.[3]

[1] The Royal Institute of International Affairs: a report by a study group of members, 'The Problem of International Investment' (for example).

[2] The opening of lines of assistance was sometimes publicised – e.g. the £m130 advanced by Paris and New York in 1931. However, the actual use made of such credits (and of assistance given by the Bank) was not made public.

[3] There was also a valuation problem which is discussed in note *h* to Table B.

SECTION 2, PART I

The contemporary figures discussed above have been revised in the light of later information. Dr Feinstein's research[1] was especially valuable in this respect (particularly for the current account), and the opportunity was also taken to incorporate several additional items. These 'best estimates' for the balance of payments as a whole are given in Table C, and everything that follows in Section 2 should be read with reference to that table.

Current account

For items in the current account Feinstein's estimates have been accepted virtually unchanged. Within visible trade, imports are thus shown f.o.b., and other adjustments have been made to allow for the creation of the Irish Free State, for net exports of second-hand ships, and for imports of diamonds.[2] Gold movements have been excluded as properly belonging to the currency flow.

Invisible items have now been grouped in accordance with current practice. All are self-explanatory except for private services and transfers, which includes shipping, travel and financial items as well as migrants' transfers. To compensate for their use of c.i.f. import figures, the B.O.T. included a corresponding credit within shipping and insurance earnings. As the lower f.o.b. figures for imports have been used here, appropriate adjustments have been made to the B.O.T.'s estimates for earnings from shipping and 'net short interest and commissions'.[3] In the light of opinion within the Bank at the time that the credit for the latter item was overstated (see p. 325 above), Feinstein's figures for financial and other services have been lowered (somewhat arbitrarily) by £m20 a year between 1920 and 1930 and by £m10 a year thereafter. Estimates for film royalties paid abroad have been included within private services and transfers, and added back to interest, profits and dividends, where Feinstein had placed them.

Government services and transfers include only current items (military spending, economic grants etc.), whereas the B.O.T.'s estimates treated all government transactions as current.

Capital account

Official long-term capital here consists of net U.K. borrowing and lending abroad. Its main constituent is repayment to the United States of loans made during the First World War: such payments terminated in 1932. The

[1] C. H. Feinstein, *National Income, Expenditure and Output of the United Kingdom 1855–1965* (Cambridge: University Press, 1972), pp. 85–8 and 110–27.

[2] A very small change has been made in 1936: £m2 has been added to imports on account of new ships delivered in Germany and bought with money already abroad (*Board of Trade Journal*, 25 Feb. 1937, p. 260). A corresponding credit has been added to other long-term investment abroad.

[3] Which included insurance companies' earnings.

special assistance granted in 1931 by the United States and France has been excluded and allocated to a separate category within official financing.

Overseas investment was described fully above. The Kindersley series have several drawbacks; in particular, dealing in existing securities is covered only very approximately under changes in other long-term investment abroad. Another important omission is any measure of direct investment inwards or outwards. There are no good estimates of the resources transferred for such investment: all that exist are annual surveys for 1932 to 1938 which show the number of 'factories established by, or with the assistance of, foreign concerns'.[1] These show that 1932 was the peak year for foreign direct investment in this country, over 20 per cent of all new factories being foreign-backed. This proportion fell to under 10 per cent in each succeeding year, but, once established, a good many factories were presumably enlarged, and there are no details on the importance of this. Nor is there any comparable information on the value of U.K. direct investment abroad.

The first figures for U.K. short-term assets and liabilities to be anything more than informed guesses were given in 1931 by the Macmillan Report, and covered the period from the end of June 1927 to the end of March 1931. They were, however, incomplete, as they excluded from liabilities the sterling bills held by London-based foreign banks, and from assets U.K. deposits held abroad. In the light of a recommendation contained in the Report, the Bank called for foreign funds returns from over 150 banks from the end of 1931 onwards. The information so gathered was combined with similar figures from the Crown Agents and overseas currency boards, and published in a White Paper in 1951.[2] The aggregate figures showed net liabilities of £m411 in December 1931, compared with Macmillan's figure for total liabilities of £m407 in March of the same year. As there were large withdrawals of funds from London in the intervening period, the Macmillan figures were cetainly too low. Williams, and Moggridge after him,[3] adjusted the figures judgmentally, using £m411 as a bench-mark. Their arguments seem plausible and their figures have been accepted.

The items that were covered by the post-Macmillan returns are given in Table F. The detail thereby available to the Bank enabled a much more comprehensive picture of the short-term position to be drawn, especially as details of currency deposits were now included (Macmillan figures had been purely sterling). A little light had thus been cast on Keynes's 'barbaric darkness',[4] though it remained confined to official quarters and did not extend to the public.

The White Paper omitted acceptances from its figures of net liabilities

[1] Board of Trade, *Survey of industrial development*, 1933–8.

[2] *Reserves and Liabilities 1931 to 1945*, Cmd. 8354, September 1951.

[3] David Williams, 'London and the 1931 Financial Crisis', *Economic History Review*, 2nd Series, April 1963, pp. 513–28. D. E. Moggridge, *British Monetary Policy*, pp. 118 and 252.

[4] J. M. Keynes, *Econ. Jnl*, December 1927, p. 565.

Table F. *Items covered in the post-Macmillan returns*

Liabilities	Assets
Foreign deposits in the United Kingdom	Deposits abroad
Advances and overdrafts from foreigners	Advances and overdrafts to foreigners
Treasury bills and other bills on U.K. residents held on foreigners' account	Bills held on foreigners, foreign governments and municipalities
Acceptances given abroad on U.K. account	Acceptances given on foreign account
British government stocks	Short-term funds employed abroad

in order to make the 1931–41 series as compatible as possible with the later series of liabilities. These are now shown separately in Table C.

Changes in holdings of British government stocks are also shown separately, as they are felt to be mostly longer-term liabilities than the remaining items reported by the banks (by definition 12 months or less). These figures for gilt-edged do not, of course, give a true representation of all movements in such securities, as they reflect only changes in holdings of stocks lodged with the banks. Holdings were also reported at nominal, and not market, values: this feature was common to other relevant items in the foreign funds returns.

The estimates for the currency flow represent the actual (as opposed to the nominal) value of changes in the country's gold and foreign exchange reserves. The main constituents of the reserves in the inter-war period were as follows:

1 gold held by the Issue Department throughout, and foreign currency (deposits and securities) held by the Department between 1928 and 1933;
2 foreign currency held by the Banking Department from 1925 onwards (although after 1933 the amount was very small and did not change); a very small gold holding has been ignored;
3 gold and foreign exchange held by the Exchange Equalisation Account from its inception in July 1932;
4 gold held until 1925 by the Currency Note Redemption Account; and
5 gold and foreign exchange held by the Treasury's Exchange Account until its assets were transferred to the E.E.A. in 1932; no details are available of changes in the years 1920–22 (any movements in these years being reflected in the balancing item), while holdings in 1928–31 have been partly estimated.

The figures given in Table C differ from Feinstein's[1] mainly because he did not include the Banking Department's currency holdings. In the present

[1] Feinstein, *National Income, Expenditure and Output*, pp. 88 and T79.

Table G. *Summary balance of payments (£ million: annual averages)*

	1920–29	1930–38
Visible balance	−205	−256
Invisible balance	+319	+216
Current balance	+114	− 40
Identified capital movements	−115	− 15
Balancing item[a]	+ 9	+ 87
Currency flow	+ 8	+ 32
Visible deficit as a percentage of G.N.P.	4.1	5.2
Current surplus or deficit as a percentage of G.N.P.	2.3	0.8

[a] Before 1928 this includes changes in short-term liabilities and acceptances.

estimates, monthly changes in the constituent parts have been converted at the average monthly gold, U.S. dollar, or French franc rates (where the figures are not already at market rates) to give a broad estimate of the cash flow in each month. Feinstein used the same method, though by quarters, and his approach has been adopted for the few components where monthly information is not available.

The United Kingdom was given special assistance from the United States and France in 1931, a facility nominally equivalent to £m130. Some of this was repaid in 1931, but most of it in the following year. As the Finance Accounts show, the equivalent of £m152 was in fact received and £m184 repaid – the 'loss' of £m32 representing changes in the exchange rate.

The balancing item is merely the amount necessary to make the identified current and capital items sum to the currency flow. It will inevitably reflect different errors and omissions at different periods, but the major omissions from the estimates (dealing in existing securities, and inward and outward direct investment) affect the balancing item throughout.

SECTION 2, PART 2: DEVELOPMENTS IN THE BALANCE OF PAYMENTS

During the two decades under review, the main components of the balance of payments changed in different ways, as summarised in Table G. First, the current balance moved progressively from surplus to deficit. In 1920 the trade deficit was comfortably covered by a large invisible surplus, ensuring a reasonable surplus on current account. By 1938, however, the position was very like the one today – a larger deficit on visible trade only partially offset by an invisible surplus, leaving the current account as a whole in deficit.

The terms of trade became increasingly favourable throughout the inter-war years; and, although, by the end of the period, the volume of exports was smaller than in 1920 and the volume of imports greater, the result was that the visible balance in cash terms did not worsen by very much. The surplus on invisibles, however, diminished. Receipts in the form of interest, profits and dividends declined in the early twenties because a large amount of British investment overseas had been liquidated to help meet the cost of the First World War. In the thirties, heavily curtailed overseas lending, larger payments for maturities and to sinking funds, and foreign default on British loans, once more reduced these forms of income. The world depression in the thirties also weakened shipping earnings, and cut fees and commissions earned by City institutions. These factors combined to change an annual average surplus on current account of well over £m100 during 1920–29 to a deficit of £m40 on average in the following nine years.

As the current balance worsened, so the capital account moved from an average outflow of over £m100 in the first period to one of under £m20 in the second. At the same time, the balancing item became much more strongly positive (the average inflow indicated for the period 1930–38 is, however, raised substantially by an exceptionally large figure in 1931). Before the First World War, the surplus on current account had financed large-scale long-term lending: the gradual erosion of this surplus meant that net inflows on capital account became necessary to prevent unacceptable loss of reserves or excessive depreciation of the currency. The reasons for the turn-round on capital account are not hard to find. A large amount of private capital seems to have been repatriated over this period, with demand even for investments on Wall Street – previously the most attractive market for foreign capital – subdued for several years after 1931. New overseas issues raised on the London market also fell off drastically in the second decade under the influence of various embargoes, while receipts by sinking funds and maturities of existing loans, raised in more favourable times, gathered momentum. In fact, in each year from 1935 to 1938 more money seems to have entered London in connection with foreign loans than left it, a most unusual development.

This reflux of capital was augmented by a large rise between 1932 and 1937 in short-term funds held in London on foreign account – a movement reflecting at various times both the surplus on the Empire's balance of payments and also the favourable covered interest rate differential between London and New York. Such short-term movements confirmed a trend already noted in the Macmillan Report[1] that 'London is now practising international deposit banking, as distinct from international acceptance business and the deposits associated with this, on a larger scale than before the War'. The attendant dangers continued to be a source of comment throughout the decade. It was perceived that, while a large proportion of U.K. holdings of foreign assets was illiquid, the increase in foreign deposits held in London – at any rate those of countries not in the Empire – was influenced primarily by short-term considerations and could be rapidly reversed.

[1] Para. 349.

Until 1930, the currency flow did not fluctuate by much from year to year. From 1932 onwards, however, fairly large inflows occurred in every year until 1938, enabling the authorities to accumulate gold and foreign exchange reserves. The crisis in 1931 had shown that the existing reserves were inadequate to support the exchange rate in the face of sustained pressure, especially when a proportion of overseas assets could not easily be mobilised. The subsequent acquisition of more reserves was thus a conscious aim, to be justified in 1938 when they were used extensively to ensure that the rate moved only slowly downwards (see Chart 2), without panic, despite the largest outflow of foreign funds since the country went off the gold standard.

SECTION 2, PART 3: QUALITY OF THE FIGURES

'All these heads are of such a nature as to make precise estimates of our receipts extremely difficult, and the amounts paid by us to foreigners for similar services are even more indeterminate.' Thus the B.O.T.[1] commenting specifically on the invisible item 'net short interest and commissions', but the remark could apply equally to many other parts of the complete balance-of-payments table. Despite the advantage of hindsight, the figures here assembled are really not much better than those available to contemporary observers – although, of course, they were never brought together in one place at the time.

Nevertheless, it is probably reasonable to assume that the trend of year-to-year movements given here is fairly accurate, though the absolute amounts may well be less so. Feinstein has given 'reliability grades' for several elements of the current account, some of which vary by up to 25 per cent on either side of his totals.[2] Capital account items are similarly uncertain. As already stated, the figures for long-term investment overseas and for short-term flows are imperfect in several ways. It is unfortunate that one of the Macmillan Report's main statistical recommendations – that brokers and banks should submit figures for deals done on behalf of U.K. residents on foreign stock exchanges and for foreign residents on U.K. exchanges[3] – was never taken any further, as it covered one of the largest omissions in the figures. Other omissions (perhaps larger than portfolio investment) are inward and outward direct investment and trade credit.

The balancing item is large in several years in relation to the net total of known capital flows. It partly reflects omissions and partly errors in the estimates, particularly in the invisible account; and, as today, a share also arises from leads and lags when making payments for goods.

[1] *Board of Trade Journal*, 27 January 1927, p. 93.
[2] Feinstein, *National Income, Expenditure and Output*, p. 115.
[3] Para. 417.

Figures for the currency flow can be considered good estimates despite the missing details of the Treasury's Exchange Account for certain years: the resources of this account were small, and movements in it would probably not have affected the totals significantly.

CONCLUSION

This appendix has sought to do two things. First, to set out the figures available to contemporary observers of the balance of payments and to comment briefly on their impact (if any) on official policy. Secondly, to assemble 'best estimates' for the balance of payments in the light of subsequent knowledge and to put them together in convenient format.

APPENDIX 33

THE BRANCHES

In the course of its history the Bank has opened seventeen Branches. Of these, fourteen were opened in the years 1826 to 1844, under the influence of government policy adopted in 1826 and outmoded after 1844. Of these fourteen, five were closed before 1873; there remained Manchester, Birmingham, Liverpool, Bristol, Leeds, Newcastle, Hull, Plymouth and Portsmouth, as well as the Western Branch, in London, opened in 1855 but sold in 1930. Also in London, in 1888 the Law Courts Branch was opened, to provide facilities for the Courts recently concentrated at the top of the Strand. Portsmouth was closed in 1914 and Hull in 1939. The last new Branch was opened in 1940, at Southampton; and for wartime purposes an Office was opened at Glasgow, but the Bank *of England* judged it politic not to characterise this as a Branch. The position at the end of the second war was thus that the Bank had eight Branches in England outside London and one in London and an Office in Glasgow. (For further detail, see the Bank's *Quarterly Bulletin*, December 1963.)

As recounted in the second section of Chapter 2 in Volume 1, the business of the Branches was in the 1890s enlivened by the Bank's need to add to its earnings. In the 1900s the Branches became less competitive in local banking business, and before the first war there was already a view in Threadneedle Street that actual withdrawal might be appropriate. It was against this background that the future of the Portsmouth Branch was reviewed. The Branch had been opened in 1834 primarily to facilitate payments at the Naval Yard, and it was always run at a loss. The naval business, though still large, could conveniently be handled from London, and in 1914 the Bank, having disposed of the premises and the goodwill of the local commercial business to the London Joint Stock Bank Ltd, closed the Branch on 30 April 1914. The shift in the Bank's general view of the business of Branches is also to be seen in a change in practice in appointing Agents (i.e. Branch Managers) and Sub-Agents. Until 1905 they were appointed from outside the Bank, and were required to be persons of considerable property, and commercial knowledge, with local experience. From 1906, however, appointments were made only from within the Bank, though it was many years before all concerned accepted the principle. Possibly the change is to be associated not only with the changing climate on the functions of the Branches but also with the reassertion, under Nairne, of the Chief Cashier's primacy in the official hierarchy of the Bank. Old-fashioned Directors continued to hanker after the old system which indeed did not expire until the retirement of the last of the old kind, in 1933.

During the first war the Bank was careful to maintain the services of its Branches, providing its customers with wartime financial facilities parallel to those available elsewhere. The attitude was not to initiate business, much less to solicit, but to respond when definite enquiries were made. After the war the position began to change, not abruptly but in the end radically. An instruction of 1 April 1920 seems to imply some regret that private accounts were being closed, but this may be regarded as a legacy of the Cokayne Governorship rather than of the Norman period which was just beginning. For under Norman the Bank quickly became self-conscious as a Central Bank and, though the Governor and his colleagues were too busy with other things to bother with minor logical untidiness, the Branches were henceforward always considered somewhat anomalous. Some value was still attached to their service as provincial nerve centres for the Bank. This feature was absent from one of the Branches very close to Threadneedle Street's eye: the Western Branch in Burlington Gardens, which did not even have the justification, in a large governmental business, that made the Law Courts Branch still useful. The Governor therefore determined to watch for his opportunity, and in 1930 the Western Branch was sold to the Royal Bank of Scotland, in the peculiar circumstances referred to in Chapter 10. In his evidence to the Macmillan Committee, Harvey dismissed the Branches in a couple of answers (to Questions 73 and 74) and they were not even mentioned in that committee's Report. The Bank, though not actually killing its commercial business, certainly did not strive officiously to keep alive, and the eight Branches scattered illogically over the English counties began to look more and more unattractive to the Directors who were called upon in regular turn to peregrinate them.

The remarks made in 1936 by one of those peregrinating Directors sparked off a major enquiry within the Bank on the usefulness of the Branches. The Deputy Governor (Catterns) defined the responsibilities of the Branches as threefold: the distribution and receipt of currency, clearing facilities for the banks, and the collection of Government revenue. He added that the number and geographical distribution of the Branches were entirely haphazard and emphasised the need for comprehensive review. The subject was then taken up with the clearing banks; the variations in their business routine, in contact with the Branches, showed that it would not be easy to settle lines of reform in the light of which the Bank might then plan the future of its Branch structure. However, the banks were at least agreed in an assurance to the Bank of the general usefulness of the facilities provided by the Branches, and attention then concentrated on one detail on which the Bank had to make up its mind urgently. This was the future of the Hull Branch, where the Bank's earnings were pitiably insufficient and rebuilding on a new site had become urgent. In effect abandoning any idea of radical reform, the Court on 21 October 1937 appointed another Special Committee, on arrangements 'consequent upon any resolution of the Court covering the retention or otherwise of the Hull Branch and the establishment of one or more new Branches'. The clearing banks had already acquiesced (by letter of 23 June 1937) in closure of the Hull Branch; the provisional view was confirmed, the Court decided on 14 April 1938 and the Branch was closed ten months later. Simultaneously with the Court's consideration of this closure, the Bank had been looking at the possibility of some new Branch: it was now thought that for reasons of public relations in the provinces the Bank should not reduce the total of its representation outside London and, reflecting the broad trend of regional development, the location should be in the south-east. Eventually the Bank fixed on Southampton, partly because through its port then passed the gold coming from South Africa and coming from or going to New York; the Bank had also an eye on the coming war. The site for the Southampton Branch was purchased on 12 May 1938; business opened on 29 April 1940. The brand-new building included a substantial vault for gold; a report twenty years later indicated that this was hardly ever used, and more generally that the superior facilities afforded were so little exercised that the Branch still hardly justified its existence.

The other important outcome of the 1937 discussions had to wait many years. The first of the Special Committees mentioned above recommended major rebuilding at Birmingham and Manchester urgently, and afterwards at Liverpool. These recommendations were the germ from which a major rebuilding programme grew in the 1960s. Meanwhile, in 1943 the Plymouth Branch was seriously damaged by bombing; when it became clear that a new building on a different site would be required, the Bank decided that the expense could not be justified, and the Branch was closed in 1949. This left the Bank with eight Branches in England and one Office in Scotland.

APPENDIX 34

THE REBUILDING OF THE BANK, 1925–41

The expansion of the Bank's functions in the first half of the twentieth century had to be matched by an enlargement of its premises, a need that could be met mainly by rebuilding on the historic Threadneedle Street site, hitherto mainly a single-storey building with vaults. The need became obvious during the first war, when the national debt broke out of its century-old limits. The Court accordingly on 16 November 1916 appointed a Committee on Building, consisting of the Governor (Cunliffe) and his Deputy, two ex-Governors, and three junior Directors: Norman, Lubbock and Tiarks. This committee recognised the exceptional nature of the architectural problem. The Bank had been well served by its own regular architects, a line unbroken since 1765, but the committee recommended that the conception of a new building on the old site should be thrown open to competition. This proposal was dropped, partly because of wartime circumstances but also on the advice of the President of R.I.B.A. (Newton). There the matter rested through the remainder of the war and the first months of peace; but the post of Architect to the Bank was allowed to lapse on the retirement of A. C. Bloomfield in 1919. On 13 May 1920, shortly after Norman became Governor, the Bank returned to the problem by appointing a Rebuilding Committee, of Lubbock, Booth and Anderson. The life of this committee ended only with the completion of the project twenty-one years later. Lubbock, the link with the earlier committee, was Chairman until 1923 when he was succeeded by Booth who held the Chair through the remaining eighteen years. George Macaulay Booth had been a Director since 1915; he had come as a young man from the shipping world, and had made a reputation as 'a man of push and go' in Lloyd George's munitions supply organisation. But he was also a man of taste, known in the world of the arts, and (he told the author) he made his Chairmanship of the Rebuilding Committee, while it lasted, the main work of his life and his special contribution to the life of the Bank. When it was all over, the architect who had seen it through with Booth spoke of his 'combination of quick insight and the understanding of complicated plans and practical problems, as well as sympathy for the artist and a genuine flair for the beautiful in art'.

First the committee sought to define the problem: Nairne (then Comptroller) estimated 3,860 as the number of staff to be accommodated. (Subsequent consideration took the committee into some overhaul of office methods, in the course of which Norman persuaded H.M. Treasury to allow typing of the government accounts and the use of loose-leaf books.) A building of several storeys covering the three acres was thought so generous that the committee entertained the idea of accommodating the Bankers' Clearing House within the building. Troup, the architect then working for the Bank on St Luke's, helped the committee to pinpoint the major planning questions. It was apparent that on this site, including an ancient burial ground, there were some awkward problems, but the biggest of all was the question whether the familiar outer screen wall, the work of Sir John Soane, should be preserved or demolished to make way for a completely new building. In 1921, at Lubbock's suggestion and with the Court's approval, the committee consulted Mr (later Sir) Herbert Baker on the major architectural questions. Baker was then working with Lutyens on the new Delhi, an association that eventually left its mark in some oddities about the interior of the new Bank. He had already behind him notable work in South Africa; there incidentally he had struck up a friendship with one of 'Milner's young men' (R. H. Brand) who was now established in the City and could therefore, Baker decided, guide him on the strength of City sentiment. Baker reported in favour of a plan 'which by the preservation and incorporation in the new building of the old external wall, of the banking halls behind it and of many other old rooms of Sir John Soane's building should go far to meet the reasonable conservative sentiment of the public and would enable your Court, while not ignoring its obligations as trustees of a precious national heirloom, to develop on its traditional site a new Bank which would be sufficiently large and efficiently planned to fulfil the new duties imposed upon it by the war; which, without any visible conflict of style, might record in its architecture...the Bank's historical periods of growth...and which might contain the elements of architectural dignity commensurate with the Bank's position and destiny in the City and the Empire'. The retention of the external walls would afford, he believed, prestige, seclusion and relief from noise; and the alternative of a free hand on a cleared site would only lead back to a similar design.

Having secured broad agreement from the Presidents of the R.I.B.A. and the Royal Academy, the Bank in 1922 published Baker's plans. A lively debate began in the Press on the merits of destroying or altering Soane's masterpiece. The Bank came under heavy fire from the Soane trustees; the City Corporation wanted to force the Bank into a withdrawal of a wall in order to widen Princes Street; and the Governor defended Baker's plan at both the General Courts in 1923. On the whole the verdict of the public was in favour of the Bank's proposals. This was sufficient to confirm the Bank in its own decided preference, and through 1923 and 1924 it felt able to go ahead with detailed development of Baker's plans. The City Corporation abandoned its attempt to widen Princes Street, but the argument on this did have an eventual result, in the reconstruction of 'the Tivoli corner' at the northern end of the Bank's Princes Street wall. The difficulty over the old churchyard within the Bank's site had been already disposed of: an Act of Parliament was necessary, and this had been obtained in July 1923. The bones thereafter disinterred proved to include, in addition to those in the graveyard of the former church of St Christopher-le-Stocks, a jumble of others probably from a plague pit. All were reinterred in vaults at Nunhead Cemetery; there they were disturbed once more, by a German bomb in 1940. The new statutory powers and the Bank's action thereunder gave the planners a free hand to use the whole site; the old churchyard was in fact eventually built over, though the present Garden Court, in a different position, in spirit continues the earlier open space.

The way was now, by the end of 1923, free for the implementation of the scheme. Baker had settled on a general plan for a building rising to seven storeys in its highest part, which was as high as it could go without seriously curtailing the lighting of the areas. Early in 1924 the Bank concluded agreements with a supervising architect, a sanitary engineer, a constructional engineer and a mechanical engineer. The decision was taken to rebuild the Bank in sectors, maintaining as much as possible of the Bank's work without removal to a different address. This decision led to the building of four separate structures, each one of which had to be completed before the next could be begun; the support of the standing portions of the Bank on the edge of a vast hole sixty feet deep gave the engineers major tasks. It was the intention at first to retain not only the Soane outer walls but also the Soane halls, but at this time the experts lost their confidence in the feasibility of preserving the halls. Facing reality, the Bank decided that the suitability of the building 'must not be jeopardised by an excess of piety for Soane's work', and eventually demolition and reconstruction of the halls was agreed. The retention of the outer walls proved difficult enough: in places the old construction was found to be flimsy, and the engineering problems of underpinning were considerable. The Bank maintained to the end its wish to preserve every feature of the old Bank for reincorporation in the new wherever possible, but compromises had to be made in order to secure at a reasonable cost a building that would efficiently serve the Bank's working purposes. When, later in 1924, Holloways Ltd were selected as builders, their contract required 'reasonable economy, excellence of workmanship and rapidity of execution'. The Bank discussed with Holloways and another firm actual quotations for the first section but, in recognition of the Bank's requirements and the nature of the task, the eventual contract for the entire project was on the basis of cost plus a fixed sum to cover overheads and profit.

At this early period the Bank envisaged a total cost of about £m5, with 1937 as the completion date. The £m5 included £200,000 to drain the Wallbrook, which was supposed to run under the Bank; the old course was found to be dry, and this was one element in reducing the estimate to £m4 in 1933, when the completion date was foreseen as 1940. By 1939, when little more had to be done, the estimate had risen to £m5.3 and the actual total was close to this. The principal increases in cost had been due to provision for mechanisation and for the greater proportion of women clerks.

The necessary approval from the Corporation of the City of London was received on 24 April 1924; the first section – the south-east – was evacuated, and handed over for demolition in February 1925; the actual rebuilding commenced on 6 April 1925. As the work proceeded on the successive sectors the various Offices had to be reshuffled and it was of course impossible to avoid some move to other buildings. The major temporary relief of space was secured by moving the Accountant's Department – the traditional and massive 'Stock Side' of the Bank – out to Finsbury Circus. This move, started in 1924, proved to mark the end of the Department's habitation of the Threadneedle Street site, for it stayed at Finsbury Circus until September 1939 when it was evacuated to Hampshire and, after the return to Finsbury Circus and the use of further temporary accommodation, its new permanent home was built at New Change near St Paul's (the move into New Change began in 1958).

One special task was provision for the safety of the bullion and securities, which were kept on the premises throughout the rebuilding. Even for temporary purposes constructional work of great strength was required and this work had subsequently to be demolished. This demolition and the final reconstruction both made a lot of noise, but the noise of other steel work was minimised by welding instead of riveting. (Welding had hitherto been used in shipbuilding but not in this country for a steel frame building of great size.) The building was provided with its own heating and lighting; also with its own water supply, drawn from nine wells most of which were sunk to a depth of eight hundred feet. A mechanical ventilation system had also to be built in: very important in a building which has more than half the 13m cubic feet of its space below the level of the street.

The Rebuilding Committee gave devoted attention to the finish and decoration of the interiors. They decided on the use of Hopton Wood stone from Derbyshire, of English oak for panelling and of Cuban mahogany for doors. They engaged the services of Charles (later Sir Charles) Wheeler, Boris Anrep and Joseph Armitage. Wheeler's work included the bronze doors, the statuary on the porches, portrait heads on corner stones, innumerable plaques over doorways, and the flying figure over the Tivoli corner. Anrep, whom Booth had come to know through the chances of wartime contacts, was responsible for the mosaic floors of the main corridors, a distinctive feature of the Bank's interior. Armitage was the chief plaster craftsman; his outstanding undertaking was the ceiling of the new Court Room. The Bank also decided to ask painters, 'preferably of the younger school, to paint portraits for the new Bank as an historical record of those who occupied representative positions in the Bank at the time of the rebuilding'. A scheme was prepared by Sir David Cameron and seven artists were engaged. Of these seven two later became Presidents of the Royal Academy, but the paintings sadly did not, in the opinion of the next generation, make an appropriate contribution to the decoration of the new Bank. Governor Norman was of course included in these portrait groups, but he was more interestingly portrayed by Anrep in a floor mosaic. This is at a corridor junction near the Princes Street entrance; it shows Norman as the two-headed god Janus, looking both backward and forward, and it is said that its subject did not approve.

In March 1940 the Rebuilding Committee considered whether the work should be stopped but, chiefly because more accommodation seemed likely to be needed and because labour and materials were still available, the decision was to press on. Eleven months later the committee brought its own work to an end. Actual building operations continued until mid-1942, when the structure was complete. A part of its east side, however, remained as a shell until after the war. Thus was brought to completion the biggest building project on which the Bank had ever embarked. Substantially the result accorded with the grand design evolved by George Booth and his colleagues more than twenty years earlier, though they had had to accept the impossibility of housing on these three acres the entire headquarters staff of the central bank.

APPENDIX 35

THE BANK'S PROFIT POSITION, 1890–1939

PROFITS AND RESERVES

The profits are shown after payment of tax but before payment of dividends and before any allowance for writing down securities. For years to 1929 profits of the Issue Department are included; thereafter they were paid to the Treasury. For *profits*, amounts are for the year ending 28/9 February in the year shown; for *reserves*, amount shown refers to 28/9 February.

(All amounts in £000)

	Profits	Reserves		Profits	Reserves
1890	1,495	3,130	1915	3,777	3,826
1891	1,488	3,308	1916	7,782	5,945
1892	1,469	3,338	1917	7,098	9,709
1893	1,376	3,342	1918	7,460	13,653
1894	1,440	3,410	1919	5,495	15,290
1895	1,375	3,485	1920	4,728	12,849
1896	1,160	3,233	1921	9,171	18,117
1897	1,339	3,348	1922	7,455	19,294
1898	1,370	3,302	1923	5,380	19,989
1899	1,477	3,433	1924	6,133	23,549
1900	1,583	3,609	1925	6,601	25,291
1901	1,678	3,838	1926	6,802	29,133
1902	1,660	3,932	1927	6,300	31,478
1903	1,592	3,737	1928	5,031	40,489
1904	1,624	3,576	1929	3,875	43,173
1905	1,540	3,820	1930	5,135	42,198
1906	1,639	4,118	1931	3,265	42,310
1907	1,944	4,121	1932	3,712	39,050
1908	2,060	3,301	1933	3,348	38,826
1909	1,684	3,487	1934	3,661	40,043
1910	1,632	3,976	1935	2,522	41,527
1911	1,808	3,875	1936	2,664	41,084
1912	1,781	3,719	1937	4,293	41,365
1913	2,065	3,522	1938	2,175	41,147
1914	2,079	3,518	1939	2,134	40,427

AMOUNTS WRITTEN OFF SECURITIES BETWEEN 1900 AND 1914 (IN £000, FOR YEARS ENDING 28/29 FEBRUARY)

1900 to 1905	nil	1909	188
		1910	144
		1911	471
1906	149	1912	631
1907	663	1913	957
1908	1,569	1914	750

APPENDIX 36

BANK RATE CHANGES, 1890–1939

	%	Page ref.
1889		
30 Dec.[a]	6	
1890		
20 Feb.	5	
6 Mar.	4½	
13 Mar.	4	
10 Apr.	3½	
17 Apr.	3	
26 June	4	
31 July	5	
21 Aug.	4	
25 Sept.	5	
7 Nov.[a]	6	
4 Dec.	5	
1891		
8 Jan.	4	
22 Jan.	3½	
29 Jan.	3	
16 Apr.	3½	
7 May	4	
14 May	5	
4 June	4	
18 June	3	
2 July	2½	
24 Sept.	3	
29 Oct.	4	
10 Dec.	3½	
1892		
21 Jan.	3	
7 Apr.	2½	
28 Apr.	2	
20 Oct.	3	
1893		
26 Jan.	2½	
4 May	3	
11 May	3½	
1893		
18 May	4	
8 June	3	
15 June	2½	
3 Aug.	3	
10 Aug.	4	
24 Aug.	5	
14 Sept.	4	
21 Sept.	3½	
5 Oct.	3	
1894		
1 Feb.	2½	
22 Feb.	2	
1895 No change		
1896		
10 Sept.	2½	51
24 Sept.	3	31n
22 Oct.	4	
1897		
21 Jan.	3½	
4 Feb.	3	
8 Apr.	2½	
13 May	2	
23 Sept.	2½	
14 Oct.	3	
1898		
7 Apr.	4	51
26 May	3½	
2 June	3	
30 June	2½	
22 Sept.	3	
13 Oct.	4	
1899		
19 Jan.	3½	
2 Feb.	3	
13 July	3½	

[a] Alteration made by the Governor and later approved by the Court.

	%	Page ref.
1899		
3 Oct.[a]	4½	
5 Oct.	5	
30 Nov.	6	51, 55
1900		
11 Jan.	5	
18 Jan.	4½	
25 Jan.	4	
24 May	3½	
14 June	3	
19 July	4	
1901		
3 Jan.	5	
7 Feb.	4½	
21 Feb.	4	
6 June	3½	
13 June	3	
31 Oct.	4	
1902		
23 Jan.	3½	
6 Feb.	3	
2 Oct.	4	
1903		
21 May	3½	
18 June	3	
3 Sept.	4	
1904		
14 Apr.	3½	
21 Apr.	3	
1905		
9 Mar.	2½	
7 Sept.	3	
28 Sept.	4	
1906		
5 Apr.	3½	
3 May	4	54
21 June	3½	55
13 Sept.	4	55
11 Oct.	5	55
19 Oct.[a]	6	55
1907		
17 Jan.	5	56
11 Apr.	4½	56
25 Apr.	4	56
15 Aug.	4½	57–8

[a] Alteration made by the Governor and later approved by the Court.

	%	Page ref.
1907		
31 Oct.	5½	58
4 Nov.[a]	6	53, 58
7 Nov.	7	43, 52–3, 58
1908		
2 Jan.	6	59
16 Jan.	5	
23 Jan.	4	52
5 Mar.	3½	
19 Mar.	3	
28 May	2½	
1909		
14 Jan.	3	
1 Apr.	2½	
7 Oct.	3	
14 Oct.	4	
21 Oct.	5	52
9 Dec.	4½	
1910		
6 Jan.	4	
20 Jan.	3½	
10 Feb.	3	
17 Mar.	4	
2 June	3½	
9 June	3	
29 Sept.	4	
20 Oct.	5	52
1 Dec.	4½	
1911		
26 Jan.	4	
16 Feb.	3½	
9 Mar.	3	
21 Sept.	4	
1912		
8 Feb.	3½	
9 May	3	
29 Aug.	4	
17 Oct.	5	52
1913		
17 Apr.	4½	
2 Oct.	5	
1914		
8 Jan.	4½	
22 Jan.	4	
29 Jan.	3	
30 July	4	71, 74, 76

[a] Alteration made by the Governor and later approved by the Court.

Bank Rate changes, 1890–1939

	%	Page ref.
1914		
31 July[a]	8	74–6
1 Aug.[a]	10	74–6
6 Aug.[a]	6	75, 77
8 Aug.[a]	5	75, 77
1915 No change		
1916		
13 July	6	95
1917		
18 Jan.	5½	96
5 Apr.	5	97
1918 No change		
1919		
6 Nov.	6	117
1920		
15 Apr.	7	118, 123, 299
1921		
28 Apr.	6½	124
23 June	6	125
21 July	5½	125
3 Nov.	5	125, 302
1922		
16 Feb.	4½	125, 302
13 Apr.	4	125, 300, 302
15 June	3½	125, 300
13 July	3	125, 300
1923		
5 July	4	119, 130
1924 No change		
1925		
5 Mar.[b]	5	144–5, 216
6 Aug.	4½	215–16, 304
1 Oct.	4	215–16, 377n
3 Dec.	5	216

[a] Alteration made by the Governor and later approved by the Court.
[b] Effective 27 February.

	%	Page ref.
1926 No change		
1927		
21 Apr.	4½	216–17, 230, 280–81
1928 No change		
1929		
7 Feb.	5½	219, 225–6, 361
26 Sept.	6½	229, 293, 362–3
31 Oct.	6	230, 283
21 Nov.	5½	230
12 Dec.	5	230
1930		
6 Feb.	4½	230–33
6 Mar.	4	232–3
20 Mar.	3½	232–3
1 May	3	232–3
1931		
14 May	2½	234, 389–91
23 July	3½	391–2
30 July	4½	393, 405
21 Sept.[a]	6	265, 412
1932		
18 Feb.	5	425
10 Mar.	4	425
17 Mar.	3½	425
21 Apr.	3	430, 436
12 May	2½	430
30 June	2	430, 439
1933 **1934** **1935** **1936** **1937** **1938**	No change	
1939		
24 Aug.	4	573–5
28 Sept.	3	574
26 Oct.	2	574, 584

[a] Approved by the Court 20 September.

APPENDIX 37

THE BANK OF ENGLAND'S HOLDINGS OF GOLD AND FOREIGN EXCHANGE, 1925–31

This table gives weekly figures of the Bank's gold and foreign exchange holdings for the seven years 1925–31, thus including the whole period of the restored gold standard.

Gold is valued as in the Bank Returns at the time, at the Bank's selling price of 77s. 10½d. per standard ounce (equivalent to 85s. per fine ounce): the holdings are mainly those of the Issue Department, but some very small holdings of the Banking Department have been added (and to this extent the figures differ from the quarterly figures given in a leaflet issued with the Bank of England's *Quarterly Bulletin* for March 1970, although the difference is never more than £m1 in rounded terms).

The figures of foreign exchange include only U.S. dollars and French francs and so do not represent a complete record of the Bank's holdings in the years shown. However, holdings of other currencies were very much smaller, and movements in them unimportant. U.S. dollars and French francs are converted to sterling throughout at the parities ruling up to September 1931 (£1 = U.S.$4.86656 and French francs 124.2134). These figures are on the same basis as those shown in the leaflet.

Slight differences may occur between figures appearing in the Appendix and those appearing in the text and there are several possible reasons for this. First, the figure in the text will be a rounded total which may not necessarily be the same as the sum of the rounded items in the Appendix; secondly, the figure in the text may relate to a date or dates not shown in the Appendix; and thirdly, the figure in the text may be quoted from a contemporary source which may take into account such things as undrawn international borrowing on the one hand or short-term international liability to repay on the other when computing a reserves figure.

Gold and foreign exchange holdings, 1925–31

(£ million)

Date (Wednesdays)		Gold	U.S. dollars	French francs
1925	7 Jan.	127	—	—
	14	127	—	—
	21	127	—	—
	28	127	—	—
	4 Feb.	127	—	—
	11	127	—	—
	18	127	—	—
	25	127	—	—
	4 Mar.	127	—	—
	11	127	—	—
	18	127	—	—
	25	127	—	—
	1 Apr.	127	—	—
	8	127	—	—
	15	127	—	—
	22	127	—	—
	29	154[a]	—	—
	6 May	153	—	—
	13	152	—	—
	20	155	—	—
	27	155	—	—
	3 June	155	—	—
	10	156	—	—
	17	156	—	—
	24	156	1	—
	1 July	156	1	—
	8	158	1	—
	15	160	1	—
	22	162	1	—
	29	163	1	—
	5 Aug.	163	1	—
	12	163	1	—
	19	163	2	—
	26	162	3	—
	2 Sept.	161	3	—
	9	160	3	—
	16	160	3	—
	23	159	3	—
	30	159	3	—
	7 Oct.	157	4	—
	14	155	4	—
	21	151	5	—
	28	149	5	—
	4 Nov.	148	5	—
	11	147	5	—
	18	146	5	—
	25	145	5	—
	2 Dec.	144	5	—
	9	144	5	—
	16	143	5	—
	23	143	5	—
	30	143	5	—

[a] Includes £m27 transferred from H.M. Treasury.

Appendix 37

(£ million)

Date (Wednesdays)		Gold	U.S. dollars	French francs
1926	6 Jan.	143	5	—
	13	143	5	—
	20	142	5	—
	27	143	6	—
	3 Feb.	143	7	—
	10	143	10	—
	17	144	10	—
	24	143	10	—
	3 Mar.	144	10	—
	10	145	10	—
	17	144	10	—
	24	146	10	—
	31	146	10	—
	7 Apr.	145	10	—
	14	145	10	—
	21	145	10	—
	28	145	10	—
	5 May	146	10	—
	12	147	10	—
	19	148	10	—
	26	148	10	—
	2 June	148	10	—
	9	148	10	—
	16	149	11	—
	23	149	11	—
	30	149	11	—
	7 July	149	12	—
	14	150	13	—
	21	151	13	—
	28	151	14	—
	4 Aug.	152	14	—
	11	153	15	—
	18	153	16	—
	25	154	17	—
	1 Sept.	154	17	—
	8	154	20	—
	15	155	17	—
	22	155	16	—
	29	154	16	—
	6 Oct.	153	17	—
	13	153	17	—
	20	153	17	—
	27	151	18	—
	3 Nov.	151	19	—
	10	151	18	—
	17	152	19	—
	24	152	19	—
	1 Dec.	152	19	—
	8	152	19	—
	15	151	20	—
	22	151	21	—
	29	150	21	—
1927	5 Jan.	150	21	—
	12	150	21	—

Gold and foreign exchange holdings, 1925–31

(£ million)

Date (Wednesdays)		Gold	U.S. dollars	French francs
1927	19	150	22	—
	26	150	22	—
	2 Feb.	150	22	—
	9	149	24	—
	16	149	25	—
	23	149	25	—
	2 Mar.	149	25	—
	9	150	25	—
	16	150	25	—
	23	149	26	—
	30	149	28	—
	6 Apr.	150	28	—
	13	152	28	—
	20	152	28	—
	27	153	28	—
	4 May	152	28	—
	11	153	28	—
	18	154	29	—
	25	151	29	—
	1 June	151	29	—
	8	151	29	—
	15	151	31	—
	22	151	30	—
	29	151	31	—
	6 July	150	31	—
	13	150	31	—
	20	150	31	—
	27	150	32	—
	3 Aug.	151	32	—
	10	151	32	—
	17	151	32	—
	24	150	33	—
	31	150	28	—
	7 Sept.	151	30	—
	14	150	38	—
	21	149	38	—
	28	150	38	—
	5 Oct.	150	38	—
	12	150	39	—
	19	150	40	—
	26	150	40	—
	2 Nov.	150	40	—
	9	150	40	—
	16	150	41	—
	23	150	41	—
	30	149	42	—
	7 Dec.	149	42	—
	14	149	42	—
	21	150	42	—
	28	152	42	—
1928	4 Jan.	152	43	—
	11	154	43	—
	18	155	43	—
	25	155	43	—

Appendix 37

(£ million)

Date (Wednesdays)		Gold	U.S. dollars	French francs
1928	1 Feb.	155	43	—
	8	157	43	—
	15	157	43	—
	22	157	44	—
	29	156	45	—
	7 Mar.	157	45	—
	14	157	45	—
	21	157	45	—
	28	157	45	—
	4 Apr.	156	45	—
	11	157	45	—
	18	157	45	—
	25	159	45	—
	2 May	159	45	—
	9	160	45	—
	16	160	45	—
	23	160	45	—
	30	161	45	—
	6 June	162	45	—
	13	166	46	—
	20	169	45	—
	27	170	45	—
	4 July	171	45	—
	11	172	42	—
	18	173	42	—
	25	173	42	—
	1 Aug.	171	42	—
	8	172	42	—
	15	171	41	—
	22	172	40	—
	29	173	39	—
	5 Sept.	174	38	—
	12	174	35	—
	19	174	36	—
	26	171	36	—
	3 Oct.	166	36	—
	10	165	35	—
	17	165	34	—
	24	165	33	—
	31	163	31	—
	7 Nov.	164	29	—
	14	161	29	—
	21	161	23	—
	28	159	22	—
	5 Dec.	158	23	—
	12	157	20	—
	19	155	20	—
	24	154	20	—
1929	2 Jan.	153	18	—
	9	154	17	—
	16	154	17	—
	23	153	17	—
	30	153	18	—
	6 Feb.	150	18	—

Gold and foreign exchange holdings, 1925–31

(£ million)

Date (Wednesdays)		Gold	U.S. dollars	French francs
1929	13	150	18	—
	20	151	18	—
	27	151	18	—
	6 Mar.	151	18	—
	13	152	18	—
	20	152	19	—
	27	153	18	—
	3 Apr.	154	18	—
	10	155	18	—
	17	156	19	—
	24	156	18	—
	1 May	158	19	—
	8	160	19	—
	15	161	21	—
	22	162	21	—
	29	162	21	—
	5 June	163	22	—
	12	163	23	—
	19	162	23	—
	26	159	23	—
	3 July	155	23	—
	10	154	23	—
	17	154	24	—
	24	149	24	—
	31	141	25	—
	7 Aug.	140	25	—
	14	139	26	—
	21	137	25	—
	28	136	23	—
	4 Sept.	136	27	—
	11	136	25	—
	18	136	25	—
	25	132	25	—
	2 Oct.	129	24	—
	9	131	24	—
	16	132	25	—
	23	132	24	—
	30	131	24	—
	6 Nov.	131	23	—
	13	132	23	—
	20	132	23	—
	27	135	20	—
	4 Dec.	134	20	—
	11	137	20	—
	18	141	19	—
	24	146	20	—
1930	1 Jan.	146	22	—
	8	149	17	—
	15	150	16	—
	22	151	17	—
	29	150	17	—
	5 Feb.	151	17	—
	12	151	17	—
	19	151	16	—

(£ million)

Date (Wednesdays)		Gold	U.S. dollars	French francs
1930	26	151	16	—
	5 Mar.	152	16	—
	12	152	16	—
	19	153	16	—
	26	155	15	—
	2 Apr.	156	14	—
	9	160	14	—
	16	160	14	—
	23	163	14	—
	30	163	14	—
	7 May	164	14	—
	14	162	14	—
	21	158	14	—
	28	157	15	—
	4 June	156	16	—
	11	156	16	—
	18	157	18	—
	25	157	19	—
	2 July	156	22	—
	9	156	23	—
	16	155	24	—
	23	154	24	—
	30	152	25	—
	6 Aug.	153	25	—
	13	153	25	—
	20	154	25	—
	27	155	25	—
	3 Sept.	154	24	—
	10	156	24	—
	17	156	24	—
	24	156	24	—
	1 Oct.	156	25	—
	8	157	25	—
	15	158	25	—
	22	159	25	—
	29	160	25	—
	5 Nov.	160	25	—
	12	159	25	—
	19	158	25	—
	26	157	25	—
	3 Dec.	155	25	—
	10	152	25	—
	17	151	25	—
	24	148	25	—
	31	148	25	—
1931	7 Jan.	146	25	—
	14	145	26	—
	21	142	26	—
	28	139	25	—
	4 Feb.	140	26	—
	11	141	27	—
	18	140	28	1
	25	141	28	1
	4 Mar.	141	29	2

Gold and foreign exchange holdings, 1925–31

(£ million)

Date (Wednesdays)		Gold	U.S. dollars	French francs
1931	11	141	30	2
	18	142	30	3
	25	144	30	3
	1 Apr.	144	30	3
	8	146	30	3
	15	145	27	4
	22	146	27	4
	29	146	27	4
	6 May	148	27	4
	13	149	26	5
	20	150	26	5
	27	151	26	5
	3 June	152	26	5
	10	155	26	4
	17	161	26	4
	24	163	26	4
	1 July	163	26	4
	8	165	24	4
	15	164	27	4
	22	149	27	4
	29	132	18	1
	5 Aug.	134	11	1
	12	132	9	24
	19	134	9	16
	26	133	9	10
	2 Sept.	134	11	3
	9	136	14	1
	16	136	14	3
	23	134	9	7
	30	135	7	2
	7 Oct.	135	9	3
	14	135	9	3
	21	136	9	2
	28	136	14	5
	4 Nov.	121	11	3
	11	121	10	3
	18	121	10	3
	25	121	11	3
	2 Dec.	121	11	4
	9	121	11	4
	16	121	13	4
	23	121	14	4
	30	121	16	4

APPENDIX 38

CHANGES IN THE BANK'S FIDUCIARY ISSUE 1844–1946

1 1844–1928

The Fiduciary Issue was fixed at £m14 by the Bank Charter Act of 1844 and can be identified in the first Bank Return under this Act, dated 7 September 1844. Increases resulting from the partial replacement of lapsed issues, and authorised by Orders in Council, were as follows:

Authorised by Order in Council dated	Date of first Bank Return showing increased Fiduciary Issue	Amended total of Fiduciary Issue (£000)
7 Dec. 1855	15 Dec. 1855	14,475
26 June 1861	10 July 1861	14,650
3 Feb. 1866	21 Feb. 1866	15,000
1 Apr. 1881	20 Apr. 1881	15,750
15 Sept. 1887	5 Oct. 1887	16,200
8 Feb. 1890	19 Feb. 1890	16,450
29 Jan. 1894	21 Feb. 1894	16,800
3 Mar. 1900	21 Mar. 1900	17,775
11 Aug. 1902	20 Aug. 1902	18,175
10 Aug. 1903	26 Aug. 1903	18,450
12 Feb. 1923	21 Feb. 1923	19,750

2 1928–1946

The amounts shown above do not include the Treasury Note Issue initiated in 1914. This Treasury Issue was amalgamated with the Bank's issue in 1928 (see Vol. 1, Chapter 12) and the Fiduciary Issue was then fixed at £m260, by the Currency and Bank Notes Act 1928. The first Bank Return to show this was dated 28 November 1928. Variations in the Fiduciary Issue above £m260 could be authorised by a Treasury Minute laid before Parliament, and variations below £m260 by a letter to the Bank from the Treasury. The duration of an increase could be extended, with or without variations in the amount, for up to two years by further Treasury Minutes: Parliamentary sanction was required for an extension beyond two years. Alterations up to the end of 1946 were as follows:

Fiduciary Issue changes, 1844–1946

Nature and date of authority[a]		Date of first and last Bank Return showing amended Fiduciary Issue	Amended total of Fiduciary Issue (£000)
TM	1 Aug. 1931	5 Aug. 1931–29 Mar. 1933	275,000
	21 Aug. 1931		
	11 Sept. 1931		
	2 Oct. 1931		
	30 Oct. 1931		
	30 Nov. 1931		
	14 Dec. 1931		
	28 Jan. 1932		
	28 Apr. 1932		
	30 June 1932		
	30 Sept. 1932		
	30 Dec. 1932		
	(Automatic reversion	5 Apr. 1933–9 Dec. 1936	260,000)
L	15 Dec. 1936	16 Dec. 1936–10 Nov. 1937	200,000
	14 Jan. 1937		
	13 Feb. 1937		
	11 May 1937		
	12 Aug. 1937		
L	12 Nov. 1937	17 Nov. 1937–12 Jan. 1938	220,000
L	12 Jan. 1938	19 Jan. 1938–30 Nov. 1938	200,000
	12 Apr. 1938		
	12 May 1938		
	11 June 1938		
	11 July 1938		
	12 Oct. 1938		
	12 Nov. 1938		
L	5 Dec. 1938	7 Dec. 1938–4 Jan. 1939	230,000
TM	6 Jan. 1939	11 Jan. 1939–22 Feb. 1939	400,000
Currency and Bank Notes Act 1939[b]		1 Mar. 1939–30 Aug. 1939	300,000
TM	6 Sept. 1939 5 Mar. 1940	6 Sept. 1939–5 June 1940	580,000
TM	10 June 1940 10 Dec. 1940	12 June 1940–23 Apr. 1941	630,000
TM	30 Apr. 1941	30 Apr. 1941–27 Aug. 1941	680,000
TM	29 Aug. 1941[c]	3 Sept. 1941–26 Nov. 1941	730,000
TM	2 Dec. 1941[c]	3 Dec. 1941–15 Apr. 1942	780,000
TM	21 Apr. 1942[c]	22 Apr. 1942–22 July 1942	830,000
TM	28 July 1942[c]	29 July 1942–25 Nov. 1942	880,000
TM	30 Nov. 1942[c]	2 Dec. 1942–7 Apr. 1943	950,000
TM	12 Apr. 1943[c,d]	14 Apr. 1943–29 Sept. 1943	1,000,000
TM	5 Oct. 1943[d]	6 Oct. 1943–1 Dec. 1943	1,050,000
TM	6 Dec. 1943[d]	8 Dec. 1943–1 Mar. 1944	1,100,000
TM	6 Mar. 1944[d]	8 Mar. 1944–26 July 1944	1,150,000

a TM = Treasury Minutes, authorising variations above £m260 (later £m300 – see note *b*). L = Letters to the Governor from the Treasury, authorising variations below £m260 (later £m300).

This Act altered the prescribed total of the Fiduciary Issue from £m260 to £m300, but did not alter the arrangements for increasing or decreasing the amount, as described above.

c The duration of the increase was extended beyond two years by authority of SRO 1941 No. 1199, 15 Aug. 1941, under the Emergency Powers (Defence) Acts 1939 and 1940.

d The duration of the increase was further extended by authority of SRO 1943 No. 1141, 10 Aug. 1943, under the Emergency Powers (Defence) Acts 1939 and 1940.

Nature and date of authority[a]	Date of first and last Bank Return showing amended Fiduciary Issue	Amended total of Fiduciary Issue (£000)
TM 1 Aug. 1944[d]	2 Aug. 1944–29 Nov. 1944	1,200,000
TM 4 Dec. 1944[d]	6 Dec. 1944–2 May 1945	1,250,000
TM 8 May 1945[d]	9 May 1945–27 June 1945	1,300,000
TM 3 July 1945[d,e]	4 July 1945–5 Dec. 1945	1,350,000
TM 10 Dec. 1945[e] 6 June 1946	12 Dec. 1945–4 Dec. 1946	1,400,000
TM 10 Dec. 1946[e] 6 June 1947 10 Dec. 1947	11 Dec. 1946–31 Dec. 1947	1,450,000

[e] The duration of the increase was further extended by authority of SRO 1945 No. 1001, 14 Aug. 1945, under the Emergency Powers (Defence) Acts 1939 to 1945, and subsequently SRO 1945 No. 1628, 20 Dec. 1945, under the Supplies and Services (Transitional Powers) Act 1945.

APPENDIX 39

LISTS 1890–1946 OF GOVERNORS, DEPUTY GOVERNORS, DIRECTORS, SENIOR OFFICIALS AND ADVISERS TO THE GOVERNORS OF THE BANK OF ENGLAND

DIRECTORS

This list enumerates those who were Directors of the Bank at some time between 1890 and 1946. To do so, it spans the years 1835–1965, but it is not, nor is it intended to be, comprehensive for the longer period. Before the Bank of England Act 1946, Governors and Directors were subject to the annual election held in late March or April; the month of assuming or relinquishing office is shown only where it differs from the customary dates.

At least in the second half of the nineteenth century, and until the adoption in 1918 of the Revelstoke Report, it was usual for a Director nominated for election as Deputy Governor to join the Committee of Treasury immediately after his nomination by the Court. Whenever this occurred or when another appointment to the Committee was made otherwise than at the first Court of the Bank's year, this is shown.

Since the list is a list and not a biographical survey, titles are given in the short form, plural honours are not recorded, nor is any honour included that does not involve a change of style. For baronets, the date is given (following 'Bt') only in the case of an honour conferred during association with the Bank. For a peer, the date (following 'Baron', 'Viscount' or 'Earl') may be either that of creation or succession, since a title does not necessarily indicate a family name.

(*T = Member of the Committee of Treasury.*)

T ADDIS, Sir Charles Stewart. May 1918–32 (*T. 1919–32*)

T AIREDALE, Baron (R. D. KITSON). 1923–47 (*T. 1941–3*)

T ALDENHAM, Baron (H. H. GIBBS). 1853–5; 1856–8; 1859–61; 1862–4; 1865–7; 1868–70; 1871–3; 1877–1900. (Dep. Governor 1873–5; Governor 1875–7) (*T. 1873–1900*)

T ANDERSON, Sir Alan Garrett. 1918–25; 1926–46. (Dep. Governor 1925–6) (*T. Nov. 1924–32*)

ARBUTHNOT, Charles George. 1884–7; 1888–90; 1891–5; 1896–Sept. 1928

BARING, Edward Charles (see REVELSTOKE, Baron, 1885)

BARING, John (see REVELSTOKE, 2nd Baron, 1897)

T BERNARD, Sir Dallas Gerald Mercer, Bt (1954). 1936–49. (Dep. Governor 1949–54) (*T. 1939–42, 1949–54*)

T BIRCH, John William. 1860–62; 1863–5; 1866–8; 1869–71; 1872–5; 1876–7; 1881–Apr. 1897 (Dep. Governor 1877–9; Governor 1879–81) (*T. Nov. 1876–1897*)

BLACKETT, Sir Basil Phillott. Jan. 1929–Aug. 1935

BLAKE, Henry Wollaston. 1848–50; 1851–3; 1854–6; 1857–9; 1860–62; 1863–5; 1866–8; 1869–71; 1872–5; 1876–9; 1880–84; 1885–9; Aug. 1889–1893

BONSOR, Sir Henry Cosmo Orme, Bt (1925). 1885–8; 1889–92; 1893–6; 1897–8; 1899–Jan. 1929

T BOOTH, George Macaulay. 1915–46 (*T. 1924–5, 1942–3*)

BROOK, Ralph Ellis. 1946–Nov. 1949

BROOKS, Herbert. 1872–4; 1875–7; 1878–81; 1882–6; 1887–90; 1891–5; Oct. 1895–Oct. 1918

BUNBURY, Evelyn James. 1937–8

CADBURY, Laurence John. 1936–8; 1940–Jan. 1961

T CAMPBELL, William Middleton. 1886–8; 1889–91; 1892–6; 1897–1905; 1909–May 1919. (Dep. Governor 1905–7; Governor 1907–9) (*T. Nov. 1904–1919*)

T CATTERNS, Basil Gage. 1934–6; Sept. 1945–1948. (Dep. Governor 1936–Aug. 1945) (*T. 1935–Aug. 1945*)

T CATTO, Baron. Apr.–June 1940 (Governor 1944–9) (*T. 1944–9*)

CATTO, Thomas Sivewright (see CATTO, Baron, 1936)

CLEGG, William Henry. 1932–7

T COBBOLD, Baron. 1938–Aug. 1945 (Dep. Governor Sept. 1945–1949; Governor 1949–June 1961) (*T. 1944–June 1961*)

COBBOLD, Cameron Fromanteel (see COBBOLD, Baron, 1960)

COKAYNE, Sir Brien (see CULLEN, Baron, 1920)

T COLE, Alfred Clayton. 1895–1909; 1913–June 1920 (Dep. Governor 1909–11; Governor 1911–13) (*T. Nov. 1908–June 1920*)

T COLLET, Sir Mark Wilks, Bt (1888). 1866–8; 1869–71; 1872–3; 1875–9; 1880–5; 1889–Apr. 1905 (Dep. Governor 1885–7; Governor 1887–9) (*T. Nov. 1884–1905*)

T COOPER, Sir Patrick Ashley. 1932–55 (*T. 1942–52*)

T CRAIGMYLE, Baron (A. SHAW). Dec. 1923–1943 (*T. 1928–35, 1936–8*)

T CULLEN, Baron. Dec. 1902–1915; 1920–Nov. 1932 (Dep. Governor 1915–18; Governor 1918–20) (*T. Feb. 1915–1932*)

T CUNLIFFE, Baron. 1895–1911; 1918–Jan. 1920 (Dep. Governor 1911–13; Governor 1913–18) (*T. Nov. 1910–Jan. 1920*)

CUNLIFFE, Walter (see CUNLIFFE, Baron, 1914)

T CURRIE, James Pattison (CURRIE-BLYTH, 1904). 1855–7; 1858–60; 1861–3; 1864–6; 1867–9; 1870–2; 1873–83; 1887–1908 (Dep. Governor 1883–5; Governor 1885–7) (*T. Nov. 1882–1908*)

T DUNCAN, Sir Andrew Rae. Jan. 1929–Jan. 1940 (*T. 1932–Jan. 1940*)

GIBBS, Henry Hucks (see ALDENHAM, Baron, 1896)

T GILLIAT, John Saunders. 1862–4; 1865–7; 1868–70; 1871–4; 1875–9; 1880–81; 1885–1912 (Dep. Governor 1881–3; Governor 1883–5) (*T. Nov. 1880–1912*)

T GLADSTONE, Sir Albert Charles, Bt. 1924–47 (*T. 1932–4, 1938–44, Sept. 1945–1947*)

T GLADSTONE, Samuel Steuart. 1881–5; 1886–9; 1890–94; July 1894–1897; 1901–May 1909 (Dep. Governor 1897–9; Governor 1899–1901) (*T. Dec. 1896–May 1909*)

T GOSCHEN, Charles Hermann. 1868–70; 1871–3; 1874–7; 1878–82; 1883–7; 1888–91; 1892–8; 1899–Mar. 1915 (*T. 1897–8, 1899–1915*)

GOSCHEN, Kenneth. 1922–July 1936.

T GREENE, Benjamin Buck. 1850–52; 1853–5; 1856–8; 1859–60; 1861–3; 1864–6; 1867–9; 1870–71; 1875–1900 (Dep. Governor 1871–3; Governor 1873–5) (*T. Nov. 1870–1900*)

GRENFELL, Edward Charles (see ST JUST, Baron, 1935)

T GRENFELL, Henry Riversdale. 1865–7; 1868–70; 1871–3; 1874–7; 1878–9; 1883–Sept. 1902 (Dep. Governor 1879–81; Governor 1881–3) (*T. Nov. 1878–Sept. 1902*)

T HAMBRO, Sir Charles Jocelyn, M.C. 1928–Aug. 1963 (*T. 1933–7*)

T HAMBRO, Sir Everard Alexander. 1879–82; 1883–6; 1887–9; Sept. 1889–92; 1893–7; Sept. 1897–Feb. 1925 (*T. 1910–24*)

T HANBURY, Col. Lionel Henry. 1908–35 (*T. 1918–19*)

T HANBURY-WILLIAMS, Sir John Coldbrook. 1936–63 (*T. 1940–63*)

T HANKEY, Thomson. 1835–7; 1838–42; 1843–5; 1846–8; 1853–Jan. 1893 (Dep. Governor 1849–51; Governor 1851–3) (*T. 1849–Jan. 1893*)

T HARVEY, Sir Ernest Musgrave, Bt (1933). Nov. 1928–1929 (Dep. Governor 1929–36) (*T. Nov. 1928–1936*)

HENDERSON, George William. July 1902–Jan. 1929.

HENDERSON, Robert. 1893–Sept. 1895

HINDLEY, John Scott (see HYNDLEY, Viscount, 1948)

HOARE, William Douro. 1898–1928

T HOLLAND, Henry Lancelot. 1844–6; 1847–9; 1850–52; 1853–5; 1856–8; 1859–61; 1862–3; 1867–Jan. 1893 (Dep. Governor 1863–5; Governor 1865–7) (*T. Nov. 1862–Jan. 1893*)

T HOLLAND-MARTIN, Edward. 1933–48 (*T. 1943–4, 1945–6*)

T HOLLENDEN, Baron (S. H. MORLEY). 1882–5; 1886–9; 1890–93; 1894–1901; 1905–21 (Dep. Governor 1901–3; Governor 1903–5) (*T. Nov. 1900–18*)

HUBBARD, Evelyn. 1890–93; 1894–9; 1900–09

T HYNDLEY, Viscount. 1931–May 1945 (*T. 1934–41, 1944–5*)

JACKSON, Frederick Huth. 1892–5; 1896–Dec. 1921

T JOHNSTON, Reginald Eden. 1893–6; 1897–Sept. 1907; 1911–Nov. 1922 (Dep. Governor Sept. 1907–9; Governor 1909–11) (*T. Sept. 1907–1918*)

KEYNES, Baron. Oct. 1941–Apr. 1946

KEYNES, John Maynard (see KEYNES, Baron, 1942)

T KINDERSLEY, Baron. 1914–46 (*T. 1924–6*)

KINDERSLEY, Sir Robert Molesworth (see KINDERSLEY, Baron, 1941)

KITSON, Roland Dudley, D.S.O., M.C. (see AIREDALE, Baron, 1944)

LEVEN and MELVILLE, Earl of. 1884–7; 1888–90; 1891–4

T LIDDERDALE, William. 1870–72; 1873–6; 1877–81; Oct. 1881–1885; 1886–7; 1892–June 1902 (Dep. Governor 1887–9; Governor 1889–92) (*T. Nov. 1886–June 1902*)

T LUBBOCK, Cecil. July 1909–1923; 1925–7; 1929–42 (Dep. Governor 1923–5; 1927–9) (*T. Nov. 1922–1933*)

T LUBBOCK, Edgar. 1890–93; 1894–9; 1900–07 (Dep. Governor 1907–Sept. 1907) (*T. Feb. 1907–Sept. 1907*)

MARTIN, John. 1937–46

MELVILLE, Ronald Ruthven Leslie (see LEVEN and MELVILLE, Earl of, 1889)

MORLEY, Samuel Hope (see HOLLENDEN, Baron, 1912)

NAIRNE, Sir John Gordon, Bt (1917). 1925–31

T NEWMAN, Robert Lydston. 1896–1913; 1915–36 (Dep. Governor 1913–15) (*T. Nov. 1912–1918*)

T NIEMEYER, Sir Otto Ernst. 1938–52 (*T. 1943–5, Sept. 1945–1949*)

T NORMAN, Baron. Oct. 1907–1918 (Dep. Governor 1918–20; Governor 1920–44) (*T. May 1916–1944*)

NORMAN, Montagu Collet, D.S.O., M.C. (see NORMAN, Baron, 1944)

T PALMER, Edward Howley. 1858–60; 1861–3; 1864–6; 1867–9; 1870–72; 1873–5; 1879–97 (Dep. Governor 1875–7; Governor 1877–9) (*T. Nov. 1874–1897*)

T PEACOCK, Sir Edward Robert. 1921–4; June 1929–1946 (*T. 1922–4, June 1929–1946*)

T PIERCY, Baron. 1946–56 (*T. 1947–56*)

PIERCY, William (see PIERCY, Baron, 1945)

PITMAN, Isaac James (K.B.E. 1961). 1941–Aug. 1945

T POWELL, David. 1870–72; 1873–6; 1877–81; 1882–6; 1887–9; 1895–Sept. 1897 (Dep. Governor 1889–92; Governor 1892–5) (*T. Nov. 1888–Sept. 1897*)

T PREVOST, Sir Augustus, Bt (1902). 1881–4; 1885–8; 1889–92; 1893–7; May 1897–1899; 1903–Dec. 1913 (Dep. Governor 1899–1901; Governor 1901–3) (*T. Nov. 1898–Dec. 1913*)

REVELSTOKE, Baron. 1879–83; 1884–7; 1888–91

T REVELSTOKE, 2nd Baron. 1898–Apr. 1929 (*T. Dec. 1915–1929*)

T ST JUST, Baron. May 1905–1940 (*T. 1918–23, 1932–6, 1937–9*)

T SANDEMAN, Albert George. 1866–8; 1869–71; 1872–5; 1876–9; 1880–84; 1885–8; 1889–92; 1893–4; 1897–1918 (Dep. Governor 1894–5; Governor 1895–7) (*T. Nov. 1893–1918*)

T SANDERSON, Baron. 1943–65 (*T. 1946–65*)

SANDERSON, Basil, M.C. (see SANDERSON, Baron, 1960)

SHAW, Alexander (see CRAIGMYLE, Baron)

T SIEPMANN, Harry Arthur. 1945–54 (*T. 1949–51*)

T SMITH, Sir Henry Babington. Nov. 1920–Sept. 1923 (*T. 1921–2*)

T SMITH, Hugh Colin. 1876–8; 1879–83; 1884–7; 1888–91; 1892–5; 1899–Mar. 1910 (Dep. Governor 1895–7; Governor 1897–9) (*T. Nov. 1894–1910*)

SPENCER-SMITH, Michael Seymour, D.S.O., M.C. 1920–Jan. 1928

T STAMP, Baron. 1928–Apr. 1941 (*T. 1929–41*)

STAMP, Sir Josiah Charles (see STAMP, Baron, 1938)

T TIARKS, Frank Cyril. 1912–45 (*T. 1920–25*)

T TROTTER, Henry Alexander. 1909–20; 1923–6; 1927–34 (Dep. Governor 1920–23, 1926–7) (*T. 1919–24, Nov. 1925–1929*)

VICKERS, Vincent Cartwright. 1910–Aug. 1919

T WALLACE, Alexander Falconer. 1887–90; 1891–4; 1895–1903; 1907–18 (Dep. Governor 1903–5; Governor 1905–7) (*T. Nov. 1902–1918*)

T WALLACE, Robert. 1919–May 1931 (*T. 1924–7*)

WANSBROUGH, Arthur George. June 1946–1949

WEDGWOOD, Josiah. 1942–6

WEIR, James George. 1935–46

T WHIGHAM, Walter Kennedy. Aug. 1919–1946 (*T. 1925–8, 1936–46*)

T WHITWORTH, Arthur. Aug. 1919–1946 (*T. 1927–9*)

T WIGRAM, Clifford. 1862–4; 1865–7; 1868–70; 1871–4; 1875–8; 1879–83; 1884–8; 1889–92; 1894–June 1894 (Dep. Governor 1892–4) (*T. Nov. 1891–June 1894*)

GOVERNORS

William Lidderdale	1889–92
David Powell	1892–5
Albert George Sandeman	1895–7
Hugh Colin Smith	1897–9
Samuel Steuart Gladstone	1899–1901
Augustus Prevost	1901–3
Samuel Hope Morley	1903–5
Alexander Falconer Wallace	1905–7
William Middleton Campbell	1907–9
Reginald Eden Johnston	1909–11
Alfred Clayton Cole	1911–13
Walter Cunliffe	1913–18
Sir Brien Cokayne	1918–20
Montagu Collet Norman, D.S.O.	1920–44
Lord Catto	1944–9

DEPUTY GOVERNORS

David Powell	1889–92
Clifford Wigram	1892–4
Albert George Sandeman	1894–5
Hugh Colin Smith	1895–7
Samuel Steuart Gladstone	1897–9
Augustus Prevost	1899–1901
Samuel Hope Morley	1901–3
Alexander Falconer Wallace	1903–5
William Middleton Campbell	1905–7
Edgar Lubbock	1907–Sept. 1907
Reginald Eden Johnston	Sept. 1907–1909
Alfred Clayton Cole	1909–11
Walter Cunliffe	1911–13
Robert Lydston Newman	1913–15
Brien Cokayne	1915–18
Montagu Collet Norman, D.S.O.	1918–20
Henry Alexander Trotter	1920–23
Cecil Lubbock	1923–5
Sir Alan Garrett Anderson, G.B.E.	1925–6
Henry Alexander Trotter	1926–7
Cecil Lubbock	1927–9
Sir Ernest Musgrave Harvey, Bt, K.B.E.	1929–36
Basil Gage Catterns	1936–Aug. 1945
Cameron Fromanteel Cobbold	Sept. 1945–1949

COMPTROLLERS

Sir John Gordon Nairne, Bt	1918–25
Sir Ernest Musgrave Harvey, Bt, K.B.E.	1925–9
Cyril Patrick Mahon	1929–32

HEADS OF DEPARTMENTS

Chief Cashier

Frank May	1873–93
Horace George Bowen	1893–1902
John Gordon Nairne	1902–18
Ernest Musgrave Harvey	1918–25
Cyril Patrick Mahon	1925–9
Basil Gage Catterns	1929–34
Kenneth Oswald Peppiatt	1934–49

Chief Accountant

Horace George Bowen	1888–93
George Frederick Stutchbury	1893–1905
Henry Ben Orchard	1905–10
Charles Northcote Latter	1910–19
William Henry Clegg	1919–21
Frank Stanley Arnold	1921
Augustus Merrifield Walker	1921–39
Edward Maitland Stapley	1939–48

Secretary

Hammond Chubb	1864–94
George Frederick Glennie	1894–8
Kenneth Grahame	1898–1908
Charles Elliot Edlmann	1908–11
Harold Stanley Inman	1911–17
Harry Tilden	1917–27
Ronald Clement George Dale	1927–34
John Arundel Caulfeild Osborne	1934–5
Edward Maitland Stapley	1935–9
Humphrey Charles Baskerville Mynors	1939–44
Walter Howard Nevill	1944–9

Chief of Establishments

Ronald Clement George Dale	1932–4
John Drysdale Mackenzie	1934–43
John Drysdale Mackenzie Eric Neale Dalton	1943–5
Eric Neale Dalton	1945–9

ASSISTANTS TO THE GOVERNORS

Leslie Lefeaux	1932–3
Ernest Harry Dudley Skinner, C.B.E.	1935–45

ADVISERS TO THE GOVERNORS

Harry Arthur Siepmann	1926–45
Sir Otto Ernst Niemeyer	1927–38
Walter W. Stewart	1927–30
Francis James Rennell Rodd	1929–32
Raymond Newton Kershaw, M.C.	1929–53
Oliver Mitchell Wentworth Sprague	1930–33
Cameron Fromanteel Cobbold	1933–8
Henry Clay[1]	1933–44
Charles Bruce-Gardner[2]	1935–8
Gilbert Edward Jackson	1935–9
Evelyn James Bunbury	1935–7
John Arundel Caulfeild Osborne	1938–45
John Bernard Rickatson-Hatt	1941–58
George Lewis French Bolton	1941–8
Humphrey Charles Baskerville Mynors	1944–9
John Stewart Lithiby	1946–55
Frederic Francis Joseph Powell	1946–51

1 Appointed a Director of the Securities Management Trust in 1930, Economic Adviser to the Governors in 1933 and an Adviser to the Governors in 1935.

2 Appointed Managing Director of the Securities Management Trust in 1930 and Industrial Adviser to the Governors in 1935.

APPENDIX 40

CHRONOLOGICAL LIST OF EVENTS WITH CHAPTER REFERENCES

This list includes the more important events, external to the Bank, mentioned in the text in the chapters indicated in italic type at the end of each entry. Their chronological order in this list will, it is hoped, facilitate reference, as well as emphasising the simultaneity of events mentioned in widely separated parts of the book.

1887	27 Jan.	Chancellor of the Exchequer G. J. Goschen
1892	27 June	The Bank Act (amends Bank's Charter) *2, 22*
	July	General Election
	18 Aug.	Chancellor of the Exchequer Sir W. Harcourt
1895	July–Aug.	General Election
	2 July	Chancellor of the Exchequer Sir M. Hicks-Beach
1896	19 Aug.	Bank of England Supplemental Charter *22*
1899	Oct.–1902 May	South African War *1, 2, 3*
1900	Sept.–Oct.	General Election
1901	22 Jan.	Death of Queen Victoria; accession of King Edward VII
1902	8 Aug.	Chancellor of the Exchequer C. T. Ritchie
1903	6 Oct.	Chancellor of the Exchequer A. Chamberlain
1904	Feb.–1905 Aug.	Russo-Japanese War *1*
1905	10 Dec.	Chancellor of the Exchequer H. Asquith
1906	Jan.–Feb.	General Election
	18 Apr.	San Francisco earthquake and fire *1, 4*
1907	Oct.	U.S. banking crisis *1, 4*
1908	12 Apr.	Chancellor of the Exchequer D. Lloyd George
1910	6 May	Death of King Edward VII; accession of King George V
	Dec.	General Election
1913	20 Jan.	Commonwealth Bank of Australia opens *8*
1914	28 June	Sarajevo – assassination of Archduke Francis Ferdinand *1*
	30 July–1915 4 Jan.	Stock Exchange closed *5*
	4 Aug.	United Kingdom declares war on Germany
	4 Aug.	Moratorium for Bills of Exchange *5*
	6 Aug.	Currency and Bank Notes Act *5*
	Nov.	Issue of $3\frac{1}{2}$% War Stock 1925–8 *5*
1915	15 Jan.	U.K. Government services agreement with J. P. Morgan and Co., New York *5*
	25 May	Chancellor of the Exchequer R. McKenna
	Oct.	Anglo-French Loan issued in New York *5*
1916	Aug.	Calais Agreement (on inter-Allied finance) *8*
	10 Dec.	Chancellor of the Exchequer A. Bonar Law

Appendix 40

1917	Jan	Issue of 5% War Loan *5, 18*
	Apr.	United States enters War *5*
	Apr.	Balfour mission to United States *5*
	7 Nov.	Russian (Bolshevik) Revolution
1918	15 Aug.	Cunliffe Committee, First Interim Report *5, 6, 7, 12*
	11 Nov.	Armistice
	14 Dec.	General Election
1919	10 Jan.	Chancellor of the Exchequer A. Chamberlain
	29 Mar.	Export of gold coin or bullion prohibited *6*
	14 Apr.	Joint Stock Banks (Amalgamation Control) Bill (withdrawn 22 Dec.) *10*
	28 June	Treaty of Versailles signed (Germany) *8*
	10 Sept.	Treaty of St Germain signed (Austria) *8*
	15 Dec.	Treasury Minute establishing the Cunliffe Limit *6, 12*
1920	10 Jan.	Versailles Treaty and League Covenant come into force *8*
	4 June	Treaty of Trianon signed (Hungary) *8*
	Sept.–Oct.	Brussels International Financial Conference *6, 8, 17*
	Dec.	Gold and Silver (Export Control etc.) Act *6, 7*
1921		South African Reserve Bank opens *8*
	1 Apr.	Chancellor of the Exchequer Sir R. S. Horne
	20 June	London Imperial Conference opens *8*
	31 Oct.	U.K. Government Loan to Austria *8*
1922	Mar.	U.S. Congress postpones its lien on Austrian assets *8*
	Apr.	Genoa – International Economic Conference *6, 8, 9, 15, 17*
	24 Oct.	Chancellor of the Exchequer S. Baldwin
	15 Nov.	General Election
1923	Feb.	Anglo-American War Debt Agreement *7*
	Mar.	Hungarian representatives seek financial aid in London *8*
	27 Aug.	Chancellor of the Exchequer N. Chamberlain
	Autumn	Bank of London and South America formed *10*
	Oct.–Nov.	London – Imperial Economic Conference *8*
	6 Dec.	General Election
	22 Dec.	Schacht appointed President of Reichsbank *8*
1924	22 Jan.	Chancellor of the Exchequer P. Snowden
	Apr.	Bank of Poland established *8*
	9 Apr.	Reparation Commission Committee (Dawes) Report published *8, 15*
	May	National Bank of Hungary established *8*
	July–Aug.	London – Inter-Allied Conference (Reparations) *8*
	1 Sept.	Dawes Plan comes into force *8*
	Oct.	Reform of the Reichsbank *8*
	18 Oct.	German External (Dawes) Loan issued (London section) *8*
	29 Oct.	General Election
	6 Nov.	Chancellor of the Exchequer W. Churchill
1925	5 Feb.	Chamberlain/Bradbury Committee Report on Note Issue *7, 12*
	13 May	The Gold Standard Act *6–9, 13, 15*
	16 Sept.	Barclays Bank (D.C.O.) formed *10*
1926	3–12 May	General Strike
	July	Belgian financial crisis *8*
	23 July	Poincaré becomes French Premier
	23 Oct.	Loans to Belgium agreed *8*
	7 Dec.	Poincaré reform of French financial system *15*

Chronological list

1927	3 Apr.	Calais meeting of Harrison, Moreau, Rist, Norman and Schacht *8*
	2–23 May	Economic Conference at Geneva
	July	New York meeting of Strong, Norman, Schacht and Rist *9, 15*
	Dec.	Italian stabilisation plan *8*
1928		Agricultural Mortgage Corporation established *20*
		Cotton Yarn Association ask the Bank for support *14*
	Jan.	Vickers-Armstrong formed with Bank support *14, 20*
	2 July	Currency and Bank Notes Act *5, 7, 12, 16, 19*
	16 Oct.	Death of Benjamin Strong *15*
	22 Nov.	Amalgamation of Treasury and Bank of England note issues *12*
	22 Dec.	Young Committee (Reparations) appointed *15*
1928–9		Rumanian stabilisation plan *8*
1929	Jan.	Lancashire Cotton Corporation registered *10*
	18 Jan.	British Italian Banking Corporation difficulties revealed *10*
	30 May	General Election *9, 16*
	7 June	Young Report published *15*
		Chancellor of the Exchequer P. Snowden
	Summer	League of Nations 'Gold Delegation' appointed *15*
	6–31 Aug.	Hague Reparations Conference – Germany accepts Young Plan *9, 15*
	14 Sept.	Onset of the Hatry crisis *9*
	24 Oct.	Wall Street crash begins *9–11*
	Nov.	Securities Management Trust established *14, 20*
1930	Jan.	Second Hague Reparations Conference *15*
	Feb.–Mar.	Geneva tariff conference
	Mar.	National Shipbuilders Security Limited registered *14*
	6 Mar.	Schacht resigns as President of Reichsbank; succeeded by Luther *9*
	Apr.	Bankers Industrial Development Company established *14, 16, 20*
	17 May	Bank for International Settlements established *8, 15*
	13 June	Young Loan (Germany), issue made on nine markets under auspices of B.I.S. *15*
	July	Williams Deacon's Bank purchased by Royal Bank of Scotland *10*
	Aug.	Lancashire Steel Corporation formed *14*
	Oct.–Nov.	London – Imperial Conference; Statute of Westminster defines status of Dominions *8*
	17–28 Nov.	Geneva – Economic Conference
1931	5 Jan.	Treasury ask Bank to assist Oceanic Steam Navigation Company *14*
	11 May	Failure of Credit Anstalt, Vienna *9, 20*
	20 June	Hoover Plan (reparations moratorium) *20*
	25 June	International credit to Reichsbank (Bank of England participates) *17*
	13 July	Central European financial crisis spreads to London *16, 17, 20*
	13 July	Macmillan Committee Report published *17–20, 22*
	20–23 July	Seven-Power Conference in London *17*
	25 July	May Committee Report published *17*

1931	11 Aug.	London Protocol on Hoover moratorium *20*
	19 Aug.	First Standstill Agreement signed *20*
	23 Aug.	Labour Government falls *17*
	24 Aug.	National Government formed *17*
	10 Sept.	Snowden's emergency Budget *17, 18*
	16 Sept.	Anglo-South American Bank asks the Bank for help *10, 20*
	17 Sept.	Standstill Agreement with creditors of Germany *20*
	19 Sept.	Gold standard suspended *17*
	21 Sept.	The Gold Standard (Amendment) Act *17*
	27 Oct.	General Election
	5 Nov.	Chancellor of the Exchequer N. Chamberlain
1932	Feb.–June	Geneva – Disarmament Conference
	13 June	Lausanne – Anglo-French friendship pact signed
	16 June–9 July	Lausanne – Conference on Reparations *10, 18*
	30 June	5% War Loan Conversion announced *18, 20*
	1 July	Exchange Equalisation Account established *18, 19, 21, 22*
	21 July–20 Aug.	Ottawa – Imperial Economic Conference *18, 20*
	8 Nov.	Roosevelt defeats Hoover in U.S. election
1933	30 Jan.	Hitler appointed German Chancellor
	4 Mar.	Inauguration of F. D. Roosevelt *18*
	9 Mar.	Roosevelt granted wide powers on currency and credit *18*
	17 Mar.	Schacht reappointed President of Reichsbank
	12 June–27 July	London – World Economic Conference *18, 19*
	27 July	British Commonwealth Declaration on monetary and economic affairs
	28 Dec.	Anglo-American war debt final payment
1934	31 Jan.	U.S.A.: Gold Standard Act *19*
	1 Aug.	Reserve Bank of New Zealand opens *20*
1935		Special Areas Reconstruction Association founded *20*
	29 Jan.	News of trouble in shellac and pepper markets *20*
	7 Feb.	James and Shakspeare (commodity brokers) failure *20*
	11 Mar.	Bank of Canada opens *20*
	25 Mar.	Belgian franc devalued *19*
	1 Apr.	Reserve Bank of India opens *8, 20*
	31 May	Central Bank of Argentina established *20*
	14 Nov.	General Election
1936	20 Jan.	Death of King George V; accession of King Edward VIII
	1 Apr.	New Zealand Reserve Bank nationalised *20*
	26 Sept.	Tripartite Agreement (Declaration) *19, 21*
	12 Oct.	Tripartite Agreement (further statement) *19*
	10/11 Dec.	Abdication of King Edward VIII; accession of King George VI
1937	May	Commonwealth Ministers in London (central bankers' discussions at the Bank) *20*
	28 May	Chancellor of the Exchequer Sir J. Simon
	July	Sino-Japanese war begins
	Nov.	Brussels – Conference of powers discuss Sino-Japanese war
1938	May	Daladier devaluation of the franc *21*
	30 Sept.	Munich Agreement signed *20, 21*
1939	21 Jan.	Schacht dismissed as President of Reichsbank
	28 Feb.	Currency and Bank Notes Act *19, 21*
	Aug.	Bank of Ceylon established *20*

1939	21 Aug.	Russo-German Pact *21*
	26 Aug.	London clearing system moves to Staffordshire *21*
	3 Sept.	United Kingdom and France declare war on Germany
	4 Sept.	Treasury Control of Foreign Exchange instituted *21*
	6 Sept.	Fiduciary Issue raised to £m580 *21*
1940	10 May	Churchill forms National Government
	12 May	Chancellor of the Exchequer Sir K. Wood
	22 May	U.K. Government granted wide emergency powers
	July	Treasury Deposit Receipts introduced *21*
1941	24 Sept.	London – Allied conference endorses Atlantic Charter
1942	1 Jan.	Washington Pact of 26 United Nations
1943	24 Sept.	Chancellor of the Exchequer Sir J. Anderson
1945	26 June	U.N. Charter signed
	27 July	Chancellor of the Exchequer H. Dalton
1946	1 Jan.	Bank of France nationalised
	14 Feb.	The Bank of England Act *22*

APPENDIX 41

LIST OF COMMITTEES (BANK, GOVERNMENT AND OTHER) REFERRED TO IN THE TEXT

The words under the dates in the left-hand column are key words to indicate the placing(s) of the committee in the Index to the text volumes.

A. BANK OF ENGLAND COMMITTEES

The committees listed in this part are, following the Bank's usage, classified as 'Standing' (i.e. permanent) or 'Special' (i.e. *ad hoc*). In times of rapid change, notably 1931, the distinction has not been consistently absolute: relevant cases are annotated below. The title shown is the formal title by which the committee was most continuously known in the Bank, important variations being indicated by annotation. Any clearly established date of termination – of a Special Committee, normally by its Final Report – is shown. The absence of any terminal date does not necessarily mean that the committee was still in existence in 1946 – committees sometimes fade away; nor may the list be taken as any indication of the titles or existence of committees after 1946.

(1) *Standing Committees*

1694 Committee	Committee of Treasury (Known by this title from 1764)
1694–1932 Daily Waiting	Committee of Daily Waiting
1730 Building	Committee on Building (Not continuous; and for some periods a Special Committee: see next part of list)
1827–1918 Branches	Committee for the Branch Banks
1894 Audit	Audit Committee
1905–18 Appointments	Committee for Appointments and Promotions of the Staff (Merged in the Staff Committee: see below)
1906 Advances	Committee on Advances and Discounts (Merger of previous separate committees)
1918 Staff	The Staff Committee (Previously a number of separate committees, some dating back to 18th century)
1919 Council	Advisory Council of Directors and Staff

1920–32
Directors
Committee for the submission to the Committee of Treasury of the names of Candidates for the Direction

1922
Committee on St Luke's
(Preceded, 1921, by a Special Committee)

(2) *Special Committees*

(All except those marked † consisted of members of the Court only.)

1902–6
Classification
S.C. on the Classification of the Staff

1903
Women
S.C. 'to consider the question of Women Clerks'

1917–18
Revelstoke
S.C. on Organisation
(Later generally referred to as the 'Revelstoke Committee')

1918
Bank Act
S.C. on...a revision of the Bank Act of 1844...
('Cokayne Committee')

1918–19
'The Profits Committee'
S.C. to consider the question of the disposal of any Special Profits of the Bank and whether an application to increase the Capital of the Bank is desirable

1918
Directors
S.C. for selection of candidates for the Direction
(Lasting only for two months, followed by a short interval, before the next S.C.)

1918–20
Directors
S.C. on candidates for the Direction
(Followed, 1920–32, by a Standing Committee)

1918
Committee
†Committee of Delegates
(Not a committee of the Court, but appointed by the Staff to bring their grievances to the attention of the chief officials and the Court)

1919
Grievances
'Grievances Committee'
S.C. appointed following the Committee of Delegates, to enquire into certain complaints on behalf of the Staff

1920–41
Building
Committee on the Rebuilding of the Bank
(Other S.C.s on building were appointed from time to time)

1921–2
S.C. on St Luke's ('finance, methods and administration')
(Followed by a Standing Committee on St Luke's)

1926–7
Trotter
S.C. on the future Government and Administration of the Bank
(The 'Trotter Committee')

1929–30
Committee
†'Organisation Committee 1929'
A Special Internal Committee appointed by Governor's Order 'on certain matters relating to the organisation of the central banking and kindred offices and their relationship to other branches of the work of the Bank and to each other'

1930 Stamp	'Stamp Committee' A Sub-Committee of Directors to advise on financial assistance to industry
1931–2 Peacock	S.C. on the Organisation of the Bank (The 'Peacock Committee')
1931 Credits	'Credits Committee' S.C. 'to deal with...credit and possible facilities...to Banks, &c.' (One of the three committees substantially but not formally 'Standing', appointed in the 1931 crisis)
1931 Foreign Exchange	†'Foreign Exchange Committee' S.C. 'to consider arrangements for handling Foreign Exchange' (Second of the three 'Special/Standing' committees appointed in the crisis)
1931 Currency	†'Currency Committee' S.C. 'to deal with questions of Currency' (Third of the three 'Special/Standing' committees appointed in the crisis)
1937	S.C. on Branches, Premises, etc.

B. GOVERNMENTAL COMMITTEES

(For relevant Reports etc. of these committees, see list 'Books and Other Publications' immediately preceding Index.)

(1) *Appointed by U.K. Government*

1878 Stock Exchange	Royal Commission on the London Stock Exchange
1913–14 Indian	Royal Commission on Indian Currency and Finance (Chamberlain)
1915–19 London	American Exchange Committee, the name of which was soon changed to London Exchange Committee (A Treasury–Bank committee, including other bankers)
1915–19 American	American Dollar Securities Committee
1915–19 Capital Issues	Capital Issues Committee (From 1916, Cunliffe; see also 1939: Capital Issues (Kennet) Committee)
1918–19 Cunliffe	Committee on Currency and Foreign Exchanges after the War (Cunliffe Committee: see Appendix 7)
1918–19 British	British Imperial Committee on Indemnity (Membership included Dominion representation)
1918 Committee	Committee on Bank Amalgamations (Colwyn Committee)

List of Committees

1918—— Amalgamation	Advisory Committee on Bank Amalgamations (Colwyn/Inchcape)
1920 Increase	Select Committee (H.C.) on Increase of Wealth (War)
1921–2 Geddes	Select Committee (H.C.) on National Expenditure (Geddes Committee)
1923 Gold Reserve (U.K.)	An informal and secret committee (Norman, Bradbury, Asquith etc.) on gold reserve, note issue etc.
1923–9 Exchange	Exchange Committee (An informal committee, consisting of representatives of Treasury, the Bank and other bankers)
1924–9 Committee	Committee on Industry and Trade (Balfour Committee)
1924–5 Chamberlain/ Bradbury	Committee on the Currency and Bank of England Note Issues (Chamberlain/Bradbury Committee)
1925–6 Indian	Royal Commission on Indian Currency and Finance
1925–6	Trade Figures Committee
1929–31 Macmillan	Committee on Finance and Industry (Macmillan Committee)
1930—— Colonial	Colonial Currency Committee
1930—— Economic	Economic Advisory Council
1931—— Economic	Committee on Economic Information (A Standing Committee of the Economic Advisory Council)
1931 May	Committee on National Expenditure (The May Economy Committee)
1931—— Exchange	Exchange Committee (Effectively a revival of the Exchange Committee of 1923–9, consisting of Treasury, Bank and other bankers to consider current operations in co-operation with the Bank of England's internal Foreign Exchange Committee)
1932 Hush	'Hush hush Committee with W.F. at Treasury' (See p. 437)
1933	Secretary of State for India's Departmental Committee
1936 Foreign Transactions	Foreign Transactions Advisory Committee (Kennet Committee: merged in Capital Issues Committee 1939)

1939—— Capital Issues	Capital Issues Committee (Kennet Committee)
1939 Savings	Committee on the Control of Savings and Investment (Phillips Committee)
1939 Exchange Difficulties	Interdepartmental Committee on Exchange Difficulties and Essential Materials
1939—— Exchange	Exchange Requirements Committee
1957–59 Radcliffe	Committee on the Working of the Monetary System (Radcliffe Committee)

(2) *International Committees and those of other governments*

1908–12 United States	National Monetary Commission, U.S.A.
1920–30 Reparation	Reparation Commission
1920—— League of Nations	Financial Committee of the League of Nations
1922 Experts	Group of Financial Experts, on stabilisation of the German mark
1923–24 Dawes Committee	First Committee of Experts appointed by the Reparation Commission (Dawes Committee)
1923–24 McKenna Committee	Second Committee of Experts appointed by the Reparation Commission (McKenna Committee)
1923 Imperial Economic	Committee, of Imperial Economic Conference, on Inter-Imperial Exchanges
1926 Kemmerer	Commission of American Financial Experts (Kemmerer), on Polish financial problems
1928–29 Young Committee	Committee of Experts appointed by various Governments (Young Committee)
1929–32 League of Nations	Gold Delegation of the Financial Committee of the League of Nations
1929–30 Bank for International Settlements	Organisation Committee for the Bank for International Settlements

1931 Wiggin	Experts Committee convened by B.I.S. following Seven-Power Conference (Variously known as Basel or Wiggin or International Bankers' Committee, and its Report as Layton–Wiggin Report)
1931–39 Arbitration	Arbitration Committee, arranged by B.I.S. under German Credit Agreement (Standstill) 1931
1932 Imperial Conference	Committee, of Imperial Economic Conference, Ottawa, on Monetary and Financial Questions
1933 Canada	Royal Commission on Banking and Currency in Canada (Canadian Macmillan Commission)
1933 Newfoundland	Newfoundland Royal Commission
1935–7 Monetary	Royal Commission on Monetary and Banking Systems in Australia

C. OTHER U.K. COMMITTEES

1821 Committee	Committee of London Clearing Bankers (Title varied slightly, but since 1895 continuously thus)
1908 Gold Reserves (U.K.) London	Gold Reserves Committee of the London Chamber of Commerce
1914–18 Discount 1919—— Discount	Discount Market Committee followed by London Discount Market Association
1914—— Accepting Houses	Accepting Houses Committee
1931–6 Foreign Exchange	[Bankers] Foreign Exchange Committee (A self-appointed committee of London foreign exchange managers from the most interested banks, through which the Treasury conveyed to the market instructions on exchange restrictions. It continued in existence after the lapse (1932) of these restrictions) (See also 1936 below)
1934 Trade	Trade and Industry Committee of the House of Commons (Non-ministerial, non-official committee of M.P.s)
—— Stock Exchange	Stock Exchange Committee (In this period the relevant committee was the Committee for General Purposes)
1935–41 London	London Pepper Sales Control Committee (Set up by the General Produce Brokers' Association)

1936—— Foreign Exchange	Foreign Exchange Committee (A committee arranged, at the request of the Governor, by the Committee of London Clearing Bankers, as a channel for conveying official requests to the market; replacing the self-appointed committee (1931–6) noted above)

APPENDIX 42

REFERENCES TO UNPUBLISHED SOURCES

Unless otherwise stated, all references are to material in the possession of the Bank. For the searches which have led the author through this labyrinth, he is especially indebted to Miss R. Heather.

ABBREVIATIONS

CLCB	Committee of London Clearing Bankers
CT	Committee of Treasury
CTM	Committee of Treasury Minutes
E.E.A.	Exchange Equalisation Account
F.R.	Federal Reserve
FRBNY	Federal Reserve Bank of New York
PDO	Principal of the Discount Office

CHAPTER 1

a Court Mins. 16 Nov. 1893, 19 July 1894, 23 Nov. 1911, 14 Nov. 1912. There is corres. Mar. 1896 Chanc. Excheq./Gov. showing that Chanc. (Hicks-Beach) was not satisfied with scope of the reforms.

b Review of internal administration: CTM 23 Nov. 1892; Report Feb. 1893.
For K. Grahame: P. Green, *Kenneth Grahame 1859–1932* (John Murray, 1959), pp. 288–9; letter Lord Courtauld-Thomson/Cobbold 1 Mar. 1949.

c Interviews with G. M. Booth (Director 1915–46), A. Whitworth (Director 1919–46), B. G. Catterns (joined Bank 1908, eventually Dep. Gov.). W. D. Hoare evidence to Revelstoke Cttee 29 Oct. 1917. Melville letter to Gov. 28 Mar. 1894.

d Memo. 30 Jan. 1894.
A. C. Cole (Gov. 1911–13) evidence to Revelstoke Cttee 21 Nov. 1917.
W. M. Campbell (Gov. 1907–9) to Cokayne 20 Oct. 1916.

e Evidence of R. L. Newman (Director from 1896 and Dep. Gov. in first 2 years of Cunliffe's Governorship) 27 Nov. 1917.

CHAPTER 2

a Funded and Unfunded Debt: figures from Bank's General Abstract in green volume 'National Debt'.
Definitions: 'The main distinction between Funded and Unfunded Debt is, that in one case provision is made for the permanent payment of interest and the date of redemption is indefinite and remote, while in the other the term of the loan is short and fixed.' (From a Bank Statement 'The Bank Capital and the Permanent Debt' Jan. 1898. Different classifications have become appropriate since 1918.)
Corres. on terms of issues: 7, 21, 27 Mar., 21 June 1890, 13 June 1894, 6 Feb., 23 July, 6 Dec. 1900.

The 1910 maturity: corres. Hamilton/Nairne expressing concern of Chanc. 27 Mar. 1906; exploring ways of dealing with this stock Apr. 1907.

b Letter Gov./Hamilton 6 Dec. 1900.

c 55 & 56 Vict. c. 48 and Treas. Min. 2 July 1892.
Hamilton's 'squeezed': letter Cole/Chalmers 9 Feb. 1912.
Dividends: the half-yearly distributions were made in respect of the half-years ending 28 Feb. and 31 Aug. each year. The 1891 distribution, e.g., related to earnings in the 12 months to 31 Aug. 1891, which included the weeks of the Baring Crisis.

d Chief Cashier memo. June 1898. Nairne note 22 Mar. 1911.

e Report Cttee for Branch Banks, Court Mins. 8 Mar. 1894.

f Court Mins. 20 June 1895. Letter Edye/Smith 9 Oct. 1902. Memo. 23 Mar. 1899.

g (Revelstoke) Cttee on Organisation 21 Nov. 1917.

h Court Mins. 6 Dec. 1894, 24 Jan., 19 Sept. 1895.
Letter Cunliffe/Bradbury 16 Feb. 1916.

i Corres. Gov./Chanc. 1896 rel. to an issue for China. Gov. corres. 1898 on a Greek loan.
Corres. B. B. Greene/Sir Mark Collet 1895–6.

CHAPTER 3

a Court Mins. 31 Dec. 1891, 8 Feb. 1894.

b In the early 1930s a brief study of the Bank's market operations in the 1890s, with figures, was prepared in the Bank. Corres. was slight: it includes Lidderdale/Waterfield corres. June, July 1890 and Gov. corres. 12 Sept. 1890.
For a study made (in 1933–4) outside the Bank, but giving all the *Economist* and *Statist* references, see Chap. II of R. S. Sayers, *Bank of England Operations 1890–1914* (P. S. King and Son, 1936).
Court Mins. 14 Feb., 5 Sept., 31 Dec. 1895, 11 Dec. 1913. Circular to Branches 18 Feb. 1895.

c Peppiatt (comment with letter) 15 Sept. 1970.

d Harvey note 1 Nov. 1933. Account books.

e For dealings with B. of Japan, corres. 8 Oct. 1902, 22 Nov. 1905; it was at the request of the Treasury that the Bank had become the issuer of Japanese Government loans (also cf. *Economist* 9 Mar. 1907). The Bank account books show that the transactions were arranged through Mullens.

f Letter Wallace/Hamilton 7 Oct. and corres. Gov./Chanc. Nov. 1905.

g Memo. 'The Bank of England as a Dealer in Bullion' by Lord Addington 6 Aug. 1889 with Supplementary Memo. 12 Aug. 1889. Addington (as J. G. Hubbard) had been Dep. Gov. when in 1852 the Bank drew up its original price schedule.

h Hankey's view: Memo. 13 June 1883; Grenfell's: 17 Aug. 1889.

i *Economist* 15 Feb. 1890, 5, 19 Nov. 1892. *Statist* 11, 18, 25 Oct. 1890, 2 Jan., 4 Feb., 12 Aug. 1893. Letter Lidderdale/Hamilton 14 Jan. 1892.

j Letter Norman/Strong 29 Aug. 1927. Cable Lubbock/Harrison 24 Jan. 1929.

CHAPTER 4

a Special operations by Bank of France, 1890, 1906 and 1907 are summarised in B. of F. memos. prepared in 1929 with translations. B. of E. memo. 8 Aug. 1930.

b Several versions of Holden's views are in Bank records; also relevant is corres. Holden/Huth Jackson/Goschen through the years 1905–10; and see numerous references in Pressnell p. 225.

c Campbell to Revelstoke Cttee 13 Oct. 1917.

d Extract from Tritton's Memo. for the bankers' Gold Sub-Cttee 31 Dec. 1913.

CHAPTER 5

a Reassuring message on 29 July: Montagu, Bradbury, Ramsay at Chanc.'s instruction visited Gov., whose view was supported by four senior Directors he had invited: M. G. R[amsay] Min. 29 July 1914, Bradbury Papers, P.R.O. T.170/14.

b Gov. remark 6 Aug. in notes of meetings of Government and bankers. For the most part, these records of the discussions in the first days of August are identical in Treas. records at P.R.O. and in Bank records.

c Court Mins. show authorities for most of these operations, and some figures. E. V. Morgan, *Studies in British Financial Policy, 1914–25* (Macmillan, 1952) has authoritative figures on this (e.g. p. 170) and other operations in this period.

d On Treas. cover for the Bank's underwriting operations, letter Gov./Chanc. 21 Feb. 1918; also Nairne's evidence to Revelstoke Cttee 12 Nov. 1917.

e On the Blackett–Paish mission, James Brown corres., Norman Papers.

f F. C. Weems, *America and Munitions* (see p. 85n of text vol.), pp. 30–31, 273–87.

g Cunliffe's complaints of the government's attitude to the exchange problem: letter Cunliffe/McAdoo 15 June 1917.
Anglo-French loan: Weems, *America and Munitions*, pp. 295–300.

h For Cunliffe's closeness, Norman Diary 19 Sept. 1916. For financing proposals generally at this juncture, Weems, *America and Munitions*, p. 312.
Letter Bank/Treas. 23 Nov. 1916.

i Letter Cunliffe/McAdoo 15 June 1917.

j Sale of yen bonds: Cokayne Diary (15 Nov. 1916) says this was solely for obtaining dollars.
Change of Bank Rate: letter Norman/Strong 24 July 1916; letter Cokayne/Cunliffe 12 June 1916.

k Letters Harvey/Treas. 20 Apr., 6 Sept. 1916. Cullen's recollection noted in 1924.

l Norman Diary 12 Nov. 1917.

m CTM 27 Aug., 14 Nov., 5 and 31 Dec. 1917, 29 May 1918. Cokayne Diary 20 Apr., 12 May 1917.
For rel. Treas. records P.R.O. T.172/906 and T.1.12316/18118.

n Norman Diary 27 Sept., 4, 27 Oct., 27 Dec. 1916, 5 Jan. 1917.

o Norman Diary 1916–18 *passim*.

p For all these events of July–Aug. 1917 CTM are an important source.

CHAPTER 6

a CTM and letter Gov./Chanc. 18 Sept. 1918.
Norman Diary 28 Feb. 1919. CTM 5 Mar. 1919.

b Norman Diary 3 June 1920. Letter to Strong 6 Nov. 1919.

c Norman Diary 30 Jan. 1919. CTM 29 Jan. 1919. Letter Gov./Chanc. 30 Jan. 1919.

d Bradbury Papers (P.R.O. T.170/140). Norman Diary 27 Mar. 1919. CTM 26 Mar., 2 Apr. 1919.

e Norman Diary 11, 17 July, 19 Sept. 1919, 9, 30 Mar. 1920. CTM 23 July 1919. Letters Gov./Chanc. 25 Sept. 1919, Norman/Hawtrey 17 July 1920. CLCB Mins.

f The Bank's view is implicit in many entries in Norman Diary and in CTM throughout the boom period; for explicit view, letters Norman/Jay 6 Sept., 25 Nov. 1920.

g For early important examples of corres. with FRBNY Strong/Cokayne 17 Oct., Norman/Strong 6 Nov. 1919, Cokayne/Jay 27 May, Norman/Jay 6 Sept. 1920, Norman/Strong 17 Feb. 1921.
Norman's visit to New York CTM 21 Sept. 1921.

h Weekly cables Bank to FRBNY 2, 8 June, 27 July 1920. Letters Norman/Jay 6 Sept.,

Norman/Addis 6 Aug. 1920. Norman Diary and CTM 4, 11 Aug. 1920. CLCB Mins. and CTM 22 Sept. 1920.

i Letter Norman/Strong 6 Nov. 1919. Cables 21, 26 Sept. 1920. CTM 6, 13 Oct. 1920. Note on Embargo on Foreign Capital Issues 18 June 1930.

j Norman Diary 23, 28 Dec. 1920.
Memo. 12 Jan. 1921. Letters Norman/Strong 17 Feb., 1, 14 Mar. 1921.

k Letter Norman/Strong 2 Apr. 1921.

l For U.S. comments on F.R. policy Dow-Jones Circular 10 June 1921. For statement of U.S. and U.K. co-ordinated policy letter Norman/Clegg 13 Oct. 1921.

m Letter Niemeyer/D. Gov. 23 Jan. 1923 and Hawtrey memo. enclosed. Note prepared for 26 May 1923 with Norman's amendments.

n Memo. 5 Mar. 1923 and rel. papers (Hawtrey, Niemeyer etc.).

o Norman Diary 4, 16 May 1923. Letter Farrer/Norman 20 May 1923 (after meetings of the Cttee on 8 and 16 May). Memo. Addis (Addis Papers) 21 May 1923.

p Letter Norman/Blackett 25 June 1923. CTM 2, 23 May, 6, 13, 20 June 1923. Norman Diary 28 June 1923. Note Addis 4 July 1923.

q Letter Cannan/Norman 11 Nov. 1923.

r Norman Diary 15 Oct. 1923. Letter Chanc./Gov. 15 Oct. 1923.
Letter Revelstoke/Addis 1 Feb. 1924 (Baring Archives: Private Letter Books of Lord Revelstoke 1916–29).

CHAPTER 7

a CTM 19 Dec. 1923.
For Bank view on prior need for settlement of reparations and war debts letters Trotter/Clegg 11 Jan., Norman/Moll 15 Feb. 1923.

b Norman Diary 16 Apr., 17 July 1924.
Note on Embargo on Foreign Capital Issues 18 June 1930.

c Letter Norman/Blackett 27 Oct. 1924. Cables nos. 15, 16 Norman/D. Gov. Jan. 1924.

d Cables nos. 54, 55, 57 (1925). Addis Diary 1924–5.
Evidence to Bradbury Cttee.

e Evidence to Bradbury Cttee. Letter Norman/Niemeyer 8 Apr. 1925.
CTM 22 Apr. 1925.

f Norman Diary 27 Feb. 1925.

g Cables Gov./Clegg 27 Feb., Norman/Strong 23 Feb. 1925.

h Letter Norman/Bradbury 24 Feb. 1925. CTM 22 Apr. 1925.

i Norman Diary 14 Apr. 1925.

j For CT meeting 22 Apr. 1925 Addis Diary.
Letter Norman/Strong 5 May 1925.

k Norman evidence to Chamberlain/Bradbury Cttee 27 June 1924.

CHAPTER 8

a Report and other papers of the International Financial Conference 1920. Letters Chamberlain/Norman 6 May, Norman/Chanc. 7 May, Cullen/Norman 9, 15 Oct., Norman/Cullen ?26 Oct. 1920.

b *The Conference Forum* 30 Sept. 1920. Letters Cullen/Norman 9 Oct., Norman/Malcolm 26 Oct., Cullen/Norman 15 Oct. 1920, Norman/Vissering 12 Oct., Norman/Clegg 13 Oct. 1921.

c Letter Skinner/Sayers 26 July 1969.

d Letter Cokayne/Strong 3 May 1917; Norman Diary. CTM 21 Sept. 1921. Letters Norman/Vissering 12 Oct., Norman/Strong 13 July, Norman/Peacock 21 July, Norman/Strong 23 July, 13 Oct. 1921. Norman corres. with various central bankers Oct., Nov., Dec. 1921.

e Interview J. A. C. Osborne 10 Dec. 1968. Norman Diary 11 Mar. 1922.

f Memos. 10 Jan. 1931 (Niemeyer/Siepmann), 19 Aug. 1932, 10 Dec. 1923, 11 Apr. 1924, 8, 9 Jan. 1931, 19 Aug. 1932. Corres. Norman/Moll and other central bankers July–Aug. 1922. Siepmann memo. 19 Aug. 1932.

g Summaries of 7 Apr. 1922, 21 June 1923, Nov. 1924. Note 11 Jan. 1927.
Memo. on the Bank's policy as regards its relationship to other central banks 7 Apr. 1922.

h Addis Papers 15 Feb. 1921. Letter Peacock/Norman 8 July 1929.

i Memo. Siepmann 19 July 1943.

j Tel. Addis/Norman 20 Apr. 1922. Note Addis 22 Apr. 1922.
Report of the Cttee of Experts 15 Apr. 1922.
Letter Norman/Clegg 1 June 1922. CTM 25 Apr. 1922.

k Letters Norman/Strong 23 June, Strong/Norman 27 July, Norman/Vissering 3 June, Norman to various central bankers June, July, Aug. 1922.

l Letters Norman/Strong 9 Aug., Strong/Norman 2 Feb., Strong/Norman 7 Sept., Trotter/Clegg 14 Sept. 1922. Other Norman letters and memo. 29 Sept. 1922.
Letter Trotter/Clegg 27 Oct. 1922.
Letters Norman/Anderson 15 July 1925, Norman/Strong 11 May, Norman/Siepmann 9 Sept. 1928. Memo. Addis 29 Dec. 1928.

m Letters Norman/Strong 8 Apr. 1927, Addis/Norman 17 Oct. 1931, Dale/Siepmann 15 June 1926, Norman/Siepmann 9 Nov. 1925, Kershaw/Dale 1929.
Memo. Siepmann 7 Jan. 1929.

n On the Austrian problem generally, note Laverack Apr. 1927.
Paper by Blackett and Monnet for Morrow 4 June 1921. L. of N. Fin. Cttee Report and Papers relative to the Financial Reconstitution of Austria 15 June 1921.
For Austrian debts to the Bank letter Norman/Robinson 9 Mar. and paper 21 Dec. 1921.

o Memo. 31 May 1921. CTM 25 May, 1 June 1921. Letter Norman/Glückstadt 1 June 1921. Notes 13 June 1921. Interview Norman/Avenol 6 July 1921. Letter Norman/Vissering 4 June 1921. Gov. corres. Balfour and Bliss July 1921. Cables and letters Norman/Strong June 1921. Additional Report on Conditions in Austria end July 1921. Cable Jay/Strong 23 Sept. 1921.

p Letter Nixon/Norman 10 Aug. 1921 with enclosures.
Treas./Bank corres. 31 Oct., 2 Nov. 1921, 16 Feb. 1922.
Letters Norman/Strong 7 Nov., Franckenstein/Norman 5 Oct. 1921.
CTM 25 May 1921.
Norman corres. with Strong, Jay, Harding June 1921–Feb. 1922.
Letter Goode/Norman with memos. 12 Mar. 1922.
Corres. with Treas., Franckenstein, Anglo-Austrian Bank Feb. 1922.
Letters Spencer-Smith/Norman Mar. 1922.

q Letters Strong/Norman 18 Feb., 22 Mar., Rosenberg/Norman 4 Aug. 1922 with memo.
Letters Bank/Treas. 5 July, Norman/Spencer-Smith 15 July 1922. Corres. with Rosenberg, Hamlyn, Benes, Franckenstein, Bark Sept. 1921–June 1922.
Letters Goode/Norman 3 Mar., Spencer-Smith/Norman 31 Mar. 1922.

r Norman corres. with Vissering, Balfour, Monnet, Spencer-Smith Oct.–Dec. 1922.
CTM 22 Nov., 13 Dec. 1922.
Norman Diary 17, 18 Oct., 17 Nov., 4, 9 Dec. 1922.
Memo. 14 Oct. 1922 and corres. Blackett, Balfour, Niemeyer.
Note Niemeyer 12 Nov. 1922. Letter Niemeyer/Norman 27 Nov. 1922.
Corres. Norman/van der Rest Nov.–Dec. 1922.
Note of meeting 12 Jan. 1923.
Corres. Norman/Franckenstein Dec. 1922–Jan. 1923.

Letters Norman/Niemeyer, Norman/Monnet 23 Dec., Norman/Spencer-Smith 6, 7 Dec. 1922.

CTM 7, 14 Feb. 1923.

Norman letters to central bankers Feb.–Mar. 1923.

s Memo. 14 Oct. 1922.

Letters Norman to central bankers Apr.–May 1923. CTM 13 June 1923, 16 Jan. 1924. Norman Diary 4 June 1923. Letter Lamont/Norman 9 Oct. 1924.

t Corres. Balfour/Norman 13 July 1921, Oct. 1922.

u Letter Strakosch/Trotter 10 Jan. 1923. Also various Norman letters Apr.–May; corres. Norman/Zimmerman July, Norman/Franckenstein Dec. 1923.

v Norman Diary 1922 and 1923. Letters Bark/Norman 29 June, Norman/Vissering 1 Mar. 1923.

w Letters Trotter/Schober, Schober/Norman (with annotations) 22 Mar. 1923. Note of meeting 27 Mar. 1923. CT 28 Mar. 1923.

x CT 28 Mar. 1923. Letters Norman/Clegg 26 May, Goode/Norman with encl. 16 Aug. 1923. This paragraph also draws heavily on Salter, 'General Survey' in League of Nations, *Financial Reconstruction of Hungary*.

y CTM 9 Jan., 7 May 1924.

Letters Niemeyer/Norman 26 Apr., Norman/Vissering 12 May, 12 June, Norman/Nathan 16 May, Norman/Robineau 19 May, Norman/Moll 5 June, Norman/Stringher 24 June 1924.

Corres. with Rothschilds June–July 1924.

z Norman Diary 21, 23 May 1924.

aa Corres. with Reichsbank 1 June–Nov. 1921. Letter Tiarks/Norman 6 June 1921.

Corres. Bank/Treas. Nov. 1921, Mar. 1922.

Norman Diary Oct. 1921.

Letters Tiarks/Norman 11 Nov., Norman/Havenstein 5, 23 Dec. 1921, Trotter/Havenstein 17 Jan. 1922, Norman/Vissering 24 Dec. 1921, Havenstein/Norman 18 Jan. 1922.

Corres. Bank/Reichsbank 1922 and 1923 and Bradbury/Norman/Trotter May 1922.

CTM 15 Mar., 20 Sept. 1922.

Memo. 15 Sept. 1922.

Letter Niemeyer/D. Gov. 16 Sept. 1922.

bb Reichsbank letters 14, 21 Apr. 1923, 16 Dec. 1922. Memo. 15 June 1923 (Schröders). Letter Havenstein/Tiarks 24 Apr. 1923. Letter Glasenapp/Norman 14 Dec. 1922.

cc Norman Diary 9 Nov. 1922, 31 Dec. 1923.

CTM 2 Jan. 1924.

Norman corres. with Vissering and other central bankers 1922 and 1923 (esp. Nov. 1922 and Nov.–Dec. 1923).

Letter Norman/Strong 25 Oct. 1922.

dd Letters Schacht/Norman 10 Jan., Norman/Schacht 14 Jan. 1924.

ee Corres. with Reichsbank Jan.–May, Norman/Vissering Jan. 1924. CTM 9, 16 Jan., 27 Feb., 5, 26 Mar., 9 Apr., 21 May 1924. Letter Lubbock/Schacht 28 July 1924.

ff Corres. Baldwin/Govs. 19, 20 Dec. 1923. CTM 20, 27 Dec. 1923. Court Mins. 27 Dec. 1923. CTM 16 Apr. 1924. CTM 17, 24 Sept. 1924.

gg Notes for CT 5 Aug. 1924.

Proceedings of the London Reparation Conference, July and August 1924 (Cmd. 2270).

CTM 17, 24 Sept., 1 Oct. 1924. Court Mins. 25 Sept. 1924.

Corres. Norman/Lamont Aug. 1924, Norman/MacDonald and Norman/Chanc. Sept. 1924. Norman Diary Sept., Oct. 1924.

hh Reports of the Expert Cttees appointed by the Reparation Commission (Cmd. 2105).
CTM 15 Oct. 1924.
Letter Addis/Norman 18 Aug. 1924.
ii Letter Peacock/Norman 30 Dec. 1929.
jj Letter Norman/Strong 4 Mar. 1926.
kk Letter Leith-Ross/Norman 8 Dec. 1927.
ll Letter Norman/Morrow 24 Dec. 1926.
CTM 27 Feb. 1924.
Letter B. of Poland/Norman 30 Apr. 1924.
Memo. 3 June 1925.
Letter Mlynarski/Norman 1 July 1925.
Letter Salter/Norman 5 Feb. 1926.
Note of meeting with Mlynarski 1 Sept. 1925.
mm Letters Norman/Schacht 12 June 1926, Norman/Morrow 16 May 1927, Norman/Salter 1 Feb. 1926.
Draft ('From G. L. H.') 24 Mar. 1927.
Letter Moreau/Norman 10 June 1927.
Agreements between central banks 9 July and 13 Oct. 1928 with corres. Lubbock/FRBNY and Norman/Moreau.
Note Siepmann 8 May 1927.
Note of conversations in Paris 19 Nov. 1927. Note 5 Dec. 1930.
Notes of meeting in Calais Apr. 1927.
Letters Moreau/Norman 10, 23 June 1927.
Interview with Auboin 24 Oct. 1972.
Note Siepmann 21 June 1927.
nn CTM 4, 20 May, 29 July, 30 Sept. 1925.
Notes of meetings with Hautain and other Belgian representative 18 May, 5, 6, 14, 16 Oct. 1925.
Norman Diary May and Oct. 1925.
Letter Strakosch/Janssen 17 Apr. 1926.
Memo. 'Belgium' 12 Oct. 1925.
Memo. Norman conversation with Leaf 23 Oct. 1925.
CTM 30 Sept., 7, 14, 21 Oct. 1925.
Cables betw. Norman and Strong Oct. 1925, Mar. 1926.
Letters Harvey/Bachmann and Harvey/Vissering, 31 Mar. 1926.
Letter Norman/Parker Gilbert 16 June 1926.
Agreements with Nat. B. of Belgium Oct. 1925, Mar. 1926.
Letters Anderson/Strong 27 Nov., Strong/Anderson 7 Dec. 1925.
Memo. Norman 26/7 Aug. 1926 (conversation with Moncheur).
Memo. Jan. 1927.
oo Letters Franck/Norman 29 Oct., Norman/Franck 9 Nov. 1926.
Note of conversations 16–18 Feb. 1926.
Letters Norman/Clegg and Norman/Smith 28 Oct. Norman/Schacht 26 Apr., Norman/Moreau 16 Oct., Norman/Strong 29 Oct. 1926.
pp Letters Norman/Strong 4 Mar. 1926, Stringher/Norman 18 Dec. 1927.
Cables Strong/Bank 19, 22 May 1926.
Letters Strong/Norman 18 Mar., 25 May 1926.
Note 9 Apr. 1932.
Memo. of interview with Nathan 23 Oct. 1926.
CTM 27 Oct. 1926.
Letters Norman/Strong 4 Mar. 1926, 26 Oct. 1927.
Norman letters to central bankers Oct.–Dec. 1926.

Notes of conversations Norman/Moreau 26 Nov. 1926, Norman/Strong 19 Nov. 1927.
Letters Norman/Salter 8 Nov., Salter/Norman 20 Nov. 1926.
CTM 27 Oct., 10 Nov., 1 Dec. 1926, 19 Oct. 1927.
Note of Siepmann conversation with Nathan 17 Oct. 1927.
Letters Strong/Norman 9 Nov., Norman/Strong 22 Nov., 26 Oct. 1927.
qq Letters Stringher/Norman 18 Dec., Norman/Franck 23 Dec. 1927.
CTM 21, 28 Dec. 1927.
Agreements 20 Dec. 1927. (Note 7 Feb. 1929.)
Norman letters to central bankers 17 Dec. 1927.
Letters Whigham/Siepmann 23 Dec. 1927, 2 Jan. 1928.
Note 9 Apr. 1930.
Norman Diary 29 Nov. 1927.
Siepmann note of conversations 29 Nov. 1927.
Letter Strong/Norman 26 Nov. 1926.
rr Norman interview with Gafenco 6 Feb. 1928.
Interviews: Auboin 24 Oct., Monnet 23 Oct. 1972.
Letters Harrison/Norman 6 June, Niemeyer/Norman 25 Jan., Strong/Norman 3 Mar. 1928.
Note of meeting 2 May 1928.
Note 'Financial Reconstruction' 4 Feb. 1928.
Niemeyer 'Various Memoranda on League and Financial Reconstruction'; other Niemeyer notes Jan.–Feb. 1928.
ss Notes and corres. Norman/Burilleanu, Niemeyer, Tiarks, Franck, Madgearu 30 Mar., various dates Oct.–Dec. 1927, Jan. 1928. Notes Siepmann 23 Jan. 1928.
Despatch by Lord Crewe 14 Jan. 1928.
Notes Siepmann 20, 23 Jan. 1928.
Cable Norman/Strong 21 Jan. 1928.
Papers handed by Moreau to Norman 27 Apr. 1928.
Letters and cables Norman, Lubbock with Strong, Harrison Feb.–Mar. 1928.
Note Siepmann conversation Mar. 1928.
Interview Auboin 24 Oct. 1972.
tt Cables Lubbock/Rist/Moreau 18, 19, 20 Feb. 1928.
Note Siepmann conversation 22 Feb. 1928.
Letter Quesnay/Siepmann 27 Feb. 1928.
Cable Strong/Lubbock 24 Feb. 1928.
Notes Siepmann conversations 2 May 1928.
Strong discussions with B. of France May 1928 (FRBNY Strong Papers 1000.9).
Norman Diary Feb.–Apr. 1928.
Cables Norman/Harrison 11 Apr., 11 May 1928.
Letters Norman/Moreau 19 Apr., 4 May 1928.
CTM 11 July, 24 Oct. 1928.
Letters Lubbock/Schacht/Stringher/Harrison 11 July 1928.
Note Siepmann 3 Oct. 1928.
Letter Schröder/Norman 16 Oct. 1928.
Letters Moreau/Norman 20 Nov., 10 Dec. 1928, 14 Feb. 1929.
Note summarising stabilisation programme 4 Mar. 1929.
Credit agreement 16 Nov. 1928.
Letter Nat. B. Rumania/Bank 4 Feb. 1931.
Note Siepmann 31 July of conversations in Paris, also 15 June 1928.
uu Letters Dreyse/Norman 7 May, Schacht/Norman 9 June, Norman/Schacht 11 June 1928.
Letters Moreau/Lubbock 6 July, Lubbock/Moreau 9 July 1928.

Lubbock corres. with Schacht June 1928. Siepmann note of conversations in Paris 19 June 1928.
Letters Bachmann/Norman 28 June, Lubbock/Bachmann 9 July 1928.

vv CTM 27 Jan., 18 Aug., 24 Nov. 1926.
League of Nations Papers 11 June, 5 Oct. 1926.
Letters Niemeyer/Norman 23 Mar., Molloff/Norman 25 Nov. 1926.
Notes 25 June, 24 Aug. 1926. Siepmann notes 22, 23 May 1928.
Agreement and tel. Siepmann/Salter 25 Aug. 1926.

ww Letter Siepmann/Barry 24 Feb. 1928.
Strong memo. 24 May 1928.

xx Letter Norman/Strong 28 Nov. 1927.

yy Corres. Norman/Clegg esp. Apr.–Aug. 1923, Mar., Apr., Sept. 1925.

zz CTM 17 Nov. 1920.
Letters Norman/Strakosch 16 Feb. 1921, Norman/Smuts 4 Feb. 1921, Peacock/White 14 Dec. 1920.
Norman corres. Strakosch, Clegg, Falk, Hunter Feb.–Apr. 1921.
Addis Papers Feb. 1921.
Letters Norman/Strong 17 Feb., Strong/Norman 21 Mar. 1921.

aaa Corres. Norman/Blackett esp. 1923.
Note Kershaw 15 Dec. 1924.
CTM 26 Oct. 1921.
Corres. Norman, Harvey, Trotter with India Office July 1922–Apr. 1923.
Tel. Trotter/Blackett 23 Jan. 1923.
Letters Norman/Vissering, Montagu, Clegg Feb. 1921, June–July 1922, Norman/Clegg 31 May 1921, Norman/Strakosch 2 Dec. 1924.

bbb Niemeyer Papers. Cttee on Inter-Imperial Exchanges 1923.
Corres. Gov./Peacock 1922.
CTM 31 Oct. 1923.
Letters Norman/Campion 11 Oct. 1924, Trotter/Harvey 25 Mar. 1927, Norman/Strakosch 14 May, Riddle/Norman 22 June 1926.
Court Papers 5 Aug. 1926.
Letters Norman/Clegg 8 Dec. 1925, 17 Aug. 1926.
Letter Harvey/Norman 21 Mar. 1927 with memo. Memo. Harvey 20 June 1927.

ccc Letter Norman/Kell 26 Aug. 1926.
Cables Clegg/Harvey, Harvey/Clegg 30 June, 2 July 1930.
Letter Harvey/Clegg 1 Oct. 1931.

ddd Letters Norman/Clegg 6 July and rel. papers Jan., Norman/Clegg 9 Jan. 1924.
Niemeyer Papers. Cttee on Inter-Imperial Exchanges 1923.
Letters Norman/Schacht 6 Dec., Norman/Strakosch 20 Oct., Norman/Clegg 27 Oct. 1924.
Cable Norman/Strong 5 Aug. 1927.
Letters Clegg/Norman 23 May, 26 June 1923.
Cables Clegg/Norman, Norman/Clegg June–July 1923.

eee Letters Norman/Clegg, Osborne Smith 28 Oct. 1926.

fff Corres. Norman/Reading May 1934–Dec. 1936.
Memo. Harvey 17 Sept. 1934.
Memo. 9 June 1937.

CHAPTER 9

a CTM 30 Nov., 7 Dec. 1927.

b Cable Norman/Clegg 19 May 1925.
Letter Norman/Blackett 27 Oct. 1925.

Letter Anderson/Norman 17 July 1925.

c CTM 25, 26 Nov. 1925.
Letters Norman/Vissering 12 Dec., Norman/Bachmann 7 Dec. 1925.
Letter Revelstoke/Baring 3 Dec. 1925 (Baring Archives: Revelstoke).

d Letters Norman/Anderson 17 Aug. 1925, Norman/Harrison 23 Aug. 1926.
CTM 4 Jan., 26 Sept. 1928.

e CTM 23 May 1927.

f Letters Norman/Strong 25 Mar., 29 Aug., Strong/Lubbock 16 Aug. 1927.
CTM 31 Oct. 1928.
Cables Norman/Harrison, McGarrah/Norman Aug. 1929.

g Norman Diary 27 Aug., frequently Nov.–Dec. 1927, Jan.–Feb. 1928.
CTM 30 Nov., 7 Dec. 1927.
Note of conversations Siepmann/Quesnay June 1927. Letter Siepmann/Norman 20 May 1927.

h Note of conversation Tetrode 31 Jan. 1928.
Note of talk Goldenweiser/Gov. Young 6 Mar. 1929. (Goldenweiser Papers Box 1, Library of Congress, Washington.)
Letter Lubbock/Strong 9 Aug. 1928 (FRBNY Strong Papers 1117.2).
Memo. on French gold demands (Siepmann) 26 Nov. 1928.
Norman Diary 13 Sept., 21 Dec. 1928.

i Norman Diary 1, 3 Jan., 19 Feb. 1929.
Cables Norman (in New York)/Lubbock Feb. 1929.
Paper for CT 13 Mar. 1929.

j Cables Norman/Harrison May 1929.

k CTM 7 Aug. 1929.
Memo. 9 Aug. 1929.

l CTM 20 Aug., 4 Sept. 1929.
Corres. Norman/Addis Aug., Sept. 1929.

m Norman Diary.
CTM 11, 25 Sept. 1929.

n CTM 30 Oct. 1929.

o Cable McGarrah/Norman 31 Jan. 1930.
CTM 26 Feb., 5, 19 Mar., 30 Apr. 1930.

p Norman Diary.
Interview G. M. Booth 4 Nov. 1969.

q Cable Norman/Harrison 27 Aug. 1930.
Memo. Sprague/Norman 14 Oct. 1930.
Norman Diary 13 Jan. 1931.
CTM 19 Nov. 1930, 7, 14 Jan., 11 May 1931.

CHAPTER 10

a CTM 10 July 1918. Norman Papers.

b Report signed 6 Mar. 1917 of a cttee appointed by the CLCB. Letter Cokayne/Strong 2 Feb. 1920. Norman Diary Feb.–Mar. 1920.

c Norman Diary 22 Feb. 1923.
Letter Niemeyer/Gov. 6 Feb. 1923. CTM 14 Feb. 1923.
Corres. Gov./Treas. 1924.

d Letter Niemeyer/Bank 5 Nov. 1923.
Norman Diary 29 Jan. 1923. CTM 7 Feb. 1923 and rel. papers. Note Unclaimed Balances 10 Jan. 1935. Letter Norman/Blackett 9 Mar. 1923.

e Note Norman of conversation with Chanc. 3 Mar. 1924. Letter Treas./Bank 15 Oct. 1924.

f Letter Norman 12 June 1925. Letter Pease/Gov. 17 Apr. 1924.
g Norman Diary 18 Oct. 1923. CTM 24 Oct. 1923. Letter Niemeyer/Pease 5 Nov. 1923.
h Letter Norman/Lubbock 6 Mar. 1925. CTM 1 Apr. 1925. CTM and Norman Diary 3 June 1925.
i Letters Wood/Norman 17 Sept., Niemeyer/Norman 1 Sept. 1925. Norman Diary 8 Oct., 5 Nov. 1925. CTM 12 Aug., 14 Oct. 1925.
CTM 3 June 1925.
Letter Norman/Niemeyer 12 June 1925. Norman Diary June–Sept. 1925.
Letter Chanc./Pease 29 June 1925. CTM 17, 24 June, 1 July 1925.
j CTM 10 Mar. 1926.
Letter Catterns/Caulcutt (Barclays D.C.O.) 4 Aug. 1939. PDO Diary 11 Dec. 1939.
Norman Diary Sept.–Dec. 1926.
CTM 24 June, 26 Aug. 1925, 15 Sept. 1926.
k Norman Diary Apr.–May 1927. CTM 28 Apr., 8 June 1927.
l Interview Gov./Nightingale 8 Dec. 1925.
m Norman Diary and CTM 23 Feb. 1927.
Norman Diary 30 Nov. 1927.
n Note of Gov. conversation with bankers 20 June 1934.
o Norman Diary throughout 1930s.
Letter Paton/Norman 31 May 1933. Norman Diary 1933–5, 1938–9.
p Harvey note of meeting 20 Dec. 1928.
Note of discussion with Dewhurst 7 Oct. 1927. Niemeyer note 2 Nov. 1927.
q Norman Diary 1, 6 Nov. 1928.
r Letter Wright/Dewhurst 11 May 1929.
CTM 23, 25 June, 27 Aug. 1930. Letter Harvey/Dewhurst 21 July 1930.
s CTM 15 Jan., 12 Mar., 23 July, 6 Aug. 1930, 21 Sept., 21 Dec. 1932, 1 Mar. 1933.
t Letter Harvey/Wright 17 Apr. 1930.
u Harvey notes of meetings 15, 22 Dec. 1930, 10 Feb. 1931.
Notes dated 6 May approved by CT 13 May, 20 May approved 27 May, 1 July approved 8 July 1931.
Memo. 8 May approved by CT 9 May 1934.
Letter Norman/Dewhurst 14 Jan. 1938.
v Memos. 25 June 1936, 9 Dec. 1937. Note 30 Jan. 1940.
w CTM 23, 30 Jan., 20, 27 Mar., 17 Apr. 1929, 10 Sept. 1930. Mins. of meetings at Bank, 18, 22 Jan. 1929, 24 Jan. 1930.
x Letter Cooper/Gov. 4 Sept. 1930. CTM 25 Apr. 1934.
y Norman Diary 16 Mar. 1931. Note Peppiatt/Sayers 19 June 1972.
CTM frequently from 16 Sept. to end Nov. 1931. Papers of Special Cttee on Credit.
z Memos. etc. Discount Office. CTM 7, 14, 21 Oct. 1931.
aa Memo. Hornsby 12 Nov. 1931.
CTM 25 Nov. 1931. Norman Diary 25, 27 Nov. 1931. Gov. corres. with Chanc. 26–8 Nov. 1931. Note 2 June 1932.
bb CTM 24 July, 18, 25 Sept. 1935. Letter Norman/Towers 5 June 1935.
CTM 21 Feb., 21 Mar. 1934.
cc CTM 24 July, 18 Dec. 1935.
dd Papers rel. to Pre- and Post-Moratorium Bills 19 July 1916, 10 Mar. 1922. Papers rel. to Huth 20, 28 Dec. 1921, 20 Feb. 1936.
CTM 24 July 1922. Notes 24, 26 July 1922.
Letter Norman/Strong 31 Oct. 1922.
ee CTM 9 Jan. 1936 and rel. papers. Court Mins. 24 Oct. 1935. Memo. Discount Office 12 Dec. 1935.

CHAPTER 11

a An illuminating source not only for this paragraph but for the whole chapter is the Diary of the Principal of the Discount Office (PDO Diary).
b PDO Diary 1 Oct. 1928.
c CTM 19, 26 Feb. 1919.
Norman Diary 6, 11 Mar. 1919.
Memo. Tiarks 25 Apr. 1927.
PDO Diary 18 Oct. 1928.
d PDO Diary 14 Oct. 1919. CTM 8 Nov. 1922.
e CTM 10 Oct. 1923, 20 Feb. 1924, 25 Mar., 1 Apr. 1925. Cttee on Advances and Discounts Mins. 26 May 1927. Memo. Norman 28 Oct. 1922.
f PDO Diary 1 Nov. 1928, 19, 30 Apr., 2, 4 May 1929.
g Letters Bull/Sayers 23 Sept., 7 Oct. 1970.
h PDO Diary 6–24 Sept., 25 Nov., 14–23 Dec. 1920.
PDO Diary 21 Apr. 1927.
i PDO Diary 12 Oct. 1928.
PDO Diary 13, 21 Aug., 6, 8 Apr. 1929.

CHAPTER 12

a Special Cttee 'to consider...a revision of the Bank Act of 1844...' Report 26 Nov. 1918 and papers. Court Mins. 12 Dec. 1918.
b CTM 23 May 1923. Letter Norman/Anderson 17 Aug. 1925.
c Letter Strong/Norman 15 Jan., Norman/Strong 10 Feb. 1925.
Letters Norman/Strong 20 Apr., Strong/Norman 30 Apr. 1925. Cable no. 92 Norman/Strong 27 Mar. 1925.
d CTM 1, 8, 15 Dec. 1926 and rel. memos. (Lefeaux).
CTM 19 Oct. 1927. St Luke's Cttee Mins. 21 Jan. 1927.
Special Cttee on profits of note issue Report 15 Nov. 1927. CTM 16 Nov. 1927. Court Mins. 17, 24 Nov., 1 Dec. 1927. Addis memo. 24 Nov. 1927.
e Special Cttee on...note issue Report and papers 1927.
f Conversation Gov./D. Gov./Hopkins 3 Feb. 1928.
g Report of Special Cttee on...note issue 1927. Addis memo. in papers of this cttee 24 Nov. 1927.
h Memo. Lefeaux 16 July 1926.
i CTM 7, 20, 28 Aug., 4, 18 Sept. 1929. Letters Addis/Norman 31 Aug., Norman/Addis 2 Sept. 1929.
j Letter Niemeyer/Leith-Ross 25 Oct. 1927. Memo. Lefeaux 16 July 1926. Memo. Mahon 9 Nov. 1925.
Gov. conversation with Treas. 8 Feb. 1928. Letters Mahon/Treas. 27 July, Hopkins/Govs. 3 Aug. 1928.
k Letter Norman/Hopkins 16 Nov. 1928.

CHAPTER 13

a CTM 16 Feb. 1921. Memo. 1 Sept. 1920.
b Norman Diary 9, 11, 30 Mar. 1920. PDO Diary 6–30 Sept. 1920.
c Memos. (Mahon) 9 Nov. 1925, 29 June 1927, 13 Feb. 1928. Note of discussion Gov./D. Gov./Hopkins 3 Feb. 1928. Letters Niemeyer/Phillips 18 Apr. 1928, Norman/Vissering 12 Dec. 1925.
d Interview Sir K. Peppiatt 15 Jan. 1969. Norman Diary 21 Nov. 1921.
e PDO Diary 10, 14 Nov. 1921, 23 Jan. 1922.

Norman Diary 21 Apr. 1922.

CTM 20 Feb. 1924. Interviews Sir K. Peppiatt 15 Jan. 1969, 28 Oct. 1971. Letter Harvey/Norman 28 June 1929.

f Peacock Cttee, evidence of D. Gov. and Chief Cashier May 1931.

Norman Diary 14 May 1923.

CTM 22 July 1925. Memo. 21 Nov. 1939.

Letter Anderson/Norman 25 July 1925.

g CTM 22, 29 July 1925. Comptroller's papers rel. to Commonwealth Bank transactions; information by courtesy of Librarian, Reserve Bank of Australia, London.

h CTM 27 July, 7 Dec. 1921, 28 Oct. 1925, 27 Apr. 1932.

i Letter Norman/Vissering 12 Dec. 1925. Memo. 28 Oct. 1925.

Memo. Some Uses of the Issue Department 1930.

j Osborne note Open Market Operations May 1932.

k CTM 18 Mar., 7 May, 19 Aug., 7 Oct. 1925. Norman Diary 17 July, 1 Oct. 1925.

l Osborne note 28 July 1930.

Peppiatt comments on Cobbold draft 1935.

m Letter Siepmann/Rooth 11 Dec. 1929.

n Letter Norman/Clegg 29 Nov. 1928.

W. Gardner memo. 16 Sept. 1929 (Board of Govs. of the Federal Reserve System).

CHAPTER 14

a Court records 21 Nov. 1929.

b Armstrong annual reports etc. (in Branch Banks Office Papers). CTM 27 Mar. 1918, 19 May 1920, 12 Dec. 1923, 22 Oct. 1924, 28 Aug. 1925. Memo. (for D. Gov.) 22 Dec. Letter Norman/Plender 6 Feb. 1934. Memo. (Skinner) 20 Aug. 1945.

c CTM 2 Sept. 1925, 26 Jan., 25 May, 28 Sept. 1927. Cable Taylor/Peacock 31 Aug. 1925. Memos. (Travers) 27 Sept. 1927, May 1930.

Letters Phillips/Norman 3 June 1937, Taylor/Norman 11 Jan. 1938. Note (Mynors) 14 Nov. 1944. Letter Skinner/Peacock 27 May 1941. Gov. interview with Taylor 1 June 1942.

d Corres. Norman/Warren Fisher/Peacock Aug. 1927. Letter Skinner/Peppiatt 28 June 1935. Reports etc. rel. to Vickers-Armstrong 1927–30. Letter Bruce-Gardner/Norman 23 Nov. 1932.

Corres. Norman/Lawrence Mar. 1936. Notes (Peppiatt) 29 Oct. 1945, (Skinner) 20 Sept. 1935. CTM 17 June 1936, 23 June 1937. Letter Bruce-Gardner/Norman 4 July 1941.

e Court Mins. 8 Apr. 1926, 6 Jan., 28 Apr., 18 Nov. 1927.

f Note (Stewart) encl. letter Niemeyer/Lady Norman 11 Apr. 1960. Letter Colwyn/Norman 13 Mar. 1928. Niemeyer corres./B. of Trade July 1928. Note (Niemeyer) 24 July 1928.

CTM 19 Sept., 24 Oct. 1928.

g CTM 24 Oct. 1928, 16, 30 Jan. 1929. Lancashire Cotton Corporation Articles of Association 23 Jan. 1929; Trust Deed 19 May 1931. Note 15 May 1929. Note (Stewart, Ryan) 9 Oct. 1930.

Note (Niemeyer) 30 Apr. 1930. CTM 7 May, 17 Dec. 1930. Letter Bank/Lancashire Cotton Corporation 29 May 1931. Note (Peppiatt) 1 Feb. 1940.

Letter Cooper/Norman 1 July 1932. Corres. Barlow/Peacock, Masters/Bank Aug. 1932.

h Letter Duncan/Norman 11 Mar. 1929. Skinner interview 3 Feb. 1971. Letter Norman/Hopkins 30 Apr. 1929. Note (Catterns) 24 Apr. 1929.

CTM 15 Jan., 23 June, 24 Sept. 1930. Letter Bruce-Gardner/Catterns 23 Sept. 1930.

i Note (Leith-Ross) 7 Dec. 1926. Beardmore Schemes of Reorganization 15 Oct. 1928,

19 July 1929. CTM 8 Dec. 1926. Note (Skinner) 2 June 1938. Draft letter Norman/Duncan 22 Aug. 1929. Norman Diary 12 June 1929. CTM 19, 26 June 1929. Cables Norman/Taylor/Norman Sept. 1929. Note (Mahon) 13 Sept. 1929. Memo. 5 Feb. 1930. Outline of Proposed Reconstruction 30 June 1938.

j Circular letter 7 Feb. 1929. Note Taylor's visit 4 Nov. 1929. Letter Taylor/Peacock 3 Dec. 1928. Brassert Reports 1929, 1930, 1932. Bruce-Gardner Report...Steel Industry 31 Dec. 1930. Corres. Taylor/Peacock/Bank 1928–9. Norman Diary 5 Nov. 1929. Letter Bischoff/Skinner 6 Mar. 1930.

Norman corres. Pam Nov. 1929, Feb. 1930. Court Records 21, 28 Nov. 1929. Memo. Bischoff/Taylor 3 Feb. 1930. Note 12 Oct. and draft 5 Dec. 1950.

k Skinner memo. 21 June; interview 13 Aug. 1969. Letters Peacock/Revelstoke 25 Oct. 1928, Norman/Dawnay 4 May 1935. Court Records 21 Nov. 1929.

l Skinner memo. 21 June 1969; interviews 13 Aug. 1969, 3 Feb. 1971. CTM 14 Nov., 5, 12 Dec. 1928, 23 Jan., 1 May, 14 Aug., 20 Nov. 1929.

m Letter Norman/Fisher 12 Sept. 1929. CTM 11, 18 Sept., 20 Nov. 1929. Norman Diary 4 Sept. 1929.

n CTM 19 June, 14 Aug., 9 Oct., 6, 20 Nov., 4 Dec. 1929. Court Records and meetings of Directors 21, 25 Nov., 2 Dec. 1929.

Meetings of S.M.T. directors.

CTM 5, 19 Mar., 2 Apr. 1930. Court Records 20 Mar. 1930.

Corres. Norman/Taylor Nov. 1929–Apr. 1930.

o Report The Bank and Industry 4 July 1933. Court Records 14, 21 Nov. 1929. CTM 16 Apr. 1930.

p CTM 19, 26 Feb., 12 Mar., 9 Apr. 1930; see also Macmillan Cttee Evidence Qus. 9029, 9030, 9035. Memo. 15 May 1930. Memo. (Skinner) 26 Apr. 1944. Letters Norman/Duncan 7 Mar., Norman/Whigham 21 Mar. 1930, Norman/Stern 10 Apr. 1935, Skinner/Peppiatt 24 Feb. 1937.

CTM 9 Jan. 1946.

CTM 16 Apr. 1930 and rel. Norman corres.

Skinner papers for Sayers 21, 26 July, 13 Aug. 1969. Court Records 21 Nov. 1929.

q Letter Norman/Peacock 14 Aug. 1929. CTM 22 Jan., 12, 19 Mar. 1930. Skinner interviews 13 Aug. 1969, 3 Feb. 1971.

r CTM 27 Nov. 1929.

s Norman Diary Mar. 1930

Corres. Norman/McLintock, 1930–37.

McLintock report 15 Apr. 1930.

t CTM 7 Jan., 25 Feb., 2 Sept. 1931, 2 Aug., 27 Sept., 18 Oct. 1933. Notes for CT (Norman) 16 Feb. 1931. Letter Hopkins/Gov. 20 Feb. 1931.

CTM 11 May 1931. Court Records 30 June 1932.

Letter Norman/Duncan 10 Mar. 1932.

Notes (Comptroller) on various schemes 1931. CTM 7 Jan., 25 Feb., 11 May 1931.

u Norman corres. Essendon, McLintock, Harvey, Baird, Barrie. Memos. (incl. 26, 29 Oct. 1934) on Royal Mail realisation etc. Memos. (Skinner etc.) 1934–7. Memo. Hopkins/Fisher/Chanc. 10 July 1934. CTM 17 Oct., 8 Nov., 12 Dec. 1934, 2 Jan. 1935.

Memo (Lefeaux) on Lord Weir's Report 14 Jan. 1933.

CTM 2 Aug. 1932, 27 Sept., 18 Oct. 1933, 5 June, 24 Oct. 1934, 24 June 1936, 6 Oct. 1937. Norman Diary Feb. 1935.

v Notes on formation of BIDCo (Skinner/Towers) 6 Oct. 1934.

Letters Schröders, Erlangers/Bank Jan.–Feb. 1930.

CHAPTER 15

a Letter Lubbock/Diomede 15 Dec. 1924. I. Rooth interview 17 May 1968. CTM 3, 28 Oct. 1928.

b Memo. 12 Nov. 1923. Letter Norman/Clegg 17 Nov. 1927. CTM 14 Apr. 1926.

c Court Mins. 22 Mar. 1923. Corres. with Netherlands Bank 1925. Letter Norman/Smith 15 June 1929. Memo. (Siepmann) 19 Aug. 1932.

d Memo. (CT 13.5.25) 7 May 1925.

e Cables Norman/Strong 4, 7 June 1927. Letter Strong/Norman 5 June 1927.

f Cable Norman/Strong 30 May 1927.

g Notes (Norman) 3–9 July 1927. CTM 8 June, 3, 17 Aug. 1927.

h L. Rist interview 24 Oct. 1972.

i Letter Norman/Strong 17 May 1924. CTM 17 Aug. 1927.

j Letters Strong/Norman/Strong 20 Oct., 4 Nov. 1927.

k Corres. and notes of conversations Siepmann/Quesnay 1927–8.
Notes of Siepmann conversations with Fuchs 11 May, Hulse 24 June, Cariguel 26 July 1929.
Memos. (Siepmann, Kay) 26, 29 Jan. 1931.

l Cable Norman/Lubbock 4 Feb. 1929.

m CTM 23 Sept. 1925.
Letters Norman/Rosenkrantz 10 Nov., Trotter/Clegg 10 Feb. 1927.

n Niemeyer memo. of discussion (Pospisil) 12 Dec.; memo. 13 Dec. 1927. Letter Norman/Strong 28 Nov. 1927. CTM 14 Nov. 1928.
Corres. Strong/Norman June–Aug. 1927.

o Siepmann note of conversation with Quesnay 18 Jan. 1928. Siepmann note of Norman/Franck conversation 28 Nov. 1927.
Letter Strong/Norman 3 Mar. 1928. Papers on Salter/Strong discussion 25 May, 30 June; note 31 July 1928. Letter Strong/Harrison 8 July 1928 (FRBNY Strong Papers 1000.9).
CTM 13 June, 14, 28 Nov. 1928.

p CTM 19 Dec. 1928, 9 Jan., 20 Feb., 6 Mar. 1929. Note (Niemeyer) 2 Jan. 1929. Norman corres. (Sprague) Oct. 1929–Jan. 1930.

q Norman corres. (FRBNY) Oct. 1929–Jan. 1930. CTM 3, 10, 17 Sept. 1930.

r Report of the Cttee of Experts (Young Plan) 1929. Norman Diary 15, 16, 17 Oct., 14 Nov., 28 Dec. 1928.
Corres. Norman/Harrison, Norman/Stringher Mar. 1930. Conversations at Bank 30 Dec. 1929. Letter Franck/Norman 1 Apr. 1930.

s Note (Siepmann) of First Official Board Meeting B.I.S. 12 May 1930.
Memo. (Norman) B.I.S. end Aug. 1929.
Note Baden-Baden negotiations 3 Dec. 1929. Letters Addis/Norman 31 Oct., 8, 10 Nov. 1929.
Letter Reynolds/Norman 13 Nov. 1929.
Norman Diary Jan., Feb., Mar. 1930. Note (Siepmann) meetings 29, 30 Apr., 3 May 1930.

t Letters Norman/Addis 15 Aug., Norman/Moreau 10 Sept. 1929.
Note conversation Norman/Snowden 4 Sept. 1929. CTM 20 Aug. 1929.

u Schacht conversations 27 Aug., 9 Sept. 1929. Letter Schacht/Moreau 12 Sept. 1929.
Notes of conversations (Siepmann) Franck 5 Sept., Moreau 30 Dec., Quesnay 13, 14 Sept. 1929. CTM 5 Mar. 1930.
Norman draft cables 18 Sept. 1929.
Letters Norman/Addis 7 Sept., Schacht/Moreau 12 Sept., Addis/Norman 8 Nov. 1929. Court Records 6 Mar. 1930. Letter Moreau/Norman 17 Sept. 1929.

Conversations Schacht/Norman/Layton 27 Aug., 9 Sept., Addis/Layton 13 Sept. 1929.

Letter Rennell/Rootham 24 Oct. 1966 with encl. Letter Addis/Siepmann 7 Sept. 1931.

v CTM 5 Mar. 1930.

Letter Harrison/Schacht 13 Aug. 1929. Mins. Meetings of Board of Directors B.I.S. 1930. Conversation Addis/Layton 13 Sept. 1929.

Corres. Norman/Addis Oct.–Nov. 1929. Note of conversation Beneduce 17, 18 Sept. 1929.

w Court Records 6 Mar. 1930. Letter Norman/Vansittart 10 Mar. 1930. CTM 23 Apr. 1930. Corres. Norman/McGarrah Apr. 1930.

Norman Diary 17 Apr. 1930. CTM 16 Apr. 1930. Letters Siepmann/McGarrah 17 Apr. 1930, Norman/Fraser 3 Dec. 1934.

Court Records 10 Jan. 1929. CTM 28 May, 23 June 1930. Report B.I.S. for period 1 Feb.–31 July 1930.

x Conversations Quesnay/Norman 24 Apr. 1930; comments Hawtrey, Niemeyer. Memo. (Rodd) 26 May 1930. CTM 20 May 1930.

Letter Lefeaux/B.I.S. 24 May 1930. Memo. 26 May 1930.

CTM 30 July 1930.

Note (Siepmann) 12 Aug. 1930. Cables Norman/Harrison/Norman Aug. 1930. Letter Norman/Luther 26 Aug. 1930.

Notes (Norman) 19 Sept., (Siepmann) 16 Sept. 1930. CTM 17 Sept. 1930.

y CTM 3, 17, 24 Sept., 1 Oct. 1930. Letters Peacock/Norman 30 Sept., Norman/Harrison 20 Sept. 1930.

Letters Norman/Clegg 10 Dec., Peacock/Norman 30 Sept. 1930.

CTM 14 Jan., 28 Oct. 1931, 8 Apr. 1936.

CHAPTER 16

a Memo. Crane/Harrison 18 Feb. 1928. FRBNY.

b Letter Harvey/Norman 12 July 1929.

c Harvey corres. with Treas. July 1929. Norman Diary 9 Aug., 14, 24, 31 Oct. 1929. Letter Norman/Treas. 30 Sept. 1929. CTM 2 Oct. 1929.

d Cable Harvey/Harrison 11 Dec. 1929. Norman Diary Nov.–Dec. 1929.

e Letter Harvey/Norman 19 Dec. 1929. Norman Diary 12 Mar. 1930. Letter Harvey/Stewart 11 Apr. 1930. Interview W. F. Crick 9 May 1973.

f CTM 2 Oct. 1929.

g Letter Norman/Ismay 2 Apr. 1930.

h Harvey notes on amendment of evidence 5 Dec. 1929.

i CTM 7 Jan. 1931.

j For this section I have drawn on a paper 'The Bank, the Press and the Public' prepared within the Bank (by Miss J. Bridges) for the purposes of this history. The paper is in two parts, the first covering the years 1890–1933, and the second covering developments to the beginning of 1941.

The most important CTM are: 22 Apr. 1925, 16 Mar., 12 Oct. 1927, 24 Oct. 1928, 25 Oct. 1933, 6 July 1932, 10 July 1935, 13, 20 June, 4 July, 5 Sept., 17 Oct. 1934, 10 Jan., 28 Aug., 4 Sept., 11 Dec. 1940. CT Records 28 Dec. 1938, 20 Dec. 1939, 22 May 1940. See also Court Records 13 Mar., and Court Mins. 17 Apr. 1941.

The more important letters are: Gibbs/Powell 27 Jan. 1894, Cunliffe/Raffalovich 16 Mar. 1915, Harvey/Norman 28 June 1929, Sprigge (*Manchester Guardian*)/Siepmann 27 June 1931, Norman/Harrison 23 Aug. 1926, Norman/Henry Bell 23 Aug. 1930, Niemeyer/Reid 28 Dec. 1931, Peat/Gov. 28 May, Kindersley/Gov. 30 Aug. 1934, Stamp/Gov. 20 July 1933, and in the Strong/Norman corres. 3 Apr. 1922, 19 Sept., 9, 21 Nov. 1927.

The more important memos. are: Dale on Press Association 28 Jan. 1927, appointment of Clay 15 Jan. 1930 and 1 June 1933, Norman/Paine 25 Oct. 1933 and note by Harvey of talk with Paine 31 May/1 June 1934, Clay on talk to Trade and Industry Cttee 20 June 1934; Statistical Summary 26 Aug. 1937, Siepmann on E.E.A. 14 Feb. 1938, Yeomans on profits of Issue Dept. 2 Sept. 1938, Temple's advice on Press relations 31 Oct. and Clay's comments 13 Nov. 1940.

CHAPTER 17

a CTM 31 Aug. 1931.
Letters Clegg/Harvey 21 Oct., reply 9 Nov.; Vissering/Harvey 21 Sept., reply 25 Sept.; Trip/Norman 27 Oct., reply 2 Nov.; Bachmann/Harvey 3 Dec., reply 21 Dec. 1931. Notes on visits Trip 23 Oct., Beneduce 2 Oct. (Siepmann note).

b Norman Diary July–Sept. 1931. Mins. Currency Cttee 6 Oct. 1931. CTM 22, 25 Aug. 1931. Clay Memos. on Gold Standard 22, 25, 26 Aug., 21, 24 Sept., 7 Oct. 1931. Note (CT) 21 Sept. 1931.

c Court Mins. 14 May 1931. CT papers on Credit Anstalt.

d Telephone Norman/Harrison 16 July 1931 (FRBNY 3115.2). Bolton account of crisis. Court Mins. 23 July 1931.
Cables Norman/Harrison 23 June, McGarrah/Bank 27 Aug., B.I.S./Bank 6/7 July 1931. Letter McGarrah/Norman 7 July 1931.
Notes (Siepmann) 16, 18, 23, 26 June 1931.

e Cable Norman/Harrison 28 July 1931. Telephone Norman/Harrison 29 July 1931 (FRBNY 3115.2).

f Cable Norman/Harrison 27 July 1931. Court Mins. 30 July 1931. CTM 27, 30 July 1931.
Letters Hopkins/Bank and Harvey/Chanc. 1 Aug. 1931. Harvey Diary 31 July 1931. Telephone Harvey/Harrison 30 July 1931 (FRBNY 3117.1).

g Siepmann conversations with Moret 5, 7 Aug. 1931. Telephone Harvey/Harrison 7 Aug. 1931. Letters Norman/Prime Minister 25 June, Strabolgi/Norman 2 July, Harvey/Chanc. 6 Aug. 1931. Memo. (Siepmann) 14 Aug. 1931.

h Norman Diary Aug.–Sept. 1931. Cables Harvey to central banks 1 Aug. 1931. CTM 14 Aug. 1931.

i CTM 27 July 1931.
Bolton account of crisis. Telephone Siepmann/Moret 5 Aug. 1931. Letter Harvey/Moret 10 Aug. 1931. Telephone Harvey/Harrison 7 Aug. 1931. CTM 6 Aug. 1931.

k Letter Norman/Niemeyer 8 Apr. 1925.

l Conversations Siepmann/Moret and Lacour-Gayet 7 Aug. 1931.

m *Ibid.* memo. (Siepmann) 12 Aug. 1931. CTM 6, 11, 12, 13, 14, 21, 22 Aug. 1931. Harvey Diary Aug. 1931. Letter Pease/Harvey 13 Aug. 1931.

n CTM 11, 14, 17, 18 Aug. 1931. Memo. 21 Aug. 1931. Note (Siepmann) 19 Aug. 1931. Letter Crane/FRBNY 16 Sept. 1931 (FRBNY Bank of England Corres. 1931 Miscell.).

o CTM 17, 19, 22 Aug. 1931. Telephone Harvey/Harrison 7 Aug. 1931. Letter Harvey/Morgan Grenfell 23 Aug. 1931. Cables Morgans NY/Morgan Grenfell 22, 23, 27 Aug. 1931.

p Thompson-McCausland account of crisis: interview Peacock/Thompson-McCausland 25 Mar. 1943.

q Bolton account of crisis. Cables Bank/Harrison 29 Aug., Harvey/Harrison 31 Aug. 1931. Telephone Harvey/Harrison 7 Aug. 1931. Note of meeting (Rodd, with comments Lefeaux) 23 Nov. 1931. Thompson-McCausland account of crisis.

r CTM Aug., Sept., Oct. 1931. Note (Phillips) 17 Sept. 1931. Notes (Siepmann, Sprague, Clay, Kershaw) Gold Standard 19–22 Aug. 1931.

Harvey Diary Aug., Sept. 1931. Notes of meetings Leith-Ross with French (Siepmann) 26, 27, 28 Aug. 1931. Harvey's corres. with Treas. 22 Aug., 17, 18 Sept. 1931. Letter Grenfell/Peacock 19 Sept. 1931.

s Mins. of Cttee on Foreign Exchange.

CTM 19 Sept. 1931. Court Mins. 20 Sept. 1931 (and papers).

t Letter Rodd/Harvey 5 Sept. 1931.

Letter Crane/FRBNY 16 Sept. 1931 (FRBNY Bank of England Corres. 1931 Miscell.).

Letters Harvey/Samuel 29 Aug., Rodd/Harvey 28 Aug., 5, 19 Sept. 1931. Cable Morgans/Morgan Grenfell 7 Sept. 1931. Harvey Diary Sept. 1931. CTM 2 Sept. 1931.

Note (Trade unionists) 3 Sept. 1931. Mins of Cttee on Foreign Exchange 16, 17 Sept. 1931. CTM 17 Sept. 1931.

u CTM 2 Sept. 1931.

v CTM 10 June, 1, 7 Sept. 1931.

Letters Rodd/Harvey 5, 19 Sept. 1931. Mins. of Cttee on Foreign Exchange 16, 17 Sept. 1931. Harvey Diary 19 Sept. 1931.

w Cable Morgans/Morgan Grenfell 7 Sept. 1931 (reply 8 Sept.). Note (Catterns) 15 Sept. 1931. Memo. (Sprague) 21 Sept. 1931. CTM 16, 21 Sept. 1931.

x Bolton account of crisis. Note (Catterns) 16 Sept. 1931. CTM 18 Sept. 1931. Telephone Harrison/Harvey 19 Sept. 1931.

y Mins. of Cttee on Foreign Exchange.

z Cables Harrison/Harvey 3 Sept. (reply 4 Sept.), Harvey/Harrison 8 Sept. 1931.

CTM 9, 16, 18 Sept. 1931. Cttee on Foreign Exchange 11, 16 Sept. 1931. Bolton account of crisis.

aa Bolton account of crisis. Note of meeting (Catterns) 3 Sept. 1931. Note (Kay) 20 Jan. 1931. Letters Harvey/Goodenough and reply 22 Sept. 1931. Note of meeting with clearing bankers 18 Sept. 1931.

bb CTM 2, 9 Sept. 1931.

cc Note (Kay) 4 Aug. 1931. Cttee on Foreign Exchange 14 Sept. 1931. Bolton account of crisis. Letter Leith-Ross/Catterns 21 Sept. 1931.

dd Letter Layton/Snowden 11 Aug. 1931. Memo. (Siepmann) 14 Aug. 1931. CTM 17, 22 Sept. 1931. Memo. Catterns/Harvey 15 Sept. 1931.

ee Bolton account of crisis. CTM 17 Sept. 1931. Letter Harvey/Clegg 9 Nov. 1931.

ff Memo. (Sprague) 21 Aug. 1931.

gg Letter (note enclosed) Treas./Harvey 4 Sept. 1931.

hh CTM 17, 19 Sept. 1931. Court Mins. and papers 19, 20 Sept. 1931. Harvey Diary 20 Sept. 1931.

ii CTM 31 Aug., 14 Oct. 1931. Court Mins. 15 Oct. 1931. Letter Harvey/Vissering 25 Sept. 1931. Cable Harvey/Vissering 29 Aug. 1931. Letter Norman/Clegg 4 Nov. 1931. Notes (London funds) 18, 19 Sept. 1931. Norman Diary Sept. 1931.

CHAPTER 18

a Mins. of Currency Cttee (and for later paragraphs of this section). Leith-Ross draft for Chanc. 26 Sept. 1931. Letter Harvey/Prime Minister 28 Sept. 1931. CTM 28 Sept. 1931.

b CTM 21 Oct. 1931.

Per Jacobsson Diary 8 July 1933.

c Mins. of Foreign Exchange Cttee and Currency Cttee (and for later paragraphs of this section). Papers rel. to Dollar Reserve Account.

d Foreign exchange cables 2–7 Oct. 1931.

e Letter Morgans/Kindersley 3 Oct. 1931. Memos. (Kay) 1, 8 Oct. 1931. Memo. Forward Exchange Operations 7 Mar. 1938.

f Letter Hambro/Leith-Ross 5 Dec. 1931.

g Norman Diary Oct.–Dec. 1931. CTM 2 Dec. 1931. Note of discussion (Chanc., Gov. etc.) 8 Dec. 1931.

h Fortnightly letters to Empire central banks Dec. 1931–Mar. 1932. CTM 9, 16 Dec. 1931.

i CTM 2 Dec. 1931. Memos. (Rodd) 31 Dec. 1931, (Clay) 4 Jan. 1932.

j Memos. (Hambro) 25 Feb., (Catterns) 5 Mar. 1932. Per Jacobsson Diary 11 Apr. 1932.

k Foreign exchange weekly reviews.

l Note on Bank's foreign exchange arrangements 29 Dec. 1928 and Note of discussion 1 Jan. 1929. Memos. (Clay) 24 Mar., (Strakosch) 31 Mar. 1932. E.E.A. Quarterly Report No. 9. Memo. (Bolton) on relations with agents 13 May 1938. Letter Bridge/Sayers 11 July 1974.

m CTM 13 Apr. 1932.

n PDO Diary 19, 12 May 1932.

o Corres. Bank/Treas. June 1932.

p Memo. (Niemeyer) 11 Nov. 1925. Letter Norman/Fisher 11 Sept. 1928. Opinion of Law Officers 13 Dec. 1928. Letter Hopkins/Norman 12 Jan. 1929.

q CTM 2 Sept. 1931. Note (4 per cent plan) 17 Feb. 1931. Letter Harvey/Clapham 12 Oct. 1944.

r Memo. (Suggested Basis) 30 May 1931. List of large holdings 22 May 1931. Note (foreign holdings) 27 May 1931. Note (tax liability) 3 June 1931. Analysis of overseas holdings 6 July 1932. Memo. War Loan (Harvey) 20 May 1931.

s CTM 21, 28 Oct. 1931.

t Norman Diary esp. 16 Mar., 2, 3, 21 May, 1 June 1932.

u Norman Diary June 1932.

v PDO Diary 29, 30 June 1932.

w Norman Diary July, 29 Sept. 1932. Letter Catterns/Burgess 6 Apr. 1933.

x PDO Diary 1–8, 19 July, 4, 9, 19 Aug., 20 Sept. 1932. CTM 20 July 1932.

y Memos. 1 Oct. 1932, 7 May 1936.

z Norman Diary 5, 6, 7, 11 July 1932. PDO Diary 6 July 1932. Note (Lefeaux) of meeting with clearing banks 6 July 1932. Memo. 7 May 1936.

Norman Diary 17 July 1919. Note (Bank Borrowings) 3 June 1932.

aa CTM 15 Mar. 1933. Proceedings of General Court 22 Sept. 1932.

bb Kershaw's Memoranda in preparation for the conference, his cables and letters to the Gov. from Ottawa, his personal diary of the conference and his notes of conversations afterwards are the principal source for the whole of this section.

Letters Norman/Smith 27 May, Norman/Hopkins 18 May 1932.

cc Note Phillips 3 Aug. 1932.

dd Letter Siepmann/Phillips 9 July 1932.

ee Cable Phillips/Hopkins, Gov. 2 Aug. 1932 (and reply). Notes on Gov. discussions with Treas. 2 Aug. 1932.

ff Phillips 27 July 1932.

gg Note Gov. comments to Treas. 3 Aug. 1932.

Norman Diary 23 Oct. 1932.

hh Telephone Harvey/Harrison 20 Dec. 1932 (important for general views).

ii Memo. (Hambro) 11 May 1933 (section 'Our Policy' may reproduce Gov.'s words).

jj CTM 1 Feb., 22 Mar., 21 June 1933 (see also League of Nations Journal of The... Conference 15 June 1933). Letter Harvey/Norman 27 Apr. 1933. Draft Declaration of Policy by central banks 8 Mar. 1933. Telephone Hambro/Lacour-Gayet 16 May 1933.

kk For discussions on Warburg and other proposals for stabilisation Apr.–May 1933 cable and letter reports from Bewley (Washington) (esp. cable 16 May), Bank comments (Hambro and others) and discussions with Treas. and Lacour-Gayet and other French representatives.

ll Letter Norman/Hopkins 27 May 1935.
Note of discussions with Lacour-Gayet 11 July 1933 and corres. with Netherlands Bank.

mm Letter Hopkins/Hambro 10 Aug. 1933.

CHAPTER 19

a Memo. Clay 12 Jan. 1934.
Norman papers, Niemeyer (*c.* 1960).

b Note Osborne/Siepmann 9 Apr. 1932.
Memo. (Clay) Credit Policy and Price Levels 26 July 1933.

c Cables and tel. conversations Norman and others/Harrison July 1933. Comments Kay and others.
For Norman on importance of franc stability Per Jacobsson Diary 8 July 1933. Comments (Kay) 12 Oct. 1933.
Report from Cariguel (B. of France) 28 Sept. 1933.
Note 29 Aug. 1933.

d Harvey note of meeting 22 Apr., Siepmann note 29 Apr. 1933.
For contacts with B. of France and changes in its Governorship, there are many notes of Cobbold's discussions at B. of France. Note (Rowe-Dutton) from Paris 3 Jan. 1935. Norman notes after Basle 14 Jan. 1935.

e Letters Phillips/Catterns 29 Jan. 1936. Corres. Norman/Tannery 17 Feb. 1936. Notes of meetings B. of France, Cobbold and Treas. Jan.–Feb. 1936.

f Tel. conversations mainly Norman/Harrison esp. 1 Dec. 1933; notes 2, 4 Dec. relating thereto.
Memo. Norman/Hopkins 25 Jan. 1934.
Kay notes 16 Aug. 1934; his reports on exchange markets throughout the period.

g Siepmann E.E.A. Report No. 7: Annex on Staffing of Exchange management.

h Memo. 7 Mar. 1938 (Bolton) with Appendix on Forward Exchange Business 1931–8.

i Letter Clay/Streat (Manchester Ch. of Commerce) 13 Mar. 1934.
Note Clay/Gov. 9 Apr. 1935.
Clay note 14 May 1935. Clay memo. 18 Jan. 1935.
Mynors/Bolton memo. 21 Feb. 1935.
Draft agreed by Phillips (Treas.) and Clay 6 Mar. 1935.

j Memo. Clay/Catterns 2 Aug. 1935.

k Purchasing Power Parity Notes – Clay/Selwyn.
Memos. (Mynors) 22 June, 16 Sept. 1937.

l The original Leith-Ross memos. 27 Nov. became the Cabinet Paper of 7 Dec. 1936. Important commentaries esp. by Stamp and Clay Dec. 1936 and Jan. 1937. Note by Gov. of agreement with Chanc. 12 Feb. 1937.

m Among the full collection of papers covering the negotiation of the Tripartite Declaration and subsequent agreement, there is an important 'Record of certain recent events' (Siepmann) covering the critical phase 22 July–3 Aug. 1936.
Norman Diary 22–8 Sept. 1936.
Interview E. Monick 7 May 1969. After this long interview M Monick agreed the author's account, reproduced in the four paragraphs following this point; and he used this account in pp. 46–58 of his book, *Pour mémoire*, privately printed in France in 1970.

n Notes Siepmann 23 Apr., Cobbold and Catterns Jan. 1936.

o Memo. (Clay) 3 Sept. 1937.
Tel. Chanc./Washington 29 Oct. 1936 and note 24 June 1938.
Memo. Siepmann for Empire Central Banks Conference 1937.
Notes Siepmann 7 Jan. 1937, 22 Apr., 4 May 1938.
E.E.A. Reports 1936–8.
Letter Siepmann/Weber 29 Oct. 1936.

p E.E.A. Report No. 6.
Note of conversation Cobbold/Fournier 23 July 1937.
Memo. The French Franc 3 Sept. 1937.
Note Cobbold 6 Aug. 1937.

q Corres. with clearing banks etc. 1935–6.
Note Mynors 27 Aug. 1937.

r Notes Cobbold, Clay, others June–July 1937. Letters and memos. from B.I.S. (Per Jacobsson).

s PDO Diary 8 Apr. 1937.
Memos. 6, 11 May 1937.

t Memo. (Clay) 1 July 1937.

u Letter Gov./Chanc. 1 Jan. 1936.
E.E.A. Quarterly Reports incl. Annex Memo. 17 Jan. 1938.
Memo. (Clay) 12 July 1937.

v Cables D. Gov. to Towers and others 6 Jan. 1939.
Several memos. by Clay on reorganisation of E.E.A. and Issue Dept. accounts 1937–8.

w On the regulation of foreign issues there is abundant documentation in the Bank, including corres. Bank/Treas., memo. (Clay) 29 Jan. 1935 and Clay corres. 1935–7.
Letter Cobbold/Bruce 7 Feb. 1938.
CTM 3 Dec. 1941 and rel. CT papers. Note (Mynors) 15 May 1943.

x Memo. (Clay) 25 Feb. 1938.
Notes (Clay, Mynors) commenting on Keynes 14 Mar. 1938.
Notes 24 Sept. 1937, 24 Feb. 1938.

y Letter Norman/Myers 5 Nov. 1935.
Memo. (Clay) 5 May 1937.

z Memos. 1 Mar. (Harvey) and 3 July 1933.
Mins. (Holland-Martin) 22, 23 Oct. 1936.
Memo. (Holland-Martin) 9 Dec. 1937.
Notes 30 Apr. 1937, 18 Jan. 1939.

aa CTM 28 July, 20 Oct. 1937.
CTM 7 Sept. 1938.
Report of discussion with Mullens and an official visitor from Paris 14 Apr. 1937.

bb Memo. (Clay) 18 Jan. 1938.
Memo. Gov./Clay and Clay reply 3 Mar. 1938.

CHAPTER 20

a This and all other paragraphs in this section are based on a research study prepared within the Bank (by Miss J. R. Cooper) for the purpose of this history. This consists of a paper entitled 'The German Standstill Agreements', with Appendix A, 'The Austrian Standstill', Appendix B, 'The Hungarian Standstill', and an Additional Note, 'The Bank's Attitude to Assistance for the Discount Market'. The sources used were exclusively those within the Bank. They included, as well as a large number of working papers, the following:

1 The formal agreements.
2 Occasional surveys, such as 'Comparative Survey of Standstill Proposals',

'A Note on Standstill Agreements' (19 Oct. 1931), 'Memorandum on the Development of Standstill Agreements' (Rodd, 2 Sept. 1932).

3 CTM and rel. notes.

4 Corres. between Bank (esp. Norman and Niemeyer) and Treas.

5 Cttee on Advances and Discounts Mins. and rel. notes.

6 Norman Diary.

7 Norman corres. etc. with Schacht.

8 Cables and tel. conversations with FRBNY.

9 Papers of the Joint Cttee of British Short-term Creditors.

b For the general interpretation in this paragraph, I have relied greatly on interviews with R. N. Kershaw, 27 Mar., 2 Apr. 1969, 9 May 1972.

CTM 4 Oct. 1933, 5, 19 Sept. 1934.

c The Canadian background, esp. the political pre-history of the Canadian Royal Commission, was discussed with Graham Towers 22 May 1968. CTM 19 July, 2 Aug. 1933. Norman Diary 28 July 1933. Letters Macmillan/Norman/Macmillan 29 July, 3 Aug. 1933.

d Letter Norman/Stewart 22 June 1934.

e Norman Diary 14 Dec. 1923. Letter Norman/Lefeaux 14 Aug. 1936.

f Cable corres. Niemeyer/Harvey June–Aug. 1930. Letters Harvey/Wilford 30 June, Niemeyer/Norman 28 Sept. 1930.

g Notes (Kershaw) for Gov. 23 Sept., 3 Oct. 1932.

Corres. New Zealand Government/Norman 17 Nov., 2 Dec. 1933.

h On the Lefeaux appointment, R. N. Kershaw interview 27 Mar. 1969 is important.

i Letter Norman/Lefeaux 30 Apr. 1936.

j CTM 13 June 1934 and rel. papers. Letter Norman/Hoare 8 Feb. 1933.

Corres. Norman/Grigg/India Office/Osborne Smith 1935–6.

k Letter Norman/Hornsby 6 Feb. 1922. Note (Niemeyer) 28 May 1929.

Gov. corres. 21 Aug.–29 Nov. 1930 rel. to E. M. Cook.

Letter Norman/Cook 17 Apr. 1939. CTM 19 Apr. 1939.

l Note (Niemeyer) 6 Sept. 1939. Letter Niemeyer/Brennan 21 Sept. 1931.

Interview Kershaw 2 Apr. 1969.

m For the general circumstances leading to the missions to South America, the opening passages of Niemeyer's Reports to the Brazilian Government 4 July 1931 and the Argentine Government 24 Mar. 1933. These Reports also contain the recommendations on the establishment of central banks, with draft statutes, referred to in the following paragraphs.

For Bank's reluctance, suggestion of B.I.S. etc., letters Niemeyer/Vansittart 17 Feb., Niemeyer/Fraser 19 Mar. 1931. CTM 19 Nov. 1930, 25 Feb., 10 June 1931.

n CTM 17 Sept., 19 Nov. 1930.

Interview F. F. Powell 26 Feb. 1969.

o Interview (Hambro) Argentine Ambassador 26 Oct. 1932. CTM 17 Feb., 12 Oct. 1932, 1 Feb. 1933.

Letter Niemeyer/Hambro 7 Apr. 1933. Draft article Overseas Activity of the Bank (for *Quarterly Bulletin*) 3 June 1966. Paper for Empire Central Bankers Conference 1937. Letter Niemeyer/Beyen 27 Jan. 1938. Memo. (Clay) 23 Feb. 1933. Letter Irving/Niemeyer 16 Jan.; memo. 28 Mar. 1935.

p CTM 4 Oct. 1933. Letter Niemeyer/Powell 31 May 1934.

CTM 15 Aug. 1934, 8 May, 24 July 1935, 17 June 1936. Letter Hopkins/Govs. 10 Aug. 1934.

O[verseas] & F[oreign] half-yearly reports 1 Aug. 1933–31 July 1934.

q CTM 1 Feb. 1933. Letter Niemeyer/Hambro 7 Apr. 1933. Cable (Niemeyer) 22 Apr. 1933.

Letters Norman/Vansittart 17 Feb., 13 Mar. 1931.
Letter Norman/Hopkins 26 Mar. 1935. CTM 24 May, 19 July 1939.

r CTM 4 Oct. 1933, 2 Sept., 25 Nov. 1936, 13 Jan., 10 Feb. 1937. Memos. prepared for 1937 discussions.

s Interview G. Towers 22 May 1968.

t Gov. corres. on Hatry crisis 20–26 Sept. 1929.

u CTM 17 Feb. 1932.

v CTM 17, 18, 22 July 1931.

w CTM 27 Apr., 26 May, 8 June 1932.
Norman Diary 17 June 1932.

x Note on Durant Radford 29 Jan. 1924. CTM 20 Oct. 1937.

y Memo. (Discount Office) 26 Oct. 1931.

z Letter Brandt/Norman and reply 26, 30 Apr. 1929.
Note (A.C.B.) 25 May 1937.

aa Gov. evidence to Treasury Cttee on Municipal Savings Banks 25 Mar. 1927.
Corres. Bank/Treas. on Building Societies 1938–9.

bb Interview G. M. Booth 4 Nov. 1969. Corres. Norman/de Stein Feb.–Mar. 1939.

cc For the whole of this section the principal sources are PDO Diary, CTM and papers of Cttee on Advances and Discounts.

dd Note (Holland-Martin) 8 Nov. 1938. CTM 16 Nov. 1938.
Cttee on Advances and Discounts Mins. 17 Oct. 1939.
For Gov.'s advocacy of amalgamation note (K.O.P.) 25 Jan. 1933.
For pressure on firm given special help notes (K.O.P.) 29 Sept. 1931–16 Jan. 1932.
CTM 23 Feb. 1927 and rel. papers.

ee Norman Diary 2, 5 Feb. 1935. PDO Diary 29, 31 Jan., 1 Feb. 1935.

ff Memos. (Peppiatt) 4, 7 Feb. 1935. Letters Norman/Accepting Houses Cttee 4 Feb. 1935. CTM 30 Oct. 1935, 19 Aug. 1936.

gg Memo. (Selwyn) Tin Scheme 12 Apr. 1935. Corres. Norman/Spens 1935. Memos. (Peppiatt) 10 Jan., 12 Feb. 1936. Corres. Norman/Demetriadi 15 Apr.–10 Aug. 1936. Letter Peacock/Norman 9 Oct. 1936. CTM 23 Oct., 4, 18 Dec. 1935.

hh CTM 17 Sept. 1930, 29 Apr. 1931. Letter Norman/Granet 18 Dec. 1930.
Also, and for the whole of this section, interviews and corres. Skinner/Sayers 1969–74.

ii Memos. 4 July 1933, 28 Aug., 11 Dec. 1934.
Report (Bruce-Gardner) 31 Dec. 1930.

jj Note (Peppiatt) 6 Feb. 1948. Note (Gibb) 12 June 1943.

kk CTM 19 May, 23 June 1937, 12 Nov. 1947. Notes (Skinner) 22 June 1937, 26 Sept. 1939.

ll Letter Richard Thomas/Bank with accounts 23 May 1940. Letters Firth/Chamberlain 11 July, Firth/Catterns 16 July, Abell/Norman 29 Apr. 1938. Note (Skinner) 2 May 1938. CTM 4 May 1938. Report (James) 24 May 1938. Note (Skinner) 30 Apr. 1938. Letter Duncan/Catterns 17 June 1938. Note 15 May 1938. Corres. Woods/Catterns 20–22 June 1938. CTM 29 June 1938.
Letter Firth/Skinner 14 July 1939. Note (Skinner) 21 Oct. 1943. Draft Mins. of Control Cttee 15 Apr. 1940. CTM 20 June 1945, 1 Sept. 1948. Memos. (Peppiatt) 19 June 1945, 13 Feb. 1948.

mm CTM 5 Oct., 9 Nov. 1938, 11 Jan. 1939. Letters Peppiatt/Skinner 1 Feb. 1939, Benton Jones/Norman 17 Jan. 1939.
Court Mins. 19 July 1945.

nn Memos. (Clay, Skinner, Mynors) Jan. 1936. Notes of meetings (Skinner) 20 Jan., 5 Oct. 1936.

oo Letter Norman/Niemeyer 20 June 1945.

pp CTM 30 Nov. 1932.

qq The examples in this paragraph are taken from earlier chapters. On 'What is a bank?' the CLCB Mins. are important, also letter Cokayne/Strong 2 Feb. 1920 and Norman Diary Feb.–Mar. 1920.

rr Chapter 7 has the background of this paragraph. An important letter Norman/Niemeyer (Treas.) 5 May 1927 illuminates Norman's position in relation to one of the Big Five banks.

ss Letter Catterns/Caulcutt (Barclays D.C.O.) 4 Aug. 1939. PDO Diary 11 Dec. 1939.

tt Letter Gov./Hamilton 18 June 1906.

Corres. Gov./CLCB June–Aug. 1929 and 1935–6. CTM 10 June 1942. Court Mins. 12 Dec. 1946.

uu Memo. (Catterns) 31 Oct. 1932 and rel. notes on discussions with CLCB.

vv Bankers' Memo. (Agricultural Credit) marked 'CT. 10.2.26'. CTM 3 Feb., 10 Mar. 1926, Feb., Mar. 1928. Note of meeting 15 Mar. 1928.

ww CTM 4, 18 Dec. 1935, 8 Jan.–8 Apr. 1936. CLCB Mins. Feb., Mar. 1934, Feb., Mar., May 1936. Letters Norman/Smith 10 Feb., Harvey/Norman 27 Apr. 1933. Memo. (Clay) 19 Jan. 1937.

xx CTM 31 Mar., 10 Nov. 1943. Internal cttee report 1943.

yy Letter Gov./Bradbury 26 Oct. 1935.

Gov. note of discussion with Bradbury and CTM 25 Mar. 1936.

CHAPTER 21

a The principal sources for this chapter are corres., notes of discussions with and comments on letters from the Treas., and E.E.A. Reports (with numerous Annexes).

Memo. (Siepmann) 12 Oct. 1938.

b Notes of discussions 23, 30 Nov. 1938. Report (Bewley/Waley) on American views 2 Nov. 1938. Memo. (Siepmann) E.E.A. gains and losses 17 Nov. 1938.

c Letter Norman/Hopkins 24 Nov. 1938 and rel. papers on the bear squeeze.

d Notes of discussion 1 Dec. 1938. Corres. Bank/Treas./Treas. representative in Washington. Memo. (Siepmann) 28 Nov. 1938. E.E.A. Report (Siepmann) 4th quarter 1938.

e Letter Norman/Hopkins 24 Nov. 1938. Note of meeting 28 Dec. 1938.

f Letters Norman/Fournier 4 Jan., Cobbold/Riksbank and other central banks 13 Jan. 1939. Note of discussion with Chanc. 29 Dec. 1938. Memos. (Clay) 29 Dec. 1938, 2, 23 Jan. 1939.

CTM 3, 4, 11 Jan., 24 Aug. 1939.

g Memo. 24 Apr. 1939.

h Letter Phillips/Catterns 3 Sept. 1937. Note on reserves 16 June 1938.

i Letter Treas./Govs. 2 Aug. 1938. Comments on 'no-blocking' view 17 May 1938.

Summary (Cobbold) on sterling area restrictions 6 Apr. 1939. Circulars for sterling countries 6 Oct. 1939.

j Interviews Sir Cyril Hawker 30 Nov. 1971, R. A. O. Bridge 8 Aug. 1969.

k Note (Cobbold) 31 Aug. with Siepmann marginalia. Siepmann draft 22 Aug. 1939.

l Norman Diary 1 Sept. 1939.

m CTM 24 Aug., 8 Nov. 1939. Note (Norman) 14 Sept. 1939.

n Norman Diary 6, 14 Sept. and notes (Norman) on bankers' queries 18 Sept. 1939.

o Note of discussion with CLCB 4 Aug. 1938.

p Letter Peppiatt/Harvey 24 Sept. 1941.

q Norman Diary Sept., Oct. 1939. Corres. Chanc./Bank/CLCB Sept. 1939.

r Review of emergency preparations (Cobbold) 18 May 1939. PDO Diary 26 May, 26–8 Sept. 1938, 30 Mar., July, 13, 21, 25, 28 Sept. 1939.

Norman Diary 13 Oct., 6 Dec. 1939.

Norman Diary 26, 29 Sept. 1939.

s Corres. Catterns, Cobbold/Stock Exchange Chairman Apr. 1938–Apr. 1939.

t Corres. and notes of discussion Bank/Stock Exchange Chairman Aug.–Sept. 1939. Norman Diary 24 Aug. 1939.

u Letters Catterns/Phillips 1, 5 Sept. 1939 and rel. papers.

v Note (Peppiatt) on interest rates 26 Apr. 1939.

w Note (Mynors) 30 Oct. and revised note 4 Nov. 1939.

x Notes (Peppiatt) 6, 15 Dec. 1939. CTM 31 Jan. 1940.

y Norman Diary 14 Mar. 1940. CTM 13 Mar. 1940.

z Letters Norman/financial institutions 5 Mar. 1940 and rel. cables to Dominion central banks.

aa Letter Catterns/Treas. 19 Oct. 1938. CTM 9 Nov. 1938.
Letter Phillips/Norman 7 Apr. 1938.

bb Cttee on Exchange Difficulties etc., Annex to Draft Mins. of 3rd meeting 9 June 1939.
Letter Norman/Chanc. 24 July 1939. CTM 26 July, 30 Aug. 1939.

cc Corres. Catterns/Phillips Mar. 1939.

dd Letters Siepmann/Branco 30 Dec. 1939, Catterns/Taylor 5 Apr. 1940.
Note Norman/Clay 9 May 1940.

ee Notes on Gov.'s discussions with Hopkins 31 Aug., with Chanc. 17 Sept. 1939. CTM 15 Nov. 1939.
CTM 4 Oct. 1939.

CHAPTER 22

a This chapter is necessarily based not only on specific papers but also on inferences from a great range of incidents, many of which have been referred to in other chapters. The principal documents are the Reports and papers relating to the major internal reviews by the Revelstoke, Trotter and Peacock Committees; and private correspondence of Norman, Addis, Anderson, Peacock, Revelstoke and other Directors, mainly with other members of the Court. Minutes of the Committee of Treasury, and sometimes of the Court, are always authoritative and occasionally illuminating. Interviews with former Directors, especially G. M. Booth, sometimes helped with the questions of constitutional practice to which much of the chapter is devoted.

b On the selection of Peacock, interviews with G. M. Booth 21 Feb., 4 Nov. 1969 were important.

c For late 1930s there are CT records on the recommendation of nominees for the Court.
Note of conversation Peacock/Norman 23 Oct. 1930. Letter Norman/Strong 28 Nov. 1927. Letter Cadbury/O'Brien 27 Nov. 1967.
Letter Catterns/Cadbury 21 Mar. 1938. Interviews Whitworth 20 May 1969, Cadbury 15 Apr. 1970.

d On Keynes with Norman, interview Booth 4 Nov. 1969.

e This section is based on a series of research papers, 'The Servants of the House' and 'Women in the Service', prepared within the Bank (by Miss J. Bridges) for the purpose of this history. Sources used included Court Mins., CTM and, from 1918, Mins. of Staff Cttee; and the Reports of the Special Cttees on Classification, as well as many working papers and memoranda prepared for these cttees or arising from problems in the day-to-day working of the offices and Departments.
Memoranda of particular importance are: that addressed to the Governors and Directors by the staff at the beginning of the New Year 1919 (printed as Appendix 5); that addressed to Sir Brien Cokayne by the 'Committee of Delegates' May 1918; those of 8 Jan., 19 Feb. and June 1894 on the employment of women, and the

report to the Deputy Governor in March 1921 on the future employment of women.

Other important papers are:

The Report of the Chief Officers upon the Internal Administration Feb. 1893; the 8th and 9th Interim Reports of the Special Cttee on Grievances July 1919 and the evidence to that cttee; corres. (1910–12) between Nairne and Waterfield on the appointment of graduates.

Many who had been employed by the Bank in these years were interviewed by R. S. S. and talked either directly or incidentally on the developments reviewed in this section. These included D. H. Allport, J. V. Bailey, P. S. Beale, Sir George Bolton, A. C. Bull, B. G. Catterns, H. S. Clarke, F. G. Conolly, L. F. Crick, A. W. C. Dascombe, C. C. Excell, J. L. Fisher, Sir Cyril Hawker, D. E. Johns, J. A. C. Osborne, Sir Maurice Parsons, Sir Kenneth Peppiatt, F. F. Powell, E. H. D. Skinner, Sir Edmund Stockdale, A. Stone, G. H. Tansley. Among former members of the Court, Sir Dallas Bernard, E. Holland-Martin and A. Whitworth were particularly familiar with staff matters.

f Quotations are from Report of the Revelstoke Cttee as submitted to Court 21 Feb. 1918.

g Note Mynors/Parsons 12 June 1966.

h Letter of appointment (Siepmann) 15 June 1926. Letters Norman/Stewart 6 June 1927, Strong/Norman 4 Jan. 1924 (FRBNY Strong Papers 1116.4).

i Interview Niemeyer 23 Jan. 1969. Note Norman/Fisher 29 Mar. 1927. Letters Norman/Strong 8, 17 Apr. 1927 (FRBNY Strong Papers 1116.7). Court Mins. 26 May 1927, 21 Feb. 1935.

CTM 3 Mar. 1926, 31 Oct. 1928. Court Mins. 10 Jan. 1929. Letter Norman/Falk 9 Jan. 1929.

k CTM 11 Nov. 1931.

l In addition to copies of the published Lawrence letters, the Bank has copies, and some originals, of corres. between Lionel Curtis, Herbert Baker and others, and important corres. between the Bank and Lord Rennell. Interview E. Holland-Martin 25 Mar. 1970. CTM 6 June, 28 Nov., 5 Dec. 1928.

m Letter Gov./Chanc. 4 Mar. 1896. Memo. on the Duties, Powers &c. of the Governors ...16 Jan. 1894.

For this section generally, the Mins. of CT itself and the Reports and other papers of the Revelstoke and Peacock Cttees are major sources. Many of the generalisations are inferences from the whole range of events surveyed in earlier chapters.

n Court Mins. 25 Jan., 28 Mar. 1894. Letter Gibbs/Powell 27 Jan. 1894. Corres. 1894 of Earl of Leven and Melville with Govs. Court Mins. 21 Mar. 1895. Note of Gov.'s interview 25 Feb. 1896 (dated 4 Mar.). Letter Greene/Gov. (Papers of Sir M. W. Collet) 11 Sept. 1896.

o Letters Gibbs/Powell 27 Jan. 1894, Campbell/Cokayne 20 Oct. 1916. Revelstoke Cttee evidence Nov. 1917.

p CTM 20 Dec. 1923. Court Mins. 27 Dec. 1923.

CTM 18 Dec. 1935. Court Mins. 3 Sept. 1942.

CT 19 July 1939.

q Note marked CT 10 Apr. 1940. Letter Dascombe/Armstrong 3 Dec. 1958. Peacock Cttee Evidence and Report.

r Letter Leven and Melville/Powell 28 Mar. 1894.

Letter Harvey/Read 31 Oct. 1929.

CT 29 Feb. 1928.

s Addis Diary 18, 25 Apr. 1924, 21, 26 Jan. 1925.

CTM Aug.–Sept. 1927. Letter Norman/Strong 29 Aug. 1927.

For the whole of this section, Reports and other papers of the Revelstoke, Trotter and Peacock Cttees.

u *E. Johnston & Co.: One Hundred Years of Coffee* (privately printed, London, 1942).

v Letter Greene/Collet 10 Dec. 1896.

w Letter Campbell/Cokayne 20 Oct. 1916.

x Norman Papers (Niemeyer, H. Wilson). Letter (Hopkins) 4 Jan. 1930.

y Note enclosed, letter Peacock/Revelstoke 27 June 1926 (Baring Archives: Revelstoke, B. of E. Affairs 1926). Letter Norman/Anderson 20 Oct. 1924 (Sir Colin Anderson's family papers). Letter Norman/Strong 30 Nov. 1924 (FRBNY Strong Papers, Strong/Norman corres.).

z Anderson corres. 1925. Anderson statement to a meeting of Directors 28 Sept. 1926 (Baring Archives: Revelstoke, B. of E. Affairs 1926). Interview Whitworth 20 May 1969.

aa Memo. of meeting of Directors 19 Oct. 1926 and rel. corres. (Baring Archives: Revelstoke, B. of E. Affairs 1926). Letters Anderson/Strong draft of 5 Feb. in Bank records, as sent 11 Feb. 1926 in FRBNY Strong Papers 1117.2; Peacock/Strong 9 Oct. 1926.

bb Court Mins. 5 July, 25 Oct. 1928 and rel. papers. Papers, Selection of Governors – Jan./Oct. 1928 and 1930–34. Evidence, Peacock Cttee. Court and CT Minutes.

cc Note of discussions 1926 (Baring Archives: Revelstoke, B. of E. Affairs 1926). Letter Peacock/Strong 25 Oct. 1926 (FRBNY Strong Papers 1112.2). Letter Revelstoke/Peacock 22 Oct. 1928 (Baring Archives: Revelstoke). Letter Peacock/Norman 27 Aug. 1937.

dd Letters Peacock/Norman 21 July, Hambro/Norman 3, 16 Sept. 1937.

ee *Thomas Sivewright Catto, Baron Catto of Cairncatto, etc. 1879–1959* (privately printed by Constable, Edinburgh, 1962). Letters Norman/Addis 21 Aug. 1930, Peacock/Norman 27 Aug. 1937. Note 'Said in CT' 17 Jan. 1940.

ff Secretary's note 'Succession – 1943' 22 June 1943. CTM 21 Oct. 1943. Secretary's note 7 Dec. 1943. Letter Towers/Sayers 10 Sept. 1974.